THE SECRET ORIGINS OF COMICS STUDIES

In *The Secret Origins of Comics Studies*, today's leading comics scholars turn back a page to reveal the founding figures dedicated to understanding comics art. Edited by comics scholars Matthew J. Smith and Randy Duncan, this collection provides an in-depth study of the individuals and institutions that have created and shaped the field of Comics Studies over the past 75 years. From Coulton Waugh to Wolfgang Fuchs, these influential historians, educators, and theorists produced the foundational work and built the institutions that inspired the recent surge in scholarly work in this dynamic, interdisciplinary field. Sometimes scorned, often underappreciated, these visionaries established a path followed by subsequent generations of scholars in literary studies, communication, art history, the social sciences, and more. Giving not only credit where credit is due, this volume both offers an authoritative account of the history of Comics Studies and also helps move the field forward by being a valuable resource for creating graduate student reading lists and the first stop for anyone writing a comics-related literature review.

Matthew J. Smith is Professor and Director in the School of Communication at Radford University in Virginia. Along with Randy Duncan, he is co-editor of Routledge's *Advances in Comics Studies* series. Previously, the two writing partners teamed with former DC Comics President and Publisher Paul Levitz to produce *The Power of Comics: History, Form, and Culture* (2nd Edition).

Randy Duncan is Professor of Communication and Director of the Comics Studies Minor at Henderson State University. He is co-editor, with Matthew J. Smith, of the Eisner-nominated *Critical Approaches to Comics: Theories and Methods*. He is a co-founder, with Peter M. Coogan, of the Comics Arts Conference and received the Inkpot Award for contributions to Comics Studies.

THE SECRET ORIGINS OF COMICS STUDIES

Edited by Matthew J. Smith and Randy Duncan

First published 2017
by Routledge
711 Third Avenue, New York, NY 10017

and by Routledge
2 Park Square, Milton Park, Abingdon, Oxon OX14 4RN

Routledge is an imprint of the Taylor & Francis Group, an informa business

© 2017 Taylor & Francis

The right of Matthew J. Smith and Randy Duncan to be identified as the authors of this work has been asserted by them in accordance with sections 77 and 78 of the Copyright, Designs and Patents Act 1988.

All rights reserved. No part of this book may be reprinted or reproduced or utilised in any form or by any electronic, mechanical, or other means, now known or hereafter invented, including photocopying and recording, or in any information storage or retrieval system, without permission in writing from the publishers.

Trademark notice: Product or corporate names may be trademarks or registered trademarks, and are used only for identification and explanation without intent to infringe.

Library of Congress Cataloging-in-Publication Data
Names: Smith, Matthew J., 1971– editor. | Duncan, Randy, 1958– editor.
Title: The secret origins of Comics Studies / edited by Matthew J. Smith and Randy Duncan.
Description: New York: Routledge, 2017.
Identifiers: LCCN 2016042603 | ISBN 9781138884519 (hardback)
Subjects: LCSH: Comic books, strips, etc.—History and criticism. | Graphic novels—History and criticism.
Classification: LCC PN6710 .S44 2017 | DDC 741.5/9—dc23
LC record available at https://lccn.loc.gov/2016042603

ISBN: 978-1-138-88451-9 (hbk)
ISBN: 978-1-315-71603-9 (ebk)

Typeset in Bembo
by codeMantra

Printed and bound in Great Britain by
TJ International Ltd, Padstow, Cornwall

Matt and Randy dedicate this book to Randy's fellow Comics Arts Conference organizers: Peter M. Coogan, Kathleen McClancy, and Travis Langley. Their hard work makes possible the conference that has, for a quarter of a century, nurtured young scholars and helped to build a Comics Studies community.

Matt also wishes to express his gratitude to Wittenberg University for its support in the initial development of this project.

CONTENTS

List of Figures   x
Foreword: Comics Studies, the Anti-Discipline   xi
Charles Hatfield
Preface   xxiii

PART 1
The Educators   1

1 Educating with Comics   3
   Carol L. Tilley

2 Educating about Comics   12
   Robert G. Weiner

   A Pioneer's Perspective: Waldomiro Vergueiro   25

   A Pioneer's Perspective: James "Bucky" Carter   28

PART 2
The Historians   31

3 The Historians of the Creators   33
   Brad Ricca

   Sidebar: Magazines and Online   36

   Sidebar: A Herstorian's Perspective   38
   Christina Blanch

   Sidebar: International Creators   40

viii Contents

4 The Historians of the Comics Industry   43
   Julie Davis and Robert Westerfelhaus

   A Pioneer's Perspective: Maurice Horn   54

5 The Historians of the Art Form   56
   Ian Horton

   Sidebar: Comic Art   57

   Sidebar: Bande Dessinée and the Problem of Form   59

   A Pioneer's Perspective: David Kunzle   67

6 The Librarians and Archivists   71
   Jenny Robb

PART 3
The Theorists   **89**

7 Literary Theory/Narrative Theory   91
   Barbara Postema

8 Semiotics and Linguistics   100
   Gert Meesters

   Sidebar: Sound Effects   101

9 Myths, Archetypes, and Religions   105
   Beth Davies-Stofka and David McConeghy

   Sidebar: Comics' Shortcut to the Sacred   105
   A. David Lewis

   Sidebar: Comics as (Pseudo-) Religion   111
   A. David Lewis

10 Ideological/Sociological   118
   Ian Gordon

   Sidebar: The Immigrant Space   121
   A. David Lewis

   Sidebar: Trauma and Disability in Comics   125
   José Alaniz

   A Pioneer's Perspective: Wolfgang Fuchs   130

11 Formalist Theory: The Cartoonists   133
   Henry Jenkins

12 Formalist Theory: Academics   150
    Ann Miller

    Sidebar: Materiality   159
    Ian Hague

13 Psychology/Psychiatry   164
    Travis Langley

    Sidebar: Martin Barker   174
    William Proctor

14 Gender Studies and Queer Studies   178
    Kane Anderson

15 Manga Studies, A History   190
    Nicholas A. Theisen

PART 4
The Institutions   **203**

16 The Organizations   205
    Jeremy Larance

    A Pioneer's Perspective: John A. Lent   221

    A Pioneer's Perspective: Peter M. Coogan   223

17 The Galleries   226
    Kim Munson

    Sidebar: Yoshihiro Yonezawa   240
    Jaqueline Berndt

18 The Conferences   246
    Julia Round and Chris Murray

    A Pioneer's Perspective: M. Thomas Inge   260

19 The Journals   262
    Alec R. Hosterman

20 The Presses   272
    Joseph Michael Sommers

    A Pioneer's Perspective: Pascal Lefèvre   281

Contributors   *285*
Index   *291*

FIGURES

6.1	Bill Blackbeard	75
6.2	Lucy Caswell with cartoonist Milton Caniff	79
10.1	Original colloquium poster	130
17.1	Promotional Poster for *Bande Dessinée et Figuration Narrative* at the Musee des Arts Decoratifs, 1967	229
17.2	Brian Walker Standing Outside of the Museum of Cartoon Art at the Mead Mansion, circa 1974	233
17.3	Lily Renee (left) and Trina Robbins signing *Pretty in Ink* at San Diego Comic Con, 2015	238

FOREWORD
Comics Studies, the Anti-Discipline

Charles Hatfield

Comics made my academic career. They inspired me to keep my nose to the grindstone long enough to become an English professor. Comics Studies gave me the means to imagine myself as a career academic and the passion to work past the hurdles, the daunting rites of passage. But they also made me impatient with doing things the conventional English studies way—that is, they either enabled or forced me to see my discipline from the vantage point of an outsider as well as insider. If comics helped place me in academia, Comics Studies has kept me continually looking for a place.

What could it mean to build a "place" for a field that cannot quite *be* placed, one that has operated on the margins and in the interstices among the disciplines—literature, art, mass communications, film and media studies, design, philosophy, sociology, and many others? Comics Studies is a liminal field, defined by the unresolved nature of its very object of study. As a social object, comics occupies many places and yet institutionally has been perfectly at home in none. Comics Studies, I would argue, is an *anti*-discipline: a way of slipping between the universes, academically speaking.[1] So what can it mean to build a place for it, and why should that matter?

I do think it matters.

To seek a place, or center, for a field that will not yield to the centripetal force of academic "disciplining": that is the contradiction from which Comics Studies speaks. That is the perspective from which the following introduction seeks to (re)tell the history of Comics Studies. My biases, of course, should be taken as just that and not the fault of my fellow contributors or our kind editors—but I hope that what I have to say will help place in perspective this very book, a timely and much-needed volume on the "secret origins" of our field.

Until recently, comics scholars have almost always become comics scholars by dint of self-directed independent study (an observation I owe, like many things, to Joseph "Rusty" Witek). Comics Studies has been an ad-hoc phenomenon, a field generated not by institutional mandate but by the eager scurrying of independent actors, opportunistically seeking niches here and there in which they can study this neglected art form and its culture. Finding ways to study comics academically has been about finding allies and protectors and about learning how to describe comics in terms that make sense within one's home discipline. In my case, I've been acutely conscious of being a literature scholar who "happens" to do comics—a matter of not only professional survival but also stubborn pride. But of course the disciplinary fit has not been easy, or seamless. For one thing, I can now see that the refusal (or mistrust) of images has been one of the basic ideological moves of literary studies. For another, the interdisciplinary field of word and image studies—which is where I have often hung my hat—is exactly that, interdisciplinary, and cannot be bound by literary study in the conventional sense that I learned as a student. Finally, my experiences at conferences such as the Popular Culture Association and the International Comic Arts Forum have often involved working with scholars from outside English, a kind of experience that has helped me see my discipline from other vantage points.

Until now, Comics Studies has been only loosely institutionalized, often through klatches of friends and colleagues. It has required much independent study by students and teachers alike. We have made it up on the go. If that has been a source of vitality for Comics Studies—and I believe it has—it has also been a source of difficulty. This has been a field without a hub, like a wheel built from its spokes alone, with no center (no place). Or perhaps there *have* been contenders for a center, but none so widely recognized as to enable the field to garner attention from the outside, and to grow. Yet now that Comics Studies is a recognized field, I believe we do need to build inward to a center—that is, we need to find and stake out some specific institutional ground.

Comics Studies is not innocent of history. A great deal of work had already been done in the field before the upsurge of the past 20 years. It's just that that work was scattered, under-recognized, and often unread; teachers and students had to do a lot of independent seeking, with few guides. Though Comics Studies is not a new academic field, until recently we have acted as if it were. The field's history is hard to trace because it happened mainly on the margins rather in the center of anything. It seems that we still often forget that history and what it might tell us—that we reinvent wheels, or that our students end up seeking to reinvent them, because we cannot see where our field has come from. This insight has been driven home to me by years of serving on committees that vetted paper abstracts in order to organize conferences and by the trouble I've had, until recently, when it comes to pointing students to the essential reference works, landmark texts, important debates, and sponsoring institutions of Comics Studies. To do even that basic work, as an advisor, has been a challenge.

Exactly when did academics begin to show interest in comics, and under what terms? The question may defy a clean and easy answer, as scattered journal articles appeared as early as the 1920s, and a few isolated theses appeared in the '30s and beyond.[2] Use of comics as instructional aides, as Carol Tilley shows in this volume, may be nearly as old as the comic strip business, and became increasingly common (and a topic of professional reflection) in the '40s. The earliest period of *sustained* academic attention to comics—that is, the first noticeable wave of academic journal articles—dates from the 1940s and on into the '50s. This wave consists mainly of pedagogically and psychologically oriented research that frames comic books in terms of their supposed effects on young readers, literacy education, and the larger social fabric. Such articles were written in response to the greater controversy, or moral panic, inspired by comic books in the '40s. In general, these articles follow what we would now call a media effects model, or focus on the way comics supposedly interfere with or retard literacy education. They sometimes target the alleged psychological or social effects of comic books, anticipating or echoing the work of Fredric Wertham; they sometimes recommend ways to wean comic book readers onto better stuff. Either way, they are topical and often polemical, in that they conceive of comic books as a moral and political problem to be dealt with. Seldom do these early articles theorize about the comics form or about the process of reading comics as anything other than a source of trouble. There is little analysis of particular examples of comics, and scant acknowledgment that one could actually ask aesthetic questions about comics. There is no recognition of the possibility of artistic autonomy or the struggle for autonomy among comics creators and no recognition that comics might speak to important questions about word and image, writing and art. The popularity of comic books posed an educational, social, moral, and psychological quandary, seen in stark terms. Beyond that, comics were of little interest as readable texts. The fact that millions of readers of diverse ages did read them seems to have been dismissed as a mere embarrassment or symptom of cultural malaise.

After the censorious early 1950s, which included the adoption of the Comics Code of self-censorship by most of the American comic book industry, the comic book retreated to a strictly policed, and marginal, corner of American culture. Meanwhile, the newspaper comic strip (entrenched since the early 1900s) continued to be a respectable medium of adult as well as children's entertainment, but no longer drew the audience of millions that once followed newspaper serials from one tense day to the next. In the wake of commercial television's rapid rise in the United States, comic books appeared less important as a target of media effects research; rather, the impact of TV became the focus of research and anxiety (just as similar panics, and research programs, have since been spurred by pop records, video gaming, and cyberculture). Comics research in the American academy dwindled and did not show an uptick until the '70s.

But something important was happening in the meantime. Unregarded by academia, the comics hobby, meaning fandom and collectordom, transformed the comic book into an object of intense nostalgia. Comic book-oriented fanzines began to sprout in the early 1960s, among the best-remembered being *Xero*, *Alter Ego*, and *Comic Art*. By mid-decade bookshops specializing in old comics (providing a public venue for the shadow economy of fandom and anticipating the later surge in comic shops) were a known if rare phenomenon. The first comic book conventions happened around the same time, with New York's conventions of 1964–65 and the Detroit Triple Fan Fair in 1965 being the most often-cited breakthroughs (regarding the rapid growth of fandom circa 1964–1965, see Schelly, 1999, particularly Chapters 6 and 7). These trends gained media attention, and a number of newspaper articles in the mid-'60s incredulously reported on the collecting hobby. All these things were signs of the growing self-awareness if not clout of organized fandom. Jules Feiffer's watershed book of 1965, *The Great Comic Book Heroes*, signaled a self-conscious nostalgia for vintage comic books, superheroes in particular, and this same emotional investment by fans actively shaped the content of the new DC and Marvel superheroes of the so-called Silver Age revival. At the same time, nostalgic kitsch, now turned ironic and neon-tinted, inspired a merchandising blitz in the form of Batmania, sparked by the campy *Batman* TV series produced by William Dozier, a fad that blazed and faded with dizzying speed from 1966 to 1968. A garish Pop Art sensibility, associated with Lichtenstein and Warhol but also trumpeted by comic book publishers themselves, fueled the partial revival of the comic book, certainly of the superhero, and foretold the nostalgic turn of American popular culture in the Nixon era. Comic books reached the early '70s with a nostalgic investment in their own history, but, truth to tell, a shrinking audience, as new comic books no longer fetched enormous profits for anyone. Despite the brief upsurge of the '60s, and the appeals of nostalgia, the industry seemed to be living on borrowed time.

This may appear unrelated to Comics Studies in academia, but consider that in 1967–68 Ray Browne founded the Center (later the Department) of Popular Culture at Bowling Green State University, as well as the *Journal of Popular Culture*, and later co-founded, with Russell Nye, the Popular Culture Association (launched in 1971). Nye's book *The Unembarrassed Muse* (1970) devotes a chapter to comics and became a touchstone in popular culture studies. These developments helped make Comics Studies possible. They happened at the same time as the nostalgic revival of interest in old comics—and ideologically the two trends were intertwined.

As Joseph Witek long ago pointed out to me, popular culture studies, as pioneered by Nye, Browne, and company, rejected the grand pessimism of the Frankfurt School and other roughly mid-century Marxist theorists of mass culture (see Witek, 1999). Instead, the new popular culture studies took a frankly celebratory view. Browne (2001) saw popular culture as "the voice of democracy, speaking and acting, [and] the seedbed in which democracy grows" (these words have been reprinted often, and Browne often returned to them). He further claimed that popular culture is a "way of living we inherit, practice and modify as we please [...]. It is the dreams we dream…" (Browne and Browne, 2001, pp. 1–2).[3] This view contrasts sharply with pessimistic analyses of the culture industry as a top-down tool of mass deception or inculcator of false consciousness. If the Popular Culture Association rejected what it saw as the elitism of academia, particularly in the fields from which Nye and Browne came, American Studies and English, it also rejected the despairing assessment of mass culture by the most influential academics and public intellectuals who had bothered examining mass culture up to that point. Nye, Browne, and their colleagues celebrated the popular as the dream-life or bedrock of American democratic culture, a position embedded from the start in the institutions of the popular culture studies movement.

That movement began in the 1960s, during America's Vietnam War nightmare, an era of wrenching social division—and it doesn't take much to see the PCA's pro-popular culture stance, in those days, as a way of healing, rejoining together, and celebrating a democracy already felt to be in crisis. Depending on your outlook, this stance was either backward-looking, a rearguard defense of America's beleaguered democratic self-image, or forward-looking, rejecting the fusty elitism of a deaf and blind academy. That debate has not been settled. Either way, this movement laid the groundwork for the academic reconsideration of comics—at precisely the time when the comic book was being salvaged, and increasingly shaped, by nostalgic hobbyists and collectors.

In the 1970s, the growth in comic book specialty stores, catering to fans, coincided with the tentative emergence of the new academic paradigm for Comics Studies that emerged through the Popular Culture movement, a paradigm that diverged sharply from earlier studies of comics as a social problem and from Marxist critiques of the culture industries. As early as 1973, M. Thomas (Tom) Inge began championing comics scholarship at the PCA, and indeed even the first PCA program in 1971 paid some attention to cartooning and comics (that program is reprinted in Browne, 2002). However, the new paradigm crystallized when the Comics (or "Comic Art and Comics") Area of the PCA launched in 1975, the very year the Association began to organize itself officially *by* Area. The establishment of that Area marked an important institutional commitment: the PCA was the first recurring national academic conference to devote a division to comics scholarship. Its sibling, the *Journal of Popular Culture,* ran articles about comics as well, but it was the conference activity within PCA's Comics Area that established the first steady venue for academic Comics Studies. Much of the work in that community went unpublished, and Comics Studies remained fairly invisible academically outside of PCA, but the Association did sustain comics scholarship, establishing a beachhead. This relationship encouraged, yet may also have isolated and cordoned off, the field, given the qualms that some academics expressed about PCA as a non-juried, populist conference (and Browne's resistance to theorizing).[4] In any case, Comics Studies developed with a pronounced populist, or anti-elitist, inclination from the first.

Despite this activity, book-length scholarship on comics during this period—from the late '60s and on through the '70s—remained mostly popular rather than academic in nature, in the tradition of Martin Sheridan's *Comics and Their Creators* (1942) and Coulton Waugh's *The Comics* (1947). Take for example the seminal *All in Color for a Dime,* a nostalgically oriented anthology of essays edited by Dick Lupoff and Don Thompson (1970). Though published by Arlington House, *All in Color for a Dime* was built out from a series of articles that ran in the SF and comics fanzine *Xero,* edited by Dick and Pat Lupoff (with art direction by Bhob Stewart) starting in 1960. On a personal note, a paperback copy of this book, along with Jim Steranko's *History of Comics* (1970–72), and eventually Feiffer's *Great Comic Book Heroes* and Maurice Horn and company's *World Encyclopedia of Comics* (1976), became my first windows onto the history of the form. All these publications benefited from a general nostalgia for old comic books, a trend that went mainstream in the '70s. *All in Color for a Dime* moved from hardback to paperback in a year and was followed in 1973 by another Arlington House collection on comics edited by Lupoff and Thompson, *The Comic-Book Book.* Interestingly, Lupoff and Thompson's introduction to *The Comic-Book Book* notes not only the advent of the annual Overstreet Price Guide for collectible comic books but also, with mixed feelings, the academic research going on at Bowling Green. They call this research "pedantic," and in a line since echoed by many comics scholars writing in and out of academia, complain that these "self-consciously scholarly publications…lose sight of the fact that [comics are] intended to be entertaining" (p. 12). These remarks testify to an already tense relationship between academic and fan-based ways of knowing.

Academic comics research in the 1970s and early '80s was largely confined to popular culture studies on the PCA model. At the same time, outside of academia, the comics hobby produced (besides ever-updated price guides) ever-more fanzine and occasional book-length work documenting the history of comics, particularly American comic books. A paper trail of comics scholarship began to build up, though of variable quality and without firm institutional footing. Much of it went out of print in short order and became hard to find.

The landmark books from this period reveal an uneasy straddling of scholarly, populist, and commercial appeals. For example, in 1967 a group of French scholars from SOCERLID (a group whose name roughly translates to the Society for Comics Study and Research) mounted *Bande Dessinée et Figuration Narrative,* an exhibition on comics at the Musée des Arts Décoratifs in the Palais du Louvre. In conjunction with that exhibition, the Society assembled a book that was then republished in an English translation by Crown the following year as *A History of the Comic Strip.* This "society" traced its roots to the French comics scholarship of the early '60s and such organizations as the *Club des Bandes Dessinées,* which arose from fandom yet sought to encourage rigorous scholarship. These were not academic organizations but did set out to garner intellectual respectability: Club became Center, then birthed a Society, and so on (a pattern that recurred in the early '70s when the fanzine *Schtroumpf* renamed itself *Les Cahiers de la bande dessinée*). Consistent with this pattern, the Society's exhibition and book seek credibility by emphasizing organizer Pierre Couperie's academic credentials. As Ann Miller (2007) has pointed out, *Bande Dessinée et Figuration Narrative* treats comics as a mass medium deserving of attention precisely because it is "mass," rather than seeking to make elevated claims for comics as capital-A Art, although appreciation of the art remains an important strand (p. 23). Of course this book belongs to the larger trajectory of French Comics Studies, which included work informed by academic theories, semiotics in particular, well before American academics took up the charge; its English translation, however, went through multiple printings, reaching a generation of Anglophone fans. Though it is not an academic text, it does seek to model smart essayistic criticism. Tellingly, *A History of the Comic Strip* was a mass-market book, sold as a brainy yet popular study of a popular form.

The French vogue for comics appreciation appears to have been part of an international fascination with the form under the warrant of Pop Art. This period produced several books on comics that sought to bridge the scholarly and the popular, such as Perry and Aldridge's *Penguin Book of Comics*, published in Britain in 1967, and Reitberger and Fuchs's *Comics: Anatomy of a Mass Medium*, published in Germany in 1970 and translated into English in 1972. Both of these are extensively researched, and *Anatomy* in particular boasts an academic style informed by mass communications studies. Like the *Penguin*, though, and like the translated French *History* too, *Anatomy* was published in an oversized trade edition in what seems to have been a bid for popular appeal. All these books, despite their serious scholarship, were published by non-academic houses, in the same period as *All in Color for a Dime* and Steranko's *History*. Yet they are informed by academic media studies, not rooted solely in fandom.

A notable academically based American book put out by a trade publisher was Arthur Asa Berger's *The Comic-Stripped American* (in 1973), published first by Walker and Company, then by Penguin. Berger offers a reflection theory of comics on ideological terms, again from the standpoint of communication studies; his outlook is sociological. This too is a book with an academic mindset that, rhetorically, attempts to address dual or multiple audiences. Yet to me the most dramatic of the early contributions to academic comics study came out of art history: David Kunzle's monograph *The Early Comic Strip*, the first volume of his monumental two-volume *History of the Comic Strip*. Published in 1973 by the University of California, *The Early Comic Strip* locates the origins of the medium in 15th-century Europe and traces its international growth as a means of popular moral and political satire to the cusp of the 19th century. Kunzle too is interested in comics as a mass medium, but from an art-historical perspective influenced by a Marxist vision of social history. If he is far from taking the celebratory stance of the popular culture movement, Kunzle also stands apart from the reflection theory of communications scholars like Berger or Reitberger and Fuchs. The academic historiography of comics essentially begins with Kunzle, though his work is an outlier to the main growth of Comics Studies in the 1970s and '80s because it does not intersect with mass communication theory, American Studies, or English. (It would be some time, 20 years or more, before comics scholars in the academy would seriously engage Kunzle.)

During this period, Comics Studies had little to do with peer-reviewed journals. The first notable example of the new Comics Studies within an academic journal was a special section in an issue of the typically un-refereed *Journal of Popular Culture* in 1971. Said section, with Arthur Asa Berger leading off, included half a dozen articles about comics. This number of the *JPC* (5.1) appears to have been the first English-language academic journal issue devoted to comics since the *Journal of Educational Sociology* published two special issues on comic books back in the 1940s. It was followed in 1979 by another special section in *JPC* (12.4) titled "The Comics as Culture," edited by Tom Inge, a pioneering effort that includes seven articles, among them Bob Harvey's "The Aesthetics of the Comic Strip" (which Harvey later worked into his book *The Art of the Funnies*). If Berger and many of the other preceding books approached comics from the standpoint of mass communication, Inge and company approach comics from a Russell Nye sort of angle, with expertise in literature and folklore (very much in the PCA vein).

In short, academic comics research at first focused on media and American Studies, but arose in step with, or even a step behind, popular scholarship that emerged from fandom under the umbrella of Pop Art. This popular scholarship at its best was *essayistic* in Craig Fischer's sense: neither narrowly fannish nor strictly academic, but written by enthusiasts with a broad frame of reference (see Fischer, 2010, par. 13). Some of it was terrific (take for example Les Daniels's book *Comix: A History of Comic Books in America*, from 1971). This popular scholarship was largely independent of established institutions and was personal, quirky, even anarchic, rooted in a club mentality rather than the University. It influenced everything to come, much as the French *Cahiers du Cinéma*, though not itself academic, changed film criticism so profoundly that it influenced academic film studies from then on (the non-academic *Comics Journal* has shaped academic discourse on comics in a similar way). As academia began to take interest, media studies provided a strong impetus, as did, belatedly, English and American Studies through their offshoot, the PCA movement. Again, faultlines appeared early on between populist studies and the so-called pedantic or allegedly joyless academic studies, yet in some cases academically trained scholars produced brightly packaged popular books on the medium. The main institution to take up comics academically, the PCA, espoused a notably *anti*-academic or at least anti-elitist line. Ray Browne's official history of the Association was originally (1989) titled *Against Academia*, even though it was published by Bowling Green State (and the line of books that Ray and Pat Browne started there is now an imprint of the University of Wisconsin Press). The fear that academic study would "lose sight" of the joy of comics and an insistence that Comics Studies take place in an environment friendly to fans and creators as well as career scholars has strongly influenced the growth of Comics Studies ever since.

It bears repeating that comics scholars have been at work for a long time. Yet the sense of Comics Studies as a brand-new undertaking, a brave, foolhardy David against academia's institutional Goliath, still persists. Part of the mythology of Comics Studies (which perhaps performs an important identity function for us) is that we are quixotic rebels, outnumbered and misunderstood. This is the story we so often tell ourselves. But why, if Comics Studies has been around for so long? Despite more than 40 years of growing academic interest in comics, despite more than a quarter century of the Comics Arts Conference, despite more than 20 years of the International Comic Arts Forum, despite the Modern Language Association's Comics and Graphic Narratives Discussion Group, founded in 2009, it appears we still have institution-building to do.

I believe that, for Comics Studies to grow, the work of scattered scholars needs to be recognized as part of a common endeavor, so that our students can get beyond the radical uncertainty and wheel-rebuilding that comes with working in a nascent field. Furthermore, the anti-academic outlook that once propelled Comics Studies is something I believe we have outgrown. Comics Studies shouldn't be "against" academia, but rather should be seeking to show what academic ways of knowing can do when they are freed of narrow, self-preserving conventionalism and elitism. Comics Studies need not hold on to a self-marginalizing identity, and indeed that kind of identity denies our field and our students the resources needed to grow. I believe we must secure those resources and provide a more stable foundation for the future of this field. The trick is, how do we do this? How do we build a hub, when our field falls between the worlds and has a history of rejecting strict disciplinarity and seeking new forms of exploration?

If Comics Studies in the United States has had an anti-institutional bias, and has insisted that scholarship stay rooted in the experiences of fans and creators, in my view we're far beyond needing to worry about that now. Often I have heard comics scholars argue that we must avoid what has happened to other academicized fields, which, so the argument goes, have abandoned vernacular criticism, fans, and creators in favor of a blanched academicism that is too narrowly specialized, too "theoretical," or too hard to read. Comics Studies ought not to worry about this any longer. First off, the field is in no danger of losing sight of the joys of comics; our history teaches us otherwise. Comics Studies will continue to include and reflect upon the experiences of creators and fans, as it must. Historically, this is so deeply engrained in our field that we need not worry about becoming remote or out of touch. Second, I do not believe Comics Studies will recapitulate the development of other, already-established fields. Comics Studies will not follow the developmental path of any existing discipline, for we are living in a changed academic world; out of necessity, our work must ally with communities and projects outside of academia. Service learning, the open-access movement, digital culture, and other innovations are opening up opportunities for academics to reach out and connect to broader publics. In any case, Comics Studies is growing up in an environment of heightened self-awareness about method, discipline, and purpose (at a moment when other, longer-established fields are starting to question *their* identity). Comics scholarship is rising up at a moment of both opportunity and crisis within higher education, so its developmental story will not be like that of film studies, American Studies, or any other discipline. Historical analogies only explain so much; we are at a moment unlike any before.

The danger we do face, though, is that we will make the job we have to do harder for our students and advisees to come, because we don't have solid institutions in our field to which they can look for encouragement and guidance. Instead, we have a track record of making things up as we go. While institutions like the Popular Culture Association have created places where our independent studies can sometimes come together, they have stopped short of asking the necessary tough questions about how to develop the field further. We would benefit from more and better institution-building and self-reflection.

If Comics Studies has been slow to develop institutionally, the most important reason for that is one that actually gives me hope. Comics scholarship has no disciplinary status in the traditional sense, no cohesive, clearly demarcated, self-contained disciplinary identity—and I would argue that it cannot have one. That is, it cannot have a disciplinary identity that serves to isolate it and shore up its borders, for two reasons: one, because the heterogeneous nature of comics itself means that, in practice, comics study has to be at the intersection of various disciplines (art history, communication, literature, design, and so forth); and, two, because this multidisciplinary nature of comics represents, in principle, *a challenge to the very idea of disciplinarity as the academy is used to practicing it.* Comics Studies forcefully reminds us that the disciplines cannot be discrete and self-contained; in effect, our field defies or at least seriously questions the compartmentalizing of knowledge that occurs within academia. Inevitably, Comics Studies will bring together various disciplines and methodologies in a workspace that is at least multidisciplinary, and, we hope, truly and deliberately *inter*disciplinary. Comics Studies can foster collaboration across disciplinary and program boundaries.

What happens when your object of study compels you to work the boundaries, margins, and overlaps between the disciplines? What *can* happen? On what grounds can we build departments, communities, programs—that demand resources—in a higher education system already in crisis, a system that has sometimes called for interdisciplinarity but seldom fostered it? The institutional life of Comics Studies going forward will depend on our ability to answer these questions: to step back far enough to see where our individual disciplines can work together, and what they can contribute to a truly interdisciplinary project of knowledge-making. Comics Studies can occupy a special place in the ecology of knowledge—a place that is no place, if you like, or many, many places. That is a complex mission, one that may complicate our institution-building, but it is an exciting one, at the intersection of fields and cultures, the crossroads of disciplines. Comics Studies can occupy such a place, if we have an honest dialogue about the history of our field. We have to learn ways to discuss and value our differences in Comics Studies and yet still band together to build that hub.

Being in Comics Studies—in my case, being an English professor in Comics Studies—means being simultaneously on the inside and the outside. My connections with scholars outside of English, I believe, have made me a better comics scholar *and* a better English professor. Of course I advise up-and-coming comics scholars to find ways to make comics answer core questions in their home disciplines; that is solid career advice, after all, and a way of bringing comics scholars from the margins to the center. But the joy of Comics Studies, for me, is partly in the way it has enabled me to pose those disciplinary questions from outside as well as within. In other words, comics has profoundly affected the way I've learned to see my discipline, and comics is my passport to working across disciplines. It has shaped how I see my role as an academic citizen.

Obviously, there is a contradiction between celebrating Comics Studies as an anti-discipline and at the same time seeking to build an institutional place for it. I have inhabited that contradiction for some time. Many of us have. In an effort to resolve it, I and many colleagues have worked together to found the Comics Studies Society, a professional association and learned society launched in 2014 and now supported by hundreds of members from diverse countries and disciplines. This society is not exclusively academic, but does have the professional needs of academics at its heart. Naturally I do not believe academics have a monopoly on useful knowledge (any survey of the history of our field would tell us otherwise), but I do believe that academic comics research needs and deserves greater institutional resources. We need more degree programs, more interdisciplinary programs, and more concerted discussion of practice. We need a refereed journal of record. We need resources for young scholars, for teachers and job-seekers. We need awards and recognitions. In short, we need the resources, traditions, and service opportunities that come with an acknowledged discipline. To build such resources requires, ironically, recognizing comics as an anti-discipline that refuses boundaries and pigeonholes. For comics scholarship in the academy to be something other than a prescription for lifelong independent study, we need to step back, reflect on the historically divided and heterogeneous nature of this field, understand our differences, and build partnerships despite, or rather because of, those differences. We need resources, and to build them we must get past the anti-academic mindset and lay claim to an actual academic identity, one with pluralism and interdisciplinarity at its core.

If Comics Studies, which has grown so spectacularly in recent years, is to survive and thrive during this time of academic crisis, it will be because we have found a way to inhabit simultaneously a space of freedom, of anti-disciplinarity, and yet of responsibility too. It will be because we have found, or rather built, a place.

Notes

1 I have taken up this issue of Comics Studies versus disciplinarity on other occasions, notably in the ejournal Transatlantica (2010) and in a plenary talk at the Rocky Mountain Conference on Comics and Graphic Novels, Denver, Colorado, in June 2014, where the present piece began to take shape. Many thanks to William Kuskin for inspiring and guiding the early revisions of this essay.

2 Tracing the rise of Comics Studies in academia remains a challenge, and I have found myself grasping at, if not straws, then the littlest clues, which come here and there, often from unexpected sources. White and Abel, 1963, approaching comics from a mass communications standpoint, declare that serious "analytic" study of the comics began in "the early 1920s" (p. 293), and offer an extensive bibliography divided into, essentially, books, professional journals, general periodicals, and theses. It contains a number of sources prior to 1940 (though these are often brief and journalistic in nature). The earliest thesis it identifies dates to 1939. Gene Kannenberg, Jr.'s expansive list of "Comics-Related Dissertations & Theses," at ComicsResearch.org, funnels together many sources and shows the richness of the field, though it finds no examples before the 1940s and very few examples from the '40s and '50s. Sol Davidson's *Culture and the Comic Strips* (NYU, 1959) has been cited as the first Ph.D. thesis on the medium (see Davidson, 2003). More recently, scholars such as Brad Ricca and Sean Howe (Ricca, 2014) and Carol Tilley (2016) have uncovered pioneering Master's theses from the '40s. Beyond theses, the backstory of Comics Studies is diffuse and hard to track. I recommend the "Pioneers of Comic Art Scholarship" series, edited by John A. Lent for the *International Journal of Comic Art*, a series that offers revealing personal accounts of what it was like to work in Comics Studies before the field had a name; see in particular *IJOCA* 5.1 (Spring 2003), 5.2 (Fall 2003), and 7.2 (Fall 2005). Speaking personally, I cannot thank enough Michael Rhode and John Bullough's online Comics Research Bibliography (1996–2011) and the massive series of print bibliographies compiled by John Lent (Greenwood Press, four vols., 1994–1996, and Praeger, six vols., 2003–2006). Lent's volumes together make up an astounding record of international comics scholarship. The global bibliography that comprises *IJOCA* 11.3 (Winter 2009), compiled by Rhode and Lent, extends that work even further. See Rhode, 2007, to put this wealth of bibliographic work into context.

3 This passage, the most quoted in Ray Browne's work, appears in numerous biographies and tributes. I have drawn it from the introduction to Ray Browne and Pat Browne's edited reference work, *The Guide to United States Popular Culture* (2001). It also occurs in, e.g., the Ray and Pat Browne-authored introduction to Browne, 2005; and, in slightly changed form, in the posthumous Browne and Urish, 2011. I first encountered the passage (unsourced) in Gary Hoppenstand's profile of Ray and Pat Browne in Browne and Marsden, 1999, p. 61.

4 Browne's resistance to what he called "fads" in theory colors a great deal of his writing about academia, but is perhaps most clearly expressed in his 1995 essay, "The Theory-Methodology Complex: The Critics' Jabberwock," which likens "structuralism," "post-modernism," and other talked-about theoretical perspectives to a devious siren song that few in popular culture studies "have fallen for." These "highly esoteric and irrelevant theories," Browne argues, make sense

to "no one but academics" (145). In general, Browne treats the word *academics*, when used in the plural to describe his profession, as a pejorative; his writings are peppered with characterizations of the academic class as narrow, elitist, unthinkingly devoted to the status quo, and prone to rarefied, hair-splitting debates, yet also flighty and faddish. When I read these passages, I feel as if I am hearing the echoes of an old and bitter quarrel – one that has perhaps also fed into elitist dismissals of the PCA. That Browne fought that fight is one of the reasons I am able to write these words at all today, though what I am recommending is that we rethink the terms of the fight.

Bibliography

Berger, A. (1973) *The Comic-Stripped American*, New York: Walker and Company.
Browne, R.B. (1995) 'The theory-methodology complex: the critics' jabberwock', *Journal of Popular Culture*, 29 (2): 143–56.
Browne, R.B. (ed.) (2002) *Mission Underway: the history of the Popular Culture Association / American Culture Association and the Popular Culture Movement 1967–2001*, Bowling Green, OH: Popular Culture Association/American Culture Association. Rev. and updated ed. of Browne, R.B. (ed.) (1989), *Against Academia: the history of the Popular Culture Association / American Culture Association and the Popular Culture Movement 1967–2001*, Bowling Green, OH: Bowling Green State University Popular Press.
Browne, R.B. (2005) *Profiles of Popular Culture: a reader*, Madison: University of Wisconsin Press.
Browne, R.B., and Browne, P. (eds.) (2001) *The Guide to United States Popular Culture*, Bowling Green, OH: Bowling Green State University Popular Press.
Browne, R.B., and Marsden, M.T. (eds.) (1999) *Pioneers in Popular Culture Studies*, Bowling Green, OH: Bowling Green State University Popular Press.
Browne, R.B., and Urish, B. (2011) 'On redefining cultural studies', *Journal of American Culture*, 34 (1): 13–15.
Couperie, P. and Horn, M. et al. (1968) *A History of the Comic Strip*, trans. E. Hennesy, from *Bande Dessinée et Figuration Narrative* (1967), New York: Crown.
Daniels, L. (1971) *Comix: a history of comic books in America*, New York: Bonanza.
Davidson, S. (2003) 'Culture & the comic strips', *International Journal of Comic Art*, 5 (2): 233–40.
Feiffer, J. (1965) *The Great Comic Book Heroes*, New York: Bonanza.
Fischer. C. (2010) 'Worlds within worlds: audiences, jargon, and North American comics discourse', *Transatlantica: revue d'études américaines.* [Online] 28 September. [Accessed 17 August 2016].
Harvey, R. (1994) *The Art of the Funnies: an aesthetic history*, Jackson: University Press of Mississippi.
Hatfield, C. (2010) 'Indiscipline, or, the condition of Comics Studies', *Transatlantica: revue d'études américaines.* [Online] 27 September. [Accessed 17 August 2016].
Horn, M. (ed.) (1976) *The World Encyclopedia of Comics*, New York: Chelsea House.
Inge, M.T. (ed.) (1979) 'The comics as culture', Spec. section of *Journal of Popular Culture*, 12 (4): 630–754.
Kannenberg, G. (2013) 'Comics-related dissertations & theses', *ComicsResearch.org* [Online] Last updated 7 July, 2013. [Accessed 17 August 2016].
Kunzle, D. (1973) *The Early Comic Strip*. Vol. One of *The History of the Comic Strip*, Berkeley: University of California.
Lent, J. (comp.) (1994–1996) *Bibliographies and Indexes in Popular Culture. Nos. 3, 4, 5, and 7*, Westport, CT: Greenwood.
Lent, J. (comp.) (2003–2006) *Bibliographies and Indexes in Popular Culture. Nos. 10, 11, 12, 13, and 14*, Westport, CT: Praeger.
Lent, J. (ed.) (2003–2005) 'Pioneers of comic art scholarship series', *International Journal of Comic Art*.
Lupoff, D. and Thompson, D. (eds.). (1970) *All in Color for a Dime*, New Rochelle, NY: Arlington House.
Lupoff, D. and Thompson, D. (eds.). (1973) *The Comic-Book Book*, New Rochelle, NY: Arlington House.

Miller, A. (2007) *Reading bandes dessinée: critical approaches to French-language comic strip,* Bristol, UK: Intellect.
Nye, R. (1970) *The Unembarrassed Muse: the popular arts in America,* New York: Dial Press.
Perry, G. and Aldridge, A. (1971) *The Penguin Book of Comics,* Harmondsworth, UK: Penguin.
Reitberger, R. and Fuchs, W. (1972) *Comics: anatomy of a mass medium,* trans. from *Comics: Anatomie eines Massenmediums* (1970), Boston: Little, Brown.
Rhode, M. (2007) 'John A. Lent's comic art bibliographies: an appreciation'. *International Journal of Comic Art,* 9 (1): 707–709.
Rhode, M. and Bullough, J. (comp.) (1996–2011) *Comics Research Bibliography.* [Online] Last major update Nov. 2009. [Accessed: 17 Aug. 2016].
Rhode, M. and Lent, J. (2009) 'Comic art, 2005–2009: a global bibliography', Spec. issue of *International Journal of Comic Art,* 11 (3).
Ricca, B. (2014) 'Unassuming barber shop: the 1st American comics scholar was a Superman artist', *The Beat: The News Blog of Comics Culture.* [Online] 14 November. [Accessed 17 August 2016].
Schelly, B. (1999) *The Golden Age of Comic Fandom.* Rev. edn, Seattle: Hamster Press.
Sheridan, M. (1942) *Comics and Their Creators,* Boston: Hale, Cushman & Flint.
Steranko, J. (1970–1972) *The Steranko History of Comics.* Two vols, Reading, PA: Supergraphics.
Tilley, C. (2016) 'Unbalanced production: the comics business in the 1940s', *The Beat: The News Blog of Comics Culture.* [Online] 1 March. [Accessed 17 August 2016].
Waugh, C. (1947) *The Comics,* New York: MacMillan.
White, D.M. and Abel, R.H. (eds.) (1963) *The Funnies: an American idiom,* London: Free Press of Glencoe.
Witek, J. (1999) 'Comic criticism in the United States: a brief historical survey'. *International Journal of Comic Art,* 1 (1): 4–16.

PREFACE
Matthew J. Smith and Randy Duncan

As an undergraduate at Indiana University in the early 1970s, Michael Uslan had an unorthodox idea: to teach a class about the comics he had grown up with and loved. Although his proposal was initially met with skepticism from the university officials reviewing it, once approved the course received a good deal of attention, both from the students who wanted to take it and the media who were fascinated by its existence. Stories about his course drew attention from media outlets ranging from the Associated Press to *Playboy* magazine. Uslan did not remain in academia, instead charting a course that would lead to success in Hollywood as a producer on virtually every Batman film adaptation since director Tim Burton's 1989 blockbuster *Batman* to director Christopher Nolan's Academy Award winning Dark Knight Trilogy and beyond.

With the contemporary media coverage of the course, his popular autobiography (*The Boy Who Loved Batman*), and his many convention appearances, Michael Uslan may be the most famous comics teacher, but he was by no means alone in those early days. It was also in 1972 that Sonia Maria Bibe Luyten developed the Comics Publishing course at Universidade de São Paulo. Luyten left the university in 1984, but the course is still taught there to this day (see Waldomiro Vergueiro's essay). It was the year before that Université Paris-Sorbonne hired Francis Laccassin to teach a course on the history and aesthetics of comics as the self-styled chaire d'histoire de la bande dessinée (see Jeremy Larance's chapter on Organizations). It was in 1967 that Arthur Asa Berger wrote to editor Stan Lee hoping to get free sets of Marvel comics for the course, The Comic Strip (and Book) and Society, he was attempting to develop at San Francisco State College (Stan Lee Archives). Berger was one of at least a dozen teachers and professors who contacted Lee in the late 1960s or early 1970s asking for free comics they could use in their classrooms (see Robert Weiner's chapter on Educating about Comics). Unfortunately, not every early contributor to Comics Studies will be mentioned in this book.

Comics Studies is an academic field maturing into its own, but one previously bereft of any authoritative account of its own history. *The Secret Origins of Comics Studies* is an in-depth study of the individuals and institutions that have created and shaped the field of

Comics Studies over the past 75 years. We believe that Comics Studies is overdue for a text that documents the emergence of our field.

Rather than attempt a single narrative of the field's emergence and development, we've elected to incorporate multiple voices in recounting how the endeavor began, welcoming the contributions of some of the leading contemporary scholars. Reading each contribution to this anthology should be like examining a facet of a gem, giving a different perspective to a structure that is, ultimately, united in the common enterprise that has become Comics Studies.

Many comics scholars will first engage with this book by turning to the index and looking for their names. If you are reading this you have probably already visited the index. It is inevitable that some people for whom we have great admiration will feel slighted. Each essay writer had to make decisions about which ideas, authors, or events to emphasize, but they also had to deal with editorial restrictions and natural barriers (language and availability).

Because the primary purpose of this work is to explore the foundations of Comics Studies rather than the recent trends, just a few years hence this work will seem to have glaring omissions. Some of the leading contemporary scholars (Bart Beaty, Jean-Paul Gabilliet, Jeet Heer, Richard Scully, Anne Magnussen, Thierry Smolderen, etc.) are scarcely mentioned, if at all. Some approaches that have been the subject of recent books—the representation of disabilities in comics, the materiality of comics—received only sidebars.

The next edition of this book, or some other work that takes up the task, will have a major essay on other perspectives. For example, a number of monographs and anthologies that examine issues of identity and representation in comics are in progress, and some of them will be published before this book goes to press.

Another emerging approach that will warrant attention is data-driven research. Neil Cohn contends that most scholarship about the structure and functions of the comics art form has been based on speculation rather than hard evidence, and he is a strong advocate for systematically gathering data to support claims. Cohn has initiated a number of ongoing research projects that range from measuring physiological reactions of people reading comics to cataloguing the linguistic content of large numbers of comics. The *What Were Comics?* project spearhead by Bart Beaty, Benjamin Woo, and Nick Sousanis challenges the traditional comics historiography that focuses on the exceptional and seeks to create a data-driven history of the typical American comic book. Carol Tilley, Kathryn La Barre, and John Walsh are developing a digital Comic Book Reader Archive that will allow research about comics readership and fandom to be based on big data gleaned from letter columns, fanzines, convention records, etc.

The language barrier has limited the scope of a number of essays. Comics scholarship produced in Japan could have figured into a variety of the essays, but little of this work has been translated and few of the contributors to this volume read Japanese. This is why we asked Nicholas Theisen to write an essay on manga scholarship. Portuguese presents another barrier. Brazilian comics historians and theorists have been actively publishing since 1970, yet they are seldom mentioned in the essays that follow. There are many multilingual comics scholars, but few of them read Portuguese.

In the final sidebar of this volume Pascal Lefèvre urges comics scholars to cross borders. He wants us to occasionally leave our "islands" of methodology or genre, but more importantly he wants us to cross (at least with Skype if not airplanes) international borders. He calls for more comparative research to be undertaken collaboratively by international teams. We hope that this book will facilitate such collaborations.

The contributions are organized according to four broad themes: the educators, the historians, the theorists, and the institutions. Within each thematic unit are several chapters that explore more specific areas within the field. Although this approach has the tendency to produce some overlap, we believe it's an exciting means to think about the interconnected ways in which the interdisciplinary movement has developed. For instance, even though the work of Donald Ault factors into the development of education, he also helped establish some of the foundational institutions in the field, including the online journal, *ImageText*.

In addition to the detailed accounts provided by our featured contributors, we are also fortunate to have brief contributions by some of the pioneers in the field. Their short essays provide perspective in looking back at what transpired in the formation of our field and look ahead to what they foresee for its growth. We are honored to have a few of those foundational figures help us to think about how we got to this point and the work that needs to be done, even as we celebrate the work that they have accomplished.

There are now hundreds of academics who self-identify as comics scholars. We hope that *The Secret Origins of Comics Studies* is a useful work for any comics scholar undertaking a review of the literature and an indispensable tool for students seeking to justify a thesis or dissertation on comics. And as Comics Studies continues to grow, we hope that those who come after us can appreciate the foundation laid before them by looking back to the ideas and institutions shaped by our predecessors.

Special thanks to David Stoddard of Henderson State University, who executed the cover concept, honoring the first issue of the comic book *Secret Origins* (1961), featuring some of the pioneering figures in Comics Studies: (left-to-right, top tier) John Lent and M. Thomas Inge, Maurice Horn and Pierre Couperie, Pascal Lefèvre, (middle tier) Trina Robbins, David Kunzle, (bottom tier) Waldomiro Vergueiro, Yoshihiro Yonezawa, Reinhold Reitberger and Wolfgang J. Fuchs. Our thanks to the pioneers who supplied reference photographs and to Kim Munson and Jaqueline Berndt for their help in securing others.

Bibliography

Berger, A.A. (1967) Letter to Stan Lee. Stan Lee Archives, American Heritage Center, University of Wyoming.

Uslan, M.E. (2011) *The Boy who Loved Batman: A Memoir,* San Francisco: Chronicle Books.

PART 1
The Educators

1

EDUCATING WITH COMICS

Carol L. Tilley

Comics have been part of classrooms for at least a century. In the early 20th century, for instance, when tuberculosis was still a prominent health threat in the United States, a writer in the *Journal of Education* proposed that having students draw comics to highlight hygienic practices related to the disease was a useful instructional strategy (Routzahn, 1910). Around the same time, an English teacher at Columbia Teachers College's Horace Mann School reflected on an instructional unit on newspapers and other periodicals. One group of students, he wrote, delivered a "highly interesting reflectoscope talk on cartoons" (Abbott, 1913, p. 423). A history teacher in Baltimore praised the use of comics in making history vital to students. He wrote, "a cartoon is, so to speak, a double exposure. It is a picture, not only of an individual, but of a public" (Millspaugh, 1914, p. 682).

This early interest in using comics as instructional aides is unsurprising. In the years after the Civil War in the United States, editorial and political cartooning flourished in popular periodicals and newspapers. In the first decade of the 20th century, newspapers' pages swelled with cartoons and the new comic strips, incurring wide readership. These developments in the comics medium coincided with an interest in the new Progressive educational techniques of child-centered instruction, active learning, and the broader use of visual aids and technologies such as comics and reflectoscope, an early opaque projector (cf. Cremin, 1961, Saettler, 2004). The result was a burgeoning interest in bringing comics into educational settings.

This chapter surveys efforts—some systematic, others more idiosyncratic—to infuse comics into teaching and learning. It will emphasize cartooning in all of its forms, unlike McCloud's *Understanding Comics* (1994), which excludes single-panel editorial and gag cartoons from comics' sphere. Furthermore, the chapter will focus on efforts to integrate comics in primary and secondary-level teaching and learning in the United States during roughly the first half of the 20th century. Rather than focus exclusively on schools, this chapter will include libraries, museums, and similar sites of informal learning for young people. Further, it extends previous work by Nyberg (2002, 2010), Thomas (2011), Tilley (2013), and Tilley and Weiner (2016).

The Pioneers: Comics as Educational Tools before 1940

The examples noted in this chapter's introduction describe some of the earliest documented uses of comics in primary and secondary school classrooms, but they are not the only ones. Of the early attempts to integrate comics into classrooms, perhaps none was as widespread or as widely known as *Texas History Movies*. The brainchild of *Dallas Morning News*' managing editor E. B. Doran, *Texas* ran Monday through Friday during the school years 1926–1927 and 1927–1928. Dallas school superintendent Dr. J. F. Kimball reportedly gave his blessing to the project and came up with the name. Through more than 400 strips, *Texas* showcased the state's history from the 16th through the 19th century. During the next several decades, these strips were collected into published volumes and distributed for use in schools throughout the state. Despite racial stereotyping common in comics of this era and an Anglo-centric focus, *Texas* seemed to be popular with teachers and students. Pulitzer Prize-winning writer Larry McMurtry recalled, "*Texas History Movies*…stopped two generations of Texas public school students dead in their tracks where history is concerned…The effect, not to mention the irreverence, of those comics would be hard to overstate" (2004, pp. 92–93).

In contrast to the widespread use of *Texas History Movie*, most other classroom applications of comics were modest and singular. Published editorial cartoons made their way into social studies classes, but at least one teacher proposed that students also draw their own cartoons to connect with current and historical events; in providing guidance to teachers who wished to emulate his practice, he encouraged them to emphasize "the idea involved and not the artistry of the production" (Wilson, 1928, p. 197). In language arts classes, comics provided opportunities for active learning. For instance, students presented on current events as expressed in editorial cartoons (Russell, 1914), gathered examples of grammar errors in comic strips and then created comics explaining preferred usage (Trovillion and Renard, 1917), and created comics for a class newspaper (Burkholder, 1914). In a secondary school English class in Athens, Ohio, students engaged in a variety of projects to help them understand *Treasure Island*. According to the teacher, one of the projects was "a booklet of the story done in pen pictures, with short sentences explaining each. The order was that of the comic strips minus the conversation" (Bryant, 1932, p. 139). Interestingly, the format Bryant described is similar to the one adopted by the artists who serialized *Treasure Island* in Malcolm Wheeler-Nicholson's National Comics publications in the mid-1930s (cf. Tilley, 2013a).

It is quite likely that comics found their way into more classrooms than one might ascertain from reports by teachers. The National Council of Teachers of English (NCTE), the key organization representing language arts teachers at primary, secondary, and collegiate levels, published its first national curriculum document in 1935. As with many standards documents, one might argue that *An Experience Curriculum in English* (Hatfield, 1935), which embodied more than five years of work, articulated current practices as much as it set expectations for teaching and learning. The NCTE document included topics and activities that integrated more traditional language arts experiences with activities representing the everyday worlds of younger students. As detailed in Tilley (2013b), *An Experience Curriculum* encouraged teachers to discuss comic strips as part of lessons on taste discrimination and humor. It also urged teachers to use then-contemporary mass media such as newspapers in the classroom, heightening the likelihood of school-based encounters with comics.

Through clubs and convocations, schools helped young people engage with comics outside of formal learning activities. For instance, junior high students in Rochester,

New York, in the 1920s could join more than five-dozen clubs (Sheehan, 1921). One of these clubs was Cartooning, which had a membership cap of 25 students and required prospective members to submit work samples for approval by the club's director. A similar club was open to students at Ambridge Junior High School in Pennsylvania (Grose, 1929), and Cartooning was one of the representative high school clubs mentioned in an educational guidance text (Hill and Mosher, 1931). In at least one school, a cartoonist was invited to speak about his work: Herbert Johnson, a conservative political cartoonist with the *Saturday Evening Post*, spoke to students about newspaper and magazine comics during a convocation at the McKinley Preparatory School in Lincoln, Nebraska (Pyrtle, 1915).

Museums and libraries capitalized on children's interests in comics to fulfill their goals for outreach and instruction. For instance, during the last half of the 1930s, the Cleveland Museum of Art began a cartooning club—for boys only—for children of members (Munro, 1936). In Chicago, the Art Institute offered occasional lectures on cartooning aimed at young people such as the one advertised for October 1927 (Bulletin, 1927). Chicago's Field Museum of Natural History created a comic strip story, Joe Elk, to go along with one of its exhibits of North American Mounds Dwellers. It justified its decision by pointing to the comic strip-like Mixtec Codexes from the 15th century that shared the story of Eight Deer Jaguar Claw (Winn, 1944). At least one library, the Enoch Pratt Free Library in Baltimore, intended to use comic strips commissioned from cartoonist Richard Yardley of the Baltimore Sun, to help educate younger library users about library practices (Wheeler, 1935).

A handful of educational researchers studied the instructional value of comics during these years. One of them, Laurance Shaffer (1930), a doctoral candidate at Columbia's Teachers College, studied more than a thousand children in grades four through twelve to understand how young people developed in their abilities to understand editorial cartoons. He found that the period of greatest development occurs in junior high-aged students and that the facility to interpret cartoons requires knowledge and skill just as progress in reading and mathematics does. In his conclusion, he recommended that cartoons be used in elementary school classrooms. A similar study by Lena Roberts Smith (1940) showed that there seems to be an association between interpretative abilities and intelligence, but that children regardless of ability would benefit from direct instruction in interpreting cartoons. Furthermore, she argued that "subject materials which may appear dull might be made to appear just a little brighter by the proper use of cartoons" (Smith, 1940, p. 67). Another researcher, Lewis Smith Jr. (1938) examined the literary merit of comic strips such as *The Gumps* and *Tarzan*. Using his analytic framework that included emotional richness and characterization, Smith determined that existing strips as a whole failed to meet the criteria of "literature." Still, he proposed that "the construction of a comic dealing with child experience and utilizing the appeals of children on a literary level would result in the placing of literature in the hands of more children. Comics could become one of the most effective non-school educational agencies" (Smith, 1938, p. 94). This early and eclectic enthusiasm for comics, though, gave way to more focused attempts.

The Legitimizers: Comics in Classrooms during the 1940s and 1950s

Comics publishers—in particular, National (DC) Comics and its sometimes affiliate All-American Comics—helped to make comics a more legitimate tool for teaching and learning. As Tilley (2013a) details, National Comics, under the direction of its founding publisher Malcolm Wheeler-Nicholson, included a number of serialized classics such as *A Tale of Two Cities* and *Ivanhoe* in the pages of its general comics magazines throughout the mid- and late-1930s. National also experimented with reviews of juvenile books and illustrated poems. In the early 1940s, National and All-American Comics, the latter helmed by M. C. Gaines, regularized juvenile book reviews, printing a contribution from Josette Frank of the Child Study Association of America in the pages of nearly every issue between 1941 and 1945. National also worked with libraries to sponsor the "Superman Good Reading" project, which used the superhero to recommend books for young readers. Although none of their endeavors lasted more than a few years, both Wheeler-Nicholson and Gaines seemed to understand the educative and communicative potential of comics. Gaines in particular strived to make comics tools for learning through his later Educational Comics (EC, which became Entertaining Comics a few years after his death) line of *Picture Stories from the Bible* and similar titles.

More than publishers' efforts, the sheer force that was comic books in the mid-20th century United States demanded that educators pay attention. The 1930s invention of comic books coincided with young people's growing economic power and leisure time, quickly making this new format a publishing phenomenon that could not be ignored. Only two years after Superman's debut in *Action Comics*, comic book sales outstripped traditional children's books by a five to one margin (Bechtel, 1941), made all the more impressive by considering comics' 10-cent cover price in comparison to the typical children's hardcover that might cost two dollars. Comic books' popularity astounded educators and educational researchers, and while many of them responded to the new format with fear and suspicion (cf. Tilley, 2007), some resolved to understand how this format might be usefully integrated into teaching and learning.

Foreign language instructors found easy purchase in comics of all kinds. A high school Spanish language instructor, for instance, reported ordering a variety of comics from Mexico, Venezuela, Cuba, Argentina, and Spain to supplement his students' regular texts. He reported that students' oral fluency had improved since reading comics, and that these books "broaden the range of pupils' vocabularies and deepen their knowledge of structure, thus increasing reading comprehension" (Vacca, 1959, p. 291). Plus, he reported that their attitudes toward the class and language improved. In another instance, a teacher from the New Mexico Military Institute enlisted the school's librarian for assistance in ordering Spanish-language Sunday newspapers so he could provide students with comics and other high-interest materials for reading (Hespelt and Williams, 1943, p. 454). Newspaper comics also found their way into college-level language classes. At the University of Cincinnati, Spanish students acted out the dialogues from the comics, taking the roles of various characters (Hutchings, 1946), while at Baldwin-Wallace College, students offered extemporaneous descriptions of action in nearly wordless comic strips like *Henry* (Sinnema, 1957).

NCTE's *Experience Curriculum* continued to hold sway during these decades, making comics a continued feature of language arts classes. Often in English and similar classes, teachers made comics the center of discussions on reading taste and aesthetic appeal, hoping to persuade impressionable and dedicated comics fans to look elsewhere for their recreational reading. The approaches differed: for example, junior high students in Pennsylvania conducted surveys, held discussions, and even created their own comic strips, all in an effort to extend their reading beyond comic books (Something Better, 1952), while elementary school students in California investigated the folkloric and literary origins of characters like

Superman, in hopes that those source texts might have greater appeal (*Santa Barbara,* 1942). A veteran high school teacher in Arizona, working from the decidedly *Experience Curriculum* strategy "to begin with the child's interests" (Kinneman, 1943, p. 331), built a unit around comics that provided opportunities for discussion, analysis of appeals, and even the production of a multi-part radio program for parents and community members on the role of comics in young people's lives. In one Buffalo, New York, classroom, the teacher even encouraged her fifth graders to read comics such as *True Comics* and *Classics Illustrated* for the purpose of preparing oral reports. These students presented their reports to an assembly of several classes, and the teacher noted that her colleagues "were impressed with the children's dramatic appeal in their manner of speaking. This apparently reflected the appealing style of the comics. Possibly the writers of children's texts may do well to study the style of the comics" (Denecke, 1945, p. 8).

Perhaps the most likely avenue for comics to enter classrooms during these years was as texts for remedial readers. Contemporary reading textbooks such as Adams, Gray, and Reese's (1949) *Teaching Children to Read* and McCullough, Strang, and Traxler's (1955) *Problems in the Improvement of Reading,* while not promoting the wholesale and indiscriminate use of comics in reading, saw value in meeting students at their current levels *even* if that meant using comics. Albert Harris, the author of *How to Increase Reading Ability* (1947), was more keen on comics: "Anything to which children respond as enthusiastically as they do to comic books must have educational values that can be developed" (p. 433). Similarly, in an article focused on specific resources for working with remedial readers at the high school level, education professor Glenn Blair (1955) specifically highlighted *Classics Illustrated* and similar comics as having "tremendous appeal" and being of "high caliber" (p. 20). Articles by school librarians Vera Elder (1947) and Merrill Bishop (1950) also saw some value in using comics as tools for connecting with disaffected readers. Classroom innovators with comics would benefit from well-placed champions for the medium.

The Champions: Advocating for the Educational Value of Comics

Trained at the University of Chicago as a sociologist and specializing in urban areas, Harvey Zorbaugh seems perhaps an unlikely person to have become one of the chief advocates for comics as educational tools. After receiving his doctorate in the late 1920s, Zorbaugh took a faculty position in the recently formed Department of Educational Sociology (DES) at New York University (NYU), where he developed an interest in the social adjustment of intellectually precocious children. Other than having had children who grew up alongside comics in the 1930s, Zorbaugh's motivation to champion comics is unclear. Yet in both 1944 and 1949, Zorbaugh dedicated full issues of the *Journal of Educational Sociology* to comics.

The 1944 issue is most salient here, as it specifically focused on comics as an educational medium and featured articles by Child Study Association of America reading consultant Josette Frank, psychiatrist Lauretta Bender, and others. Those readers expecting hard-hitting research on comics would be disappointed in the issue's offerings: most of the contributions are catalogs of examples, rather than empirical research, and none of the articles is critical of comics to any meaningful extent. The lack of criticism is not unexpected, as most of the contributors had formal ties to mainstream comics publishers. For instance, Frank, Bender, and W. W. D. Sones were on the editorial advisory board of National

Comics (DC), while Zorbaugh and Sidonie Gruenberg held similar positions at Fawcett Comics. Although these affiliations are not obvious in the *Journal*, the members of the editorial advisory boards were prominently listed in the comics.

Three pieces in this *Journal* issue touch directly on the role of comics in teaching and learning. One by W. W. D. Sones (1944), a former high school science teacher turned college education professor, offered an overview of how comics had been applied in various instructional settings. As such, he touched on initiatives such as the *Superman Work Book*, which was developed jointly between the character's publisher and a Massachusetts teacher in an attempt to make grammar and language study more enjoyable. Sones also provided a brief synopsis of a study he had undertaken on reading comprehension and comics. Although he provided few details, Sones asserted that the images in comics contributed to higher comprehension among less skilled readers. A second came from Zorbaugh (1944) himself. This article was wide-ranging, befitting his training as a descriptive sociologist, and described readership and fandom, comics integration in contemporary society and culture, and the medium's educational potential. Reading researcher Paul Witty (1944) provided the third article, which highlighted various visual aids used for military training. Comics in the form of a specially created strip featuring "Private Pete" were used to share information in the monthly *Our War* magazine.

At the time Witty contributed the article to Zorbaugh's special issue, he was serving in the US Army as an instructional developer, but his other job was as an education professor at Northwestern University. Witty's training was as a school psychologist, and he applied that training to both the study of intellectually gifted children and reading. Witty believed that "reading is not an isolated phenomenon and that the term itself can be broadly interpreted in relation to all that is visually perceived" (Weingarten, 1957, p. 483), so comics were a natural part of his study. Through several large-scale surveys (e.g. Witty, 1941a; Witty, 1941b; Witty, Smith, and Coomer, 1942) and a popular textbook on reading (Witty, 1949), Witty provided a more positive view of comics than could be found in many other education-centered texts at the time. For instance, Witty (1941b) argued that reading comics was not in itself indicative of a paucity of more traditional reading. He cited as one example a sixth grader "who reported that he read 28 comic magazines *occasionally* and more than 20 strips *regularly* [and] listed 30 books which he had read voluntarily during the few months preceding the investigation" (Witty, 1941b, p. 108). Witty (1949) proposed that teachers and librarians must seek to understand young people's interests in reading comics if they want to be successful in offering reading guidance.

In the late 1940s, Zorbaugh capitalized on his enthusiasm for the educative potential of comics. He organized a comics workshop that was billed as the "first comprehensive analysis of the comics as a medium of communication and a social force" (School of Education at New York University, n.d.). As part of its work, the Workshop on the Cartoon Narrative brought together cartoonists, publishers, teachers, and similar professionals to explore how comics might contribute to education (Tilley and Weiner, 2016). In particular it focused on five facets including research (such as on the effectiveness of comics in communicating ideas), consultation with agencies wishing to integrate comics for instruction, and production guidance for writers and artists who wanted to create educational comics. The full extent of the Workshop's impact is unknown, as there seem to be few extant records of its work. Still, as Tilley and Weiner (2017) argue, its activities over a several-year period make the Workshop "the earliest example both of a comics studies program in higher education and of a cohesive program to investigate the role of comics in teaching and learning" (np).

One of the few concrete examples of the Workshop's activities is found in a study conducted by Pittsburgh elementary school teacher Katharine Hutchinson (1949). Writing in Zorbaugh's second comics issue of the *Journal of Educational Sociology*, Hutchinson describes the results of a survey of more than 400 teachers who used the Workshop's *Comics in the Classroom* manual (more than 2000 teachers requested this manual, but only a fifth of them returned the questionnaire) and accompanying newspaper strips from *Puck Weekly* / King Features Syndicate. Based on teachers' responses, Hutchinson concluded that middle-school classrooms were optimal for integrating comics. Over a span of 13 weeks, teachers reported using comics to teach reading, social studies, art, and other subjects. Strips like *Tillie the Toiler* spurred discussions on personal and social relations, while others like *Flash Gordon* encouraged reluctant and poor readers. One teacher reported that *Prince Valiant* served as a useful adjunct for geography and history. Of particular note, Hutchinson's survey data established that for more than one-third of the respondents, comics had been part of their instructional repertoire on other occasions.

A Caveat and Looking Forward

The examples of educating with comics provided in this chapter indicate that using comics in classrooms is not a recent development, as the comics medium has long been part of work in schools. This effort to foreground early examples of curricula and initiatives should not be regarded as evidence that comics played a normative or positive part in teaching and learning for most of the 20th century. The story is complicated. As Tilley (2007) indicates, some teachers and librarians went against conventional wisdom to see value in comics as a communications medium and an element in young people's print culture. Frank Cutright, Jr. (1942) was one of those educators who offered a resounding "Yes!" to comics as reading and instructional materials. Alluding to Aristotle's *Poetics* on the role of literature in providing pleasure, Cutright argues that comics can serve that function, as well as offer spurs for teachable moments (e.g. "How does Superman jump that high?") and platforms for "teaching tolerance and understanding" (1942, pp. 166, 167). Cutright blames his fellow educators' reluctance to use comics on "that part of American literary and moral heritage which is derived from the Puritan suspicion of anything pleasurable" (1942, p. 166).

That suspicion, if Cutright is correct, created far more educators and educational researchers who for decades viewed comics as an enemy to overcome in battle rather than as a tool to enhance learning. Certainly the broader social and cultural war waged against comics in the 1940s and 1950s—a war in which many teachers and librarians actively fought against comics—kept comics from achieving a more valued pedagogical role (cf. Nyberg, 2002; Tilley, 2007). Although there continued to be occasional missives and studies from the 1960s through the 1990s that highlighted the instructional possibilities that comics afforded, it was not until the turn of the new century that the educational community saw sustained work on comics (Tilley and Weiner, 2016). Recent works by scholars and practitioners such as Michael Bitz (2010), James 'Bucky' Carter (2007), and Dale Jacobs (2013) are aiding the cause of comics and helping them find their roles in classrooms and libraries as instructional aides and reading texts.

Bibliography

Abbott, A. (1913) 'A high-school course in periodical literature', *The English Journal*, 2 (7): 422–27.
Adams, F., Gray, L. and Reese, D. (1949) *Teaching Children to Read*, New York: The Ronald Press.
Bechtel, L.S. (1941) 'The comics and children's books', *Horn Book*, 17: 296–303.
Bibliography. (1944) *Journal of Educational Sociology*, 18 (4): 250–55.
Bishop, M. (1950) 'The school library and remedial reading', *Wilson Library Bulletin*. 25: 254–55.
Bitz, M. (2010) *When Commas Meet Kryptonite: classroom lessons from the Comic Book Project*, New York: Teachers College Press, Columbia University.
Blair, G.M. (1955) 'Reading materials for pupils with reading disabilities', *The High School Journal*, 39 (1): 14–21.
Bryant, W.M. (1932) 'Off for Treasure Island', *The English Journal*, 21 (2): 137–39.
Bulletin of the Art Institute of Chicago (1927) 21 (5): 67.
Burkholder, E.C. (1914) 'An eighth-grade newspaper. An experiment in English involving unity of purpose as against individual effort', *The Elementary School Teacher*, 14 (9): 418–22.
Carter, J.B. (2007) *Building Literacy Connections with Graphic Novels: Page by Page, Panel by Panel*, Urbana, IL: National Council of Teachers of English.
Cremin, L. (1961) *The Transformation of the School: Progressivism in American Education 1876–1957*, New York: Knopf.
Cutright, Jr., F. (1942) 'Shall our children read the comics? Yes!' *Elementary English Review*, 19 (5): 165–67.
Denecke, L. (1945) 'Fifth graders study the comic books', *Elementary English Review*, 22 (1): 6–8.
Elder, V. (1974) 'The library and the retarded reader', *Wilson Library Bulletin*, 21: 661–65.
Grose, C.H. (1929) 'Ambridge Junior High School social activities period', *The Junior High Clearing House*, 3 (7): 28–32.
Harris, A.J. (1947) *How to Increase Reading Ability: A Guide to Individual and Remedial Methods* 2d edn, New York: Longmans.
Hatfield, W.W. (1935) *An Experience Curriculum in English: a report of the Curriculum Commission of the National Council of Teachers of English,* New York: D. Appleton.
Hespelt, E.H. and Williams, R.H. (1943) 'Questions and answers', *Hispania*, 26 (4): 453–62.
Hill, C.M. and Mosher, R.D. (1931) *Making the Most of High School: a textbook in educational guidance for junior-high-school pupils*, New York: Laidlaw.
Hutchings, C. (1946) 'How to use a newspaper in foreign language classes', *Hispania*, 29 (3): 394–97.
Hutchinson, K.H. (1949) 'An experiment in the use of comics as instructional material', *Journal of Educational Sociology*, 23 (4): 236–45.
Jacobs, D. (2013) *Graphic Encounters: comics and the sponsorship of multimodal literacy*, New York: Bloomsbury Publishing USA.
Kinneman, F.C. (1943) 'The comics and their appeal to youth', *English Journal*, 32: 331–35.
McCloud, S. (1994) *Understanding Comics: the invisible art*, New York: Morrow.
McCullough, C., Strang, R. and Traxler, A. (1955) *Problems in the Improvement of Reading* 2d edn, New York: McGraw Hill.
McMurtry, L. (2004) *Sacagawea's Nickname: essays on the American West*, New York: New York Review of Books.
Millspaugh, A.C. (1914) 'Notes on history-teaching', *The School Review*, 22 (10): 678–85.
Munro, T. (1936) 'Educational plans for 1936–37 first half year', *The Bulletin of the Cleveland Museum of Art*, 23 (8): 119–22.
Nyberg, A.K. (2002) 'Poisoning children's culture: comics and their critics', in L.C. Schurman and D. Johnson (eds.) *Scorned Literature: essays on the history and criticism of popular mass-produced fiction in America*, Westport, CT: Greenwood, 167–86.
Nyberg, A.K. (2010) 'How librarians learned to love the graphic novel', in R.G. Weiner (ed.) *Graphic Novels and Comics in Libraries and Archives: essays on readers, research, history and cataloging*, Jefferson, NC: McFarland, 26–40.
Pyrtle, E.R. (1915) 'McKinley Preparatory School', *The Elementary School Journal*, 16 (1): 49–52.
Routzahn, B.G. (1910) 'Some methods for teaching tuberculosis in the schoolroom', *The Journal of Education*, 71 (10): 262.

Russell, L.M. (1914) 'Some experiments in oral English in the high school', *The English Journal*, 3 (3): 176–80.
Saettler, P. (2004) *The Evolution of American Educational Technology*. Charlotte, NC: IAP.
Santa Barbara County Teachers Develop Builders in Daily Democratic Living Volume 6: Elementary (1942) Santa Barbara: The Schauer Printing Studio.
School of Education at New York University (nd). Workshop on the cartoon narrative. Box 111, Folder 4, *Fredric Wertham Papers*. Manuscripts Division. Library of Congress. Washington, D.C.
Shaffer, L. (1930) *Children's Interpretations of Cartoons (Teachers College Contributions to Education NO. 429.)* New York: Teachers College, Columbia University.
Sheehan, M.A. (1921) 'Clubs: a regular social activity', *The High School Journal*, 4 (6): 132–35.
Sinnema, J.R. (1957) 'Cartoons in conversation classes', *The Modern Language Journal*, 41 (3): 124–25.
Smith, L.R. (1940) 'The interpretation of newspaper cartoons by sixth grade children', MA thesis, the Ohio University, Athens, OH.
Smith, Jr., L.C. (1938) 'Comics as literature for children', MA thesis, Colorado State College of Education, Greeley, CO.
'Something better than the comics'. (1952) In *Course of Study in English for Secondary Schools. A Progress Report* (Bulletin 280), Harrisburg, PA: Commonwealth of Pennsylvania, Department of Public Instruction, 147–50.
Sones, W.W.D. (1944) 'The comics and instructional method', *Journal of Educational Sociology*, 18 (4): 232–40.
Sperzel, E.Z. (1948) 'The effect of comic books on vocabulary growth and reading comprehension', *Elementary English*, 25 (2): 109–13.
Thomas, P.L. (2011) 'Adventures in genre!: rethinking genre through comics/graphic novels', *Journal of Graphic Novels and Comics*, 2 (2): 187–201.
Tilley, C.L. (2007) 'Of Nightingales and Supermen: how youth services librarians responded to comics between the years 1938 and 1955', Ph.D. dissertation, Indiana University, Bloomington.
Tilley, C.L. (2013a) 'Superman says 'read': national comics and reading promotion', *Children's Literature in Education*, 44 (3): 251–63.
Tilley, C.L. (2013b) 'Using comics to teach the language arts in the 1940s and 1950s', in C. Syma and R.G. Weiner (eds.) *Graphic Novels and Comics in the Classroom: essays on the educational power of sequential art*, Jefferson, NC: McFarland, 12–22.
Tilley, C.L. and Weiner, R.G. (2017) 'Comics and education', in F. Bramlett, R. Cook and A. Meskin (eds.) *Routledge Companion to Comics and Graphic Novels*, New York: Routledge.
Trovillion, M.C. and Renard, H.E. (1917) 'Cartooning grammar', *The English Journal*, 6 (7): 472–73.
Vacca, C. (1959) 'Comic books as a teaching tool', *Hispania*, 42 (2): 291–92.
Walters, P.B. (2007) 'Betwixt and between discipline and profession: a history of sociology of education', in C. Calhoun (ed.) *Sociology in America: a history*, Chicago: University of Chicago Press, 639–65.
Weingarten, S. (1957) 'Pioneers in reading III: Paul Witty', *Elementary English*, 34 (7): 481–84.
Wheeler, J.L. (1935) 'Methods for making known to inexperienced readers the resources and facilities offered by American public libraries', *Library Quarterly*, 5 (4): 371–406.
Wilson, H.E. (1928) 'Cartoons as an aid in the teaching of history', *The School Review*, 36 (3): 192–98.
Winn, M. (1944) 'Front views and profiles', *Chicago Tribune*, April 29: 10.
Witty, P.A. (1941a) 'Children's interest in reading the comics', *Journal of Experimental Education*, 10 (2): 100–104.
Witty, P.A. (1941b) 'Reading the comics—a comparative study', *Journal of Experimental Education*, 10 (2): 105–109.
Witty, P.A. (1944) 'Some uses of visual aids in the army', *Journal of Educational Sociology*, 18 (4): 241–49.
Witty, P.A. (1949) *Reading in Modern Education*, Boston: Heath.
Witty, P.A., Smith, E. and Coomer, A. (1942) 'Reading the comics in grades VII and VIII', *Journal of Educational Psychology*, 33: 173–82.
Zorbaugh, H. (1944) 'The comics—there they stand!', *Journal of Educational Sociology*, 18 (4): 196–203.

2

EDUCATING ABOUT COMICS

Robert G. Weiner

It is hard to imagine that there was a time when teaching and studying comics, graphic novels, funny books, graphic narratives, or sequential art in higher education was a radical idea or something new, especially in today's world (2016–2017), when it seems like one hears about professors offering a new class related to comics practically every day. One can find courses coming from a variety of departments including: Anthropology, Cultural Studies, Electronic Media and Communications, English, Film Studies, Honors, Library and Information Science, and Philosophy. There are degree programs in Comics Studies at University of Florida, University of Oregon, and Scotland's University of Dundee.

One could argue that Comics Studies is where Film Studies was 40 years ago. There were those pioneering professors who used comics in the classroom during the 1960s, '70s, '80s, early '90s, and beyond. This essay attempts to document a few of those individuals through the use of oral history interviews and other sources. This is not meant be an exhaustive picture or narrative, but a snapshot of a few pioneers and innovators who taught. This article will close with a few contemporary individuals who have made an impact on bringing comics education to a wider audience.

As early as 1968, comic writer and Marvel Universe co-creator Stan Lee talked about how "… more than a dozen college professors now use Marvel mags in their English Litt [sic]. courses as supplemental material" (1968, n.p.). If Stan Lee is to be believed, and this is not just hyperbole, then perhaps most of these pioneering professors have been lost to history. Nevertheless, the fact that Lee would even make such a statement shows that something was going on and that he was beginning to champion comics as worth more than simple disposable entertainment. However, William David Sherman, an English Professor at New York University, wrote to Stan Lee in 1966 asking for extra copies of *Fantastic Four 46* to use in his Contemporary American Literature Course. As documented in a well-known article about Marvel and the appeal of comics among college students from the September 1966 issue of *Esquire* magazine, Sherman was among the first professors to use comic book superheroes to explain to students "various archetypal and mythological patterns at work which would give them better insight to where things are today" (*Esquire*, 1966, p. 115). In a different section, numerous college professors are profiled and given superhero costumes drawn by artist

Marie Severin. They are described as "Super-Profs," and although there is no indication that these professors used comics in any of their classes, *Esquire* guaranteed that they would not be boring. These "Super-Profs" included folks like physics Professor Richard Feynman who was dressed in a "Thor-like" costume and psychology Professor David LaBerge who is dressed in a Shazam-like (Captain Marvel) costume (1966, pp. 122–123). A year earlier, however, an article from the *Village Voice* boasted that a nameless Cornell physics professor was "pointing" things out about Marvel Comics "in his classes" (Kemptor, 1965, p. 5).

The academic relevance of comics was also evidenced by the fact that literary intellectuals, such as Ken Kesey in the 1960s, talked about how characters based on comic superheroes like Captain Marvel, Plastic Man, Batman, and others were "honest American myths" (Wolfe, 1986, p. 39). Ray Browne documented in *Against Academia* how comics were being studied and presented when the Popular Culture Movement, in academic circles, was in its infancy. This was also a time when studying anything related to popular culture was often suspect and looked down upon by much of higher education. Browne's volume describes in detail how difficult it could be to be taken seriously when teaching popular culture. Stan Lee apparently attended some of the early Popular Culture Association academic meetings and was a popular speaker on university campuses in the late 1960s and early 1970s (Browne, 1989, pp. 27–28, 30, 37, 51, 129, 140). As many of the interviewees document here, comics were not often taught as a class by itself, but rather were incorporated into a larger subject area. In 1973, *College and Research Libraries* documented that popular culture courses were being taught in "over 500 schools" and that undergraduates could be expected to "delve into dime novels and comic books" for their "class assignments" (Clarke, 1973, p. 217).

Perhaps the most notable person in the history of teaching Comics Studies is Michael Uslan, who has written for DC Comics, Archie Comics, Dynamite Comics, and is the producer of the *Batman* feature films including 2008's *The Dark Knight*. In 1972 at Indiana University, Uslan taught the "first accredited [three-hour] college course [solely] on comic books" (Uslan, 1974, p. 26). He had been teaching about comics the year before through an experimental program known as the "The Free University" (Uslan, 2011, p. 100). His contemporary at Indiana and future comics writer Roger Stern had also been teaching a "one-hour credit experimental course on comic book history and art" (Uslan, 1974, p. 26). Uslan found a faculty sponsor in the folklore department and through some quick thinking convinced the Dean of Arts and Sciences that the course had merit (2011, p. 1974). He wanted the class to be taken seriously and for it to be "as important as history, physics, or chemistry," so making sure the class was given that three-hour credit designation was vital (Uslan, 1974, p. 26). In his study guide *The Comic Book in America*, he admonished students to have a "responsible and scholarly attitude on your part toward comic books," so that they would take seriously the study of comics and not think of them as lesser form (Uslan, 1973, p. v). In his course Uslan discussed everything from comics, including folklore, history, cultural mirrors to our society, contemporary relevance, psychological relationships, other media and comics, comics as art, censorship, the educational potential of comics, and how comics are created (Uslan, 1973). The course created quite a stir, and Uslan was interviewed by various media outlets including print and television. He eventually had to weed out students who were not serious, as over 200 wanted to take the class, and there were only 35 spots (Uslan, 2011, pp. 103–105). The course was originally called "Comic Book in Society" but changed to "The Comic Book in America" to reflect the title of the text. Uslan was able to garner interest from folks like Stan Lee, Denny O' Neil and others in the industry and eventually went to write for DC in 1975. In 2012 he received an honorary doctorate of Fine Arts from Monmouth University and in 2015 he taught a MOOC (Massive Open Online Course) sponsored by the Smithsonian Institution called "The Rise of Superheroes and Their Impact on Pop Culture" with Stan Lee.

One scholar who incorporated comics into the curriculum as early as 1969 was literary scholar M. Thomas Inge in "what some have identified as the earliest course on American Humor" at Michigan State University. He offered this course at the various universities he taught at over the years which "always included a segment on comics," reasoning that there was no way one could "teach American Humor without including comics" (Inge, 2015). Over the years he would teach George Herriman's *Krazy Kat*, Charles Schulz's *Peanuts*, and Bill Watterson's *Calvin and Hobbes*, together with Mark Twain, James Thurber, Woody Allen and other masters of American Humor. Inge has been a mover and shaker in the field of comics scholarship for over 40 years. A few of his comics-related works include *Comics as Culture* (1990), *Charles M. Schulz: Conversations* (2000), and a booklet on teaching produced by the Smithsonian, *Comics in the Classroom* (1989). He edited a special section of the *Journal of Popular Culture* (Spring 1979) devoted to comics, and edited or wrote more than 60 other publications including *The Greenwood Guide to American Popular Culture* (2002). In 1974 at Virginia Commonwealth University, he taught a several-week continuing education course on American Comic Art—one of the first of its kind. Through his painstaking scholarship and work, he gradually built up a reputation as a scholar whose work on comics should be taken seriously, but it was not an easy road. Rather than "force" his idea that comics should be taught as a legitimate subject area by itself, Inge took the stealth approach:

> When I first started encouraging the study of comics, I realized that I could do one of two things—but not both. Either I could start the arguments that would eventually lead to the grudging acceptance of comics in the curriculum (from which I might emerge without a job or considered insane), or I could start to build the body of scholarship, biography, and history necessary to begin serious scholarship. Without the availability of a sound and substantial body of history and criticism, effective teaching could not begin anyway. So I thought I would devote a large part of my career to such work and let the others, surely coming, attend to the curriculum matters. Besides, the approval of the academy is in no way necessary to understand or appreciate the power and beauty of the graphic narrative. That said, I must add that I have been teaching comics bootleg for over 45 years. (2015)

It was this stealth approach that allowed Inge to continue advocating for the legitimacy of the comics art form, while continuing to teach without interference from those administrators and colleagues who considered his study of comics a lesser form of academic pursuit. There was "little toleration for what I wanted to do" as most of them "looked on in amused disbelief" with comments like, "I think it's nice you have a hobby, Tom." He continued to pursue the study and teaching of comics and found some like-minded academics in the Popular Culture Movement. However, Inge knew he was onto something because whether his colleagues respected his work on comic art or not, the students did, and he found that whenever he lectured on comics and the comic strip, those lectures were appreciated by those in the audience (Browne, 1989, p. 75). Although Professor Inge has been incorporating comics into his teaching for over 45 years, it was not until 2013 that he taught his first academically credited class devoted solely to comics studies, called the "Graphic Narrative."

Donald Ault is another key figure in putting the teaching of comics on the academic landscape today. He was instrumental in establishing the Comics Studies program at the University of Florida and founded the online peer reviewed journal *ImageText,* which publishes articles related to visual texts including comics, animation, illustrated children's literature, and digital content. Will Eisner once called the journal the "Manhattan Project of comics studies" (Ault, 2015). *ImageText* is published by the University of Florida; Ault also edited *Carl Barks: Conversations* (2003a). Ault directed Joseph Witek's dissertation on comics at Vanderbilt, which was eventually published as *Comic Books as History* (1989), known as "one of the best books ever on the analysis of comics" (Ault, 2003b, p. 250). In 1969, while teaching at Berkeley, Ault began incorporating comics into his freshman composition courses and used Disney, Marvel, and underground comix (Ault, 2003b, p. 242). Comics provided a way to teach students various "verbal/visualizations and a range of narrative possibilities in panel format." With comics, Ault "taught them to read and write in very precise forms" (Ault, 2015). He began to take a keen interest in the work of Disney writer and artist Carl Barks and wanted to teach his work but couldn't "propose a course in Donald Duck" as he knew colleagues would not view that as a worthy academic subject (Ault, 2003b, p. 243). Nevertheless, while still teaching at Berkeley in 1972, he proposed a special topics course "Literature and Popular Culture," which was a way for him to teach comics directly:

> The meeting was interesting. The first question was "why should we give standing status to a course that only one professor can teach?" Then about 10 faculty members put up their hands, affirming that they wanted to teach such a course, and the course went through.
>
> *(Ault, 2015)*

In 1973, he co-taught an evening extension course with Thomas Andrae on "American Popular Culture" which included comics (Ault, 2003b, pp. 244–245). When Ault moved to Vanderbilt in the mid-1970s he had had "11 long years of teaching as a 'Special Topic' until 1987" when a comics-specific course was officially approved (Ault, 2003b, p. 250). He was looked down upon by some of his colleagues for teaching such low-brow material, with one colleague calling him "the Departmental trash man." Vanderbilt had hired him as a William Blake professor, but "had it written into my contract" that he would teach comics classes (Ault, 2015). Professor Ault knew that if he kept teaching comics as though they were worth of study "by treating comics with respect and intellectual rigor" time would eventually prove him right (Ault, 2003b, p. 251). Despite this, even the mainstream media often treated Ault with disdain and did not take him seriously. "Most of the articles treated teaching comics as a symptom of the final deterioration of the American academy. Several television news anchors attacked the idea of the course." Even when Ault was interviewed by *Entertainment Tonight,* the broadcast on October 5 & 6, 1985, was not sympathetic (Ault, 2003b, pp. 252–253). Eventually though when he moved to the University of Florida in 1988, he found an "atmosphere entirely different from Vanderbilt," and was able to foster comics studies there (Ault, 2003b, p. 254). He again had teaching comics written into his contract and the UF faculty "[was] glad to have a comics professor," but he still had to contend with a "huge swatch of extremely right wing senior faculty who fought the idea of having a standing course that contains Mickey Mouse. This went on until the last year I taught there. It was finally approved when enough of the faculty retired" (Ault, 2015). Ault's tenacity and passion for teaching comics has continued to make an impact today even though he has now retired: "The value of using comics in the academy returns unexpected rewards often many years down the line" (Ault, 2003b, p. 256).

Another early pioneer is Thomas Andrae. He is a cultural and film historian. He wrote *Carl Barks and the Disney Comic Book* (2006), co-authored *Walt Kelly* (2012), and worked with Batman co-creator Bob Kane on his autobiography, *Batman and Me* (1990). In addition, he co-produced with Donald Ault a documentary on Carl Barks. Over the course of nearly 40 years, Andrae has interviewed many legendary comics' creators including Jerry Siegel, Will Eisner, Harvey Kurtzman, Floyd Gottfredson, and Jerry Robinson. He also discovered and published a "lost" interview with Bill Finger. Many of these interviews can be found in *Creators of Superheroes* (2011). In July 1974, he taught "The Contemporary American Comic Book" at University of California, Berkeley. It was a weekend extension course that surveyed some of the key figures in comic art, early animation related to comics, comics as social history, women's comics, and superheroes. The response was very positive among students because "people were not used to this," and they were fascinated to see a new take on something that for so long had been considered a lesser form of artistic endeavor (Andrae, 2015). In 1976, Andrae started teaching general courses on American popular culture in which he incorporated comics:

> I lectured on Disney comics and superheroes, based upon my articles and books. I used a cultural studies approach that combined production, textual analysis, and consumption. This involved historical contextualization, psychoanalysis, and textual exegesis and genre theory, along with visual semiotics.
>
> *(Andrae, 2015a)*

His classes were popular, and the use of comics in the classroom did not cause much controversy or dissent among students or the administration. Andrae also taught one of the first classes on superhero-related films at San Francisco State University in 2001. He continued to integrate comics as part of cultural studies classes. While among students he often did not have much opposition, Andrae's scholarly work in the larger community of fans and reviewers has come under fire, in particular his application of psychoanalysis to the study of comics:

> Some fans were intolerant of scholarly analyses of comics and pop culture, especially the use of psychoanalysis, and discussions of racism in fan favorites like Walt Kelly's early work. Much of my early work was pretty groundbreaking, before comics had been that established in the academy, or by the public.
>
> *(Andrae, 2015a)*

Reviewers would often give his commentaries "a negative review, claiming that the stories could stand on their own and didn't need any scholarly analysis" (Andrae, 2015a).

One example from Popular Culture studies is Jack Nachbar. He is considered one of the founding fathers of the Popular Culture Movement in higher education. He is the co-author of one of the most highly regarded preparatory Popular Culture textbooks, *Popular Culture: An Introductory Text* (1992), co-editor of the *The Popular Culture Reader* (1983), and *Focus on the Western* (1974) among many other articles and books on various aspects of Popular Culture, including comics. While at the University of Minnesota in Morris during the late 1960s, his teaching of comics was "at best incidental." It was really when Professor Nachbar was at Bowling Green State University in the Department of Popular Culture that the use of comics was incorporated into the classroom "whenever appropriate in general courses." In the "Introduction to Popular Culture Course," comics was incorporated into the "section on Popular Heroes" (Nachbar, 2015). In the late 1970s and again in the early 1980s he taught a graduate "Comics and Culture class covering the 1920s to the present. ..." The students would use the special collection of "comics materials" at the Popular Culture Library at Bowling Green for their analysis and research. Some of the highlights of the course were visits to both the DC and Marvel offices and the Museum of Cartoon Art. What is interesting is that Nachbar taught these courses because the students from the Popular Culture department requested that he do so. The "evaluations were very enthusiastic" and the only negative responses he ever received in teaching about comics were from the "oversell department" (Nachbar, 2015).

The development of Comics Studies is not limited to English departments. For example, David Kunzle is an art historian and philosopher known for his books on the innovators of the early comic strip and in particular Rodolphe Töpffer. He published several groundbreaking early academic studies, *The History of the Comic Strip* (1973) and *Father of the Comic Strip: Rodolphe Töpffer* (2007), and translated the biting Marxist critique of capitalism, *How to Read Donald Duck* (1975). As a professor at UCLA in the late 1970s, Kunzle would introduce comics as part of his art, philosophy, and aesthetics (usually graduate) courses. He would use the early masters of the comic strip to teach students to "speak nonsense words" as an exercise in understanding how to see the world in a different way. As creators like Töpffer were producing "satires on education," it was only natural to try and see if students could interpret comic art in this way. Kunzle wanted to incorporate this to show that although most "art isn't funny," the comic strip turned art into something of a "hybrid" by combining it with language to show art and humor are juxtaposed together. Students had a hard time "speaking nonsense words" in using comic strips as examples, but it was a useful exercise in getting students to think critically about comics in the world of what one would call "Art" (Kunzle, 2015).

Since the 1980s, David Huxley, a library scholar and historian, has been the editor and co-founder of the *Journal of Graphic Novels and Comics* and author of a seminal work on British underground comics, *Nasty Tales* (2001). He first taught a comics-related course in 1981 at Manchester Polytechnic for Graphic Design. At this early stage one did not have to consider things like learning objectives or outcomes and "essentially you could offer a unit in an area that interested you—I'd been drawing and writing about comics since the early 1970s and I was just able to provide a basic outline and go from there" (Huxley, 2015). Since comics were in the special collections at universities like Newcastle and Manchester, Huxley made use of these collections, applying his training as a librarian in his approach to teaching. He notes: "librarians were ahead of academics" since they saw comics "as another part of popular culture (posters, postcards, etc.) that were already pretty respectable as fields for study" (Huxley, 2015). In his teaching he chose the visual and historical approach to teaching comics since his early courses were offered in the art department (and then later in film and media). His coverage focused on UK and European comics as well as important American comics. While he didn't have many problems from administration, there was a "small amount of carping from some of the more traditional art historians," who held the belief that this was a lesser form of artistic endeavor (Huxley, 2015). Huxley remembers that one of his colleagues at Manchester (Victoria) had a difficult time getting a course approved, and the use of the term "graphic novel" finally got his course accepted. He also found that the student response was quite good even if a few female students felt as though comics "were boys' stuff." Ultimately, however, students liked working with the images that Huxley showed in class and "were amazed by the breadth and quality of the work" the comics had to offer (Huxley, 2015).

Another pioneer from the 1980s is Martin Barker, a cultural studies critic, film theorist, and philosopher whose monographs on comics include *Comics: Ideology, Power and the Critics* (1989), *Action: The Story of a Violent Comic* (1990), and *Haunt of Fears: The Strange History of the British Horror Comics Campaign* (1992). Unlike many other comics scholars, Professor Barker was not a fan of comics growing up, and even today he is very particular about what sequential art he reads and studies. While teaching cultural studies at Bristol Polytechnic in the early 1980s, Barker wanted students to look at various media materials from television, the press:

> to popular stories, whatever. I became absorbed with finding materials that would do three things simultaneously: still stay in the classroom (tricky with TV, film, etc.); exist in several versions/formats, so comparisons could be directly made; and deal with stories, because I was becoming fascinated with the additional problems raised for cultural theory by fiction, story-telling. (2015)

While at a comic book store in Bristol, he came across a box of *Classics Illustrated* and found several versions of *Last of the Mohicans* and "That was it—I had my teaching materials" (Barker, 2015). Previously, though, he had a student named Irena who wanted to study the character of Superman from a Jungian perspective, and Barker became frustrated because he realized he didn't have a reference point to apply such an approach to something as seemingly arbitrary as Superman. When he tried to research the scholarly material related to comics that could be found at the library, he found there wasn't much available (late 1970s) (Barker, 2002, p. 65). When Barker started incorporating comics into his cultural studies classes they were "first as bits within a wider module, then in a module called Studies in Comics (though I don't think we used the word module in those days)." He didn't really encounter any resistance or controversy in teaching comics. He realized that at the time it was unusual to be teaching this type of subject matter "providing we met general university criteria, we were given a fairly free hand in things of this kind." This does not mean that students expecting a "soft option" would take Barker's class as a blow off, "it wasn't." His students would:

> study how comics work, talk to fans and collectors, talk to their parents about their recollections of comics, and so on-as well as studying them textually and to some degree historically. But we also dealt closely with claims and debates and over them so they could think about the *issues they raised.*
>
> *(Barker, 2015)*

Ultimately, Professor Barker sees himself as someone who "taught about comics, rather than teaching comics" (2015).

The 1990s saw Roger Sabin, a cultural studies critic and journalist whose comics-related works *Adult Comics* (1992) and *Comics, Comix & Graphic Novels: A History of Comic Art* (1996) have become standards in the history of comics studies. He first taught comics in 1993 at the London Art School Central Saint Martins as a result of the notoriety received from his book *Adult Comics*. "If I am a pioneer then it was due to that book- and the fact that I was lucky enough to catch the 'graphic novel' wave (i.e., *Maus, Watchmen* and *The Dark Knight Returns* had just happened, and the academy was interested)" (Sabin, 2015). There was enthusiasm about teaching something that was still considered unique in higher education and "talking about graphic novels in a systematic way-both in the book and in my subsequent teaching-it did feel like I was doing something unprecedented" (Sabin, 2015). As *Adult Comics* was published by a first-rate academic press (Routledge) as part of a series that itself was considered "pioneering ('New Accents'), it kind of 'gave permission' for comics to be taught in higher education" and in academic circles. He acknowledges there were many "comic scholars before me" who laid the groundwork in other places, but at Central Saint Martins College his course "was the first of its kind" (Sabin, 2015). His next book, "*Comics, Comix, & Graphic Novels* became the basis of a three-part BBC documentary." He states, "for a while, I ended up as an academic spokesperson for the field, which I guess was 'pioneering' in its own way" (Sabin, 2015). He has taught at numerous institutions including Kingston University, Camberwell College of Art, and University of London. In addition to teaching students the historical context of comics based around material from his monographs, he devised a way for students to present information about the comics that were meaningful to them so a true dialogue between professor and student could take place:

> I started out by teaching the content of my book - i.e. UK comics one week, US comics the next, manga the next, underground comix the next, etc. - which was horribly dull, and a beginner's mistake. Over time, I learnt to let the students do more of the talking, and I devised my classes around 'them teaching me' about comics that were meaningful to them. You have to remember that in London, the student body is incredibly diverse, and so I was getting student presentations about comics from every corner of the globe. What a luxury!
>
> *(Sabin, 2015)*

Unfortunately, despite the acclaim both from the academic and the general press, the response from the "college high ups wasn't always quite so positive. They didn't really understand comics, and I was always considered 'non-serious.'" Although Comics Studies has gained some respectability throughout the academy in some places in the world, even today Sabin feels the sting of slow progress. In a 2014 staff meeting, Professor Sabin "was laughed at openly … when somebody discovered I taught comics." It's something he has perhaps gotten used to (Sabin, 2015).

Gene Kannenberg Jr. is an educator, scholar, and author, who, in 2002, completed a dissertation on the use of text and image in comics narrative at the University of Connecticut where he first used comics in teaching in the early 1990s. His work includes the groundbreaking website *ComicsResearch.org,* the books *500 Essential Graphic Novels* (2008), and two volumes (with Tim Pilcher) looking at the history of *Erotic Comics* (2008/2009). He first taught as a graduate student using Alan Moore and David Lloyd's *V for Vendetta* for a freshman composition class that had a "utopia/dystopia theme." He continued to teach comics at various institutions including some New England and NYC colleges, University of Houston, and College of Saint Rose in Albany and has guest lectured at Harper College and St. Louis Community College among others (Kannenberg, 2015). He used comics initially for composition classrooms "where there was a lot of freedom to design loose curriculums." Kannenberg was eventually able to expand his scope to incorporate works like Herge's *Tintin in Tibet* and Sendak's *In the Night Kitchen* into his Children's and Young Adult literature classes. At the University of Houston, he taught a "Comics and Visual Literature" course and "needed to get the word literature in there" in order to give the course legitimacy with others in the department (Kannenberg, 2015). At first he found that the college students were a little puzzled when asked to read comics thinking that it was "simplistic stuff." However, after the discussions and projects started and students started really examining the material, they were "always positive if not enthusiastic" (Kannenberg, 2015).

At the University of Connecticut, Kannenberg found that support for those studying comics while in graduate school was quite encouraging. He was fortunate to be with a good group of graduate students possessing similar interests. He and classmate Charles Hatfield both became "active in comics scholarship, running conferences and publishing a good bit." There were other students before and after who have gone on to do a great deal of comics scholarship like Wendy Goldberg, Kate Laity, and Brian Cremins. If there was any question about the legitimacy of comics scholarship at UConn those detractors just "stepped out of the way, while others embraced what we were doing and helped whenever they could" (Kannenberg, 2015). A professor he worked with at the institution (and who worked with Hatfield and many other scholars who are currently active in comics studies today) was Tom Roberts. Roberts had been teaching a comics and graphic novels course for "quite some time already." It was a "Special Topics" course and was "offered very regularly and was always very popular." Kannenberg and Hatfield were sometimes given the opportunity to be guest lecturers in Roberts' course. It is a testament to Roberts' teaching that he helped put the passion to study comics into so many future comics scholars (Kannenberg, 2015).

It's important to mention the spread of Comics Studies on a global scale. An example of someone instrumental in the globalization of teaching comics is John Lent. He is the author of *Comic Art of the United States through 2000* (2005) and the editor of *Southwest East Asia Cartoon Art* (2014) and *Animation in Asia and the Pacific* (2001) among many other books, articles, and bibliographies looking at worldwide comic art. Lent has taught in universities all over the world including the Philippines, Malaysia, Canada, and China as well as all over the United States including Wyoming, West Virginia, and Wisconsin. While teaching in Malaysia around 1972–1974, he began the country's first mass-communications program in a university where he "encouraged a few students to research Malaysian comics" for the class projects (Lent, 2015). Most of his direct teaching of comics started in the 1980s at Temple University and began as a weekly evening class open to "Temple students and adult-non students." Since then until his retirement in 2011 he continued to teach comics-related courses all over the world. Lent encouraged his undergraduate and graduate students to study comic art. His former students study comic art throughout the world including Taiwan, Cuba, Korea, China, Turkey, Kenya, and Japan and under his "guidance at Temple" graduate students from Thailand, Nepal, India, China, Taiwan, Korea "also researched comic art" (Lent, 2015). In addition to comics-related courses, he taught animation courses and in mid-2005 "started perhaps the first comics and animation center in China" where he is part of the animation faculty at Communication University of China and continues to "supervise Ph.D. dissertations." Lent has "taught students mainly foreign comic art, because in those days, comics studies usually was only US superhero-oriented. I taught from an historical, industrial perspective" (Lent, 2015). Lent also incorporated comics and animation into his general popular culture courses and rarely found any opposition to his teaching comics among students or faculty. He founded the *International Journal of Comic Art* in 1998 because when he was "taking students to conferences in the 1990s, I heard young doctoral students and others say a journal was needed for comic art" (Lent, 2015). He announced the birth of the journal at 1998 International Comic Art Forum and most of the original funding came out of Lent's bank account. The goal of the journal was to cover all aspects of comics worldwide. It would be an independent publication free from the meddling of outside sources and interests and "issues contained academic-type articles, interviews, profession-oriented content, book and exhibition reviews, a portfolio of cartoons, and other features" (Lent, 2015).

One recent example of an educator who has been influential in the last 15 years is Michael Bitz. His life's work has been educating children and adults with comics, and his Comic Book Project (CBP) has gained him renown worldwide among educators and scholars. He discovered comics when he was already an educator; rather than growing up reading comics, he preferred "chapter books and novels." He found that comics were "not just great literature, but also a way to motivate and excite kids about literacy and language." Bitz created the CBP in 2001 as a way to engage "children in writing and designing their own comic books and then publishing those works in the students' own schools and communities" (Bitz, 2015). With the help of Teachers College, Columbia University, and Dark Horse Comics, the CBP became an educational tool that served children who often felt left out "find a voice in the learning process by creating original writing and artwork about important issues in their lives," helping over 200,000 youths find a personal way to express themselves. When he first surveyed students, he found that in creating comics "four elements—characters, plot, design, and publishing—" had to become the major "backbone" of the CBP (Bitz, 2015). He was able to take lessons he learned from this trailblazing venture and publish them in *When Commas Meet Kryptonite* (2010). The goal of the CBP has always been to teach that creating comics is "a conduit for creativity, critical thinking, identity exploration, and community engagement" (Bitz, 2010, p. 5). By having students create their own comics professor Bitz is teaching about the comics form in a unique way that allows students to appreciate the complexities of sequential art. Bitz has also taught at Ramapo College, Manhattanville College, Columbia University, and Teachers College. His contribution to Comics Studies and to the world of education cannot be overestimated, and scholars and educators can use Bitz's example to create programs of their own.

Carl Potts is one of the few professionals (writer, editor, artist, and professor) who has straddled the line between the industry and the academy. He is known for his work at Continuity Studios, Marvel Comics, DC Comics and for writing the textbook *The DC Comics Guide to Creating Comics: Inside the Art of Visual Storytelling* (2013). In it, he outlines his unique theory of visual narrative, which he calls "Sequential Visual Storytelling (SVS)." "SVS is the art at the heart of comics and other sequential visual media" and it is important for artists to grasp the importance of storytelling technique just as it is for writers to be able to communicate this and work with artists. They both need to understand how the visual, the framing, the juxtaposition, and the relationship between the visual elements all work together (Potts, 2013, p. 14). He states that SVS contains the following:

> Three major creative elements: Narrative (usually a story), Visuals (photography, drawings, etc.) and Sequential Visual Storytelling: SVS consists of –
> - The visuals a creator chooses to show - and those he/she chooses not to show
> - The framing, angle, layout and rendering of the visual elements
> - The juxtaposition, order and sequence of the visual elements
> - The way the visuals and dialogue or text affect each other through juxtaposition
> - The emphasis given the visual elements relative to each other.
>
> *(Potts, 2015a)*

Potts had given seminars "a few times in artist/writer Walt Simonson's class at the School of Visual Arts in New York when he was teaching there." He met with artist/writer Klaus Janson over lunch in the mid-2000s and mentioned that "he was interested in teaching a class" at the SVA where Janson had been teaching for a "long time." The turnover for teaching comics at SVA is very low, but when Janson was asked to teach a second senior portfolio class, he put in a "good word" for Potts, and they co-taught the course. After that, Potts began teaching the course on his own (Potts, 2014). He is quick to point out, however, that he has been "teaching comics since he was an editor at Marvel where I found and trained a lot of new talent" (including Jim Lee) (Potts, 2015a). In his senior portfolio class for comics majors he takes a practical approach to teaching students:

> I begin with a four page assigned story that includes perspective scenes, everyday people, a dinosaur, an alien, a super heroine, cars, foliage, horses and dogs. Since comics artists have to be able to draw everything real or imagined at the same level of convincingness, I want to see where each student has strengths and weaknesses in their drawing skills. Students then work on a short original story to improve on their drawing, story structure and visual storytelling. They then launch into a longer original story for their portfolios.
>
> *(Potts, 2015b)*

He's also taught at schools such as SUNY Purchase and Academy of Art University, given seminars at Roy H. Park School of Communications, Montclair State University, College of Mount Saint Vincent, New York University, Fashion Institute of Technology, and Savannah College of Art and Design, and spoken at Pixar, Psyop, Ogilvy & Mather, Google's New York Office, and the Society of Illustrators, among others. Potts has given teaching colloquiums at Blue Sky Studios and Blizzard Entertainment.

These are just a few of the pioneering educators and innovators in comics studies surveyed for this project. There are, of course, people such as Arthur Asa Berger, Terry Zwigoff, Jeff Brown, Bonnie Gabawitz, Larry Landrum, Milton Plesur, Maurice Horn, Don LoCicero, William Savage, Alexander Simmons, Beverly Penny David, and countless others whose ground breaking work paved the way for so many educators who now teach comics in higher education and other educational realms (note: the author of this essay was not able to interview the above-mentioned individuals but thought acknowledging them was important). Oftentimes, it was just a matter of stealthily incorporating comics into a larger course of study such as literature or media studies. Although rare, there were occasional stand-alone comics courses. Many fought against the prejudices for studying, researching, and teaching these funny books despite being looked down upon for doing so. These pioneers understood how comics (e.g., from the strips to the funny animals to the superheroes and alternative comics) were rich in content and were much more complicated than a casual glance at them would offer. Teaching comics provided a mirror into humanity's collective memory, and it was worth fighting for its justification.

It's hard to imagine that there is still some resistance in higher education to the study of sequential art. As Stephen Tabachnick noted in his excellent 1994 article "A Course in the Graphic Novel," he didn't find as much resistance to teaching graphic novels from his departmental colleagues as he did from his "English majors, who have been taught all their lives that comics are a low level form suitable only for children and teenagers" (1994, p. 144); however, many pioneers discussed above have revealed the opposite to be true. In the last 20 years, great strides have been made as comics and graphic novels continue to make their way into mainstream culture and films based on comic properties rise in popularity. Resistance in some academic circles still exists. If there is anything to be learned from these pioneers, it is that while one should not have to justify teaching Comics Studies, more education about why the discipline is important to administrators, departmental colleagues, students, and even parents may be required.

Acknowledgments

Special thanks to Randy Duncan and Matthew J. Smith for their kind encouragement and assistance. Thank you to readers and reviewers Kimberly Vardeman, Matthew McEniry, Marilyn Weiner, and Alicia Goodman; thank you for your insights.

Please note the interpretations are my own. This essay is dedicated to all those who've taught comics studies in higher education and in particular those pioneers discussed here. A big thank you to those who agreed to be interviewed for this project including Donald Ault, Thomas Andrae, Thomas Inge, David Huxley, Roger Sabin, Martin Barker, John Lent, Michael Bitz, Carl Potts, Jack Nachbar, David Kunzle, and Gene Kannenberg. Thank you for taking the time out of your busy schedules to talk to me. It is your work that has paved the way for so many.

Bibliography

Andrae, T. (2006) *Carl Barks and the Disney Comic Book: unmasking the myth of modernity*, Jackson: University of Mississippi Press.
Andrae, T. (2011) *Creators of Superheroes*, Neshannock, PA: Hermes Press.
Andrae, T. (2012) *Walt Kelly: the life and art of the creator of Pogo*, Neshannock, PA: Hermes Press.
Andrae, T. (2015a) Email Interview with Author, 26 June.
Andrae, T. (2015b) Telephone Interview with Author, 1 July.
Ault, D. (2003a) *Carl Barks: conversations*, Jackson: University of Mississippi Press.
Ault, D. (2003b) 'In the trenches, taking the heat: confessions of a comics professor', *International Journal of Comic Art*, 5 (2): 241–60.
Ault, D. (2015) Email Interview with Author, 21 July.
Barker, M. (1989) *Comics: ideology, power and the critics*, Manchester: Manchester University Press.
Barker, M. (1990) *Action: the story of a violent comic*, London: Titan.
Barker, M. (1992) *A Haunt of Fears: the strange history of the British horror comics campaign*, Jackson: University of Mississippi Press (note: originally published in 1984 by Pluto Press).
Barker, M. (2002) 'Kicked in the gutters: my dad doesn't read comics, he studies them', *International Journal of Comic Art*, 4 (1): 64–77.

Barker, M. (2015) Email Interview with Author, 7 July.
Bitz, M. (2010) *When Commas Meet Kryptonite: classroom lessons from the Comic Book Project*, New York: Teachers College Press, Columbia University.
Bitz, M. (2015) Email Interview with Author, 9 June.
Browne, R. (1989) *Against Academia*, Bowling Green, OH: Popular Press.
Clarke, J. (1973) 'Popular culture in libraries', *College and Research Libraries*, 334 (3): 215–18.
Dorfman, A. and Mattelart, A. (1975) *How to Read Donald Duck*, trans. by D. Kunzle, New York: International General.
Four Ways to Go: a road map to super prof (1966) *Esquire*, September LXVI (3): 122–23.
Geist, C.D. and Nachbar, J. G. (eds.) (1982) *The Popular Culture Reader*, Bowling Green, OH: Bowling Green State University Popular Press.
Hergé. (1975) *Tintin in Tibet*, New York: Little Brown and Co.
Huxley, D. (2001) *Nasty Tales: sex, drugs, rock 'n' roll, and violence in the British Underground*, Manchester: Critical Vision.
Huxley, D. (2015) Email Interview with Author, 2 July.
Inge, T.M. (1989) *Comics in the Classroom*, Washington D.C.: Smithsonian Institution.
Inge, T.M. (2000) *Charles M. Schulz: conversations*, Jackson: University of Mississippi Press.
Inge, T.M. (2015) Email Interview with Author, 14 June.
Inge, T.M. and Hall, D. (eds.) (2002) *The Greenwood Guide to American Popular Culture*. Westport, CT: Greenwood Press.
Kane, B. and Andrae, T. (1989) *Batman and Me: an autobiography*, Forestville, CA: Eclipse Books.
Kannenberg G. Jr. (2008) *500 Essential Graphic Novels*, New York: Harper Collins.
Kannenberg, G. Jr. (2015) Email Interview with Author, 8 July.
Kemptor, S. (1965) Spiderman's dilemma: super-anti hero in Forest Hills, *Village Voice*. 1 April: 5, 15–16.
Kunzle, D. (1973a) *The Early Comic Strip: narrative strips and picture stories in the European broadsheet from c.1450 to 1825,* Berkeley: University of California Press.
Kunzle, D. (1973b) *History of the Comic Strip*, Berkeley: University of California Press.
Kunzle, D. (2007) *Father of the Comic Strip: Rodolphe Töpffer*, Jackson: University of Mississippi Press.
Kunzle, D. (2015) Telephone Interview with Author, 15 May.
Lee, S. (1968) Stan's Soapbox!, *Marvel Tales*, 1 (4), n.p.
Lent, J.A. (ed.) (2001) *Animation in Asia and the Pacific*, Bloomington, IN: Indiana University Press.
Lent, J.A. (2005) *Comic Art of the United States through 2000, Animation and Cartoons: an international bibliography*, Westport, CT: Praeger.
Lent, J.A. (ed.) (2014) *Southeast Asian Cartoon Art: history, trends and problems*, Jefferson, NC: McFarland.
Lent, J.A. (2015) Email Interview with Author, 17 July.
Moore, A. and Lloyd, D. (2005) *V for Vendetta*, New York: DC Comics.
Nachbar, J.G. (1974) *Focus on the Western*, Englewood Cliffs, NJ: Prentice-Hall.
Nachbar, J.G. (2015) Email Interview with Author, 4 July.
Nachbar, J.G. and Lause, K. (1992) *Popular Culture: an introductory text*, Bowling Green, OH: Bowling Green State University Popular Press.
O.K., You Passed the 2-S Test-Now You're Smart Enough for Comic Books (1966) *Esquire*, September LXVI (3): 114–15.
Pilcher, T. and Kannenberg Jr., G. (2008) *Erotic Comics: a graphic history from Tijuana Bibles to underground comix,* New York: Abrams.
Pilcher, T. and Kannenberg Jr., G. (2009) *Erotic Comics 2: a graphic history from the liberated '70's to the Internet*, New York: Abrams.
Potts, C. (2013) *The DC Comics Guide to Creating Comics: inside the art of visual storytelling*, New York: Watson-Guptill Publications.
Potts, C. (2014) Podcast episode 266: Carl Potts *Sidebar Nation.com,* 14 April. http://www.sidebarnation.com/my_weblog/2014/04/podcast-episode-xxx-carl-potts.html.
Potts, C. (2015a) Email Interview with Author, 2 June.

Potts, C. (2015b) Email Interview with Author, 17 August.
Sabin, R. (1993) *Adult Comics: an introduction*, London: Routledge.
Sabin, R. (1996) *Comics, Comix & Graphic Novels*, London: Phaidon Press.
Sabin, R. (2015) Email Interview with Author, 5 July.
Sendak, M. (1970) *In the Night Kitchen*, New York: Harper & Row.
Tabachnick, S. (1994) 'A course in the graphic novel', *Readerly/Writerly Texts*, 1 (2): 140–55.
Uslan, M. (1973) *A Study Guide for P.C. 1: the comic book in America*, Bloomington, IN: Indiana University Press.
Uslan, M. (1974) 'Confessions of a comic book professor', *Amazing World of DC Comics*, 1 (3): 26–29.
Uslan, M. (2011) *The Boy Who Loved Batman: a memoir*, San Francisco: Chronicle Books.
Wolfe, T. (1968) *The Electric Kool-Aid Acid Test*, New York: Farrar, Straus and Giroux.

A PIONEER'S PERSPECTIVE: WALDOMIRO VERGUEIRO

Brazil has a long tradition in the publishing and reading of comics. Prototypes of the comics' language have appeared in Brazilian newspapers since 1869, and the first magazine to publish comics on a regular basis was released in 1905. *O Tico-Tico* was a hugely popular children's magazine. By the mid-20th century, the arrival of North American syndicated characters, followed by comic-book heroes, largely contributed to enhancing the popularity of comics in the country, soon encouraging native authors to develop their efforts toward an autochthonous production.

Some Brazilian comics' artists and enthusiasts were more active than others. In fact, it is possible to say that the first theoretical approach to comics in Brazil was due to these enthusiasts' efforts. A group of idealistic young men organized the First International Comics Exhibition in the city of São Paulo in 1951. Álvaro de Moya (journalist), Reynaldo de Oliveira (graphic professional), Syllas Roberg (writer and bank employee), Miguel Penteado (graphic professional and publisher), and Jayme Cortês (comics artist, the only non-Brazilian in the group, who emigrated from his home country, Portugal, during his teens) wanted to make the exhibition the first favorable approach to comics open to the public. They gave space to original art from the most important North American artists of the time (who were very flattered when they received letters asking for their original pages, and who sent them to Brazil free of charge). The exhibition also presented critical analysis of comics' pages, elaborated by the organizers.

It was not a very big event. However, it had a strong media impact, not only due to the boldness of the organizers, but also to their intuitive marketing sense. The exhibition represented the first foray toward giving comics a scientific view, using techniques of image analyses similar to those used for cinema and aiming to identify the main characteristics of Brazilian production. One of the main revelations of the group was that the famous and popular "Brazilian" comics character Chiquinho, published in the above mentioned magazine *O Tico-Tico*, was in fact a local version of the North American Buster Brown, created by Richard Felton Outcault, in 1902 (Vergueiro & Santos, 2005).

All of the organizers of the 1951 Comics Exhibition continued to work in the comics field in the following decades. However, only Álvaro de Moya entered the academic environment, becoming a faculty member at Escola de Comunicações e Artes (School

(Continued)

of Communications and Arts) of the Universidade de São Paulo (University of São Paulo). He worked there from 1970 to 1991, when he retired. However, he preferred to maintain his relationship with the comics, film, and television industries, working as a part-time lecturer for 21 years. Notwithstanding, he developed an intense independent research of comics, giving his attention to the historical and industrial development of comics, especially to Brazilian production. He organized the book *Shazam!* (1970), the first anthology of critical texts on comics published in Brazil. The book had articles by psychiatrists, educators, journalists, architects, artists, and publishers. It is still in print and is used by Brazilian students as their introduction to Comics Studies.

Outside the academic field, Herman Lima published an important book for the study of graphic humor in Brazil, *História da Caricatura no Brasil* (*History of Cartoons in Brazil*), focusing on several comics artists. He was a literary critic and intended to follow a historical approach to the study of cartoon art in Brazil. His masterpiece had four volumes and presented a large and comprehensive survey of the production of cartoons and caricature in Brazil in the 19th and first half of the 20th centuries. It was the result of almost 20 years of independent research, which received financial support from Brazilian publisher José Olympio, finally published in 1963. Even if Lima's and Moya's written production lacked the scientific rigor expected in academic texts, their books and—especially in the case of the latter—dozens of national and international newspaper articles were very important in encouraging what can be called a dilettante production about comics in Brazil.

Comics entered the academic environment in Brazil in 1967. Professor José Marques de Melo, of the Centro de Pesquisas da Comunicação Social (Center of Researches for Social Communication) of the Faculdade de Jornalismo Casper Líbero (Faculty of Journalism Casper Líbero), coordinated the first formal research on comics in the city of São Paulo. With his undergraduate students, Marques de Melo used a functionalist approach in order to better understand the world of comics in Brazil. He composed a very detailed overview of the production of comic books at the time. In practice, the study consisted of both a survey on the comic books (number of published titles, of copies, distribution channels, workers, productive process, rules, comics code and consumers), as well as a content analysis of 25 randomly selected comic books. It was included as a chapter of one of Melo's first books (1970).

The following decade represented the effective inclusion of comics in the field of Communication Sciences in Brazil. Two academic courses about comics were created in two Brazilian universities in this decade. Francisco Araújo gave the first course on comics in the Universidade Federal de Brasília (Brasília Federal University) in 1970. However, it was short lived, lasting only for a few years. The second course, specifically on Comics Publishing, began in 1972 and remains active today. Sonia Maria Bibe Luyten, one of the first scholars on comics in Brazil, proposed the course at the Escola de Comunicações e Artes of Universidade de São Paulo. Luyten left the university in 1984, but the course continued in other lecturers' hands. It is, as far as we know, the longest-lasting academic course on comics in the world, representing a model for other academic courses in Brazil.

The work of the first Brazilian comics' academic scholars began in the 1970s. Besides the above-mentioned Sonia Luyten, who is the biggest specialist in the Japanese comics' production in Brazil, that decade also saw the first works of Antonio Luis Cagnin and Moacy Cirne. The latter was the most conspicuous representative of the critical theory and the Marxist approach for the study of comics in Brazil, following a predominance present in most of the South American universities. A Lecturer at the Departamento de Comunicação Social (Social Communication Department) of Universidade Federal Fluminense (Federal Fluminense University), Cirne was secretary of the scientific periodical *Revista de Cultura Vozes* during the 1970s and edited several issues about comics, focusing specifically on the ideology of comics and the world of superheroes. He was the author of the first academic book on comics to be published in Brazil, *A Explosão Criativa dos Quadrinhos* (*The Creative Explosion of Comics*), in 1970, a few months earlier than the already-mentioned *Shazam!* It was the first title in his prolific academic production on the subject over the next 40 years, establishing the prototype for academic books on comics in Brazil. On the other hand, Cagnin was the author of the first master's dissertation on the language of comics in Brazil, published in 1975. Working initially as a high school teacher, Cagnin entered the Universidade de São Paulo as a lecturer in the 1980s, where he concentrated his research on the beginning of comics in Brazil, especially on the work of the Italian-Brazilian Angelo Agostini.

The 1970s also saw the first doctoral research on comics in Brazil. It happened in Faculdade de Psicologia (Faculty of Psychology) of Universidade de São Paulo, by Zilda Augusta Anselmo, focusing on the production of comic books for children and their influence on Brazilian children, especially regarding the relationship of comics with education. One of the first reception studies on comics, Anselmo's study concluded that comics do not have a bad influence on children's study habits. Her thesis was the second academic book on comics published in Brazil. Originally titled *Histórias em Quadrinhos e Adolescentes* (*Comics and Teenagers*), it was published in 1975.

Comics' scholarship reached its maturity in Brazil in the 1980s and '90s. In that period, the first research groups appeared. Papers on comics were presented in the annual congresses of the Intercom—Sociedade Brasileira de Estudos Interdisciplinares de Comunicação (Brazilian Association of Interdisciplinary Studies in Communication) practically since its creation in 1977. The presence of professor José Marques de Melo in the leadership of that non-profit organization, whose aim is to gather researchers and professionals of communications under an interdisciplinary perspective, can probably explain the presence of comics research there. Anyway, the space was formally occupied in 1995, when Flávio Calazans proposed the Grupo de Trabalho Humor e Quadrinhos (Working Group on Humor and Comics), always attracting great interest from the communications scholars and encouraging the constitution of a community of comics scholars in Brazil. The group remained active until the first decade of the 2000s.

The most important research group on comics in Brazil appeared in the University of São Paulo, where three lecturers were working at the Escola de Comunicações e Artes in the 1980s and 1990: Antonio Luiz Cagnin, Alvaro de Moya, and Waldomiro Vergueiro. They proposed the creation of a research group on comics to their school in 1990, which was initially denominated Núcleo de Pesquisa de Histórias em Quadrinhos (Research Nucleus on Comics) and later assumed its current denomination, Observatório de Histórias em Quadrinhos (Observatory of Comics). Settled in the most important university of Brazil, the Observatório is now a very active research center, making possible the development of researchers (undergraduate and graduate), as well as the organization

(Continued)

of books and scientific congresses (national and international). The center serves as a model for the establishment of similar initiatives in other Brazilian universities.

Today, comics is a very popular subject for research projects in Brazilian universities. Each year, students of all fields of knowledge present dozens of master's dissertations and doctoral theses focused on the subject (Vergueiro, Ramos, & Chinen, 2011).

Bibliography

Anselmo, Z.A. (1975) *Histórias em quadrinhos*, Rio de Janeiro: Vozes.
Cirne, M. (1970) *A explosão criativa dos quadrinhos*, Rio de Janeiro: Vozes.
Lima, H. (1963) *História da caricatura no Brasil*, Rio de Janeiro: Ed. José Olympio. 4v.
Melo, J.M. (1970) 'Quadrinhos no Brasil: estrutura industrial e conteúdo das mensagens', in J.M. Melo (ed.) *Comunicação social: teoria e pesquisa*, Petrópolis: Vozes.
Moya, A. (1970) *Shazam!*, São Paulo: Perspectiva.
Vergueiro, W., Ramos, P. and Chinen, N. (2011) *Intersecções acadêmicas: Panorama das 1as Jornadas Internacionais de Histórias em Quadrinhos*, São Paulo: Criativo.
Vergueiro, W. & Santos, R.E. (2005) *O Tico-Tico: Centenário da primeira revista de quadrinhos do Brasil*, São Paulo: Opera Graphica.

A PIONEER'S PERSPECTIVE: JAMES "BUCKY" CARTER

What are the emerging frontiers in comics and education? Several must garner consideration from educators. For one, as publishers seek to diversify their talents, characters, and stories further from paradigms of whiteness and male identities, educators must key in to how comics' evolving readership and authorship change long-held beliefs about comics storytelling. Especially, teachers should study how or if voices that are more diverse and a more diverse readership than has previously appeared challenge longstanding tropes within the myriad genres the comics medium supports.

As a new wave of comics journalists, bloggers, and critics emerges to voice opinions and make claims, an ardent rhetorician's skepticism behooves teachers who must facilitate critical eyes and ears in their students as well, lest comics history becomes distorted by those eager to revise it for their own aims; villainize it without scholarly understandings in literature, art, and comics culture; and praise its latest texts and makers as revolutions or revolutionaries without situating them in relation to the previous story arcs, trends, tropes, and people who built comics foundations and pushed sequential art narrative storytelling.

Further, teachers should consider how comics facilitate discourse around issues of social justice and equity. Creators and characters are more openly showing diversity in gender, sexuality, religion, and other aspects of plurality. Readers, media figures, and scholars helping to usher in the wave of progress associated with 2015's watershed moments in comics history, which saw women garner recognition like never before through critically acclaimed titles, awards like the Eisners and Ignatzs, and other honors, may be investigating fissures in the social commentary emerging throughout comics. Educators *must* investigate these fissures. Where do comics fail to express certain voices, even as the stories change? Does a single narrative predominate still? Who remains invisible between the covers, in the panels, and on the credits pages? Do comics appear to expand the range of voices or simply "appear" some and "disappear" others whom might have been dominant in previous generations? While comics have always illustrated and will continue to reveal aspects of the cultures in which they are embedded, when do they move beyond base representation? Will they push boundaries even as boundaries are redefined? (or will they settle into a new normal?), and who will be marginalized in what many, including me, feel is the most democratic of mediums? Via engaging in these questions, teachers help students connect comics to ongoing social concerns regarding equity and representation, equality and justice.

Much attention is given to critical race studies, gender studies, ethnic studies, and safe spaces now. Comics will mirror this attention. So, it is imperative that educators make concerted efforts to note who gains privilege and who loses it in comics texts and creative circles. Particularly, educators should push themselves and their students to examine socioeconomic conditions, statements, and omissions. What do comics say about the working poor, for example, and about growing mobility and opportunity gaps in societies? If they say little, how do readers and scholars push creators to focus new energy on those frontiers?

Connected, perhaps opaquely at first, to comics' emerging sociocultural representations and social justice manifestations or exclusions, is the emerging realm of abstract comics. Comics scholars/creators such as Andrei Molotiu and Gene Kannenberg, Jr. must be included not just in Comics Studies courses but in any course seriously investigating comics. Abstract comics acknowledge elements of comics form, history, and theory but deconstruct them simultaneously, offering commentary and critique that rattles even the sharp mind from preconceived notions of form, reader interaction, and analysis. As such, they are prime texts for developing a critical consciousness of comics and the subjects they broach. Molotiu's *Abstract Comics: The Anthology* and Kannenberg's *Comics Machine* and work of other abstract comics makers may hold the intellectual key to keeping comics and pedagogy properly situated *while* properly unraveled.

Poetry comics are not new, nor are abstractions in comics art or *as* comics, as Molotiu's anthology illustrates, but critical attention to poetry comics remains emergent. Perhaps abstract comics are their own entity. Perhaps they join with poetry comics, or *visual poetry*, or *graphic poesy*, as a subgenre of comics that retains the ability to frazzle stolid conventions of the forms they combine while also reifying conventions inherent in both poetry and comics. Many common conventions exist, which may surprise some educators. Surely there is merit in studying abstract and poetry comics in and of themselves, but as teaching is political, and certainly the study of pedagogy undergirds policy (and vice versa), these two genres have utility in helping teachers and students find and examine ruptures and fissures too. Michael Chaney's pedagogy deserves attention, as he has taught the study and creation of comics poetry. Also worthy of attention are longtime comics poetry craftspeople Joe Brainard, Warren Craghead, Julie Delporte, Kenneth Koch, and Gary Sullivan. Crag Hill and Nico Vassilakis' *The Last Vispo Anthology: 1999–2008* and *Ink Brick: A Journal of Comics Poetix* must accompany

(*Continued*)

Eisner's *Comics & Sequential Art* and *Graphic Storytelling & Visual Narrative*; McCloud's *Understanding Comics*; and Abel and Madden's *Drawing Words & Writing Pictures* and *Mastering Comics: Drawing Words & Writing Pictures Continued* as intellectual craft texts central to discourse on comics, teaching with them, and teaching through them.

What's more, educators must work to move beyond instances of comics integration as a means of teaching other ideas—of teaching *through* or *with* comics—and make space for studying comics *as* comics, not just as means of conveying a theme or illustrating a social issue, but as a distinctive medium of communication itself. Teachers must make efforts to bridge pedagogical theory and comics theory. Dale Jacobs' *Graphic Encounters: Comics and the Sponsorship of Multimodal Literacy* and Nick Sousanis' *Unflattening* are helpful texts for such bridging.

Finally, to embrace a model of teaching that favors taxonomies of learning like the Bloom's and Marzano/Kendall scales, in which creation is viewed as the apex of understanding, instructors must make room for students to illustrate their thinking via making comics.

Bibliography

Abel, J. and Madden, M. (2008) *Drawing Words & Writing Pictures*, New York: First Second.
Abel, J. and Madden, M. (2012) *Mastering Comics: drawing words & writing pictures continued*, New York: First Second.
Anderson, L.W. and Krathwohl, D.R. (eds.) (2001) *A Taxonomy for Learning, Teaching, and Assessing: a revision of Bloom's Taxonomy of Educational Objectives*, New York: Longman.
Eisner, W. (1985) *Comics & Sequential Art*, Tamarac, FL: Poorhouse Press.
Eisner, W. (1996) *Graphic Storytelling & Visual Narrative*, Tamarac, FL: Poorhouse Press.
Hill, C. and Vassilakis, N. (eds.) (2012) *The Last Vispo Anthology: 1999–2008*. Seattle: Fantagraphics.
Ink Brick: A Journal of Comics Poetix. [Online]. Available from: http://www.inkbrick.com [Accessed 2 December 2015].
Jacobs, D. (2013) *Graphic Encounters: comics and the sponsorship of multimodal literacy*, New York: Bloomsbury.
Kannenberg, Jr., G. (2015) *Comics Machine* [Online]. Available from: http://comicsmachine.tumblr.com/ [Accessed 2 December 2015].
Marzano, J. and Kendall, J.S. (2007) *The New Taxonomy of Educational Objectives*, Thousand Oaks, CA: Corwin.
McCloud, S. (1993) *Understanding Comics*, Northampton, MA: Tundra.
Molotiu, A. (ed.) (2009) *Abstract Comics: the anthology*, Seattle: Fantagraphics.
Silverstein, H. (2014) 'English professor's students publishing 'graphic poems'', *Dartmouth Now*, 5 December. [Online] Available from: http://now.dartmouth.edu/2014/12/english-professors-students-publishing-graphic-poems. [Accessed 2 December 2015].
Sousanis, N. (2015) *Unflattening*, Cambridge, MA: Harvard University Press.

PART 2
The Historians

3

THE HISTORIANS OF THE CREATORS

Brad Ricca

Comics creators have always been keen subjects of reader curiosity, but they have not always been the most popular subjects for critical work. Artistically, historically, and commercially, the role of the comics creator has traditionally come second to the product itself, creators left behind the curtain of fascination that is the initial experience of reading comics. Creators have also tended to be seen, especially by young readers, as romanticized author figures. This layover from the pulp magazine era, where fans built letter-column shrines and letter-writing clubs devoted to Robert E. Howard, E. E. "Doc" Smith, H.P. Lovecraft, and others, helped to foment an atmosphere where the genre creator was seen as a fictional hero rather than a historical subject. To make things even more difficult, while some early comics publishers did acknowledge their workforce, many did not. Because of a variety of factors, most notably anonymous production methods via shops and ghosts as well as the complicated ownerships of many of the characters, readers and critics were always only given partial information on who exactly was making what. Early comics publishers either changed or outright neglected bylines, further building a curiosity over the process of comics creation that proved irresistible to readers who wanted to learn more. This vacillation—between acknowledgment and denial, fandom and fact—is what makes the study of comics creators as a historical subject so important—and so difficult.

A variety of writers—among them creators, historians, fans, and academics—have contributed to the important rediscovery of these creators. More importantly, these writers have shown us that reading comics through contexts of history, biography, and culture unveils rich new meanings in the work itself.

The first major book to take a comprehensive look at comics creators was Martin Sheridan's *Comics and their Creators: Life Stories of American Cartoonists* (1942). Sheridan, a WWII newspaper correspondent who served in both theaters of the war, returned home and got a job at the studio of Russ Westover, the artist of the *Tillie the Toiler* newspaper strip. Sheridan met many other cartoon strip artists at this job and was astounded at the popularity of the comics, which inspired him to begin amassing information for a book. Sheridan's work consisted of short biographies accompanied by self-caricatures, exclusive sketches, photos, and other ephemera. Sheridan titled each entry with the comic character's name, but focused much of his attention on the creators themselves. Among those included in Sheridan's history (which was more of a snapshot of working creators) were Superman, Krazy Kat, Walt Disney, Tarzan, Popeye, Dick Tracy, Buck Rogers, Flash Gordon, Blondie, and many more. Sheridan's book was the first to actually show these creators (albeit exaggerated) alongside a slightly anecdotal, but overall journalistic, short biography of their lives. Sheridan's book, which was reprinted several times, was popular in the '40s simply because comics were. This relationship, between creator history and comics popularity, is one that would be repeated.

Coulton Waugh, like Sheridan, became interested in the history of comics after firsthand experience in the field. Waugh was an artist who worked under Milton Caniff on the newspaper strip *Dickie Dare*, which he eventually took over from Caniff in 1934. Waugh left to work on another strip, the artistically experimental *Hank*, before returning to *Dickie Dare*. Excited by his work in the comics field, Waugh researched and wrote *The Comics* (1947), which is largely acknowledged as the first history of newspaper comics. His approach in the book differed from Sheridan's in that Waugh's work was more of a chronological history, working its way from *The Yellow Kid* in 1895 to the first true comic books of *Famous Funnies* and *New Fun*. Waugh foregrounded the strips themselves but also incorporated creator histories (many of them the first published) of the "great, single personalities" of the field, including Richard F. Outcault, Bud Fisher, and George Herriman, among many others (Waugh, 1947, p. 115).

Once the popularity of comics waned after World War II, critical interest in creators also waned, only to be rekindled in the '60s and '70s. The timing was right for a renaissance in creator history at that time because not only were the young readers who had read Golden Age comics now grown up (and still fascinated by the comics they had absorbed), but the counterculture climate of the '60s and '70s was certainly favorable to rediscovering artists who had been cheated—as the stories went—out of their fortunes by rich corporations.

Sam Moskowitz was another writer who began his career as a young reader, in his case, as an early pioneer and organizer of science-fiction fandom. Like many of his peers, Moskowitz soon found himself actively working in the field he had consumed by getting involved in editing anthologies of science-fiction as well as writing about the genre from the perspective of history. In his book *Seekers of Tomorrow: Masters of Modern Science Fiction* (1965), Moskowitz spotlighted the work and lives of the major S-F authors. The book was, in his words, "a webwork history of science fiction ... told through the lives, works, and influences" of its greatest authors (Moskowitz, 1974, p. 4). Most important to Comics Studies, Moskowitz included a section about Superman and editor Mort Weisinger, which also had a substantial section on Siegel and Shuster that included new details on their process in creating Superman. Though this was the only major comics entry, its inclusion was a victory for legitimacy because Moskowitz placed these comics creators among such luminary authors as Isaac Asimov, Robert A. Heinlein, and Edmond Hamilton.

Similarly, cartoonist Jules Feiffer's *Great Comic Book Heroes* (1965) was a short, funny, and thought-provoking interpretation of the classic superheroes. Feiffer's semi-autobiographical memoir is some of the first true cultural analysis of superheroes, including some creator information and anecdotes. The book, which was very popular due to its nostalgic content, also included a reprint of an entire *Spirit* story, which helped introduce a new generation to the artistry of Will Eisner.

Richard A. Lupoff and Don Thompson's edited collection *All in Color for a Dime* (1970) contained reprints of articles from the early fanzine *XERO* but gave some coverage to early creators in essays by Dick Lupoff, Ron Goulart, Ted White, and others. In particular, it was Lupoff's investigation of Captain Marvel that was one of the first historical looks at Billy Parker and C. C. Beck, who created the popular (albeit controversial) character. The book's subsequent mass-market publication later that year further opened up comics history to several generations of comic book readers who were interested in the subject.

Arguably the most influential of these new works on creator history was Jim Steranko's two-volume *The Steranko History of Comics*, published by Supergraphics Press (Steranko's own imprint) in 1970 and 1972, boasting a foreword by Italian filmmaker Federico Fellini. Steranko, who at that time was already an accomplished artist and painter best known for his surrealist version of *Nick Fury Agent of S.H.I.E.L.D.*, decided to undertake a history of the medium, which was the first of its kind. Though only two of a planned six volumes were ever produced, the work combined fact with anecdote, art with artifact, to produce what might best be understood as an art history of the comics medium in an oversized, tabloid form.

Though frustratingly uncited, *The Steranko History of Comics* was the first work to make real cross-cultural connections between comics and other mediums, especially to the pulp magazines of the '20s and '30s, whose rich relationship to comics was supported with striking visual and textual evidence. The work's real contribution, though, was the inclusion of facts and stories of the early creators of comics, including Siegel and Shuster, Kane and Finger, Will Eisner, Jack Kirby. Not only did *The Steranko History* provide never-before-published, anecdotal stories about these figures, but it also reprinted original drawings, prototype art, and another *Spirit* story in order to make the point that superhero comics were an evolving genre, not instantaneous, self-contained works of art. Steranko's fascination that comics "were produced for kids BY KIDS!" layered itself into his work in a way that made comics and youth seem, for the first time, inseparable (Steranko, 1970, p. 4). Steranko offered the first wholesale cultural analysis of the genre as a history of its creators rather than of its characters.

Steranko's work was also important because of its audience. His two books—wrapped in bright full-color artwork depicting every major comics character—were marketed and sold to comics readers. Steranko, as a respected artist himself, not only assured comics fans that it was important to know their history, but legitimized a new way of researching that seemed indebted to the medium itself. Using images to make points of connection rather than dry academic quotes, Steranko, without any formal training in history, in many ways began the study of cultural historicism in comics by making his process plain. His method of understanding comics history—by hunting for cultural forebears, swipes, artifacts, and stories—is still very much in practice today.

As former fans and artists were writing—and rewriting—comics history by focusing on its creators, there was one man working on a decades-long project that would become the touchstone of the overall enterprise of understanding comics creation. Like those before him, Jerry Bails began his historical work on comics from the perspective of an ardent fan. A particular aficionado of Golden Age comics and, in particular, the Justice Society of America, Bails began his career as a young fan writing to editors, writers, and people like himself. He founded the fanzine *Alter Ego* with Roy Thomas in 1961, among many other publications and fan groups.

But Bails' most important work concerning comics was yet to come. Bails worked at night with his friend Hames Ware on their *Who's Who* series of comics history books.

From 1973 to 1976, they published the four-volume *Who's Who of American Comic Books*, which attempted to be an index of comic books not only by year, but also by artist, writer, inker, and so on. In short, it was the first comprehensive study of comics creators with a data-driven approach. Bails' goal was simple: he wanted to discover who did what. It is hard to imagine how difficult historical work on comics would have been before this project.

Bails' methodology was drastically different from Steranko's cultural approach, but has proven invaluable. Bails' biggest obstacle was authentication, mostly because many of the early comics he was indexing did not have bylines. So Bails, just as he had done as a young comics fan, wrote to creators, talked to them, and tried to reach as definitive a truth as he could.

But Bails' methodology now had an academic sharpness that his old fan letters had lacked. Due to his training as a Ph.D. (he worked by day as a Professor of Natural Sciences at Wayne State University), Bails developed an elaborate questionnaire that asked pointed questions of creators and placed their contributions in categories such as Name, Credit, and Tenure. Bails also showed the non-comics work of these creators, which would help later scholars make inroads into larger biographical analyses.

Bails also microfilmed an estimated 500,000 pages of old comic books to not only ascertain their credits, but also subject them to the expertise of his partners and consultants, including Hames Ware, who was an expert on identifying art styles, and Martin O'Hearn, who could identify Silver Age writers by their dialogue alone.

Even more important was Bails' decision, even in the dark days of dial-up, to put the *Who's Who* online. Though technologically frustrating at times, Bails' online www.bailsproject.com gave free access to creator information that, though certainly not devoid of fan passion in its creation, removed the romanticism of other comics histories. Bails' work remains probably the most important work on comics creators ever attempted. Its goal, as "a database designed to document the careers of people who have contributed to or supported the publication of original material in US comic books in the years 1928–99" professionalized the work of not only these creators, but of the very scholars working on them (Bails, 2006). Bails' work has continued in spirit through similar projects such as The Grand Comics Database, which is a massive online database of comics "sequences" that are indexed by creator, theme, and several other criteria.

SIDEBAR: MAGAZINES AND ONLINE

Brad Ricca

The built-in fan communities of comics led to an easy transition to more temporary publishing ventures such as magazines and the Internet. Though many have come and gone (and have been largely fan-based), several remain significant for their treatment of comics creators in particular. Jerry Bails' first partner, Roy Thomas (see main entry), later became Mort Weisinger's assistant editor at DC, which he successfully parlayed into a long, very popular career as an editor and writer at Marvel, DC, and elsewhere. Thomas continued to produce the fanzine, then magazine *Alter Ego* through a series of volumes alongside others such as Bill Schelly and publisher John Morrow. Thomas made sure that creator interviews, biographies, and artifacts would always have a place in *Alter Ego*, no matter the pedigree of the writer. Throughout its long history, *Alter Ego* has run important interviews with creators such as Gil Kane, Bill Everett, and Joe Kubert, among many others. TwoMorrow's list has expanded to include *Comic Book Artist*, *Comic Book Creator*, *Jack Kirby Collector*, and the *Modern Masters* series, which focuses on individual artists, often showcasing rare process work and interviews.

The Comics Journal, since its inception in 1976, has been outspoken in its ongoing discussion of comics creators. This focus has usually taken the form of lengthy interviews with people like Charles Schulz, Robert Crumb, Gil Kane, and Jerry Robinson, among many others. In addition, the *Journal* has, under the direction of editor Gary Groth, reprinted entire depositions of creator lawsuits. Though the print version has necessarily adapted to an annual showcase journal, the website remains a current source of news and long-form comics criticism. Tom Spurgeon, a former editor at *TCJ*, left to run *The Comics Reporter*, an online blog dedicated to comics. The site contains a breadth of archived, lengthy interviews, especially with new, sometimes unknown, creators. Spurgeon's commitment to independent creators allows him to showcase many contemporary artists who do not get covered elsewhere.

Unlike the *TCJ*, the *International Journal of Comic Art* is a publication that is much more academic in spirit. The *IJOCA*, one of the first English-language journals in the field, was founded and edited by John A. Lent in 1999. The *Journal* frequently runs essays devoted to comics creators, especially international ones.

Unfortunately, some periodicals have ceased publication and remain available only in archives. Jud Hurd's *Cartoonist PROfiles* was one such magazine that ran from 1969 to 2005. Consisting of creator biographies and illustrations, the magazine was famous for its "shop talk" that provided a unique look at the process life of the individual cartoonist. Hurd, a cartoonist himself and one-time Hollywood reporter, provided equal parts anecdote and lesson in *PROfiles* to make it a vital part of the cartooning community for over 25 years—making it indispensable to historians.

Trina Robbins is a comics artist-herstorian who became an influential figure in recognizing and rescuing creators of the past, particularly female ones disregarded by previous scholars. In the San Francisco underground comix scene, Robbins was active co-producing the first all-woman comic book *It Ain't Me, Babe* (1970) and the comics anthology *Wimmen's Comix* (1972–1992). In 1986, Robbins was also the first woman artist to officially draw *Wonder Woman* for DC Comics.

Robbins also researched and wrote, with Eclipse Comics editor Catherine Yronwode, *Women and the Comics* (1985), the first book dedicated to the history of female newspaper strip and comic book creators. The book, which uncovered a wealth of names and comics new to modern readers, was very popular with general audiences. After the success of the book, Robbins found there was much more to say on the subject. Her research has since produced a number of subsequent studies on women creators including *A Century of Women Cartoonists* (1993), *The Great Women Superheroes* (1996), *From Girls to Grrrlz: A History of Women's Comics from Teens to Zines* (1999), and *The Great Women Cartoonists* (2001). Her more recent work, *Pretty in Ink* (2013), is her most comprehensive, covering 1896 to the present-day. Robbins' approach is largely research based as she uncovers artists, illustrators, and writers who contributed to the medium, in major newspapers or sometimes small, forgotten magazines. She presents her work in a way similar to Steranko: as art placed alongside textual analysis. She is also careful to place these creators in the historical times they worked in, particularly in feminist contexts. Throughout her career, she has focused in particular on illustrators Rose O'Neill, Nell Brinkley, and popular characters such as Dale Messick's Brenda Starr and Tarpe Mills' Miss Fury.

SIDEBAR: *A HERSTORIAN'S PERSPECTIVE*

Christina Blanch

Trina Robbins not only edited the very first all-woman comic book, *It Ain't Me, Babe*, drew the first comic about a lesbian, and became the first woman to draw a published Wonder Woman comic, she is also the preeminent comics scholar focusing on women and feminism. Penning such books as *Women and the Comics* (1985 with Cat Yronwode), *From Girls to Grrrlz: A History of Women's Comics from Teens to Zines* (1999), *The Great Women Cartoonists* (2001), and *Pretty in Ink: North American Women Cartoonists 1896–2013* (2013), no one can deny that Trina is a triple threat—a comic book writer, artist, and scholar. Yet, she is so much more. And recently, Trina has been inducted into the Will Eisner Hall of Fame.

Starting her path into comics in the late 1960s, Trina has been an unstoppable force for the place of women within the comic book industry. She attends multiple conventions every year, publishes constantly, and maintains a blog about her life. She is a true pioneer of comic book scholarship. She refers to herself as a "Herstorian," and in that very act of renaming her role, she both fits—and defies—the definition of a comic book scholar.

In *The Great Women Cartoonists* and *Pretty in Ink*, Trina shined a spotlight on the history of women cartoonists. She notes that "as many woman cartoonists break the mold as fit into it, with as many different styles as there are artists" (Robbins, 2001, p. 130). These woman artists vary as widely as do those of us that study their work.

She not only writes about female cartoonists, but her writings also give great insight into the representation of men and women in comics. While talking about how comics reveal more about the creator than is sometimes intentional, she brings up the point that how genders are portrayed in comics reveals how the authors/artists see themselves and the opposite sex. In her article "Gender Differences in Comics" (2002), she writes "both genders are fantasies for young male readers, the women representing sex fantasies of adolescent boys who have little or no experience with real women."

In *From Girls to Grrrlz* she not only gives a history of comics featuring women, but also refers to the women and girls that were reading them. Pointing out that "there once was a time when more girls than boys read comics, a time when comics for girls sold in the millions, outnumbering every other kind of comic book" (Robbins, 1999, p. 7), she made many readers sit up and take notice of the sizable portion of the comics audience that the women and girls have been historically.

Without Trina insisting that people remember the female creators of comics and the girls and women that were reading them, the changes happening in the world of comics might not be happening today. As an academic focused on women in comics myself, I know if I had not picked up *From Girls to Grrrlz*, I would most likely not have bent my teachings toward gender.

Bibliography

Robbins, T. (1999) *From Girls to Grrrlz: a history of women's comics from teens to zines,* San Francisco: Chronicle Books.

Robbins, T. (2001) *The Great Women Cartoonists,* New York: Watson-Guptill Publications.

Robbins, T. (2002) 'Gender differences in comics', *Image [&] Narrative: Online Magazine of the Visual Narrative,* 2(2). [Online] Available from: http://www.imageandnarrative.be/inarchive/gender/trinarobbins.htm [Accessed 16 July 2016].

Robbins, T. (2013) *Pretty in Ink: North American women cartoonists 1896–2013,* Seattle: Fantagraphics.

Robbins, T. and Yronwode, C.T. (1985) *Women and the Comics,* Forestville, CA: Eclipse Books.

Like Robbins, Robert C. (R.C.) Harvey was a freelance cartoonist before he started writing about comics for *The Menomonee Falls Gazette.* Starting out, Harvey's niche of knowledge was the cartoon strip, which led him to write *The Art of the Funnies* (1994) and *The Art of the Comic Book* (1996). He also wrote *The Genius of Winsor McCay* (1998) and contributed to *Comics PROfile.* Harvey's most creator-focused work was on Milt Caniff, the creator of one of the most popular newspaper strips of the 20th century, *Terry and the Pirates.* Harvey edited *Milton Caniff: Conversations* (2002) and wrote the nearly 1,000 page *Meanwhile... A Biography of Milton Caniff, Creator of Terry and the Pirates and Steve Canyon* (2007). His most recent work is *Insider Histories of Cartooning* (2014), which deals with short anecdotal histories of largely (and almost completely) forgotten cartoonists.

As superheroes became popular again in the '80s and '90s, comics became a subject eligible for all types of writers, not just former cartoonists. Les Daniels was a novelist and journalist who had written *Comix: A History of the Comic Book in America* (1971), a general history of the medium. Daniels was asked to contribute the text to three books from DC Comics about their trinity of superheroes: Superman (1998), Batman (1999), and Wonder Woman (2000). In these *Official History* books, which combined high-quality photography and design by Chip Kidd, each character's visual history was showcased and chronicled. Daniels' text, somewhat surprisingly, also contained a significant amount of newly published information on the creators of these characters: Siegel and Shuster, Finger and Kane, and William Moulton Marston, much of it in very un-romanticized terms. Like Steranko, Daniels and Kidd also used never-before-seen art to unveil a creator process that was evolutionary—with stops and starts—as opposed to revolutionary perfect.

Daniels' contributions to creator history were important because the books sold very well to general audiences. For the first time, a new generation of comics fans was introduced to the creators of their favorite superheroes in an officially licensed product that placed them on the same page.

Thomas Andrae was one of the first trained academics to approach comics from a literary and cultural perspective. Early in his career, he recorded interviews with important comics creators such as Bob Kane, Siegel and Shuster, Jack Kirby, Jerry Robinson, Carl Barks, and many others, asking questions about culture, history, inspiration, and process instead of the usual fan-driven queries. These interviews, which are mostly reprinted in his *Creators of the*

Superheroes (2011) and *Carl Barks and the Disney Comic Book* (2006), remain some of the best primary source material in existence for many of these creators.

In 2000, it was a bestselling novel that may have helped contribute to a new popularity in long-form cultural and biographical narratives about comics creators. Michael Chabon's *The Amazing Adventures of Kavalier & Clay* (2000) was a fictional story of two immigrant boys who became superhero comics creators in Depression-era New York. An imaginary pastiche of the lives of Siegel, Shuster, Eisner, and Steranko (among others), the novel was an enormous bestseller and served as an introduction to many non-comics readers to some of the stories and drama of the early comics creators. Though Chabon's work was fictional, it opened the marketplace door to longer, general audience books about comics creators.

After the success of Chabon's novel, a number of readers, fans, and scholars took up this banner of understanding comics creators through narratives that took place on a much longer, grander scale. Gerard Jones, a comics writer turned cultural historian, wrote *Men of Tomorrow: Geeks, Gangsters, and the Birth of the Comic Book* (2004), the first large-scale telling of the birth of the Golden Age of comics as a product of a shady network of creators, publishers, and economic pressures. A book that took a similar approach to different eras was David Michaelis' *Schulz and Peanuts: A Biography* (2007), an unauthorized biography of Charles Schulz that read individual panels of his work in terms of exact biographical facts.

For young adults, Marc Tyler Nobleman's picture books *Boys of Steel* (2008) and *Bill the Boy Wonder* contained extra-textual chapters with extensive never-before-published information on the creators of Superman and Batman. Sean Howe's book *Marvel Comics: The Untold Story* (2012) was a company history overlaid with rich new information from meticulous research and creator interviews. More recently, Jill Lepore's *The Secret History of Wonder Woman* (2014) analyzed the feminist icon through the remarkable biographical details of her creator William Moulton Marston, as well as his interaction with the works of Margaret Sanger.

SIDEBAR: INTERNATIONAL CREATORS

Brad Ricca

Scholarship about comics creators is by no means isolated to North America and the English language. In fact, the rich traditions of comics in western Europe and Japan—especially those produced by comics auteurs—have yielded important creator scholarship in both English and their respective native languages.

Several scholars have written on creators working in the rich Franco-Belgian (*bande dessinée*) tradition of comics. Thierry Groensteen, the French language scholar of comics best known for his theoretical work *The System of Comics* (2007), also produced a book on Rodolphe Töpffer, the 19th-century teacher and artist who produced, arguably, some of the first comics. Groensteen's book *Töpffer, l'invention de la bande dessinée*, co-written with Benoît Peeters (1994), went into detail about not only Töpffer's early cartoon work, but also his fascinating theoretical writings about producing images for children. David Kunzle's *Father of the Comic Strip: Rodolphe Töpffer* (2007) provided another biography of Töpffer that also included first-ever English translations of strip facsimiles.

> Harry Thompson's book *Tintin: Hergé and His Creation* (1991) was the first comprehensive biography of Georges Prosper Remi, otherwise known as Hergé, the 20th-century cartoonist who produced the massively popular *The Adventures of Tintin* series. Thompson's book, in English, went into detail about Hergé's guarded personal life—and the sometimes difficult values portrayed in his comics. A later work on Hergé was Benoit Peeters' *Hergé: Son of Tintin* (2011), a shorter, more artifact-based study that provided a very useful companion to Thompson's longer biography.
>
> Jacques Tardi, the famous French cartoonist, produces work over a broader range—from documentary comics to serial adventure, including his famous heroine, Adèle Blanc-Sec. Several French studies of Tardi, well known for his deliberate intersection of comics and outspoken politics, include Thierry Groensteen's *Tardi* (1980), Olivier Maltret's *Presque tout Tardi* (1996) and Michel Boujut's *Tardi par la fenêtre* (1996). For those interested in an overview of the *bande dessinée* movement, consult Matthew Screech's *Masters of the Ninth Art: Bandes Dessinées and Franco-Belgian Identity* (2005).
>
> In Japan, individual comics creators (*mangaka*) have long been revered alongside their creations, as the production of Japanese manga is largely an apprentice system of significant, respectable work. In English, Natsu Onoda Power's *God of Comics: Osamu Tezuka and the Creation of Post-World War II Manga* (2009) is a biography of Tezuka, the creator of *Astro Boy*, *Kimba the White Lion*, and the longer *Phoenix* series of graphic novels. Though there is a great deal written on mangaka in Japanese, there is precious little in translation, and even less in English. More full-length work needs to be done, especially on such creators as Naoko Takeuchi (*Sailor Moon*) and Masamune Shirow (*Ghost in the Shell*), among others.

Substantial work has been done by scholars and experts such as Carol Tilley, Craig Yoe, Denis Kitchen, Tom Heintjes, Mark Evanier, Charles Hatfield, Bill Schelly, Arlen Schumer, Nicky Wheeler Nicholson, J. David Spurlock, Jeet Heer—in articles, on panels, and in discussion boards online—as we continue in our attempt to understand the process and ramifications of comics creation. The University Press of Mississippi continues to publish important books in their Great Comics Artists Series and Conversation with Comic Artists Series. The Ohio State University Billy Ireland Cartoon Library & Museum has also been influential in foregrounding creators both known and esoteric through its various public exhibitions. The curtain has certainly begun to be lifted, but there are many more layers to excavate. There will also always be a certain level of romanticism to dispel for our new, best historical narratives to take hold. Though our study of the major superheroes has yielded interesting results, historical studies of creators of color, LGBTQ creators, non-traditional creators, and the histories of editors and publishers all remain rich places for us to engage the lengthy process by which comics are both imagined and made.

Bibliography

Andrae, T. (2006) *Carl Barks and the Disney Comic Book*, Jackson: University Press of Mississippi.
Andrae, T. (2011) *Creators of the Superheroes*, Timonium, MD: Hermes.
Bails, J. (2006) *Who's Who in American Comic Books 1928–1999*. Available from: http://www.bailsproject.com. [Accessed 27 July 2015].

Daniels, L. and Kidd, C. (1998) *Superman: the complete history*, San Francisco: Chronicle.
Daniels, L. and Kidd, C. (1999) *Batman: the complete history*, San Francisco: Chronicle.
Daniels, L. and Kidd, C. (2000) *Wonder Woman: the complete history*, San Francisco: Chronicle.
Feiffer, J. (2003) *The Great Comic Book Heroes*, Seattle: Fantagraphics. Reprint.
Harvey, R.C. (2007) *Meanwhile... A Biography of Milton Caniff, Creator of Terry and the Pirates and Steve Canyon*, Seattle: Fantagraphics.
Harvey, R.C. (2014) *Insider Histories of Cartooning*, Jackson: University Press of Mississippi.
Howe, S. (2012) *Marvel Comics: the untold story*, New York: Harper.
Jones, G. (2004) *Men of Tomorrow: geeks, gangsters, and the birth of the comic book*, New York: Basic.
Kunzle, D. (2007) *Father of the Comic Strip: Rodolphe Töpffer*, Jackson: University Press of Mississippi.
Lepore, J. (2014) *The Secret History of Wonder Woman*, New York: Knopf.
Michaelis, D. (2007) *Schulz and Peanuts: a biography*, New York: Harper.
Moskowitz, S. (1974) *Seekers of Tomorrow: masters of modern science fiction*, New York: Hyperion Press. Reprint.
Nobleman, M. and MacDonald, R. (2008) *Boys of Steel: the creators of Superman*, New York: Knopf.
Nobleman, M., MacDonald, R. and Templeton, T. (2012) *Bill the Boy Wonder: the secret co-creator of Batman*, Watertown, MA: Charlesbridge.
Peeters, B. (2011) *Hergé: Son of Tintin*, Baltimore: Johns Hopkins University Press.
Power, N. (2009) *God of Comics: Osamu Tezuka and the creation of post-World War II manga*, Jackson: University Press of Mississippi.
Robbins, T. (1993) *A Century of Women Cartoonists*. Northampton, MA: Kitchen Sink.
Robbins, T. (1997) *The Great Women Superheroes*, Northampton, MA: Kitchen Sink.
Robbins, T. (1999) *From Girls to Grrrlz: a history of women's comics from teens to zines*, San Francisco: Chronicle.
Robbins, T. (2001) *The Great Women Cartoonists*, New York: Watson-Guptill.
Robbins, T. (2013) *Pretty In Ink: North American women cartoonists 1896–2013*, Seattle: Fantagraphics.
Robbins, T. and Yronwode, C. (1985) *Women and the Comics*, Forestville, CA: Eclipse Books.
Screech, M. (2005) *Masters of the Ninth Art: Bandes Dessinées and Franco-Belgian identity*, Liverpool: Liverpool University Press.
Sheridan, M. (1942) *Comics and Their Creators: life stories of American cartoonists*, Boston: Hale Cushman & Flint.
Steranko, J. (1970, 1972) *The Steranko History of Comics*, Reading, PA: Supergraphics. 2 vols.
Thompson, H. (1991) *Tintin: Hergé and his creation*, London: Hodder and Stoughton.
Waugh, C. (1947) *The Comics*, New York: Macmillan.

4

THE HISTORIANS OF THE COMICS INDUSTRY

Julie Davis and Robert Westerfelhaus

The first product of the U S comic book industry comprised of entirely original material, *New Fun Comics*, was published in 1935. Until then, the content of comic books was commonly recycled from the Sunday "funny pages," which as an art form are not much older than comic books. An early and classic example, *The Yellow Kid*, debuted as a Sunday supplement strip in 1895 in Joseph Pulitzer's popular *New York World*. Despite its status as a relatively new medium, the comic book industry has spawned a robust and specialized cadre of historians dedicated to studying its past (Schumer, 1988). Whether members of this group are teaching at universities, writing scholarly books and articles, posting popular blog posts, speaking at academic or fan conventions, or discussing comic books in the industry press, they all owe a debt to those pioneers who thought systematically studying comics' past was a worthwhile enterprise even at a time when the medium was still derisively considered ephemeral children's fare, as disposable as the cheap paper upon which the garishly colored magazines were printed. This chapter identifies the attributes that define someone as a historian of the comic book industry, then sketches the background and contributions of several key historians of the industry, and finally offers a brief look at contemporary and possible future trends in the field.

Defining Characteristics of Comic Book Historians

Unlike many professions, there are no set educational or licensing requirements defining who can call him- or herself a comic book historian. As a result, individuals with a wide range of backgrounds, experiences, and expertise are referred to, and refer to themselves, as comic book historians. Interestingly, this lack of standardization is not limited to historians who study comic books. Indeed, historians representing many differing methodological approaches and a wide range of diverse foci have lacked established and recognized definitional criteria since Herodotus penned the first history text two and a half millennia ago.

A set of such criteria can be found not in the work of a historian but rather in a lengthy 200-page ruling penned on April 11, 2000, by Judge Charles Gray regarding the case of Irving v. Penguin Books, Ltd., in which David Irving unsuccessfully sued Professor

Deborah Lipstadt and her publisher in the Royal Courts of London for libel because she referred to him as a Holocaust denier in her 1996 book *Denying the Holocaust* (Goodman, 2010). The judgment, which favored the defendants, hinged upon the definition of an "Objective Historian." The definition pointed to was not derived from established law or academic scholarship, but was based instead upon the testimony of an expert witness (Schneider, 2001). Although Judge Gray's ruling did not explicitly lay out the definition of a historian per se, Schneider (2001) argues that based upon the judge's finding regarding the case "one can distill a code of conduct for the objective historian" (p. 1534), which includes:

- treating source material with a proper degree of skepticism;
- fairly evaluating and interpreting all data without bias, without "cherry-picking," without materially relevant omissions, and with a willingness to take into consideration any counterevidence to one's cherished views; and,
- clearly distinguishing between objective fact and subjective speculation.

These same definitional criteria are certainly applicable to all historians regardless of the specific subject matter they study. Barry Pearl (2012), author of a Marvel reference book, lays out additional criteria that, he argues, are defining characteristics of true comic book historians. According to Pearl, they should:

- be passionate about the medium;
- specialize, rather than attempt to cultivate a general knowledge of the field as a whole;
- enjoy easy and regular access to an extensive and well organized collection of comic books with which they are intimately familiar;
- collect fanzines, magazines, newspaper articles, and other writings focused upon comic books;
- collect books about comics;
- read, re-read, and make substantive use of the comics, books, and other textual materials they have collected;
- cultivate reliable sources within the industry, from whom they can obtain information and check facts;
- follow the facts, avoid speculation, and substantiate claims; and, most importantly, comic books historians should
- be fans first and foremost.

Although some of Pearl's (2012) criteria could easily apply to historians in general (one would hope that historians enjoy their subject matter, be organized, and be familiar with the materials they study), others are specific to the study of comics (e.g., most historians are not be able to personally possess an extensive collection of original artifacts). The last criterion listed above deserves brief consideration. At the very least, the notion that a comic book historian should be a fan complicates the expectation that a historian should be objective. Moreover, one can be interested in studying someone or something for whom or for which she is not an ardent admirer. For example, a historian need not be a fan of Hitler or the Ku Klux Klan in order to invest the time, energy, and expertise required to systematically study them from a historical perspective. Why, then, must a comic book historian necessarily be a fan of Superman or Ms. Marvel to be considered a legitimate authority regarding those characters?

Pearl (2012) also makes it a point to note that being a well-informed industry insider renders one a witness to history but does not necessarily make one a historian. This point draws an important distinction, but one that is ironic given the professional identity of the earliest historians of the comic book industry, such as Jules Feiffer and Jim Steranko, who were witnesses to and chroniclers of the history of the very industry in which they were employed.

Early Comic Book Historians: Industry Insiders

While it may seem odd for someone to choose to chronicle the history of a relatively new medium, Jules Feiffer did just that when in 1965 he published his groundbreaking *The Great Comic Book Heroes*. In that book, he coupled superhero origin stories with commentary about the works in which they are featured. This work has been called "The granddaddy of all books about comic books" (Carlson, 2008). Within a few years, a wave of comic book histories followed in the wake of the publication of Feiffer's book, beginning with the release of the first volume of Jim Steranko's *The Steranko History of Comics* in 1970. The second volume was published in 1972. This set bookended an extremely prolific 1971, which saw the publication of Maurice Horn's *Seventy-Five Years of the Comics*, which discussed both newspaper comic strips and comic books, and Les Daniels' *Comix: A History of Comic Books in America*.

Many of the early comic book historians were not only observers of the industry, but often members of it as well. Thus, each offers a uniquely situated insider's view. Jim Steranko, for instance, worked for Marvel, writing and drawing a variety of different titles (Howe, 2012). Jules Feiffer spent years as a syndicated newspaper cartoonist before and after producing his groundbreaking work. This industry experience enabled such situated authors to provide some context to their explanations about the industry.

Jules Feiffer (1929–)

Like many early comic book illustrators, who typically referred to themselves as cartoonists or commercial artists, Jules Feiffer grew up in the New York City metropolitan area. He was raised in the Bronx, where he spent much of his youth reading comic books and drawing on the sidewalk (Groth, 2004). Early in his career, Feiffer worked for almost a decade as an assistant to Will Eisner on *The Spirit* while also creating his own strip, *Clifford*, a one-page addition to Eisner's *Spirit*. Later, he wrote and drew a long-running strip that appeared for 42 years in the *Village Voice* (1956–1997). Originally titled *Sick, Sick, Sick*, the strip's name was later changed to *Feiffer's Fables* and then simply *Feiffer*. This strip earned him the Pulitzer Prize for editorial cartooning in 1986 (Wepman, 1990). In addition to comics, Feiffer's creative output includes writing plays, children's novels, and picture books. Feiffer also produced an animated film, *Munro*, based upon his cartoons, for which he won an Academy Award for Best Short-Subject Cartoon in 1961.

The only non-fiction work in Feiffer's prolific career, *The Great Comic Book Heroes* (1965), combined origin stories of iconic heroes, often stories that had not been re-released since their debut decades earlier, coupled with critical and biographical essays about the comic book industry and a discussion of the impact of comic book narratives and characters upon the public as well as Feiffer himself (Carlson, 2008). In an interesting twist, it is worth noting that this work revived the career of celebrated cartoonist, and early Feiffer supervisor, Will Eisner. *The Great Comic Book Heroes* was well received, with *New York Times* book reviewer Eliot Fremont-Smith (1965) describing Feiffer's introduction as "marvelous, knowing, pungent and very funny" and offering only one "complaint about this book: there isn't enough of it" (p. 35). Gabilliet (2010) called this work "the foundational text with regard to superheroes of the first generation" (p. 361).

Perhaps the best-known, and certainly the most cited, passage in the book is an almost celebratory description of comic books as a lower form of culture. As described by Feiffer (1965):

> Comic books, first of all, are junk. To accuse them of being what they are is to make no accusation at all: there is no such thing as uncorrupt junk or moral junk or educational junk—though attempts at the latter have, from time to time, been foisted on us. But education is not the purpose of junk (which is one reason why True Comics and Classic Comics and other half-hearted attempts to bring reality or literature into the field invariably looked embarrassing). (p. 4)

In contrast, Feiffer (1965) argues, "Junk is there to entertain on the basest, most compromised of levels. It finds the lowest phantasmal common denominator and proceeds from there" (p. 4). However, according to Feiffer (1965), relegating comics to the category of junk literature has cultural and creative advantages. As he explains:

> Junk is a second-class citizen of the arts; a status of which we and it are constantly aware. There are certain inherent privileges in second-class citizenship. Irresponsibility is one. Not being taken seriously is another. Junk, like the drunk at the wedding, can get away with doing or saying anything because, by its very appearance, it is already in disgrace. It has no one's respect to lose; no image to endanger. Its values are the least middle class of all the mass media. That's why it is needed so. (p. 4)

Thus, Feiffer suggests, as junk art comic books can create characters, tell stories, and make statements that would not have been permitted by those creating or consuming other ostensibly more established and better respected art forms. In promoting this perspective he raised appreciation for comic books as a legitimate art form capable of conveying serious content and with a history worthy of study. While he was the first to chart that history, Feiffer did not have to wait long for others to join him.

James Steranko (1938–)

Indeed, Feiffer was not the only comic book insider of his era to author an early chronicle of the medium's history. James (Jim) Steranko is possibly the best-known artist and writer who was also a pioneer historian of comic books. In contrast to the New York City upbringing typical of his contemporary colleagues, Steranko grew up in the industrial city of Reading, Pennsylvania. The son of poor immigrants, he lived in poverty for much of his youth. Prior to entering the comics industry, Steranko earned his living in a variety of ways. He performed as a magician and escape artist and as a musician in a rock band, and he worked in advertising, designing ads and producing product illustrations (Howe, 2012).

Steranko is best known for his celebrated work on Marvel's *Nick Fury, Agent of S.H.I.E.L.D*. He is credited with infusing a pop-art sensibility into the famous Marvel style during his brief initial turn (1968–1969) working as an artist for that publisher (Howe, 2012). Steranko claims that experts have discerned 150 new narrative devices in the 29 comic books he drew during that time (Ross, 2010). He was certainly innovative with respect to style (his work referenced psychedelic, op, and pop art), layout (he made productive use of one- and two-page spreads, and introduced the first four-page spread), and even title treatment (his blend of text and image for the title of the Nick Fury story "Today the Earth Died" in *Strange Tales* #168 was a factor in his winning the 1968 Alley Award for Best Feature Story). After leaving Marvel in 1969, Steranko opened his own publishing company, Supergraphics. He continued to work in commercial art, creating comic book covers, posters, graphic novels, a magazine, and anti-drug comic books (Goulart, 1990; Ross, 2010). With Supergraphics, Steranko began an ambitious project: a proposed six-volume chronicle of the history of the comic book industry. However, only two of these volumes were published: *The Steranko History of Comics*, Volume 1 in 1970 and Volume 2 in 1972. Duncan and Smith (2009) argue that these works were "the first serious attempts to preserve the history of the comic book medium, and they mark the first time that the comics scholarship of the fanzines was available to a wider audience" (p. 185).

Over the years, the two volumes have received mixed reviews. Some authorities call them "well-researched" (Goulart, 1990, p. 347) and "the canon of the Golden Age" (Gabilliet, 2010, p. 303). Highsmith (1987) claims that, despite its limitations, "it is nonetheless a source that has yet to be fully superseded or matched" (p. 206). Other experts are less flattering, calling the volumes "an exciting, if not always accurate exploration of comic book history" (Duncan & Smith, 2009, p. 185) or advising readers to "avoid basing any analysis on the details offered by" the work (Gabilliet, 2010, p. 358).

Despite the lack of additional volumes examining the field after the 1940s, and inconsistent reviews, Steranko's two volumes, coupled with that of Feiffer, are credited with sparking interest in the comic industry's past that inspired the work of later historians, who took the torch from him and Feiffer and have continued to carry it. In doing so, they too argue for the significance of comic books' aesthetic innovations, their contributions to the broader culture from which they draw inspiration, and their potential to provide serious sociopolitical commentary. In doing so, they have improved upon the anecdotal and episodic approach employed by Feiffer and Steranko, been more rigorous in identifying and using primary sources, and have expanded the scope of comic book history well beyond the familiar confines of the medium's popular costumed superheroes.

Denis Gifford (1927–2000)

Denis Gifford, an Englishman born in London, was a prolific creator and chronicler of a variety of genres of British popular culture. He published his first comic book at age 14; wrote more than 50 books on a variety of popular culture topics, including comics, film, and nostalgia; and created radio and television programs (Denis Gifford, 2000). Within the comic book industry, in which he was active from the mid-1940s until the early 1970s, Gifford worked as a writer and artist on diverse material ranging from humor strips and science fiction to such action genres as superhero narratives and the Western. Early in his career, he created several of Britain's Golden Age superheroes, including Mr. Muscle and Tiger-Man. He also adapted such Western staples as Roy Rogers and Annie Oakley for the British market. Gifford wrote for his entire working life, phoning in his final work on the day he is believed to have passed away (Holland, 2000).

In describing his career arc, Gifford explains that he started "out as a cartoonist and comic strip artist/writer" and then "my career switched in midstream so that my hobby, which had been collecting and researching cinema history, became my livelihood, and my cartooning and collecting of comics became my hobby. All my books reflect my twin interests, and my main aim is to rescue and restore past achievements in both fields, and record for today and posterity the work of forgotten artists in popular entertainment" (Denis Gifford, 2002). That he succeeded in achieving those twin goals is reflected in Gifford's being known by such appellations as "Britain's most eminent comic historian" and "Mr. Nostalgia" (Holland, 2000).

Gifford was an archivist as well as historian. He possessed an extensive comic book collection, consisting of more than 20,000 issues. This collection included complete runs of many, but not all, popular British comics. By the time of his death in 2000, his collection had taken "over his whole house until he could not even open the oven" (Denis Gifford, 2000). Gifford certainly met Pearl's (2012) criterion that comic book historians should possess a substantial personal collection of primary sources. He put his knowledge of this collection to good use, writing and editing numerous books about comics. In doing so, Gifford earned the reputation as "a custodian of the British comic, a one-man archivist, consulted ever more frequently on matters of fact and authenticity by writers and historians" (Morehead, 1976, p. 14). His expertise was also pressed into service with the writing of obituaries of prominent figures associated with British popular culture, including those connected with comic books. These obituaries were published in *The Guardian* and other national newspapers.

Gifford also shared his encyclopedic knowledge of comic book history as a prolific author. He wrote encyclopedia entries, edited anthologies, and authored a dozen books in which he covered the history of British comic books and newspaper strips. Morehead (1976) describes Gifford's book, *The Complete Catalogue of British Comics and Price Guide* published in 1975, as "a labour of love of great value to nostalgic fans and social historians, but of little interest to casual readers" (p. 14). However, as Morehead (1976) notes, Gifford also produced books with a more popular appeal. And, in such books as *Happy Days: 100 Years of Comics* and *Run Adolf Run: The World War Two Fun Book*, both 1975, he published compilations with full-sized facsimile reproductions drawn from his extensive personal collection, making a wide range of out-of-print material available to a broad audience that otherwise would not have had access to it. This alone assures his place among the preeminent historians of the comic book medium.

Gifford, like Feiffer and Steranko, was a comic book insider, although these three were so much more as well. As gifted creators, each played a prominent role in the history of the comic book. Collectively, these three pioneers also legitimized the pursuit of comic book history and laid the foundations for its future. In doing so, they preserved print sources and oral histories that most likely would have been lost to posterity without their efforts. In addition, they served as devoted and articulate apologists for the aesthetic, cultural, and political relevance of the art form to which they devoted much of their working lives. Of course, this defense of comic books' significance is in part self-serving, given their personal and professional involvement; but it also argues for the value of studying the medium's history, as there is little point in spending time and energy studying irrelevant ephemera.

The Next Generation: Fans as Historians

The critical and commercial response to the historical work done by Feiffer, Steranko, and Gifford proved beyond a doubt that there is deep interest in the history of comic books on the part of not only core fans, but also the medium's more casual readers and the creators and consumers of other popular culture texts, as well as cultural critics, media scholars, and assorted other academic specialists. This interest continues to spark research into comic books' past. In contrast to those comic book historians previously sketched, however, most of the later historians are fans who lack direct experience working in the creative side of the industry. Their lack of personal involvement with, and investment in, the production and distribution of comic books has imbued these historians with a critical distance and resultant objectivity absent in the subjective narratives and analyses of the early pioneering histories.

Les Daniels (1943–2011)

Leslie Noel Daniels III, or simply Les, was born in Danbury, Connecticut. He grew up in Newberry, Connecticut (Hevesi, 2011), attended Brown University, taught film classes at Rhode Island College, and "lived his entire adult life on Benefit Street" in Providence (Booth, 2012). His was a decidedly different, and considerably more academic, upbringing than that of the industry insiders who also chronicled comic book history. Daniels did not have the art school, military, or performance backgrounds common to many other comic book historians. Gabilliet (2010) describes Daniels as "a rock musician with a master's degree in English literature" (p. 303). While his musical talent did not do much to inform his work as an author, his experience with literature helped him write seven comic book histories, as well as five horror novels, a history of horror in the media, and numerous short stories.

Daniels is perhaps best known among comic book aficionados for his first book, *Comix: A History of Comic Books in America* (1971). This work differed from earlier efforts at charting the history of comics in terms of conveying the medium's broad scope. In it, Daniels discussed different genres of comic books (romance, war, and superhero, among others) as part of greater cultural forms (Gabilliet, 2010). This starkly contrasts with earlier histories of the medium, which focused primarily, if not exclusively, on the superhero genre. Daniels also expanded the scope of comic book history by looking beyond the comics produced by DC and Marvel. His scope extended so far as to include a discussion of underground comics, which were then gaining in popularity. In *Comix*, Daniels also examined the issue of censorship with respect to the Comics Code of America. His interest in and concern about censorship permeates much of the book. This was a longtime interest of Daniels, who once noted in an interview: "when I was a boy in the 1950's, the horror comics were more or less banned in the United States" (Ward, 1995). The tone of Daniels's work also differed from that of the few earlier works on the subject available. Gabilliet (2010) describes it as "the first true attempt at a general history of comic books, from their origins to the end of the 1960s" (p. 303). He goes on to note that it was also "written in a more scholarly spirit" (p. 303). *The Comics Reporter* (2011) agreed, arguing that the work "was a groundbreaking, widely disseminated volume, best remembered for the nuances of its approach compared to other early comic book histories" (Spurgeon, 2011).

Daniels' *Comix* impressed those working in the comic book industry so much that decades later Marvel approached him about writing its own official history. Later, DC did the same and followed up by commissioning him to write histories of some of its most iconic characters: Superman, Batman, and Wonder Woman. According to Mark Evanier, comic book writer and historian, Daniels was the "guy that publishers hired to come in and figure out the histories of their own companies ... and he produced major works upon which all future histories will be built" (cited in Hevesi, 2011). *The Complete History of Wonder Woman* (1991) earned Daniels an Eisner Award, the highest honor in the comics industry. Despite such accolades some in the comic industry felt that Daniels' later works, those commissioned by Marvel and DC, did not provide complete and unvarnished accounts, leaving out elements that would have reflected badly upon the companies. Stephen Bissette (2011), a comic artist and friend of Daniels, noted that by sanctioning the works, Marvel and DC limited the types of information that could be included, saying, "Les often bemoaned the great stories he wasn't permitted to share about comics history and there were some doozies." Still, as Paul Levitz, a former president and publisher of DC Comics observes, "Daniels made an important contribution documenting the history of an American art form. ... And this was 30 years before the Metropolitan Museum of Art began acknowledging comics as an art form" (cited in Hevesi, 2011).

In currying the favor of Marvel and DC and earning commissions for sanctioned histories from them, Daniels enjoyed insider access to information he would not otherwise be privy to; but as noted above this access came at a cost: his ability to provide full and unfettered histories was compromised. The next historian, Maurice Horn, is decidedly not an insider.

Maurice Horn (1931–)

Maurice Horn is arguably the most prolific historian of the comic book industry to date. Somehow, while researching and writing about the comic book industry, Horn also found the time to write three French-language mystery novels under the pseudonym Franck Sauvage. But he did not work in the industry he studies. Gorner (1976) notes that by not writing, drawing, or selling comics, "he has become a leading expert precisely because he is Mr. Outside. ... Horn basically is a buff who was drawn into comics criticism by ... friends" (p. Tempo 1). Horn is also from France, which cultural background adds to his outsider status and enables him to look at the comic book industry in general, and the American industry in particular, with an outsider's objectivity that often results in a unique perspective. One area where Horn differs from other comic book historians, for example, is in dating the beginnings of comics. While some experts date the introduction of the comic strip to the 1895 publication of *The Yellow Kid*, Horn argues instead that that newspaper comic strips did not acquire their defining characteristics until a year later, in 1896 ("Centennial in '96," 1996). However, he dates the origins of the art form out of which the comic book emerged back to the Italian Renaissance (Gorner, 1976, Tempo 1). Horn's challenge against what was once established orthodoxy illustrates the difficulty of determining a definitive date for the origin of comic books as well as the debatable definitions concerning the core constitutive elements of the medium.

As Highsmith (1987) observes, although Maurice Horn is "occasionally idiosyncratic in his approach to and opinions about comics [he] is one of the few writers who have attempted a both comprehensive and scholarly overview of the comics field" (p. 205). He has done so as the author, co-author, and editor of numerous books, encyclopedias, and other works. Horn's magnum opus is *The World Encyclopedia of Cartoons*, an 800-page behemoth he edited that was first published in 1976 and has since been re-issued in multiple editions. The encyclopedia is noteworthy for being among the first books to look at the comic book industry as an international, and not just an American, phenomenon. According to Gorner (1976), with this work "he has assured his reputation" (p. Tempo 1). Horn's effort in promoting appreciation for comic books and newspaper funnies is not limited to his written work or the lectures he has delivered. Indeed, as Kim Munson notes elsewhere in this volume, he was part of a group of French comic book enthusiasts, SOCERLID, that was responsible for organizing an exhibition of the art form at the Louvre in Paris. This exhibition is regarded as the first of its kind at a major museum.

Current and Potential Future Trends

Today, fans and scholars alike can avail themselves of electronic, print, and online materials covering various and sundry aspects of the still-evolving history of comic books. Some of these materials are aimed at the casual reader, some at hardcore fans, and others at serious scholars of popular culture. These histories range from accounts of the development and widening influence of non-Western comic books, such as Japanese manga (Koyama-Richard, 2014; McCarthy, 2014), to Jon Morris' (2015) *The League of Regrettable Superheroes*, a humorous and informative survey of failed costumed characters who never enjoyed the popularity of DC and Marvel's iconic superheroes.

Jill Lepore (1966–)

While there is still a strong market for comic book histories that engage in industry gossip, that praise or castigate individuals or companies, or cater to nostalgia, there has been a growing number of histories that offer interested readers the product of solid scholarly research. Jill Lepore's (2014) *The Secret History of Wonder Woman* is a good example of the kind of rigorous historical scholarship and cultural criticism now devoted to the study of comic books and those who create them. This work earned Lepore, a history professor at Harvard, the prestigious American History Book Prize in 2015. Such recognition is illustrative of the respect that studying comic books now enjoys in at least some quarters of the academy, and by extension it affirms comic books as an art form worthy of serious study.

The comic book industry is not an impersonal entity that works in a vacuum but is rather the product of people—working as individuals and collectively—who labor within the historic sociocultural context in which they reside. In her history, Lepore (2014) offers a nuanced feminist reading of Wonder Woman that situates the character, her creation, her reception, and her enduring pop-culture influence within cultural, social, and political currents that have their genesis in the early 20th century's suffragist, birth control, and women's rights movements; that then flowed through the shifting gender landscape of Rosie the Riveter's America during World War II; continued to flow through the placid and prosperous post-war years of the 1950s, the turbulence of the 1960s, and the decadence of the 1970s; and which continue to inform public discourse and private life today.

Lepore (2014) couples this cultural history with a description of the domestic life of Wonder Woman's creator, William Moulton Marston, and of his unconventional family. Most informed comic book fans are aware that Marston was a Harvard educated experimental psychologist who contributed to the development of the polygraph machine (lie detector) and was one of the leading proponents of the device. But, as Lepore (2014) reports, Marston was also a complex and contradictory man: a proto-feminist, a polyamorous bigamist, and a fetishist interested in bondage and submission, among other things. Ironically, these salacious revelations would have come as no surprise to Dr. Fredric Wertham (1954), author of *Seduction of the Innocent*, who argued in that book and as a congressional witness that the salacious and violent content of comic books—such as the bondage, spanking, and other fetishistic practices frequently featured in Marston's Wonder Woman narratives—was a corrupting influence upon America's youth. But then, Marston is not a fictional character who can be expected to possess the same unambiguous and puritanical moral clarity as his classic Golden Age creation, Wonder Woman.

The Future

Future historians of the comic book industry will of course continue to plow much of the same ground already covered by historians discussed above, as well as many others. As Lepore (2014) has deftly demonstrated, there is still much of interest to be mined from that familiar terrain. But no doubt historians will also explore new terrain as well. As the social and mass media, migration, and other factors continue to render Marshall McLuhan's (1962) global village a lived reality, consumers will come into contact with and develop interest in the comic books of other cultures and languages, as will historians of the industry. As the commercial success and aesthetic influence of manga in America demonstrates, there is a ready market for alternative comic book formats, characters, and narratives.

Perhaps the biggest shift distinguishing the work of past and present comic book historians from those of the future will be the nature of the media they will study. The old pulp paper, four-color comic books no longer possess their former popularity. The same is true of their glossy paper cousins as well as the graphic novel. Indeed, comic books have disappeared from many of the places they used to be routinely sold to the general public, such as drugstores and newsstands; and, the number of specialty shops catering to comic book fans is now modest when compared to the glory days of the 1980s, when such shops were at the peak of their popularity. While DC and Marvel continue to publish conventional comic books, they have clearly moved the bulk of their creative and commercial attention to other more popular—and thus more lucrative—media. Now, most consumers encounter iconic comic book characters depicted in films, television series, and video games. The *Avengers* and *Dark Knight* film franchises; television series such as *Agent Carter*, *Arrow*, and *Gotham*; and, video games ranging in tone from the dark-hued hyper-violence of *Batman: Arkham Asylum* to the colorful kid-friendly *Lego Marvel's Avengers* all enjoy great commercial success and critical acclaim. Indeed, these media have increased the popularity and extended the influence of characters and narratives that originated on the pages of pulp magazines but will remain of vital interest to historians regardless of the media through which they are conveyed because of how they shape and are shaped by the cultural interests, social arrangements, and communication technology of the various historical periods in which they are produced.

Bibliography

Bissette, S.R. (2011) So long, Les Daniels … [sic]. Weblog. [Online] Available from: http://srbissette.com/?p=13498 [Accessed 25 November 2015].

Booth, B. (2012) The official web site of Les Daniels: horror author & comic book historian. Weblog. [Online] Available from: http://www.lesdaniels.com/index.html [Accessed 25 November 2015].

Carlson, K.C. (2008) The well-stocked comic book bookshelf. Weblog. [Online] Available from: http://westfieldcomics.com/comics-feature/KC-The-Well-Stocked-Comic-Book-Bookshelf-200 [Accessed 25 November 2015].

'Centennial in '96?' (1996) *Editor & Publisher*, 30 March, 129 (13): 36.

Duncan, R. and Smith, M. (2009) *The Power of Comics: history, form, and culture*, New York: Continuum.

Feiffer, J. (1997) '[The] Great Comic Book Heroes: Intro & Afterword', *The Comics Journal #200*. [Online] Available from: http://www.tcj.com/the-great-comic-book-heroes-intro-afterword-by-jules-feiffer/ [Accessed 26 November 2015].

Fremont-Smith, E. (1965) 'What the—?' [sic], *New York Times*, Monday 22 November: 35.

Gabilliet, J.P. (2010) *Of Comics and Men: a cultural history of comic books*, trans. B. Beaty and N. Nguyen, Jackson, MS: University Press of Mississippi.

Gifford, D. (2000) *The Telegraph*. May 25 [Online] Available from: http://www.telegraph.co.uk/news/obituaries/1366811/Denis-Gifford.html [Accessed 26 November 2015].

Gifford, D. (2002) *Contemporary Authors Online*. [Online] Available from: http://go.galegroup.com/ps/i.do?id=GALE%7CH1000036474&v=2.1&u=cofc_main&it=r&p=CA&sw=w&asid=50f895326acf7cf71079a39c78ab66a2. [Accessed 26 November 2015].

Goodman, M.D. (2010) 'Slipping through the gate: trusting *Daubert* and trial procedures to reveal the 'pseudo-historian' expert witness and to enable the reliable historian expert witness—troubling lessons from Holocaust related trials', *Baylor Law Review*, 60 (3): 824–79.

Gorner, P. (1976) 'To a connoisseur, 'funnies' are classics—not comics', *Chicago Tribune*, Tuesday 9 November: Tempo, 1 & 4.

Goulart, R. (1990) 'Steranko, James', in R. Goulart (ed.) *The Encyclopedia of American Comics From 1897 to the Present*, New York: Promised Land Production, 347.

Groth, G. (2004) 'Prophet of failure: a conversation with Jules Feiffer', *The Comics Journal Special Edition*, 4: 32–43.

Hevesi, D. (2011) 'Les Daniels, historian of comic books, dies at 68', *The New York Times*, Friday 18 November: B9.

Highsmith, D. (1987) 'Comic books: a guide to information sources', *RQ*, 27 (4): 202–209.

Holland, S. (2000) 'Obituaries: Denis Gifford', *The Guardian*, Thursday 25 May, [Online] Available from: http://www.theguardian.com/news/2000/may/26/guardianobituaries. [Accessed 25 November 2015].

Horn, M. (2001) *Contemporary Authors Online*. [Online] Available from: http://go.galegroup.com/ps/i.do?id=GALE%7CH1000036474&v=2.1&u=cofc_main&it=r&p=CA&sw=w&asid=50f895326acf7cf71079a39c78ab66a2 [Accessed 26 November 2015].

Howe, S. (2012) *Marvel Comics: the untold story*, New York: Harper.

Koyama-Richard, B. (2014) *One Thousand Years of Manga*, Paris: Flammarion.

Lepore, J. (2014) *The Secret History of Wonder Woman*, New York: Alfred A. Knopf.

McCarthy, H. (2014) *A Brief History of Manga*, London: Ilex Press.

McLuhan, M. (1962) *The Gutenberg Galaxy: the making of typographic man*, Toronto: University of Toronto Press.

Morehead, C. 'Lord Snooty and Desperate Dan win an honourable mention in British art history', *Times* [London, England] 20 Mar. 1976: 14.

Morris, J. (2015) *The League of Regrettable Superheroes*, Philadelphia: Quirk Books.

Pearl, B. (2012) The new historians: what is a comic book historian? [Online] Available from: http://comicbookcollectorsclub.com/the-new-historians-what-is-a-comic-book-historian/ [Accessed 26 November 2015].

Ross, J. (2010) 'Jonathan Ross meets Jim Steranko, his comic-book hero', *The Guardian*. 20 July [Online] Available from: [Online] Available from: http://www.theguardian.com/books/2010/jul/21/jim-steranko-comics-jonathan-ross. [Accessed 25 November 2015].

Schneider, W.E. (2001) 'Objective historian standard applied to determine libel in Irving v. Penguin Books Ltd.', *Yale Law Journal June*, 110 (8): 1531–45.

Schumer, A. (1988) 'The new superheroes: a graphic transformation', *Print*, 42 (6): 112–31.

Ward, K. (1995) 'Living with fear: an interview with Les Daniels', *Tabula Rasa* #7. [Online] Available from: http://www.tabula-rasa.info/Horror/LesDaniels.html. [Accessed 25 November 2015].

Wepman, D. (1990) 'Feiffer, Jules', in R. Goulart (ed.) *The Encyclopedia of American Comics from 1897 to the Present*, New York: Promised Land Production, 127.

Wertham, F. (1954) *Seduction of the Innocent: the influence of comic books on today's youth*, New York: Rinehart & Company.

A PIONEER'S PERSPECTIVE: MAURICE HORN

From prehistoric time to digital time, the story of man groping toward a language uniting word and image, with its ups and downs, reads like a soap opera. Cave paintings, Roman columns, church windows (take your pick) are all antecedents, images that may be suggestive or evocative but remain quiescent. Those were epiphenomena unconnected from one another in space and time, and too inchoate to actually constitute a formal language.

The situation was to change radically with what Canadian theorist Marshall McLuhan was to call "the Gutenberg galaxy," a new era ushered in by the invention of the printing press. This industrialized process brought about an unprecedented integration of word and image into a distinct language variously denominated "picture story," "illustrated story," etc. The result of Johannes Gutenberg's revolutionary printing press was a growing galaxy of authors all over Europe who blended together text and picture, notably in England with William Hogarth and Thomas Rowlandson, who made distinctive use of the "speech balloon," and later with the Swiss Rodolphe Töpffer and the German Wilhelm Busch.

Yet these efforts remained largely desultory and unconnected; the real breakthrough, however, came from an unexpected place. American artists had contributed their share of graphic stories and illustrated tales in a number of lively humor magazines, but their audience remained limited, as it had in Europe. This situation changed radically with the introduction of the color Sunday supplement to American newspapers that featured serial illustrated stories later to be called "comics." A new and wide readership was thus created, turning what had been a novelty into a mass medium that soon found counterparts all over the world, such as France ("bande dessinée"), Japan ("manga"), Brazil ("quadrinho"), and others.

In his celebrated collection of essays on popular culture, *The Mechanical Bride*, McLuhan predicted that American comics would be recognized by the French ten years hence. That was in 1951, and his prediction proved uncannily accurate; in 1961, precisely, there sprang up in France several organizations dedicated to proving just that in a series of essays, lectures, public debates, and notably exhibitions, culminating in the 1967 "Bande Dessinée et Figuration Narrative," which garnered worldwide acclaim and gave rise to similar exhibitions all around the globe.

The section of the show reserved for "figuration narrative" (the French equivalent of the American "pop art") spawned a large number of exhibits in the same spirit associating comic art and pop art. The most recent example of this craze is the London Tate Gallery's "The World Goes Pop" that was introduced in October 2015 in those terms: "Whaam! Pop! Kapow!"—exclamations clearly borrowed from the comics' lexicon.

Now, with the development of electronics, the Gutenberg Galaxy has come to an eclipse, if not to an end, resulting in the shift from the domination of the word to the reign of the image (words themselves become images on the computer screen and in e-books). This expands exponentially the possibilities of comic art creation, since comics can now be created entirely on a computer or digitized from existing print comics. Furthermore, these resources can now be shared by the members of an established pool of users ("cloud computing").

That was in the past. What of the future? Now that it has been accepted as a universal medium, comic art will become more and more integrated into modern art and thus go into directions far beyond comic strips and comic books. While storytelling in print or on the web will remain its main form, it will also deal with biography, science, music, even politics. A new mythology will be born carried by young authors equally at ease with the virtual and the concrete, the word and the image. Enjoy!

5

THE HISTORIANS OF THE ART FORM

Ian Horton

The idea that there are art-historical precedents for the comic book form is now commonplace, and many popular books on the subject, from the USA and Europe, give an overview of earlier artistic practices that used sequential images to tell stories. Such books include George Perry and Alan Aldridge's *The Penguin Book of Comics* (1967, England), Jacques Marny's *Le Monde étonnant des bandes dessinées* (1968, France), Scott McCloud's *Understanding Comics* (1993, USA) and Kees Ribbens and Rik Sanders' *Getekende Tijd: Wisselwerking tussen geschiedenis en strips* (2006, Netherlands). They all trace back the origins of the comic book form to Palaeolithic cave paintings, Egyptian papyri, Trajan's Column, and the Bayeux Tapestry. They all additionally examine the development of popular religious, political and satirical prints from the 15th to the early 19th century as precursors to the comic book form. The fact that these populist works highlight the origins of the form is welcome, but it must be noted that they are underpinned by scholarship that has used the discipline of art history to analyze the comic book medium in more depth.

This overview will compare and contrast the development of critical discourses, in both French and English, concerning the origins of the formal aspects of comic books in earlier artistic practices. The key texts examined here show how art-historical approaches toward the study of comic books developed in the 1960s in France and in the 1970s in the English-speaking world.[1] Central to any evaluation of art-historical approaches to the study of comic books are the two volumes of David Kunzle's *The History of the Comic Strip*, published in 1973 and 1990, respectively, which still stand out as the most substantial body of scholarship on the emergence of the form in any language. The concluding sections of this overview consider the continuing impact of this early scholarship and how the ideas presented have been critically revised in academic texts from the 1990s to the present day as Comics Studies has emerged as a discipline internationally.

The debates around the origins of the comic book form and the search for examples of proto-comics are here evaluated in relation to two main issues: the specific art-historical methods and methodologies used and the desire to elevate the status of comic books by establishing a canonical lineage for the form. It additionally considers how such approaches have led to recent developments in comic scholarship that see some comic book practices as forms of art themselves.

SIDEBAR: COMIC ART

Ian Horton

Recent comic scholarship has stressed the notion that comic books can be considered an artistic practice and has promoted the work of practitioners such as Robert Crumb, Art Spiegelman, and Chris Ware as leading this development. It is significant that Crumb emerges from the underground comics scene of the 1960s and that Spiegelman before the fame of *Maus* was co-editor (along with his wife Françoise Mouly) of the avant-garde comic book anthology *Raw*. This notion of comics existing outside the mainstream has been most notably analyzed in English by the Canadian comic scholar Bart Beaty in his works *Unpopular Culture: Transforming the European Comic Book in the 1990s* and *Art versus Comics*, where he analyzes the factors of production and consumption that allow works to be considered as art practice rather than popular culture (Beaty, 2007, 2012). More recently this idea of comic books as art has been promoted by Paul Gravett in the British Library exhibition *Comics Unmasked: Art and Anarchy in the UK* and the book *Comic Art* published by the Tate Gallery (2013).

In France the idea of comics as art has its roots in some of the ideas of Couperie and Moliterni from the 1960s and has mainly been promoted since the 1980s by Thierry Groensteen, who as editor of *Le Cahier de la Bande Dessinée* was keen to stress the avant-garde potential of the medium. More recently he has written about the need to include small press work in the definition of the medium and considered the potential of abstract comic books to break new ground for the form (Groensteen, 2007, 2012).

Francophone Origins

In 1975 when giving an account of the shifts that had occurred in the production, consumption, and critical engagement with comics in France since the 1960s, Luc Boltanski noted that

> The care that is taken to establish a connection between high culture and comics, and to confer on comics the antiquity that is constitutive of every legitimate cultural tradition, accounts for the tendency (found primarily among internal commentators), to relocate the origins of comics to the greatest possible historical distance...
> *(Boltanski, 1975, p. 288)*

The desire for the cultural recognition of comic books in France described by Boltanski emerged with the formation of the *Club des Bandes Dessinées* (CBD) in 1962 and they directly promoted the legitimacy of comic books in their fanzine-like journal *Giff-Wiff*. Key founding members of the CBD included Francis Lacassin, a journalist and filmmaker, and Pierre Couperie, who had studied art history at the Sorbonne. In 1964 the group changed its name to the *Centre d'études des littératures d'expression graphique* (CELEG) so emphasizing the need to give academic legitimacy to the study of the medium. This group also included many members working in the film industry, and this may have been one of the factors behind a schism in 1964 with some members leaving to form *La société civile d'études et de recherches des littératures dessinée* (*SOCERLID*). This new group included amongst its members Couperie and Claude Moliterni, who were both on the editorial board of *Phénix*, the new journal published by *SOCERLID* (Grove, 2010, pp. 234–240; Miller, 2007, pp. 23–24.). One of the most significant activities of *SOCERLID* was the 1967 exhibition *Bande dessinée et figuration narrative* held at the Musée des Arts Décoratifs in Paris, which was curated by Couperie and Moliterni and attended by half a million people during the three months it was open. The exhibition displayed enlarged reproductions of comic strips and contextualized these in relation to the current art movements of Nouveau réalisme and Pop Art (Grove, 2010, pp. 236–238). Although not an attempt to explore the origins of the form, it was clear that the curators wanted to raise the status of the medium through association. Ann Miller's analysis of the catalogue accompanying the exhibition, which was also edited by Couperie, suggests that this link to contemporary art was not a reasoned argument but rather a polemical stance and that the authors were just as keen to make links back to the art of the Renaissance as to the present (Miller, 2007, p. 23). A more detailed overview of the critical writings of Couperie and other members of *CBD* and *SOCERLID* reveals that there is some substance to both aspects of their arguments.

In 1972 Couperie wrote two articles, "Antecedents and Definition of the Comic Strip" and "Echoes of Modern Art in the Comic Strip," for publication in a special issue of the bi-monthly, tri-lingual Swiss magazine *Graphis,* which was devoted to graphic and applied arts (1972a, 1972b). These articles advance similar arguments to those promoted in the 1967 exhibition by directly linking comic books to modern and contemporary art. Couperie is explicit in explaining his methodology:

> In reality it is quite possible to follow the evolution of comics in the sequence (or co-existence) of the trends that have characterized art from 1880 to the present day. This sequence and coexistence are very clearly defined in the comic strip if it is subjected to the same critical methods as are applied to painting and other established arts, i.e. if attention is paid only to a minority of important artists, instead of considering the total production at a given point in time.
>
> *(Couperie, 1972b, p. 14)*

In emphasizing key individuals and referencing the formal features of canonical works that stand apart from the mainstream, he takes a very traditionalist art-historical approach to the subject of comic books. The sections outlining the origins of the form also highlight canonical works from the past that are linked to the present by referencing *Narrative Figuration*, a specifically French art movement of the 1960s that promoted a return to critically engaged realist painting. Couperie references Classical, Mannerist, and Baroque traditions throughout these articles, particularly when discussing the forms used in American newspaper strips. This highlights the fact that these art-historical categories were privileged by the academic Beaux-Arts tradition still dominant in France during the 1950s and 60s.

The American newspaper strip was also an important reference point for Couperie and Maurice Horn's *A History of the Comic Strip* (1968), an English translation of *Bande dessinée et figuration narrative*, the volume published in connection with the 1967 Musée des Arts Décoratifs exhibit (Couperie and Horn, 1968). This is one of the earliest sources to bridge the gap between French and English-speaking comic book histories, and Horn, a founding member of *SOCERLID,* was an important figure in linking these two cultures. In the essay

"The Magic of Burne Hogarth," which prefaced a new edition of Hogarth's comic strip work on *Tarzan of the Apes*, Horn drew extensively on French sources such as *Giff-Wiff* and references both Couperie and Lacassin (Horn, 1972, pp. 5–31). Horn quotes directly from Lacassin to emphasize the artistic traditions Burne Hogarth draws on.

> Hogarth is fascinated by…the suffering portrayed by Grunewald, by the vitality of Rubens' compositions…by the classicism of Greek sculpture, and by the ideas of German expressionism.
> *(Lacassin, 1971a as quoted in Horn, 1972, p. 16)*

In contrast to the loose art-historical approaches used by the circle that emerged out of *Giff-Wiff* and *SOCERLID*, art historian Gerard Blanchard's *Histoire de la bande dessinee* from 1969 gave a detailed and nuanced account of the origins of the key features of comics form. Blanchard specifically focused on image-text relationships from the medieval period and examined the importance of methods of reproduction including woodcut, engraving, and letterpress printing. Even when examining pre-linguistic cave paintings, Blanchard's emphasis is on the iconic symbols and signs that surround the more representational imagery. This theme of image-text relationships is evident throughout Blanchard's study, and debates surrounding the integration of image and text in defining the comic book form are legion within comic book scholarship and form a backdrop to the issues explored throughout this chapter. Blanchard avoided the rather basic interpretations that might follow from seeing the scrolls that appear in medieval sculptures and illuminated texts as being early forms of speech balloons even when the form suggests this might be the case. He relied instead on detailed scholarship of the period to place the works and image-text relationships in context (Blanchard, 1969).

Another feature of Blanchard's analysis is the focus on framing devices borrowed from architecture in these illuminated manuscripts and how they made their way into engraved images in early printed books in the 15th century. He notes that such books remained the preserve of an elite class of society and that there was a parallel development of underground satirical political and religious pamphlets. He ends this section of his study by suggesting that "The history of this activist imagery remains to be written" (Blanchard, 1969, 36). Unknown to Blanchard the writing of this history was already in progress and would be published by the British art historian David Kunzle in 1973.

SIDEBAR: BANDE DESSINÉE AND THE PROBLEM OF FORM

Ian Horton

The term *bande dessinée* is now universally accepted within the French-speaking world, but this was not always the case. Jean-Claude Glasser has traced the use of the term to the 1930s but notes that it only gradually emerged as standard terminology and was initially reserved for the newspaper strip and not the comic book album that has become the mainstay of the Franco-Belgian publishing industry (Glasser, 1988, p. 8). This term's disputed nature in Francophile comic book scholarship relates directly to the idea of the strip as opposed to page layout with the strip being privileged over the comic book in the period when the origins for comics form were most keenly pursued. As Couperie

(Continued)

> suggested in the fanzine cum journal *Giff-Wiff* in 1964, "The comic book is not a bande dessinée, it succeeds in being at once an inferior by-product of the newspaper, an inferior product of the comic and an inferior by-product of the book" (Couperie quoted in Groensteen, 2012, p. 97).
>
> The primacy given to the idea of the bande dessinée, or comic strip as opposed to the comic book page, has implications for tracing the origins of the medium. If the strip is seen as more culturally significant, then sources that reflect this interpretation might be more dominant. This might go some way to explaining why the Bayeux Tapestry and Trajan's Column are constantly referenced as examples of proto-comics when other less linear forms might be just as important (Fresnault-Deruelle, 1976, pp. 121–138).

Anglophone Origins

David Kunzle's two volumes on the origins of comic form still stand as the most significant and scholarly of works on the topic, or as Scott McCloud put it in when referring to the first volume: "Kunzle's book…has gone virtually unnoticed by the comics community but it is an enormously important work. Check it out!" (McCloud, 1993, p. 216).

The first of Kunzle's books, *History of the Comic Strip, Volume I, The Early Comic Strip: Narrative Picture Stories in the European Broadsheet from c. 1450 to 1825,* was published in 1973. It had been in preparation since the early 1960s when Kunzle was a Ph.D. student at the University of London under the supervision of the art historian Ernst Gombrich. As noted in Kunzle's Preface the book was essentially a revised and reorganized version of his doctoral thesis submitted in 1964. It is a monumental work, some 467 pages in length, and examines pamphlets and broadsheets that displayed formal features of modern comic strips and comic books from across Europe over four centuries.

In the introduction to this volume, he examines the origin of the term *comic strip* and then provides his own terms for these proto-comics, which he calls variously *narrative strip, narrative sequence, picture story,* or *picture sequence*. He goes on to note the fact that contemporary books on the comic strip contain only brief overviews of the prehistory and that these give the general impression that the comic strip only starts in the 1890s (Kunzle, 1973, pp. 1–2). Interestingly he does not refer to these contemporary books by name or include any existing histories of the 20th century comic book in his introduction (or bibliography) apart from John Paul Adams' *Milton Caniff, Rembrandt of the Comic Strip* from 1946 and Stephen Becker's *Comic Art in America* from 1960. The lack of references to the increasing number of books on comics produced in the late 1960s and early 1970s suggests that this volume was substantially completed by 1968 when the Preface was written but only published in 1973.

The introduction to this volume also outlines Kunzle's definition of the medium in which he highlights four key features.

> …I would propose a definition in which a comic strip of any period, in any country, fulfills the following conditions: 1) There must be a sequence of separate images; 2) there must be a preponderance of image over text; 3) The medium in which the strip appears and for which it is originally intended must be reproductive, that is in printed form, a mass medium; 4) The sequence must tell a story which is both moral and topical.
> *(Kunzle, 1973, pp. 2–4)*

This definition is often referenced and equally as often criticized, but these criticisms can say more about the position of the commentators than Kunzle's work itself. For example, Thierry Groensteen has recently taken Kunzle to task for the insistence that comics are mass produced only because he wants to include contemporary limited edition small press works within the scope of comics rather than being seen within the tradition of the artist's book (Groensteen, 2012, pp. 93–114).

Some of the conditions Kunzle used for his definition were necessary to set the scope of his study. The idea that works must be in reproducible printed form was essential if they were to be distinguished from earlier illustrated manuscripts. It also sets the starting date for his study as 1450 in a post-Gutenberg world of the mass media, a point he emphasized at some length. A more difficult aspect of the definition is the idea that these proto-comics must be both moral and topical. Kunzle is quite specific in considering modern and contemporary comic strips to have a strong moral content and justifies the idea of topicality by stressing the transformative potential of narrative strips that comment on social and political issues and thereby excluding traditional subjects such as biblical stories. These approaches are reflected in the organization of the book, which has major headings such as "Politics" and "Personal Morality."

Kunzle directly acknowledges the influence of his Ph.D. supervisor Ernst Gombrich on his choice of subject, and he was equally influential in terms of Kunzle's choice of arthistorical methods. Best known as author of *The Story of Art* (1950), Gombrich's greatest impact within the discipline of art history was in promoting a new approach to cultural history. Previously culture was seen as a universal and consistent whole within any one period that could therefore be represented by a small body of canonical artworks. Gombrich rejected this idea in favor of a more fractured conception that required a detailed knowledge of all aspects of a culture if one was to gain any understanding of its key aesthetic features. One result of this new idea of culture was the fact that popular imagery, once rejected by art historians as insignificant, became worthy of attention (Gombrich, 1979).[2] In the introduction to *Art and Illusion* (1960) Gombrich directly referenced the value of comic books as an object of study and included a chapter titled "The Experiment of Caricature," which examined the work of the Swiss cartoonist Rodolphe Töpffer, who developed new formal devices in his innovative proto-comic books published in the early 19th century (Gombrich, 1960, pp. 7, 279–303). The implications of this new art-historical approach for the study of the origins of the comic book form in popular print are evident in Kunzle's work.[3]

Although studying popular culture and comics books was new within art history, Kunzle used traditional art-historical archival research in terms of the methods employed when contextualizing the prints that form the core of his study. He specifically used the iconographic methodology of the German art historian Erwin Panofsky, which relied on a detailed use of documentary sources to establish the content and context of the works being examined.[4] Following this iconographic methodology, Kunzle made a detailed analysis of the imagery employed in the printed works but always in relation to the social and political context of the period using available documentary sources. This focus on the social became even more important in his second book, *History of the Comic Strip, Volume II: The Nineteenth Century* published in 1990. There is a clear tension in this volume between the traditional art-historical methods used and his social and political concerns. Kunzle is quite explicit about this problem in the introduction.

> Even art history, that most recalcitrant of disciplines, has begun to engage in the 'social history of art' and to become tainted with questions of ideology and sociopolitical

contexts of production and reception. This volume is intended as a 'social history of art' but not of art as defined by our vanguard social art historians, for whom art is still painting and sculpture, the media that commanded such bounteous criticism. The comic strip, however (which is certainly a distinct – perhaps distinguished – genre, if not art), is déclassé.

(Kunzle, 1990, p. xix)

His new allegiance to the social history of art, an approach drawing on Marxist theory and exemplified by the German art historian Arnold Hauser, shows how far he had moved away from Gombrich who was one of the most critical opponents of this ideological approach to the discipline (Gombrich, 1963, pp. 86–94).[5] Kunzle's new volume had sections titled: Politics and Farce; The "Lower-class" Audience; Means of Distribution; and The Artist and Conditions of Work, all of which reveal his ideological concerns. In terms of his methods the new volume was remarkably consistent with the previous one, the imagery was again analyzed in detail, but now the magazines that published these early comic strips provided much of the documentary context.

There were also some differences between the two volumes. The introduction and conclusion to the second volume give more attention to the context in which these comic strips were sold, bought, and most importantly read than was evident in the first volume. However, the most significant differences between the two volumes lie in their concluding sections. The first volume highlights the lack of information on the authors, artists, and publishers of these proto-comic strips before noting the key themes of political violence and social criticism that run throughout them. In contrast, the second volume has a section where Kunzle, for the first time, directly examines the visual languages employed in the early comic book and focuses specifically on the representation of movement. The conclusion also has significant sub-sections on viewpoint, framing, sound, and captions, which are contextualized in relation to ideas of mechanical movement as exemplified in the 19th century by the coming of the railways.

When considering the critical reaction to Kunzle's work, it is worth remembering that there were no academic journals devoted to comics scholarship at the time. The first volume was reviewed in the journals *Art Bulletin* (Adhmar, 1975, pp. 301–302), *The American Historical Review* (Mayor, 1975, p. 960), *The Burlington Magazine* (Fox, 1976, p. 38), *Eighteenth-Century Studies* (Paulson, 1975, pp. 479–489), and *The Journal of Modern History* (Wellman, 1977, pp. 301–303). This indicates the range of different academic disciplines taking an interest in the emerging subject of comics studies and the clearly art-historical discourses within which it was positioned. The second volume was also reviewed in *The American Historical Review* (Smith Allen, 1991, pp. 1508–1509) but was additionally examined in *The Journal of Popular Culture* (Browne, 1992, p. 174) and the *Journal of Social History* (Rearick, 1992, pp. 661–663). The fact that it was reviewed in these new academic contexts parallels the changes in art-historical discourse noted earlier and demonstrates the emergence of popular culture as an academic discipline.

Impact and Reappraisal

Kunzle continues to have a significant impact on both British and European scholarship in Comics Studies. In a British context this is openly acknowledged by Roger Sabin in both

Adult Comics: An Introduction (1993) and *Comics, Comix and Graphic Novels: The History of Comics Art* (1996), both of which clearly adopt a cultural history approach to the subject, as exemplified by Kunzle and with its roots in Gombrich's writings.[6] Other scholars such as Martin Barker take their cue from Kunzle by focusing on production, consumption, and audience reception and share his ideological concerns if not his art-historical methods (Barker, 1989). More recently James Chapman references Kunzle and uses his work to look at 19th-century comic books but again draws not specifically on his art-historical approach but on a broader application of the idea of cultural history (2011, pp. 14–29).

In recent scholarship, there has been a shift to focus primarily on the 19th century and not go back to earlier periods when examining the origins of the form. This is evident in the title of Pascal Lefèvre and Charles Dierick's *Forging a New Medium: The Comic Strip in the 19th Century* (1998) and was also the focus of a special issue of the journal *European Comic Art* titled "The Nineteenth Century and Beyond" (Grove, McKinney, and Miller, 2009, pp. v–viii). Kunzle himself has contributed to this shift and has in recent years published articles and books that both examine and reprint work by Töpffer from the early 1800s (Kunzle, 2007a, 2007b). Töpffer has now become the much-disputed focus for many historians looking for an originary point for the "Modern" comic book form, and his work is examined in many articles and conference papers.[7]

Kunzle's work is also a key reference point for the French language comic-book scholar Thierry Smolderen in *The Origins of Comics: From William Hogarth to Winsor McCay* (2014). At one level he is referencing the final section of Kunzle's first volume in choosing William Hogarth as a focal point. More interestingly, he takes Kunzle's ideas about comics form in the 19th century being intrinsically linked to technological innovation based around movement, sound, and time and extends these to include other developments such as x-rays and the phonograph. Smolderen also considers comic books to be a graphic hybrid form owing much to caricature and cartooning rather than sequential imaging and is building a new framework for understanding the medium in the cultural context of the 19th century (2014b, pp. 47–61).

In contrast to this increasing focus on the 19th century, one of the few writers to have extended the debate around the emergence of proto-comic books in the medieval period is Laurence Grove. He explicitly acknowledges Kunzle as the foundation on which much of his research is built and applies many of the same methodologies in outlining the tradition of text and image relationships through detailed archival research. In effect he utilizes the iconographic approach of earlier art historians such as Panofsky but is also influenced by the cultural studies and social history of art approaches of Kunzle.[8] There are also differences in his approach in that he primarily confines himself to those works produced in French-speaking countries and is concerned with the emergence of formal devices regardless of medium and so includes illuminated manuscripts as well as printed materials in his studies (Grove, 2005b, 2010, pp. 59–92).

Potential Futures

Scholarship from the 1960s and 1970s is still relevant today as the issue of the origin(s) of comic book form(s) and the medium's relationship to art history continue to be debated within Comics Studies.[9] In 2015 two of the keynote speakers at the inaugural Amsterdam Comic Conference, titled *Comics Interaction,* examined some of these issues. In "Hollow Man,

Modernity, and Comics" Joyce Goggin examined the continuing impact of William Hogarth on our understanding of comic book form drawing on many of the same ideas as Kunzle and Smolderen. In contrast, Bart Beaty's talk "Comics Studies, Here Be Dragons" looked at the marginal status of Comics Studies as a sub-category of literary studies. He concluded by noting that comics books have even less cultural capital within the discipline of art history and that there is much potential value in drawing on art-historical methods to advance the study of the medium.[10]

In 2010 two panels on *Comics in Art History* were included in the *College Art Association Annual Conference* in Chicago in 2010. This is the major art-historical conference in the USA, and the inclusion of comic books is a significant nod by art historians to their position within the canon. Two of the papers presented, one by joint panel organizer Patricia Mainardi titled *From Popular Prints to Comics* and Marianna Shreve Simpson's *Comics in 3-D from the Medieval Islamic World*, directly engage in debates around the origin of the form. However, the majority of papers presented show how art history has developed as a discipline in the last 50 years. These papers stressed the importance of theoretical approaches to art history, using ideas such as appropriation and conceptualism that would have been unimaginable in the 1960s, and focus on the relationship between comics and contemporary art practices.[11]

Focusing on the contemporary was also central to the art-historical approaches suggested by Pierre Couperie and Claude Moliterni in the 1960s and 1970s where they also compared comics form directly with current art practices in an attempt to elevate its status as a medium. Couperie, along with Maurice Horn and Francis Lacassin, also applied terms such as *Classical, Baroque,* and *Expressionist* to comics from the 1930s to the 1970s. Subsequently, these categories have only been very loosely applied in comics studies, and there is some future potential in applying art-historical methodologies in a more systematic way to examine the medium of comics.

Notes

1 Until recently many of these texts have not been available to English-speaking scholars. This has changed with the emergence of a substantial body of work on French comic books in English since the mid-2000s, including Miller and Beaty's recent *The French Comics Theory Reader* containing translations of key texts into English and the formation of the *International Bande Dessinée Society* and the *European Comic Art* journal. I personally would not have been able to write this chapter without the assistance of these translations and new research in the area. This overview focuses entirely on Francophile and Anglophile texts, but I am aware that there are sources in Spanish (both European and South American), Italian, and German that deal with the origins of the art form, but they are not translated into English and consequently their impact on the international field of Comics Studies is more limited.
2 For an overview of Gombrich's contribution to art history and reevaluation of cultural history see Eric Fernie (1995) *Art History and Its Methods: A Critical Anthology*, London: Phaidon, pp. 223–226.
3 Töpffer continues to be a key figure for Kunzle, who has published two books about his work and reprinted his cartoons and writings.
4 For an overview of Panofsky's approach to iconography as an art-historical method see Eric Fernie (1995) *Art History and Its Methods*, pp. 181–195; 345–346.
5 For an overview of Hauser and the social history of art see Andrew Hemmingway (ed.) (2006) *Marxism and the History of Art: From William Morris to the New Left*, London: Pluto Press. Interestingly, Kunzle was appointed to a professorship at the University of California, Los Angeles, 1977, and worked alongside Albert Boime and O.K. Werckmeister, both instrumental in the emergence of social history of art in the discipline in the USA.

6   I am indebted to Roger Sabin for our discussions about the impact of Kunzle on his own research and comic scholarship in general.
7   See for example Laurence Grove "Töpffer's Travels" presented at *Voyages* (*Sixth International Graphic Novel and Comics Conference* and *Ninth International Bande Dessinée Society Conference*), which specifically built on Kunzle's ideas in relation to modernity and the emergence of new visual forms in the early 19th century. Töpffer is also central to a forthcoming chapter by Grove titled "Ferdinand de Saussure's Unknown *Bande Dessinée*" in the forthcoming volume of *Yale French Studies*: L. Grove and M. Syrotinski (eds.) (2017) *Bande Dessinée: Thinking Outside the Boxes*, New Haven: Yale University Press.
8   Interview with Laurence (Billy) Grove conducted at *Voyages* on 24/6/2015 in which we discussed the impact of Blanchard, Couperie, and Kunzle on his own work and the discipline of Comics Studies in general.
9   Interestingly, Thierry Groensteen will publish a re-appraisal of Blanchard's ideas titled "From Stories in Pictures to *Bande Dessinée*: Questioning the Blanchard Theory" in the forthcoming volume of *Yale French Studies*.
10 Two other papers at the conference, Barbara Uhlig's "The Art of Comics: References to 20th Century Art and their Narrative Significance in Lorenzo Mattotti's Comics" and Patricia Ayala's "Sequentiality in Three Paintings of The Renaissance" developed art historical themes, and one of the round table discussions examined the cultural capital of comics in relation to exhibitions and notions of art history.
11 These two panels were organized by Andrei Molotiu and Patricia Mainardi. See Programme for the College Art Association Annual Conference 2010 (Download of the Conference sessions available at http://www.collegeart.org/conference/history). I would like to thank Maggie Gray for drawing my attention to these panels.

Bibliography

Adams, J.P. (1946) *Milton Caniff, Rembrandt of the Comic Strip*, Philadelphia: David Mackay Company.
Adhmar, J. (1975) 'Review: David Kunzle', *History of the Comic Strip, Vol. I, The Early Comic Strip: Narrative Picture Stories in the European Broadsheet from c. 1450 to 1825*. Art Bulletin 57 (2): 301–302.
Barker, M. (1989) *Comics, Ideology, Power and the Critics*, Manchester: Manchester University Press.
Beaty, B. (2007) *Unpopular Culture: transforming the European comic book in the 1990s*, Toronto: University of Toronto.
Beaty, B. (2012) *Comics versus Art*, Toronto: University of Toronto.
Becker S. (1960) *Comic Art in America: a social history of the funnies, the political cartoons, magazine humor, sporting cartoons, and animated cartoons*, New York: Simon and Schuster.
Blanchard, G. (1969) *Histoire de la bande dessinee* (*The History of Comics*), Verviers: Marabout Universite. Edited extracts translated in A. Miller and B. Beaty (eds.) (2014) *The French Comics Theory Reader*, Leuven: Leuven University Press, 25–37.
Boltanski, L. (1975) 'The constitution of the comics field. Originally published as La constitution du champ de la bande dessinee', *Actes de la recherche en sciences sociales*, 1: 37–59. Translated in A. Miller and B. Beaty (eds.) (2014) *The French Comics Theory Reader*, Leuven: Leuven University Press, 281–301.
Browne, R.B. (1992) 'Review: *The history of the comic strip: the nineteenth century*, by David Kunzle', *Journal of Popular Culture*, 25 (4): 174.
Chapman, J. (2011) *British Comics: a cultural history*, London: Reaktion Press.
Couperie, P. (1972a) 'Antecedents and definition of the comic strip', *Graphis*, 28 (159): 8–13, in W. Herdig and D. Pascal (eds.) (1972) *The Art of the Comic Strip*, Zurich: The Graphis Press.
Couperie, P. (1972b) 'Echoes of modern art in the comic strip', *Graphis*, 28 (159): 14–25, in W. Herdig and D. Pascal (eds.) (1972) *The Art of the Comic Strip*, Zurich: The Graphis Press.
Couperie, P. and Horn, M. (1968) *A History of the Comic Strip*, New York: Crown.
Fernie, E. (1995) *Art History and Its Methods: a critical anthology*, London: Phaidon.
Fox, C. (1976) 'Reviews: *Political Prints in the Age of Hogarth*, by Herbert M. Atherton, and *The Early Comic Strip: Narrative Strips and Picture Stories in the European Broadsheet from c.1450 to 1825*, by David Kunzle', *The Burlington Magazine*, 118 (874): 38.

Fresnault-Deruelle, P. (1976) 'From Linear to tabular' (Originally published as Lineaire au tabulaire), *Communications,* 24: 121–38, translated in A. Miller and B. Beaty (eds.) (2014) *The French Comics Theory Reader,* Leuven: Leuven University Press, 221–38.

Glasser, J. (1988) 'Origin of the term 'bande dessinée'' (Originally published as 'Courrier' [Mail]), *Les Cahiers de la bande dessinée,* 80: 8, translated in A. Miller and B. Beaty (eds.) (2014) *The French Comics Theory Reader,* Leuven: Leuven University Press, 21–23.

Gombrich, E.H. (1950) *The Story of Art,* London: Phaidon.

Gombrich, E.H. (1960) *Art and Illusion,* London: Phaidon.

Gombrich, E.H. (1963) *Meditations on a Hobby Horse,* London: Phaidon.

Gombrich, E.H. (1979) 'In search of cultural history', *Ideals and Idols: essays on values in history and in art,* London: Phaidon, 42–59.

Gravett, P. (2013) *Comics Art,* London: Tate Publishing.

Groensteen, T. (2007) *The System of Comics,* Jackson, MS: University Press of Mississippi.

Groensteen, T. (2012) Definitions (Originally published as Definitions), in Ory, Pacal; Martin, Laurent; Venayre, Sylvain (eds.) *L'art de la bande dessinée (The Art of Comics),* Paris: Citidelles et Mazenod, translated in A. Miller and B. Beaty (eds.) (2014) *The French Comics Theory Reader,* Leuven: Leuven University Press, 93–114.

Grove, L. (2005a) 'BD theory before the term BD existed', in C. Forsdick, L. Grove and L. McQuillen, L., (eds.) *The Francophone Bande Dessinée,* Amsterdam-NewYork: Editions Rodolphi.

Grove, L. (2005b) *Text/Image Mosaics in French Culture: emblems and comic strips,* Ashgate: Aldershot.

Grove, L. (2010) *Comics in French: the European bande dessinée in context,* New York-Oxford: Berghahn Books.

Grove, L., McKinney, M. and Miller, A. (eds.) (2009) 'The nineteenth century and beyond', *European Comic Art,* 2 (2): v–viii.

Grove, L. and Syrotinski, M. (eds.) (2017) *Bande Dessinée: thinking outside the boxes,* New Haven: Yale University Press.

Hemmingway, A. (ed.) (2006) *Marxism and the History of Art: from William Morris to the New Left,* London: Pluto Press.

Herdig, W. and Pascal, D. (eds.) (1972) *The Art of the Comic Strip,* Zurich: The Graphis Press.

Horn, M. (1972) 'The magic of Burne Hogarth', in B. Hogarth *Tarzan of the Apes,* London: Pan, 5–31.

Kunzle, D. (1973) *The History of the Comic Strip. Volume I. The Early Comic Strip: narrative picture stories in the European broadsheet from c. 1450 to 1825,* Berkeley: University of California Press.

Kunzle, D. (1990) *The History of the Comic Strip. Volume II. The Nineteenth Century,* Berkeley: University of California Press.

Kunzle, D. (ed. and translator) (2007a) *Rodolphe Töpffer: the complete comic strips,* Jackson, MS: University Press of Mississippi.

Kunzle, D. (ed. and translator) (2007b) *Father of the Comic Strip: Rodolphe Töpffer,* Jackson, MS: University Press of Mississippi.

Lacassin, Francis. (1971a) *Tarzan or the Intense Knight,* Paris: Union Generale Editions.

Lacassin, Francis. (1971b) 'Dictionary definition' (Originally published as Definition pour le larousse), *Pour une 9e at, la bande dessinee (For a 9th Art, Comics),* Paris: 10/18. Translated in A. Miller and B. Beaty (eds.) (2014) *The French Comics Theory Reader,* Leuven: Leuven University Press, 39–46.

Lefèvre, P. and Dierick, C. (eds.) (1998) *Forging a New Medium, The Comic Strip in the 19th Century,* Brussels: VUB University Publishers.

Marny, J. (1968) *Le Monde étonnant des bandes dessinées (The Amazing World of Comics),* Paris: Le Centurion.

Mayor, A. Hyatt. (1975) 'Review: David Kunzle, *History of the Comic Strip. Vol. 1, The Early Comic Strip: Narrative Strips and Picture Stories in the European Broadsheet from c. 1450 to 1825',* American Historical Review, 80 (4): 960.

McCloud, S. (1973) *Understanding Comics,* Northampton, MA: Kitchen Sink Press.

Miller, A. (2007) *Reading Bande Dessinée: Critical Approaches to French Language Comic Strip*, Bristol: Intellect.
Miller, A. and Beaty, B. (eds.) (2014) *The French Comics Theory Reader*, Leuven: Leuven University Press.
Moliterni, C. (1972) 'Narrative technique', *Graphis*, 28 (159): 26–43, in W. Herdig and D. Pascal (eds.) (1972) *The Art of the Comic Strip*, Zurich: The Graphis Press.
Paulson, Ronald. (1975) 'Political cartoons and comic strips (review of *Political Prints in the Age of Hogarth* by H.M. Atherton and *History of the Comic Strip, Vol.1* by D. Kunzle)', *Eighteenth-Century Studies*, 8 (4): 479–89.
Perry, G. and Aldridge, A. (1967) *The Penguin Book of Comics*, Harmondsworth, Middlesex: Penguin Books Ltd.
Rearick, C. (1992) 'Review: Kunzle, David *The History of the Comic Strip*', *Journal of Social History*, 25: 661–63.
Ribbens, K. and Sanders, R. (2006) *Getekende Tijd: Wisselwerking tussen geschiedenis en strips* (*Drawn Time: Exchanges between history and comics*), Utrecht: Matrijs.
Sabin, R. (1993) *Adult Comics: an Introduction*, London: Routledge.
Sabin, R. (1996) *Comics, Comix & Graphic Novels*, London: Phaidon.
Smith Allen, J. (1991) 'Review: David Kunzle. *The History of the Comic Strip: The nineteenth century*', *American Historical Review*, 96 (5): 1508–1509.
Smolderen, T. (2014a) *The Origins of Comics: from William Hogarth to Winsor McCay*, Jackson, MS: University Press of Mississippi.
Smolderen, T. (2014b) 'Graphic hybridisation: the crucible of comics' (Originally published as L'Hybridation graphique,creuset de la bande dessinee), in L. Gerbier (ed) *Hybridations texte et image* (*Text Image Hybridizations*), Tour: PUFR, translated in A. Miller and B. Beaty (eds.) (2014) *The French Comics Theory Reader*, Leuven: Leuven University Press, 47–61.
Wellman, K. (1977) 'Review: *History of the Comic Strip. Volume 1: The Early Comic Strip: Narrative Strips and Picture Stories in the European Broadsheet from 1450 to 1825*, by David Kunzle', *The Journal of Modern History*, 49 (2): 301–303.

A PIONEER'S PERSPECTIVE: DAVID KUNZLE

Secret 1. The war (WW II) was still on, but it was deemed safe to return to my native city, Birmingham, England. My first promise of a career, at age seven, as an archaeologist, was aborted when my mother refused to bring to our new home my large box of crockery fragments previously dug up in a neighbor's garden. I was quickly consoled and diverted on discovering a huge book, Hogarth's *Complete Works* as republished (elephant folio, original plates restruck) in 1822. This album, originally bought by an uncle who died young of polio and remained a secret to us, I discovered kept in a huge magical cupboard in a back room at my grandfather's. This place and this work became my secret refuge and a window onto real life: death, disease, sex, and vices of many kinds, all topics taboo next door, at home.

Secret 2. Seventy years after Hogarth gave me a real and somehow present world opening vast historical horizons, he divulged another secret. I dragged the Hogarth volume, the binding desiccated and collapsed in a Los Angeles climate, to the binder. He returned it to me, saying "by the way I found these two engravings inside a well-hidden slip pocket at the front. Do I put them back?" I had never discovered that clever pocket,

(*Continued*)

concealing the two naughty prints, "Before" and "After," that it was assumed I wouldn't, in a (pre-) Victorian age, want my daughters to see. My (female) Hogarth class at UCLA, so much later, was much more curious than shocked.

Secret 3. I was redirected by Ernst Gombrich, from an adolescent, proto-research project on the erotic Fuseli, to the picture story (comic strip) from Hogarth to Töpffer. I never got seriously to Töpffer until much later, after discovering centuries of historic pre-, proto- and post-Hogarthian graphic narrative from various European countries secreted in archives all over. This became a Ph.D. and a very large book called *The Early Comic Strip*. Wrong title: I should have called it "Hogarth Before and After," if only because Hogarthians have largely ignored it ever since it was published in 1974. Hogarth was, by the way, the only model for moral, graphic narrative recognized by Töpffer.

Now I got into trouble, no secret here, now buried by time, with Washington, no less, and then my own university (University of California Santa Barbara). The year was 1967: shortly after arriving in California, I found myself the winner of a federal grant, from the first-ever allocation of federal funds for scholarship in the humanities (National Endowment for the Humanities), a brand-new program conceived under Kennedy and realized by the Johnson administration. The grant, for $8,780, was for a follow-up book on the history of the comic strip in the 19th century (Töpffer et al.). I had by then distinguished myself as the author of several letters to the local newspaper condemning the Vietnam War, which earned me some angry rebuttals, death threats, a treasured missive addressed to the "Santa Barbara Branch of the Communist Party, Attn D. Kunzle" (me who had never even met a Communist), a letter of approval from a retired U S Brigadier General—and, more worryingly, ten minutes of fame.

Washington, April 1967: Representative Durward Hall of Missouri raised in Congress the absurdity of government subsidy to so trivial and "anti-intellectual" a project as the study of comics, singling out this grant among others also deemed absurd. Hall soon found another reason to denounce my grant in particular: it had gone to a recent immigrant who had made known, in the local (only) Santa Barbara paper, his opposition to the war in Vietnam, a war then enjoying a massive escalation, with corresponding protest against it. This little academic ruffle suddenly became news, with headlines in the press and syndication all over the country. The local paper tried to remain neutral and spoke positively of the author taking seriously the comics. So Vietnam helped launch comics study in the public arena.

Congressman Durward Hall had his own view of serious issues, which put my project in good company. A John Bircher, he opposed, according to syndicated columnist Drew Pearson, the United Nations, The Peace Corps, Medicare, and erecting a memorial to Eleanor Roosevelt. It was widely, but falsely, reported that the Endowment was investigating the award and considering Hall's demand it be rescinded. More credibly, the Endowment was expected to face a reduced budget next year. *The New Republic* pointed out, helpfully, that comics are not trivial but indeed political, just look at *Terry and the Pirates*, *Steve Canyon*, and *Little Orphan Annie* (all rightwing war-mongers I should add). I was even invited to be grilled on the notorious *Joe Pyne Show* (the Bill O'Reilly of the time).

This little fracas soon fizzled out, of course, and I spent the grant time (improperly?) rewriting my *Early Comic Strip*. It took five years, from submission in 1968 to 1973, for the UC Press to get it into print: one year of this tiresome delay was not the fault of the publisher but entirely my own, having innocently/greedily given the whole book, text and innumerable photographs, to Kunstverlag in Dresden (E. Germany), at the behest of a redoubtable small Italian publisher called La Pietra who happened to be my brother-without-the-law and who personally knew the Dresden editor. The pair committed us all to a trilingual edition: Italian, German, and English (this latter still from UC Press). WOW: my first book as a trinity! Not to be: The German editor was demoted for not being nice enough to the Russians in a book called *Art in Resistance*. Another political obstruction.

Meanwhile, UCSB had been busy trying to fire me. I knew this was due to a variety of small political actions against the Vietnam War, most of them of the conventional extra-curricular kind. I was for four successive years almost unanimously recommended by my department for tenure. One of the last things the Art History chair, Alfred Moir (bless his cotton socks) said to me when the final denial came through in 1973, was "Get a lawyer." So I did, with the help of my then compañera, the poet and novelist Deena Metzger, and the lawyer fighting her case, which was about dismissal from a Los Angeles college for the outrage of reading a pornographic poem of her composition to a class on pornography. (This was by the way the age of *Zap Comix* and Robert Crumb.) I found a different lawyer, from the American Federation of Teachers, a union to which I had paid my dues and financed my suit. The officially given grounds of my own dismissal had been the grandly vague "inadequate scholarship." No details were given by the dean—I had three books, one out (*Posters of Protest*), one written and contracted for, one (the *ECS*) in press, nearly out; while the dean who fired me, also a senior professor, had only one.

Now, back to the Congressman Hall affair: After my firing I was out of real teaching work for four years, although happily busy with translating and researching *How to Read Donald Duck* by Ariel Dorfman and Armand Mattelart, just out in Chile. But I had leisure for the lawsuit. Summoned by my lawyer to produce every scrap of evidence, for and against me, I mentioned the winning of the grant and the ensuing publicity without at the time thinking for a moment that it could have had any greater effect than to publicize and raise my status as a scholar, while arousing the ire of a cultural philistine in Congress. "Did you keep the newspaper cuttings?" I had, after I received a whole package of them from a thoughtful UCSB administration. "Aha," says the canny lawyer. "This is the university showing you what a deal of trouble you caused them." Really? As I return to them now, I am astonished at their extent, though incomplete, thanks to the university's press clipping agency: 31 different newspapers, including big ones like *The New York Times*, *The Wall Street Journal*, *The Los Angeles Times*, as well as magazines such as *Science* and *The New Republic*, and on the TV front, NBC. Most of the fuss was printed in the *Congressional Record*, where I found over 18 separate citations on different dates, giving a total of 156 column inches devoted to the Kunzle, Hall, and NEH affair.

Still, I could not imagine that I was actually being fired for studying comic strip "trivia," although in hindsight I suppose that may have been part of it. More significant, probably, was another comics–related project, an exhibition of *Posters of Protest* in the University Art Gallery (with catalog, 1971), which then traveled to New York and Europe. This, a friend told me (later) had aroused some concern with the chancellor who, while he could not forbid it, found the "timing wrong." It did not help, I suppose, that one student who was condemned and jailed for helping burn down the UCSB branch of the

(*Continued*)

Bank of America had written to the student newspaper claiming he had been inspired by my exhibition—not to do the burning, at which he was present without having instigated it or even actively helping—but to give him the courage to continue protesting.

Meanwhile, another government agency, U S Customs and Border Protection, took up the cudgels against the serious study of comics. My English edition (translation, introduction) of the intellectually and morally inflammatory Chilean *How to Read Donald Duck* by Dorfman and Mattelart, was held up at the port, on behalf of Disney. It was finally argued into the country by The Center for Constitutional Rights.

I daresay all of this is not so secret, just rather small in the grander scheme of academic history, and the ongoing persecution of intellectuals and scholars in the US, which is, anyway, no great shakes by global standards. There have been plenty of US aggressive wars, indeed, continuously since then, without their coinciding like this with comics scholarship, or a warrior Congress finding occasion to denigrate its status. Such scholarship has won the day, no doubt of it, with cartoonists Garry Trudeau and Art Spiegelman winning a Pulitzer Prize.

If I may end here on this personal "secret" accolade, which I much treasure and would like to be remembered by: On July 11, 1975, Carl Maven in the *Santa Barbara News and Review* drew up a list of his (fictive) "UCSB Fired Professors Alumni Association." This included me, Sociology Professor Maurice Zeitlin (now also UCLA), and Linus Pauling, "First President of the FPAA," Professor of Chemistry at Stanford, and winner of two Nobel prizes. Could one be in better company?

6

THE LIBRARIANS AND ARCHIVISTS

Jenny Robb

In 1993, historian William W. Savage Jr. (1993, p. 90) wrote this indictment of the libraries that had failed to collect comics, in spite of decades of growing interest from scholars and researchers: "The comic books I cited in my book, *Comic Books and America, 1945–1954* (Norman: University of Oklahoma Press, 1990), were begged, borrowed, or bought (and usually that) from dealers in Oklahoma, Kansas, Texas, and California over a period of ten years; and in no case were the research facilities available to me of any blessed use whatsoever." Savage had to become his own archivist in order to gain access to the primary source materials he wanted to research. After he finished his book, he offered the comic book collection he had acquired to a library, presumably in his area, and it was turned down because, he was told, "nobody cared" (Savage, Jr., 1993, p. 90).

For most of the 20th century, librarians—both public and academic—shunned the idea of spending precious financial, staff, or space resources on collecting, preserving, and cataloging comics and cartoons. In his print "Lead Pipe Sunday," Art Spiegelman described comics as "the bastard offspring of art and commerce" who "murder their parents and go off on a Sunday outing." The prevailing opinion was that comic strips, comic books, and other print cartooning were mostly poorly drawn and poorly written drivel created to entertain children and the masses in order to make a profit. Highly educated adults might laugh at the comics on Sunday morning; they might give an appreciative nod to the more artistic and poetic specimens like George Herriman's *Krazy Kat* or Walt Kelly's *Pogo*, and they might even look the other way when their kids brought home *Archie*, *Donald Duck* or *Spider-Man* comic books, but they saw little in comics worthy of investigation or serious analysis. Librarians were trained to choose the best literature, art, and scholarship to be included in their hallowed halls of learning and culture. Comics, like other forms of popular or alternative culture media, simply did not belong. As Allen Ellis and Doug Highsmith (2000, p. 21) posit in their study of library literature about comics, "A dismissive, often actively hostile, attitude toward the comics medium was accepted as a matter of course by many members of the academic community—with a substantial majority of librarians among them."

In addition to the general prejudice against collecting comics, there were practical problems. Comics were fragile and difficult to preserve. They created unique challenges to the established system for cataloging, which was designed for more traditional media. And it seemed impossible for any library to try to keep up with the sheer mass of comics being produced, let alone have the resources to acquire historical primary sources in a comprehensive way. In the end, it was left largely to private collectors and fans of comics to do the work of collecting and cataloging popular culture materials for much of the 20th century.

The anti-comics attitudes at universities and libraries in the U S showed early signs of change in the 1960s and '70s. The study of comics as a legitimate academic pursuit started to surface during an era defined by its counterculture and the rebellion of its youth against conservative social norms. At the academy, against the backdrop of campus anti-war and other social protests, scholars in the humanities continued to place increasing emphasis on social history, the experiences of the common man (and woman), and the culture of the masses, a departure from the traditional focus on the powerful, the elite, and the canonized in history, art, and literature. Interest in investigating comic books and strips in a serious way grew in traditional academic fields like History, English, Communication, Religion, Philosophy, and Sociology as well as newer cross-disciplinary fields such as American Studies, Women's Studies, and, most importantly, Popular Culture Studies.

Librarians and archivists—both professional and amateur—responded to these changes in two important ways. Some wrote and spoke about the need to collect and preserve these materials in institutions and encouraged their colleagues to act on the growing demand for access. They provided the necessary justification and rationale for others, who began the hard work of actually gathering popular culture materials and cataloging them. In this chapter, I'll give an overview of the history of institutional cartoon and comics collecting with a special focus on three critical pioneers in the United States whose work left a lasting legacy for comics scholars. Then I'll discuss international efforts and end with some reflections on the current status of institutional collecting.

The earliest efforts to collect comics material were somewhat haphazard, and few resources were put into making them discoverable or accessible. As the copyright depository, the Library of Congress acquired a massive and relatively comprehensive comic book collection, but it did little to catalog them or make them available to researchers until the 1990s. Starting in the 1950s, the Center for Research Libraries in Chicago had been purchasing a sampling of popular magazines and comics semi-annually from the largest wholesale distributor in Chicago. In this way, it had amassed a representative sample of comic books published since 1950, although they weren't cataloged individually (Clarke, 1973, p. 216). In the area of archives, Syracuse University Library's Special Collections division, under the leadership of Chancellor William Tolley, actively sought the papers and art of cartoonists during the 1950s and '60s. They acquired many collections that may otherwise have been lost, but they eventually stopped collecting in the area and did not have the resources until recently to fully process their collections and publish their holdings.

The birth of Popular Culture Studies was an important turning point. In the mid-1960s, Dr. Ray Browne, a pioneer in the study of popular media, began to organize conferences focused on popular culture at Purdue University when he was part of the English Department there. After moving to Bowling Green State University in 1967, he founded the *Journal of Popular Culture* and the Center for the Study of Popular Culture. Two years later, Brown, with the help of Russell Nye at Michigan State and Marshall Fishwick at Lincoln University, also founded the Popular Culture Association, which held its first meeting at Michigan State University in April 1971. While no papers at the inaugural conference focused on comics, the issue of collecting popular culture materials in libraries was addressed during a panel entitled "Archiving Popular Culture" (Browne, 1989, p. 115). Another panel focused on curriculum and popular culture, indicating the growing inclusion of the subject, once shunned by educators and librarians alike, in the classroom at the high school and college levels (Browne, 1989, p. 106).

Browne recognized early that academic libraries would need to begin collecting primary sources of popular literature, music, and art if people were going to be able to write and teach about them. A library devoted to the collection of popular culture materials was a critical part of his multi-pronged approach to establishing Popular Culture Studies as an academic field. He found a willing partner in Bowling Green librarian William Schurk, whose primary interest was popular music, and they started building a collection. "Sometimes in varying combinations, Pat [Browne] and Bill and I merely went to flea markets, to second-hand book stores and stocked-up" (Browne, 1989, p. 87). They also relied heavily on donations to grow the collection. In 1969, Browne and Schurk (pp. 723–724) published a report of the "Popular Culture Collections" at Bowling Green, which included a summary of current collections, noted recent donations, and outlined their collecting policy. "Comic books" are listed as one of the "special collections to be developed," and a gift of 50 comic books by Susan E. Kinch was mentioned. Browne (1989, p. 89) acknowledges a number of librarians who advanced the Popular Culture Library over the years including Nancy Lee, Evron Collins, Jean Geist, and Brenda McCallum. By 1989, the library listed among its holdings 35,000 comic books, as well as the Allen and John Saunders Collection of more than 20 linear feet of original comic strip art and archival materials, indicating a very proactive program of collecting comics material during its first two decades (Geist, 1989, p. 120).

Following Browne and Bowling Green's lead, forward-thinking librarians and archivists, including several professors of library science, began sounding the call for librarians, especially those at research and academic libraries, to begin collecting popular culture materials such as comics in a serious and systematic way. One of the earliest was Jack A. Clarke, a professor at the University of Wisconsin Library School. He published an article in *College & Research Libraries* in 1973 outlining early library efforts to respond to the growing scholarly interest in popular culture. Clarke pointed out that over 500 colleges already offered courses in the new discipline, including small liberal arts schools and academic giants. Clarke (1973, pp. 215–216) advocated for inter-institutional cooperation, or collective collecting, since "the sheer mass and variety of these publications is so vast that it is beyond the physical capacity of even the largest library to acquire more than a fraction of the total output."

Another pioneer, Gordon Stevenson, Professor at the School of Library and Information Science at SUNY/Albany, debuted a course called "Popular Culture in the Library," in 1972. He also wrote a thorough survey for *Library Trends* in 1977 in which he outlined the rise of popular culture studies and examined the home disciplines of popular culture researchers, the topics they studied, their methodologies, and the types of resources they used, as well as how popular culture was being incorporated in university teaching. The purpose of the article was to help inform fellow librarians what materials they should consider collecting and what services they should provide to the growing field of Popular Culture Studies. Stevenson (1977, p. 782) argued that "besides whatever long-range responsibilities librarians have to document our times (constructing that social memory, which has long been considered to be one of the more enduring cultural functions of the library), there are the practical issues of dealing with the demands of faculties and students as the library responds to or anticipates the changing climate of research and teaching." In his opinion, the direction of the climate change was clear: "I am firmly convinced that popular culture studies will continue on their present course, although at an accelerated rate. ... Attempts to understand popular culture and to study it in some systematic fashion will remain an important challenge to scholarship as long as popular culture continues to play such an important role in shaping our society" (Stevenson, 1977, p. 814).

Wayne A. Wiegand and Barbara Moran also took up the crusade. Wiegand served on the faculty of the College of Library Science at the University of Kentucky from 1976 to 1986. During that time, he wrote a number of articles on popular culture and libraries (Wiegand, 1979). In 1981, Wiegand (p. 189) wrote that "academia is beginning to show signs of accepting popular culture studies as culturally valuable, pedagogically viable conduits to advancing knowledge and augmenting societal self-awareness." As such, he insisted, "It is time for academic librarians to fall in line."

Moran, who served as Dean and Professor at the School of Information and Library Science, University of North Carolina at Chapel Hill, frequently wrote and spoke about the issue in the 1980s and '90s, arguing that, "despite the tightness of budgets, despite the lack of familiarity with the material, despite problems associated with such collections, academic librarians should be working collectively to assure that collections of popular materials are being amassed today that will be needed for scholars of the future" (Moran, 1993, p. 8).

In the last decade of the 20th century, more and more librarians and archivists responded to the clarion calls of Browne, Clarke, Stevenson, Moran, Wiegand, and others. Allen Ellis, professor of Library Services at Northern Kentucky University, organized and served as first Chair of the "Popular Culture and Libraries Discussion Group" within the Association of College and Research Libraries in 1988. Five years later, the journal *Popular Culture in Libraries* was launched to "provide information and act as a forum for the exchange of ideas about the evaluation, acquisition, organization, preservation and utilization of popular culture concepts and materials in a wide array of print, audiovisual and three-dimensional formats" (Hoffmann, 1993, p. 1). The new publication was "geared primarily to librarians, archivists, educators, and other professionals dealing with these collections," while "the journal will also endeavor to combat traditional biases against popular culture held by many academics as well as library users and students" (Hoffmann, 1993, p. 1). The premier issue featured the transcript of a panel held at the Popular Culture Association Conference in 1991 with two scholars and two librarians. They discussed the prejudices against collecting popular culture materials that many librarians and archivists faced, along with other challenges and ideas for overcoming these obstacles. Collecting comics in particular was one of the featured topics in that first issue of *Popular Culture in Libraries*. It included an essay by librarian Randall Scott, entitled "Comics and Libraries and the Scholarly World," detailing his efforts to collect and catalog comic books and related materials at Michigan State (of which we will hear more later in this chapter).

Pioneering Special Collections Librarians and Archivists

Against this backdrop, three individuals in the U S actually began tackling the daunting task of collecting, preserving, and cataloging comic books, comic strips, and related material: Bill Blackbeard, Randall Scott, and Lucy Shelton Caswell. Each recognized a need early on and set to work in their own individual ways, using whatever resources they could manage to procure. They focused on different and complementary aspects of collecting comics. In the end, each created an amazing legacy by amassing distinctive collections of comics and cartoon materials that are indispensable to the work of researchers, scholars, and students from all over the world today. The second part of this chapter will explore the journeys of these three leaders and pioneers of the field.

Bill Blackbeard and the San Francisco Academy of Comic Art

Blackbeard's interest in comics began when he was a child.[1] The arrival of the Sunday comics was the highlight of his week, but then he discovered something that transformed him from enthusiastic consumer to collector. Before anyone thought of recycling, people kept large collections of newspapers in their basements or garages for various uses. Young Blackbeard rescued the comics pages from these caches held by neighbors, reading them and keeping them organized in stacks. After serving in the military in World War II and attending Fullerton College, Blackbeard continued to develop his interests in the humanities and popular media. He became particularly curious about comics as an art form and a business and about the ways comics related to other popular literature and art. In 1967, the same year Ray Browne founded the *Journal of Popular Culture*, Blackbeard decided to write a scholarly history of the newspaper comic strip, and he reportedly sold the concept to Oxford University Press (Lewis, 1984).

In the course of his research, he learned that libraries around the country were starting to discard their bound volumes of old newspapers, which contained the daily and Sunday printed comics, and replacing them with microfilm. Blackbeard recognized that microfilm, which only recorded black and white images, would be insufficient to document the beautiful Sunday color comics that he had treasured as a kid and continued to appreciate as an adult. His local library, the San Francisco Public Library, was in the process of getting rid of

FIGURE 6.1 Bill Blackbeard.
Source: Photo courtesy of the Billy Ireland Cartoon Library and Museum.

a number of their bound volumes, so Blackbeard offered to take them. The library's policy prohibited them from giving away material to an individual, so Blackbeard had the idea to become a non-profit. "I never did anything so ... fast in my life. In less than a week, I was the San Francisco Academy of Comic Art," Blackbeard recalled in 2007.

Blackbeard didn't stop with this first transfer. Over the years he continued to take in unwanted bound newspaper volumes from libraries around the country, including the Library of Congress, the Chicago Public Library, the Los Angeles Public Library and more. He kept the material at his home in San Francisco. He saved some of the older volumes intact, but he removed the comics pages out of most and discarded the rest of the newspaper material. He and his wife and various volunteers cut out individual strips to create complete chronological runs of hundreds of titles. In the 1990s, he estimated that the collection contained 350,000 Sunday and 2.5 million daily comic strip clippings (n.d. [c.1997]), all meticulously arranged and organized despite the fact that he did not have professional training as an archivist or librarian.

Although the focus of the San Francisco Academy of Comic Art was on newspaper comic strips, Blackbeard recognized that all forms of popular culture were interrelated, so he decided to expand his collection to include all of popular narrative. He acquired penny dreadfuls, dime novels, pulp magazines, and comic books. He believed that comics should be examined in the larger context of all the art and literature that was created for the masses so that scholars and students could understand how these different media informed and influenced each other and society.

In 1997, Blackbeard lost the lease on the home that had served as his residence and had housed his massive collection for decades. At the same time, he recognized that the collection would eventually need to be transferred to a larger institution that could continue to preserve it and make it accessible to future generations of comics scholars. Lucy Caswell at Ohio State University worked with Blackbeard to make the necessary arrangements to purchase the collection and ship it across the country. Six large semi-trucks were required to transport the 75 tons of material to their new home (Caswell, 2008).

In 1980, Blackbeard wrote, "It is my conviction that the present and long-extended determination of most American libraries to dump their often literally priceless printed newspaper files[2] upon 'replacement' by microfilm is nothing less than an archival disaster." Thanks to Blackbeard's visionary work, such a disaster was largely averted in regards to the comic strips contained in those bound newspaper volumes. He made it his life's mission to rescue the comics that libraries around the country were discarding. Although he never completed the book for Oxford University Press that started him on his journey, he did go on to write, edit, or contribute to more than 200 books about comics and cartoons. He represents the private popular culture collector who ultimately institutionalized his collection in order to support his own scholarly efforts and those of other comics scholars.

Blackbeard died in 2011, but his legacy lives on. Historian R. C. Harvey (1997) stated, "Blackbeard, without question or quibble, is the only absolutely indispensable figure in the history of comics scholarship for the last quarter century." The collection, now housed at the Billy Ireland Cartoon Library & Museum, is used by researchers from a wide variety of disciplines, and scholars from around the world regularly travel to Ohio to access the unique materials.

Randall Scott and the Comic Art Collection at Michigan State University

Independent collectors like Blackbeard played a crucial role in collecting and preserving comics materials that most libraries and museums long thought were not worth collecting. Indeed, with few exceptions, most comics collections at academic institutions began with a single donated collection from a private collector or creator. In the case of Michigan State University and Ohio State University, visionary librarians Randy Scott and Lucy Caswell saw the potential for their institutions to build on those founding collections in order to respond to the growing academic demand to make popular culture materials, including comics, available in a way they never had been before.

In 1970, Russel B. Nye, an English professor at Michigan State University, published his ground-breaking book, the *Unembarrassed Muse*, which explored the "popular arts" created to please a mass audience. He included a chapter on comic strips and books entitled "Fun in Four Colors: The Comics." Once the book was published, Nye convinced the Michigan State Library Special Collections division to accept a collection of 6,000 comic books (along with similar collections of other popular media he had used for the book), so that others could check or reproduce his scholarly work on the subject.

An avid comic book reader as a child, Scott's interest was rekindled while working in a comic book store in the early 1970s. After receiving a B.A. in humanities from Michigan State in 1972, he worked as a typist at the Michigan State University Library. In the summer of 1974, he started a card file index of about 20 cards for his personal comic book collection. "The whole concept suddenly seemed exciting. Then I put them away and went camping in Canada for a long weekend, with the understanding that if it still seemed exciting when I got back I'd work on it for a few years. Well, it still seemed like the right thing to do. Before long I was in library school, and the card file had grown to 74,000 cards when I quit typing them in 1978" (Scott, 2010a, p. 127).

In 1975, Nye came looking for a student librarian to nurture the comic book collection at MSU. Scott volunteered and embarked on a project that resulted in the publication of "A Subject Index to Comic Books and Related Material" (Scott, 1975). This very early effort provided an inventory of MSU's comics holdings and outlined a card catalog system Scott had developed for comic books.

Scott received an M.S. in Library Service from Columbia University in 1977 and returned to work at MSU, this time as a general humanities and German language cataloger. The advent of MARC (MAchine Readable Cataloging) and OCLC (Online Computer Library Center—a cooperative library effort to share computerized cataloging), which had come to MSU in 1975, paved the way for professional cataloging of MSU's comic book collection. For Scott, this was a critical turning point in the acceptance of comics in academic libraries. Prior to this, with the exception of MSU, even the few libraries that had collections of comics (the Library of Congress most notably) had made no serious attempts to catalog them, thus ensuring they were all but invisible to potential researchers. Scott had found his cause.

In 2010, Scott (2010b, p. 124) wrote, "Why is cataloging so important? Because cataloging is the first order of research after accumulating; cataloging begins to make sense of piles of stuff. And if you can't say what you have, why would scholars visit, or why would donors donate?" Over the years, Scott developed a system for cataloging comic books that included robust descriptive information including Library of Congress subject headings. This level of cataloging not only made the materials truly accessible for the first time, but also contributed significantly to the growth of the collection. "The ability to point with pride to the catalog spilled over into a kind of trust between our library and prospective donors. In the twenty years from 1975 to 1995, the collection grew from about 5,000 unique items to about 100,000 items, and almost every one was donated" (Scott, 1998, p. 50).

In 1990, Scott published a ground-breaking book entitled *Comics Librarianship: A Handbook*. He stated, "this volume asserts that comics are a communications medium within human culture that touches millions of lives daily and is therefore important to understand. This volume is dedicated to the collecting and study of comics at an institutional level, where there is some hope that funds and space can be made available to do the job well" (Scott, 1990, p. 10). The book offers practical suggestions for building and cataloging a comics collection, including a detailed explanation of the cataloging system that Scott had developed. Reviews called the book "an invaluable guide...to all librarians who deal with popular culture materials" (Stevens, 1991, pp. 125–126) and "highly recommended" for any librarians adding comics to their holdings (Shoptaugh, 1991, p. 237). The handbook served to further legitimize the idea that comics belonged in academic libraries. For Scott (1990, p. 10), it was a serious crusade: "For librarians or prospective librarians who have an interest in comics, there is a cause here that can be taken up, and a struggle to be won that can only take place in research libraries."

Scott's efforts were not without detractors. In 1993, he wrote "since popular collections tend to be massive and very visible, however, there is a potential for trouble. We can find ourselves isolated from teaching faculty and administrators, and we may discover that we are exercising leadership in an organization that hadn't intended to be led.... In the eyes of some, our comics collection grew like a weed and was no less welcome" (Scott, 1993, p. 81). Nevertheless, in 1992, Scott's position was transferred to the Special Collections Department, where he was now able to focus his cataloging efforts. His pace increased dramatically, but so too did the size of the collection. "It seems that this frenzy of cataloging was so encouraging to bibliographers and donors that our acquisitions program almost literally exploded" (Scott, 1998, p. 51).

The Comic Art Collection was originally intended to be a "sample" collection, so that researchers from a variety of disciplines could find evidence within popular culture to support their theses, whatever those might be. In the 1980s, the collection scope expanded with a goal to collect comic books as comprehensively as possible, given the constraints of budget and storage space. However, the collection intentionally excluded original art and most archival material, such as the papers of cartoonists. "Libraries are designed to collect books, and we collect comics as books, not as curiosities or as objects of art. We are not an archive or a gallery or a museum" (Scott, 2010b, p. 123). The collection was also largely restricted to narrative comics and did not focus on editorial cartooning, magazine cartooning, illustration, caricature, or the prehistory of comics (prior to 1895). Historically, the three main strengths of the collection were U S comic books, U S newspaper comic strips, and the history and criticism of comics, but in 1995, MSU decided to invest in a purchase of 11,000 European comic books, thus truly widening the scope of the collection to be international.

Another important contribution to comics studies was the Reading Room Index of the Comic Art Collection. Scott saw the need to go beyond standard cataloging to provide additional points of access to advanced researchers. Topics of particular interest were identified based on patrons' reference questions, and indexes for those topics were created covering the comic books and major journals and comics reference books in the Comic Art Collection. The Reading Room Index, which started as loose-leaf notebooks in the reading room and then moved to the Internet, was invaluable to researchers in the days before most journals and magazines were digitized and searchable online, and even now it is still a useful and much-used resource.

Forty years have passed since Scott first started working with the Comic Art Collection. He continues to serve as the Assistant Head of Special Collections and Comic Art Bibliographer at Michigan State, presiding over what has become the largest, and best-cataloged, collection of comic books in the world.

Lucy Caswell and the Billy Ireland Cartoon Library & Museum at Ohio State University

At about the same time as Scott started working with the comic books at Michigan State, the Billy Ireland Cartoon Library & Museum began in the Journalism School of Ohio State University with the papers and artwork of famous OSU alumnus, Milton Caniff, the creator of the phenomenally successful adventure comics *Terry and the Pirates* and *Steve Canyon*. According to Caswell (2008), Caniff offered his collection to the University Libraries, perhaps at the behest of President Novice Fawcett, but the Libraries director, Hugh Atkinson, declined it. William Hall, who was the Director of the School of Journalism, accepted it. Caniff was a saver, and the collection was massive, documenting many aspects of comics that would provide rich material for future scholars in areas ranging from the evolution of art styles on the comics page to the business of syndication. The first installment of his collection arrived in 1974. It was followed in 1975 by the papers of Jon Whitcomb, a successful illustrator who had also graduated from Ohio State.

FIGURE 6.2 Lucy Caswell with cartoonist Milton Caniff.
Source: Photo courtesy of the Billy Ireland Cartoon Library and Museum.

Caswell had always been a consumer of comics, especially newspaper comics, and had received her degree in Library Science from the University of Michigan in 1970. After graduating, she worked as the Ohio State University Journalism Librarian but had left in 1975 over differences with the direction the director was taking the library. After a leadership change, she was subsequently hired in 1977 on a temporary basis to survey and catalog the Caniff and Whitcomb collections, which were housed in classrooms in the Journalism building named the Milton Caniff Research Room.

She began to realize the collection was something special when she tried to determine how other universities were handling similar collections. "When I started, being a good librarian, one of the things you do is find out how other people do things" (Caswell, 2008). She went to the print directories available at the time and tried to find other special collections of comic strips, comic books, underground comics, or editorial cartoons. She wrote to the handful she could find. "As the answers trickled in, it was really clear that nobody had anything like the Caniff Collection, which was huge and comprised of not only original art but also all the related materials to the art" (Caswell, 2008).

Caswell saw an opportunity for Ohio State to lead the way in collecting comics, including original cartoons and archival materials. Much of the history of cartoons and comics had already been lost—original cartoon art wasn't valued after it was photographed for print, and the correspondence and papers of cartoonists generally weren't being collected by libraries and other cultural institutions. In her first annual report dated July 17, 1978, she wrote:

> The potential of The Milton Caniff Research Room can be enormous if it receives adequate permanent funding.... The key to enhancing the collection lies in enlarging the holdings to include the works of other cartoonists and, perhaps, papers from the National Cartoonists Society to complement those in the Caniff Collections. The Caniff Collection is a 'first' of its kind and presents a unique opportunity to the University for the development of a research facility.

Permanent funding was one of the key areas of focus in the early years. Caswell's efforts to grow and promote the collection enjoyed considerable support from the School of Journalism and from the Library's new director, William Studer, but there was resistance from other departments at Ohio State that did not acknowledge that what she was doing was important. For the first five years, Caswell's staff position was temporary and had to be renewed each year. Finally in 1982, her position was made permanent and she joined the OSU Libraries faculty in 1983, with a joint appointment in the School of Journalism.

Caswell understood the importance of cultivating relationships within the cartoon and comics community for the purpose of both collection development and fundraising. Shortly after the Milton Caniff Research Room was formally dedicated on May 19, 1979, an endowment fund was started and Caswell reported calling on potential donors and writing grant applications. She also founded the Festival of Cartoon Art in 1983, an event that brought many people from the cartoon community to Columbus as speakers or attendees. In addition to celebrating the artform and its creators, the Festival, held triennially, helped to raise awareness of her efforts to collect and preserve cartoons and comics materials.

The Association of American Editorial Cartoonists placed its archives at Ohio State in 1984 (Caswell, 1984), and the National Cartoonists Society followed suit in 1985 (Caswell,

1985). Lucy attended the annual meetings of both organizations each year, which gave her the opportunity to spread the word to professional cartoonists around the country that Ohio State was interested in collecting their papers and art. Many expressed surprise that an academic institution would even want their collections. Undoubtedly, much of their material would have been lost, had Caswell not taken proactive steps to acquire it.

Caswell's efforts were remarkably successful, and the collection grew rapidly through donations of books, art, and manuscript materials. She was also able to make strategic purchases with the small acquisitions budget she was given, occasionally supplemented by OSU Libraries' funds when special opportunities arose. Having completely outgrown the classrooms in the Journalism Building, a new facility was built for the library, which was renamed the Cartoon, Graphic and Photographic[3] Arts Research Library when it opened in 1990. In 1998, as discussed earlier in this chapter, she successfully lobbied for Ohio State to acquire the massive San Francisco Academy of Comic Art Collection. Later, the Library also acquired the collection of the International Museum of Cartoon Art, a museum founded in 1974 by Mort Walker, the creator of *Beetle Bailey*. Its mission focused on exhibitions, and as such the institution had amassed one of the largest collections of original cartoon art in the world. In 2002, the museum closed its location in Boca Raton, Florida, and when efforts to reopen in New York were unsuccessful, the board decided to transfer the collection to Ohio State in 2008. This acquisition doubled the Library's already substantial original art collection, which now numbers in the hundreds of thousands.

Another major contribution was Caswell's founding of the journal *Inks: Cartoon and Comic Art Studies* in February 1994. Caswell wrote in the inaugural issue, "Recently, journalism historians, political scientists, art historians, sociologists and others have begun to examine cartoons and comic art, seeking to understand their development, the role they have played in society, the values and opinions they represent and the techniques and artistry they embody" (Caswell, 1994, p. 1). The journal provided an outlet for comics scholarship from inside and outside the academy. It also featured book reviews, reviews of cartoon exhibitions, cartoon-related bibliographies, and information about comics research collections. Although the journal only lasted for 3 years, it made a substantial contribution to legitimizing Comics Studies.

By 2005, the Library's collection storage area was once again at capacity. Caswell's careful attention over the years to building positive relationships with the cartoon and comics community resulted in a successful capital campaign to build a new facility. In 1980, Caswell had published a book about Milton Caniff's mentor, *Columbus Dispatch* cartoonist Billy Ireland. Ireland had given Caniff the job that enabled him to attend Ohio State, and he encouraged young Caniff to pursue cartooning as a career. The foundation started by Ireland's daughter, the Elizabeth Ireland Graves Foundation, gave the lead gift of $7 million for the new building. In honor of the donation and Ireland's important role as mentor to Milton Caniff, the Library was renamed the Billy Ireland Cartoon Library & Museum. Jean Schulz, the widow of *Peanuts'* creator Charles Schulz, followed with a $3.5 million gift. Of that, $2.5 million was a matching grant, so an additional $2.5 million needed to be raised. Donors from the cartoon and comics community joined Ohio State alumni, faculty, and staff and fans of the art form from all over to help meet Mrs. Schulz's challenge. In all, a total of $13,000,000 was raised to build the special collection a new home.

The resulting facility included a museum with three exhibition galleries, a state-of-the-art storage facility, new collections processing and office space, and a new dedicated reading room where researchers could access the rare and unique materials in the collection. It opened with great fanfare in October 2013. Bill Kartalopoulos wrote in the *Comics Journal*, "There can be no doubt that the Billy Ireland Cartoon Library & Museum is the foremost repository of comics' material history in North America, and is now uniquely equipped to curatorially perform ongoing historical and critical practice in its well-conceived gallery spaces and auxiliary facilities. The Museum offers peerless resources to comics artists and collectors who wish to deposit their work for posterity, and holds the potential to continue to place the great works of the present and the future into intelligent, ongoing, public conversation with the great works of the past." Some heralded the new facility as a critical moment for comics studies and the growing number of scholars working in the field. Charles Hatfield (2013), Professor at California State University, summed up the excitement felt by many: "the transformation and reopening of the Library, I believe, mark a signal moment, a turning point, in the institutional support for cartoon and comic art studies" (Hatfield, 2013).

Caswell attributes her success in building the Library in spite of the many challenges she encountered to tenacity and stubbornness. She refers to it as the dripping water theory—slowly but surely wearing people down (Caswell, 2008). Undoubtedly, her actions in establishing and nurturing the Library had a positive impact on the growing understanding that cartoons and comics do have a place at the academy and, in turn, the Library benefited from those changing attitudes. On the occasion of Caswell's semi-retirement in 2010, editorial cartoonist J. P. Trostle said, "Lucy's work here means that the life's work of a lot of other talented people will not simply blow away, but will be seen and celebrated by future generations."

The International Scene

The movement to preserve and catalog primary and secondary sources of comics in the US has its equivalent in other parts of the world, particularly those with strong cartoon and comics traditions. Perhaps the earliest institutional effort in Europe was the British Cartoon Archive (BCA) at the University of Kent at Canterbury, founded in 1973. It was previously called the Centre for the Study of Cartoons and Caricature. "The Cartoon Centre began more like the flu than a broken leg. With a leg, one minute it is not broken and the next minute it is. Flu, in contrast, creeps up on you. Thus did the idea of the Centre gradually take shape in the mind of its founder, Dr. Graham Thomas, a member of Kent's Politics department" (Seymour-Ure, 1997, p. 9). The BCA is dedicated to documenting the history of British cartooning over the last 200 years, although its focus is on political and magazine cartoons rather than comics. The collection includes 140,000 pieces of cartoon art supported by holdings of books, catalogues, magazines, and clippings. Many of the cartoons have been digitized and are available in their impressive online database. Another pioneer was Goethe University's Instituts für Jugendbuchforschung (Institute for Children's Book Research) in Frankfurt, Germany, which began developing a comic archive of German-language comics and complementary English and French works in the 1960s and '70s.

Several other European collections started in the 1980s. The Cartoonmuseum Basel (formerly known as the Karikatur & Cartoon Museum Basel) was founded by a private collector who wanted to make his collection more accessible to the public and produced its first exhibition in 1980. The organization also includes a library with a variety of comics materials. The Belgian Center for Comic Strip Art, which includes a study library containing comic albums, magazines, and reference works, was founded in 1984. The Cité International de la bande dessinée et de l'image in Angoulême, France, originated in 1989 and includes a research library with extensive holdings of French and Belgian comics materials. It is now the copyright depository for French comic books.

As in the U S, there has been a significant increase in comics festivals, comics-focused organizations, and specialty museums, collections, and archives in Europe in the last 20 years. Some notable examples include the Serieteket, "Sweden's only specialist library for comics," which was founded in 1996 by Kristiina Kolehmainen as a branch of the Stockholm Public Library but is now part of the Kulturhuset Stadsteatern, a publicly funded cultural institution devoted to all forms of art. The Comics and Visual Culture Center, which is part of the Russian State Library for Young Adults, was established in 2010 and is dedicated to collecting comics, manga, and other types of visual narrative. Aalto University School of Art and Design in Helsinki, Finland, houses the comics collection of the Finnish Comics Society (founded in 1971), which includes thousands of Finnish and foreign comics as well as secondary comics literature. In 2011, it launched "a project for establishing a comics archive…, the purpose of which is to collect and archive original comics material in a centralised manner."

In Canada, the Library and Archives Canada (formerly the National Library of Canada and the National Archives of Canada), has been collecting comic books and related publications as the copyright depository for all Canadian publications. In 1996, its Rare Book Collection acquired the first of several installments of an extensive collection of Canadian comic books, mini-comics, original art, and archival materials from John Bell, a historian and expert on Canadian comics and a former archivist at the LAC. The collection is not yet catalogued, but an inventory list is available. Bell (n.d.) explained why he donated his collection in an interview with Ivan Kocmarek:

> First of all, for nearly twenty years I had endeavoured to collect all comics published in Canada. By the mid-1990s, with the proliferation of small-press comics, this self-imposed mandate was becoming a burden, and I was starting to suffer from collecting fatigue. Secondly, a new rare-books librarian, Michel Brisebois, had arrived at LAC. A former book dealer, Michel was himself a collector and respected the passion and obsessive drive required to build a collection. He also recognized the importance of documenting our popular culture. So, I knew that under his direction the Rare Books section at the National Library would offer a good home to the collection, one where it would not only be preserved, but also made available to other researchers. I am pleased to see that more and more people are now consulting the collection.

Similarly, the National Library of Australia acquired the John Ryan Collection in the 1980s. Like Blackbeard and Bell, Ryan was an individual collector and comics historian who amassed an important and rare collection of comic books before passing it on to a larger institution.

David Hopkins discusses the status of manga in Japanese libraries in the 2010 book *Graphic Novels and Comics in Libraries and Archives*. He mentions several institutions with substantial collections, including the National Diet Library (the Japanese equivalent of the

Library of Congress) and the Kyoto International Manga Museum, which opened in 2006 with the mission to collect, preserve, and exhibit manga materials, as well as to promote the study of manga and manga culture. Meiji University in Tokyo also recently opened the Yoshihiro Yonezawa Memorial Library of Manga and Subcultures as part of its initiative to develop a manga, anime, and video game archive that will be the largest of its kind in the world. Hopkins (2010, pp. 17–18) concludes that, given the international popularity of manga and anime, "the rise of dedicated manga museums and research centers is, however, surprisingly late on the scene. ..." The President of Meiji University, Hiromi Naya (n.d.), acknowledges this in a statement on the Yonezawa Memorial Library's website: "Manga and anime, which are two Japanese subcultures, have in the past both deeply penetrated our lives and played an important role in drawing overseas interest to Japan. However, despite their significance—perhaps because they are truly subcultures—preservation of manga and anime documents has very rarely been carried out systematically, even by public institutions." The university's new library is intended to address this oversight. "The purpose of this facility is to... bring together and preserve in one integrated location materials that have until now been collected and preserved mainly through the individual efforts of experts and volunteers, as well as to broadly contribute to research and the cultural utilization of manga, anime, and other subcultures" (Naya n.d.). The Meiji University library began with the private collection of Yoshihiro Yonezawa, the founder of the Comic Market (Comiket), the largest fair or convention for dōjinshi (self-published comics) in the world.

In Korea, the KOMACON (the Korean Manhwa Contents Agency) was founded in 1998 "to tell the world about Korea's Manhwa, to bring fun and happiness to readers, and to support the comics industry and its future growth" (Lee, n.d.). Its services and programs include a museum, a library, and the "Korean Manhwa Digital Archiving Project," which strives "to systematically preserve cultural assets and provide a database service to the nation by collecting manhwa materials and converting them into database format and to further the cultural and commercial value creation of Korean manhwa, through systematic online and offline manhwa archiving." According to the website, it collects and preserves materials such as early and rare manhwa, as well as modern published manhwa (including individual volumes, magazines, theoretical monographs, and foreign material, among others) (KOMACON).

Conclusion

In the 21st century, the climate for collecting comics and cartoons in libraries continues to become more favorable, in large part because of the pioneering work of the librarians and scholars discussed in this book, combined with other factors such as the recent rise of the graphic novel and its library-friendly book format as well as the proliferation of tools that help librarians with selection and acquisition of comics (Nyberg, 2010). These developments have led to the acceptance of comics and cartoons as worthy of study both because of their status as a popular medium consumed by millions and their development as a serious art form with distinct aesthetic and literary merits. Public and academic libraries have embraced comics (or at least graphic novels). In 2010, Alicia Houston (p. 9) wrote, "At this juncture, it is not a question of whether to include graphic novels in libraries, but where to begin." Many more university libraries have started collecting in this area, including both circulating and special collections. Notable comics collections can now be found at the University of Missouri's Special Collections and Rare Books Library, Duke University's Rubenstein Library, Brown University's John Hay Library, Iowa State University Library, Virginia Commonwealth University, the University of Wyoming American Heritage Center, Indiana's Lilly Library, Columbia University (which has developed a large circulating collection and started to acquire art and archival materials in its Rare Book and Manuscript Library), and the University of Florida's Smathers Library (UF boasts the first Comics Studies program in the United States). This is by no means an exhaustive list. At the same time, private collectors and fans continue to play a critical role. More often than not, their collections still provide the seeds or contribute to the substantial growth of the institutional collections.

Early proponents of collecting popular culture materials recognized that no one institution could do it all. Suggestions were made to establish regional centers or to develop an inter-institutional cooperative collecting program. While nothing of this kind emerged at the national level, there was a regional effort undertaken called the Consortium of Popular Culture Collections in the Midwest. The original members were (not surprisingly) Bowling Green State University, Michigan State University, and Ohio State University. Some of the ambitious goals outlined in the original prospectus (Berg, Caswell, and McCallum, 1993) failed to come to fruition, but there have been lasting successes with regards to comics in the areas of shared cataloging and cooperative collection development. Although there is some duplication among the libraries, there were efforts to divide up the acquisition of materials by genre, format, and geographic region, particularly between the two libraries whose focus was on comics and cartoons. For example, Michigan State collects U S and foreign comic books as comprehensively as possible, while Ohio State only collects representative samples of comic books. Ohio State's collection includes original art and archives, while Michigan State's does not. Internationally, Michigan State focuses on documenting European comics while Ohio State collects Japanese manga. Ohio State's scope includes editorial cartoons, magazine cartoons, and illustration while Michigan State focuses on comic books and strips. As Scott (2010a, p. 125) notes, the arrangement "isn't rigid, or binding, or inhibiting in any way… each library's first responsibility is to its own patrons." Although the Consortium has been inactive for several years, the principles established between these institutions continue to help shape their collection develop policies.

With more and more libraries collecting comics materials and the promise that digitization brings for making them accessible anytime and anywhere, there is still great potential for inter-institutional cooperation on a national level in collection development and providing access. Thanks to the leadership of the individuals discussed in this chapter, the pioneering work of establishing comics collections at research libraries has made it possible for the current generation of librarians and archivists to better serve the scholars and students of Comics Studies.

Notes

1. Unless otherwise noted, all biographical information and quotes from Blackbeard, 2007.
2. Blackbeard referred to bound newspaper volumes as "files."
3. At the time, the library included several important photograph and film poster collections. These have since been moved to other special collections at Ohio State University.

Bibliography

Bell, J. (n.d.) John Bell interview by Ivan Kocmarek, September 10. Available from: http://www.comicbookdaily.com/collecting-community/whites-tsunami-weca-splashes/john-bell/. [Accessed 19 August 2015].

Berg, P., Caswell, L. and McCallum, B. (1993) 'Consortium of popular culture collections in the Midwest: prospectus', *Popular Culture in Libraries,* 1 (1): 91–100.

Blackbeard, B. (1980) Letter to Charles Blitzer of the Smithsonian Institution, 15 February, *San Francisco Academy of Comic Art Collection,* The Ohio State University Cartoon Library & Museum.

Blackbeard, B. (n.d. [c. 1997]) The San Francisco Academy of Comic Art: the comic strip collection in detail. *Bill Blackbeard Donor File,* The Ohio State University Cartoon Library & Museum.

Blackbeard, B. (2007) Unpublished interview by Jenny E. Robb, May 14, 2007, Billy Ireland Cartoon Library & Museum, Ohio State University.

Browne, R.B. (1989) *Against Academia: The History of the Popular Culture Association/American Culture Association and the Popular Culture Movement, 1967–1988,* Bowling Green, OH: Bowling Green State University Popular Press.

Browne, R.B. and Schurk, W.L. (1969) 'Bowling Green University: popular culture collections', *Journal of Popular Culture,* 2 (4): 723–25.

Caswell, L.S. (1978) Annual report of the activities of The Milton Caniff Research Room, 1977–1978. Billy Ireland Cartoon Library & Museum archives, The Ohio State University.

Caswell, L.S. (1984) Annual report. Billy Ireland Cartoon Library & Museum archives, The Ohio State University.

Caswell, L.S. (1985) Annual report. Billy Ireland Cartoon Library & Museum archives, The Ohio State University.

Caswell, L.S. (1994) 'Introduction', *Inks: cartoon and comic arts studies,* 1 (1): 1–2.

Caswell, L.S. (2008) Unpublished interview by Jenny E. Robb on February 19, 2008, Billy Ireland Cartoon Library & Museum, Ohio State University.

Clarke, J.A. (1973) Popular culture in Libraries', *College and Research Libraries,* May: 215–18.

Ellis, A. and Highsmith, D. (2000) 'About face: comic books in library literature', *Serials Review,* 26 (2): 21–43.

Geist, C.D. et al. (1989) *Directory of Popular Culture Collections,* Phoenix, AZ: The Oryx Press.

Harvey, R.C. (1997) 'Milestones at two score and one', *Comics Journal,* 200, 78–84.

Hatfield, C. (2013) 'Comics heaven in Columbus', *See Hatfield* blog. Available from: https://seehatfield.wordpress.com/2013/11/18/osufest2013/. [Accessed 18 November 2013].

Hoffmann, F. (1993) 'Editor's note', *Popular Culture in Libraries,* 1 (1): 1–3.

Hopkins, D. (2010) 'Manga in Japanese libraries: a historical overview', in R.G. Weiner (ed) *Graphic Novels and Comics in Libraries and Archives: essays on readers, research, history and cataloging,* Jefferson, NC: McFarland & Company, Inc., 17–25.

Houston, A. (2010) 'A librarian's guide to the history of graphic novels', in R.G. Weiner (ed) *Graphic Novels and Comics in Libraries and Archives: essays on readers, research, history and cataloging,* Jefferson, NC: McFarland & Company, Inc., 9–16.

Kartalopoulos, B. (2013) 'A landmark in comics history: The Billy Ireland Cartoon Library and Museum opens in Columbus, Ohio', *The Comics Journal.* Available from: http://www.tcj.com/a-landmark-in-comics-history-the-billy-ireland-cartoon-library-and-museum-opens-in-columbus-ohio/. [Accessed 20 November 2013].

KOMACON (n.d.) Expansion of the cultural infrastructure for Manhwa. Available from: http://www.komacon.kr/komacon_en/project/overview02.asp. [Accessed 8 August 2015].

Lee, H. (n.d.) Welcome message. Available from: http://www.komacon.kr/komacon_en/about/welcome.asp. [Accessed 8 August 2015].

Lewis, J.D. (1984) 'The man who's serious about the funnies', *Ford Times,* January: 28–30.

Moran, B. (1993) 'Going against the grain', *The Acquisitions Librarian,* 4 (8): 3–12.

Naya, H. (n.d.) Yoshihiro Yanazawa Memorial Library of Manga and subculture message. Available from: https://www.meiji.ac.jp/manga/english/yonezawa_lib/message/. [Accessed 1 June 2015].

Nyberg, A.K. (2010) 'How librarians learned to love the graphic novel', in R.G. Weiner (ed) *Graphic Novels and Comics in Libraries and Archives: essays on readers, research, history and cataloging*, Jefferson, NC: McFarland & Company, Inc., 26–40.

Nye, R.B. (1970) *The Unembarrassed Muse: the popular arts in America*, New York: Dial.

Savage, Jr., W.W. (1993) 'Research and comic books: a historian's perspective', *Popular Culture in Libraries*, 1 (1): 85–90.

Scott, R.W. (1975) *A Subject Index to Comic Books and Related Material*, East Lansing, MI: Michigan State University Libraries Special Collections.

Scott, R.W. (1990) *Comics Librarianship: a handbook*, Jefferson, NC: McFarland & Co.

Scott, R.W. (1993) 'Comics and libraries and the scholarly world', *Popular Culture in Libraries*, 1 (1): 81–84.

Scott, R.W. (1998) 'A practicing comic-book librarian surveys his collection and his craft', *Serials Review*, 24 (1): 49–56.

Scott, R.W. (2010a) 'Comic art collection at Michigan State University libraries', in R.G. Weiner (ed) *Graphic Novels and Comics in Libraries and Archives: essays on readers, research, history and cataloging*, Jefferson, NC: McFarland & Company, Inc., 123–26.

Scott, R.W. (2010b) 'Interview with Randall W. Scott by Nicholas Yanes and Robert G. Weiner', in R.G. Weiner (ed) *Graphic Novels and Comics in Libraries and Archives: essays on readers, research, history and cataloging*, Jefferson, NC: McFarland & Company, Inc., 127–30.

Seymour-Ure, C. (1997) 'The Centre for the Study of Cartoons and Caricature and the University of Kent', in *A Sense of Permanence? Essays on the Art of the Cartoon*, Canterbury: The Centre for the Study of Cartoons and Caricature, 9–10.

Shoptaugh, T.L. (1991) 'Review of *Comics Librarianship: A Handbook* by Randall W. Scott', *Journal of Academic Librarianship*, 17 (4): 237.

Stevens, N.D. (1991) 'Review of *Comics Librarianship: a handbook* by Randall W. Scott', *Wilson Library Bulletin*, 65: 125–26.

Stevenson, G. (1977) 'The wayward scholar', *Library Trends*, April: 779–818.

Wiegand, W. (1979) 'Popular culture: a new frontier for academic libraries', *Journal of Academic Librarianship*, 5 (4): 200–204.

Wiegand, W. (1981) 'The academic library's responsibility to the resource needs of the popular culture community', in F.E.H. Schroeder (ed) *Twentieth Century Popular Culture in Museums and Libraries*, Bowling Green, OH: Bowling Green University Popular Press, 187–98.

PART 3
The Theorists

7
LITERARY THEORY/NARRATIVE THEORY

Barbara Postema

Introduction

The increasing popularity of the term "graphic narrative" in reference to comics, or in some cases more narrowly as a synonym for graphic novels, shows the easy fit that literary or narrative studies have as an approach to studying comics. This approach comes all the more naturally since the disciplinary background of many comics scholars is in literary studies, for some national literature or another, or in some cases Comparative Literature. However, this focus has not generally translated into a strict narratological focus or an approach deeply rooted in literary theory, even when a scholar is discussing the stories of various comics. For example, in the special issue of *Modern Fiction Studies*, edited by Hillary Chute and Marianne DeKoven, the topic of which was "Graphic Narrative" (2006), only a few of the diverse articles collected engage narrative theory in a strict way. This is in contrast to the special issue of *SubStance* (2011), which engages narrative theory as it applies to comics specifically. In the introduction, editors Jared Gardner and David Herman lay out various special considerations that graphic narrative theory raises in the context of multimodal narratives and accounts of narrative in various media. While stories have been of longstanding interest to comics scholars, recent scholarship has taken narratology and literary theory and applied it very specifically to the study of comics, often with results that expand our understanding of both comics and the theory in question.

Practice-Based Discussion of Comics Narrative

Will Eisner discusses comics as a "form of reading" in *Comics and Sequential Art* (1985, p. 7). He is interested in the ways that text in comics reads visually (Eisner, 1985, p. 10), but even more in the ways that images read as text, or rather the ways in which images take on the burden of meaning-making, of storytelling. To this end, Eisner draws a distinction between images in comics as "illustration," where they reinforce a textual narrative, or as "visual," where they carry the narrative, replacing the text (Eisner, 1985, pp. 127–128). In *Graphic Storytelling and Visual Narrative* Eisner goes into more detail regarding what a story is and how images can carry the narrative. However, sections such as "Images as Narrative

Tools" (Eisner, 2008, p. 11), in which Eisner addresses the topics "Stereotypical Images" and "Symbolism," show that he is more interested in the particular effects of drawings than in an analysis of the particular structures or breakdowns that might be involved in narrative in a visual form, despite the many examples he provides. He spends significant time on storytelling technique, on ways to flesh out characters, setting, atmosphere, and not so much on structure or genre.

Scott McCloud too sets out to explain the way that comics tell stories using images, in *Understanding Comics: The Invisible Art*. He acknowledges his indebtedness to Will Eisner's work and takes up his notion of sequential art (McCloud, 1993, p. 5). While narrative is not one of the defining features of comics in the definition of the form that McCloud settles on (1993, p. 9), most of the comics he subsequently discusses in the book are narrative in nature, while his discussion of closure in Chapter Three mainly explains how readers make sense of comics in a narrative way. Furthermore, he breaks down this process on a micro-level, between two panels at a time, rather than across the full range of panels that compile a text. Hannah Miodrag convincingly argues the limitations of this approach in her book *Comics and Language* (2013, p. 118). McCloud draws attention to the time that is elided between panels as well as to how time can be captured in varying ways within panels. He equates the passing of time and the representation of action with narrative, but he offers tools for creating narrative in the form of comics, rather than tools to analyze comics narratives. McCloud's work introduced the notion of analyzing the comics form to a broader audience, but within academic circles, the analysis of comics had been ongoing for some time, and the focus on narrative in particular was about to explode.

From Comics as Narrative to Comics as Literature

Much of the work on comics over the course of the twentieth century applied approaches based in social, historical, or educational interests. The narratives of comics, and certainly the ways in which comics created narrative, were often not considered with much attention. However, it was often taken as a given that comics were narrative in their form and intention, as is evident from David Kunzle's definition of the comic strip in his history of early comics. He makes sure to "stress the *narrative* role of the medium, which [he] consider[s] primary" (Kunzle, 1973, p. 1) and mentions narrative as one of the four elements of his definition of the (early) comic strip: "the sequence must tell a story which is both moral and topical" (p. 2). While analyzing narrative is not his main interest, he does go so far, by the end of the second volume of the history, as linking the abbreviated and fragmented form of narrative in comics to the frenetic and fragmented experience of train travel, the environment where, according to Kunzle, many readers read their comics (1990, p. 377).

The Argentine-Chilean literary critic and novelist Ariel Dorfman analyzes comics narratives, notably American comics for children, to make overt the underlying ideologies of these stories, in particular the cultural imperialism of the United States. Together with Armand Mattelart, he demonstrates the presence of this ideology in the adventures of Donald Duck, a type of analysis that he continues in *The Empire's Old Clothes*, where he also discusses the underlying meaning of the narratives of *Superman* and the Chilean children's magazine and eponymous comic series *Mampato*. In the preface Dorfman explains that he wants to expose the hidden social and political messages of popular fiction, even if such messages are uncomfortable to acknowledge (1983, p. ix). Ariel Dorfman's narrative analyses are given extra force due to his own exile from Chile after President Salvador Allende was ousted and killed by the U S-government-supported coup led by General Pinochet in 1973.

Joseph Witek, in *Comic Books as History: The Narrative Art of Jack Jackson, Art Spiegelman, and Harvey Pekar*, was probably the first American academic to explicitly call for the sustained critical analysis of comics based in literary theory (1989, p. 3). He argues that this kind of attention "is especially necessary now, when a growing number of contemporary American comic books are being written *as* literature" (1989, p. 3). In his readings of Jackson's works, Spiegelman's *Maus*, and Pekar's *American Splendor*, Witek models this critical analysis. He also contextualizes the newly popular "true stories" (p. 154) told in comics form for adults, by situating them within comics history such as the establishment of the Comics Code and the underground comix movement. Witek has gone on to combine his interests in the materiality and formal structures of comics, and his advocacy for comics studies in the academy, with articles such as "The Arrow and the Grid" (2009) and "Comics Modes: Caricature and Illustration in the Crumb Family's *Dirty Laundry*" (2012), which offer tools for reading comics narratives through attention to page structure and rendering styles, as well as the article "American Comics Criticism and the Problem of Dual Address" (2008) in which he considers how academics discuss their research with different audiences.

European Narrative and Semiotic Comics Theory

Witek may have taken a cue for his attention to the literary side of comics from an article he cites by Lawrence L. Abbott, "Comic Art: Characteristics and Potentialities of a Narrative Medium." Abbott states that "the comic art drawing, as a narrative element must conform to an order of perception that is essentially literary" (1986, p. 156). Abbott himself was referencing European book-length studies on comics, mainly in German, that have gone more or less unnoticed in North America. Abbott's sources include several European texts on comics and narratology from the 1970s: *Strukturen des Comic Strip: Ansätze zu einer textlinguistisch-semiotischen Analyse narrativer comics* by Wolfgang K. Hünig (1973) uses structuralist and semiotic approaches to look at narratives told in comics form, in particular *The Adventures of Phoebe Zeit-Geist* by Michael O'Donoghue and Frank Springer; Ulrich Kraft's *Comics lesen: Untersuchungen zur Textualität von Comics* (1978) expands on Hünig's work, applying an approach based in textlinguistics to the semiotic analysis of comics; and Alain Rey's *Les spectres de la bande: essai sur la B.D.* (1978), which is a highly idiosyncratic reading of the comics form based, as the book's cover blurb summarizes, in "quasi-psychiatry, pseudo-sociology, and almost semiology." Much of this work has not been translated into English, but in Europe it was part of the corpus that served as the basis of the robust scholarly debate on narratology and semiotics in comics that has been going on between mainly Belgian and French comics theorists since at least the 1980s. Some of the results of this ongoing discussion are now available in English, such as the translations of Thierry Groensteen's books (2007 and 2013), Thierry Smolderen's history of comics's origins (2014), and notably *The French Comics Theory Reader* edited and translated by Ann Miller and Bart Beaty (2014), which introduces a range of French comics theorists to English speakers, some of them for the first time.

French comics theory was introduced to the English-language academy mainly through the work of Thierry Groensteen, and as a result gained a certain notoriety, in part because his work *The System of Comics* (2007) was seen as dense and needlessly convoluted, and perhaps also because for his examples he used mainly Franco-Belgian comics that were unknown to English readers, making his analyses that much harder to follow. Despite such perceived barriers, his work has been very influential, leading to a new rigor in the use of academic language related to comics and offering a number of concepts that have been taken up by English-language scholars and have influenced their own narratology-based analyses of comics. In *The System of Comics*, Groensteen approaches comics in a very broad, formalistic way, laying a foundation for the study of comics with concepts such as the spatio-topical system (Chapter One), restrained arthrology or the sequence (Chapter Two), and general arthrology or the network (Chapter Three). On the way he breaks down functions of various elements of the page layout, including panels, frames, and word balloons. Groensteen's work is clearly in dialogue with other comics scholars, and he refers frequently to the work of for example Pierre Fresnault-Deruelle, perhaps the first French scholar to work on comics in a sustained way (2007, p. 1), and Benoît Peeters, a French comics scriptwriter and critic who has written on comics using a structuralist approach. Groensteen also builds on the work of narrative theorists working outside of comics such as Roland Barthes, who developed strict structuralist methodologies for analyzing narrative as well as various approaches to visual semiotics, and André Gaudreault, a film theorist who was interested in how images narrate.

Groensteen wields a specialized vocabulary in order to discuss comics in very specific detail. For some of this vocabulary he draws on existing terminology, for example applying "monstration," which is originally taken from film studies: André Gaudreault used the term to denote how film and drama communicate narrative through showing rather than telling, which applies in comics as well (2013, p. 84), when images further the action without the use of captions. In other cases, Groensteen creates new terminology as needed. An example of the latter is the term *tressage* or braiding, which refers to the way comics images exist in a network, with certain design elements or motifs reoccurring throughout a work. It is a feature in comics narrative that is hard to translate to other forms or media and is one of the areas in which Groensteen's influence can be seen. Thus, Craig Fischer and Charles Hatfield apply the concept in their reading of Eddie Campbell's collected work, where they point out that "braiding in comics does something medium-specific: it confers unity via fragmentation, or, to put it another way, exploits fragmentation-in-unity, a fragmentation enacted literally on the comics page" (2011, p. 85). Barbara Postema's *Narrative Structure in Comics* is another study that is clearly influenced by Groensteen's system, in addition to the more traditional narratology and semiotics of Gérard Genette and Roland Barthes. Postema breaks down various levels of signification in comics—i.e. the image, the panel, the sequence—and examines how meaning is generated there, based for example on Groensteen's spatio-topical system and the notion of iconic solidarity: images coexist on the same page but are at the same time separated by gutters and frames. Postema tries to make Groensteen's Franco-Belgian approach more accessible to an English readership in part by using a variety of North American comics as her primary texts, including *Peanuts* and Lynda Barry's work.

If Groensteen's first translated work was seen as hermetic, he is much more accessible in his second book in English, *Comics and Narration* (2013). This work is less formalist in focus than the previous and seeks to clarify some of the confusion that *System* might have allowed to linger, and it is also more narratological in focus, devoting chapters to the narrator in comics, and to how comics show characters' interiority. *Comics and Narration* also draws on a wider range of texts for its examples, including manga, American graphic novels, and digital comics. The critical conversation in which the work is engaged no longer includes only Franco-Belgian scholars, but also Europeans from across the continent and North Americans.

Other European theorists who have had an impact on narratological comics theory are Jan Baetens and Pascal Lefèvre, who are both Belgian. They wrote a book-length study of a literary approach to comics in 1993, published simultaneously in Dutch and French, and excerpts of this work are included in *The French Comics Theory Reader*. More importantly, Jan Baetens is the long-time editor of the Leuven University-based journal *Image & Narrative*, which publishes articles both in English and in French and focuses on visual narratology and word and image studies. The journal is not devoted exclusively to comics, but it has served to introduce European scholarship on comics to English-language scholars since 2000. Early issues took up topics such as cognitive narratology, the fantastic, and gender in comics but also photography and time, Autofiction and/in the image, and the digital archive. Contributors to the journal who work on literary or narrative theory and comics specifically have included Jan Baetens himself, Pascal Lefèvre, Aarnoud Rommens, Marie-Laure Ryan, Kai Mikkonen, Raphaël Baroni, Barbara Postema, and Nancy Pedri.

Both Jan Baetens and Pascal Lefèvre have made significant contributions to narrative and literary approaches to comics through their individual publications, many of them in English. Lefèvre's work is especially striking for the range of comics that he uses for his analyses. He has discussed framing in comics using a manga series (2012), diegetic and extradiegetic space in comics with reference to newspaper strips, BD, alternative comics, and manga (2009), while for a discussion of schemata used by readers of comics he draws on an avant-garde Canadian comic and a Flemish strip by Willy Vandersteen from 1947 (2000). He is perhaps most wide-ranging in his corpus in an article on medium-specific qualities of sequences in comics for a special issue on graphic narrative theory of the journal *SubStance*. Jan Baetens' eclecticism in his choice of source materials runs more in a formal range, covering for example avant-garde wordless comics (2002, 2009, and 2011), North American graphic novels (2015), and mainstream Franco-Belgian comics (2002 and 2003). His co-written study *The Graphic Novel* (2015) contains a striking chapter that addresses the influence that the graphic novel as a "medium" has had on literary fiction and vice versa, though this section doesn't so much go into narrative strategies per se, apart from describing a kind of inter-textuality between the two fields (Baetens and Frey, 2015, pp. 193–195). Other contemporary French comics scholars whose work is based in narrative and literary studies are Benoît Peeters (*Lire la bande dessinée*, 2010) and Harry Morgan (*Principes des littératures dessinées*, 2003).

Literary Comics Studies in English

In part under the influence of Continental comics criticism such as that in *Image [&] Narrative* and Groensteen's work, but also due to a growing confidence in its own disciplinary standing, Comics Studies in North America has become increasingly rigorous and steadily more specialized. Thus, journal issues devoted to comics have gone from general topics related to comics, such as the special issue of *Modern Fiction Studies* on Graphic Narrative, to issues with a much narrower disciplinary scope, such as the special issue of *SubStance* on Graphic Narratives and Narrative Theory (2011). This issue was co-edited by comics scholar Jared Gardner and narrative theorist David Herman, and articles in this special issue demonstrate a great range in the ways that narrative theory is applied in comics scholarship. Besides using the concept of braiding, as discussed above, Fischer and Hatfield's analysis of the single-volume collection of the *Alec* comics by Eddie Campbell exemplifies how considerations of the materiality of comics can add interesting wrinkles to discussions of long-form comics narrative. By drawing attention to processes including artistic creation and publishing history and practices, Fischer and Hatfield consider concepts such as focalization and narrative braiding, for which the two scholars also draw attention to Campbell's range of visual styles. Jared Gardner (2011), too, pays attention to visual styles, discussing linework in comics as a storytelling tool. Suzanne Keen's and David Herman's articles consider various ways in which characters, especially non-human characters, affect narrative, while Karin Kukkonen considers transmedial narratology by looking at comics as a multi-modal form. Thus this special issue, while seemingly narrow in scope, showcases the range of work possible under the disciplinary umbrella of literary or narrative theory. In addition, the issue strengthens the dialogue between U S and European comics scholarship by including articles by Jan Baetens and Pascal Lefèvre.

Other scholars who have been writing studies of comics using approaches based in narrative theory are Marc Singer, Richard Walsh, and Thomas A. Bredehoft. Singer's chapter on *The Invisibles* in *Critical Approaches to Comics* (2012) demonstrates the applicability of several of Gérard Genette's concepts from *Narrative Discourse* to Grant Morrison's comic book series. Furthermore, he argues that reading the series, and in particular the issue "Best Man Fall," is aided by following Genette's distinction between discourse and story, the way that narrative events are presented and the narrative that readers construct out of that representation. This is especially effective for Morrison's narrative in order to make sense of its non-linear and fragmented structure (Singer, 2012, p. 63). Richard Walsh discusses how the particular media in which it is presented affects narrative imagination, using an issue of *Sandman* as his illustration, while Thomas Bredehoft has written about the comics of Chris Ware and elsewhere about Harvey Pekar, to discuss topics as wide-ranging as narrative voice and representations of narrative time. Walsh and Bredehoft each have an article in the Graphic Narrative issue of *Modern Fiction Studies* exploring narratological concepts in various comics works and thus adding to the growing disciplinary corpus of comics narrative theory.

Contemporary Directions

Narrative theory continues to be influenced by Gérard Genette but is also seeing directions based in cognitive and linguistic approaches. Genette's presence can be felt in the growing body of work that deals with focalization in comics, a topic that is of particular interest in Comics Studies given the visual basis of the term itself. Work on focalization includes articles by Kai Mikkonen (2008), Silke Horstkotte and Nancy Pedri (2011), and the monograph *Contemporary Comics Storytelling* by Karin Kukkonen (2013). Kukkonen's work in particular makes its alliances explicit. She writes, "This book…has a narratological and literary agenda" (1) and is interested in "meaning-making processes" (3). A striking quality of Kukkonen's book is that she draws the corpus for her case studies from mainstream comics series rather than graphic novels, as is a common tendency amongst scholars with a literary approach. Thus the comics that Kukkonen writes about include the series *100 Bullets*, *Fables* and *Tom Strong*. In the conclusion of her study, Kukkonen lays out where she feels important work is to be done in terms of the narratological and literary study of comics: "The story/discourse distinction, the narrator, and focalization are the crucial problems that a narratology of comics would have to engage with before it can call itself by this name" (p. 184).

Also related to Gerard Genette's work, particularly his discussion of paratexts and the broader concept of frame narratives, is Eric Berlatsky's 2009 article "Lost in the Gutter," which uses the panels and gutters of comics as an analogy to discuss ways and forms of framing in literature. This is one of the few examples of comics theory being used to elucidate narrative theory, as opposed to the other way around.

Hannah Miodrag's book *Comics and Language: Reimagining Critical Discourse on the Form* (2013) takes a somewhat combative stance toward previous work in Comics Studies, taking issue for example with the way that scholars have used the word "language" imprecisely in their discussions of comics texts and questioning the applicability of the term "sequence" in the way that it has been used to describe comics. However, her call for a more precise use of terminology in Comics Studies is not a bad idea, and many of her readings are insightful. Miodrag's work has a distinctive linguistic and, like Kukkonen's, cognitive thrust, and she frequently cites Neil Cohn's work on cognitive linguistics. One notable point Miodrag makes is the distinction between literary value and narrative content. She claims that frequently, comics that are lauded for their literary worth in fact do not contain any particularly sophisticated language. Instead, these comics are considered literary due to their intricate narratives and structure. As an example here, she mentions Alan Moore's work. On the other hand, there are comics that use language in highly idiosyncratic and thoughtful ways that are not seen as "literary" comics at all, including Herriman's *Krazy Kat* and Lynda Barry's *Freddie Stories*. Thus Miodrag's call to distinguish between narrative and language in noting the "literariness" of comics is an interesting challenge.

In *Alternative Comics*, Charles Hatfield discusses graphic novels as "an emerging literature," grounding himself in his own disciplinary background in literary studies. One area he discusses in detail is the notion of (self)representation of the narrator, which he looks at specifically in autobiographical comics such as those by Harvey Pekar (2005, p. 110) and Art Spiegelman (p. 139). Hatfield's discussion has implications for discussions of narration and point of view in comics more broadly. Simultaneously, Hatfield traces the origins of alternative comics through underground comix and the changes in the comic book market, adding a historical perspective to the literary analysis. Even as *Alternative Comics* provides insightful readings of works by Gilbert Hernandez and Justin Green, and demonstrates with relish what makes comics so interesting for analysis in the chapter "An Art of Tensions," the work is also evidence of a certain anxiety about the place of comics in literary studies, claiming the graphic novel as a "bid for the recognition of comics as a literary form" even though comics themselves may not seek that recognition at all.

Even as the term "graphic novel" was originally received with some cynicism, as a form, the graphic novel has firmly established itself, and with it the narrative and literary approaches to comics the form attracts, as Baetens and Frey's discussion demonstrates. Furthermore, these approaches have extended beyond graphic novels to all kinds of comics forms, including comic strips, comic books, and webcomics, which in their own diverse ways spin narratives and invite analysis. As scholars are increasingly studying comics using sophisticated narratological and literary approaches, they are also bothering less with trying to make arguments that the comics they are working on warrant this treatment, since the studies themselves are evidence enough.

Bibliography

Abbott, L.L. (1986) 'Comic art: characteristics and potentialities of a narrative medium', *Journal of Popular Culture*, 19: 155–73.
Baetens, J. ed. (2001) *The Graphic Novel*, Leuven: Leuven UP.
Baetens, J. (2002) Hergé, écrivain à contraintes. *Hergé. Colloque de Chaudfontaine*, ed. Marion, P. Liège: Ed. de la Bibliothèque des Paralittératures, n.p.
Baetens, J. (2003) 'Comic strips and constrained writing', *Image [&] Narrative*, 4 (1): n.p. [Online].
Baetens, J. (2009) 'A cultural approach to nonnarrative graphic novels: a case study from Flanders', in S. Tabachnick (ed) *Teaching the Graphic Novel*. New York: MLA, 281–87.
Baetens, J. (2011) Abstract comics, *SubStance*, 40 (1): 94–113.
Baetens, J., and Frey, H. (2015) *The Graphic Novel: an introduction*, Cambridge: Cambridge University Press.
Berlatsky, E. (2009) 'Lost in the gutter: within and between frames in narrative and narrative theory', *Narrative*, 17 (2): 162–87.
Bredehoft, T.A. (2008) 'Comics architecture, multidimensionality, and time: Chris Ware's *Jimmy Corrigan: The Smartest Kid on Earth*', *Modern Fiction Studies*, 52 (4), 869–90.
Bredehoft, T.A. (2011) 'Style, voice, and authorship in Harvey Pekar's (auto)(bio)graphical comics', *College Literature*, 38 (3): 97–110.
Chute, H. and DeKoven, M. eds. (2006) *Graphic Narrative*, spec. issue of *Modern Fiction Studies*, 52 (4).
Cohn, N. (2013) *The Visual Language of Comics: introduction to the structure and cognition of sequential images*, London: Bloomsbury.
Dorfman, A. (1983) *The Empire's Old Clothes: what the Lone Ranger, Babar, and other innocent heroes do to our minds*, New York: Pantheon.
Dorfman, A. and Mattelart, A. (1971/1975) *How to Read Donald Duck: imperialist ideology in the Disney Comic*, trans. D. Kunzle, London: International General.
Eisner, W. (1985/2001) *Comics and Sequential Art*, Tamarac, FL: Poorhouse Press.
Eisner, W. (1996/2008) *Graphic Storytelling and Visual Narrative*, New York: W.W. Norton & Co.
Fischer, C. and Hatfield, C. (2011) 'Teeth, sticks, and bricks: calligraphy, graphic focalization, and narrative braiding in Eddie Campbell's *Alec*', *SubStance*, 40 (1): 70–93.
Gardner, J. (2011) 'Storylines', *SubStance*, 40 (1): 53–69.
Gardner, J. and Herman, D. (2011) 'Graphic narratives and narrative theory: introduction', *SubStance*, 40 (1): 3–13.
Gardner, J., and Herman, D., eds. (2011) *Graphic Narratives and Narrative Theory*, spec. issue of *SubStance*, 40 (1).
Groensteen, T. (2007) *The System of Comics*, trans. B. Beaty and N. Nguyen, Jackson: University Press of Mississippi.
Groensteen, T. (2011/2013) *Comics and Narration*, trans. A. Miller, Jackson: University Press of Mississippi.
Hatfield, C. (2005) *Alternative Comics: an emerging literature*, Jackson: University Press of Mississippi.
Heer, J. and Worcester, K., eds. (2009) *A Comics Studies Reader*, Jackson: University Press of Mississippi.
Herman, D. (2011) 'Storyworld/Umwelt: nonhuman experiences in graphic narratives', *SubStance*, 40 (1): 156–81.
Horstkotte, S. and Pedri, N. (2011) 'Focalization in graphic narrative', *Narrative*, 19 (3): 330–57.
Hünig, W.K. (1974) *Strukturen des Comic Strip: Ansätze zu einer textlinguistisch-semiotischen Analyse narrativer comics*, Hildesheim: Georg Olms Verlag.
Krafft, U. (1978) *Comics lesen: Untersuchungen zur Textualität von Comics*, Stuttgart: Klett-Cotta.
Kukkonen, K. (2011) 'Comics as a test case for transmedial narratology', *SubStance*, 40(1): 34–52.
Kukkonen, K. (2013) *Contemporary Comics Storytelling*, Lincoln: University of Nebraska Press.
Kunzle, D. (1973) *History of the Comic Strip Vol. 1: The Early Comic Strip*, Berkeley: University of California Press.

Kunzle, D. (1990) *The History of the Comic Strip (Vol. 2): The Nineteenth Century*, Berkeley: University of California Press.
Lefèvre, P. (2000) 'Narration in comics', *Image [&] Narrative*, 1 (1), n.p. [Online].
Lefèvre, P. (2009) 'The construction of space in comics', in J. Heer and K. Worcester (eds) *A Comic Studies Reader*, Jackson: University Press of Mississippi, 157–62.
Lefèvre, P. (2011) 'Some medium-specific qualities of graphic sequences', *SubStance*, 40 (1): 14–33.
Lefèvre, P. (2012) 'Mise en scène and framing: visual storytelling in *Lone Wolf and Cub*', in M.J. Smith and R. Duncan (eds) *Critical Approaches to Comics: theories and methods*, London: Routledge, 71–83.
Lefèvre, P., and Baetens, J. (1993) *Strips Anders Lezen [Pour une lecture moderne de la bande dessinée]*, Amsterdam: Sherpa / Bruxelles: CBBD.
McCloud, S. *Understanding Comics: The Invisible Art*, New York: HarperPerennial.
Mikkonen, K. (2008) 'Presenting minds in graphic narratives', *Partial Answers: journal of literature and the history of ideas*, 6 (2): 301–21.
Miller, A., and Beaty, B., eds. (2014) *The French Comics Theory Reader*, Leuven: Leuven University Press.
Miodrag, H. (2013) *Comics and Language: reimagining critical discourse on the form*, Jackson: University Press of Mississippi.
Morgan, H. (2003) *Principes de littératures dessinées*, Angoulême: Éditions de l'An 2.
Morgan, H. (2009) 'Graphic shorthand: from caricature to narratology in twentieth-century bande dessinée and comics', *European Comic Art*, 2 (1): 21–39.
Peeters, B. (2010) *Lire la bande dessinée*, Paris: Flammarion.
Postema, B. (2013) *Narrative Structure in Comics: making sense of fragments*, Rochester: RIT Press.
Rey, A. (1978) *Les spectres de la bande: essai sur la B.D.* (Series: Critique), Paris: Éditions de Minuit.
Round, J. (2007) 'Visual perspective and narrative voice in comics: redefining literary terminology', *International Journal of Comic Art*, 9 (2): 316–29.
Singer, M. (2012) 'Time and narrative: unity and discontinuity in *The Invisibles*', in M.J. Smith and R. Duncan (eds) *Critical Approaches to Comics: theories and methods*, London: Routledge, 55–70.
Smith, M.J., and Duncan, R., eds. (2012) *Critical Approaches to Comics: theories and methods*, London: Routledge.
Smolderen, T. (2000/2014) *The Origins of Comics: from William Hogarth to Winsor McCay*, trans. B. Beaty and N. Nguyen, Jackson: UP Mississippi.
Walsh, R. (2008) 'The narrative imagination across media', *Modern Fiction Studies*, 52 (4): 855–68.
Witek, J. (1989) *Comic Books as History: the narrative art of Jack Jackson, Art Spiegelman, and Harvey Pekar*, Jackson: UP of Mississippi.
Witek, J. (2008) 'American comics criticism and the problem of dual address', *International Journal of Comic Art*, 10 (1): 218–25.
Witek, J. (2009) 'The arrow and the grid', in J. Heer and K. Worcester (eds) *A Comic Studies Reader*, Jackson: University Press of Mississippi, 149–56.
Witek, J. (2012) 'Comics modes: caricature and illustration in the Crumb family's *Dirty Laundry*', in M.J. Smith and R. Duncan (eds) *Critical Approaches to Comics: Theories and Methods*, London: Routledge, 27–42.

8
SEMIOTICS AND LINGUISTICS

Gert Meesters

Semiotics and linguistics both deal with understanding systems of human communication, and as sciences, they share a common foundation. Twentieth- and twenty-first-century research in both disciplines owes a strong structural foundation to Fernand de Saussure's seminal teaching as published in *Cours de linguistique générale* (1916). Nevertheless, the disciplines have evolved so much that their contributions to Comics Studies can better be described separately. It is essential to avoid confusion because of the widely used metaphor of comics as a language. As Miodrag (2013) has argued persuasively, the differences between a natural human language and the communicative system in comics are too important to use one term for both without clarifying the differences.

Semiotics

The beginning of Comics Studies in Europe is closely linked to the emergence of semiotics as a separate scientific discipline. Two figures have been of primordial importance to the rise of comics as a subject fit for academic study: Umberto Eco and Pierre Fresnault-Deruelle. The Italian Umberto Eco, world famous since the 1980s as the writer of the novels *The Name of the Rose* and *Foucault's Pendulum*, was among other things, an avid reader of comics and one of the first to publish about them at the university. As early as 1964, in his *Apocalittici e integrati*, he made a case for the serious study of mass media such as television and crime or science fiction novels, but his main subject was comics. In analyses of *Superman* and *Peanuts*, he touched on the most diverse aspects of comics. In the book, he even published a provisional programme for Comics Studies that the field is still carrying out today. The most important pages of the book in relation to the role of semiotics in Comics Studies are his analysis of the first page of Milton Caniff's *Steve Canyon*. Long before other comics scholars, he made an inventory of the conventions of what he called the comics "language" or "code": the balloons, the frames, and differences from and similarities with film. Eco's writing was accessible and innovative, the work of a true *uomo universale*.

Maybe even more influential in the development of comics theory in Europe than Eco's book were the writings by Pierre Fresnault-Deruelle in the early 1970s. At a time when formal structural semiotics was soaring, Fresnault-Deruelle published several seminal texts about comics: *La bande dessinée, essai d'analyse sémiotique* (1972), *Dessins et bulles. La bande dessinée comme moyen d'expression* (1972), and *Récits et discours par la bande. Essais sur les comics* (1977). Fresnault-Deruelle and his fellow French semioticians had a major influence on the later work of francophone scholars coming from the comics field itself, like Thierry Groensteen (especially in *Système de la bande dessinée* (1999)) and Benoît Peeters (*Case, planche récit* (1991), see Ann Miller's chapter in this volume). Another seminal semiotic text that is often cited, e.g., by Groensteen, is *Traité du signe visuel* (1992) by the Mu group. This collective of semioticians from Liège was not interested in comics per se but wanted to provide for a method to interpret images, a visual semiotics. In the US, W.J.T. Mitchell has played a similar role, providing a ground for comics researchers to stand on by putting forward a theory of images. In his books *Picture Theory* (1994) and *Iconology* (1986), he argues that modern society has taken a "pictorial turn," and he famously defends an interpretation of the image as a living thing. As can already be gathered from the previous description, Mitchell's writings differ greatly from the more formalist European tendencies in semiotics. In addition to Fresnault-Deruelle, the Mu group and Mitchell, Peirce's (1931–1935; 1958) distinction among icon, index, and symbol has been used by many comics scholars to understand visual signification in comics, but Anne Magnussen (2000) was certainly a pioneer. She pointed out that Peirce's (1931–1935; 1958) terminology was not meant to be exclusive and that comics can be better understood when signs in panels can be iconic, indexical, and symbolic at the same time. To understand the connection between panels and page structure, she built on an inference process suggested by Van Dijk and Kintsch (1983).

SIDEBAR: SOUND EFFECTS

Gert Meesters

One characteristic of many comics that attracted the attention of linguists and semioticians early on was sound effects. Not only do comics provide an incessant stream of written sounds that can rarely be found in other texts, onomatopoeias are also a fascinating exception to the arbitrariness of the sign that has been widely accepted as a principle in human language since the Saussurean revolution in linguistics. Contrary to most simple words, sound effects are motivated: they are coined to imitate sounds from the "real" world.

Almost every early book about comics has a small section about sound effects, including Benayoun's 1968 book with the telling title *Vroom Tchac Zowie*. French semiotic comics pioneer Fresnault-Deruelle (1970) touched upon them in an article about language in comics and wrote an entire article about sound effects afterward (Fresnault-Deruelle, 1971), in which he collected examples in French and English. Mansat (1972) did not mention comics in the title of his article, but like Fresnault-Deruelle, he analyzed sound effects from French and English comics.

As early as Fresnault-Deruelle and Mansat's articles were, a comprehensive view of sound effects in comics (*Astérix*, *Tintin* magazine, and *Spirou* magazine) and other sources had already been published in 1969 by a scholar from Ghent, Jean-Pierre Reynvoet. He

(Continued)

had devoted his Ph.D. thesis in Romance Languages to onomatopoeias in 1967 and published a seminal article about the different types of sound effects two years later. Reynvoet (1969) may still have the most interesting linguistic take on sound effects, almost 50 years after the fact. He established distinct categories among onomatopoeias. An important difference is between "unpolished" sound effects on the one hand, coined to imitate a sound as closely as possible without necessarily respecting word structure (e.g., *brroamm*), and sound effects that behave like other words and can often be found in dictionaries, on the other hand (e.g., *to clap*). Reynvoet also distinguished between human sounds such as snoring and laughing, which he called "mimologies" and other onomatopoeias, as the first are usually not imitations, but sounds produced by the human body itself. Like the "real" sound effects, they can be hard to write down, but imitating them with the phonemes of a language is usually fairly easy because they were originally produced with speech organs in the first place.

Although in principle every language user and therefore every cartoonist can create his or her own onomatopoeias, this is not what happens in most cases. Sound effects that stand for frequent noises in comics, like gunshots or explosions, have been standardized, i.e., some forms have been adopted by many cartoonists. Interestingly, this can happen across languages. One would maybe expect this because the sounds are not language-specific, but in reality, the specific phoneme inventory of a language mostly plays an important role in the creation of sound effects. Nevertheless, in comics, compared to literature, for instance, onomatopoeias are more easily borrowed from other languages. Infrequent as they may be in language outside of comics, sound effects have become a flexible international inventory in comics. This does not mean that any sound effect can function in any language. The standardization and the competition between loans and language specific coinings have, among other reasons, incited scholars to make lists of sound effects in comics. Most publications cited so far include these, but some scholars have gone further and have become lexicographers of onomatopoeias. The first systematic dictionary of sound effects was Havlik's. For his 1981 book, he excerpted 40 German language comics. It was the work of a pioneer without much linguistic background. By comparison, similar works in other languages often focus less on quantity and representativeness of the selection and more on showing the artwork, like Gasca and Gubern (2008) for Spanish sound effects. The visual aspects of onomatopoeias in comics are as important as the reference to sound itself, but scholars in general have written less about the graphics of sound effects. A notable exception is Pollman (2001), who claims that the visual effect of writing letters in the images may have contributed to the extension of this practice to inaudible things such as feelings in Japanese.

Bibliography

Benayoun, R. (1968) *Vroom Tchac Zowie. Le ballon dans la bande dessinée*, Paris: André Balland.

Fresnault-Deruelle, P. (1970) 'Le verbal dans les bandes dessinées', *Communications*, 15: 145–61.

Fresnault-Deruelle, P. (1971) 'Aux frontières de la langue: quelques réflexions sur les onomatopées dans la bande dessinée', *Cahiers de lexicologie*, 18 (1): 79–88.

Gasca, L. and Gubern, R. (2008) *Diccionario de onomatopeyas del comic,* Madrid: Catedra.

Havlik, E.J. (1981) *Lexikon der Onomatopöien. Die lautimitierenden Wörter im Comic,* Frankfurt am Main: Fricke.

Mansat, A. (1972) 'De Ah à Erk. Contribution à une étude de l'interjection', *Les Langues Modernes,* 66 (4): 109–18.

Pollman, J. (2001) 'Shaping sounds in comics', *The International Journal of Comic Art,* (3): 9–21.

Reynvoet, J.-P. (1969) 'Contribution à l'étude de l'onomatopée brute', *Travaux de Linguistique,* 1: 99–128.

Linguistics

Scholar Neil Cohn is probably the best proof that the boundaries between semiotics and linguistics can depend on your definition of language. Since the beginning of his academic career around the turn of the millennium, this long-time comics reader has called himself "the visual linguist" and has kept publishing texts (e.g., Cohn, 2003, 2013) that deal with how comics narration works and the way comics are processed in the brain. Although the word "language" may cause confusion as a name for the communicative system underlying the reader's comprehension of comics, the link with linguistics is very real. Cohn's tree structures remind linguists of the early stages of Noam Chomsky's Transformational Generative Grammar (starting with *Syntactic Structures* in 1957). He has also worked with one of the early mainstays of this linguistic framework: Ray Jackendoff. Cohn does not restrict himself to the structure of comics, its arthrology, as Groensteen would put it, but he has also published empirical research based on experiments conducted by psycholinguists in order to comprehend how comics are processed in the brain. His broad interpretation of the term *language* and his curiosity about mechanisms in the brain link his work to the popular framework of cognitive linguistics. Inspired by diverse frameworks and subdisciplines of linguistics, Cohn may be the first linguist to devote the majority of his work to comics, even though he only started writing about comics less than 20 years ago.

Cognitive linguistics, especially the theories of metaphor that are arguably its most popular and fruitful line of research, have led many other linguists to explore visual communication through comics. Most of this work is fairly recent, but especially interesting have been the attempts by Charles Forceville (e.g., 2005, 2010, 2011) to metaphorically explain visual aspects of comics narration, such as the shape of balloons or visual metaphors for showing feelings.

Although much of the linguistic interest in comics is quite new, Frank Bramlett (2012) in the introduction to his seminal collection *Linguistics and the Study of Comics* uncovered some very early linguistic books on comics. His earliest reference is from 1935, an article about the English in "comic cartoons" by H. T. Tysell. Most of these early papers were not specifically aimed at a better understanding of comics but used comics as a specific corpus that allowed for the discovery of language phenomena that were more difficult to unearth in other media and in other registers of spoken or written language.

Bramlett's collection also shows how varied contemporary linguistic approaches to comics can be. Apart from cognitive approaches to comics narration and metaphors, linguistics can provide insight into identity marking and linguistic stereotyping in dialogues, into the functioning of humor in comics, and into multilingualism and code switching in comics.

Linguistics not only brings a different set of research topics to Comics Studies, but also a different research methodology. I have shown (2000, 2011) that quantitative methods from corpus linguistics can be used not only to analyze the evolution of language in long-running popular comics, but also to compare stylistics. Stylistic devices such as onomatopoeia or speed lines can be used to differentiate between genres of comics or to show evolutions within a certain body of work.

As can be gathered from the dates of publication in this linguistic section, comics have only recently become a popular research corpus for linguistic research, so the diversity of the subjects may continue to increase.

Bibliography

Bramlett, F. (ed.) (2012) *Linguistics and the Study of Comics*, London: Palgrave Macmillan.
Chomsky, N. (1957) *Syntactic Structures*, The Hague/Paris: Mouton.
Cohn, N. (2003) *Early Writings on Visual Language*, Carlsbad: Emaki Productions.
Cohn, N. (2013) *The Visual Language of Comics. Introduction to the Structure and Cognition of Sequential Images*, London: Bloomsbury.
De Saussure, F. (1916) *Cours de linguistique générale*, Paris: Payot.
Eco, U. (1964) *Apocalittici e integrati. comunicazioni di massa e teorie della cultura di massa*, Milan: Bompiani.
Forceville, Ch. (2005) 'Visual representations of the idealized cognitive model of anger in the Asterix album *La Zizanie*', *Journal of Pragmatics*, 37 (1): 69–88.
Forceville, Ch. (2011) 'Pictorial runes in 'Tintin and the Picaros'', *Journal of Pragmatics*, 43 (3): 875–90.
Forceville, Ch., Veale, T. and Feyaerts, K. (2010) 'Balloonics: the visuals of balloons in comics', in J. Goggin and D. Hassler-Forest (eds) *The Rise and Reason of Comics and Graphic Literature: Critical Essays on the Form*, Jefferson, NC: McFarland & Co., 56–73.
Fresnault-Deruelle, P. (1972) *La bande dessinée, essai d'analyse sémiotique*, Paris: Hachette.
Fresnault-Deruelle, P. (1972) *Dessins et bulles. La bande dessinée comme moyen d'expression*, Paris/Brussels / Montréal: Bordas.
Fresnault-Deruelle, P. (1977) *Récits et discours par la bande. Essais sur les comics*, Paris: Hachette.
Groensteen, Th. (1999) *Système de la bande dessinée*, Paris: PUF.
Group Mu [F. Edeline, J.-M. Klinkenberg and Ph Minguet] (1992) *Traité du signe visuel. Pour une rhétorique de l'image*, Paris: Seuil.
Magnussen, A. (2000) 'The semiotics of C. S. Peirce as a theoretical framework for the understanding of comics', in A. Magnussen and H.-C. Christiansen (eds) *Comics and Culture: analytical and theoretical approaches to comics*, Copenhagen: Museum Tusculanum, 93–207.
Meesters, G. (2000) 'Convergentie en divergentie in de Nederlandse standaardtaal. Het stripverhaal Suske en Wiske als casus', *Nederlande taalkunde*, 5 (2): 164–76.
Meesters, G. (2011) 'La narration visuelle de L'Association. De *Tintin à Lapin*', in E. Dejasse, T. Habrand, G. Meesters and Acme (eds) *L'Association. Une utopie éditoriale et esthétique*. Brussels : Les Impressions Nouvelles, 123–31, 218–19.
Miodrag, H. (2013) *Comics and Language*, Jackson: University Press of Mississippi.
Mitchell, W.J.T. (1986) *Iconology*, Chicago: University of Chicago Press.
Mitchell, W.J.T. (1994) *Picture Theory. Essays on Verbal and Visual Representation*, Chicago: University of Chicago Press.
Peeters, B. (1991) *Case, planche récit. Comment lire une bande dessinée*, Paris: Casterman.
Peirce, C.S. (1931–1935; 1958) *Collected Papers*, Cambridge: Harvard University Press.
Tysell, H.T. (1935) 'The English of the comic cartoons', *American Speech*, 10 (1): 43–55.
Van Dyck, T. and Kintsch, W. (1983) *Strategies of Discourse Comprehension*, London: Academic Press Inc.

9
MYTHS, ARCHETYPES, AND RELIGIONS

Beth Davies-Stofka and David McConeghy

Introduction

In its origins, scholarship in religion and comics was far-flung and widely varied. Seminal contributions were made by practitioners, journalists, writers, and independent scholars, as well as students and professors working in multiple academic disciplines. As diverse as the original studies were, early interest in the subject breaks into three general areas: myths and archetypes, comics and religion, and the relationship of Jewish artists and visionaries to the creation of the medium and the industry.

The year 2008 might be regarded as a turning point in the field, when scattered interests converged in conferences and publications reflecting the passion shared by diverse scholars and communities. Hence, the "secret origins" of our field lie in the years prior. At present, this is a busy and dynamic field in which new lines of inquiry are regularly established. In this chapter, we discuss seminal works in in the studies of myths and archetypes, Jews and comics, and comics and religion, and weigh their influence. We conclude with a brief synopsis of emerging trends in the field.

SIDEBAR: COMICS' SHORTCUT TO THE SACRED

A. David Lewis

Comics are never to be mistaken for reality. That is, while a film may want the viewer to feel immersed in the cinematic environment and, as far as is possible, forget that he or she is in a theater, even the most compelling comic book will never fully dupe the reader into believing similarly. The pages, the panels, and the cerebral mechanics involved in moving through a comics narrative never entirely disappear. This, far from being a weakness, is among comics' greatest strengths: what Will Eisner called its "special reality" (qtd in Versaci, 2007, p. 37), its obvious representationality.

(Continued)

> Consider the theories of Mircea Eliade (1987), author of numerous books on philosophy and myth criticism but most especially *The Sacred and the Profane: The Nature of Religion*. In this particular work, Eliade outlines the core of a sacred space, act, or item being its connection to the "real" that lies behind/above/beyond the tangible, common, or everyday. A church, for instance, might be sacred not because of its geographical space or its patrons but because of its purported access to the transcendent, to the eternal, or to the divine. These are the "real," argues Eliade, not the brick and mortar of the church's walls and foundations.
>
> Given Eliade's perspective, then, comics could be perceived as a shortcut to the sacred. The medium's lack of verisimilitude, relatively speaking, could place it a step closer to Eliade's real in that it makes no argument for being real. This is not to say comics are sacred; rather, they could be viewed, even as a product of pop culture, as a medium less bound to the profane.
>
> **Bibliography**
>
> Eliade, M. (1987) *The Sacred and the Profane: the nature of religion*, New York: Harcourt.
> Versaci, R. (2007) *This Book Contains Graphic Language: comics as literature*, New York: Continuum.

Comics as/and Myths

The earliest studies of myth in relation to comics divide into three broad areas. Some, such as Umberto Eco and Richard Reynolds, argued for the significance of comics as myth from the perspective of structuralism and semiotics. Working from a Jungian-Campbellian perspective, Robert Jewett and John Shelton Lawrence developed the influential theory of the "American monomyth." In a third approach, Reinhold Reitberger and Wolfgang Fuchs sketched an initial taxonomy of comic book characters and their mythic counterparts.

The idea that superheroes could be theorized as myth first appeared in Umberto Eco's short essay "The Myth of Superman" (1962, English translation 1972), although Eco's chief concern was not Superman, or even comics, but modern thought. Eco argued that Superman was a response to an early 20th-century need for powerful heroes. Average citizens of industrialized societies were experiencing feelings of powerlessness, and in response developed a deep yearning for personal power. However, the principal literary form of industrialization was the modern novel, which tended to emphasize the powerlessness of the individual through its characteristically unpredictable outcomes. People needed a new myth, appropriate to the times.

Superman fulfilled this need. He was bound by universal laws, rendering him predictable and unchanging. The medium of comics could do what the novel could not, using serialization to guarantee a return to the status quo at the end of an adventure. Each issue had its own beginning and end and resulted in a predictable outcome—a victory for truth and justice.

Thirty years later, the first book-length analysis of the mythological nature of superhero comics appeared: Richard Reynolds' famous and oft-cited *Super Heroes: A Modern Mythology*.

Published first in the United Kingdom in 1992, University Press of Mississippi published an expanded edition in the United States in 1994. Reynolds began his short and significant study by defining the superhero genre, listing seven "laws" or "features" of superhero stories. He then presented a close reading of superhero comics by combining the structuralist theories of myth developed by Claude Lévi-Strauss and Roland Barthes with the semiological approach to the comics form developed by Pierre Fresnault-Deruelle in his pivotal 1976 essay "From Linear to Tabular."

Reynolds argued that the plots of comics, communicated through sequential panels on pages, represent a collaboration of story and medium where common superhero conventions such as costume, identity, and villainy continually reinforce an ideology of social control and order. In a related argument, Reynolds connected "continuity" (a comic's ongoing "back story") to Barthes' concept of inter-textuality, demonstrating how it reinforces the genre's central message that the social order is good and worth preserving and protecting.

Super Heroes has been continually in print, yet it has received less scholarly attention than is warranted for its sophisticated use of structuralism. When interviewed on May 15, 2015, Reynolds observed:

> I think now that the word 'mythology' has caused a certain amount of confusion about my intentions. Some people see that word in the title, and expectations are raised that the book is going to be something like Frazer's *Golden Bough* in miniature - an account of how traditional mythology has informed the superhero genre. This wasn't my intention at all...I think that - very broadly - those who are familiar with [Barthes'] use of the word 'mythology' also tend to understand what *Super Heroes* is trying to do.

Still, Reynolds' influence in two other respects is undeniable. First, many scholars have found his seven "laws" of superhero stories to be useful, and Reynolds' definition is commonly cited (see Coogan, 2006, or Lewis, 2014). Second, his thesis regarding the social function of the superhero mythos has begun to inform new studies of comics in society and culture (as in Fingeroth, 2004, and Roth, 2008).

If Reynolds did not systematize comics and cultural myths into original taxonomic descriptions (like Frazer's *Golden Bough* in miniature), research duo Reinhold Reitberger and Wolfgang Fuchs did. In *Comics: Anatomy of a Mass Medium* (1972), they listed and catalogued superheroes, superpowers, and supervillains, aligning them with their counterparts in ancient myths and legends. Seeing explicit roots for the "modern myths" in Norse, Roman, Egyptian, and other cultures' mythologies, they argued that superheroes "express in today's idiom the ancient longing of mankind for a mighty protector, a helper, guide, or guardian angel who offers miraculous deliverance to mortals" (p. 100).

Reitberger and Fuchs articulated an impulse that saw comics reinvesting present-day heroes with ancient tropes, but this came long after the publication of Joseph Campbell's *The Hero with a Thousand Faces* (1949). Indeed, the allure of an archetypal heroic was initially not so much a springboard for new material as a tried-and-true template to produce "acceptable" moral tales. Campbell argued that all heroic myths were part of a single world "monomyth" that expanded the "formula represented in the rites of passage: separation—initiation—return" (p. 30). However, this age-old model was endangered by the modern world and its erosion of the power of symbolism. Before Reitberger and Fuchs found the answer in comics superheroes, Campbell had wondered if any modern heroes would answer the call.

Campbell was influential, but his fears about the loss of symbolic value in the modern world also made him part of a rising jeremiad against moral decay. During the Second Red Scare of 1950s America, Fredric Wertham's *The Seduction of the Innocent* (1954) argued that comics were to blame for the erosion of youth values. This helped establish the Comics Code Authority, a mirror to the Motion Picture Production Code (or Hays Code of 1930–1968) and led to comic publishers being coerced to regulate the moral content of their comics. Robert Jewett and John Shelton Lawrence's *The American Monomyth* (1977) deals primarily with movies, but their *tour-de-force* about the narrative consistency of American movies was strongly influential on comics and equally forceful in its claims that Campbell's monomyth is ever-present. "The result of [Wertham's] crusade," they argued, "was the codification of the monomythic values in the Comics Code Authority, whose conventions paralleled those of the movie industry" (p. 223). Those values were central to the restoration of the kind of symbolism that Campbell feared had been lost. Jewett and Lawrence argued that narrative tropes in film and comics coalesced to outline the set of morals society desires but is unable to realize. Society's dysfunction became an opportunity for "one man [to serve] as rescuer for no reason but his devotion to abstract justice" (p. xv). More broadly, the American Monomyth became not the formula of initiation–separation–return but the story of when "a community threatened by evil is redeemed through superheroism" (p. 249).

As it had in Eco's work and would later in Reynolds' work, Jewett and Lawrence's use of comics saw superhero stories as conduits for moral and social conventions. Superman, Spider-Man, and others demonstrated "sexual segmentation" or the differentiation of heroic virility from what, especially due to the Comics Code Authority's restrictions, were necessarily chaste do-gooders. Superman, for instance, was offered as a mirror for readers to see themselves not as the feeble Clark Kent who pines *for* Lois but as his empowered alter ego who is desirable *to* Lois. This sense of comics as surfaces for reader projection not only follows theoretical works by Carl Jung and Sigmund Freud, but also became a mode of interpretation. To psychologize the dynamics of the influence of comics on readers—as Wertham and Jewett and Lawrence had done in contradictory ways—was to see comics scholarship as penetrating not only the myths of the comics narrative but also those held by their readers.

By the time the authors rewrote *The American Monomyth* as *The Myth of the American Superhero* (2002), the monomyth had become a staple of interpretation for the origin stories and adventures of nearly all heroic characters. Recent works like A. David Lewis' *American Comics, Literary Theory, and Religion* (2014) follow both a Campbellian theoretical orientation—that the narrative structure of heroic stories is consistent enough to merit typology—and proceed to work within the subset of the monomyth by detailing the ways comics plots have used initiation in the afterlife to deal with issues of identity. Campbell opened the door to humanity's mythical past while decrying its present decay. The present-day application of the American monomyth, on the other hand, has been more influential in positively articulating the power of mythical tropes as models not only for comic narratives but also for their interpretation.

Structuralism regards myth as medium and message, linguistically contextualized and historically conditioned, while Campbellian-inspired psychology regards myths as ahistorical is one word vehicles for eternal truths. These contradictory positions were first harmonized in Danny Fingeroth's innovative book *Superman on the Couch: What Superheroes Really Tell Us about Ourselves and Our Society* (2004). A former Marvel editor and writer, Fingeroth combined an intricate analysis of superheroes as myth with a speculative psychological discussion of superheroes and their readers into a concept he called "superhero comic consciousness." Why do we need superheroes? What needs do superhero fantasies fulfill? What social function is met by our participation in the telling and retelling of these stories? Superheroes, he concluded, are a transcendent and permanent form of cultural expression. They embody ideas that are "constants in our society's collective needs and desires, in our very dreams themselves" (p. 172). They are eternal, like myths, *and* offer therapeutic benefits and social commentary.

When interviewed on June 5, 2015, Fingeroth explained that he was inspired by Jules Feiffer's influential 1965 essay, "The Great Comic Book Heroes." Feiffer may have been the first writer in the English language to suggest a meaningful connection between superheroes and mythology, opening an intriguing line of inquiry into what might be hidden behind a secret identity and what could be revealed through psychoanalysis (pp. 18–21). Fingeroth stressed that Feiffer's influence cannot be overemphasized: "That book was an influence on me and on many, many comics creators, scholars and fans of the era it came out, and well beyond. It answered questions we didn't even know we had. For comic lovers, it was *the* holiday gift of 1965. It remains relevant and fascinating 50 years later. And it was the first place many of us had ever heard of Will Eisner and *The Spirit*, so you could even credit it with leading eventually to *Contract With God* and all that followed."

Over the last half century, studies of comics as myth have tended to prefer the model of the monomyth. At least in American scholarship, Jewett and Lawrence's appropriation of Campbell has been much more widely influential in allowing comics to be seen as iterations of pervasive cultural tropes such as the American Dream or the principle that justice will prevail. Linguistics, anthropology, and continental philosophy have not yet been mined in the United States with as much alacrity, yet interest in their potential is growing.

Jews and Comics

In contrast to the interest in comics as myth, early scholarship on Jews and comics centered on the role of Jews in the origins of American comics and the comic book industry and in the interpretation of a variety of related concepts, including the identity and psychology of various individual superheroes; the influence of the Jewish immigrant experience on the subjects and concerns of comics and graphic novels; the recurrence of Jewish themes (such as social consciousness and civil rights, biblical metaphors, *Kabbalah*, Yiddishisms, and *Yiddishkeit*) in comics and graphic novels; and the significance of history and memory, especially as represented in attitudes regarding the Jewish Holocaust and the State of Israel.

Early studies emerged mostly from outside of the academy. In the spirit of Feiffer's 1965 essay, Canadian novelist Mordecai Richler titled his 1972 essay "The Great Comic Book Heroes." Richler connected his own Jewish identity to the superheroes:

> Although the original boyhood appeal of the comic books was all but irresistible to my generation, I have not gone into the reasons until now for they seemed to me obvious. *Superman, The Flash, The Human Torch,* even *Captain Marvel*, were our *golems*....There is no doubt, for instance, that *The Green Lantern* has its origins in

Hassidic mythology. Will Eisner's *The Spirit*, so much admired by Feiffer, is given to cabalistic superstitions and speaking in parables. (p. 52)

Feiffer and Richler each proposed a number of provocative ideas, yet the subject of Jews and comics did not attract significant attention until the new millennium, with only two notable exceptions (see Brower, 1979, and Brod, 1995). Then the century's first Pulitzer Prize went to Michael Chabon's *The Amazing Adventures of Kavalier and Clay* (2000). Chabon's acclaimed fictional work focused on the creation of the American comic book by Jewish immigrants, but it mirrored the factual history of the medium. Gerard Jones' meticulously researched *Men of Tomorrow* (2004) explored this same subject, and in the wake of these two books, it was no longer possible to ignore the importance of Jewish creators and publishers in the birth and development of the American comics industry.

In "After Maus: The Jewish Experience in American Graphic Novels," published in *The Jewish Quarterly* (2001), Paul Gravett presented a history of the graphic novel centered on the medium's ability to deal "powerfully and imaginatively with aspects of the Jewish condition" (p. 22). He focused on Jewish creators of comics from the 1930s to the 1990s, illuminating the ways in which the American graphic novel has served as a sophisticated medium for reflecting on such themes as fascism, the Holocaust, discrimination, antisemitism, God and evil, *Yiddishkeit*, history, memory, and loss, in a manner of nuance and immediacy not afforded by "the indistinguishable grey columns of typeset text in a standard novel" (p. 21).

In *Disguised as Clark Kent: Jews, Comics, and the Creation of the Superhero* (2007), Danny Fingeroth combined an interest in the Jewish origins and creators of the superhero genre, shared by Chabon and Jones, with Gravett's interest in Jewish themes and experiences. Building upon his interest in the social and psychological features of superheroes, first explored in *Superman on the Couch* (discussed above), Fingeroth revealed the often-hidden connections between Judaism and American superheroes, including parallels between Superman and Moses and similarities in the moral messages of the Torah and Spider-Man. Where Mordecai Richler saw golems in the superheroes, Fingeroth saw Jewish history, culture, experiences, and concerns and argued for them eloquently through close reading and an artist's testimony.

Paul Buhle's *Jews and American Comics: An Illustrated History of an American Art Form* (2008) was the first scholarly effort to produce a comprehensive history of its subject from the earliest days, including Yiddish material. Beginning with the newspaper strips of the early 20th century, Buhle connected these comics to their roots in Yiddish literary culture and declared comics to be "*the* vernacular form in which Jewish genius (or, at least, the genius of some hundreds of Jewish artists) found its true mass audience" (p. 10). He provided short and informative essays but largely allowed the more than 200 comics included in the book to speak for themselves. The range of original art in *Jews and American Comics* is startling in its purpose and power, describing a century-long search for identity conducted between readers and creators.

Also in 2008, Arie Kaplan's influential trade volume *From Krakow to Krypton: Jews and Comic Books* was published with an innovative foreword supplied in graphic form by Harvey Pekar and J. T. Waldman. The book is a detailed historical account of the Jewish creators and publishers of American comic books, beginning with 1933's *Famous Funnies* #1 and concluding with a look at the innovative work of such contemporary creators as Trina Robbins, Neil Gaiman, and French comics artist Joann Sfar. *From Krakow to Krypton* is invaluable for the stories it tells and the memories Kaplan obtained by interviewing many of the artists and writers that were his subjects.

This body of work on Jews in comics has revealed the previously hidden or unacknowledged contributions that Jews have made to American culture. Recent work, theoretically rich and historically nuanced, builds upon this pioneering work. Examples include Baskind and Omer-Sherman's edited volume *The Jewish Graphic Novel: Critical Approaches* (2010) and Stephen Tabachnick's *The Quest for Jewish Belief and Identity in the Graphic Novel* (2014). The formative relationship between Jews and comics continues to spur contemporary scholarship, but it also influenced the growing body of work on comics and other religions, to which we now turn.

SIDEBAR: COMICS AS (PSEUDO-) RELIGION

A. David Lewis

Starting as early as M. Thomas Inge's *Comics as Culture* (1990) and continuing with Matthew Pustz's *Comic Book Culture* (1999), the intriguing possibility of comics *as* religion has operated at the margins of scholarly discussion. Certainly, if the precepts of Victor Turner (1969) were to be applied to the self-identification, habits, and actions of comics fans, then, as a group, they frequently enter into a liminal space, perform rituals, and share in valued narratives together—all hallmarks of a religion by his account. Or, take it from the theories of Clifford Geertz (1960), where religion is meant to establish a communal effect that, in turn, aids in shaping the participants' view of existence: do the best comics not accomplish that, informing and even creating a shared worldview for its audience? Add to this the qualifiers proposed by Ninian Smart (1968) in terms of the identifiable dimensions of a religion, and comics fandom scores quite high (having a Practical/Ritual Dimension, Experiential/Emotional Dimension, Narrative/Mythic Dimension, Ethical/Legal Dimension, Social/Institutional Dimension, and Material Dimension). Only what Smart would call its Doctrinal/Philosophical Dimension may be up for debate (i.e., what do comics fans, as a whole, jointly believe?), but that could be more a matter of no attempts at consensus ever having been undertaken than the easy dismissal of its being an impossible or flawed concept. Even as an inter-religious entity, comics as pseudo-religion (rather than an accidental quasi-religion) remain a tantalizingly open question.

Bibliography

Geertz, C. (1960) *The Religion of Java*, Glencoe, IL: Free Press.
Inge, M.T. (1990) *Comics as Culture*, Jackson, MS: University Press of Mississippi.
Pustz, M. (1999) *Comic Book Culture Fanboys and True Believers*, Jackson, MS: University Press of Mississippi.
Smart, N. (1968) *Secular Education and the Logic of Religion*, New York: Humanities Press.
Turner, V. (1969) *The Ritual Process: structure and anti-structure*, Chicago: Aldine Publishing Co.

Comics as Religious and Comics for Religion

As authors and audience, Jews have a special relationship with comics, but other religious groups have increasingly tried to use or see comics as a religiously significant medium. In this section, a distinction evolves in scholarship surrounding religion and comics—are comics an object through which religious themes can be read, or are comics a religious product in their own right? Are comics intended to be reduced to the preexisting monomyth, or are they actively shaping the cultures that consume them? Much like scholarship on Jews and comics came to embrace the medium as a tool for dealing with Jewish identity, emerging religious studies scholarship on comics has developed myth as comics' particular genius for religion. That is, myth is not simply code for fictional, traditional stories. Myth is now a medium used by creators and embraced by audiences for the advance of religion as a specific social and cultural phenomenon. Some say this does not go far enough and insist all (superhero) comics are religious, full stop.

With the exception of Robert Short's religiously motivated *The Gospel According to Peanuts* (1965) and its sequel *The Parables of Peanuts* (1968), systematic work in English on comics and religion is only about 15 to 20 years old. Short employed this popular strip as a shortcut to religious insight, an enterprise shocking in its day, but which we now take for granted. The commercial success of *The Gospel According to Peanuts* spawned a rash of imitators, none of which did as well. From a scholar's perspective, the most notable item from this lineage is B. J. Oropeza's *The Gospel According to Superheroes: Religion and Popular Culture* (2005). This often-cited edited volume collects academic essays on mostly Christian theological subjects and is evidence that the legacy of "The Gospel According to …" titles is likely far from finished.

In Gregg Garrett's *Holy Superheroes!* (2005), religious interpretation expanded beyond theological canon. Garrett argued instead that superheroes are templates for better humans. "We look for heroes as examples of how we're supposed to live," he wrote, "and we can take that example into the ongoing struggle to redeem this world" (p. 119). Garrett, a Professor of English and lay Episcopal preacher, reflected a nominally Judeo-Christian sensibility that avoided offense but also excluded diversity. The result was a moral commentary framed in religious language, referencing elementary religious narratives. In some ways, Garrett took Eco's and Campbell's claims to their logical extension: if our age is one threatened by secularization's effects, then what our society needs is secularly situated gods to replace those we have lost.

Garrett's book was an incremental step beyond insider perspectives that became a giant, occult leap in Christopher Knowles' *Our Gods Wear Spandex* (2007). Knowles' eccentric volume argues, like Reitberger and Fuchs, that superheroes are the gods reborn for a new age. They "fill the role in our modern society that the gods and demigods provided to the ancients" (p. xv). Just as our religious needs are diverse—much more diverse than someone like Garrett allows for—Knowles' volume describes an esoteric religious pantheon inscribed in comics as "the collision of science, morality, and magic" whose influences are not just Christian or Jewish, but Rosicrucian, occultist, and mystical (p. 221). In a similar vein, in *Superheroes and Gods: A Comparative Study from Babylonia to Batman* (2007) Don LoCicero argued for an archetypal reading of modern superheroes as ancient mythological characters. Eco and Campbell's influence remains significant.

The idea that comics could be seen as more than allegory also appealed to Ben Saunders, whose *Do the Gods Wear Capes?* (2011) follows Knowles in regarding comics as religious products. Saunders wrote, "I have simply tried to approach superhero comics as fantastic, speculative, and distinctly modern expressions of a perhaps perennial human wish: the wish that things were otherwise" (p. 3). (Students of the theory of religion could productively apply their reading of Jonathan Z. Smith's in "The Bare Facts of Ritual" (1982) to Saunders' findings.) If comics express our wishes, then some creators also saw comics as a medium to fulfill their personal religious agendas. More than one scholar has seen Alan Moore's *Promethea* as a work of magic (in line with Moore's intent) (see Kraemer and Winslade, 2010, and Howell, 2015). Though they were often a source of ridicule, something similar could be said of Jack Chick Tracts, short comics designed to advocate for their author's conservative Christian morals. These were fundamentally religious creations—created and distributed for evangelism—and the trend of using comics for such purposes is only increasing (Bivins, 2008 and Lund, 2015).

While Judaism and Christianity stood out as early subjects of study, scholars of the 1990s were also laying the initial foundations for the study of comics produced outside the west, particularly in India and Japan. Indian comics are diverse, but a major subject of interest was the long-running and best-selling Indian series *Amar Chitra Katha*, often known simply as ACK. ACK first received scholarly attention in 1995 when Frances W. Pritchett and John Stratton Hawley each contributed essays about the series to the edited volume *Media and the Transformation of Religion in South Asia*.

Pritchett's essay "The World of Amar Chitra Katha" provided a history of the series and its mission to raise children who value India as a positive, multicultural nation, concluding that ACK is largely constructive, despite gaps where Indian Muslims and Indian Islamic traditions have received short shrift. Hawley's essay "The Saints Subdued: Domestic Virtue and National Integration in Amar Chitra Katha" discussed the ways in which ACK adapts classic Indian myths to modern comics in order to rewrite and perhaps even reinvent Indian religion as inclusive.

The years 2008 to 2010 saw the publication of three book-length studies of ACK: Nandini Chandra's *The Classic Popular: Amar Chitra Katha, 1967–2007* (2008), Karline McLain's *India's Immortal Comic Books: Gods, Kings, and Other Heroes* (2009), and Deepa Sreenivas' *Sculpting the Middle Class: History, Masculinity and the Amar Chitra Katha*, indicating that scholarly work in Indian comics is gaining steam alongside the growing Indian comics industry. When interviewed on November 23, 2015, Indian comics expert Corey Creekmur explained that writing about the industry presents a challenge because scholarship can be out of date almost as soon as it is published.

Japanese-language scholarship on manga and religion is largely inaccessible to English-language readers, but work in English also began in the 1990s, notably in Mark Wheeler MacWilliams' "Japanese Comic Books and Religion: Osamu Tezuka's Story of the Buddha" published in *Japan Pop!: Inside the World of Japanese Popular Culture* (2000). MacWilliams analyzed Tezuka's almost 3,000-page manga to highlight the ways in which Tezuka altered the sacred story to make it more appealing and relevant for a modern Japanese audience. *Budda* (as it is spelled in the manga) is not a conventional retelling of the Buddha's life. It is an adventure tale, set in Japan and told using both manga conventions and traditional devotional images communicated through Tezuka's innovative "cinematic style."

In 2012 the first English-language monograph devoted to Japanese religion in manga appeared, Jolyon Baraka Thomas' *Drawing on Tradition: Manga, Anime, and Religion in Contemporary Japan*. Thomas analyzed the interaction between creators and readers and argued that this ongoing relationship, avidly pursued by each, enables the construction of what he termed "religious frames of mind" (p. 27). Thomas' engagement with manga appears to be an essential platform for future studies as it suggests a deeper appreciation of the connection among creator, creation, and audience. Serious scholarship now routinely rejects the idea that comics are mere lenses through which religious themes outside of comics can be found.

Ongoing Trends and Current Research

Since the work of myth and religion on comics scholarship is rapidly expanding today, this essay concludes by surveying the diverse English-language scholarship in two key areas. First, religion as an object for study in comics has begun to diversify beyond the superhero genre. Second, in the aftermath of the Danish *Jyllands-Posten* Muhammad cartoons controversy of 2005, the representation and use of Islam in comics is among the most dynamic areas of studies today.

A. David Lewis and Christine Hoff Kraemer's *Graven Images: Religion in Comic Books and Graphic Novels* was a watershed moment for the field (2010). The collected essays, many presented first at a conference at Boston University in 2008, carved a space for an identification of comics as "one site where individuals grapple with issues of ethics, meaning and values; engage in ritualized behavior and explore both traditional and new religious traditions" (p. 3). The collection's diverse authors—both scholars and creators—are an influential community today. Perhaps because the collection focuses primarily on creations beyond DC and Marvel, it also suggests another emerging trend: scholarship on religion and non-superhero comics, as more than half the contributions deal with non-superhero comics. The diversity of the subjects studied reflects not only the contemporary climate of religious pluralism, but also a serious approach to all religious claims found in comics and graphic novels.

This widened gaze means many comics remain ripe for study. Early newspaper comic strips have received almost no attention, even though Hal Foster's *Prince Valiant* (ongoing since 1937) may be a treasure trove of religious themes surrounding the not-yet King Arthur. Political cartoons—especially in the wake of 9/11 and the Muhammad cartoons controversy—have not been studied sufficiently either. The thriving market of contemporary online cartoons like Mike Stanfill's Gary Larsen tribute *The Far Left Side* (now called *Raging Pencils* and located at ragingpencils.com) is overflowing with religious themes but remains unanalyzed. The explosion in religiously themed comic publications from Avatar, Oni Press, and Image Comics (including *The Life After, East of West, God Is Dead*, and *The Wicked and the Divine*) is so recent that no peer-reviewed publications have appeared yet to account for the sub-genre's sudden popularity. And the religious connections of Fredric Wertham's *Seduction of the Innocent* to the Catholic League remain largely unexplored.

The rise of discourse and dialogue on Islam in the 15 years since 9/11, however, undoubtedly represents the most pressing area of scholarship. Early pieces examining the "Danish Cartoon Controversy" appeared online and in print journalism immediately and so widely that it may have obscured the subsequent wave of political science, media studies, and legal examinations of the event. Philosophical analyses soon followed from Talal Asad, Wendy Brown, Saba Mahmood, and Judith P. Butler (2013) in the form of a dialogue on the limits of free speech and the secular sphere. Academic approaches qualified to speak to both the context of Islam in Europe and the history of Muslim and non-Muslim representations of Muhammad have been few. In the wake of the *Charlie Hebdo* attacks in Paris in January 2015, Hussein Rashid, associate editor at *Religion Dispatches*, wrote a widely shared piece for Emory University's *Sacred Matters* blog on "Images of Muhammad" that remains one of the few public academic responses to the fundamental issue of visual representation in Islam.

Within this context, Islamic artists have begun to embrace comics for spreading positive messages about Islam to Muslims and non-Muslims. There are webcomics about confronting Islamophobia drawn by an Egyptian woman—*Qahera: The Superhero*—and full-fledged superhero teams like *The 99* that embody the 99 attributes of God found in the Qur'an. The collection of the first story arc of G. Willow Wilson's *Ms. Marvel*, a Muslim Pakistani-American superhero, won the 2015 Hugo Award for Best Graphic Story. A planned edited volume from A. David Lewis and Martin Lund on Muslim superheroes will attempt to broaden the discourse on representations of Islam—looking at both these success stories as well as the many challenges that remain for representations of Islam regarding gender stereotypes, Islamophobia, and orientalism.

Still, the most fundamental problem of the expansion of this scholarship remains not cross-cultural appreciation nor better critical paradigms to analyze myth and religion, but rather the barrier of language. While English-language comics remain the focus of scholarship in English, this is to the great detriment of comics from the rest of the world. The future of studies of myths, archetypes, and religions in comics will undoubtedly embrace these new reading communities and the items they cherish. Religious studies scholarship on comics will be limited only by the interests of our global and multilingual community of scholars. American religious pluralism may have pushed the scholarship into a diverse relationship with the world's myths and religions, but the future will see an expansion of interest by scholars all over the world who will study comics and religion in their myriad forms, themes, and purposes. As in all aspects of religious studies, our challenge is to learn how to communicate the best of what we discover with one another.

Bibliography

Asad, T. et al. (2013) *Is Critique Secular? Blasphemy, Injury and Free Speech*, New York: Fordham University Press.
Babb, L.A. and Wadley, S. S. (eds.). (1995) *Media and the Transformation of Religion in South Asia*, Philadelphia: University of Pennsylvania Press.
Baskind, S. and Omer-Sherman, R. (eds.). (2010) *The Jewish Graphic Novel: critical approaches*, New Brunswick, NJ: Rutgers University Press.
Bivins, J.C. (2008) *Religion of Fear: the politics of horror in conservative evangelicalism*, New York: Oxford University Press.
Brod, H. (1995) 'Of mice and supermen: images of Jewish masculinity', in T.M. Rudavasky (ed.), *Gender and Judaism: the transformation of tradition*, New York: New York University Press, 279–94.
Brower, J.K. (1979) 'The Hebrew origins of Superman', *Biblical Archaeology Review*, 5.03 (May/Jun): 22–26.
Buhle, P. (ed.). (2008) *Jews and American Comics*, New York: New Press.
Campbell, J. (1949) *The Hero with a Thousand Faces*, 2nd edn [1968], Princeton, NJ: Princeton University Press.
Chabon, M. (2000) *The Amazing Adventures of Kavalier and Clay*, New York: Random House.

Chandra, N. (2008). *The Classic Popular: Amar Chitra Katha, 1967–2007*, New Delhi, India: Yoda Press.
Coogan, P. (2006) *Superhero: the secret origin of a genre*, Austin, TX: Monkeybrain Books.
Eco, U. and Chilton, N. (1972) 'The myth of Superman', *Diacritics* 2:1 (Spring): 14–22.
Feiffer, J. (2003) *The Great Comic Book Heroes*. Reprint [1965], Seattle, WA: Fantagraphics.
Fingeroth, D. (2004) *Superman on the Couch: what superheroes really tell us about ourselves and our society*, New York: Bloomsbury.
Fingeroth, D. (2007) *Disguised as Clark Kent: Jews, comics, and the creation of the superhero*, New York: Continuum.
Fuchs, W.J. and Reinhold, R. (1972) *Comics: anatomy of a mass medium*, London: Little Brown.
Garrett, G. (2008) *Holy Superheroes! Exploring the Sacred in Comics, Graphic Novels, and Film*. Revised edn, Louisville, KY: Westminster John Knox.
Gravett, P. (2001) 'After *Maus*: graphic novels confront the Jewish experience', *Jewish Quarterly*, 49.4: 21–28.
Howell, T.L. (2015) 'The monstrous alchemy of Alan Moore: *Promethea* as literacy narrative', *Studies in the Novel*, 47.3 (Fall): 381–98.
Jewett, R. and Lawrence, J.S. (1977) *The American Monomyth*, Garden City, NY: Anchor/Doubleday.
Jones, G. (2004) *Men of Tomorrow: geeks, gangsters, and the birth of the comic book*, New York: Basic Books.
Kaplan, A. (2008) *From Krakow to Krypton: Jews and comic books*, Philadelphia: Jewish Publication Society.
Knowles, C. (2007) *Our Gods Wear Spandex: the secret history of comic book heroes*, San Francisco, CA: Weiser Books.
Kraemer, C.H. and Winslade, J.L. (2010) "The magic circus of the mind': Alan Moore's *Promethea* and the transformation of consciousness through comics', in A.D. Lewis and C.H. Kraemer (eds.) *Graven Images: religion in comic books and graphic novels*, New York: Continuum: 274–91.
Lewis, A.D. (2014) *American Comics, Literary Theory, and Religion: the superhero afterlife*, London: Palgrave Macmillan.
Lewis, A.D. and Kraemer, C.H. (eds.) *Graven Images: religion in comic books and graphic novels*, New York: Continuum.
Locicero, D. (2007) *Superheroes and Gods: a comparative study from Babylonia to Batman*, Jefferson, NC: McFarland.
Lund, M. (2015) "[A] Matter of SAVED or LOST': difference, salvation, and subjection in Chick Tracts', in R.P. Cortsen, E.L. Cour and A. Magnussen (eds.) *Comics and Power: representing and questioning culture, subjects and communities*, Newcastle upon Tyne, England: Cambridge Scholars.
MacWilliams, M.W. (2000) 'Japanese comic books and religion: Osamu Tezuka's story of the Buddha', in T. Craig (ed.) *Japan Pop!: inside the world of Japanese popular culture*, London: Routledge.
McLain, K. (2009) *India's Immortal Comic Books: gods, kings, and other heroes*, Indianapolis: Indiana University Press.
Oropeza, B.J. (ed.) (2005) *The Gospel According to Superheroes: religion and popular culture*, New York: Peter Lang.
Rashid, H. (2015) 'Images of Muhammad', *Sacred Matters: Religious Currents in Culture*, 4 April 2015. Available from: https://scholarblogs.emory.edu/sacredmatters/. [Accessed 1 December 2015].
Reynolds, R. (1994) *Super Heroes: a modern mythology*, Jackson: University Press of Mississippi.
Richler, M. (1967) 'The great comic book heroes', *Encounter* (May): 46–52.
Roth, L. (2008) 'Contemporary American Jewish comic books: abject pasts, heroic futures', in S. Baskind and R. Omer-Sherman (eds.) *The Jewish Graphic Novel: critical approaches*, New Brunswick, NJ: Rutgers University Press, 3–21.
Saunders, B. (2011) *Do the Gods Wear Capes? Spirituality, Fantasy, and Superheroes*, New York: Continuum.
Short, R.L. (1965) *The Gospel According to Peanuts*, Louisville, KY: Westminster John Knox Press.
Short, R.L. (1968) *The Parables of Peanuts*, New York: HarperOne.

Smith, J.Z. (1982) *Imagining Religion: from Babylon to Jonestown*, Chicago: The University of Chicago Press.
Sreenivas, D. (2010) *Sculpting the Middle Class: history, masculinity and the Amar Chitra Katha*, New Delhi: Routledge India.
Tabachnick, S.E. (2014) *The Quest for Jewish Belief and Identity in the Graphic Novel*, Tuscaloosa: University of Alabama Press.
Thomas, J.B. (2012) *Drawing on Tradition: manga, anime, and religion in contemporary Japan*, Honolulu: University of Hawai'i Press.
Wertham, F. (1954) *Seduction of the Innocent*, New York: Rinehart.

10
IDEOLOGICAL/SOCIOLOGICAL

Ian Gordon

In the early 1980s, a search for comics scholarship would have revealed a fairly limited set of works, many of which had only appeared in the previous ten years. Certainly no field of comics scholarship existed, and a student trying to think about comics would most likely have read whatever was available. So while from a 2017 perspective David Kunzle's 1973 volume *History of the Comic Strip: The Early Comic Strip: Narrative Strips and Picture Stories in the European Broadsheet from c. 1450 to 1825* clearly seems history, in the 1980s scholars were just as likely to mine it for the materialist ideological underpinnings it offered. Likewise, Umberto Eco's finely crafted semiotic reading of Superman, which originally appeared in Italian in 1962 but became broadly known to English-speaking audiences through its 1972 translation, offered an ideological view of the 1950s Superman as locked in a timeless state that denied the possibility of change (Eco, 1972). These are just two examples of scholars whose work had a clear ideological dimension but whose discipline or methodology makes them better discussed elsewhere in this volume. Eco had another early impact on comics scholarship since in 1963–1964 he encountered the 30-year-old Arthur Asa Berger in Milan, Italy, and helped the latter feel assured enough of the scholarly merits of scholarship on comics that he decided to do his doctoral dissertation on the Al Capp comic strip *Li'l Abner* (Berger, 1969, pp. 172–173).

It is fairly easy to determine work that is sociological in nature. Such work tends to be produced by scholars trained in sociology who see in comics a way of discussing social issues of one sort or another. Such approaches bleed into ideological approaches, often because a scholar will come to the issue with the notion that comics are the carriers of ideological freight. There is no ideological approach, *per se*, save for examining a comic for the ideology it may contain and unpacking that for an audience. The strength and coherence of such readings tend to rest on the reading itself rather than the application of some particular theoretical approach.

Berger's 1969 *Li'l Abner* book, drawn from his 1965 dissertation, displays many of the nascent issues for the comics scholarship that came later. Berger related that he faced four issues: a perceived need to justify writing about comics, the particular comic strip he chose, the specific episodes he chose, and the desire to examine "the relationship between Al

Capp's subject matter and technique and American society" (Berger, 1969, pp. 14–15). Berger's answers to these issues became the opening rhetorical gambit of much comics scholarship for a good number of years. Popular culture, he said, could not be overlooked because of its abundance, and the importance of Capps's work on *Li'l Abner* was "that it mirrors many of the tensions that exist in our thinking and reflects many of our ideological commitments and values" (Berger, 1969, p. 15). The defensive pose of justifying a study of comics by reference to their popularity became all too familiar in years to come. The appeal to popularity as a reason for examining a subject seems a little obtuse because potentially anything, popular or not, is worthy of study. The point is to show that worth in the quality of the study—in the case of comics whether it is, for instance, a formal account of the properties of comic art or a historical study of the social relevance of comics. Berger offered a reason for studying comics beyond their popularity, suggesting that comics are a mirror of society, and this reason became an all too familiar go-to defense for scholars of comics. Certainly comics reflect society, but so do all cultural artifacts, and the point is to say something about how they might have shaped people's lives and society not just reflected it. Berger's reading of *Li'l Abner* strips and Capp's art, though, went beyond his *raison d'être*, and he offered suggestive readings of the connection between the strip's humor and earlier forms of American dialect jokes. Perhaps most importantly, Berger examined Capp as a caricaturist deftly linking the form of humor to not just the dialogue, but to the manner in which Capp and his ghost artists drew the strip.

A flurry of general works on comics appeared in the five years between 1967 and 1972 and the most substantial of these was the volume by Reinhold Reitberger and Wolfgang Fuchs, *Comics: Anatomy of a Mass Medium* (1972), translated from the original German. Returning to this work more than forty years since its publication is a small revelation. Unlike so many of the general histories of comics that appeared at the same time, Reitberger and Fuchs methodically footnoted their argument and provided a useful chronology and a bibliography. This marked the volume as a work of scholarship. Moreover, the authors believed that "a work dealing with comics does not need to begin by justifying its subject matter." For them the triviality of comics was "sufficient justification" (Reitberger and Fuchs, 1972, p. 8). They rejected attempts to link comics to a range of visual narratives like cave drawings, hieroglyphics and the Bayeux tapestry, seeing instead the "immediate forerunners of the comic strip" as having "much more influence on its present shape and form than these early ancestors." And they saw the humor magazines *Puck, Judge,* and *Life* as of "paramount importance to the further development of the comic strip" (Reitberger and Fuchs, 1972, p. 11).[1] In this argument Reitberger and Fuchs were years in advance of many comics scholars who continued to feel a need to ground comics in antiquity.

Comics: Anatomy of a Mass Medium has a broad scope. Rather than writing a linear history, Reitberger and Fuchs—both then not yet 30 years old—offered a thematic account of comics. Both had experienced the American occupation of Germany post-World War II first hand and as a consequence they grew up with ready access to American comics. Fuchs trained in media studies and Reitberger in American Studies. The prime focus of their book was American comics, but they also offered a chapter on the European scene. Other chapters dealt with "Humour and Everyday Life," "Adventure and Melodrama," "Criticism and Censorship," "Sex and Satire," "The Art of the Comics," the to-be-expected chapter on "Super-heroes," and a conceptually innovative "Inter-Media Dependencies" chapter. Reitberger and Fuchs used the anti-comic book campaign of Fredric Wertham, and the enactment of the Comics Code, as a framing device for their chapter on censorship. Their argument took issue with the "worn-out anti-comics arguments fashionable" in Wertham's time, but rather than simply lambast Wertham, they offered a nuanced account of the reaction of readers to crime and violence in comics. It may seem like common sense, but their observations that readers of comics' responses depended on their "psychological state" and that an individual's reaction might "vary considerably at different times" were points not generally made in the brouhaha over comics (Reitberger and Fuchs, 1972, p. 130). The pair did not shy away from agreeing that some of Wertham's examples were "horrific," and indeed stated that "no child could remain untouched by such horrors." But for Reitberger and Fuchs much of this debate about the impact of comics was too simplistic because the cause and effect Wertham offered failed to take account of other factors and most particularly neglected that "a child's fundamental character traits are moulded by the parents" (Reitberger and Fuchs, 1972, pp. 132–133). The chapter also raised the important issue of self-censorship and the limits it places on expression especially when commercial interests want to attract mass audiences for their products. They noted that although storytelling and artwork improved as the market contracted, the absence of violence led to rather boring stories (Reitberger and Fuchs, 1972, p. 138).

In a chapter called "Society as Portrayed in Comics," Reitberger and Fuchs discuss the social influence of comics, the readership they attract, and the ideologies they display. Their reading is at base a Marxist interpretation noting as they do "the conditions of production overrule most other considerations, for the contents of popular escapist media reflect the economic background of the nation. If a mass medium initiates new trends ... such moves are dictated by the opportunities the market offers, not by any deeper sociological reason" (Reitberger and Fuchs, 1972, p. 152). It was not all that uncommon for early 1970s works on media to be tinged with Marxist ideology. However, not all authors were as astute as Reitberger and Fuchs or as grounded in their subject and able to produce something truly innovative.

Reitberger and Fuchs' chapter on "Inter-media Dependencies" may seem old hat now, but in 1972 it was fresh. Rather than seeing comics simply as a medium that stood in clear distinction to other media, the pair understood the inter-connectedness of comics and other media forms. They connected comics to popular serial literature like dime novels and pulps and to radio serials, many of which shared characters with pulps and/or comic strips. They noted the large number of 1950s and early 1960s comic books based on television series such as *77 Sunset Strip* and *Gunsmoke*. They discussed cartoon animations with comic book tie-ins from *Felix the Cat* to Disney's *Snow White*. They also noted the success of the early Charlie Brown television specials using the characters from *Peanuts*. And in Marvel's *Nick Fury—Agent of S.H.I.E.L.D.* they saw the influence of the James Bond spy craze of the 1960s. To be sure much of Reitberger and Fuchs' book is descriptive, and each of the chapters is a sketch of what could be a book-length study. The strength of the work is twofold: the breadth and depth of their knowledge and their conceptualization of how comics should be studied.

A more formal scholarly piece by another German, Wolfgang Max Faust, appeared in a 1971 issue of the *Journal of Popular Culture*. Faust, who later shaped a career as an art historian and critic, took it as self-evident that comics served as both entertainment and transmitters of ideology. He found it difficult to attribute greater emphasis to one or the other as far as producers' intent was concerned. Faust highlighted the absence of an adequate conceptual language to talk about comics, as no rigorous analysis of the relationship between "formal composition and mythical content existed" (1971, p. 195). Likewise, concepts that read comics with attention to the dynamic relationship between images and words had not as yet developed. Faust proposed a reading of a single issue of *Action Comics* through "syntactical and rhetorical concepts" (1971, pp. 195–196). Faust then performed a very close reading of the cover page of *Action Comics* #368 (October 1968), breaking down its visual and textual organization and arguing that such a reading reveals the underlying ideological function of the comic: to remind readers that their "satisfaction is dependent on the editorial authority" (1971, p. 202). For Faust, the point is that "the presentation to the reader of a world dependent on a hero who coerces society into a totally passive role forces upon the reader, too, the realization that he can exert no formative influence on the world around him" (1971, p. 201). Faust's position had much in common with an earlier piece of work by the American scholar and priest Walter Ong, although there is no indication that he had read Ong's work.

Writing in the *Arizona Quarterly* in 1945, Walter Ong's concerns centered on what he called "the super state," a term that was roughly interchangeable with totalitarianism. Ong equated Superman with Hitler and Mussolini and wrote, "the Superman of the cartoons is true to his sources," which for Ong were Nietzsche's philosophy and his concept of the *übermensch*. The herd followed such heroes not through rational engagement, but because they put on a show or mesmerized their audience (Ong, 1945, p. 35). Faust and Ong then saw comic book readers as passive, rendered so in Faust's view primarily through the political economy of the comic book industry and Ong through the *a priori* existence in any story with a super hero of a debilitating fascist ideology. Ong's analysis is rather limited, and much of his essay is mocking and scornful rather than tightly reasoned. He seems to have missed for instance that the creators and publishers of these "fascist" superheroes were often Jews, which on the surface at least would seem to make his argument, such as it was, rather thin. Ong, though, had some useful undeveloped points. He noted that defenders of comics liked to equate them with folklore and that by doing so all criticism evaporated. Ong worried about equating comics with folklore because of the association with *"das Volk."* The piece appeared in 1945 when German = Nazi, so he settled the matter with a rhetorical flourish rather than pursuing an argument that might have been useful. Also, he lampooned a writer who dismissed critics of comics as snobs, saying that the writer had determined the argument before the comics were examined, something Ong himself had done and ascribed them a fascist ideology. Here again, Ong could have made something of an argument about the relentless need to see anything that was popular as reflecting some sort of democratic value, as if popularity equaled democracy. Moreover, for an article written in a scholarly tone, and with direct quotations, it is unsettling that Ong did not cite his sources or name directly those he criticized.

SIDEBAR: THE IMMIGRANT SPACE

A. David Lewis

The legacy of Jewish immigrants and first-generation American families raises both an opportunity and conundrum in contemporary culture. In his book, *Disguised as Clark Kent* (2007), Danny Fingeroth notes the appeal, conscious or otherwise, of the superhero to new US arrivals from overseas. The Depression-era fringe medium and its unpoliced

(Continued)

content granted young Jewish artists the freedom to indulge in power fantasies, morality plays, flights of fantasy, and more. As Fingeroth and many others have noted, the Golden Age generation of comics creators fashioned some of the most enduring icons out of epic immigrants, such as Superman, Wonder Woman, or any number of strange visitors.

Shouldn't, then, the post-9/11 uptick in Muslim superheroes have been seen as overdue rather than as a cultural consequence? Certainly, not all Muslims are foreign nationals or immigrants—far from it. Some are internationals, like the X-Man Dust (Sooraya Qadir) or the Batman-ally Nightrunner (Bilal Asselah), and some are native-born Americans, such as the newest Green Lantern (Simon Baz) or Avengers recruit Ms. Marvel (Kamala Khan). Yet, Islam's inclusion in the genre was not seen as a consequence of the religion's becoming part of the great American story; nor were the characters welcome newcomers. In all likelihood, for better or for worse, their boosted profile in the genre comes from the raised Western media presence of Islam globally and domestically.

Why hasn't the superhero genre, a narrative space shaped largely by immigrants for and arguably about immigrants, been perceived as hospitable to subsequent iterations of immigrants? Are the Jewish roots of these comics a fluke of history or did they establish a space for other religions' expressions of narrative acculturation?

Bibliography

Fingeroth, D. (2007) *Disguised as Clark Kent: Jews, comics, and the creation of the Superhero*: New York, Continuum.

When it came to comics, Ong was not alone in taking a lackadaisical attitude about sources of evidence and citations and about shaping an argument rather than relying on forceful or fanciful rhetoric. In his second work on comics, *The Comic-Stripped American* (1973), Arthur Asa Berger provides references to his sources, but not always, and his work is more a series of observations—some of them fanciful—than a sustained interpretative argument. So for instance, in his chapter on the comic strip *Krazy Kat* he writes that "recent evidence suggests that Herriman was a Negro posing as a white" without providing any source (Berger, 1973, p. 69).[2] On the whole, Berger's argument in this work is rather thin. While criticizing earlier works on comics for being far too general and acclaiming himself as the first to "investigate this virgin land of the American imagination with any thoroughness" (Berger, 1973, p. 2), his work too is very general, consisting of 16 chapters analyzing various comics across 200 pages set in a large font. The book is composed of a set of sketches rather than a sustained argument. Berger tosses off observations, such as Krazy Kat's unwillingness to acknowledge "Ignatz's ill will" in throwing bricks as reflecting an American "tendency to value illusion over fact," that are not argued but simply asserted (Berger, 1973, p. 67). Given Berger's knowledge of Eco's work, the chapter on Superman in this book is rather weak. He equates Superman with Puritans, leaving a corrupt old world for a new world. Hence Superman's susceptibility to Kryptonite is similar to the American need to avoid contact with the corrupting influence of the old world and for a "repudiation of the past" and an American mindset that is "ahistorical." Like Ong, Berger saw a super state as limiting the individual, but for Berger in 1973 this was the United States, and his account offered no coherent explanation of Superman's connection to this state of being (Berger, 1973, pp. 156–159). Berger tried to combine a critique of mass culture with an appreciation of comics as a form. However, Reitberger and Fuchs were more convincing and credible in that undertaking.

Ariel Dorfman and Armand Mattelart's *How to Read Donald Duck: Imperialist Ideology in the Disney Comic* (1973) is the work of comics scholarship that is perhaps most explicit in its ideology. It is a difficult work to read, not so much because of its rudimentary economic Marxism as because of its horrible typeface and design. It is hard to know how much of the polemically charged language is its authors' (Dorfman and Mattelart had apparently enjoyed Disney comics as children) or its translator David Kunzle's. As Kunzle notes, he worked "on the translation in intensely emotional circumstances" (Kunzle, 2012, p. 3). Kunzle had been in Chile and met Dorfman shortly before the 1973 coup that deposed the elected government of Salvador Allende and installed Augusto Pinochet as the head of a brutal military junta that murdered thousands. By Kunzle's own account it was a tumultuous time in his life; not least of all he had been recently fired from his job at UC Santa Barbara, and he was in the process of becoming "a true Marxist art historian" (Kunzle, 2012, p. 4). As Kunzle told it in 1976 the book was his effort at throwing in his "lot with the Third World" (Kunzle, 2012, p. 4). Indeed, the book's subtitle in English is Kunzle's addition (Kunzle, 2012, p. 3).

The core argument of the book is that Disney comics are a form of American cultural imperialism. The expression and concept are familiar enough and as a concept carry enough veracity that less Marxist-inclined commentators on the impact of American media internationally refer to it as "soft power."[3] For Dorfman and Mattelart, Disney comics presented the citizens of the third world as childlike. In their view Chileans and others internalized such representations from Disney and this legitimated American power. This is a rather bare summary, but it gets to the heart of the argument and the problems with the work.

Thomas Andrae in his book on Barks addresses some of the problems with *How to Read Donald Duck*. One problem with the work is that it projects what was rather particular about editions of Disney comics in Chile to the total output of Disney across the globe. In doing so they misunderstood some of the work of Carl Barks, creator of Scrooge McDuck, and an author/artist who had a somewhat free reign in the stories he told. Much of Barks' work was satire, and Dorfman and Mattelart, working without access to the original US editions, did not grasp this aspect. Andrae also points to the problem of attributing a media effect of influence on an audience's values. Andrae argues that audiences are not "passive dupes," but play an active role in constructing meaning around media texts. Andrae suggested that a Gramscian model of hegemony provided a better guide to understanding a comics effect and that such things are a process, not fixed, and depend on "a sociohistoric context" (Andrae, 2006, pp. 12–16). Andrae, writing in 2006, offers a sophisticated critique, and indeed he cites Dorfman who on reflection thought he had "not been true to the complexity of cultural interchange [and] the fact that not all mass-media products absorbed from abroad are negative" (Dorfman, 1999, pp. 252–253). People, Dorfman came to understand, are "tangled, hybrid, wily creatures ready to appropriate and despoil the messages that come their way, relocate their meaning, reclaim them as their own by changing their significance" (Dorfman, 1999, pp. 252–253). But in 1975 when the book appeared in English, it was something of a sensation among left-leaning comics aficionados. Here was a book seemingly deeply informed about comics that criticized them from a left-wing anti-imperialist perspective. Kunzle's introduction set the work within the context of the political economy of the Disney corporation. Despite its many shortcomings, the book helped spark interest in the way American culture circulated internationally and impacted other nations. It also alerted would-be scholars of comics of the need to be attentive to underlying ideologies therein.

Thomas Andrae's *Carl Barks and the Disney Comic Book* (2006) came later in his career, but Andrae was an innovator in comics scholarship. Andrae studied at Berkeley first as an undergraduate in the 1960s and later as a graduate student. In 1979 Andrae was a founding member of the Editorial Board of *Discourse*, an academic journal best described as an interdisciplinary journal focused on cultural communication and with which he is still associated in 2015. From 1984 to 1990 Andrae worked as an editor on the seven-volume *Carl Barks Library* published by Another Rainbow. From July 1983 to February 1989, he also appeared on the masthead of *Nemo*, a magazine devoted to the history of comic art, to which he contributed several pieces. Andrae's interests extended from television and film, to superheroes and funny animal comic books, and a wave of cultural studies theory. As can be seen from his critique of *How to Read Donald Duck*, Andrae brought a finely tuned sensibility about comics and culture to his work. His 1980 piece in *Discourse*, "From Menace to Messiah: The Prehistory of the Superman in Science Fiction Literature," was a model in comics scholarship. He thought scholars like Reinhold Reitberger and Wolfgang Fuchs, and DC Comics editor E. Nelson Birdwell were wrong to suggest that superheroes were modern incarnations of ancient mythological gods. Andrae's argument is that Superman is a character born of science fiction, which, as a form that created characters with superhuman strength engendered by science rather than nature or the supernatural, dated from Mary Shelley's 1818 novel *Frankenstein*. He unpacks this argument and links it to the Great Depression as a moment when collectivist action drew wide support and the changing nature of individualism. The comics scholar N. C. Christopher Couch recently labeled Andrae "the best unsung comics scholar in the field" (2015). When rereading his Superman piece in its original form in *Discourse*, rather than the abbreviated version in the collection *American Media and Mass Culture*, one is struck by the prescience of Andrae, whose argument predated similar work by Peter Coogan and Aldo Regaldo tracing the origin of superheroes and Superman respectively. Andrae was also the first scholar to provide an account of Superman's early history as an agent of social justice before Siegel's success at attracting a large audience with this sort of story proved its undoing, drawing attention to Superman's anti-establishment activities and causing DC to feel compelled to reign in the character. The piece contextualizes Superman's actions in a time and place and the process of change in his character.

Another early piece of Andrae's scholarship, an interview with Superman's creators Jerry Siegel and Joe Shuster published in *Nemo*, has become a go-to piece for those writing on the history of Superman. In that interview Jerry Siegel outlined Superman's creation, or at least his memory of the process. The interview piece also reprinted Siegel and Shuster's original, non-heroic, "The Reign of the Superman" story that first appeared in a mimeographed science fiction fanzine they produced in January 1933. In this story "the superman" is a product of science not the sole survivor of another planet. Andrae's *Discourse* article draws on this short story to make his point that Superman was a product of science, both in terms of the milieu of science fiction and originally as a fictional character as the outcome of a scientific experiment, much like Frankenstein's monster. Jerry Siegel's memory was not always accurate in the interview; for instance, he does not mention the work Russell Keaton did on an attempted comic strip version of Superman in mid-1934, which calls into question the story he told of developing the finalized version of Superman one restless night in 1934. Nonetheless, the interview is a key text in the historiography of Superman's creation, even if as a document to be refuted through cross-checking facts.

Martin Barker's *Comics: Ideology, Power & the Critics* (1989) is a work often overlooked by comics scholars but widely cited in cultural studies work. It is a rich and complex book, although written in a conversational tone, with many useful cautions about drawing conclusion based on methodology that *a priori* sets up the conclusion as the only possible outcome of the research. Barker addresses ideology in comics directly and takes issue with many scholars' readings of ideology into comics. Barker's absence from so much comics scholarship is perhaps explained by his primary focus on British comics and his explicit exclusion of superhero and underground comics from his analysis. Barker criticizes scholars' too-easy use of a notion of identification, the resort to media effects as a justification for moral panics on both the left and the right, develops his own approach to ideology, and brings this all together as a theory and a method in a case study application in reading *How to Read Donald Duck*.

One reason Barker is not so widely cited in comics scholarship is that he is not a theory builder but rather a careful critic of theory who avoids totalizing statements and generalizations. To demonstrate the weak points of Dorfman and Mattelart's work he offers three other interpretations of Disney that "appeal to exactly the same evidence from the stories" (1989, p. 287). As he tells it "for Reitberger and Fuchs ... capitalism is mocked by being made absurd," for another critic Dave Wagner "if we were not able to laugh at Scrooge, he could not survive to be the object of our derision" and for Michael Barrier "the humour is a parable of human absurdity"—how we are undone by our obsessions (Barker, 1989, p. 287). For Barker it is not that comics do not have an ideology, but that such is not singular, even within, say, Uncle Scrooge comics and that getting at this requires more than a reading of a comic or set of comics. What he calls the production history of comics is also important. For Barker the Scrooge comics oscillate between "two poles of American middle-class ideology: a self-congratulatory but humourous desire for wealth; and an obsessive fear of power-politics" (Barker, 1989, p. 299). Barker's views here are predicated on his belief that comics establish a contract with their readers in which various negotiations of topics and content occur, negotiations somewhat observable through circulation figures and changes in plot devices, tropes, and the like in comics. In Disney's case, the Scrooge comics are absent the awful lack of play induced by Disney's creation of theme parks where all the work of play has been done already, and they also lack the horrible prettiness of Disney's nature films where "animals end up performing to a Disney script with a voice-over narration making then cutely, dehumanised humans" (Barker, 1989, p. 290). Barker saw his work as "hints and gestures" and that "new kinds of research" was necessary to do more.

SIDEBAR: TRAUMA AND DISABILITY IN COMICS

José Alaniz

Modern comics, like myriad other aspects of human existence, have reflected the experiences of trauma and disability at least since Slippy Dempsey, the boy perpetually falling out of upper-story windows in Richard F. Outcault's *Hogan's Alley*; the nightmare visions

(Continued)

in Winsor McCay's *Dreams of the Rarebit Fiend;* and Krazy's abreactions to repeated bricks to the head in George Herriman's *Krazy Kat* (to restrict ourselves to three early examples). Yet, while often linked, these two facets of life yield important differences that have led to disparate approaches in Disability Studies and Trauma Studies. This sidebar takes up these divergences in the course of discussion.

Trauma (from Greek, "wound") first underwent scrutiny in the medical-clinical literature (especially in the wake of World War I) and later from Holocaust Studies and feminist scholars, among them Dominick LaCapra and Cary Caruth. Its theorists concentrate on "the actuality and force of the traumatic event" (Berger, 2015, p. 181), which overwhelms the subject's capacity to process, leading to a destabilization of self. Key to trauma's shattering power is its resistance to representation and inaccessibility via language (Gilmore, 2000, p. 6).

Comics representations of trauma would here seem to hold an advantage over strictly textual media in that the former's image-text hybridity allows for "theorizing trauma in connection to the visual" (Chute, 2010, p. 4). As Susan Squier puts it, "Comics can show us things *that can't be said,* just as they can narrate experiences without relying on words" through verbal/visual, juxtapositional, and other strategies (2008, p. 131, emphasis in original).

For example, comics' page design may evoke the fragmentation and will to coherence of the narrativizing traumatized subject (Dony & Van Linthout, 2010, p. 180). This seems the case in a nine-panel page from Keiji Nakazawa's autobiographical *I Saw It* (1982), in which the author in present-day Hiroshima contemplates his childhood experience of the US bombing at the end of World War II, which killed several family members. As he stares into a still pond, lily pads suggest mushroom clouds, the texture of bricks evokes irradiated ash, a pebble impacting the water resembles a devastating explosion, with ripples reverberating across panels and gutters. The sequence disrupts barriers among space, time, history, and the now; its last three panels depict a full-blown return to the painful wartime past of our narrator's memory. Artists have similarly tapped comics' legacy of cartooning and caricature techniques to limn traumatic personal and historical events, as when Marjane Satrapi, in her memoir *Persepolis* (2003), utilizes a black panel to signify a childhood friend's mangled remains after a bombing raid during the Iran-Iraq War.

Other notable comics artists whose works often involve trauma include Art Spiegelman: "Prisoner on the Hell Planet" (1972), *Maus* (1986–1991), and *In the Shadow of No Towers* (2004); Joe Sacco: *Palestine* (2001/2007), *Safe Area Goražde* (2000/2010) and *Footnotes in Gaza* (2009); and those who address sexual abuse within families, such as Phoebe Gloeckner (material collected in *A Child's Life and Other Stories,* 1998/2002) and Debbie Drechsler in *Daddy's Girl* (1996). Trauma also figures as a primary component in the origin stories of superheroes since the genre's inception, e.g., the murder of Batman/Bruce Wayne's parents.

For sociohistorical and cultural reasons, comics' representation of disability reflects very different political stakes from those of trauma. Whereas clinicians and therapists have traditionally applied a model of "cure" and "healing" to the individual's experience of trauma, global disability rights movements since the 1970s have resisted such medicalization in favor of variations on "social" and identity politics models that aim to emancipate a marginalized minority of the "differently abled." These efforts have been codified in such official discourses as the UN Convention on the Rights of Persons with Disabilities (2006) and, in the US, the Americans with Disabilities Act (1990).

In practice, this has meant that Disability Studies sees "the event" very differently from Trauma Studies, de-emphasizing its significance and displacing it with a much more intense focus on the social, cultural, and ideological *responses* to physical/cognitive difference, i.e., the ways in which disability is socially constructed, regardless of any precipitating "event." As Berger notes, "disability studies is marked by an inability to mourn, and trauma studies by an inability to *stop* mourning" (Berger, 2014, p. 173, emphasis in original).

The case of Oracle/Barbara Gordon is instructive in this context. The former Batgirl, paralyzed as the result of a shooting in Alan Moore/Brian Bolland's graphic novel *A Killing Joke* (1988), would go on to become the wheelchair-using heroine Oracle: cyberhacker, information broker, and leader of the Birds of Prey. This situation persisted until 2011, when DC Comics "retconned" Gordon to her former able-bodied self as Batgirl—prompting both an outcry from the disabled community and accolades from other readers (many arguing from feminist premises) who had never accepted Gordon's "diminished" status as a woman crippled by male violence (Alaniz, forthcoming). In contrast, a Disability Studies reading would see nothing "disempowering" about a woman in a wheelchair and resist any metaphor-driven, "narrative prosthesis" approach to the character (Mitchell & Snyder, 2000, pp. 6–7).

Mainstream depictions of the disabled span the history of the superhero genre, as seen in such Golden Age figures as the lame Freddie Freeman, alter-ego of Captain Marvel, Jr.; the partially blind Dr. Mid-Nite; and the blind Daredevil. However, disability as a fully fledged facet of identity was not systematically worked into these early narratives; only with the advent of the so-called Silver Age were disabilities foregrounded in something other than a binary model, in both civilian and superheroic guise, through characters like Thor/Donald Blake (lame), Iron Man/Tony Stark (heart condition), Daredevil/Matt Murdock (blind), The Thing/Ben Grimm (disfigured), the X-Men and Doom Patrol (Alaniz, 2014).

Key works of alternative comics that privilege the social, "dys-appearance" model of the disability/illness experience (El Refaie, 2012, p. 61) include Justin Green's *Binky Brown Meets the Holy Virgin Mary* (1972), on obsessive compulsive disorder; Richard and Renee Jensen's *Amputee Love* (1975); Al Davison's *The Spiral Cage* (1988/2003), on spina bifida; Harvey Pekar and Joyce Brabner's *Our Cancer Year* (1994); David B.'s *Epileptic* (2003); Ellen Forney's *Marbles: Mania, Depression, Michelangelo, and Me: A Graphic Memoir* (2012), on bipolar disorder; and the Belgian collective Fremok's Match de Catch project, which publishes the work of mentally disabled artists (launched in 2009).

In response to changes in sociocultural life since World War II, as well as to the rise of disability rights movements, the depiction of trauma and disability has blossomed in Western comics. It represents a significant portion of post-*Maus* production in graphic narrative.

(Continued)

Bibliography

Alaniz, J. (2014) *Death, Disability and the Superhero: the silver age and beyond*, Jackson: University Press of Mississippi.

Alaniz, J. (2016) 'Standing Orders: oracle, disability and retconning' in C. Foss et al. (eds.) *Disability in Comic Books and Graphic Narratives*, London: Palgrave.

Berger, J. (2014) *The Disarticulate: language, disability, and the narratives of modernity*, New York: New York University Press.

Berger, J. (2015) 'Trauma', in R. Adams et al. (eds.) *Keywords for Disability Studies*, New York: New York University Press.

Caruth, C. (1996) *Unclaimed Experience: trauma, narrative, and history*, Baltimore: Johns Hopkins University Press.

Chute, H.L. (2010) *Graphic Women: life narrative and contemporary comics*, New York: Columbia University Press.

Dony, C. and Van Linthout, C. (2010) 'Comics, trauma, and cultural memory(ies) of 9/11', in J. Goggin and D. Hassler-Forest (eds.) *The Rise and Reason of Comics and Graphic Literature: critical essays on the form*, Jefferson, NC: McFarland & Co.

El Refaie, E. (2012) *Autobiographical Comics: life writing in pictures*, Jackson: University Press of Mississippi.

Foss, C., Gray, J.W. and Whalen, Z. (eds.) (2016) *Disability in Comic Books and Graphic Narratives. (Literary Disability Studies)*, New York: Palgrave Macmillan.

Gilmore, L. (2000) *The Limits of Autobiography: trauma and testimony*, Ithaca: Cornell University Press.

LaCapra, D. (1994) *Representing the Holocaust: history, theory, trauma*, Ithaca: Cornell University Press.

Mitchell, D.T. and Snyder, S.L. (2000) *Narrative Prosthesis: disability and the dependencies of discourse*, Ann Arbor: University of Michigan Press.

Squier, S. (2008) 'Literature and medicine, future tense: make it graphic', *Literature and Medicine*, 27 (2): 124–52.

Most of the figures discussed in this chapter have proved to be inspirational rather than aspirational for comics scholars. Of those that held academic jobs and might have attracted graduate students and so produced a school, neither Berger nor Barker seems to have produced a student who is a comics scholar. Barker to be sure has worked closely with Roger Sabin and is accorded much respect by British-based comics scholars. Berger is seldom referenced. Andrae spent a career between academia and the semi-professional community of comics enthusiasts who produced reprints of important comics and early serious, but not scholarly, studies of comics. Of these he was clearly the most talented, but without tenure and research funding his output was limited. After the coup in Chile, Mattelart worked in France for many years as a Communication scholar but seems to have not pursued an interest in comics, at least in terms of publishing and mentoring students. Dorfman remains in academia at Duke University but likewise is mostly not engaged with comics. Reitberger and Fuchs worked in publishing and design and not academia. So comics scholarship did not develop directly out of this work. If the origins of comics scholarship are "secret" it is perhaps because not enough of this work has been read, a complaint of scholars like Bart Beaty, who often bemoans younger comics scholars' inattention to earlier work in the field. Not all this work offers a payoff intellectually, but a field that does not know and read its own history is impoverished.

Notes

1 Although listed in the bibliography of my *Comic Strips and Consumer Culture* (1998) I do not cite this volume in the body of the work. I had read it in 1986, but as far as I recall, had not returned to it during my own research in 1991–1992. Clearly though it left its mark since the observations about the early history of the American comic strip are things I fleshed out in a chapter.
2 A reader interested in verifying this information can check it in Patrick McDonnell, Karen O'Connell, and Georgia Riley de Havenon, *Krazy Kat: the comic art of George Herriman* (New York: Harry N. Abrams, 1986), p. 30. It is more accurate to say that Herriman was of mixed ancestry (most likely including French, Spanish, and African Americans in his lineage), but if this had been common knowledge he would not have been able to pass as white in American society of his day, as it policed such matters strictly.
3 The term is generally thought to have originated with Joseph Nye in the 1980s.

Bibliography

Andrae, T. (1980) 'From menace to messiah: the prehistory of the superman in science fiction literature', *Discourse*, 2: 84–112; reprinted in Lazure, D. (ed.) *American Media and Mass Culture: left perspectives*, Berkeley: University of California Press, 124–38.
Andrae, T. (1983) 'Of Superman and kids with dreams: an interview with the creators of Superman, Jerry Siegel and Joe Shuster', *Nemo*, 2: 6–19.
Andrae, T. (2006) *Carl Barks and the Disney Comic Book: unmasking the myth of modernity*, Jackson: University Press of Mississippi.
Barker, M. (1989) *Comics: ideology, power, and the critics*, Manchester: Manchester University Press.
Barrier, M. (1973) 'The duck man', in D. Thompson and D. Lupoff (eds.) *The Comic-Book Book*, New York: Arlington, 210–27.
Berger, A.A. (1969) *Li'l Abner: a study in American satire*, Jackson: University Press of Mississippi.
Berger, A.A. (1973) *The Comic-Stripped American*, New York: Walker and Company.
Coogan, P.M. (2006) *Superhero: the secret origin of a genre*, Austin: MonkeyBrain Books.
Couch, N.C.C. (2015) Personal correspondence with author, May 28.
Dorfman, A. (1999) *Heading South, Looking North: a bilingual journey*, New York: Penguin.
Dorfman, A. and Mattelart, A. (1973) *How to Read Donald Duck: imperialist ideology in the Disney comic*, New York: I. G. Editions.
Eco, U. (1972) 'The myth of Superman', *Diacritics*, 2: 14–22.
Faust, W. (1971) 'Comics and how to read them', *Journal of Popular Culture*, 5 (1): 94–202.
Kunzle, D. (1973) *History of the Comic Strip / Vol. 1, The Early Comic Strip: narrative strips and picture stories in the European broadsheet from c. 1450 to 1825*, Berkeley: University of California Press.
Kunzle, D. (2012) 'The parts that got left out of the Donald Duck book, or: how Karl Marx Prevailed over Carl Barks', *ImageTexT: Interdisciplinary Comics Studies*, 6 (2). http://www.english.ufl.edu/imagetext/archives/v6_2/kunzle/. [Accessed May 25, 2015.]
Ong, W. (1945) 'The comics and the super state', *Arizona Quarterly*, 1 (3): 34–48.
Regalado, A. (2015) *Bending Steel: modernity and the American superhero*, Jackson: University Press of Mississippi.
Reitberger, R. and Fuchs, W. (1972) *Comics: anatomy of a mass medium*, Boston: Little Brown.
Wagner, D. (1973) 'Donald Duck: an interview', *Radical America*, 7 (1): 1–19.

A PIONEER'S PERSPECTIVE: WOLFGANG FUCHS

Our book *Comics—Anatomy of a Mass Medium* came into being as the result of a colloquium at the Department of American Studies at LMU (Ludwig Maximilians University of Munich, Germany). A colloquium was ranked as a pre-seminar. Attendance of two pre-seminars was necessary to be able to attend full seminars. Our colloquium was part of a series of activities analyzing various aspects of popular culture initiated by Professor Werner Friedmann who, at the time, headed the department. He knew of our interest in comics and therefore asked us to head the colloquium.

FIGURE 10.1 Original colloquium poster.
Source: Photo courtesy of Wolfgang Fuchs.

For the weekly sessions of the colloquium on "Comics"—subtitled: "The Function of a 'Popular Art' within American Society"—we prepared papers on various aspects of the comics as a basis for discussions. We also prepared a reading list of books (Stephen Becker, Fredric Wertham, etc.) to be read for the discussions. They could be found in a special section of the department library. There, we also offered for perusal a selection of comic books as well as one or two volumes of Sunday comic sections especially bound for the occasion. For one session, we even invited a representative of a German comics publisher as guest speaker. Ultimately, Professor Friedmann suggested that, having invested so much work in the project, we should turn it into a book.

The *Anatomy* was written at a time when most German books dealing with comics considered them as something potentially harmful, culturally or politically. There was a slight indication of a changing of opinion when the comics exhibition shown at the Louvre in the late 1960s was shown in Berlin with a German translation of the catalogue.

We concocted an outline for the book and a first draft of the chapter on superheroes on the grounds of a public swimming pool. This earned me a slight case of sunstroke. We then discussed and rearranged our ideas with actual cut-and-paste procedures (as there were not yet computers to facilitate that task). We then typed a final draft, which we illustrated with several xeroxes. We also did additional research contacting American comic publishers and cartoonists like Charles Schulz and Walt Kelly to flesh out our findings. Ultimately, we also asked permission to use any borrowed material.

Nevertheless, the first publisher who looked at our book rejected it on the grounds of its being too "balanced." He probably would have liked less history and a more leftist slant. We had the good luck of finding a publisher, though, who felt at ease with our presenting comics as a medium with a history. The result was overwhelming. Not only was the book immediately reprinted and then turned into a paperback, but it also was published in Great Britain, the United States, the Netherlands, and Spain (in serialized form in the magazine *Zeppelin*). The book was reviewed in most national and local papers and magazines. Some journalists even turned the book into full-page articles about comics without mentioning the book.

All of a sudden, comics were a focal point of interest that, while still being eyed somewhat suspiciously, was also beginning to be considered as something one could accept culturally and even use in politics. Many theses about comics were now being written by students aspiring to get their M.A. or Ph.D. The German department at the University of Frankfurt held a symposium about comics and started a collection of comic books. As I found out later, one publisher even used our book as a kind of catalogue to decide what comics to select to enlarge his company's comics offerings.

So, basically, besides giving comics a chance to be considered with less prejudice, our book helped widen the scope of comics published in Germany and furthered a general acceptance of the medium. Comics were now being researched in religious as well as academic circles while fans started having conventions and publishing fanzines that brought out interesting facts about the history of comics that had been overlooked by academia up to this point.

(Continued)

There are all kinds of academic and non-academic research going on these days. A number of historically important comics of postwar Germany have been reprinted and analyzed. What seems to be lacking, though, is a look at the history of German comics in correlation to historic events that, by and large, reflected on the perception of comics.

For quite a while now annual publications about research of German comics history are putting the medium in a culturally more relevant perspective. However, many authors still begin with excuses for touching on the subject or with the Adams and Eves of comic history before proceeding to what they really want to say about comics. The fact that there now is a budding scene of aspiring German comic artists should help change that in time.

11

FORMALIST THEORY

The Cartoonists

Henry Jenkins

Some of the most important writing about art comes from artists themselves, expert practitioners who develop theories to help explain and perhaps perpetuate their own creative practice. For a fuller discussion of the value of such perspectives, see McLaughlin, 1996. Practitioner discourse may take the form of manifestos or theoretical works, how-to guides, or even informal interviews. If, for example, we consider the history of cinema, examples might include Sergei Eisenstein's *Film Form* (1949), John Alton's *Painting with Light* (1985), Francois Truffaut's book-length interview/conversation with Alfred Hitchcock (1967), or Andrei Tarkovsky's justification of his long-take aesthetic in *Sculpting in Time* (1989). Such writing may emerge spontaneously when media are new (as with more recent work on game design) or when it is under attack by outside forces (again, game theory). In the case of comics, both factors play a role.

Comic artists have theorized their own practices going back to Rodolphe Töpffer, who wrote a noteworthy illustrated essay on "physiognomie" in 1845. Töpffer's essay was intended to provide a rationale for an emerging genre—"the picture-story" with "its unique advantages of brevity and consequently, of clarity" (Wiese, 1965, p. 4), which he saw as a form uniquely suited for moral instruction and popular education. Such work, he felt, did not require master craftsmen in perfect control of their art as much as the capacity to think and express one's ideas through words and pictures. Indeed, for this Swiss pioneer, the most productive thinking might emerge through doodles or what he calls "simple line drawing": such an approach, he argues, requires the artist to cut to the core of an image, to focus only on its broad outlines, and thus to bring out its expressive potential. His is not quite an argument for abstraction, but it certainly is an argument about the kinds of legibility that can be achieved by breaking the world down to its core elements and representing them in broad outline. He stresses the ways that the human mind would fill in missing elements within a visual image in a way that readers would be much less able to do in responding to a prose description. His emphasis on physiology—which he describes in terms of a focus on human expression—as opposed to phrenology—which he discusses in terms of a means of reading moral character and intelligence from fixed physical features—grows out of this emphasis on improvising through line-drawing in the hopes of identifying striking images that may most directly convey underlying ideas and tones. The best pictorial ideas, he suggests, emerge from the artist playing around with their tools rather than from careful formal planning and technical skills.

In their introduction to *The French Comics Theory Reader*, Ann Miller and Bart Beaty (2014) suggest that such border crossing has played a key role in shaping comics theory and criticism in Europe:

> Perhaps following Töpffer, French comics theorists are much more likely than their Anglo counterparts to be involved in the comics industry as creators. From this volume alone, Thierry Smolderen, Thierry Groensteen, Jean-Christophe Menu, Barthélémy Schwartz and Benoît Peeters have all published comics as well as important scholarship on the form, and Groensteen and Menu both work full-time as editors and publishers. This may explain why the structural and formal emphasis that is common to a great deal of French comics scholarship has had a larger impact on the traditions of French-language comics production than English-language comics scholarship has had on the shaping [sic] British and American comics traditions. (p. 12)

Contrary to the national distinction they are drawing, theoretical works by comics artists in the American tradition have also articulated core aesthetic principles shaping this evolving medium while comparing and contrasting comics to other artistic practices and shaping the critical acceptance of "sequential art" and "graphic storytelling" in the academy and the art world alike. For a discussion of the role comic artists have played in theorizing manga, see Nicholas A. Theisen's essay in this volume.

My primary focus here will be on the ways comics artists have theorized and conveyed their own ideas about their "poetics" to readers, often imagined to be other comic book artists in training but also comics fans and readers. As David Bordwell (1989) has explained, "The poetics of any medium studies the finished work as the result of a process of construction—a process which includes a craft component (e.g., rules of thumb), the more general principles according to which the work is composed, and its functions, effects, and uses" (p. 371). Studies on aesthetics may abstract from the completed work to explore larger questions around the nature of beauty or what makes an artwork culturally valuable; studies on poetics explore how a work is made and what principles might guide future artists. This strong emphasis on craft helps to distinguish the work of the expert practitioners I am discussing here from other kinds of formalist analysis. By comparison, Thierry Smolderen's magisterial *The Origins of Comics* (2014) is a far more academically focused text. Smolderen traces the historic emergence and evolution of representational codes within comics "from William Hogarth to Winsor McCay," often through comparisons to other examples from media and art history. Robert C. Harvey's *The Art of the Funnies* (1994), on the other hand, offers an "aesthetic history" of comic strips from the vantage point of a fan, collector, or connoisseur, helping to explain why certain artists are valued for their contributions to an emerging mode of expression. Both Smolderen and Harvey brought valuable perspectives to these projects, based on their own practical experiences as cartoonists, but they each framed their books for a different kind of audience than the theorists I am discussing here—as one more invested in appreciating specific texts than in mastering the language of the medium. The same would be true of Coulton Waugh, a comic-strip veteran, whose 1947 book, *The Comics*, helped to map some key figures and texts in the US comic strip tradition: Waugh offers critical insights about specific artists and their work, but he avoids larger claims about how the medium operates. Waugh gave us a history and a criticism of American comic strips, but not yet a theory.

Examinations of the poetics of comics by expert practitioners can be understood as theory in the sense that they make meaningful and shareable generalizations about how comics work. In many cases, such writings rely on metaphors of comics as a language and reading comics as a literacy, which implies a vocabulary understood by readers and artists alike. These theorists differ in terms of how they understand the reading process, in what mix exists between the normative and the descriptive, in whether the focus is on medium-specific arguments or on arguments that link comics to a range of other storytelling practices, and upon what other kinds of knowledge (for instance, anthropology, media theory, psychology, art history) the artists rely for support. Part of what interests me here is the ways that comics artists have used comics (literally in the case of Scott McCloud, or as part of a larger hybrid work in the case of Will Eisner and others) in order to explain comics. In some cases, this involves the production of original comics intended to illustrate core principles of graphic storytelling, often in the process advancing the medium by experimenting with its form. In other instances, these works redirect our attention onto existing works, helping readers to see them through a new critical lens.

Mort Walker

Comics artists, especially early on, had difficulty taking their creative work seriously as art. Mort Walker's *Lexicon of Comicana*, published in 1980 by the Museum of Cartoon Art, was intended as a parody of the very idea of creating a theory of comics. Walker makes several tongue-in-cheek comments about the value of his collection, including an invoice recounting how much time and money readers wasted or a section parodying "art-speak" via a mock critique of one of his own *Hi and Lois* cartoons: "The all over effect is one of direct immediacy, not implying any subtle inferences, nor requiring any degree of sophistication for cognizance" (1980, p. 87).

Walker, best known for his work on *Beetle Bailey*, cataloged the core clichés and stereotypes of the American comic strip tradition. Along the way, he invented terms—such as *plewds, grawlizes,* and *emanata*—that have been widely used by subsequent generations of writers who wanted to know what to call those darned things, and his account takes us from facial expressions (what he calls Teteology) through word balloons (Fumetti) to what he calls Emanata, which provide external correlates for internal emotional states. He seems to have chosen terms for their humorous effect, but the work proceeds from a belief that a shared vocabulary or lexicon of such devices insures greater clarity of expression and economy of effort. Walker introduces the book by referencing the connections between the stylized expression of cartooning and children's first drawings. He also stresses the ways that visual language is helping to facilitate communication across national and language boundaries, though also acknowledging that many such devices require familiarity with local cultural conventions in order to be deciphered. However uncomfortably, Walker was opening the door for the study of comics in relation to visual literacy.

Will Eisner

Like Walker's, Will Eisner's efforts to theorize his own practice suggest a deep ambivalence about the value of articulating insights that have often emerged through creative experimentation and intuitive practice. He explains early on in *Comics and Sequential Art* (1985), "Traditionally, most practitioners with whom I worked and talked produced their art viscerally. Few ever had the time or the inclination to diagnose the form itself. In the main, they were content to concentrate on the development of their draftsmanship and their perception of the audience and the demands of the marketplace" (p. xii). In *Graphic Storytelling and Visual Narrative* (1996), Eisner worries that too much attention to the technical dimensions of graphic art ("the packaging effort") may "deflect" from the storytelling (p. xi). Yet, in other passages, Eisner is much more decisive in justifying a theory of comics: "This work is intended to consider and examine the unique aesthetics of sequential arts as a means of creative expression, a distinct discipline, an art and literary form that deals with the arrangement of pictures or images and words to narrate a story or dramatize an idea" (Eisner, 1985, p. xi). If Eisner saw theory as of limited value to those making comics, his belief that comics justified as much serious reflection as any other medium never faltered.

Eisner wrote three books spelling out his core approach: *Comics and Sequential Art* (1985); *Graphic Storytelling and Visual Narrative* (1996); and *Expressive Anatomy for Comics and Narrative* (2008), published posthumously. Eisner helped to pioneer the instructional use of comics while with the U S military during World War II and, after, working for commercial clients of the American Visuals Corporation. For a sample of this instructional work, see Eisner 2011. His ideas about the formal properties of comics were shaped by his experiences teaching an early class in Sequential Art at the School of Visual Arts in New York City (originally established as the Cartoonists and Illustrators School), which has at one time or another been home to many of those whose work we are discussing here (Art Spiegelman, Jessica Abel, Matt Madden, Paul Karasik, and Mark Newgarden among them). Eisner's original formulations of these ideas were first published in the back pages of *The Spirit Magazine* (where he also shared interviews and advice from comics industry veterans such as Milton Caniff, Gil Kane, Joe Simon, Jack Kirby, and Joe Kubert). Eisner's books were initially self-published but are today published by W.W. Norton, a major textbook publisher, suggesting how influential Eisner has become in the classroom. Perhaps as much as anything else, these books called attention to Eisner's own mix of craft and experimentation, getting people to sample his oeuvre and cementing his critical reputation. Eisner's detailed commentary on his own work, integrated across these books, provides useful guidance for everyone else who has tried to explain his techniques and practices. Producing these books also gave the industry veteran a chance to demonstrate that he still had chops as an artist and designer. Eisner has credited his time in the classroom and writing these materials with helping him to reflect on where he had gone as an artist over many decades in comics and inspiring him to do the more experimental, often more autobiographical work that would dominate the final phases of his career (Schumacher, 2010).

If Will Eisner, as Greg M. Smith (2010) has argued, is both a "modernist extraordinaire" and a throwback to 19th-century melodrama and vaudeville, his comics theory simultaneously encourages expressive freedom and advances a classical conception of comics art. As Eisner (1985) explains, "In sequential art the artist must, from the outset, secure control of the reader's attention and dictate the sequence in which the reader will follow the narrative.

The limitations inherent in the technology of the printed comics are both obstacle and asset in the attempt to accomplish this. The most important obstacle to surmount is the tendency of the reader's eye to wander" (p. 40). And, as a consequence, there is a crisis each time a reader flips forward: "On any given page, for example, there is absolutely no way in which the artist can prevent the reading of the last panel before the first. The turning of the page does mechanically enforce some control, but hardly as absolutely as in film" (Eisner, 1985, p. 40). Later, he explains, "Keep in mind that when the reader turns the page a pause occurs. This permits a change of time, a shift of scene, an opportunity to control the reader's focus. Here one deals with retention as well as attention" (Eisner, 1985, p. 65).

For Eisner, the breakdown of the action into discrete segments through framing allows the artist to direct the reader's attention onto narratively salient details, a process Eisner calls *containment*. I use the term *classical* to describe Eisner's model here because it is hard to escape the parallels with the ways analytic editing works in Classical Hollywood Cinema: a means of both focusing attention and decreasing distraction. A passage in *Graphic Storytelling* (1996) suggests a somewhat more ambivalent attitude toward the interpretive process: "Film requires nothing more than spectator attention, while comics need a certain amount of literacy and participation. A film watcher is imprisoned until the film ends while the comics reader is free to roam, to peak at the ending, or dwell on an image and fantasize" (p. 71). We should, perhaps, not expect too much consistency in these writings, which evolved over time and reflected his own growing understanding of his medium; Eisner rewrote this material multiple times, and Norton has adapted some of the materials since his death, making tracing the evolution of any given passage an archeological exercise. But we can see this process as, in part, Eisner working through how much freedom readers should enjoy and how much control authors/artists should exert over their wandering attention.

Perhaps Eisner's most original contribution was his focus on the gestalt of the page as opposed to the focus on the individual panels. For Eisner (1985), the poetics of comics involves how the artist (and, through the artist, the reader) exploits the relationships between two different frames: "the total page ... on which there are any number of panels and the panel itself, within which the narrative action unfolds" (p. 41). The reader takes in the "shape of the page" at once, forming a larger, but somewhat inchoate, impression. But, at the same time, the reader focuses on only one panel at a time, situating the depicted action into an evolving comprehension of the work as a whole. This focus on "the shape of the page" (or what he elsewhere calls "the page as meta-panel") helps us to understand the highly layered, almost collage-like compositions that Eisner had developed through his work on *The Spirit* and subsequently. Because these images can be taken in all at once to create an overall effect, they have as much to do with the role of superimpositions or dissolves in cinema than with montage and decoupage.

Eisner struggles with how to distinguish the distinctive kinds of juxtapositions enabled by comics from those found in other media, especially cinema. He writes about "comic's singular ability to allow a reader to consider many images at the same time, or from different directions, a capability film lacks" (Eisner, 1985, p. 20). At the same time he is making medium specificity arguments (see Carroll, 1996), Eisner situates comics on a continuum with other means of representing the human condition, comparing comics to pictographs or hieroglyphics, even Morse Code or musical notation. In *Graphic Storytelling* (1996), Eisner traces the roots of storytelling back to our primitive origins, using recurring images of cavemen to convey the timeless quality of entertainment experiences. These ideas reflect the artist's engagement with the media theories of Marshall McLuhan (specifically, *The Medium Is the Massage* [McLuhan and Fiore, 1967]; see Eisner, 1996, p. xv.), as well as a range of different experts on primitive art (for instance, Ladislas Segy) and the mythmaking process (such as Joseph Campbell and Roger D. Abrahams).

Throughout, Eisner returns again and again to the ways human brains operate. Drawing on ideas popular in art theory and cognitive psychology, such as E. H. Gombrich's focus on "the viewer's share" (1960) or Jerome Bruner's focus on how readers "go beyond the information given" (1973), Eisner celebrates the work the reader does in processing the signs comics artists produce in their effort to shorthand human emotion and bodily movement. Images, Eisner (1985, pp. 147–148) argues, are "specific" and "obviate interpretation," compared with literary texts, and thus "allow little input of an imaginative nature from the reader." However, the reader pieces together "in-between" actions "out of his own experiences and thus must actively contribute to making sense of what is being depicted" (Eisner, 1985, p. 148). Eisner (1996, p. 49) speaks about an informal or implicit "contract" between reader and storyteller: "the storyteller expects that the audience will comprehend, while the audience expects the author will deliver something that is comprehensible." Make no mistake, Eisner the classicist reminds us, "in this agreement, the burden is on the storyteller" (1996, p. 49).

Comics require a basic literacy because their language built up over time: "In its most economical state, comics employ a series of repetitive images and recognizable symbols. When these are used again and again to convey similar ideas, they become a distinct language—a literary form, if you will. And it is this disciplined application that creates the 'grammar' of sequential art" (Eisner, 1985, p. 2). The notion of literacy would have been a particularly sensitive one for comics artists and writers of Eisner's generation because of the ways that critics, such as Fredric Wertham (1954; see also Beaty, 2005) described comics as a threat to the ability of youth to acquire literacy or the ways that even defenders of comics had often stressed their appeal to illiterate or semi-literate populations—immigrants and children (a connection Eisner himself makes early in *Graphic Storytelling*; see Eisner, 1996, p. xv). Eisner defiantly situated comics as "at the center" of the increasingly important role visual literacy was playing in the late 20th century.

Expressive Anatomy (2008) consolidates another important strand within Eisner's comic theory—metaphors of theatricality. For example, Eisner describes his book as "a basic guide of body grammar for the depiction of people as characters and their manipulation as actors in the service of a drama," further explaining "the artist functions like a theater director choreographing the action" (Eisner, 2008, p. xi) (note, again, the literacy metaphor in the use of the term *grammar*). This process often requires a reliance on more codified or stylized postures, gestures, and expressions to convey particular affective states (what he calls "expressive anatomy"). Throughout, there is a blurring between the terms *character* (as in a fictional construct) and *actor* (the physical body through which the character is conveyed to the reader), with character design choices likened to casting decisions. Eisner, elsewhere, uses the term *pantomime* to refer to comics without words (Eisner, 1985, p. 10) and refers to visual narratives as a "theater of our comprehension" (p. 24). Near the end of *Expressive Anatomy*, Eisner links his "expressive anatomy" to the efforts of Francois Delsarte in the late 19th century to codify and teach a gestural language for popular stage melodrama (2008, pp. 161–163). *Expressive Anatomy* reproduces several pages from Delsarte's guidebooks for theatrical actors alongside a passage from Eisner's *The Big City* showing the persistence of those gestures in his graphic novels (pp. 162–167).

We can see similar ideas about the power of codified gestures in "Hamlet on the Rooftop" in *Comics and Sequential Art*. Here, a Brando-like punk walks us through "To Be or Not To Be," constructing a distinctive interpretation of the soliloquy (Eisner, 1985, pp. 115–124). If Eisner's experimentation with framing is what gives his comics their modernist feel, his reliance on melodramatic vignettes and codified gestures can make these same pieces seem quaint to some contemporary readers. Yet, we should note how many of the characters in contemporary mainstream comics—from Batman to Wolverine—have characteristic stances or gestures reproduced by a range of artists to shorthand who they are and how they relate to their surrounding environment. The particulars of Eisner's "body grammar" may have dated, but the quest for the right gesture to convey the larger emotional context remains a constant in graphic storytelling.

Scott McCloud

Scott McCloud has described the deep influence Eisner exerted on his own thinking about comics. In many ways, he can be seen as having carried forward that particular torch. In personal correspondence I had with McCloud, he said of Eisner:

> His early work on *The Spirit* embraced the whole page and its compositional possibilities in a way that very few of his peers were willing to do. Every new installment felt like a new door opening. Even 40 years later, when young artists like me stumbled across reprints of the strip, it felt that way. I can only imagine what it felt like for young cartoonists in the early '40s. ... I was especially swayed by his assertion that we'd only seen the tip of the iceberg when it came to using comics to convey ideas, not just stories. It was true then, and it probably still is, but people are only just now waking up to what Eisner was saying decades ago ... . Finally, anyone from my generation who knew him—as a lot of us did—were impressed by his open-mindedness and enthusiasm for the work of young cartoonists; as well as a refusal to give in to some of the calcified prejudices of others from his generation. I can think of at least three occasions where I saw Eisner debating other older cartoonists, and he always came across as the youngest man in the room. (Scott McCloud, email message to author, May 26, 2015)

By the time McCloud published *Understanding Comics: The Invisible Art* in 1993, he had already established his critical reputation via the genre-breaking *Zot!* series and his intellectual leadership through his strong advocacy for a creator's rights movement.

McCloud's work gained visibility in the context of the rise of alternative comics and the artistic ambitions of Art Spiegelman. Spiegelman used the cultural capital he gained through writing his Pulitzer Prize-winning *Maus* to advocate for greater recognition of comics as an art form. Spiegelman's public lectures and occasional writings, not to mention his curatorial and editorial work, reconstructed a canon of neglected comics artists working outside the mainstream superhero tradition (For a fuller discussion, see Jenkins, 2015.). Spiegelman (2013) has long promoted the concept of the "co-mix," which he defines in terms of the mixing of words and pictures, often in unanticipated and surprising ways, as a way of explaining what his medium can achieve that no other can. Spiegelman's own creative practice, in turn, often relied on the creative reworking of earlier comics—whether his creative defacing of a Rex Morgan comic strip in "The Malpractice Suite" or his incorporation of images from Happy Holligan or the Katzenjammer Kids in *In the Shadow of No Towers*—which have further called attention to what contemporary graphic artists owe to earlier generations of experimenters and pioneers.

Meanwhile, in *Understanding Comics*, McCloud advanced the core idea that comics were not a genre (limited to men in capes) but rather a medium that could be used to tell all kinds of stories in all kinds of styles for all kinds of audiences: "There are NO LIMITS to what you can fill that BLANK PAGE with—once you understand the PRINCIPLES that all comics storytelling is built upon" (McCloud, 1993, p. 5). With his more expansive notion of the medium, McCloud traces its historical roots much earlier than early 20th-century newspapers or late 19th-century humor magazines, calling attention to similarities with the Bayeaux Tapestry, Trajan's Column, Egyptian hieroglyphs, or Mayan codex, a move that both parallels and adds greater nuance to Eisner's attempts to trace comics back to cave paintings. If Eisner is a classicist, McCloud is much more invested in experimentation, in pushing the limits of current comics language.

That said, McCloud's approach was deeply informed by Eisner's concept of "sequential art" from which he would generate his own more expansive (and yet also carefully delimited) notion of what constitutes comics: "juxtaposed pictorial and other images in deliberate sequence, intended to convey information and/or to produce an aesthetic response in the viewer" (1993, p. 20). The focus on sequential art meant, however, that McCloud placed far less emphasis on mise-en-scène than he did on the relationship between panels, a choice that is also partially reflected by his argument that single-frame cartoons are not comics *per se*. Eisner and McCloud arguably overemphasize the importance of breakdown to the aesthetic experience of comics: certainly, the flow of information across sequential panels is a distinctive element of comics as compared with other media such as painting, but there may also be meaningful juxtapositions within a single panel—and, perhaps most importantly, these two forms of juxtaposition do not represent an either-or stylistic choice of the kind that debates between *mise-en-scène* and montage in cinema have classically imagined. The same panel may invite slow scrutiny and also initiate a dramatic sequence.

Much like Eisner, McCloud is interested in how comic conventions structure the reading process. Drawing on semiotics, he seeks to explain the iconic nature of comic representation: humans anthropomorphize almost everything in their surroundings and are apt to develop stronger feelings toward cartoonish images because the simplification of their rendering helps to universalize them. Like Eisner, McCloud sees the comic's artist as shaping and controlling the reader's perceptions: "In comics, you can do a lot of that 'cutting' BEFOREHAND to insure that the flow of images readers see are exactly the ones you WANT them to see in the ORDER that best serves your STORYTELLING GOALS" (1993, p. 35). For McCloud, comics work both by identifying key moments and then structuring in gaps—the gutter—between images: "Comic panels FRACTURE both TIME and SPACE, offering a JAGGED, STACCATO RHYTHM of UNCONNECTED MOMENTS, but closure allows us to CONNECT these moments and MENTALLY CONSTRUCT A CONTINUOUS, UNIFIED REALITY" (1993, p. 67). McCloud also suggests that comics artists shape the speed with which a reader moves across the pages by the amount of visual density contained within each panel: a panel that includes a simple, easy-to-recognize, iconic image can be moved past fairly rapidly as we are eager to discover what happens next, whereas a much more dense composition may require us to slow down and pay more attention. Artists also control reading speed through the number of panels they use to break down an action.

McCloud catalogs different kinds of juxtapositions between images (not unlike the Soviet film theorists who sought to understand different logics of montage). Here, McCloud distinguishes culturally specific patterns of juxtaposition, noting that American comics (especially in the Jack Kirby tradition) tend to stress direct action-to-action, moment-to-moment transitions, while the Japanese manga tradition introduces more aspect-to-aspect juxtapositions, thus placing greater emphasis on tone and process. Across the book, McCloud identifies other potential means of artistic expression—including the use of color or line—which might broaden the vocabulary of contemporary comics, looking for exemplars among his contemporaries. McCloud's desire to think globally about comics goes hand in hand with his eagerness to explore alternative possibilities that have been constrained within the American tradition.

In a critique of *Understanding Comics*, published in *The Comics Journal* in 2001, the New Zealand-based comics creator Dylan Horrocks notes that the book has become "something of a manifesto for many in the comics community. It constructs a way of talking about comics that affirms and supports our longing for critical respectability and seems to offer an escape from the cultural ghetto" (p. 1). Horrocks, however, called attention to the ways McCloud's otherwise expansive definition also set borders and boundaries and directed attention away from other possible understandings of the medium: "Nowhere in *Understanding Comics* does Scott attempt to justify why 'Sequential Art' should be seen as the one definitive element in comics to the exclusion of all others: the combination of words and pictures, the use of certain conventions (e.g., speech balloons, panel borders), particular formats, styles, genres, etc." (2001, p. 2). Horrocks, for example, explores the consequences of McCloud's emphasis on the pictorial rather than the verbal dimensions of comics or his insistence that children's picture books or single-panel cartoons do not constitute sequential art.

McCloud was the only one of the artist/theorists discussed here to explore his ideas via fully adopting the comic book format (which he used with self-conscious wit), rather than a more traditional mix of texts and illustrations. All of these works are multi-modal, in the sense that they use words and images, in various combinations, to explore their ideas. As such, they exist alongside other multi-modal works of art criticism and theory such as, say, John Berger's *Ways of Seeing* (1990) and Marshall McLuhan and Quentin Fiore's *The Medium Is the Massage* (1967), both of which used collages of images to convey far more than the authors could express through words. There are certainly examples of filmmakers who have used the cinema to help people look at moving images in new ways—works by Noel Burch (*What Do These Old Films Mean?*), Jean-Luc Goddard (*Letter to Jane, Histoire du Cinema*) and Martin Scorsese (*A Personal Journey through American Movies*) come to mind here—but there seems to be a unique opportunity in the case of comics to combine texts and images to advance critical understanding or applied practice. McCloud was able to use comics to demonstrate his core thesis about their unrealized potentials, creating his own examples to illustrate what could not be shown through existing exemplars. Witness his experiments in *Understanding Comics* with non-linear storytelling (1993, p. 105) and with the mixed cues about time that might occur within a single frame (p. 95), to cite two examples. The book also incorporates, for example, a two-page spread charting the ways that 116 different comics artists strike a balance between realism and iconicity within their work (pp. 52–53). Here, McCloud was literally mapping the experimentation taking place in comics in the late 1990s and providing a catalog for readers interested in finding where the interesting work was.

From the start, McCloud signaled that current comic conventions were compromises with particular technological affordances, stressing in his definition "Nothing is said about PAPER and INK. No PRINTING PROCESS is mentioned. Printing ITSELF isn't even specified!" (1993, p. 22). With his second book, *Reinventing Comics* (2000a), McCloud encouraged comics artists to use the emerging potentials of digital media to move beyond current constraints: "the page is an artifact of print, no more intrinsic to comics than staples or india ink. Once released from that box, some will take the shape of the box with them but gradually, comics creators will stretch their limbs and start to explore the design opportunities of an infinite canvas" (2000a, p. 222). Describing comics as a "map of time," an attempt to translate temporal events into spatial representations, McCloud revisits his prehistory of comics: "The ancestors of printed comics drew, painted and carved their time-paths from beginning to end, without interruptions" (2000a, p. 220).

Through his blog, McCloud's ideas about the "infinite canvas" (which McCloud defined in terms of "treating the screen as a window rather than a page") became a movement, with the author showcasing a range of other creators experimenting in new spatial configurations, again serving as a curator of experimental work that might define "the future of comics." McCloud also used his blog to share his own experiments with new screen configurations, including new *Zot!* stories (McCloud, 2000b), which took advantage of long scrolls and the use of blank space between panels to create meaningful time lapses; "My Obsession with Chess" (McCloud, 1998–1999), where sideways and top-to-bottom scrolling between panels were modeled loosely on moves on the game board; and "The Right Number" (McCloud, 2003–2004), where the panels were embedded in each other so moving forward involved drilling deeper into the screen. Looking back, McCloud (2009) confesses, "A handful of cartoonists and developers have taken up that challenge in the decade since I started beating the drum on my own site, with occasionally impressive results, but it's been a rocky road. By the early '00s, most using the term had only a sketchy idea of what it meant, and such formats are still a poor fit for most readers' day-to-day reading habits" (n.p.).

McCloud also acknowledges that perhaps the most persuasive critique of the "infinite canvas" model came from those who felt that artists needed limitations to do their best work and that conventions are enabling mechanisms as much as or more than they are constraints on creative experimentation. As such, it is interesting that each of McCloud's own experiments set its own limits on what formal choices he made. While McCloud celebrated the emergence of alternative spatial configurations of comics, he was far more conservative in terms of how comics dealt with time, seeing comics as essentially a medium of static images and rejecting motion comics and other uses of animation within digital comics as moving toward a different kind of medium altogether: "Additive approaches sidestepped the question of comics' own evolution by letting comics become an undigested lump in multimedia's stomach without ever expanding on the ideas at comics' core" (2009, n.p.).

Across *Reinventing Comics*, McCloud made a range of other speculations—some prescient, some outlandish—about the future of comics in the digital age. Perhaps his most impactful prediction was the idea that, freed of specialty shops where only people already seeking their current content are apt to venture, creators would be free to explore a broader range of content than before, and a range of other niche interests—his examples is chess—might find their audience. Here, McCloud anticipates the web comics movement that has substantially broadened today's comics in terms of the range of content, the diversity of creators, and the dispersion of readers, all central themes for *Reinventing Comics*. (For McCloud's further reflections on how comics have changed in the digital era, see Jenkins, 2014.) McCloud's defense of the digital made him a lightning rod for debates among comics artists, authors, and theorists about how new media might impact their work. (For a useful overview of these debates, see Bukatman, 2002.)

Jessica Abel and Matt Madden; Carl Potts; Paul Karasik and Mark Newgarden

If Eisner's *Comics and Sequential Arts* paved the way for McCloud's *Understanding Comics*, McCloud's *Making Comics* (2006) helped to prepare the way for Jessica Abel and Matt Madden's *Drawing Words & Writing Pictures* (2008) and its follow-up book, *Mastering Comics* (2012). Inspired by how his books had been taken up for instruction, McCloud shifted from speculative aesthetics to a more applied approach in *Making Comics*, offering "storytelling secrets" to those seeking to enter the "comics profession." Here, he consolidated and built upon many of his earlier theories but also tackled more practical questions about tools and techniques and included exercises through which readers could apply his ideas.

Abel and Madden are married independent comics creators who regularly taught comics design and production through the School of the Visual Arts. Abel is best known for such works as *Life Sucks* and *La Perdida* and Madden for *Black Candy* and *Odds Off*. Consequently, Abel and Madden developed their project explicitly as a textbook, "a definitive course from concept to comic in 15 lessons" (Abel and Madden, 2008, subtitle), adopting a visual style throughout which reflects the "multimodal" characteristics Gunther Kress (2009) has identified in contemporary pedagogical works rather than trying (as McCloud had) to fit their ideas into a comic book format. Abel and Madden do use some comics segments, featuring two would-be artists, Craig and Junko, who bring different expectations about the medium and different skills to their work. This allows the duo to model different ways students might learn from their text.

Eisner needed to make the case that comics should be taken seriously as an artform; McCloud took that as a given and used his works to advocate an expanded conception of what that medium could do. Abel and Madden, in turn, were able to take McCloud's more expansive vision as a starting point: "The outer limits of the medium have yet to be discovered; there is a vast incognita waiting for pioneering cartoonist-explorers" (2008, p. xiii). Abel and Madden are able to explicitly build on what has come before, critiquing the definitions of comics offered by Eisner, McCloud, and David Kunzle (whose inclusion hints at the ways academic theory has started to enter into the conversations of comics artists).

Their book's title, *Drawing Words & Writing Pictures*, signals Abel and Madden's recurring focus on the ways that comics integrate words and images:

> Drawing words means to think of the letterforms as a part of the visual language of the comic. Writing pictures means to think of the images as carrying meaning as much as language does. Comics has been compared to calligraphy in the blending of word and image, and to music notation in the visual translation of time passing and emotion written in ink. Making comics requires creators to think fluidly of words and images, to smudge the boundaries, and to artfully blend the two usually distinct forms of communication into a synchronized whole. (p. xiv)

Throughout, the focus is on the techniques artists would need to create their own comics, yet they illustrate their arguments with sophisticated close readings of examples drawn from the canon of historical and contemporary "masters of the comic arts." And they consistently display an interest in comics as a medium that contrasts sharply with other how-to books, such as Nat Gertler and Steve Lieber's *The Complete Idiot's Guide to Creating a Graphic Novel* (2004), which is more narrowly focused on business and craft concerns.

A more interesting and productive contrast might be made with Carl Potts' *The DC Comics Guide to Creating Comics: Inside the Art of Visual Storytelling* (2013). Potts worked for several decades as a trainer of new comics artists for Marvel, became a consultant for DC and other publishers, and developed his ideas about visual storytelling from a presentation he gave on the subject at the 1993 Comics Arts Conference. Unlike Eisner, Spiegelman, McCloud, or Abel and Madden, Potts maintains a strong focus on superhero comics (reflecting his particular set of experiences in the industry), with an emphasis on the ways that the visual presentation of the material "affects the audience" (2013, p. 33).

Much of his vocabulary for discussing visual storytelling derives from established film-making practices (close-ups, zooms, tracking shots, montage), rather than the development of a medium-specific vocabulary. For example, Potts describes the comics artist as fulfilling the roles that might be served in film by the director, the cinematographer, the casting director, the lighting director, the set designer, the editor, and so forth (2013, p. 33). As with the traditions of classical Hollywood style, Potts argues that comics technique serves the story best when it is essentially invisible: "The creators' choices and execution will appear seamless—seemingly self-evident as the best way to execute the stories!" (2013, p. 24) For Potts, visual storytelling in comics is less an art than it is a craft—a means of engaging and entertaining a mass audience with stories that are immediately accessible and comprehensible. By contrast, most of the examples that Abel and Madden draw upon come from the alternative comics tradition; their examples reflect their belief that the most innovative and interesting work was coming from artists who enjoyed some degree of freedom from the major publishers.

Perhaps the most distinctive feature of Abel and Madden's work is a focus on permutations of basic story types or the different possibilities that an artist might explore in translating a core action into a single panel (2008, p. 153). Madden has taken this idea of permutation even further in his *99 Ways to Tell a Story: Exercises in Style* (2005), a work inspired by Raymond Queneau—a French novelist and poet who was active in the Ouvroir de littérature potentielle (Oulipo) movement. Here, Madden introduces what he calls a "template story" involving a man working late, checking the time, and looking for a snack in his refrigerator and redraws it to explore a range of different narrational techniques, visual styles, and genre conventions. As he explains, "Suddenly it's clear that what appear to be merely 'stylistic' choices are in fact an essential part of the story. In reading these comics you have the opportunity to question the effects that ways of telling have on what is being told, and just as important, to enjoy the rich variety of approaches available to the artist in comics and in other media" (Madden, 2005, p. 1).

Madden's focus on how visual storytelling can add greater dynamism to what remains a fairly basic narrative structure, consciously or not, echoes a much earlier piece, "Wally Wood's 22 Panels That Always Work!!" Wood is best known today for his contributions to EC horror comics and *Mad* in the 1950s and can be seen as emblematic of the kinds of mastery over craft that emerged from decades of work-for-hire within the industry. No one is sure when Wood produced his "22 Panels," which seeks to demonstrate a range of techniques artists might use "to get some variety into those boring panels where some dumb writer has a bunch of lame characters sitting around and talking for page after page!" But, the piece resurfaced in 1980 and has been widely circulated amongst artists working in the industry, many of whom have adopted his panels into their own projects or have published their own versions as homage.

Abel and Madden's focus on permutations within the comics language will be pushed even further by the yet-to-be published *How to Read Nancy: The Elements of Comics in Three Easy Panels* (Karasik and Newgarden, forthcoming). Paul Karasik is perhaps best known for his collaboration with David Mazzucchelli on *City of Glass*, and Mark Newgarden is part of a generation of new artists introduced to the world through *Raw*. Their book will be based on a 1988 essay they co-authored that shows how these two veteran comics artists, both noted for their experimental approaches, seek to understand what may seem on the surface to be a simple, even simple-minded, comic strip: Ernie Bushmiller's *Nancy*. But, they argue, "like architect Mies Van Der Rohe [or others they compare him to, such as Buster Keaton or Jacques Tati] the simplicity is a carefully designed function of a complex amalgam of formal rules laid out by the designer" (1988). By comparing similar gags across a range of daily strips, the authors are able to explore themes and variations (for example, the different uses he made of recurring props, such as a bathroom plunger) to illustrate the kinds of complex "problem solving" that enabled Bushmiller to create work that achieved its desired impact, "the gag reflex," for decades.

Ivan Brunetti and Lynda Barry

I will close my essay with two recent works—Ivan Brunetti's *Cartooning: Philosophy and Practice* (2011) and Lynda Barry's *Syllabus: Notes from an Accidental Professor* (2014)—both of which might be described as "anti-theory" or "anti-formalist" textbooks, in that their pedagogy strips aside preconceptions and encourages students to rely more fully on their unconscious minds through acts of improvisation. Brunetti and Barry both are veterans of the underground comics movement, which has stressed pushing past some of the taboos that shaped earlier work in the comics medium, and they are known for their uninhibited and, in the case of Barry, increasingly experimental art practice. Celebrating the untutored nature of earlier moments in the history of comics, Brunetti writes, "Cartoonists of my generation and earlier at least had something to work against (disdain or outright indifference towards cartooning as a potential art form), which forced upon them a certain obsessive quality, as they pluckily created their own rules; this, in turn, made their work unique, visceral, and compelling" (2011, p. 3). He does recognize a place for craft, which involves mastery over basic tools and techniques: "Rules are really just a safety net that allows us to get started; once the pencil hits the paper, everything changes, and one has to allow the ideas, characters, and stories to take on a life of their own" (Brunetti, 2011, p. 6). But he quickly pushes toward a more intuitive understanding of cartooning as "a translation of how we experience, structure, and remember the world" (Brunetti, 2011, p. 8). Brunetti's advice stresses letting go of conscious problem solving: "let your stream of consciousness guide you" (2011, p. 28), "let your mind and hand wander" (p. 34), draw "whatever strikes your fancy" (p. 40). He celebrates Chris Ware's idea that cartooning is "dreaming on paper" (Brunetti, 2011, p. 49). Art, he tells us in wrapping up the book, is "somewhat like spit.

It does not repulse or even worry us while it is still inside of us, but once it exits our body, it becomes disgusting" (Brunetti, 2011, p. 73). Such primitivist turns are familiar in avant-garde discourse, though this focus on uncensored personal expression runs counter to the commercial history of comics as a popular art form.

Similarly, Lynda Barry stresses that the only way to understand how comics work is "by making things. Thinking about it, theorizing about it, chatting about it will not get you there" (2014, p. 72). Elsewhere, she suggests, "They don't involve the talking part of us which is a part that came after we could already use the languages of music and dancing and pictures. Every baby old enough to hold a crayon can already use and understand these 3 languages, sometimes all at once" (Barry, 2014, p. 14). Like Eisner and McCloud, Barry is interested in how we might connect theories of the mind to theories of artistic practice, but her version is less about the cognitive than the more affective dimensions of art, taking its inspiration from the work of psychologist Ian McGilchrist (2012): "How do images move and transfer? Something inside one person takes external form—contained by a poem, story, picture, melody, play, etc.—and through a certain kind of engagement is transferred to the inside of someone else" (Barry, 2014, p. 9).

Barry dedicated her book to her own art teacher, Evergreen State University's Marilyn Frasca, who "showed me ways of using these simple things—our hands, a pen, and some paper—as both a navigation and expedition device, one that could reliably carry me into my past, deeper into my present, or further into a place I have come to call 'the image world'—a place we all know, even if we don't notice knowing until someone reminds us of its ever-present existence" (2014, p. 4). Once again, the visual is seen as pre-articulate, if not pre-literate, a space within the unconscious mind we can only reach by pushing away rational analysis. Barry calls this space "the unthinkable" (2014, p. 10). If McCloud represents himself across his work as a kind of professorial figure (one who grows old as the artist himself has matured), Barry depicts herself variously as a monkey or Chewbacca, figures that suggest a reliance on instinct and impulse rather than knowledge. Her approach is closely linked to the associative writing practices of the surrealists: "I know if I can just keep them drawing without thinking about it too much, something quite original will appear ... almost by itself" (Barry, 2014, p. 21).

Both Brunetti and Barry do not speak about visual literacy but rather see comics as tapping something more basic—an extension of the ways humans think. Brunetti sees "doodling" as the roots of cartooning: "As the simplest doodle emerges, when we really have too little time to think about the drawing, we get closer to the 'idea' or essence of the thing being drawn. Here we begin to see the universal, latent, symbolic, visual, mnemonic language that is comics" (2011, pp. 66–67). Brunetti's focus on the doodle harkens back to Töpffer, who, as David Kunzle (2007) notes, used doodled faces to show how the simplest set of lines could nevertheless be deployed to communicate human emotion and personality. Barry focuses on the vitality of children's art (long a source of inspiration for modern artists) and the ways the naturalness and spontaneity of such work gets lost as adults convince themselves they do not know how to express themselves through drawing. To get her students back to this state, she gave them endless activities involving coloring books or rewarded their efforts with popular children's candies. In a similar vein, Brunetti's *Aesthetics* reproduces some of his own childhood drawings, suggesting they represented his "best period as an artist" because "the drawings are careful, sincere, and free of pretension" (2013, n.p.) This focus on free association is reflected in the design of Lynda Barry's pages, which include both artwork produced by her students through her in-class experiments and her own free drawing in a range of different styles. Her pages do rely on juxtaposition between words and texts but are non-linear, refusing to work in relation to predictable grids or patterns, and there is little interest here in how comics might function beyond the level of the individual image.

The alternative examples offered by Brunetti and Barry help us to understand how the other comics artists and theorists discussed here might be seen as fitting within a coherent tradition, each building on the other's work, as they fostered greater acceptance of comics as an art form and recognition of its unrealized potentials as a medium. They each proposed a language or lexicon of comics, emphasizing the conscious design choices through which graphic artists structure our sense of time and space or convey narrative information. They each stressed core literacies that allow readers to go beyond the visual data provided, to make meaning from "expressive anatomy" or to navigate the complex interplay of words and images. They map core codes and conventions through which contemporary comics operate as well as outline possible permutations on the level of different national traditions, different genres, and different artistic priorities and temperaments. They sought to train readers in the core elements of their craft (increasingly within a formal educational context, as many comics artists support themselves through their teaching), but they also sought to develop a deeper critical appreciation for the still-evolving canon of landmark comics. A core tension in this tradition centers on the difference between classicists (such as Potts and, to some degree, Eisner), who emphasize the craft of visual storytelling, and experimentalists (such as McCloud, Abel and Madden, etc.), who seek to expand opportunities for self-expression and experimentation within the medium.

Brunetti and Barry also see their books as an extension of their teaching: Brunetti at the Columbia College Chicago and the University of Chicago and Barry at the University of Wisconsin-Madison. But they both seek to strip away intellectual pretensions and get back to the core building blocks of cartooning, which for them have to do with a human urge to communicate their perceptions of the world to someone else through simple and direct drawings. Their focus is on expression rather than on convention, and experimentation for them is about finding the most direct way back to pure perceptions.

Bibliography

Abel, J. and Madden, M. (2008) *Drawing Words & Writing Pictures*, New York: First Second.
Abel, J. and Madden, M. (2012) *Mastering Comics*, New York: First Second.
Alton, J. (1985) *Painting with Light*, Berkeley: University of California Press.
Barry, L. (2014) *Syllabus: notes from an Accidental Professor*, Montreal: Drawn and Quarterly.
Beaty, B. (2005) *Fredric Wertham and the Critique of Mass Culture*, Jackson: University Press of Mississippi.
Berger, John. 1990. *Ways of Seeing*, New York: Penguin.
Bordwell, D. (1989) 'Historical poetics of cinema', in R. B. Palmer (ed.) *The Cinematic Text: methods and approaches*, New York: AMS Press, 369–98.
Bruner, J. (1973) *Beyond the Information Given: the psychology of knowing*, New York: W.W. Norton.
Brunetti, I. (2011) *Cartooning: philosophy and practice*, New Haven: Yale University Press.
Brunetti, I. (2013) *Aesthetics: a memoir*, New Haven: Yale University Press.
Bukatman, S. (2002) 'Online comics and the reframing of the moving image', in D. Harries (ed.) *The New Media Book*, London: British Film Institute, 133–43.
Carroll, N. (1996) *Theorizing the Moving Image*, Cambridge: Cambridge University Press.

Eisenstein, S. (1949) *Film Form: essays in film theory*. Edited and translated by Jay Leyda, New York: Harcourt.
Eisner, W. (1985) *Comics and Sequential Art*, New York: W.W. Norton.
Eisner, W. (1996) *Graphic Storytelling and Visual Narrative*, New York: W.W. Norton.
Eisner, W. (2008) *Expressive Anatomy for Comics and Narrative*, New York: W.W. Norton.
Eisner, W. (2011) *PS Magazine: the best of the preventive maintenance monthly*, New York: Harry N. Abrams.
Gertler, N. and Lieber, S. (2004) *The Complete Idiot's Guide to Creating a Graphic Novel*, New York: Alpha.
Gombrich, E.H. (1960) *Art and Illusion: a study in the psychology of pictorial representation*, Princeton: Princeton University Press.
Harvey, R.C. (1994) *The Art of the Funnies: an aesthetic history*, Jackson: University Press of Mississippi.
Horrocks, D. (2001) 'Inventing comics: Scott McCloud's definition of comics', *Comics Journal* 234, June, as posted at: http://www.hicksville.co.nz/Inventing%20Comics.htm.
Jenkins, H. (2014) 'Scott McCloud reimagines the future of comics', *Confessions of an Aca-Fan*, November 7. http://henryjenkins.org/2014/11/scott-mccloud-reimagines-the-future-of-comics.html.
Jenkins, H. (2015) 'Archival, ephemeral, and residual: the functions of early comics in Art Spiegelman's *In The Shadow of No Towers*', in D. Stein and J. Thon (eds.) *From Comic Strips to Graphic Novels: contributions to the theory and history of graphic narrative*, Berlin: Walter de Gruyter, 301–22.
Karasik, P. and Newgarden, M. (1988) How to read *Nancy*. Available online at *Laffpix*, http://www.laffpix.com/howtoreadnancy.pdf. Originally published in Walker, B. (1988) *The Best of Ernie Bushmiller's Nancy*, Wilton, CT: Comicana, 98–105.
Karasik, P. and Newgarden, M. [Forthcoming] *How to Read Nancy: the elements of comics in three easy panels*, Seattle: Fantagraphics.
Kress, G. (2009) *Multimodality: a social semiotic approach to contemporary communication*, New York: Routledge.
Kunzle, D. (2007) *Father of the Comic Strip: Rodolphe Töpffer*, Jackson: University Press of Mississippi.
Madden, M. (2005) *99 Ways to Tell a Story: exercises in style*, New York: Chamberlain Brothers.
McCloud, S. (1993) *Understanding Comics: the invisible art*, Northhampton, MA: Tundra.
McCloud, S. (1998–1999) 'My obsession with chess', *Scott McCloud*. http://scottmccloud.com/1-webcomics/chess/index.html.
McCloud, S. (2000a) *Reinventing Comics*, New York: DC.
McCloud, S. (2000b) *Zot!* online: hearts & minds. *Scott McCloud*. http://scottmccloud.com/1-webcomics/zot/index.html.
McCloud, S. (2003–2004) 'The right number', *Scott McCloud*. http://scottmccloud.com/1-webcomics/trn-intro/index.html.
McCloud, S. (2006) *Making Comics*, New York: Harper.
McCloud, S. (2009) 'The 'Infinite Canvas'', *Scott McCloud*. http://scottmccloud.com/4-inventions/canvas/index.html.
McGilchrist, I. (2012) *The Master and His Emissary: the divided brain and the making of the western world*, New Haven: Yale University Press.
McLaughlin, T. (1996) *Street Smarts and Critical Theory: listening to the vernacular*, Madison: University of Wisconsin Press.
McLuhan, M. and Fiore, Q. (1967) *The Medium Is the Massage*, Berkeley: Ginko Press.
Miller, A. and Beaty, B. eds. (2014) *The French Comics Theory Reader*, Leuven: Leuven University Press.
Potts, C. (2013) *The DC Comics Guide to Creating Comics: inside the art of visual storytelling*, New York: DC.
Schumacher, M. (2010) *Will Eisner: a dreamer's life in comics*, New York: Bloomsbury.
Sims, D. (2012) 'Wally Wood's 22 panels that always work!!', *A Moment of Cerebus*, July 15. http://momentofcerebus.blogspot.com/2012/07/wally-woods-22-panels-that-always-work.html.

Smith, G.M. (2010) 'Will Eisner: vaudevillian of the cityscape', in J. Ahrens and A. Meteling (eds.) *Comics and the City: urban space in print, picture and sequence*, New York: Continuum, 183–98.
Smolderen, T. (2014) *The Origins of Comics from William Hogarth to Winsor McCay*, Jackson: University Press of Mississippi.
Spiegelman, A. (2013) *Co-Mix: a retrospective of comics, graphics, and scraps*, Montreal: Drawn and Quarterly.
Tarkovsky, A. (1989) *Sculpting in Time: the great Russian filmmaker discusses his art*, Austin: University of Texas Press.
Töpffer, R. (1845) *Essai de Physiognomonie*, Geneva: Schmid.
Truffaut, F. (1967) *Hitchcock*, New York: Simon and Schuster.
Walker, M. (1980) *The Lexicon of Comicana*, Lincoln, NB: Authors Guild.
Waugh, C. (1947) *The Comics*, Jackson: University Press of Mississippi.
Wertham, F. (1954) *The Seduction of The Innocent*, New York: Amereon.
Wiese, E., trans. (1965) *Enter: the comics: Rodolphe Topffer's essay on physiognomy and the true story of Monsieur Crepin*, Lincoln: University of Nebraska Press.

12
FORMALIST THEORY
Academics

Ann Miller

My title is not an inviting one: it suggests a sterile concern with the technical aspects of a medium that is beloved above all for its unruliness and uninhibited imagination. The effort to catalogue formal resources has, moreover, often been coupled with a search for definitions, and definitional debates have escalated into skirmishes over origins, with starting points determined on the basis of the presence (or absence) of certain components. For example, those for whom speech balloons are a defining feature disqualify the claim of the Swiss schoolmaster Rodolphe Töpffer to be regarded as the inaugurator of the medium in the 1830s, on the grounds that the texts in his sequential satirical cartoon stories are set out beneath the images. They prefer to anoint instead the American cartoonist Richard Outcault, who used speech balloons in his strip *The Yellow Kid* in 1896. Although they had appeared in single-image political cartoons since the 18th century, this was the first time speech balloons had been used in a sequential comics narrative (Blackbeard, 1995, p. 70).

These demarcation disputes may now appear pedantic and unproductive, but they were perhaps a necessary stage in the constitution of comics as a recognized art form. The earliest definition of the medium is that of Töpffer himself, a contender, in the view of some, for not only founding father but also for first comics theoretician. While eschewing speech balloons, he nonetheless insisted in 1837 on the "mixed" nature of his "stories in engravings" (qtd. in Groensteen, 2014, p. 219), an "invention," a "discovery," that, as he alleged with mock hyperbole in 1842, would "change the face of the universe and the future of humanity" (p. 227). Thus it was, that, according to the major French-language comics theorist Thierry Groensteen, comics "achieved self-awareness" and "came to exist as a cultural object" (Groensteen, 2014, p. 103). It would, though, be a long time before that object attained anything approaching acceptance as a medium of artistic expression. By the 1970s, it had attracted the attention of French-language academics, who approached it through the discipline of semiology (or semiotics), the science of signs. Their concern through that decade and the next to identify the specific signifying practices of comics, sometimes in contrast with other media such as cinema (see, for example, Lacassin, 1971; Fresnault-Deruelle, 1972; Masson 1985), can be attributed, according to French media sociologist Éric Maigret, to the need for valorization: comics still suffered from a lack of cultural self-assurance

(Maigret, 2012, pp. 6–7). If Anglo-Saxon critics were less preoccupied with formal aspects of the medium at that time, this is because they were not embarking on a bid for legitimization: Italian "fumettologo" (comics expert) Matteo Stefanelli points out that comics were first visible in Anglo-Saxon academe as a branch of mass communications research and of the nascent discipline of cultural studies (2012, pp. 37–39). It was from outside the portals of the university that American critics entered the definitional fray: while cartoonist Scott McCloud, following on from his illustrious predecessor Will Eisner, who had coined the term "sequential art" (Eisner, 1985), famously proposed "juxtaposed pictorial and other images in deliberate sequence" (McCloud, 1993, p. 9), fellow cartoonist Robert C. Harvey asserted that the "essential character of the medium" lay in the mix of verbal and visual content (1996, p. 246).

More recent critical work, both European and American, has disentangled formal concerns from the essentializing compulsions that drove the wrangling over definitions and origins. In 1999, Thierry Groensteen (at that time the director of the comics museum that was part of the French national comics center in Angoulême) produced his key theoretical study, *Système de la bande dessinée* [The System of Comics], based on the doctoral thesis that he had defended at the University of Toulouse three years earlier. Groensteen, who, during his period as editor of the influential journal *Cahiers de la bande dessinée* [Notebooks on Comics] from 1984 to 1988, had invited, and contributed to, a series of articles that examined the "specificity" question, now comprehensively demonstrated the ultimate futility of the quest for definitions. He did so by drawing up a list of works that most of us would describe as "comics" although they lack some element that has been categorized as essential by one or another theorist (Groensteen, 1999, pp. 14–21). Groensteen ended by proffering, as the only ontological principle that he was prepared to admit, the minimalist "iconic solidarity": in other words, comics is a medium made up of images that are brought together in a non-random way (1999, p. 21).

A decade later, attempts to construct a definitive narrative of origins for the medium were dealt a decisive blow by the publication of an important book by Belgian comics historian Thierry Smolderen, with a significant plural in its title, *Les Naissances de la bande dessinée* [The Origins of Comics]. In this book, Smolderen contests any conception of comics as a medium existing in isolation from others, having progressed toward a stable, describable form whose origin can be retrospectively pinpointed. On the contrary, he argues that its history is one of hybridization, its devices drawn from a variety of sources including medieval phylactera (repurposed from their original labeling function) and single-image cartoons (Smolderen, 2009). Smolderen's findings are corroborated by some research that had been undertaken by American comics scholar Joseph Witek a decade earlier, in a paper that was presented at the International Comic Arts Forum in 1999, but that was more widely circulated in *A Comic Studies Reader* published in 2009, the same year as Smolderen's book. Witek investigated two features, panel numbers and directional arrows, that were in common use in the 19th and early 20th century, and whose emergence and subsequent disappearance testify to a shifting horizon of reader expectations. He postulates that "comicsness" may simply reside in "a historically contingent and evolving set of reading protocols," and proposes his own pithy (anti-)definition: "to be a comic text means to be *read* as a comic" (Witek, 2009, p. 149).

The urge to delimit "comicsness" or to track the chimera of a "true" lineage has faded as the need to secure the cultural legitimacy of the medium has become less pressing, partly as a result of the small-press explosion of the 1990s, which brought an aura of intellectualism and a new readership, and partly as a result of a blurring of the boundaries not only between "high" and "low" cultures, but also among different media, as comics have migrated to phone or tablet screens and undergone various forms of adaptation. Maigret, introducing an edited volume on comics as a media culture, argues that any ontology must be open ended, and must situate comics within a media landscape that includes transmediality and convergence culture (Maigret, 2012). This does not, though, mean that critics have lost interest in investigating the formal properties of comics. In the same volume, Belgian communications theorist Philippe Marion proposes a (plural) poetics of comics that would acknowledge its intersection with other cultural traditions, but that would nonetheless investigate the phenomenon of "médiagénie": the inter-penetration between an expressive project and the potential of the medium (Marion, 2012), in other words, the nitty-gritty of pages, panels, and graphic lines.

In my present enterprise of trying to summarize formal approaches to the medium, I will be concerned, like Groensteen (in what he calls a "neo-semiotic" approach), with comics as "a set of mechanisms that produce meaning" (however contingent they may be) with the aim of elucidating the "intelligibility" of the medium (Groensteen, 1999, p. 2). The "reading protocols" alluded to by Witek are not just historically variable but must surely also be a function of how alert each reader is to the operation of the "mechanisms" that the medium brings into play. For the American comics theorist Charles Hatfield, the reader's response (which he defines as participation and interpretation) is structured by a set of tensions: between codes of signification (image and text); between single image and image in series; between narrative sequence and page surface; between reading as experience and text as material object (Hatfield, 2005, p. 36). He stresses that he is not setting out an empirical, experimentally verifiable model of reading, but aiming to establish the complexity of the form (2005, p. 36), and so, it might be added, enabling us to become more observant and expert readers. I propose to borrow Hatfield's categories. My account will be highly selective and, like the medium itself, will have many gaps and silences. French-language theorists will feature more strongly than their English-language counterparts, for the good reason that many of the latter are dealt with elsewhere in this volume under different headings.

Code vs. Code (Word vs. Image)

According to Groensteen, the "impossible marriage" between text and image is responsible for the cultural disdain in which comics was long held (Groensteen, 2006, p. 23). The hugely influential American theorist of word and image, W. J. T. Mitchell, refers to the "rhetoric of purity," from Gotthold Ephraim Lessing in the 18th century to Clement Greenberg, the 20th century advocate of high modernism, that has objected to the contamination of the image by language (Mitchell, 1994, pp. 96–97). This rhetoric is challenged, argues Mitchell, by the "collapse of the distinction between writing and drawing" in the illuminated books of William Blake (1994, p. 91). His wording is interestingly echoed by Hatfield, for whom comics "collapse the word/image dichotomy," given that "words can be *drawn* and images *written*" (Hatfield, 2005, pp. 36–37). The term "collapse" may be overstating the case, however. On closer inspection, Hatfield does not in fact claim that words and images are interchangeable. He argues instead that there is a tension between them, in that they often "play against each other" and that the tension is made more complex by the tendency of images toward abstraction, and of words to be visually inflected (Hatfield, 2005, pp. 36–37).

These two aspects of word/image hybridity, functional tension and visual convergence, are both, in fact, present in the writings of Rodolphe Töpffer. The Swiss theorist elucidates the first aspect, the tension between verbal and visual elements, in an oft-quoted statement published in 1837, in which he maintains that the drawings without the text "would have only an obscure meaning," and "the text, without the drawings, would mean nothing" (qtd. in Groensteen, 2014, p. 219). Töpffer's insight is essentially into the device responsible for much of the comic appeal of his own work, the counterpoint between exuberant drawings of improbable occurrences and sober, understated text, given that he was as yet the sole exponent of the new medium of "stories in engravings."

A century and a half later, for the American Robert C. Harvey, the "blending of word and picture to the degree that neither makes sense without the other" becomes a defining principle of the now long-established (albeit critically undervalued) medium of comics, although Harvey tends to focus on inter-dependence rather than tension (Harvey, 1996, p. 51). For Harvey, a wordless comic fails fully to exploit the nature of the medium, but so does a comic in which images are merely illustrative, a consequence, he argues, of the division of labor between artists and writers in the comics industry, until the balance was altered by the more dynamic collaboration, as from 1960, of Stan Lee with Jack Kirby and other artists (1996, p. 44). The Belgian cultural theorist Jan Baetens has written extensively on the text/image relationship. In an important book written with fellow Belgian comics theorist Pascal Lefèvre in 1993, a chapter devoted to this question stresses, as Harvey does, the importance of avoiding mere illustration or word/image redundancy and then notes the striking effects achieved by disjunction between words and images, as in the work of the coolly ironical French political comics artist Régis Franc (Baetens and Lefèvre, 1993, pp. 15–25). In 2015, in a book co-written with British cinema and comics historian Hugo Frey, Baetens argues that the advent of the graphic novel has introduced more complex word/image relationships to comics, "not just irony but also unreliable storytelling, multiple storytelling, and self reflectivity" (Baetens and Frey, 2015, p. 149).

Töpffer was similarly prescient of future critical concerns in his remarks on the second aspect of hybridity, the continuity between the style of the drawings and the lettering of the text. In 1844, in correspondence with the artist Cham, who was commissioned to produce a wood-engraved version of one of Töpffer's stories, the Swiss artist deplores the fact that the captions will be type-set rather than handwritten as they had been in his own work, a recognition that the text is itself a visual element, intended to harmonize with the images (qtd in Groensteen, 2014, p. 233). In relation to the drawings, he stresses the importance of speed and spontaneity and of the clarity of the idea. Only essential elements should be kept in, and in this the graphic line resembles spoken or written language, he says (2014, p. 283). He notably prefigures the work of 20th-century semiologists/semioticians through his observation that the graphic line works by convention, not by imitation of nature (2014, p. 281), representing an idea by signs (p. 219).

As a 19th-century writer, Töpffer was unencumbered by the model based on Saussurian linguistics that led some 1970s and 1980s comics semiologists to postulate a "language of comics" by seeking discrete units within the image, like Guy Gauthier's identification of a "digitalized code" based on a paradigm of five versions of Charlie Brown's eyeline, at differing angles from the horizontal (Gauthier, 1976, pp. 117–118). Others, though, such as

Fresnault-Deruelle and Pierre Masson, doubted whether the rigid application of linguistic concepts was appropriate, given the continuous, non-discrete, nature of the visual image (Fresnault-Deruelle, 1972, p. 20; Masson, 1985, pp. 15–16). Their use of the term "language" or "code" differs from that of Gauthier, therefore, and refers simply to the signifying practices that they aimed to illuminate in a medium that had long languished in critical neglect.

Semiologists had a particular fascination for what Fresnault-Deruelle called the "imaging function" of the text (Fresnault-Deruelle, 1972, p. 36), and Bernard Toussaint its "ideogrammaticization" (Toussaint, 1976, p. 82), that is to say the tendency for comics lettering to become not merely a transparent transmitter of linguistic meaning, but a graphic signifier in its own right, unlike the self-effacing typeset lettering to be found in print media. Writing in the 1970s and 1980s, the semiologists tended to focus on the work of Belgian artists such as Hergé, Jacques Martin, or André Franquin who had observed, and in some cases laid down, a number of conventions. These included variations in the shape of speech balloons (such as the wavy outline indicating "thinks"); the use of iconic symbols within them (such as the cog wheels representing the psychic mechanism that conjures up a whiskey bottle in one of Captain Haddock's dreams); and the distortion of words, inside the balloons as dialogue or outside them in the form of onomatopoeic sounds, which could become fat-lettered or jagged at moments of intensity (Fresnault-Deruelle, 1972, pp. 19–40). More recently, work by artists such as the American Chris Ware and the Belgian Dominique Goblet, extreme in its foregrounding of words through their striking visual qualities and in its disruption of the conventional division of the comics page into textual and visual zones, has engendered a new critical vocabulary. Baetens extends Marion's term "graphiation," which refers to the drawing style of the individual artist (Marion, 1993), to cover the highly idiosyncratic and occasionally illegible lettering used by Goblet, the "awkward form of handwriting" that becomes a formal design element of the page (Baetens, 2011, p. 82). Baetens has, in addition, borrowed the term "grammatextuality" from French literary critic Jean-Gérard Lapacherie, in order to denote the "various mechanisms that enhance the visibility of the material qualities of the text" (2011, 82). Words, whose characteristic in Lessing's view was—and should only be—their extension in time, can, in comics, be thoroughly and inventively spatialized.

Narrative Sequence and Page Surface

This heading concerns the tension between the two fundamental comics operations: layout (the design of panels over the page as a whole) and breakdown (the articulation of the narrative sequence into separate and successive panels). The ur-text in which the dual reading process of the comics page was first expounded in detail appeared in 1976 in an article in a special edition of the prestigious semiological journal *Communications* devoted entirely to comics. The author, Pierre Fresnault-Deruelle, had been a pioneer of academic comics study in France with the publication in 1972 of his thesis on the semiotic analysis of comics. Four years later, in his ground-breaking article, he notes that the arrangement of formal features on the flat surface of the page may create what he calls a "tabular effect," whereby the page as a whole is perceived as a *tableau*, a unified composition. This effect tends to break up the linear narrative flow between panels invested with perspectival depth and so threatens the fictional illusion for the reader. Fresnault-Deruelle's insight that the comics page tends simultaneously to the "mosaic" and the "frieze" (1976, p. 23) has remained influential.

The linear/tabular distinction was subsequently taken up by Benoît Peeters, French comics scriptwriter (collaborator of Belgian artist François Schuiten on the *Cities of the Fantastic* series), novelist, and cultural commentator, in his 1991 book *Case, Planche, Récit* [Panel, Page, Narrative]. Peeters' classification posits four types of comics page, according to the dominance of the temporally ordered linear narrative (along which the reader "slides") or the spatially arranged tabular surface (at which the reader may "stare"), and the relationship of dependency or autonomy between the two opposing tendencies (Peeters, 1991, pp. 34–53). The dominance of the linear dimension will produce either a "rhetorical" grid in which the size and shape of frames are adjusted according to the needs of the story (as in *Tintin*), and which is therefore "dependent" on it, or a "conventional," "waffle-iron" grid, which pre-exists narrative breakdown and is therefore "autonomous" in relation to the narrative. The conventional grid, often imposed on artists in the early days of comics, tends to become transparent, Peeters argues, although he notes that the immobility of framing can be used to great effect (as it is in the satirical comics of Clare Bretécher, which draw attention to the smallest of changes in expression or posture of her Parisian would-be intellectuals). The dominance of the tabular dimension will produce a "decorative" grid if it has no narrative relevance (as in the aesthetic experimentation of science fiction comics artist Philippe Druillet, author of the *Lone Sloane* saga, whose flamboyant compositions tend to arrest the progression of the story), and a "productive" grid if the arrangement of panels actually engenders the story (as in an example from Winsor McCay, where panels framed in a descending-stair pattern determine the height of characters: this can be contrasted to the "rhetorical" grid used by Hergé, where the size and shape of panel frames are adapted to their contents). In the second edition of his book, published in 1998, Peeters acknowledged that the "conventional" grid, by exacerbation of the constraint, could itself become productive, as in "Demi-Tour," a comic he himself scripted, based on a thematic principle of parallelism.

Peeters' typology has since given rise to much debate (although he anticipates in his book the charge that the boundaries between categories are not always clear). The first important response was that of Groensteen, in 1999. He argues that Peeters does not take sufficient account of the perceptual and cognitive activity of the reader (1999, p. 110) and goes on to propose a different typology, based on the objective criterion of regularity versus irregularity and the subjective judgment of the reader as to whether the page is ostentatious or discreet. These two categories are independent of each other: for example, a regular framework, as in *Watchmen*, can be highly ostentatious. On the other hand, although Peeters' "rhetorical" category is irregular, it is so common as to be the default category and is therefore unremarkable, or, in Groensteen's term, discreet. In the case of an ostentatious layout, the artist's motivations should be evaluated, Groensteen suggests: is the page intended to be merely decorative, or is it rhetorical (by resonating with the subject matter)? He offers the example of a dislocated layout that may correspond to a chaotic situation or the madness of a protagonist. He sums up his approach as having taken account of the objective evidence of regularity or irregularity, the reader's subjective appreciation of ostentatiousness or discreetness, and the (presumed) intention of the author (1999, pp. 108–119).

The "reader" is of course an abstraction, constructed by the text but not bound by it, whether sliding or staring. In his monumental work on "drawn literatures," which contextualizes comics in relation to their literary antecedents and contests the claims and conclusions of comics semiologists, Harry Morgan (French novelist, artist, and cultural theorist) argues that the constraint is a loose one. He maintains that since the reader is not obliged to follow the path laid out by the artist, the linear/tabular distinction is irrelevant and that, moreover, where writing is always "a question of thread," drawing, even when arranged into discontinuous units, is "always a question of surface" (Morgan, 2003, pp. 34–35).

It is true that we cannot know to what extent the comics reader's itinerary over the page is conditioned by the artist's choices. (The American cognitive psychologist Neil Cohn has carried out empirical experiments with eye-tracking, but he is not concerned with layout in relation to an artistic project. See, for example, Cohn, 2014.) The French theorist Renaud Chavanne, while admitting that "grazing" is always an option, insists nonetheless that the emergence of meaning depends on the structuring by the artist of the reader's trajectory. Chavanne, who has had a long involvement with small-press comics theory journals, and who since 2011 has organized an annual comics festival in Paris dedicated to productive dialogue between artists and theorists, developed his own approach in the course of writing a first book based on analysis of the intricate page compositions of Belgian artist Edgar P. Jacobs (Chavanne, 2005). On the basis of the subsequent study of thousands of comics of varying national origins, he elaborated a framework and notation system that builds on the Peeters/Groensteen notions of regular and rhetorical composition but brings considerable precision to the description of the comics page (2010). For Chavanne, the strip, rather than the page, is fundamental in organizing the reading path, although it is made more complex by "fragmentation," which allows for the inclusion of smaller, vertically aligned panels (that may then be further split). Strip-by-strip progression does not exclude appreciation of the composition in its totality, and certain patterns particularly emphasize symmetry or other spatial relationships. The visual distinctness of strips may be diminished (for example in the "ultra-strip" where smaller panels are overlaid onto a large background image, exemplified by a Mike McMahon *Judge Dredd* page, or through the hyperfragmentation deployed in Chris Ware's *Jimmy Corrigan*), without jeopardizing their role in determining the reading order, especially as the eye is in any case guided by compositional features of the image and by the positioning of gutters and narrative boxes. However, certain types of layout based on the inter-meshing of frames from different strips, or a centripetal construction around a central frame, will tend to disrupt linear reading protocols. Chavanne goes on to consider a small number of comics that adopt much freer ways of occupying the compositional space, such as Ware's use of "aggregates" (images grouped together coherently, but not organized into strips), and plurilinear pathways in *Quimby the Mouse* that emulate the non-linear workings of memory.

Single Image and Image in Series

Under this heading, I will look first at attempts by theorists to account for the way in which readers make sense of images as part of a sequence, second at analyses of the relations of both difference and sameness between panels, third at approaches to the question of rhythm in comics, and finally at the question of non-narrative links between images, threaded through an entire work.

As readers, we may be tempted to "build our nest" in a single panel, as Belgian art historian and playwright Pierre Sterckx puts it in his contribution to a series on "memorable panels" that ran in *Les Cahiers de la bande dessinée* (Sterckx, 1984, p. 67), but we are always conscious of the surrounding images, or "perifield," in the useful term coined by Peeters: the panel not only seizes a moment and frames it but also displays its nature as a fragment of a greater whole (Peeters, 1991, p. 15). Some theorists have focused on the gutter as a site of meaning production. Peeters postulates it as the locus of a "ghost-panel" the reader constructs (1991, p. 27), and McCloud's use of the term "closure" to describe the reader's activity in creating continuity across frame boundaries has had considerable currency among comics theorists (McCloud, 1993, pp. 60–93). Indeed, Hatfield's choice of the word "series" rather than "sequence" relates to the division of labor between the artist, whose task is breakdown, and the reader, whose task is closure: the former creates a "series" that the latter translates into a "sequence" (Hatfield, 2005, p. 41). However, others have rejected the "over-valuation" of the gutter, which Morgan compares to the obsession with montage of early cinema theorists (Morgan, 2003, p. 356). Groensteen emphasizes that an articulated discourse is constructed from the images, not the gaps (Groensteen, 1999, pp. 131–135). The sequence is given an internal dynamic by a process of *mise-en-scène,* involving the selection of angles, composition, and other parameters of the image, even if the semantic richness of a panel is not reducible to its function within the narrative (Groensteen, 1999, pp. 142, 150). Moreover, he points out that meaning may be established retroactively: reading is, in that sense, always multidirectional, or "plurivectoral" (Groensteen, 1999, pp. 127–130). In 2011, Groensteen revisited the question of sequentiality and this time set out to analyze how readers make sense of the inter-frame hiatus. He refers to McCloud's notion of closure but sees it as too limited, concerning only the way that links are made between objects in the story world. Groensteen argues instead that different modes of reading are required by different kinds of artistic project: out of what is *shown,* readers may simply need to infer what has *intervened.* In more complex or poetic comics, however, interpretation of what is *signified* will be required, as the juxtaposition may be based on stylistic, metaphorical, or rhythmic associations (Groensteen, 2011, pp. 36–41).

The comics grid, or "multiframe," in the term coined by Belgian philosopher Henri Van Lier (1988, p. 5) is a mechanism designed both for transformation and iteration, with a built-in dialectic between movement and immobility. Art historian David Kunzle's work on early comics referred to the "graphic speed-up" of 19th-century visual narratives inaugurated by Töpffer's action-packed travel tales, in which his hapless heroes get caught up in manifold chases and catastrophic chain reactions, liberated from the dense background detail of their graphic predecessors, like the protagonists of Hogarth's moralistic etchings series, in which each episode of their "progress" is separated from the next by weeks or months (Kunzle, 1973, pp. 360–363). The capacity of comics for rapidity and transmutation was stressed by much early theoretical work. Van Lier memorably described the medium as "mutational and permutational" (1988, p. 5), and Peeters called it a "theatre of specific metamorphoses," citing *Little Nemo* for its virtuoso exploitation of this principle (Peeters, 1991, pp. 6, 23–24). However, the semiologist Masson, writing in 1985 and drawing on the hyperactive heroes of Franco-Belgian comics for most of his examples, had already observed a tendency toward stationary characters and reflection in a small number of works such as *Peanuts* or the comic strips of Jules Feiffer (1985, p. 77). The noticeable slowing-down of 21st-century comics, most obviously those of Chris Ware, has given rise to a new theoretical focus on visual strategies, such as static scenes and repetition, for conveying the subjective experience of the passing of time (see for example Conard and Lambeens, 2012). This change of pace is particularly associated with the thematic of everyday life as portrayed, for example, by French artist Lewis Trondheim or Norwegian artist Jason, in whose work, as the Brazilian scholar Greice Schneider (who has particularly investigated the representation of boredom in comics) notes, causality gives way to "non-eventness." Feelings of inertia and ennui are evoked by Ware or the Finnish comics artist and underground publisher Tommi Musturi, best known for *The Last Book of Hope* series and a more contemplative mood by one of the greatest French exponents of autobiographical comics, Fabrice Neaud, or by manga artist Jiro Taniguchi, often through scenes in which the reader is invited to share the protagonist's viewpoint (Schneider, 2010).

The question of time in comics is complex and has been theorized by Baetens and Lefèvre (1993), and subsequently by Groensteen (2011) as a matter of rhythm. The three theorists agree that the rhythm of narrating is not determined by time elapsed within the diegesis, since duration can be accelerated between frames but also dilated. In Groensteen's example of Robert Crumb's *Mr. Natural*, days and weeks go by between panels, or, conversely, the recounting of a few seconds takes up as many as six panels. Baetens and Lefèvre demonstrate how a visual rhythm can be created by patterning on a page, as in the checkerboard design of *Watchmen*. Groensteen offers a more detailed analysis: the basic cadence provided by the regular grid is accentuated by repetition and alternation (of iconic content or other features such as color, framing, and angle), while a more complex rhythm is created by periodic alternation, where a group of panels, identifiable by some visual feature (such as the vertical alignment that Chavanne calls "fragmentation"), form a "stanza" that stands out against the background beat (2011, p. 162). In the case of a rhetorical grid, there is no background beat, but instances of localized regularity, such as "serial effects" of identical framing akin to a sequence shot in cinema, may stand out (2011, p. 160). Groensteen is clear that these rhythmic effects are not measurable but felt. Of course, neither diegetic time nor rhythm of recounting can determine the rhythm of reading, a function of the level of the reader's engagement with a text that is more or less dense (2011, pp. 148–151), although the artist can attempt to delay us, through the inclusion of text or by framing some element of décor that might otherwise have escaped our attention (1999, pp. 64–68). Groensteen refers to this strategy as exploiting the "reading function" of the frame, one of a series of functions that he enumerates (1999, pp. 49–68).

Beyond layout and breakdown, panels may enter into what Baetens and Lefèvre have called "translinear" relationships (1993, pp. 72–74) and Groensteen has called "braiding" (1999, pp. 95–97). Overlaid onto the narrative sequence may be an infra-narrative series of images that are linked through iconic, semantic, or formal correspondences, forming networks across the page or through the book, such as the motif of the circle in *Watchmen* (1999, p. 173). These resonances are not essential to narrative development (and so may go unnoticed without detriment to understanding at the level of plot), but they can "texturize" it and enrich reading (1999, pp. 174, 181). To the tensions between narrative sequence and page surface, and between single image and image in series, we can, then, add a supplementary tension: between narrative sequence and braided series.

Text as Experience vs. Text as Object

Harry Morgan has referred to the "codexité" of comics (2003, pp. 61–63), which we might translate as "bookness," an acknowledgement that the materiality of the comic as object is part of our experience of reading it. Baetens and Lefevre have noted the particular importance of the paratext in setting up expectations: unlike the covers of novels, comics covers are often used as marketing devices, asserting the album as part of a series, for example, although some more ambitious works have integrated the paratext into their artistic project: Martin Vaughn-James, for example, creates an ambiguity in his wordless comic *La Cage*, in which a mysterious space undergoes a gradual metamorphosis, as to the point where the reader leaves the preliminary pages and enters the fictional world (Baetens and Lefèvre, 1993, pp. 75–85).

The book as object was crucial to the change in the comics landscape brought about by the emergence of small presses in Europe in the 1990s, which differentiated themselves from the mainstream commercial norm of "48CC" (48-page, hard-covered, color) albums by adopting soft covers, a variable number of pages, and a black-and-white sobriety of cover design. Jean-Christophe Menu has expounded the politics of L'Association, the press that he co-founded, in this respect, and has railed against the practice of commercial publishers who create imprints with an "alternative" look, but of mediocre quality, far from the beautiful objects the small presses prided themselves on producing (Menu, 2005).

The material conditions of reading comics have of course undergone a radical change with the advent of digital media, and this revolution in comics production and consumption has been widely theorized, including by Groensteen, who regrets the loss of the self-contained reading experience and the spatial memory provided by the book. He doubts whether the incorporation of multimedia content constitutes an enrichment of a medium wrongly assumed to be handicapped by the absence of sound and motion. In fact, he argues, the innate temporality of added sound and motion disrupts the spatially engendered rhythm of comics, and voiceover and sound effects detract from text/image integration. As for interactivity, it is already a property of the comic book (Groensteen, 2011, pp. 67–83). The attachment to comics as material objects is perhaps inextricable from the sensory experience of reading them. In a recent book, Ian Hague has set out to analyze comics in their auditory, olfactory, and tactile aspects: while the latter in particular may be fetishized by comics scholars, he points out that digital comics are very much associated with touch (Hague, 2014, pp. 92–96).

SIDEBAR: MATERIALITY

Ian Hague

The study of materiality in Comics Studies involves looking at the physical "stuff" that comics are made from and thinking about how it might impact upon experiences of reading or making comics. Subjects that are of concern to scholars interested in materiality include: comparisons between printed and digital comics, processes of production, comics formats (size, shape, arrangement of pages, etc.), comics and the senses, and aspects of the sociology and economics of comics.

Materiality has always played an important role in the ways in which comics have been created and distributed. For example, early Swiss comics pioneer Rodolphe Töpffer's work was facilitated by the development of autography, a variant form of lithography that allowed him to produce images from pen drawings. Not only did this help him to work despite failing eyesight, it also represented a material operation (or perhaps a constraint) that determined what images in his early *bandes dessinées* would, and could, look

(*Continued*)

like (Kunzle, 2007, pp. 77–78, but cf. Grove, 2010, pp. 86–88 and 96–97). Similarly, the American comic book developed from newspapers: four Sunday supplement pages were folded in half and then in half again to create a 32-page booklet (Gabilliet, 2010, p. 9). Again a material constraint, a physical format, determined to a large extent the types of stories that could be told in comics, and the comic book remains a common format even today. As each of these examples demonstrates, the material composition of comics can have a big impact upon their stories and their storytelling, and it can affect the ways in which comics circulate in society, how they are sold (and for how much), and the types of experiences readers have as well.

Because these material elements are so fundamental to comics, they have long been aspects of comics scholarship, even if only implicitly. Histories of the form, for example, have necessarily paid attention to the ways that form has developed, a development that has taken place not only in terms of artistic and writerly style and technique, but also in physical formats and systems of distribution—concerns that are inextricably bound up with comics' materialities. Similarly, literary studies of comics and other approaches that privilege the development of the graphic novel as a key moment in the history of the form pay attention to materiality in their argument that comics improved their sociocultural standing through the repackaging of graphic narrative in hardback and paperback books as opposed to the more ephemeral comic book. This move arguably allowed comics to be understood as "literature" by enabling them to move out of the magazine rack and into the bookshop, where they are sold alongside more "established" forms such as prose. Here, though, the focus on materiality is generally implicit as opposed to being the main area of interest.

More recently, materiality has become an explicit focus in studies of comics as well. In 2005 Charles Hatfield's *Alternative Comics: An Emerging Literature* stressed the importance of the relationship between the story and the page it is printed on, identifying a "tension" between "reading-as-experience and text as material object." Hatfield was not the first to discuss the materiality of comics (there are examples of materiality-oriented criticism at least as early as 1940, when Sterling North described comic books as "pulp-paper nightmares" [see Hague, 2014, pp. 41, 43–44]), but he is an important contributor to modern discussions of the subject in comics scholarship. Hatfield wrote: "Broadly, we may say that comics exploit *format* as a signifier in itself; more specifically, that comics involve a tension between the experience of reading in sequence and the format or shape of the object being read. In other words, the art of comics entails a tense relationship between perceived time and perceived space" (52).

Other academics have also concentrated on the ways in which materiality is involved in the experiences and processes that surround comics reading. Ernesto Priego (2010), for example, has developed a model of materiality that draws on four important elements: text, physical interface, human body, and space/habitat. These categories allow for studies of comics that include the text (i.e., the written and drawn visual element of comics) but do not exclude other concerns in doing so. Importantly, these categories implicate not only the material form of comics, but also the reader's physical body and the spaces in which comics are consumed as important aspects of materiality. *The International Journal of Comic Art* (IJOCA), a pioneering publication in the field, has also developed some of these themes in publishing articles by authors such as Pascal Lefèvre (1999) and Marco Pellitteri (2007), on the ways in which comics' materiality allows for the communication of sensory effects to readers, something I also developed in my own work on comics in the 2014 book *Comics and the Senses*.

Finally, as digital comics continue to develop and establish a place in the comics "ecosystem," scholars have begun to focus on the ways in which a shift from the printed page to the digital screen is affecting the texts that are being produced, as well as the various ways in which those texts are consumed. Although the digital media landscape is changing and evolving rapidly, academic research is maintaining an interest in the changes that are taking place, and it therefore seems likely that as a research topic materiality is here to stay.

Bibliography

Gabilliet, J. (2010) *Of Comics and Men: a cultural history of comic books*, Jackson: University Press of Mississippi.

Grove, L. (2010) *Comics in French: the European bande dessinée in context*, New York: Berghahn.

Hague, I. (2014) *Comics and the Senses: a multisensory approach to comics and graphic novels*, New York: Routledge.

Hatfield, C. (2005) *Alternative Comics: an emerging literature*, Jackson: University Press of Mississippi.

Kunzle, D. (2007) *Father of the Comic Strip: Rodolphe Töpffer*, Jackson: University Press of Mississippi.

Lefèvre, P. (1999) 'Recovering sensuality in comic theory', *International Journal of Comic Art*, 1 (1): 140–49.

Pellitteri, M. (2007) 'Pornography and sinaesthesia in manga: multi-sensorial reception of eros in Japanese comics', *International Journal of Comic Art*, 9 (2): 425–40.

Priego, E. (2010) 'On cultural materialism, comics and digital media', *Opticon1826*, 9: 1–3.

I hope to have shown that formal theories, far from fixing and containing the protean object that is comics, have renewed themselves as the medium has expanded its own resources. But anyone seeking a profound understanding of the artistic potential of comics might turn first to the brilliant formal experiments of the OuBaPo [Workshop for Potential Comics] group who, following on from their literary predecessors such as Raymond Queneau and Georges Perec in Oulipo, founded in 1960, have, since 1992, created comics texts based on constraints, such as the iteration of the same image throughout or the banning of certain elements such as characters or on the transformation of existing texts by verbal or visual substitution, drastic reframing or reduction (see, for example, the collectively edited *OuBaPo 2*: 2003). The result is the exacerbation or disruption of the fundamental signifying devices of the medium. Comics has always been a self-reflexive art. With OuBaPo it becomes metatheoretical, as theory becomes inextricable from artistic enterprise. Matt Madden's *99 Ways to Tell a Story (Exercises in Style)* (2005) is based on Queneau's literary *Exercices de style* (1947), in which the same, slight, story is retold 99 times in different styles. Madden's comics version offers a virtuoso demonstration of the range of formal resources upon which the medium draws. The greater the formal awareness of the reader, the greater, perhaps, is the pleasure to be had from comics. OuBaPo offers both at once. Why deny yourself?

Bibliography

Baetens, J. (2011) 'Dominique Goblet: the list principle and the meaning of form', in M.A. Chaney (ed.) *Graphic Subjects*, Madison: University of Wisconsin Press.

Baetens, J. and Frey, H. (2015) *The Graphic Novel, an Introduction*, Cambridge: Cambridge University Press.

Baetens, J. and Lefèvre, P. (1993) *Pour une lecture moderne de la bande dessinée* [Toward a modern reading of comics], Brussels: CBBD.

Blackbeard, B. (1995) *R.F. Outcault, The Yellow Kid*, Northampton, MA: Kitchen Sink Press.

Chavanne, R. (2005) *Edgar P. Jacobs et le secret de l'explosion [Edgar P. Jacobs and the Secret of the Explosion]*, Montrouge: P.L.G.

Chavanne, R. (2010) *Composition de la bande dessinée* [The Composition of Comics], Montrouge: P.L.G.

Cohn, N. (2014) 'The architecture of visual narrative comprehension: the interaction of narrative structure on page layout in understanding comics', *Frontiers in Psychology* 5. http://journal.frontiersin.org/article/10.3389/fpsyg.2014.00680/full.

Conard, S. and Lambeens, T. (2012) 'Duration in comics', *European Comic Art*, 5 (2): 92–113.

Eisner, W. (1985) *Comics and Sequential Art*, Tamarac, FL: Poorhouse Press.

Fresnault-Deruelle, P. (1972) *La Bande dessinée: essai d'analyse sémiotique [Comics, a semiotic analysis]*, Paris: Hachette.

Fresnault-Deruelle, P. (1976) 'Du linéaire au tabulaire' [From linear to tabular], *Communications*, 24: 7–23.

Gauthier, G. (1976) 'Les Peanuts: un graphisme idiomatique' [Peanuts: an idiomatic graphic style], *Communications*, 24: 108–39.

Groensteen, T. (1999) *Système de la bande dessinée* [The System of Comics]. Paris: PUF.

Groensteen, T. (2006) *Un object culturel non identifié [An unidentified cultural object]*, Angoulême: Éditions de l'an 2.

Groensteen, T. (2011) *Bande dessinée et narration [Comics and Narration]*, Paris: PUF.

Groensteen, T. (2014) 'Definitions', in A, Miller and B. Beaty (eds) *The French Comics Theory Reader*, Leuven: Leuven University Press, 93–114.

Hague, I. (2014) *Comics and the Senses, a Multisensory Approach to Comics and Graphic Novels*, New York: Routledge.

Harvey, R.C. (1996) *The Art of the Comic Book. An Aesthetic History*, Jackson: University Press of Mississippi.

Hatfield, C. (2005) *Alternative Comics. An Emerging Literature*, Jackson: University Press of Mississippi.

Hatfield, C. (2014) *M.Töpffer invente la bande dessinée [M.Töpffer invents comics]*, Brussels: Les Impressions nouvelles.

Kunzle, D. (1973) *The Early Comic Strip: narrative strips and picture stories in the European broadsheet from c. 1450 to 1825*, Berkeley: University of California Press.

Kunzle, D. (2001) 'The voices of silence: Willette, Steinlen and the introduction of the silent strip in the *Chat Noir*, with a German coda', in R. Varnum and C.T. Gibbons (eds.) *The Language of Comics*, Jackson: University Press of Mississippi, 3–18.

Lacassin, F. (1971) *Pour un neuvième art, la bande dessinée [Toward a Ninth Art, Comics]*, Paris: 10/18.

Madden, M. (2005) *99 Ways to Tell a Story (Exercises in Style)*, New York: Chamberlain Brothers.

Maigret, E. (2012) 'Introduction: Un tournant constructiviste' [Introduction: a constructivist turn], in E. Maigret and M. Stefanelli (eds.) *La Bande dessinée: une médiaculture [Comics, a mediaculture]*, Paris: Armand Colin, p. 5–13.

Marion, P. (1993) *Traces en cases. Travail graphique, figuration narrative [Framed Traces. Graphic Work, Narrative Figuration]*, Louvain-la-neuve: Academia.

Marion, P. (2012) 'Emprise graphique et jeu de l'oie. Fragments d'une poétique de la bande dessinée' [Graphic grip and chequered board. Fragments of a poetics of comics], in E. Maigret and M. Stefanelli (eds.) *La Bande dessinée: une médiaculture [Comics, a mediaculture]*, Paris: Armand Colin, 175–99.

Masson, P. (1985) *Lire la bande dessinée* [*Reading Comics*], Lyon: Presses universitaires de Lyon.
McCloud, S. (1993) *Understanding Comics*, New York: Harper Collins.
Menu, J-C. (2005) *Plates-bandes* [*Flower beds/Flat strips*], Paris: L'Association.
Mitchell, W.J.T. (1994) *Picture Theory*, Chicago: University of Chicago Press.
Morgan, H. (2003) *Principes des littératures dessinées* [*Principles of Drawn Literatures*], Angoulême: Éditions de l'an 2.
OuBaPo collective (2003) *OuBaPo 2*, Paris: L'Association.
Peeters, B. (1991) *Case, planche, récit* [*Panel, page, narrative*], Tournai: Casterman.
Schneider, G. (2010) 'Comics and everyday life: from ennui to contemplation', *European Comic Art*, 3 (1): 37–63.
Smolderen, T. (2009) *Naissances de la bande dessinée, de William Hogarth à Winsor McCay* [*The Origins of Comics, from William Hogarth to Winsor McCay*], Brussels: Les Impressions nouvelles.
Stefanelli, M. (2012) 'Un siècle de recherches sur la bande dessinée' [A century of research into comics], in E. Maigret and M. Stefanelli (eds.) *La Bande dessinée: une médiaculture* [*Comics, a mediaculture*], Paris: Armand Colin, Maigret and Stefanelli, 17–49.
Sterckx, P. (1984) 'Les Cases mémorables de Pierre Sterckx' [The memorable panels of Pierre Sterckx]. *Les Cahiers de la bande Dessinée*, 56: 67–69.
Toussaint, B. (1976) 'Idéographie et bande dessinée' [Ideography and Comics]. *Communications*, 24: 81–93.
Van Lier, H. (1988) 'La Bande dessinée, une cosmogonie dure' [Comics, a hard cosmogony], in T. Groensteen (ed.) *Bande dessinée, récit et modernité* [*Comics, Narration and Modernity*], Paris: Futuropolis, 5–24.
Witek, J. (2009) 'The arrow and the grid', in J. Heer and K. Worcester (eds.) *A Comic Studies Reader*, Jackson: University Press of Mississippi, 149–56.

13
PSYCHOLOGY/PSYCHIATRY

Travis Langley

A psychologist created the world's most famous superheroine. A psychiatrist specifically and harshly criticized that character in the course of making his broader attack on the comic book business as a whole. One helped bring the Golden Age of Comics to life, one played a critical role in killing it, and scholars in their areas have felt their repercussions ever since, as has the comics industry itself. After the 1950s, psychologically oriented comics scholarship—*comics psychology*—largely disappeared until the 21st century. Now, a growing number of psychology professionals analyze comics, with some making fresh marks on the medium.

The Golden Age

The comic book as a medium was new in the 1930s. The public barely had time to start pondering the medium's effects, implications, and sheer worth when Superman burst onto the scene in 1938's *Action Comics* #1 and the superhero arrived. At no other point in comics history have scholars played as much of a direct role in shaping comic books as psychologist William Moulton Marston and psychiatrist Fredric Wertham did during the Golden Age, for reasons both good and bad.

War and Wonders

The Harvard-trained psychologist who would later create a heroine who wielded her Lasso of Truth first made a name for himself as an early pioneer in the science of truth. William Moulton Marston became fascinated with the detection of deception during his undergraduate years under experimental psychologist Hugo Munsterberg, a man known as the father of forensic psychology and the broader field of applied psychology (Huss, 2009). While working on his law degree, Marston wrote an article proposing that systolic blood pressure will go up when people lie and that investigators might therefore identify deception by measuring increases in blood pressure (Marston, 1917). Shortly after also receiving his Ph.D. in psychology (Daniel, 2000), he played a critical role when called upon to assess a defendant's honesty in *Frye v. US* (1923). That landmark legal case established the standards by which expert testimony would be permitted in court—most notably through the ruling that expert testimony should be based on generally accepted scientific practices and, therefore, so-called lie detection would *not* be admissible in court (Meyer & Weaver, 2006). Although references to Marston as the "inventor of the lie detector" are imprecise, they are not wholly unwarranted either. While many other researchers' efforts contributed to the eventual development of the polygraph as a "lie detector," Marston was the most vocal and visible of its early proponents. Despite its lasting inadmissibility in court, the allure of an infallible measure of discerning truth remained popular and carried over into Marston's comics.

During his time as a consulting psychologist for *The Family Circle* magazine, Marston was interviewed in a 1940 issue by Olive Byrne (under the pen name Olive Richard) about his views on the recent popularity of comic books. He spoke glowingly of their "great educational potential" and specifically praised publisher Max Gaines (Richard, 1940). When the article caught the publisher's attention, Gaines hired Marston onto the editorial advisory board for All-American Publications and its sister company National Comics, which would merge and eventually become DC Comics.

Presented by editor Sheldon Mayer with the opportunity to create a new character for All-American, Marston wanted to introduce a superhero motivated by love instead of violence. His wife Elizabeth, who similarly held advanced degrees in both law and psychology, said he had better make the character a woman: "Come on, let's have a Superwoman! There's too many men out there" (Hanley, 2014, p. 18). Under the pen name Charles Moulton, which combined his and Max Gaines's middle names, the psychologist became a comic book writer. His creation, Wonder Woman, debuted as the Justice Society's secretary in *All-Star Comics* #8 (December, 1941) but quickly became a bestselling character as the star of *Sensation Comics* and then her eponymous title *Wonder Woman* within a few months.

In addition to the pursuit of truth, two other key aspects of Marston's approach to psychology would form the cornerstones of his superhero creation: more obviously, his reverence for womanhood and less obviously, his belief in the value of loving submission. Years before, writing about one heroic Amazon, he had predicted that "the next hundred years will see the beginning of an American matriarchy—a nation of Amazons in the psychological sense rather than physical sense" (New York Times, 1937). He believed women to be psychologically stronger than men. Where he saw weakness and aggression driving so many of the male heroes, he made her strong and caring. He noticed that the superheroes often suffered from tragic origins or became superheroes to overcome their own weaknesses—the way frail Steve Rogers would scientifically become Captain America or the boy Billy Batson would magically become fully grown Captain Marvel, transformed in ways that fulfilled wishes to become larger, stronger, mightier. Wonder Woman's background derived from neither personal tragedy nor weakness. Permeating Marston's work was his belief that the world would become a better place through women's empowerment.

Although not obvious to younger readers, elements of bondage and discipline in Marston's stories caused concern for the same advisory board of which Marston had been a member. Gaines assigned Dorothy Robicek, the All-American main office's first female assistant editor, to handle their advisory board's stern objections to possibly fetishistic content in *Wonder Woman* (Hanley, 2014, p. 18). Because Wonder Woman lost her powers when bound by a man or by anyone using her own magic lasso, she often found herself bound in Marston's stories. She bound others as well and "played many binding games" (*Sensation Comics* #35, 1942) telling her Amazon sisters, "Bind me as tight as you can, girls, with the biggest ropes and chains you can find!" (*Wonder Woman* #13, 1943). In his 1928 book *Emotion of Normal People*, Marston introduced his DISC theory, positing that dominance, inducement, submission, and compliance (DISC) are important to all human relationships—whether romantic, friendly, parental, occupational, or otherwise (Marston, 1928). He believed that dominating without aggression, inducing behavior without manipulating, submitting in love and trust, and complying with directions from others could all be good, healthy, and normal. "Comic books aren't psychology texts," comic book historian Tim Hanley (2014, p. 17) said of the relationship between Marston's theory and his comics. "Though inspired by DISC theory and the dubious implications therein, the nature of comic books simplified these messages. They were adventure stories for kids that presented simple, surface-level messages about a strong and capable heroine, and children flocked to the book."

William Moulton Marston died of cancer on May 2, 1947, a week short of his 54th birthday and too soon to challenge the psychiatrist whose campaign would damage the industry Moulton had helped build. Although the bondage elements would fade from Wonder Woman's stories after her creator's passing, Wertham would wield them like a weapon through the decade that followed.

The Post-War Backlash

At the time of Marston's death, psychiatrist Fredric Wertham was in the process of conducting a two-year study on juvenile delinquents. Researchers across the Atlantic came to attribute the post-war increase in juvenile delinquency to wartime disruption in family bonds (Ainsworth & Bowlby, 1965; Bretherton, 1992), while Wertham in New York placed the blame squarely on comic books. "So far we have determined that the effect is definitely and completely harmful," he said of the medium (Crist, 1948, p. 22).

In 1948, ten months after Marston died, Wertham led a symposium titled, "The Psychopathology of Comic Books." Symposium speaker Marvin L. Blumberg speculated briefly on the so-called bad influence of comic books (1948). Hilde Mosse, in condemning comic books for their violence, described at length how they related to Sigmund Freud's unprovable theory of death instincts. Although also engaging in some Freudian conjecture, Paula Elkisch offered speculations based on empirical data, a survey of children's reading habits. Based on the fact that out of 18 who preferred comic books to other books, nine said that parents and teachers should discourage the reading of comic books, Elkisch (1948, pp. 485–486) perceived a "peculiar conflict the children seem to be caught in, in relation to the effects of comic books: it is the concept of the *identification with the aggressor*." (The survey did not ask any question regarding identification with characters.) Gerson Legman (1948, p. 475) asserted that "comic books have succeeded only in giving every American child a complete course in paranoid megalomania such as no German child ever had, a total conviction of the morality of force such as no Nazi could ever aspire to." Wertham's own remarks from the symposium appeared in a *Saturday Review of Literature* article titled, "The Comics—Very Funny!" as if in long-delayed response to *The Family Circle* interview that first brought William Moulton Marston to Gaines' attention, "Don't Laugh at the Comics."

Wertham's campaign against comic books had begun. It would culminate in a bestselling book and his testimony before the Senate. Like Marston, Wertham had also helped pioneer courtroom use of expert witnesses. Wertham's testimony always related to his concern for social issues. After his early work in court regarded the evaluation of insanity (1941), he went on to provide information that helped the Supreme Court end desegregation (*Brown v. Board of Education*, 1954) and to testify before the US Senate's Committee on the Judiciary Subcommittee to Investigate Juvenile Delinquency. Along the way he told the Senate, "I think Hitler was a beginner compared to the comic book industry" (1954, US Senate).

Wertham's 1954 book *Seduction of the Innocent* condemned comic books for causing juvenile delinquency. In the tome, Wertham described crime, gore, sexual content, drug use, and other adult material that appeared in comics either overtly or, to his eyes, through undertones. Based on his work with troubled youth, Wertham made generalizations about all young readers with no control (comparison) group. Because the delinquents had all read comic books, comic books had to be a causal factor. Given that they had all eaten candy and watched baseball games, he might just as easily have blamed candy or baseball. The book concentrated on horror and crime comics. Superhero comic books, which Wertham considered to be a type of crime comics, became the focus of only one chapter—titled, "I Want to be a Sex Maniac," supposedly based on a quotation from a child he had treated. In that chapter, he described the homosexual subtext he saw in the stories of Batman and Robin and called Wonder Woman "the Lesbian counterpart of Batman" (Wertham, 1954, p. 192). His accusations that Wonder Woman stories included bondage elements were a decade out of date.

Seduction of the Innocent, which came out at a time of flagging comic book sales, paved the way for the creation of the Comics Code Authority, which developed guidelines for the comic book industry to police itself and regulate content. Even though Wertham had rallied the opposition to violence and sexual content, he also objected to censorship. He neither endorsed nor opposed the Authority's creation.

As it turned out, Wertham's tendency to reach convoluted and sometimes unfounded conclusions may not have been the greatest of his scientific sins. Decades later, after careful examination of Wertham's records, scholar Carol Tilley accused him of fraud. Tilley reported that he apparently exaggerated the number of participants, misstated ages, omitted information about other influences like family violence and parental drug use, combined quotes from different children as if they had come from the same child, attributed a single child's quotes to multiple children when that suited his purposes instead, and invented details outright. Tilley (2012, p. 383), concluded, "Wertham manipulated, overstated, compromised, and fabricated evidence—especially that evidence he attributed to personal clinical research with young people—for rhetorical gain."

Nevertheless, during Wertham's own time, the damage was done. The Golden Age of Comic Books was over.

Later 20th Century: The Dark Ages of Comics Psychology

Through the Silver and Bronze Ages of comics (mid-1950s to mid-1980s), psychologists and psychiatrists stayed fairly silent even as the medium matured over that span of time. DC Comics revitalized their flagging superhero line, starting with a new Flash in 1956. At Marvel Comics, Stan Lee, Jack Kirby, Steve Ditko, and other co-creators brought depth to superheroes and their stories at a time when comic book characters' depictions had been rather flat. DC would slowly follow suit once a drop in sales after the campy *Batman* TV series led to the editorial perception that readers were ready for comics they could take more seriously. The early 1970s shift from less heavy Silver Age to more serious Bronze Age attracted no consequent rush of psychological analysis.

The success of the 1989 *Batman* motion picture directed by Tim Burton proved that the world could take comic book stories—or at least superheroes—more seriously and elicited some psychological analysis at the time. Journalists invited psychologists to comment on Batman's mental health, and a few professionals in other areas such as communication applied psychology in analyses of the film (e.g., Collins, 1991; Terrill, 1993), but then interest among the professionals died out. The brief burst of interest inspired no ongoing scholarship in comics psychology.

21st Century: The Renaissance of Comics Psychology

In his 2004 book, *Superman on the Couch: What Superheroes Really Tell Us about Ourselves and Our Society*, comic book writer and editor Danny Fingeroth observed that there had been "little written in recent decades by mental health professionals about superheroes. There is much literature about fairy tales and mythology, including works by Bruno Bettelheim, Rollo May, C. G. Jung, and Joseph Campbell, but no major specific studies of superheroes by psychiatrists or psychologists" (p. 23). Fully half a century after psychiatrist Fredric Wertham's book *Seduction of the Innocent* critically wounded the comic book industry, Fingeroth braced himself for a deluge of experts berating him for not knowing about the many great works that had appeared during that time (personal communication). No such deluge befell him, because no such great works existed. Soon, though, some psychology and psychiatry returned to Comics Studies. The reasons are manifold.

The superhero, a character type that first appeared when the world was heading to World War II, saw a surge in popularity after the attacks of September 11, 2001, left people yearning for heroes great enough to help fix the modern world and believable enough in cynical times. By then, the CGI-enhanced motion pictures *Blade* (1998) and *X-Men* (2000) had proven that audiences would welcome new kinds of comic book stories on film, but the even greater success soon achieved by *Spider-Man* (2002) confirmed that fantastic heroes were welcome in the post-9/11 world. Christopher Nolan brought Batman into the most realistic world that the Dark Knight had ever occupied on screen in a trilogy of films that examined terrorism. *Slate* called *The Dark Knight* (2008), in particular, "a bleak post-9/11 allegory about how terror (and, make no mistake, Heath Ledger's Joker is a terrorist) breaks down those reassuring moral categories" (Stevens, 2008). That same year, *Iron Man* depicted a man with plausible weaponry taking on modern terrorists, grounding what would become an increasingly incredible Marvel Cinematic Universe in a veneer of reality. The proliferation of superhero motion pictures also inspired professionals to discuss how realistically the films depicted an ever-increasing variety of psychologically relevant issues like Iron Man's personal growth (e.g., Brix & Connor, 2011) and posttraumatic reactions (e.g., Letamendi, 2013; Plein, 2013). Films based on comic books inspired writers in psychology, and whatever *Zeitgeist* led to greater depth in comic book films and increased their popularity likely inspired the psychology scholars as well. A large audience for comic book films and television series created cultural demand for commentary.

Writers in other areas helped pave the way by offering their own examinations of comic book characters through the lenses of their respective professions. Authors applied physical sciences such as physics to superheroes, teaching science by describing ways in which superheroes were realistic or not (Gresh & Weinberg, 2002, 2004; Kakalios, 2006). Open Court Publishing Company launched a successful series on popular culture and philosophy, eventually with more than 100 books, and other publishers like Wiley-Blackwell soon did, too. Early entries included philosophical looks at cartoon characters (e.g., Irwin, Conard, & Skoble, 2001) and fantastic heroes (e.g., Baggett & Klein, 2004; South, 2003), and superheroes soon followed (e.g., Morris & Morris, 2005). Books on supervillains did, too (e.g., Dyer, 2009). As a discipline, psychology has always wrestled with its place as the hardest of the soft sciences, the one most likely to follow scientific method and conduct empirical tests on the relationship between concrete reality and abstract subject matter like love, thought, or the nature of the "mind" itself. Perhaps psychology, the offspring of physiology and philosophy, first needed its parent disciplines to embrace Comics Studies and prove that comics psychology could be taken seriously.

While the late 20th century's age of communication may have yielded little in comics psychology, the age of the Internet led to a proliferation. Writers who might have hesitated to devote themselves to the arduous process of submitting content to professional journals could quickly post online, and those concerned about risking their reputations could create online personas of which their officemates might be unaware. Through blogs, social media, podcasts, YouTube, and more, people were sharing ideas on the widest array of topics, and they received feedback in this realm of instant exchange (e.g. Broken Brain, 2015; DeFife, 2012). People opened up even on topics that may have gotten them ostracized elsewhere in their lives, and they shared a message: Geek is good.

Geek gatherings provide opportunities for "psych geeks" to meet, share ideas, and support each other's efforts to expand comics psychology. The Comics Arts Conference, the scholarly conference-within-the-convention held twice yearly in conjunction with San Diego Comic-Con and WonderCon, provides a meeting ground for comics scholars. Although founded in 1992, the conference did not regularly receive psychologically oriented submissions before 2002. From that point on, the Comics Arts Conference consistently featured panels related to psychology, with Neil Cohn and then also Travis Langley presenting most often.

Thinking with Comics

Cognitive scientist Neil Cohn studies the psychology of how people read comics, applying science of cognition and linguistics. Based on surveys, observation, brain scans, and other empirical investigations (e.g., Cohn, Paczynski, & Jackendoff, 2012), Cohn argues that visual languages develop according to which individuals in different cultures learn to process visual stories in different ways, particularly noting distinctions between Japanese Visual Language and American Visual Language, and that these follow structure and constraints akin to those in spoken and sign languages (e.g., Cohn, 2012, 2013). In other words, different people grow up learning different ways to read comics, depending on their cultures and the kind of comics they grow up reading. They will have difficulty adapting to comics presented the "wrong" way, even something as seemingly simple as turning pages from right to left instead of left to right.

Cohn's research into how people read comics is unusual for psychological science, though. Most psychological examinations of comics focus on in-story content, whether that means using psychology to look at the characters and stories or using the characters and stories to say something about psychology.

Teaching with Comics

After non-psychologist Danny Fingeroth speculated on the nature of fictional superheroes and what they mean for people in the real world in *Superman on the Couch*, psychologists began writing more on this themselves. The first 21st-century book by psychologists completely contemplating comic book characters was 2008's appropriately titled *The Psychology of Superheroes*, which Robin S. Rosenberg edited. In its chapters, psychologists explored questions such as why superheroes choose to be superheroes, how the X-Men might cope with prejudice against them, and family dynamics in the Fantastic Four. A History Channel documentary, *Batman Unmasked: The Psychology of the Dark Knight* (2008), featured comic book professionals and a number of psychologists, including Rosenberg, as a special in conjunction with the theatrical release of *The Dark Knight* motion picture. Rosenberg would go on to edit works aimed at defining superheroes (Rosenberg & Coogan, 2013) and understanding why superheroes fascinate people (Rosenberg, 2013).

The first book on the psychology of a specific superhero was *Batman and Psychology: A Dark and Stormy Knight* by Travis Langley (2012), who had become one of the organizers of the Comics Arts Conference. In addition to examining mental health issues among Batman and his foes, the work applied psychological theories and empirical research findings to consider how those characters and also Batman's partners could be used to demonstrate real cognitive, social, and developmental concepts in psychology. One segment of the 2013 documentary *Legends of the Knight* showed how Langley would use fictional characters like Batman to teach real psychology. Langley later edited a series of books on the psychology of comic books and other popular culture topics (2015, 2016).

Rosenberg and Langley each write about superheroes and other fictional characters online for *Psychology Today*. Around the Internet, psychologists such as Ali Mattu (brainknowsbetter.com), Andrea Letamendi (underthemaskonline.com), and others blog about comic book characters—again, especially superheroes. In her weekly podcast, "The Arkham Sessions," Letamendi presents analyses of *Batman: The Animated Series* designed to be "nostalgic, humorous, and even a little educational" (Letamendi, n.d.). In a sign of how comics psychology had shed some of the Wertham blemish, both Letamendi and Langley appeared among the interviewees featured prominently in Warner Bros./DC Comics' 2013 documentary *Necessary Evil: Super-Villains of DC Comics*.

A few psychiatrists began studying comics, too. Sharon Packer looked at the culture, history, and mythology of superheroes in the book *Superheroes and Superegos: Analyzing the Minds Behind the Masks* (2009). The Broadcast Thought group of forensic psychiatrists—H. Eric Bender, Praveen R. Kambam, and Vasilis Pozios—delved into characters' in-story mental states as part of their ongoing endeavor to educate the public about mental health through popular culture examples. They have diagnosed Gotham City's criminals (Pozios, Kambam, & Bender, 2015), assessed whether the supervillains committed to Arkham Asylum really should be found legally insane (Bender, Kambam, & Pozios, 2012), and debated whether *The Walking Dead*'s zombies would be culpable for their destructive actions (Bender, Kambam, & Pozios, 2013). "Passionate about reducing the stigma associated with mental illnesses and their treatment through more accurate depictions of mental health issues in the media" (Pozios, quoted by Shannon, 2014), they also rubbed some industry professionals the wrong way (Uslan, 2012) with a *New York Times* op-ed piece that called for such accuracy in comic books (Bender, Kambam, & Pozios, 2011). Whereas William Moulton Marston's praise of comic book publisher Max Gaines helped land Marston an advisory job, naming DC Comics' publishers and calling upon them to change how DC depicted mental health did not bring the Broadcast Thought psychiatrists into the company fold. Pozios actively did what he called upon the comics industry to do, though, when he authored the Prism Award-nominated story "Aura," about a bipolar superhero, for a Grayhaven Comics anthology (Scarlet, 2014b).

Healing with Comics

A growing number of mental health professionals have found ways to use comics therapeutically. Psychologist Lawrence Rubin integrated superheroes into mental health sessions with youth and adolescents, as he described in *Using Superheroes in Counseling and Play Therapy* (2006), one of his several books on incorporating popular culture topics into therapy. Several therapists at the Southeast Psych practice in Charlotte, North Carolina (southeastpsych.com), use superheroes and comic books to open dialogue with clients. Southeast Psych founding partner Frank Gaskill authored the graphic novel *Max Gamer*, starring an autistic superhero (Gaskill & Kelly, 2011).

In addition to using comic books, video games, and other artifacts of geek culture both to teach and to interact with clients, Patrick O'Connor operates the Comicspedia database (comicspedia.net) to help other therapists interested in attempting the same. The online database catalogues hundreds of comic book issue summaries, tagging each with psychological themes. The website provides O'Connor's suggestions to help therapists open dialogue with clients and individuals gain greater understanding on their own. Therapists Josué Cardona and Lara Taylor similarly find "positive uses of Geek culture staples such as comic books, video games, superheroes, geek narratives, and tech" in therapeutic situations through Geek Therapy (Cardona & Taylor, n.d.).

Janina Scarlet brings it all together in her book, *Superhero Therapy* (Scarlet, in press). Scarlet's "Superhero Therapy" incorporates comic book characters as well as other fantastic characters into evidence-based therapeutic techniques such as cognitive-behavioral therapy (CBT) to treat a variety of conditions such as anxiety, stress, and depression. As Scarlet (2014a) describes it, "Superhero Therapy can refer to either psychoanalyzing Superheroes or to using Superheroes in therapy in order to facilitate recovery."

Conclusion

Whereas psychologist William Moulton Marston's optimistic critique led to his employment within the comic book industry, he enjoyed the luxury of working during the decade before psychiatrist Fredric Wertham wounded that industry. Wertham tainted the way many people would view both comics scholars in general and mental health professionals in particular. Comics psychology lay dormant for half a century, through the area's dark ages. For a myriad of reasons that included 9/11, CGI, comic cons, and the Internet, comics psychology reawakened with innovative new methods and applications in its 21st-century Renaissance. Comics psychology looks likely to continue to grow.

Bibliography

Ainsworth, M., and Bowlby, J. (1965) *Child Care and the Growth of Love*, London, UK: Penguin.
Baggett, D. and Klein, S.E. (2004) *Harry Potter and Philosophy: if Aristotle ran Hogwarts*. Chicago, IL: Open Court.
Bender, H.E., Kambam, P.R., and Pozios, V. (2011, September 20) 'Putting the Caped Crusader on the couch', *New York Times*: http://www.nytimes.com/2011/09/21/opinion/putting-the-caped-crusader-on-the-couch.html?_r=0.
Bender, H.E., Kambam, P.R., and Pozios, V. (2012) Unlocking Arkham: the forensic psychiatry of Batman's rogues' gallery. Panel presented at San Diego Comic-Con International, San Diego, CA.
Bender, H.E., Kambam, P.R., Pozios, V., Daily, J., and Davidson, R. (2013) Not guilty by reason of zombification? Law and forensic psychiatry after the zombie apocalypse. Panel presented at WonderCon, Anaheim, CA.
Blumberg, M.L. (1948) 'The practical aspects of the bad influence of comic books', *American Journal of Psychotherapy*, 2 (3): 487–88.
Bretherton, I. (1992) 'The origins of attachment theory: John Bowlby and Mary Ainsworth'. *Development Psychology*, 28 (5): 759–75.
Brix, C. and Connor, J. (2011) 'Review of *Iron Man 2* movie'. *Journal of Feminist Family Therapy*, 23 (1): 66–68.
Broken Brain, The (2015, July 9) *Superhero psychology*. The Broken Brain: http://brokenbrain.libsyn.com/superhero-psychology.
Cardona, J. and Taylor, L. (n.d.) *Welcome to Geek Therapy!* Geek Therapy: http://www.geektherapy.com/about.html.
Clyman, J. (2010, May 25) 'Iron Man on the couch: The psychological hang-ups of this year's hottest superhero' *Psychology Today*: https://www.psychologytoday.com/blog/reel-therapy/201005/iron-man-the-couch.
Cohn, N. (2012) 'Explaining "I can't draw": parallels between the structure and development of language and drawing' *Human Development*, 55: 167–92.
Cohn, N. (2013) *The Visual Language of Comics: introduction to the structure and cognition of sequential images*, London, UK: Bloomsbury.
Cohn, N., Paczynski, M., Jackendoff, R., and Holcomb, P.J. (2012) '(Pea)nuts and bolts of visual narrative: structure and meaning in sequential image comprehension', *Cognitive Psychology*, 65: 1–38.
Collins, J. (1991) 'Batman: the movie, narrative: the hyperconscious', in R.E. Pearson and W. Uricchio (eds.), *The Many Lives of the Batman*, New York: Routledge, Chapman and Hall, 164–81.
Crist, J. (1948, March 27) 'Horror in the nursery', *Collier's Weekly*: 22–23, 95.
Daniel, L. (2000) *Wonder Woman: the complete history*, San Francisco, CA: Chronicle.
DeFife, D. (2012) *A Psychoanalysis of Bruce Wayne (Batman)*, Emory University: https://www.youtube.com/watch?v=eRlbV8tNILg.
Dyer, B. (2009) *Supervillains and Philosophy: sometimes, evil is its own reward*, Chicago, IL: Open Court.
Elkisch, P. (1948) 'The child's conflict about comic books', *American Journal of Psychotherapy*, 2 (3): 483–87.
Fingeroth, D. (2007) *Disguised as Clark Kent: Jews, comics, and the creation of the superhero*, New York, Continuum.
Gaskill, F. and Kelly, R. (2011) *Max Gamer*, Charlotte, NC: Hero House.
Gresh, L.H. and Weinberg, R. (2002) *The Science of Superheroes*, New York: Wiley.
Gresh, L.H. and Weinberg, R. (2004) *The Science of Supervillains*, New York: Wiley.
Hanley, T. (2014) *Wonder Woman Unbound: the curious history of the world's most famous heroine*, Chicago, IL: Chicago Review.
Huss, M.T. (2009) *Forensic Psychology: research, clinical practice, and applications*, Malden, MA: Wiley-Blackwell.
Irwin, W., Conard, M., and Skoble, A. (eds.) (2001) *The Simpsons and Philosophy: the d'oh! of Homer*, Chicago, IL: Open Court.
Kakalios, J. (2006). *The Physics of Superheroes*, New York: Gotham.
Langley, T. (2012). *Batman and Psychology: a dark and stormy knight*, New York: Wiley.

Langley, T. (2013, May 4). 'Does Iron Man 3's hero suffer posttraumatic stress disorder?', *Psychology Today*: http://www.psychologytoday.com/blog/beyond-heroes-and-villains/201305/does-iron-man-3s-hero-suffer-posttraumatic-stress-disorder.

Langley, T. (ed.) (2015) *The Walking Dead Psychology: psych of the living dead*, New York: Sterling.

Langley, T. (ed.) (2016) *Captain America vs. Iron Man: freedom, security, psychology*, New York: Sterling.

Legman, G. (1948) 'The comic books and the public', *American Journal of Psychotherapy*, 2 (3): 473–77.

Letamendi, A. (2013, May 10) 'Iron Man: a terrible privilege', *Under the Mask*: http://www.underthemaskonline.com/iron-man-a-terrible-privilege/.

Letamendi, A. (n.d.) 'The Arkham sessions', *Under the Mask*: http://www.underthemaskonline.com/the-arkham-sessions/.

Letamendi, A., Rosenberg, R., Langley, T., and Wein, L. (2011, July) The superhero battlefield. Panel presented at San Diego Comic-Con International, San Diego, CA.

Lyubansky, M. (2010, January 27) 'The Zen of watchmen', *Psychology Today*: https://www.psychologytoday.com/blog/between-the-lines/201001/the-zen-watchmen.

Lyubansky, M. (2012, February 6) 'How super is superhero justice?' *Psychology Today*: https://www.psychologytoday.com/blog/between-the-lines/201202/how-super-is-superhero-justice.

Marston, W.M. (1917) 'Systolic blood pressure symptoms of deception', *Journal of Experimental Psychology*, 2 (2): 117–63.

Marston, W.M. (1928) *Emotions of Normal People*, Torquay, UK: Devonshire Press.

Meyer, R.G. and Weaver, C.M. (2006) *Law and Mental Health: a case-based approach*, New York: Guilford.

Morris, T. and Morris, M. (2005) *Superheroes and Philosophy: truth, justice, and the socratic way*, Chicago, IL: Open Court.

Mosse, H. (1948) 'Aggression and violence in fantasy and fact', *American Journal of Psychotherapy*, 2 (3): 477–83.

New York Times (1937, November 11) 'Marston advises 3 L's for success: "Live, love and laugh" offered by psychologist as recipe for required happiness', *New York Times*: 27, C7. http://query.nytimes.com/gst/abstract.html?res=9D06E0D8133DE23ABC4952DFB767838C629EDE.

Packer, S. (2009) *Superheroes and Superegos: analyzing the minds behind the masks*, Santa Barbara, CA: Praeger.

Plein, A. (2013, July 16) 'Using comic books and games to help treat PTSD', *Superhero Therapy*: http://www.superhero-therapy.com/2013/07/using-comic-books-and-games-to-help-treat-ptsd/.

Pozios, V.K., Kambam, P.R., and Bender, H.E. (2015, January 13) 'We asked psychiatrists to analyze Gotham's unhinged villains', *Wired*: http://www.wired.com/2015/01/gotham-villain-psychoanalysis/.

Richard, O. (1940, October 25) 'Don't laugh at the comics', *The Family Circle*: 10–11, 22.

Rosenberg, R.S. (ed.) (2008) *The Psychology of Superheroes*, Dallas, TX: BenBella.

Rosenberg, R.S. (ed.) (2013) *Our Superheroes, Ourselves*, Oxford, UK: Oxford University Press.

Rosenberg, R.S. and Coogan, P. (eds.) (2013). *What Is a Superhero?*, Oxford, UK: Oxford University Press.

Rubin, L.C. (2006). *Using Superheroes in Counseling and Play Therapy*, New York: Springer.

Scarlet, J. (2014a, May 14). 'What Is Superhero Therapy?', *Psychology Today*: https://www.psychologytoday.com/blog/beyond-heroes-and-villains/201405/what-is-superhero-therapy.

Scarlet, J. (2014b, September 28). 'Aura—the superhero with mental illness and migraines', *Superhero Therapy*: http://www.superhero-therapy.com/2014/09/aura-the-superhero-with-mental-illness-and-migraines/.

Scarlet, J. (in press) *Superhero Therapy*, New York: Little, Brown.

Sergi, J. (2012, June 8) '1948: the year comics met their match', *Comic Book Legal Defense Fund*: http://cbldf.org/2012/06/1948-the-year-comics-met-their-match/.

Shannon, H.M. (2014) 'Mental illness, superheroes, and stereotypes—Vasilis Pozios on his new comic aura', *Bleeding Cool*: http://www.bleedingcool.com/2014/09/16/mental-illness-superheroes-and-stereotypes-vasilis-pozios-on-his-new-comic-aura/.

South, J.B. (ed.) (2003) *Buffy the Vampire Slayer and Philosophy: fear and trembling in Sunnydale*, Chicago, IL: Open Court.

Stevens, D. (2008, July 17) 'No joke: The Dark Knight, reviewed' *Slate*: http://www.slate.com/articles/arts/movies/2008/07/no_joke.html.

Terrill, R.E. (1993) 'Put on a happy face: Batman as schizophrenic savior', *Quarterly Journal of Speech*, 79 (3): 319–35.

Tilley, C.L. (2012) 'Seducing the innocent: Fredric Wertham and the falsifications that helped condemn comics', *Information & Culture: A Journal of History*, 47 (4): 383–413.

U.S. Senate (1954) *Hearings before the Subcommittee to Investigate Juvenile Delinquency of the Committee on the Judiciary, United States Senate*. https://archive.org/stream/juveniledelinque54unit/juveniledelinque54unit_djvu.txt.

Uslan, M. (2012) 'Foreword', in T. Langley (Author) *Batman and Psychology: a dark and stormy knight*, New York: Wiley, xi–xii.

Wertham, F. (1941) *Dark Legend*, New York: Duell, Sloane, & Pearce.

Wertham, F. (1948, May 29) 'The comics—very funny!' *Saturday Review of Literature*: 6.

Wertham, F. (1954/2004) *Seduction of the Innocent*, New York: Rinehart.

Wertham, F., Legman, G., Mosse, H.L., Elkisch, P., and Blumberg, M.L. (1948, March). The Psychopathology of Comic Books. Symposium presented at the meeting of the Association for the Advancement of Psychotherapy.

SIDEBAR: MARTIN BARKER

William Proctor

In an academic career spanning over four decades, Martin Barker has covered a lot of ground. Following his first monograph, *A New Racism* (1981), Barker has primarily been involved with audience and reception studies, and it is within this ambit that his research into comics are seminal contributions to what we now describe as "Comics Studies."

By his own admission, Barker's interest in the medium happened quite by accident: "just about everything about me indicated against it. I didn't much read comics as a child…and didn't at all as an adult, apart from a brief period of reading *2000AD*" (2002, p. 64). Why, then, the sudden and unexpected turn? At the center of Barker's project, firmly encapsulated in *A Haunt of Fears* (1984) and *Comics: Ideology, Power and the Critics* (1989), is a preoccupation with those unacknowledged forces that discursively surround certain comics publications, as well as a commitment to challenging those widespread assumptions about the influence and effects of comics on behavior.

In *A Haunt of Fears* (*AHOF*), Barker mounted a scathing examination of the horror comics campaign in the UK between 1949 and 1955, a campaign that led to the passing of the Children and Young Persons (Harmful Publications) Act of 1955. Yet, "[t]he campaign against the comics was not *about* the comics, but about a conception of society, children and Britain" (1984, p. 6). Campaigns of this kind, of course, are not a new phenomenon, then as now. But at the epicenter of such wrathful moralizing stands the figure of "the child": vulnerable, pliable, and, above all else, *innocent*. "Like a garden pruned to make it safe, the only things allowed will be those which the adults see as good for the children" (1989, p. 280).

The horror comics campaign had its roots in the USA and reached its zenith with the publication of Fredric Wertham's famous (and most infamous) *Seduction of the Innocent*

(1954), but was also "a truly international fever," a moral virus that sent shockwaves of hostility in Ireland, Canada, Australia, New Zealand, Denmark, Germany, Italy, and Holland (1989, p. 14). Given that the campaign, on both sides of the Atlantic, "made such powerful claims about what a 'horror comic' is and what it could do to a child-reader," Barker "had to find ways of evaluating the comics to see what all the fuss was about" (p. 7).

Rather than the comics themselves, then, that simply "couldn't have affected them in ways that were claimed" (ibid), Barker unmasks the political and ideological thrust that governs and surrounds the campaign (especially since a close reading of *The Orphan* swiftly dispatches the moralizers' complaints almost from the off). As a self-confessed "contrarian swine," Barker sought to demonstrate that "the campaigners' accounts of their own motives and purposes could not be trusted" (2002, p. 70) and that the spark of hostility lay elsewhere. "Only when I dug behind their claims," explains Barker, "did the *politics* of the campaign come into view" and "the leading role in the entire campaign had been taken by the British Communist Party" (ibid). Fearful of the "barbarians" of American Imperialism storming Britain's cultural ramparts, however, "they ended up attacking the very comics which…were among the few popular cultural materials of that period to resist the McCarthyite paranoia about 'communists'"(ibid).

But what also emerges from *AHOF* is a manifesto about readers and audiences. In order to analyze a text, whatever its genre or medium, we need to understand "what is involved in the act of reading it, and how it builds a relation with its readers, and what impact is thus possible" (1984, p. 90). Barker's next book, *Comics: Ideology, Power and the Critics,* originally titled *Zapping Their Brains* and sadly out of print, is in some ways a thematic sequel to AHOF, but expands and further develops Barker's hermeneutics as he turns toward a wider selection of comic material, the bulk of them British. Beginning with another unacknowledged history, Barker looked into the curious tale of British weekly comic, *Action* (1976), which was canceled after only eight months. Once again, the figure of the child stands at the center as an open vessel for harmful and insidious media influence. And, once again, Barker drills down deeply to demonstrate how ill founded and steadfastly *political* the campaign against *Action* was. "Here is a comic that went-over-the-top," wrote Barker, summarizing the views of the censors. It was a "brimful of violence, perhaps even directly inciting delinquency" (1989, p. 23). It wasn't the "violent" content, however, that was a cause for concern—and Barker has repeatedly stressed that that "'violence' is not some singular 'thing' which might grow cumulatively like poison inside of people' (2001, p. 3), but means different things in different contexts—but that the comic "stood at the edge of a very radical politics—and that couldn't be allowed' (p. 49).

Comics: Ideology, Power and the Critics is a landmark text in the field of Comics Studies (which was emergent, even nascent, at the time of publication, especially in the Anglo-American sphere). What is central to the study is the concept of ideology, and it is here that Barker throws down a gauntlet: what would enable us to "test" prevalent theories of ideology? If the ideology of "violence," "romance" or what have you, and its direct consequences—its "effects"—is what concerns the "contemporary witch-hunters" (2001, p. 2), how come they have got it so wrong, especially when so much counter-evidence

(*Continued*)

is ignored? Such theories, Barker argued, are inherently political: "it commits them to assumptions which not only precede their evidence, but shape it" (1989, p. 3).

It is not only "the establishment" that gets Barker's goat. Academics, too, have fallen into the "effects" trap, none more so than Angela McRobbie's study of UK girl's comic, *Jackie*, wherein she sees as "an ideological bloc of mammoth proportions" (p. 155) that "stereotype[s] girls, restrict[s] them to feminine careers, [and] enforce[s] an ideology of romance on them" (p. 135). Barker's chagrin comes from a number of places. First, McRobbie fails to cite her sources, and this set Barker on a trail to search through editions of *Jackie* to uncover the stories examined. Second, the analysis is based on a parochial reading that ignores any evidence that might serve as a contradiction paralleled by an "un-transparent" methodology (2002). Third, the essay has been "quoted, feted, reprinted—and ultimately wrong" (ibid). It is not that Barker "present[ed] the magazine as a source of hidden virtues," but that it is "far more complicated than the critics have made out" (1989, p. 134). Part of Barker's project is to challenge analyses that read texts via pre-judgements that lead to "ideology-spotting," while ignoring the role of the reader:

> [w]e will only make progress...if we can uncover such implicit theorisations and develop appropriate tests. The tricky part is that it involves an interplay between studying the texts, and thinking about their readers. Any research which claims to stay on one side of the divide only, will be silently making assumptions. (1989, p. 247)

Other topics tackled in the book include the UK comic strip, *Scream Inn*. In a nutshell, *Scream Inn* is about a "grotesque Gothic Hostelry [which] held a haunted room in which no one had managed to stay the whole night. A challenge: any creature that did succeed in staying the night would win a million pounds!" (p. 62). Children were invited to write into the comic to propose challengers for the Inn, and Barker was able to gain access to 618 such proposals, which granted him access to "a kind of information rarely available about children's relations with a comic," relations that "were a product of their actual live relations...not of an artificial recall" (ibid). It is through this analysis that Barker began building his theory of "the contract" as a dialogic relationship between texts and readers by drawing upon the work of Valentin Voloshinov (1973):

> The idea of a 'contract' suggests that a magazine like *Jackie* is more than just a body of contents looking for a mind to invade. It suggests that it offers a kind of relationship to its readers. We might say that *Jackie* extends an invitation to readers to join in and use its contents in particular ways.
>
> (Barker, 1989, p. 257)

Barker's use of Voloshinov is certainly interesting but one that requires further development. The concept of the "contract" as a site whereby readers orient themselves to the material has plenty of potential. Comics "have to have a logic to which particular groups of readers are capable of orienting themselves" (p. 274), whether that logic involves fantastic elements, such as magic, or narrative sleight-of-hand (as in the *Scream Inn* strip). But the idea of "natural reader[s]," that is, "those whose typified life-experience makes them most able to become its implied audience" (p. 277) is problematic or, at least, undeveloped. Is there only *one* "contract" offered by the text and only *one* kind of "natural reader," for example? Moreover, as Strinati (2004, p. 232) states in his discussion of Barker's work, "we might ask what part power has to play in the forming of contract between texts and audiences," and is this relationship an equal one? The comics that Barker analyzes are not produced by readers, "but are the result of industrial and cultural production" (ibid). In this way, Barker's dialogical approach "is still a long way from considering how the relationships he discusses are influenced by the way popular culture becomes a commodity" (p. 233).

Although comics have historically—and unfairly—been accused of delinquency and of little cultural value, Barker concluded by stating: "let us have as many of the things as we possibly can. In the face of the capital-calculating machine called Thatcherism which uses morality like murderers use shotguns, all the little things like comics matter" (p. 301). Although he was writing in the 1980s, a period marked by neoliberalism and conservative governments on both sides of the Atlantic, Barker's words ring as true today as they did then.

Bibliography

Barker, M. (1981) *The New Racism: conservatives and the ideology of the tribe,* London: Junction Books.
Barker, M. (1984) *A Haunt of Fears,* London: Pluto Press.
Barker, M. (1989) *Comics: ideology, power and the critics,* Manchester: Manchester University Press.
Barker, M. (2002) 'Kicked into the gutters: or, "My dad doesn't read comics, he studies them'. *International Journal of Comic Art,* 4 (1): 64–77.
Barker, M. and Petley, J. (2001) *Ill Effects: the media/violence debate* 2nd edn, London: Routledge.
Strinati, D. (2004) *An Introduction to Theories of Popular Culture* 2nd edn, London: Routledge.
Voloshinov, V. (1973) *Marxism and the Philosophy of Language,* New York: Seminar Press.
Wertham, F. (1954) *Seduction of the Innocent,* London: Museum Press.

14

GENDER STUDIES AND QUEER STUDIES

Kane Anderson

STEVE TREVOR: Where am I?
PRINCESS DIANA: You're the only man on an island full of women!
TREVOR: …sounds like paradise.
DIANA: So you've heard of it… We've got to get you patched up.
TREVOR: Say, you're pretty strong for a girl.
DIANA: No, I'm just pretty strong.
TREVOR: I didn't mean to offend. …
DIANA: That doesn't mean you didn't.
—"The Secret Origin of Wonder Woman" in *Secret Origins* #6 (2014).

In studying comic books, a medium wherein characters' identities potentially shift and change from panel to panel, questions of identity and its stability come to the forefront for many scholars. The passage above from DC Comics' *Secret Origins* (2014) introduces the revised origin of Wonder Woman and offers us an example of the assumptions made on the basis of gender and sexuality. Steve Trevor, with dialogue that seems like a throwback to Wonder Woman's 1940s origins, states, "Say, you're pretty strong for a girl." Her correction that she is "just pretty strong" calls attention to the seeming expectations of Princess Diana's gender: she should be weak, or at least weaker than any man. Trevor calling an island full of women a "paradise" further frames the interaction in terms of his own heterosexuality. That Diana calls him out for his line of essentialist thinking on the basis of gender points to important questioning of how her identity is—or perhaps should be—considered.

As approaches to studying comic books, Gender Studies and Queer Studies unhook identity from the moorings of social constructions surrounding gender expression, gender identity, biological sex, and sexual orientation. These postmodern hermeneutics uncover and deconstruct social hierarchies to challenge assumptions of what is natural, normal, and privileged. Queer theory has always had as its central discourse a critique of what Michael Warner (1993) identifies as "regimes of the normal" (p. xxxvi); thus queerness can be read as that which is non-normative, or that which has been labeled abnormal with much of the negative connotation that word carries. Both Gender and Queer Studies scholars confront marginalization. They critique power relationships. They locate for those left out of the history and canon. Analyzing graphic literature with attention to gender roles and sexuality illustrates that identity is not static; rather, such scholarly strategies identify the fallacy of stability and point to how a dominant social position allows for the marginalization or disappearance of others. With the comic book industry largely dominated by heterosexual maleness (in America, at least), debunking the binaries of masculinity/femininity, straightness/queerness, and the limits/potential of biologies helps us understand how comic books may transmit certain ideological "truths" that are anything but true.

I want to offer an analogy here that may help clarify Gender Studies and Queer thinking in relation to comic books. Judith Butler's (1990) conception of gender performativity points to how a series of citational performances over time ultimately build toward a collection of narratives, signs, and behaviors that we recognize as gender. For our purposes, we might consider this similar to the character-building process enacted when a serially published superhero comic constructs what we know as "Superman" over issue after issue of stories about that character. Though we may recognize "Superman" as a particular creation in the popular sense, there are in fact many different articulations and interpretations constructing that concept.[1] Gender and Queer Studies approaches to Comics Studies function like retcons (retroactively revising narrative continuities). Retcons break such citational chains both by calling attention to the incongruities and by intentionally making them. In simplest terms, Gender and Queer Studies are often used to intervene in the perceived solidity (and perhaps simplicity) of established narratives to mine value from their contradictions. If DC Comics' *Crisis on Infinite Earths* (1985) meant to collapse that company's complicated histories into one single understanding of the DC Comics universe, then these approaches to Comics Studies mean to do the opposite: they break open narratives, they complicate histories, and they reveal alternate—but no less viable—realities existing alongside cultural hegemonies constructed in concepts like gender expression and sexuality.

My analogy is sure to rile up some *aca-fans* (even if they identify as fanboys, fangrrls… etc.). Much existing scholarship conflates Gender Studies with Feminist Studies and Queer Studies with LGBTQIA studies.[2] Certainly, a reciprocity exists, and my project here will indulge in some of this mixing as I frame gender and queerness as processes existing in the becoming; I do this because even defining the terms remains a contentious and ongoing project. Queerness as I use it here involves examining comic books as queer in terms of both content—i.e., LGBTQIA stories, characters, readings—and form. I argue that comic books themselves are queer. Despite leaping tall prejudices in multiple bounds (thanks in part to books like this one), comics are essentially still a queer medium operating on the fringes of more accepted art forms. More than the bastard child of literature and pictures, more than the progenitor of film-like storytelling in frames, comic books embrace their hybridity and defy easy classification in terms of existing media.

Grouping together discussions of gender expression, biological sex, and sexual orientation may be contentious to some as we should recognize that these are very different constructs. Though this chapter addresses some instances of sexuality in comics, I ask that we consider that sex in comics is always queer. From the strangely non-sexual forms of desire in early superhero stories, to the intentionally bold explicitness of underground erotica, to the more banal representations offered in some autobiographical comics, depictions of sexuality and sexual acts are divorced from actual bodies in favor of visual representations. These multifaceted images come to the reader mediated along a continuum of intents and deserve scrutiny for their implied situating of cisgender norms and often-compulsive heteronormativity.[3] My discussion means to touch on these varied issues as means of providing inroads to those seeking to take more directed research paths.

The bulk of comics scholarship viewing the medium and its narratives through the frames of gender and queerness concerns breaking down assumptions that sexuality, biological sex, and gender necessarily exist in patterns of normality versus abnormality. Still, Gender Studies, Queer Studies, Comics Studies, and the discourses among them, are still relatively new. Constructing a clear history of how they interact is difficult given the amount of inquiry still needing to be done. Certainly, some prominent scholars of gender theory exist and will appear in this chapter; still, queer approaches remain largely scattered. As such, in this chapter I aim to demonstrate which vectors scholars have taken in analyzing comics rather than attempting to construct a strict chronology of the applications themselves. What follows then is an attempt to reconcile these interdisciplinary networks in the becoming; as I discuss, they continue to develop as means of understanding comic books, graphic narratives, and the identity politics of characters, creators, and fans.

Comic books continually raise questions of gender construction and representation. Though considered by many a medium primarily made by and for the male gender, graphic literature offers a productive access point to discussing power relationships, identity politics, and the performance of gender beyond the false benchmarks of what is acceptable, deviant, or idealized. However, Gender Studies approaches are still relatively new in Comics Studies, and understandably so. Amy Kiste Nyberg's (1995) "Comic Books and Women Readers: Trespassers in Masculine Territory?" argues that expectations of gender norms permeate not only comic books but the creation, distribution, and purchase of them. In the context of the supposedly masculine milieu of comic book fandom, voices that question this dominance are in a sense going against the grain of the medium. Thankfully, the rise of acceptance of comic books as cultural artifacts invites deeper critique of their origins and interpretations and stake new claims for the characters and stories.

Admittedly, much early scholarship on comic books in their area conflates Gender Studies with Feminist Studies. While these discourses are certainly linked, the focus of Gender Studies considers the constructedness of gender roles in the false binaries of masculine versus feminine. This hermeneutic points to the panorama of gender positions and performances, often denying their stability and immutability. Given the absence in comics, or at least decreased visibility and perhaps viability, of gender articulations outside of a heteronormative, patriarchal gaze, much of the existing scholarship invoking these approaches still considers a Feminist perspective in recognizing how often problematic depictions of women occurred in the larger history of graphic literature.

The construction of the superheroine exists on a continuum of subversion of normative gender roles and reinforcement of hegemonic norms. In her book *Tough Girls: Women Warriors and Wonder Women in Popular Culture*, Sherrie A. Inness (1999) locates action heroism as traditionally belonging to the male gender. She complicates uninformed attempts to label heroism a masculine trait while also arguing that "toughness" breaks through gendered stereotypes. "Toughness," as Inness uses it, "always carries the threat of chaos, the breakdown of 'civilized' society," and is worshipped "because of its association with success and strength" (p. 14). Denying toughness as an exclusively male trait, Inness (2004) writes in her later book *Action Chicks: New Images of Tough Women in Popular Culture* that the female action heroines coincide with new expectations with the "tough aesthetic" for the female body in terms of blending the feminine with traditionally masculine behaviors like weightlifting. Comic book heroines therefore reconcile power and femininity in a medium that historically renders that relationship a paradox.

This relationship between the body and gender plays out significantly in comic books where the drawn body often reflects idealizations of masculinity and femininity in accordance with a male gaze. From the vantage point of a fan-scholar, Mike Madrid's publications begin to unpack some of these issues. His (2009) *The Supergirls: Fashion, Feminism, Fantasy, and the History of Comic Book Heroines* and its sequels chiefly historicize representations of women in popular comics. Madrid passionately brings greater visibility to these characters as he narrates the evolutions and trends of the female body amid the changing gender politics of American comic books. As a resource, his books provide an accessible introduction to some of the gendered power dynamics entrenched in comic book mythologies.

Cultural anthropologist Jeffrey A. Brown tackles these questions with greater depth, though. His research into popular culture looks to understand the placement of the subaltern groups as lacking in social status in relationship to mainstream society. Though perhaps best known for his book *Black Superheroes: Milestone Comics and Their Fans* (2001), Brown's contribution to comics scholarship excavates gender constructions as well as how race functions in relation to comic book characters and fan behaviors. In discussing what he calls "comic book masculinity," he challenges heterosexual masculinity as gender identity characterized by its naturalness and stability. Brown (2003) argues, "In general, masculinity is defined by what it is not, namely 'feminine,' and by all its associated traits—hard *not* soft, strong *not* weak, reserved *not* emotional, active *not* passive" (p. 168, emphasis in original). He exposes these false binaries, noting that comic book superheroes from Milestone Comics represent a complication of traditional forms of black masculinity by exercising as much, if not more, brain than brawn in their characterizations.

Brown continues to delve into issues of gender in his *Dangerous Curves: Action Heroines, Gender, Fetishism, and Popular Culture* (2011). He argues that the female action hero is necessarily "[…] overburdened as both a symbol of feminist agency in a genre rooted in masculine power fantasies and as a sexual fetish in visually oriented mediums that continue to present women as erotic ideals above all else" (p. 235). Looking beyond comic books to other popular culture media as well, this text challenges the objectification of female action heroes by considering how the dominant male gaze can subvert feminine and female power. He argues that female characters, often situated as sexualized object despite operating as primary antagonists, actually embody ongoing cultural change in terms of socially acceptable and celebrated femininities.

The push and pull between acceptable and deviant articulations of gender in comics extends to scholarship on creators as well as characters. Literary critic and English scholar Hillary Chute addresses the construction of gender and the presence of women in comic book autobiographies and documentaries. Her projects often negotiate how personal histories become publicly accessible graphic narratives. In *Graphic Women: Life Narrative and Contemporary Comics* (2010), Chute focuses on the autobiographical comics of Aline Kominsky-Crumb, Phoebe Gloeckner, Lynda Barry, Marjane Satrapi, and Alison Bechdel. Significantly, Chute's approach pays great attention to the construction of comic book storytelling in terms of words and images but also in dialectics of absence versus presence. Her scholarship follows a feminist trajectory as she brings female authors to the forefront of her discussions, arguing that much of current "feminist cultural production is in the form of accessible yet edgy graphic narratives" (p. 2). Chute further specifically considers comic book narratives in relation to the drawn body on the page as a means of analyzing identity politics when she argues, "[t]hus, while we may read comics' spatializing of narrative as a hybrid project, we may read this hybridity as a challenge to the structure of binary classification that opposes a set of terms, privileging one" (p. 10). In other words, comic books, even on a purely structural level, invite and support research agendas that are diverse and multivalent.

As cultural artifacts with decades of continuity, comic books can also serve as means to measure and evaluate these changes in gender and identity politics over time. Best known as the editor of the series of *The Ages of...* anthologies analyzing popular superheroes, Joseph J. Darowski is an American Studies scholar who examines how the changes in comic book characters reflect changing cultural mores in American culture.[4] His research examines these characters while recognizing gender as a narrative of ongoing development. In his book, *X-Men and the Mutant Metaphor: Race and Gender in the Comic Book* (2014), Darowski identifies Marvel Comics' characters the X-Men as exemplars of perceptions of gender. In discussing the pattern of X-Men heroes becoming villains (Jean Grey to Dark Phoenix, Professor X to Onslaught, etc.), Darowski locates within the transformation from good to evil an altered articulation of the characters' genders. Jean Grey becomes hyper-sexualized while Onslaught is an over-muscled, violent aggressor in direct contrast to the wheelchair-bound professor. However, the consequences of evil acts see females die versus males imprisoned and soon pardoned. The upshot: female sexuality is evil and unforgivable while some problematically hyperbolic masculinity is easier to accept. Framing such reoccurring narratives as spaces from which we may recognize the overlap of objectification and idealization, Darowski points to the problematically ingrained assumptions of power articulated in gender. His project also provides a statistical analysis of how the X-Men, known for supposed diversity, at many times prove less than representative of difference.

Significantly, these changes in representing and understanding the plurality of gender identities extend to fandom as well. Alongside the evolution of scholarship critiquing comics books through the lens of Gender Studies, there evolved the study of comics fandom as a gendered entity. As a "geektavist" and founder of Seattle's GeekGirlCon convention celebrating the intersections of women and geek culture like comics fandom and gaming, Jennifer K. Stuller looks for greater diversity in comics and fandom. Stuller explores how female heroes in modern mythologies like comic books break through gender barriers. She highlights the reciprocal relationship between pop culture and sociopolitical ideologies to reclaim the positions of diverse populations as media makers in their own rights. She seeks to return those of subaltern gender, race, or status to the discussion. Her *Ink-Stained Amazons and Cinematic Warriors* (2010) harks back to Nathaniel Hawthorne of *The Scarlet Letter* fame decrying female writers as "damned scribbling women" and "ink-stained Amazons." *Ink-Stained Amazons* further introduces a plurality to the concept of heroes. Reframing the discussion in terms of heroisms opens up traditional representations of popular heroes to a more diverse panorama of experiences. In doing so, she reclaims the fan position as one that includes a plurality of races and genders as well. Somewhat extending this discussion, Mel Gibson (2015) primarily delves into how younger readers—particularly females—negotiate narratives in graphic literature. While she primarily looks at British and American comic books, her theorizing on audience reception identifies how childhood may be constructed alongside strict gender divides—arguing that comics are more often linked to boyhood than girlhood. Her research further reveals how reading the mainstream comics aimed at boys becomes a transgressive act for some female readers. Breaking down imposed gender barriers via comic books and their culture allows scholars to mark the broader social issues of equality and representation in not just comic book narratives, but also in comic book consumerism and fandom. It demonstrates that Comics Studies *is* Cultural Studies.

A developing vector of Comics Studies investigates the utility of comic books as a pedagogical tool, particularly in regards to gender. Breaking down the potentially problematic introduction of comic book material to younger female readers in her 2004 book, Inness uses female action figures to illustrate how children bring new narratives to life by defying the expectations of manufacturers, pointing to how gender may be performed critically and innocently simultaneously. Anne H Thalheimer's (2009) "Too Weenie to Deal with All of This 'Girl Stuff': Women, Comics, and the Classroom" takes this further, attesting to the value of graphic novels in opening up difficult conversations on feminism, gender inequality, and women's history. In part because of the cultural bias about and within comics, comic books can appear innocent or ephemeral when they actually communicate highly complex narratives that illustrate how normative views on gender and sexuality can seem natural when they are in fact not so. Christina Blanch, a comic book creator and scholar, deploys this assumed ambiguity in examining the functions and methods of comics scholarship, particularly in relation to gender. Her 2013 Super MOOC (massive open online course) "Gender through Comics" attracted thousands of students and introduced them to comic books as means to track changes in the perceptions of gender over time. Intentionally stepping away from often-examined staples like *Persepolis* (Satrapi, 2000) and *Fun Home: A Family Tragicomic* (Bechdel, 2006), Blanch demonstrates how Gender Studies can operate as a lens through which to understand any comic book. Of particular value is her argument that the 1990s saw an obsession with male strength versus female frailty in many mainstream comic books. Recognizing this as a reaction to third wave Feminism, Blanch (2013) identifies how a focus on physical stature, even hyperbolic articulations thereof, may reinforce gender norms and stereotypes. Her approach of integrating interviews with comic book creators with scholarly texts on gender and sexuality opens up discussions on the continuum of masculinity and femininity in contemporary graphic literature. One innovative and generative approach of Blanch's involves asking comic book creators and students to score the Bem Sex Role Inventory test on well-known comic book superheroes. The resulting placements—including Batman as hyper-masculine and Superman as more feminine—demonstrate the ongoing negotiation of these popular characters in the gender spectrum.

This gender spectrum is of course fluid and unstable, especially when it intersects the spectrum of sexual orientation. Therefore, the reciprocity between Gender Studies and Queer Studies exists in overlapping narratives and hermeneutics. Largely emerging from the rise of feminist thought that questions the constructedness of gender roles as well as a reaction to the dehumanizing rhetoric against homosexuality during the 1980s AIDS crisis, queer theory seeks to reexamine identity politics by both disrupting those discursive tropes of sexuality and gender by which we categorize ourselves and others and by revealing the once-suppressed existence of gay, lesbian, and transgendered individuals in our cultural narratives. In her entry on comic books in the *Encyclopedia of Lesbian, Gay, Bisexual and Transgendered History in America*, Thalheimer (2004) argues that queer characters have likely existed in comics since the medium's inception, albeit mostly in the background (p. 250). However, most queer characters, creators, and storylines were largely invisible in mainstream American comics for much of the medium's history. Underground comic books, or comix, offered some representation but were even more ephemeral and disposable than their supposedly more legitimate cousins. Until relatively recently, comics scholarship followed this trajectory with many scholars even forgoing the words "gay" or "queer" in their supposedly inclusive looks at graphic literature. This "presence-by-absence"—understood in the context of how Eve Kosofsky Sedgwick (2008) debunks the assumed coupling of queer sexual activities with preconceived, non-sexual behaviors at times labeled similarly "suspect" or "abhorrent"—points to the value of these approaches to studying comics: at the intersection of Queer Studies with graphic literature, then, is a project of legitimizing queer characters, their explicit or implicit narratives, and also the contributions of queer creators and fans.

Perhaps controversially, I see the earliest of instances of the Queer Studies of comic books in the work of infamous anti-comics crusader Fredric Wertham. When Wertham attacked the comic book industry in the 1950s for its supposedly insidious potential to corrupt America's youth, he claimed comics taught children homosexuality by essentially queering some of the comic book industry's most famous characters.[5] To queer something is to deconstruct its singular homogeneity in favor of more diverse, inclusive, and unstable readings. However, in a more literal usage of that concept, by queering a character or story, a scholar excavates the seemingly absent LGBTQIA narrative within a supposedly heteronormative work. Famously, Wertham (1954) identifies Batman and Robin as "like a wish dream of two homosexuals living together" (p. 190). As a psychologist, Wertham points to the characters' lavish lifestyle as confirmed bachelors living in sumptuous Wayne Manor, arguing, "Only someone ignorant of the fundaments of psychiatry and of the psychopathology of sex can fail to realize a subtle atmosphere of homoeroticism which pervades the adventures" of the Caped Crusaders (pp. 189–190). While we should certainly recall that Wertham aimed to denigrate comics as a whole in a particular sociotemporal moment when LGBTQIA individuals suffered great discrimination, his strategy noticeably relies on queerness as a cultural boogeyman. Still, he imposes a queer narrative atop superheroes at a time when superhero comics were decidedly heteronormative.

In critiquing Wertham's argument, Mark Best (2005) rejects the conflation of homosociality with homosexuality. Instead, Best asserts that superhero comics in the 1950s played with the divide between the two inherent in the hyperbolic masculinity and male fantasy as represented by the superhero. This push and pull on the relationship among masculinity, homosociality, and homosexuality encourages the use of queerness as a lens with which to analyze comics when we consider that many genres of comics—war, Westerns, superhero—all articulate versions of maleness based on ideals of how manliness was constructed in the 1940s and 1950s. The coding of queerness exists in those comics even if their stories are ostensibly heteronormative.

Indeed, the controversial essay "Batman, Deviance and Camp" by Andy Medhurst (1991) aligns Batman squarely with homosexuality and gay culture, arguing that gay audiences, denied supportive images that reflect their own sexuality and culture "had to fashion what [they] could out of the images of dominance, to snatch illicit meanings from the fabric of normality, to undertake a corrupt decoding for the purposes of satisfying marginalized desires" (p. 153). Despite some problematic value judgments in his phrasing, Medhurst points to queering as a fan practice long before it was a scholarly practice. He makes a provocative point that the introduction of queerness by Wertham likely influenced the

1960s *Batman* television show's camp sensibility. The lasting associations between Batman and gayness continue to play out in popular culture and as a lens in which to read Batman's comic book stories.

The recognition of explicit, implicit, and disappeared sexuality is a significant part of Queer Studies' approaches to studying comics. Andréa Gilroy's (2015) "The Epistemology of the Phone Booth: The Superheroic Identity and Queer Theory in *Batwoman: Elegy*" argues that the popular press' titillation of a lesbian Batwoman is far less important than the manner in which sexuality and physical prowess are linked. Gilroy's application of theories of drag performance frames Batwoman's lesbianism, her sexualized depiction, and her at times heteronormative flirtations as dynamic and overlapping gendered performances. Such performances of gender, according to Gilroy, aren't meant to "fool" audiences; instead, they hyperbolically depict the complexity of gender and queerness amid the characters' (and creators') carefully deployed strategies of enacting feminine gender. By demonstrating how easily assumptions of normativity may miss queer narratives at play in comics, scholars like Gilroy point to the expectations of heteronormativity embedded in most mainstream comics.

When considered as a popular medium reflective of American culture, such comic books reflect a compulsive heterosexuality at work in society across multiple forms of entertainment. At stake in such theorizing is the legitimacy of comic books as a medium accessible and meaningful to diverse readerships. Media artist and scholar Rob Lendrum (2004) addresses, among other things, the "ownership" of masculinity. His analysis of Marvel's 2003 series *The Rawhide Kid* "Slap Leather" argues that the gunslinger is a distinctly American idealization of masculinity. Marvel Comics reinvented their character the Rawhide Kid as a gay character, with author Ron Zimmerman invoking some stereotypes of queer men in his portrayal of the Western hero. Lendrum aims to expose the fallacy in the largely unquestioned link between such masculinity and heteronormativity. His work breaks down the assumption that gay characters may not be masculine characters even while he also acknowledges an entrenched narrative of queer deviance at work in many comics.

This association between queer and deviance seems to be fading as mainstream comics incorporate LGBTQIA characters into stories in popular comics. The rise of queer characters accompanies an appreciation for using queer formats in mainstream comic books. As a comics scholar, Paul Petrovic's work intersects queerness in relation to content as well as form. He pays particular attention to borders and frames as means of queering the comics page. When discussing DC Comics' lesbian Batwoman (2011a), he argues that artist J. H. Williams III's art breaks the traditional form so as to challenge the character's previous incarnations as heteronormative. In his essay "'It Came Out of Nothing Except Our Love': Queer Desire and Transcendental Love in *Promethea*" invoking Thierry Groensteen's theorizing on comic art, Petrovic (2012) argues that the panels and borders of the comic "are gendered as normative and heterosexual, while the foregrounding of gaps acts to queer and liberate…" (pp. 163–164). The recognition of the border and frame as a construct that shapes readers' reception of narrative echoes Queer Studies in considering how language has been subtly used to define and contain gendered and anti-queer thought through imposed normatizing.

Scrutinizing and deconstructing the concept of normalcy is particularly provocative in scholarship surrounding superhero comics. The secret identity and the stakes of its revelation make a suitable analogy for LGBTQIA individuals hiding in the closet considering that superheroes hid their true identities in elaborate performances of normalcy. That Wertham queers Batman, Robin, and Wonder Woman should come as no surprise in that sense. In contrast to my earlier argument that queerness was hidden and only recently came to the forefront of writing and researching comic books, Noah Berlatsky (2012) asserts that the absence of queerness in American comic books is something of a fallacy. His article "Comic Books Have Always Been Gay" on *Slate.com* points to an undercurrent of queerness at work in American comics for most of their existence:

> According to the companies [DC and Marvel Comics], and of course, conservative groups, this [storylines featuring gay content] is a significant step—forward or backward, depending on your politics. But the truth is, comic books have been gay from the genre's inception.

Indeed, Berlatsky speaks to comics addressing queerness and sexuality with surprising openness as far back as the 1940s. His book *Wonder Woman: Bondage and Feminism in the Marston/Peter Comics, 1941–1948* (2014) interrogates the history of Wonder Woman and her creators in relation to feminism, gender, and queerness. Debunking the often assumed simplicity of Golden Age comic books, Berlatsky locates the stakes of queerness in Wonder Woman, an icon amid phallic imagery, bondage fantasies, and, most striking, rape. He complicates the binaries of masculine/feminine and gay/straight in critiquing the campy stories of early *Wonder Woman* comics and their explicit and implicit allusions to kink, lesbianism, and the fluidity of sexual identity. Most provocatively from a scholarly perspective, Berlatsky puts Wonder Woman's creator William Moulton Marston in conversation with contemporary gender and queer studies scholars like Judith Butler and Julia Serrano in order to position Marston as feminist and queer theorist in his own right.

Recognizing the existence of queerness and how it functions as a project of social change remains at the heart of these hermeneutics. Perhaps the most direct application of Queer Studies on comic books is Ramzi Fawaz's (2015) book *The New Mutants: Superheroes and the Radical Imagination of American Comics*. Fawaz employs queer theory as a lens to look at comic books—particularly the X-Men—in relation to civil rights movements and social justice. Critiquing comic book narratives in relation to radical politics like the Gay Liberation Movement, he considers how many readers of comics find themselves identifying with characters for their outcast status. Fawaz recognizes not only how gay and lesbian readers feel distanced from the normative mainstream, but also how comics provided cultural access points to other marginalized groups who faced discriminatory practices in post-World War II America. His work situates popular culture as a means of helping to activate and illustrate the movements of gender, sexual, and racial equality.

The scholars mentioned above each contribute to the developing scholarly narrative that expands the reach of Comics Studies. Like Superman's "Never-Ending Battle for Truth, Justice, and the American Way," the nature of Gender and Queer Studies approaches is that they always exist in the becoming. Gender and Queer Studies will never arrive, never be finished; they are always and only ways toward something else. In this chapter, I've attempted to demonstrate how scholars situate comic books as a fertile ground for that something else. Whether we locate "Superman" in his near-saintly lust for Lois Lane or his more contemporary and sexualized relationship with Wonder Woman—or in the slash narratives of the Man of Steel in sexual congress with Batman or Jimmy Olsen—Gender and Queer

Studies approaches to studying comics reveal an ever-developing panorama of conflicting stories and images that potentially provide deeper understanding of the character, the medium, and its fans.

Notes

1 This says nothing of how television shows, cartoons, films, Internet content, novels, and many more media further coalesce into what we know popularly to be "Superman."
2 For purposes of this narrative, I occasionally use LGBTQIA as shorthand for Lesbian, Gay, Bisexual, Transgender, Queer, Intersex, and Asexual (and sometimes Ally). By no means do I mean to ascribe any sort of universality to these positions; throughout this chapter I will use "queer" as shorthand and will use more specific terms when they are called for.
3 Cisgender, a relatively new term, refers to one whose gender identity corresponds to what was assigned at birth. Commonly, it is used as opposed to the term "transgender." However, this terminology continues to develop.
4 Each published by McFarland, *The Ages of… Superman* (2012), *Wonder Woman* (2013), *Avengers* (2014), *X-Men* (2014), *Iron Man* (2015), *Incredible Hulk* (2016).
5 Comics scholar Carol L. Tilley largely debunks much of Wertham's evidence and methods, noting his deep-seated biases. See "Seducing the Innocent: Fredric Wertham and the Falsifications That Helped Condemn Comics" (2012).

Bibliography

Azzarello, B., Chang, C. (writers) and Sudsuka, G. (artist). (2014) 'The secret origin of Wonder Woman', *Secret Origins #6*, New York: DC Comics.
Bechdel, A. (2006) *Fun Home: a family tragicomic*, Boston: Houghton Mifflin.
Berlatsky, N. (2012) 'Comic books have always been gay', *Slate.com*. [Online] Available from: http://www.slate.com/blogs/xx_factor/2012/06/01/gay_comic_books_have_been_around_since_the_birth_of_wonder_woman.html. [Accessed 11 July 2015].
Berlatsky, N. (2014) *Wonder Woman: bondage and feminism in the Marston/Peter comics, 1941–1948*, New Brunswick: Rutgers University Press.
Best, M.T. (2005) 'Domesticity, homosociality, and male power in superhero comics in the 1950s', *Iowa Journal of Comics Studies*, 6: 80–99.
Blanch, C.L. (2013) 'What do comic books teach us about gender attitudes?', *Forbes.com*. [Online] Available from: http://www.forbes.com/sites/forbeswomanfiles/2013/01/23/what-do-comic-books-teach-us-about-gender-attitudes/#6e2743c916ac. [Accessed 11 July 2015].
Blanch, C.L. and Mulvihill, T.M. (2015) 'Do serenity comics forecast our pedagogies of identity and construction?', in V.E. Frankel (ed.) *The Comics of Joss Whedon: critical essays*, Jefferson, NC: McFarland.
Brown, J.A. (2001) *Black Superheroes: Milestone Comics and their fans*, Jackson: University Press of Mississippi.
Brown, J.A. (2011) *Dangerous Curves: action heroines, gender, fetishism, and popular culture*, Jackson: University Press of Mississippi.
Brown, J.A. (2013) 'Comic book masculinity', in C. Hatfield, J. Heer and K. Worcester (eds.) *The Superhero Reader*, Jackson: University of Mississippi Press.
Brown, J.A. and Loucks, M. (eds.) (2014) 'A comic of her own: Women writing, reading and embodying through comics', *ImageText*, 7 (4). [Online] Available from: http://www.english.ufl.edu/imagetext/archives/v7_4/. [Accessed 11 July 2015].
Butler, J. (1990) *Gender Trouble: feminism and the subversion of identity*, New York: Routledge.
Chute, H. (2010) *Graphic Women: life narrative and contemporary comics*, New York: Columbia University Press.
Chute, H. (2012) 'Graphic narrative', in J. Bray, A. Gibbons and B. McHale (eds.) *The Routledge Companion to Experimental Literature*, New York: Routledge.

Chute, H. (2016) *Disaster Drawn: visual witness, comics, and documentary form*, Cambridge: Harvard University Press.
Chute, H. and Jagoda, P. (eds.). (2014) 'Comics & media', *Critical Inquiry*, 40 (3).
Darowski, J.J. (ed.). (2013) *The Ages of Wonder Woman: essays on the Amazon Princess in changing times*, Jefferson, NC: McFarland.
Darowski, J.J. (2014) *X-Men and the Mutant Metaphor: race and gender in the comic books*, Lanham, MD: Rowman & Littlefield.
Fawaz, R. (2011) '"Where no X-man has gone before!" Mutant superheroes and the cultural politics of popular fantasy in postwar America', *American Literature*, 83 (2): 355–88.
Fawaz, R. (2015) *The New Mutants: superheroes and the radical imagination of American comics*, New York: New York University Press.
Gibson, M. (2010) 'What Bunty did next: exploring some of the ways in which the British girls' comic protagonists were revisited and revised in Late twentieth-century comics and graphic novels', *Journal of Graphic Novels & Comics*, 1 (2): 121–35.
Gibson, M. (2011) 'Cultural studies: British girls' comics, readers and memories', in M.J. Smith & R. Duncan (eds.) *Critical Approaches to Comics: theories and methods*, New York: Routledge.
Gibson, M. (2015) *Remembered Reading: memory, comics and post-war constructions of British girlhood*, Leuven: Leuven University Press.
Gilroy, A. (2015) 'The epistemology of the phone booth: The superheroic identity and queer theory in *Batwoman: Elegy*', *ImageTexT*, 8 (1). [Online] Available from: http://www.english.ufl.edu/imagetext/archives/v8_1/gilroy/. [Accessed 11 July 2015].
Inness, S.A. (1999) *Tough Girls: women warriors and Wonder Women in popular culture*, Philadelphia: University of Pennsylvania Press.
Inness, S.A. (ed.). (2004) *Action Chicks: new images of tough women in popular culture*, New York: Palgrave Macmillan.
Kosofsky Sedgwick, E. (2008) *Epistemology of the Closet*, Berkeley: University of California Press.
Lendrum, R. (2004) 'Queering super-manhood: the gay superhero in contemporary mainstream comic books', *Journal for the Arts, Sciences, and Technology*, 2 (2): 69–73.
Lendrum, R. (2005a) 'Queering super-manhood: superhero masculinity, camp and public relations as a textual framework', *International Journal of Comic Art*, 7 (1): 287–303.
Lendrum, R. (2005b) 'The super black macho, one baaad mutha: black superhero masculinity in 1970s mainstream comic books', *Extrapolation: Journal of Science Fiction and Fantasy*, 46 (3): 360–72.
Madrid, M. (2009) *The Supergirls: fashion, feminism, fantasy, and the history of comic book heroines*, Ashland, OR: Exterminating Angel Press.
Madrid, M. (2013) *Divas, Dames & Daredevils: lost heroines of Golden Age comics*, Ashland, OR: Exterminating Angel Press.
Madrid, M. (2014) *Vixens, Vamps & Vipers: lost villainesses of Golden Age comics*, Ashland, OR: Exterminating Angel Press.
Medhurst, A. (1991) 'Batman, deviance and camp', in R.E. Pearson and W. Uricchio (eds.) *The Many Lives of the Batman: critical approaches to a superhero and his Media*, New York, Routledge.
Nyberg, A.K. (1995) 'Comic books and women readers: trespassers in masculine territory?', in P.C. Rollins and S.W. Rollins (eds.) *Gender in Popular Culture: images of men and women in literature, visual media and material culture*, Cleveland: Ridgemont.
Petrovic, P. (2011a) 'Queer resistance, gender performance, and 'coming out' of the panel borders in Greg Rucka and J.H. Williams III's *Batwoman: Elegy*', *Journal of Graphic Novels and Comics*, 2 (1): 67–76.
Petrovic, P. (2011b) 'The culturally constituted gaze: fetishizing the feminine from Alan Moore and Dave Gibbons's *Watchmen* to Zack Snyder's *Watchmen*', *ImageTexT* 5 (4).[Online] Available from: http://www.english.ufl.edu/imagetext/archives/v5_4/petrovic/. [Accessed 27 June 2015].
Petrovic, P. (2012) 'It came out of nothing except our love': queer desire and transcendental love in *Promethea*', in T.A. Corner and J.M. Sommers (eds.) *Sexual Ideology in the Works of Alan Moore: critical essays on the graphic novels*, Jefferson, NC: McFarland.

Satrapi, M. (2000). *Persepolis,* Paris: L'Association.
Stuller, J.K. (ed.). (2010) *Ink-Stained Amazons and Cinematic Warriors: superwomen in modern mythology,* New York: I.B. Tauris.
Stuller, J.K. (2011) 'Feminism: second-wave feminism in the pages of *Lois Lane*', in M.J. Smith and R. Duncan (eds.) *Critical Approaches to Comics: theories and methods,* New York: Routledge.
Stuller, J.K. (2013) 'Love will bring you to your gift', in C. Hatfield, J. Heer and K. Worcester (eds.) *The Superhero Reader,* Jackson: University of Mississippi Press.
Thalheimer, A.N. (2004) 'Comics and comic books', *Encyclopedia of Lesbian, Gay, Bisexual and Transgendered History in America, Vol. 1,* Detroit: Charles Scribner's Sons.
Thalheimer, A.N. (2009) 'Too weenie to deal with all of this 'girl stuff': women, comics, and the classroom', in S.E. Tabachnick (ed.) *Teaching the Graphic Novel,* New York: Modern Language Association.
Tilley, C.L. (2012) 'Seducing the innocent: Fredric Wertham and the falsifications that helped condemn comics', *Information & Culture: A Journal of History,* 47 (4): 383–413.
Warner, M. (1993) 'Introduction', in M. Warner (ed.) *Fear of a Queer Planet,* Minneapolis: University of Minnesota Press.
Wertham, F. (1954) *Seduction of the Innocent,* New York: Rinehart.
Wonder Women! The Untold Story of American Superheroines. (2012) Film. Directed by Kristy Guevara-Flanagan. [DVD] US: New Day Films.

15
MANGA STUDIES, A HISTORY

Nicholas A. Theisen

The history of manga[1] studies has to be regarded as a persistent question—what is it exactly? And when did it begin?—that swiftly dissolves into a number of related, fundamental, and arguably tedious questions. This oft-untraveled mode of inquiry, though, undermines the composition of a clear vector of a critical tradition with an obvious or at least consensual point of departure arriving over many pages at its terminus in the here and now. If what is desired is the account of a more-or-less self-sustaining critical discourse surrounding manga in Japan, then I would direct the reader to Jaqueline Berndt's already excellent but not quite up-to-date "Considering Manga Discourse: Location, Ambiguity, Historicity" from 2008. Berndt's somewhat narrow purview for dealing with the "what is manga studies?" question is especially apt, when considering how the moment one steps out of this localized framing, the questions of where to begin and where to stop become increasingly fraught. On the one hand, it might strike the reader as rather unreasonable—perhaps not—to begin with Katsushika Hokusai's[2] prefaces to the several volumes of his *Hokusai manga* (1814) that make clearly programmatic claims about the nature of illustration and therefore manga. Likewise, it seems odd to ignore Kitazawa Rakuten's similarly programmatic claims in the early 20th century or Okamoto Ippei's systematic conceptualization of manga in his how-to-draw manual from 1928.[3] Yet, I am not going to discuss Hokusai's claims here, though they are worthy of discussion, even as I treat Rakuten and Ippei in depth, even though all three fall rather easily into the category of "creator" or "artist" and only uneasily into those of "critic" or "scholar," upon which we regularly depend to separate disciplines from the vast expanses of anyone saying anything whatsoever. My justification for making this arbitrary split within the category of, shall we say, critically engaged practitioners of earlier manga history lies in how Rakuten and Ippei represent an alternative conceptualization of what manga is. For most of the 20th century, this [pre]conception of manga was largely forgotten or ignored. Of late, though, manga studies within Japan and without has, almost accidentally, come back to it as a means of integrating a field, if not a discipline, that has developed an international interest, yet for some time only in relatively isolated pockets. In the earliest days of what might be recognized as "international" manga studies, many non-Japanese critics of manga demonstrated little interest in the Japanese language discourse of *mangagaku* ("manga studies"), and, coincidentally, scholars and critics writing in Japanese quite often demonstrated little if any interest in Comics Studies outside Japan's national boundaries.

This chapter, then, is bookended by early and latter-day "internationalizations" of manga studies. It will also recount the "four stages" of manga discourse in Japan that Berndt (2008) treats, by her own admission, perfunctorily and fill in a number of gaps in her account. This discussion will point to the necessity for expanding the manga studies temporal window to include, at least, Rakuten, Ippei, and Tezuka Osamu in the critical discourse that "begins" in the 1960s. I also intend to present a "history" of manga studies as wildly divergent along a number of paths that periodically overlap and persist even as later critical movements appear to obviate them. It is, perhaps, more correct to speak of four zones of manga discourse than four stages, as the second term implies a certain trajectory, a movement away from rather than within a realm of possibilities. Finally, I hope this history, imperfect and far from comprehensive as it may be, opens up rather than closes off any ready sense of what manga might be as well as the study thereof. Because more and more Japanese critics produce work in English, my main focus will be on the Anglophone critical sphere. As more non-Japanese critics involve themselves outside their native milieu and as more translated work crosses the substantial language barrier between Japanese and non-Japanese Comics Studies, any strict sense of manga as uniquely Japanese, be it in terms of language or culture, breaks down. Coincidentally, this "broken down" *manga* is far more in keeping with how the word is used in the Japanese language.

Early Japanese Comics Theory

Miyamoto Hirohito (2009) has identified two broad categories of manga historiography: one that emphasizes the post-war history of manga as significantly breaking with the medium as understood thereto and one that sees manga or something profoundly manga-like in any of a number of art forms going back more than a thousand years, typically beginning with the *Chōjū jinbutsu giga*—a set of four illustrated scrolls from Kōzan-ji in Kyoto that depict anthropomorphized animals in a satire of contemporary social mores. The archetype of the ancient history school of manga and of the numerous manga histories to later take this tack is Hosokibara Seiki's *Nihon manga-shi [History of Japanese Manga]*[4] from 1924. He was the first to make an explicit connection between the still somewhat new *manga*, even though the word dates back to the very end of the 18th century, and the long-established *giga*, a then catchall term for amusing illustrations, but especially with the aforementioned *Chōjū giga* in mind. Hosokibara was not, strictly speaking, a scholar, but rather an artist and poet whose *manga* appeared in the newspapers *Keijō nippō*, *Tōkyō nichi-nichi shinbun*, and *Ōsaka asahi shibun*, so his critical work falls quite clearly into that category also occupied by Rakuten, Ippei, and Tezuka, amongst many others. In fact, what is typically regarded, at least among academics, as the "beginning" of manga studies in the overly schematic "four stages" is merely the beginning of a kind of manga critique practiced by those who were not also producing manga in some capacity. Moreover, as Hosokibara's example makes clear, these practitioner-critics established the baseline, the fundamental presumptions of which those critics of the now-consensual tradition operated and largely still operate, even though nowadays those presumptions do not always go unchallenged.

However, the "long history" conceptualization of manga was not the only one in play in the 1920s. Kitazawa Rakuten conceived of manga as completely divorced from this tradition. As Ron Stewart (2013) notes in "Manga as Schism," "Rakuten did not think of *manga* as the outgrowth of a Japanese tradition and did not feel much value could be learned from Japanese artists of the past" (p. 34). The manga that appeared in Rakuten's *Tokyo Puck*, the magazine he created in 1905 once he was free from the constraints imposed by his work at the newspaper *Jiji shinpō*, were quite often tri-lingual—Japanese, English, and Chinese. This trio of languages reflected not only an international orientation for manga but also a grounding in *recent*, not distant, Japanese history, in particular the treaty port culture of Yokohama, where Rakuten had his first job as an illustrator for E.V. Thorn's trade publication *Box of Curios* and where those three languages were in regular circulation. Rakuten perceived manga as "an international visual language" that was "universal and modern" (Stewart, 2013, p. 34), not uniquely Japanese. From the beginning, Rakuten's models were for the most part Euro-American, not Japanese, meaning manga according to this cast was fundamentally transnational. This is a key difference from Hosokibara and those who follow him—and even many who do not—because the long history posits an essentially Japanese base upon which non-Japanese comics may exhibit an influence and result in recognizable deviations, as is often asserted with regard to manga in the immediate post-war period under the Allied occupation of Japan. Rakuten turns this notion on its head: manga is what resists Japanese essentialism and does so by drawing upon an entire world of comic art.

At first glance, Okamoto Ippei's conceptualization of manga in his *Shin manga no kakikata [How to Draw the New Manga]*[5] from 1928 might align well with Hosokibara's long history, though Ippei arguably exposes what may, in fact, be profoundly arbitrary in drawing a connection between manga and illustrated text more generally, for Ippei expands manga precursors to include classical Japanese authors such as Sei Shōnagon and Yoshida Kenkō, who were literary and not visual artists. Moreover, Ippei looks well beyond Japan for ancient precursors. In a section on "Western manga" [*ōbei manga*], Ippei (1990) reproduces a famous illustration from the interior of a Greek drinking vessel in which a woman holds a man's head as he vomits (p. 186). The thread connecting all of these examples Ippei draws together in his text is not a localized culture and its history or the rejection thereof but a sense of manga as an attitude or orientation toward the world. For Ippei, manga is a form of "illustration wherein one freely observes and freely depicts" (p. 9) the world and in so doing represents human experience in its full range of ambiguities and contradictions. Ippei elaborates upon this notion of manga as free observation and depiction, by juxtaposing manga with original works of art [*honga*] and later with *ponchi*, the form of exaggerated comic illustration often involving elaborate visual-verbal interplay that emerged in the latter half of the 19th century. Manga here is neither ideal, as in a work of art, nor hyperbolic, as in caricature, but rather considered and polysemous, susceptible to divergent readings that may contradict but never overrule one another. Manga is a matrix of possibilities as wide as the world, not a representation of any one particular idea.

If each of these conceptualizations of manga was available prior to World War II and prior to the establishment of a stable manga studies discourse in the 1960s, the question remains as to why both Rakuten and Ippei were largely forgotten as manga theorists and potential progenitors of later manga criticism. The answer is, in part, Tezuka Osamu, who, in addition to creating works such as *Manga daigaku [Manga University]* (1950) that sought to explain comic art to the masses, tried to control how manga history was perceived and especially who should and should not be considered proper *mangaka*. In an interview with

Ishiko Jun, later published as *Tezuka Osamu - manga no ōgi [Tezuka Osamu—The Secret to Manga]* (interviewed 1988, printed 1997), Tezuka regards both Rakuten and Ippei as only partially *mangaka*, more akin to journalists, especially since both worked for newspapers and addressed current affairs in their work, than to comic artists. To this end he identifies a number of arbitrary criteria for *mangaka* status, some more and some less convincing (such as needing to draw with a pen rather than a brush), which appear to justify, after the fact, a sequestration already accomplished before the criteria were named (p. 28). This might pass as a mere curiosity, except for the fact that some later manga critics actually make serious use of Tezuka's criteria. Takeuchi Ichirō, for example, in 2006 relied on Tezuka's own criteria in an attempt to reestablish the artist as preeminent in a scholarly environment that has in recent years worn away his supposedly godlike status.

More to the point, though, in the same interview with Ishiko (1997), Tezuka identifies Miyao Shigeo as the first true or "100%" *mangaka* and his debut title *Manga Tarō* as the seminal manga text, both for the reason of its being pen-generated line art and, less ridiculously, for being the seminal narrative manga for children (p. 28). Tezuka's assumption is that the essence of all manga lies in *kodomo manga*, comics for children, while not entirely denying the designation of comic art to the more politically and socially observant manga of artists who preceded Miyao but still regarding them as deviations from manga's core. In addition to the ersatz originator, Miyao was also the author of a history published in 1967 of the aforementioned *giga* (*Nihon giga – rekishi to fūzoku* [*Japanese Cartoons – History and Manners*]), of the "long tradition" of Japanese illustrated texts in which manga figures prominently. Though a clear descendant of Hosokibara's text, Miyao's history considers manga within the context of a larger, though still transhistorical, cartooning tradition rather than projecting a contemporary perception of manga back onto the past. It was also influential for the "first" generation of critics to emerge in the 1960s. Tsurumi Shunsuke, for instance, in the introduction to his *Manga no sengo shisō [Thoughts on Manga in the Postwar]* (1973), works from Miyao's conceptualization of *giga*, agreeing with some points and taking issue with others, precisely in the mode of an ongoing critical discourse. Miyao's history both looks back to the emergence in the early 20th century of a certain transhistorical preconception of manga and fits into the critical tradition that is presumed to appear much later. Far from being a prehistory of manga studies as we now know it, this early period of mostly practitioners writing and speaking in a scholarly mode in fact establishes the baseline of critical assumptions from which latter-day manga studies operates and, as we will see, an international conception of comics/manga to which the discourse will return.

A Revised Four Stages of Manga Criticism

What follows is, perhaps, overly schematic and, given the previous discussion of manga practitioners theorizing their art form, something of an illusion, but the "four stages" story needs first to be understood in order to contemplate its faults. Also, the shift is not entirely illusory. I have already noted how this discursive space is occupied mostly by those who have little or no experience producing comic texts and a few who do. In a sense, the discourse becomes an admixture of readers and creators, even though one might argue that creators are always readers as well. This discursive space is also marked by a larger degree of obvious interaction and stability due to the establishment of institutions, in particular journals and academic programs in which critical work can be circulated and reviewed.

The nature of these institutions and the effect they have had on the development of manga criticism demand greater consideration in light of this story in which a litany of critics figure prominently.

To that end, I mean to approach this middle period, if you will, as a series of amendments to Berndt's (2008) already lucid account of the four stages.

> In the early 1960s, some essays about manga appeared in the journal *Shisō no kagaku* (The Science of Thought, 1946–1996). Cultural sociologist [Tsurumi Shunsuke], along with [Fujikawa Chisui] and film critic [Satō Tadao], first treated manga, from caricatures and newspaper strips to entertaining stories, as an object worthy of intellectual investigation. They also discussed it as part of a specifically Japanese popular culture. (p. 303)

What Berndt does not note, though, is the fact that while the founders of *Shisō no kagaku* contributed a large number of articles to the publication in addition to writing books of their own, they also solicited articles from the larger public, making it, in the main, a populist periodical at its core. Moreover, it published far more than just manga-related criticism, on all aspects of contemporary Japanese culture, meaning manga was understood as one aspect of that culture—an important one, to be sure. So Berndt's claim that Tsurumi et al. refashioned manga as a worthy object of serious critique is apt; nevertheless, this refashioning was part of a larger program of cultural studies. This populism carries over explicitly into Tsurumi's manga criticism, for instance, in the way he valorizes artists popular across broad swaths of society, such as Tezuka, Mizuki Shigeru, and Hasegawa Machiko, and focuses on the reading experiences of the working class. As Berndt (2008) says, "[f]or Tsurumi, manga did not belong to either 'pure art' (*junsui geijutsu*) or 'mass art' (*taishū geijutsu*), but rather to what he called 'liminal art' (*genkai geijutsu*)," which grew out of folk culture and united the interests of creators and the public they address.

> The second stage began around the time [Ishiko Junzō], [Gondō Susumu], [Kaiji Jun], and [Yamane Sadao]... founded the review journal *Mangashugi* (*Manga-ism*, 1967–1978). Like earlier critics, they were primarily interested in comics as a medium of communicating social experiences, and they favorably discussed "anti-authoritarian" comics like those by Sanpei Shirato and Yoshiharu Tsuge. In contrast to the critics from the early 1960s, these commentators did not believe that such comics were read by ordinary Japanese people.... (ibid.)

Not only did the critics of *Mangashugi* eschew *Shisō no kagaku*'s populist conception of the manga readership in favor of something resembling what might nowadays be called fan communities centered around the rental book shops that experienced a boom in the post-war era, Ishiko in particular, as CJ Suzuki (2014) has noted, "considered manga as a *modern* product: mass produced via reproduction technology, thus disavowing the uncritically repeated contention of previous scholarship that regarded manga as an extension of traditional pictorial art." Though Tsurumi's and Ishiko's communities of critics regarded similar ranges of texts as worthy of serious study, their orientations toward those texts were fundamentally different, and those differences are eerily analogous to the historiographic divide between long tradition and post-war valorization that Miyamoto identifies. This latter-day critical antagonism finds its clear analogue in a period of manga criticism regularly sequestered as a "pre-history," if not entirely disregarded.

> In the 1970s, a generation of critics, born in the 1950s and the very first to be raised on manga, rejected [Tsurumi Shunsuke] and [Ishiko Junzō] alike. These new critics, who included [Murakami Tomohiko], [Nakajima Azusa], and [Yonezawa Yoshihiro], argued that Tsurumi and Ishiko paid too much attention to the societal roles of certain manga and to groups which they did not belong… [t]hey claimed that the proper approach for critics was to question themselves as individual readers.…
> *(Berndt, 2008, pp. 303–304)*

This generation of critics came to be known as "I narrators" [*boku-gatari*], who, even though they rejected Ishiko's fannish communities, represents a later point along the potential trajectory in conceiving of manga readership as first large social classes, then smaller groups, and now individuals. This movement toward faithfully expressing one's own experience as reader led to an opening of manga criticism to a number of modes that previously had been passed over: subjective criticism, the expression of affective response, and, as a result of those two, a critical space in which *shōjo manga* could be taken seriously rather than denigrated. Well into the 1980s, *shōjo manga* was regarded as opaque at best with visual and narrative forms of romantic tropes meant to cater to the "simple" and therefore nonintellectual interests of teenage girls. Critics of *shōjo manga*, rather than accepting the terms of this critique and arguing, as with the previous generations of critics, that *shōjo manga* truly was worth analysis, in fact, assumed the claim of *shōjo manga*'s opacity as indicative of an inner world of feminine subjectivity specifically available to female readers and therefore only explicable by them. Takahashi Mizuki does precisely this in her 2008 article "Opening the Closed World of *Shōjo Manga*":

> While many critics have disparaged *shōjo manga* for the lack of sophisticated action or plot, they have not understood that it is not so much the story, but the emotive power of the images that appeals to fans. As a reader who has been deeply influenced by *shōjo manga*, I will concentrate on explaining the pictorial features that made this genre distinct and powerful for me. In contrast, comparatively little attention will be paid to its "literary" particularities. (p. 115)

Takahashi's still current use of this critical mode that emerged in the 1970s demonstrates a point I have yet to make entirely explicit, that these stages or generations do not supplant one another but rather overlap and speak to one another, just as you might assume for any engaged scholarly domain.

Finally, Berndt (2008) identifies a fourth generation of critics whose work might be understood as broadly formalist.

> In the early 1990s, the semiotic investigation of manga's representational conventions began to flourish under the rubric of studying manga as a medium of expression (*manga hyōgenron*). [Yomota Inuhiko]… and [Natsume Fusanosuke], who pioneered this movement, disdained the extremes of both politically motivated criticism and extremely subjective criticism. (p. 304)

While the rejection of subjective criticism may be true of Natsume (2003) and Yomota, it is less true of other formalist critics such as Takeuchi Osamu who, like Takahashi, locates his formative experiences in the reading of a particular kind of manga, Tezuka's, in Takeuchi's case, which spoke directly to his interest in the "cinematic" qualities of the artist's work.[6] In the history of manga criticism, Tezuka is much more than just an important artist; he has become, as I have previously argued, an entire domain upon which formalist theories are quite often based and that has subsumed even critiques of his importance within the history of manga criticism.

What emerges in the 1990s is not merely a turn in manga criticism toward dissecting and explicating what one sees on the page, where formalism seems to supplant subjective criticism, just as it supplanted a focus on small reader groups, but rather a fleshing out of manga studies into a variety of areas that might be treated separately on occasion but that, nevertheless, grossly overlap. While on the one hand, there is Yomota's, Natsume's, and Takeuchi's emphasis on manga expression [*manga hyōgen*], there is also nowadays a greater interest in media studies and semiotics and a more systematic approach to historiography and gender studies, to name a few, all of which are indicative of how, as manga criticism has become more academic in its institutional orientation, it has also become characterized by an interdisciplinary eclecticism involving literary criticism, art history, cinema studies, communication studies, and history. Within this framework, movements toward one theoretical framework and away from another represent less a seismic shift in the totality of manga studies and more the inclinations of individual critics adopting a particular methodology for a desired end. The manga criticism of Ōtsuka Eiji, for instance, in *Manga no kōzō [The Structure of Comic]*[7] (1987) approaches manga from a number of different angles, including but not limited to analysis of industrial constraints, narratology, consumer practices, theory of adaptation (between manga and anime, for instance), etc. However, his 2013 book, *Mikkī no shoshiki [The Form of Mickey (Mouse)]*, is more straightforwardly historiographic, even though it seeks to illuminate a period in manga history, the immediate prewar and wartime, that is so often shrouded in speculation and misunderstanding.

Even the historiographic enterprise comprises a number of divergent approaches. On the one hand, there is Shimizu Isao, a collector/fan/historian, whose now-numerous works on various aspects of manga history, Stewart (2013) reminds us in an article for *Comics Forum*, are indicative of a continuity among manga artists of the 19th and 20th centuries (contra Tezuka) with the "long tradition" one can trace back to Hosokibara's history. Additionally, Shimizu is responsible for editing a number of volumes, the *Manga zasshi hakubutsukan [Manga Periodical Museum]* series in particular, that provide access to historical manga examples difficult to come by outside of private collections and archives. Unlike the "long tradition" approach his work seems analogous to, Shimizu's historiography is coupled with a curatorial impulse meant as much to explain what the history of manga is as to ensure that the documentary evidence of that history survives and is disseminated. On the other hand, there is the aforementioned Miyamoto Hirohito (2009), who has not only written metacritically on manga historiography but whose own work highlights the discontinuities in Japanese comic art that undermine histories like Shimizu's.

This sense of rupture with tried and true practices within manga scholarship is perhaps best exemplified by Itō Gō's provocative 2005 book *Tezuka izu deddo [Tezuka Is Dead]*. In this work, Itō endeavors to accomplish two important critical tasks, the first being to deconstruct the Tezuka-as-critical domain upon which modern manga formalism is built.

The second task is to highlight aspects of Tezuka's work the critical tradition overlooks or diminishes and that reveal his manga to be not basic and fundamental but rather remarkably avant-garde. Itō's explicit and lengthy critique of manga scholarship concerning Tezuka led to a public spat with Takeuchi Osamu, when the latter criticized *Tezuka izu deddo* in his amateur journal *Biranji*. The Tezuka mythos has taken a number of hits in recent years: from not only Itō but also Nakano Haruyuki, perhaps best known for his work on the manga publishing industry, who produced a critical biography of Sakai Shichima, Tezuka's collaborator on the seminal manga text *Shin takarajima [New Treasure Island]*, in 2007 (*Nazo no mangaka Sakai Shichima den [The Mysterious Manga Artist, Sakai Shichima]*). The biography had the doubled effect of rehabilitating Sakai's reputation and demonstrating why he is a more likely candidate for being the creator of formal innovations more commonly attributed to Tezuka. Given this recent state of affairs, one can imagine the Tezuka stalwarts feeling rather embattled, but perhaps this is the clearest sign of manga studies' having become a true discipline in Japan: a scholarly domain large enough now to encompass a wide variety of critical attitudes in, quite often heated, conversation with one another, whereas in the earliest days, as I nominate them here, manga practitioners largely labored in theoretical isolation.

The Internationalization of Anglophone Manga Studies

Perhaps the most blistering critique of Tezuka's unique genius in the artist's earliest work has been Ryan Holmberg's (2012) several pieces for *The Comics Journal*. Holmberg, despite producing excellent manga scholarship engaged with both English and Japanese language Comic Studies discourses, has had a difficult time finding himself an institutional home, as have many like him, due in no small part to the general conservatism of Asian studies programs in North America and the United Kingdom. This has meant, rather paradoxically, that Anglophone manga studies has developed for the most part outside those programs, either abroad in Europe and Asia or in academic environments such as art schools whose curricula are far less tied to the presumptions of what Japanese studies properly ought to be in colleges and universities. Also, like the "pre-history" of manga studies in Japan, English language *mangagaku* began in isolated pockets, with individual scholars whose work may be taken up by later writers but may also as easily be passed over. For example, Tsurumi spent a number of years teaching at McGill University in Montreal and produced several works in English, one of which, *A Cultural History of Postwar Japan* from 1987, contains an entire chapter on manga in addition to references to manga texts throughout other chapters. Yet, this work is not cited much at all by those who would come to write about manga in Europe and North America. Moreover, it is rather common even today to find critical treatments of manga in English that make no reference whatsoever to Japanese scholarly sources. How the emerging Anglophone criticism integrated with existing Japanese discourses has been entirely haphazard.

The first major scholar to synthesize these discourses in English was, arguably, Frederik Schodt (1983) in *Manga! Manga!*, which, though somewhat dated now due simply to the three decades of manga history that have transpired since its publication, remains useful precisely for its broad engagements. For Schodt's critical purview is not limited to criticism, but as a translator of both manga and works on Japanese media (Miyazaki Hayao's (2009) *Starting Point*, for instance) he has, like Shimizu above, provided access to texts that might not otherwise be available to English readers. This is best exemplified by his translation of and lengthy introduction to Henry Yoshitaka Kiyama's *Manga yonin shosei [The Four Immigrants Manga]* (1931), which Schodt discovered in 1980, a rare contemporary comic documentation of the immigrant experience in the United States. While Reginald H. Blyth's (1959) chapter on Japanese caricature in *Oriental Humor* predates *Manga! Manga!* by many years, Schodt's work did far more to establish a base upon which later English language manga studies could build and expand. Sharon Kinsella's *Adult Manga* from 2000 engages largely with Japanese-language manga criticism, not merely because her book focuses on the interconnections between manga texts and the publishing industry in Japan but also because a decade and half after Schodt's *Manga! Manga!* Anglophone manga studies had yet to arrive.

For that arrival to occur, there needed to be an institutional framework in which manga studies might develop, but given the conservatism noted above, the pressure to form that institution had to come from outside the academy as traditionally understood. The first Schoolgirls and Mobile Suits conference was held at the Minneapolis College of Art and Design (MCAD) in 2001, and the first *Mechademia* volume appeared in 2006, though, according to Christopher Bolton (xi), the idea for an anime- and manga-focused journal was first proposed by Frenchy Lunning in 2003. In its earliest iterations, *Mechademia* devoted far more space to anime than to manga, and, in many ways, the inclusion of manga in *Mechademia*'s purview was due to the series embrace of Japanese popular culture in general. Unlike Japan, where the critical discourses of animation and manga are fundamentally separate from one another, the scholarly community that grew up around MCAD enforced no such strict disciplinary divisions, in part because there was at the time a real vacuum when it came to outlets for academic work on Japanese popular media. Along those lines, *Mechademia* also provided a consistent outlet for translations of Japanese language criticism, sorely needed to provide not only an institutional base for Anglophone manga-within-Japanese-media studies but also a bridge to a native critical tradition already well established.

Another art school, Kyoto Seika University in Japan, provides the basis for both the Manga Culture Research Institute, created in 2001, as well as a manga studies faculty in 2006. Affiliated with Kyoto Seika is the International Manga Research Center (IMRC), also established in 2006, headed by Jaqueline Berndt, which holds a number of workshops as well as a yearly conference and contributes content to and manages the Kyoto International Manga Museum. Part of the IMRC's stated mission is to not only produce publications about manga but also facilitate networking among interested parties both within Japan and abroad. Both the Mechademia and IMRC conferences have brought together scholars from the Americas, Europe, and Asia and serve as a nexus of contact for critics otherwise far flung, such as Deborah Shamoon in Singapore and Marco Pellitteri in Italy. For, as manga studies has increasingly internationalized, the need to develop and maintain institutions that provide lines of communication between Japanese and non-Japanese critics has increased as well. This is true as well of the resources necessary to perform the kind of research that might communicate effectively across this divide. The recent agreement between the Kyoto International Manga Museum and the Billy Ireland Cartoon Library & Museum at Ohio State University has created an avenue for materials normally only found in Japan to be used and studied outside that country.

Interestingly, this broadening of the manga studies footprint has had a particular effect on the discipline as it develops within Japan and has revealed a number of conceptual blind spots. Natsume, in the preface to a recent translation of selections from his book *Tezuka Osamu wa doko ni iru [Where Is Tezuka Osamu?]* (1992), recognizes how formalist criticism in Japan, though it has pretensions toward universality, is, in fact, rather parochial.

> At the time I wrote this book, my interests generally centered on postwar Japanese manga, and the scope of my inquiry was almost entirely limited to Japan. If we were to consider European and American influences on manga from the Meiji period, the discussion in this book on transformations related to time and panel articulation would link to world-historical questions of modernity (changes in the expression of time and space in modern times).... Future research will surely depend on sharing knowledge and intellectual exchanges between scholars in different countries. (pp. 91–92)

In 2013, when this statement was published, the future had already arrived for non-Japanese scholars trying to work with Japanese language materials, both manga and criticism, but Japanese manga studies was somewhat slow to accept the need not only to maintain contact with scholars abroad and but also to import the critical work of comic studies in Europe and North America, just as the Anglophone sphere was slow to integrate critical work in Japanese. The language barrier works both ways, but as recent developments have shown, it is not an insurmountable impediment to the broadening of manga studies throughout the world.

So, we have come full circle back to Rakuten's early 20th-century conceptualization of manga—should we now say comics?—as a fundamentally international artistic form. Rakuten's rather bare assertion was susceptible to yet another, the historiographic, presumption, following Hosokibara, that manga is something distinctly Japanese and tied to a specifically Japanese tradition. The recent return to an international notion of manga and manga studies should prove to be far more resilient, precisely due to the creation of institutions and lines of contact between scholars throughout the world that cannot be undermined by any one person's assertion of a contrary critical attitude. In fact, given the current state of affairs, a return to conceiving of manga as essentially Japanese is far more likely to become subsumed within manga studies' international orientation, just as critiques of the Tezuka mythos once were and perhaps still are woven into what Thomas Lamarre has referred to as the "long unending Tezuka" (50).

Notes

1 In my most recent work, I have come around to bracketing the word [manga] because its use in English is ambiguous at best and inextricable from presumptions of Japanese cultural identity that ought to be, yet so rarely are, called into question. I leave the word here unmarked, though it should become clear why any firm sense of "manga" ought to be held at arm's length.

2 For the most part, I will adhere to Japanese name order, family then given name, as is now standard practice in Japanese studies. That said, certain names pose difficulties in this regard, in particular Kiyama Yoshitaka, who, as an immigrant to the United States, stylized himself as Henry Y. Kiyama, with his given name serving as the middle initial. Also, some scholars who work consistently in English and Japanese, such as CJ (Shige) Suzuki, prefer one name in English and another in Japanese. Where no such circumstances attain, I adhere to the conventions of Japanese Studies, but where they do, I have endeavored to honor the choices of particular artists and critics. Even though this may cause some difficulty making cross comparisons with previous

work published in English, recent trends attempt to make such references consistent across all languages, including Japanese.

It is also worth noting that while in the main Japanese writers are referred to by their family names, in some cases (Okamo Ippei, for instance), it is more common to refer to them using their given names. That practice has been adopted here.

3 For a more extensive consideration of Rakuten's theoretical perspective on manga, see Stewart (2013, 2014). For Okamoto Ippei, see Theisen (2015).
4 "Japanese manga" may strike the reader as redundant, and yet that is one crucial way to read *Nihon manga*, since, at that time, *manga* was used as mostly synonymous with contemporary usage of "comic" or "cartoon" in English.
5 On its own, Ippei's title is somewhat ambiguous and could be read either as above or as *The New How to Draw Manga*, which, incidentally, is how the title is typically rendered. I prefer this far less common reading, given Ippei's sense of manga as being distinct from certain humorous visual forms, such as ponchi, which precede it.
6 c.f. especially Takeuchi's *Tezuka Osamu ron* (*On Tezuka Osamu*) which preface locates his first conceptualization of manga in the context of his childhood reading experiences of the "master's" work.
7 This is not my translation but rather Ōtsuka's own English title.

Bibliography

Berndt, J. (2008) 'Considering manga discourse: location, ambiguity, historicity', in M.W. Williams (ed) *Japanese Visual Culture,* London: M.E. Sharpe.
Bolton, C. (2014) 'Introduction', *Mechademia Vol. 9: Origins,* Minneapolis: University of Minnesota Press.
Blyth, R. (1959) *Oriental Humour,* Tokyo: Hokuseido Press.
Holmberg, R. (2012a) 'Tezuka Osamu & the rectification of Mickey', *The Comics Journal*. [Online] Available from: http://www.tcj.com/tezuka-osamu-the-rectification-of-mickey/ [Accessed 27 September 2015].
Holmberg, R. (2012b) 'Tezuka Osamu and American comics', *The Comics Journal*. [Online] Available from: http://www.tcj.com/tezuka-osamu-and-american-comics/ [Accessed 27 September 2015].
Holmberg, R. (2012c) 'Manga finds pirate gold: the case of *New Treasure Island'*, *The Comics Journal*. [Online] Available from: http://www.tcj.com/manga-finds-pirate-gold-the-case-of-new-treasure-island/ [Accessed 27 September 2015].
Hosokibara, S. (1924) *Nihon manga-shi,* Tokyo: Yūzankaku.
Itō, G. (2005) *Tezuka izu deddo: Hirakareta manga hyōgenron e,* Tokyo: NTT Shuppan.
Katsushika, H. (1814/2005) *Hokusai manga (zen),* Tokyo: Shōgakkan.
Kinsella, S. (2000) *Adult Manga: culture and power in contemporary Japanese society,* Honolulu: University of Hawai'i Press.
Kiyama, H.Y. (1999) *The Four Immigrants Manga: a Japanese experience in San Francisco, 1904–1924,* trans. by F. Schodt, Berkeley: Stone Bridge Press.
Lamarre, T. (2010). 'Speciesism, Part II: Tezuka Osamu and the multispecies ideal', *Mechademia Vol. 5: Fanthropologies,* Minneapolis: University of Minnesota Press.
Miyamoto, H. (2009) 'Rekishi kenkyū', in N. Fusanosuke and T. Osamu (eds) *Mangagaku nyūmon,* Kyoto: Mineruva shobō.
Miyao, S. (1967) *Nihon giga – rekishi to fūzoku,*. Tokyo: Daiichi hōki shuppan.
Miyazaki, H. (2009) *Starting Point: 1979–1996,* trans B. Cary and F. Schodt, San Francisco: Viz Media.
Nakano, H. (2007) *Nazo no mangaka Sakai Shichima den: "Shin takarajima" densetsu no hikari to kage,* Tokyo: Chikuma shobō.
Natsume, F. (2003) 'Where is Tezuka? A Theory of manga expression', trans M. Young, in *Mechademia Vol. 8: Tezuka's Manga Life,* Minneapolis: University of Minnesota Press.
Okamoto, I. (1990) 'Shin manga no kakikata', *Ippei zenshū, Vol. 13,* Tokyo: Ōzorasha.
Ōtsuka, E. (1987) *Manga no kōzō: shohin tekisuto gensho,* Tokyo: Yudachisha.

Ōtsuka, E. (2013). *Mikkī no shoshiki: sengo manga no senjika kigen*, Tokyo: Kadokawa gakugei shuppan.
Schodt, F. (1983). *Manga! Manga! The World of Japanese Comics*, New York: Kōdansha.
Shimizu, I. (1991). *Manga rekishi*, Tokyo: Iwanami Shoten.
Shimizu, I. (2007). *Nenpyō Nihon mangashi*, Kyoto: Rinsen Shoten.
Stewart, R. (2013) 'Manga as schism: Kitazawa Rakuten's resistance to 'old-fashioned' Japan'', in J. Berndt and B. Kümmerling-Meibauer (eds) *Manga's Cultural Crossroads*, New York: Routledge.
Stewart, R. (2014) 'Manga history: Shimizu Isao and Miyamoto Hirohito on Japan's first modern 'manga' artist Kitazawa Rakuten', *Comics Forum*. [Online] Available from: https://comicsforum.org/2014/06/14/manga-studies-2-manga-history-shimizu-isao-and-miyamoto-hirohito-on-japans-first-modern-manga-artist-kitazawa-rakuten-by-ronald-stewart/. [Accessed 31 May 2015].
Suzuki, S (CJ). (2014) 'Traversing art and manga: Ishiko Junzō's writings on manga/gekiga', *Comics Forum*. [Online] Available from: https://comicsforum.org/2014/08/11/manga-studies-4-traversing-art-and-manga-ishiko-junzos-writings-on-mangagekiga-by-shige-cj-suzuki/. [Accessed 31 May 2015].
Takahashi, M. (2008) 'Opening the closed world of Shōjo Manga', in M.W. Williams (ed) *Japanese Visual Culture*, London: M.E. Sharpe.
Takeuchi, I. (2006) *Tezuka Osamu = sutorī manga no kigen*, Tokyo: Kōdansha.
Takeuchi, O. (1992) *Tezuka Osamu ron*, Tokyo: Heibonsha.
Tezuka, O. (1950) *Manga daigaku*, Tokyo: Kōdansha.
Tezuka, O. and Jun, I. (1997) *Tezuka Osamu – manga no ōgi*, Tokyo: Kōdansha.
Theisen, N. (2015). *Manga [Comics] as Reading, or A Theory of Alter-textuality*. [Online] Available from: https://whatismanga.wordpress.com/comics-as-reading-or-a-theory-of-alter-textuality/. [Accessed 22 November 2015].
Tsurumi, S. (1973). *Manga no sengo shisō*, Tokyo: Bungei shunju.
Tsurumi, S. (1987) *Cultural History of Postwar Japan, 1945–1980*, New York: KPI.

PART 4
The Institutions

PART 4

The Institutions

16

THE ORGANIZATIONS

Jeremy Larance

In a 2011 article published on the *Comics Forum*, Randy Duncan and Matthew J. Smith lamented the fact that "one of the most notable shortfalls" in Comics Studies remained the lack of "self-sustaining organizations" dedicated to the field. There is, after all, something to be said for strength in numbers, but more importantly, especially in academia, organizations provide structure and legitimacy to new movements in a profession largely steered by publication trends and the relative scarcity of full-time (let alone tenure-track) teaching positions. Despite hundreds of scholars interested in the subject matter and legions upon legions of fans, Comics Studies has weathered decades of sporadic development, and—like Film Studies before it—the pedagogy of comics has been sluggish and sporadic, making it all the more difficult for would-be scholars to maintain their focus. As Duncan and Smith note, "Without the ability to pass along the lessons learned about organization and advocacy from one generation to the next, the field is locked into a situation where the proverbial wheel must be continually reinvented." This is not to say that organizations did not exist before 2011, nor is it necessarily a critique of the current state of Comics Studies. One could easily argue that this is simply a natural growing pain, one—once again—previously endured in Film Studies, which struggled for years to be recognized as an independent, legitimate field on its own merits.

There is, in fact, an interesting history of organizations dedicated to "Comics Studies," although many of those groups would never have imagined the current theoretical concepts related to that term nor, for that matter, would they have come to an easily agreed-upon definition of what "Comics Studies" means. In the beginning, organizations interested in what we now refer to as Comics Studies were not, necessarily, interested in promoting the academic reputation of comics as much as they simply wanted to find others who shared their love of the medium. Eventually, however, scholars in want of academic respectability and support found that they, too, could find solace in numbers, using academic organizations to validate their need to both deepen their own appreciation of comics and pass this knowledge on to their students. In many ways, one can learn quite a bit about Comics Studies by seeing how organizations dedicated to the study of that field have evolved over the years.

Early "Comics Studies" Organizations

One of the first major organizations dedicated to the study of comics began, not surprisingly, in France in 1962 when a group of science fiction enthusiasts founded "Le Club des Bandes Dessinées" [The Comics Club], later renamed the "Centre d'études des littératures d'expression graphique" (CELEG or CBD) in 1964. The club, chaired by Francis Lacassin, is credited with popularizing the term *"un neuvième art"* [the "ninth art"] in its fanzine, *Giff-Wiff*, which frequently included articles about the history and scholarship of comics, including a translation of Umberto Eco's "Le Mythe de Superman et la dissolution du temps." Still, according to Laurence Grove (2010), for many of the CBD members, *Giff-Wiff* was more like "a shared nostalgic hobby" than a professional organization, "even if two if its leading members, Lacassin and [Pierre] Couperie, were academics" (p. 235). As such, most of the CBD's early efforts focused on defining the language of comics and preserving its history.

Like several members of the CBD, Lacassin began as a film scholar; working primarily as a journalist and freelance writer, he made a name for himself as a specialist of popular culture. The University of Paris Sorbonne hired him as a professor to teach "the history and aesthetics of comics" (Magnussen, 2000, p. 12) in 1971, the same year he published *Pour un neuvième art, la bande dessinée [For a Ninth Art, the Comic Strip]*, a book that would become one of the earliest examples of Comics Studies in France to have a major impact on American scholarship. Translated by David Kunzle and published in *Film Quarterly* in 1972 under the title "The Comic Strip and Film Language," Lacassin argues that the "shared" language of comics and film may owe more to the development of the former than to the latter, although the opposite is often said to be the case. For Lacassin (1972), the argument was worth making if it helped legitimize comics as a true art form. "Which of the two arts borrowed this structure, this language from the other?" he asks. "While the cinema has been for nearly forty years an art recognized and sanctioned by the cultural critics, the comic strip was—at least until recently—ignored or scorned" (p. 11). Ultimately, he argues that, "with a few rare exceptions, the comic strip gathered most of its basic expressive resources without recourse to the cinema, and often even before the latter was born" (p. 14). With the help of the CBD, Lacassin made great strides in legitimizing the "ninth art" as a viable field of study with a rich history worthy of scholarly attention.

The CBD's predilection for the "nostalgic" nature of comics, however, eventually led to a schism in 1964 when a group, led by Pierre Couperie and Claude Moliterni, broke off to form its own organization, the "Société civile d'étude et de recherche des littératures dessinées" (SOCERLID), in order to focus more on the "literary attributes" of the *bande dessinée*. Two years later, SOCERLID began its own periodical, *Phénix*, a quasi-academic journal that included a mixture of scholarly articles, interviews, and book reviews. As noted by Joel Vessels (2010), to differentiate itself from the CBD, SOCERLID "aggressively sought to push awareness of the medium as a complicated and nuanced mass-cultural form" (p. 206). The group helped organize the *Bande dessinée et figuration narrative* exhibit in the Musée des Beaux Arts in 1967, attracting more than 500,000 visitors (Miller, 2007, p. 23). In years to follow, SOCERLID would continue its support of scholarly events, such as the "La convention de la bande dessinée" in Paris in 1969, as well as popular fairs like the Angoulême Comics Festival in 1972. More importantly, at least in terms of Comics Studies, SOCERLID played a major role in publishing Couperie and Maurice Horn's *Bande Dessinée et Figuration Narrative*, a book written as a result of the exhibit at the Musée des Beaux Arts, which would become a "foundational" manifesto of Comics Studies (Groensteen, 2007, p. 23).

In the following decade, similar organizations began to appear in other countries around the globe, including Belgium (La Bande Dessinée en Belgique, founded in 1968), Brazil (Centro Brasileiro de Pesquisas sóbre Histórias em Quadrinhos, founded in 1966), France (Federation Internationale des Centres de Recherches sur les Bandes Dessinées, founded 1966), Italy (Centro di Studi Iconografici, founded in 1967, and Club Anni Trenta, founded in 1969), Japan (Japan Cartoonist Association, founded in 1965, and Manga Communication Group, founded in 1971), Spain (Centro de Expresión Grafica, founded in 1963), and Switzerland (Groupe d'Etudes des Littératures Dessinées, founded in 1966, and Svenska Serieakademin, founded in 1965). As John A. Lent (2010) notes, "The burgeoning research generated by these centres and associations resulted in a sharp increase in the number of books and journals published on comic art" (p. 27). Nevertheless, unlike traditional academic organizations, Comics Studies was, for many years, a movement still largely propelled by groups made up mostly of amateurs who, although less credentialed, were far more influential members of these groups than their academic counterparts. This trend, according to Lent (2010), was especially true in the United States where the less-than-rigorous reputation of comics "by some purists in the academy" meant that Comics Studies was driven mainly by the efforts of professionals and fans of the medium whose work, he argues, "though considered less rigorous and scholarly...has been grossly understated" (p. 23).

In 1962, for example, a fan organization in the United States named the Academy of Comic Book Arts and Sciences (ACBAS) formed through a "ratification" process signed by 92 fans (Lopes, 2009, p. 94). In an effort to emulate the success and respectability of the Academy of Motion Picture Arts and Sciences, the ACBAS gave out its own version of the Oscars, called the Alley Awards, to comic book artists and publishers. In 1970, when industry professionals rallied together to form their own organization, they adapted the name of the ACBAS (which went defunct in 1969) by simply dropping the "and Sciences" to become the Academy of Comic Book Arts (ACBA). Once again, the initial objective of the organization was to use the motion picture industry as a model, and between 1970–1975 the SHAZAMS (the ACBA's version of the Oscars) were given out during an annual award show in New York City. There was, however, almost from the beginning, a tension between the artists and the publishers, with some even going as far as to protest the membership of Stan Lee who was, nevertheless, elected as the ACBA's first president (Roach & Cooke, 2001, p. 104). One young artist in particular, Neal Adams, was especially vocal about using the ACBA guild to protect the creative rights of comic-book artists and writers, and over the years the organization did earn a few minor victories including, for example, the right to maintain ownership of their own original artwork (Cassel, Sultan, & Trimpe, 2015, p. 33) and insurance plans for freelancers (Wright, 2001, p. 256). But, as Bradford Wright (2001) notes in *Comic Book Nation*, the overall efforts of the ACBA "to garner popular respect for comic books" failed, "some of which degenerated into farce" (p. 256). By 1975, the last year of the ACBA's existence, the organization could not even afford to purchase plaques for the winners of the SHAZAM awards, asking, instead, that winners choose to pick up the tab on their own (Wright, 2001, p. 256).

Nevertheless, despite the ACBA's failure to garner as much public notice and respect as the Academy of Motion Picture Arts and Sciences, the fan culture of comics was still strong enough to produce regional organizations and establish comics as an undeniably vital part of American popular culture. In academia, however, scholars interested in the aesthetic and cultural value of comics still found it difficult to find support in their institutions, and in the years before the Internet, finding like-minded scholars in the field remained a difficult task for scholars like Donald Ault (2003), who characterized the stigma attached to Comics Studies as a "deeply entrenched ideological opposition to making comics a central focus of academic study" (p. 250). This stigma began to change in the mid-1990s when scholars across the United States who were interested in comics started to make concerted efforts to strengthen their numbers, and reputation, by establishing their own organizations dedicated to the field. For many would-be scholars in Comics Studies, the burgeoning field of Popular Studies in the 1970s was one of the only viable outlets for "scholarly" activity and, perhaps more importantly, a means for further organization.

When Ray Browne from Bowling Green State University founded the Popular Culture Association (PCA) in 1971, for example, paper topics on comics were frequently included in the program, and in 1974 Stan Lee was among the "luminaries" who attended the annual conference (Browne, 1989, p. 27). One of the earliest and most prolific contributors to the PCA was Thomas Inge, who originally solidified his reputation in the pop-culture field by editing the University of Mississippi's "Studies in Popular Culture" series in the late 1980s. However, before making his name in academia, Inge had already spent much of the previous decade producing books and essays promoting the scholarship and criticism of comics, including collaboration with comic-book artist Bill Blackbeard and articles for *The Comic Book Price Guide* (Browne & Marsden, 1999, p. 123). As one of the PCA's pioneers, Inge continued his scholarly interest in comics, producing many of the field's most important and groundbreaking publications, including *The American Comic Book* in 1985 and *Comics as Culture* in 1990. In 1996, members from the "Comic Art & Comics Area" of the Popular Culture Association/American Culture Association (PCA/ACA) started giving out the annual "M. Thomas Inge Award for Comics Scholarship," a prize given to the best comics-related paper presented at the PCA/ACA conference. Over the years, this large platform provided by the PCA/ACA has played an invaluable role in strengthening the legitimacy of Comics Studies in the United States.

One of the earliest groups dedicated explicitly to the study of comics was the International Comic Arts Forum (ICAF) founded at Georgetown University in 1995 by Tristan Fonlladosa, a visiting scholar from the Cultural Service of the French Embassy, and Guy Spielman, a native of France and faculty member in the Department of French. Together, the two organized what was originally conceived as a one-time event, the International Comics & Animation Festival, featuring invited cartoonists and professionals from the field of comics. To coincide with a traveling exhibit from the Centre national de la bande dessinée et de l'image (CNBDI), the event was repeated the following year but expanded to include an international call for papers. After Fonlladosa returned to France in 1996, Spielman (with the help of a newly formed Executive Committee) took over much of the organization's logistical work, including several collaborations with Small Press Expo (SPX), a non-profit organization in Bethesda, Maryland, created in 1994 to promote artists and publishers of independent comics. The annual "Festival" continued to expand for a decade before being renamed the International Comic Arts Forum in 2006, a change made in large part to "reaffirm and strengthen its academic focus" (International Comic Arts Forum, 2015). The following year, the Executive Committee adopted its first formal bylaws, "with the hopes of recruiting new scholars and engaging in continual reinvention," before accepting an offer from the School of the Art Institute of Chicago to host the conference in 2008. Since that time, the responsibilities of hosting the ICAF's conference have rotated among various scholars at academic institutions across the United States.

For academics in the United States, the ICAF played a major role in bringing scholars together in an organization dedicated to the advancement of Comics Studies, particularly for those interested in the interdisciplinary appeal of the medium. The ICAF emphasizes this point in its "Mission" by drawing attention to the organization's international and multidisciplinary approach to Comics Studies on the organization's website:

- to foster recognition of comic art as an international phenomenon, both by seeking common ground between various world traditions and by exploring the crucial differences between them;
- to welcome a multidisciplinary and pluralistic approach to the study of comic art, with due attention to larger cultural, political, literary, and artistic contexts;
- to encourage discussion and collaboration among academics, independent scholars, comics professionals, and the wider public;
- to provide an accessible showcase for innovative comics scholarship and comic art, with special emphasis on traditions hitherto neglected in English-language studies (International Comic Arts Forum, 2015).

For years, the ICAF was one of the few organizations in the United States where comics scholars could meet with like-minded individuals who shared their commitment to a field that still did not offer many tenure-track positions for those who specialized in "comic books." As successful as the ICAF was, the field of Comics Studies was still very much a fringe area of study in the United States throughout much of the 1990s, but by the end of the decade, Comics Studies had evolved enough to warrant further calls for unity. Participants in the Comics and Comic Art area of the PCA/ACA created a style guide for writing about comics and published those guidelines in the inaugural issue of the *International Journal of Comic Art* in 1999, and, one year later, they produced one of the first comprehensive copyright guides designed specifically for scholars in the field of Comics Studies (Kannenberg, Srinivasan & Witek, 2003).

In recent years, efforts such as these have made it easier for scholars in North America to create organizations that are more like traditional professional organizations in academia, organizations that—although still multidisciplinary—can more easily build their field upon a shared scholarly foundation. In 2008, for example, Peter Coogan, author of *Superhero: The Secret Origin of a Genre*, founded the Institute for Comics Studies (ICS), a non-profit organization described by Coogan as a "'think tank' of comics scholarship" (qtd. in Davis-Stofka, 2015) where scholars and industry professionals could come together to promote "the study, understanding, recognition, and cultural legitimacy of comics" (Institute for Comics Studies, 2015). According to Coogan, the ICS mission revolves around four major areas of emphasis: communication, knowledge, expertise, and support, four areas he believes are critical to the success of the organization and the future of Comics Studies:

> Communication is the building of relationships between and within the comics academy and the industry, and communicating with the public about comics. Knowledge is the creation of new knowledge and understanding via scholarly activity, including

publications and conferences. Expertise is the promotion of comics scholars in the academy, the media, and the professional world. And support is the development of collections, funding, faculty, and programs in academia.

(qtd. in Davis-Stofka, 2015)

In addition to supporting academic programs, the ICS is also very active at comics conventions and trade shows, often using these venues as locations for panels, symposia, and more traditional academic conferences. At its core, however, the ICS is a unique organization in that it makes a collaborative effort to bridge the gap between scholarship and industrial expertise. The institute's bylaws, for example, stipulate that the Board of Directors must consist of both industry professionals and scholars, a symbiotic and symbolic structuring that further emphasizes the mission of the ICS.

In 2009, comics scholars attending the Annual Convention of the Modern Language Association (MLA), started a Discussion Group on Comics and Graphic Narratives, "a body [with] aims to bring greater focus and attention to comics studies within the Association, and within literary studies more broadly" (Modern Language Association, 2015). The petition to create the group was written by Hillary Chute, an Associate Professor in the Department of English at the University of Chicago, and one of Comics Studies most accomplished scholars. In an essay published in 2008 titled "Comics as Literature? Reading Graphic Narrative," Chute argued that *"now* is the time to expand scholarly expertise and interest in comics [emphasis added]" (p. 462). Specifically, "Critical approaches to literature," she added, "as they are starting to do, need to direct more sustained attention to this developing form—a form that demands a rethinking of narrative, genre, and, to use James Joyce's phrase, today's 'ineluctable modality of the visible'" (p. 462). Consequently, the 2009 creation of the discussion group at MLA appears to have been brought about largely by Chute's insistence that Comics Studies was reaching a critical stage in its development, particularly in the United States. For members of the Discussion Group on Comics and Graphic Narratives, the group's very existence in the MLA became a "helpful" and "overdue acknowledgment" of Comics Studies, "a diverse range of scholarship spanning themes, motifs, periods, and languages, as well as multiple disciplinary perspectives—and in particular the growing importance of comics to the literary field" (Modern Language Association, 2015).

One of the founding members of the MLA discussion group was Charles Hatfield, an Associate Professor in the Department of English at California State University, Northridge, who previously served on the executive committee of the ICAF. In 2010, Hatfield published an article titled "Indiscipline, or, The Condition of Comics Studies," in which he, like Chute, suggested that the "nascent academic field" of Comics Studies in North America was nearing a turning point in regard to its reputation and productivity (2). For both Chute and Hatfield, one of the few remaining obstacles for Comics Studies remained its natural tendency to be approached as an "intersection of various disciplines" (Hatfield, p. 2), a problematic strength that made it that much more difficult to establish Comics Studies as a legitimate and independent field of study. "In order to reach critical mass intellectually and professionally," Hatfield argued, "comics studies has to take a multidisciplinary perspective, yet the overlap and tension between the various participating disciplines has not yet led to a concerted discussion, much less a coherent model, of interdisciplinarity" (Hatfield, p. 3). Having served on the executive committee of the ICAF, Hatfield was undoubtedly also well aware of how relatively uninformed many American scholars were compared to their European counterparts, yet one more obstacle in the production of regular and vigorous scholarship in Comics Studies in America. The push to include Comics Studies in the MLA network of organizations, therefore, played a key strategic role in focusing American eyes and minds on the possibilities of working together, across disciplines and borders, to bring together like-minded scholars interested in the promotion of Comics Studies in the United States. In other English-speaking countries, the momentum continued, as organizations like the British Consortium of Comics Scholars, the Scottish Centre for Comics Studies, and the Canadian Society for the Study of Comics—all of which were founded in the past five years—have done much to ease the interdisciplinary "tensions" Hatfield discussed in his 2010 article.

In the United States, organizations like the ICAF continue to forge connections with Comics Studies scholars internationally, and, perhaps more importantly, online organizations such as the Comix-Scholars Listserv, housed on servers at the University of Florida, greatly expedited this process of legitimization by bringing together comics scholars from multiple fields into manageable communities. During an impromptu session at the International Comic Arts Forum in 2014, Charles Hatfield made a motion to create the Comic Studies Society, an association that, as the name implies, would go on to become the first major academic society in the United States to focus on the scholarship of comics. While earlier organizations, such as the ICAF and the ICS, made conscious efforts to maintain a strong balance between professional and academic interests, the bylaws ultimately approved by the CSS's founding members made it clear that many scholars in the field were looking for something more akin to traditional academic associations:

> The Comics Studies Society (CSS) is an interdisciplinary learned society offering scholars and teachers, (including academics, non-academic or independent scholars, instructors at all levels, and students) the opportunity to promote the critical study of comics as an art and a communicative form, improve classroom teaching, and engage in open and ongoing conversations about the media, means, and cultures of comics.
> *(Comic Studies Society, 2015)*

The CSS's mission, in other words, clearly defines itself as an organization interested more in the study of the medium (i.e., criticism and research) than the actual production of comics. Although the professional aspect of Comics Studies is certainly still a major consideration, the CSS's move toward a more scholarly focus is indicative of the great change in perception of Comics Studies in academia, particularly in the United States.

Only time will tell if the CSS will be successful in its mission to make Comics Studies a viable and more traditional discipline of academic study, but there are indications that colleges and universities are becoming more open to the idea themselves. Following their discussion of the sustainability of Comics Studies through professional organizations, Duncan and Smith suggest that Comics Studies will truly come unto its own "once degrees are offered," thus supplying the need and expertise to introduce the field into college curriculums on a more regular basis. Despite the call by some, such as Henry Jenkins (2012), to keep Comics Studies "radically undisciplined" (6), the serious application of comics in the academy is arguably a necessary step in advancing the study of the medium beyond its present, somewhat stagnant, state. Over the decades, countless colleges and universities have offered courses specifically dedicated to the study of comics in a wide variety of disciplines, including art, history, communication, literature, popular culture, and psychology. Unfortunately, only a handful of institutions presently offer entire degree programs in Comics Studies, and—much like the professional organizations discussed above—their various approaches say much about the field's natural diversity.

Colleges and Universities

Donald Ault is largely credited with developing the first degree program in Comics Studies when he created the "Comics and Visual Rhetoric" tracks for the M.A. and Ph.D. programs in the Department of English at the University of Florida in 2011. Ault first taught courses on comics at Berkeley in the 1970s and at Vanderbilt University in the 1980s before ending his career at the University of Florida, where he joined the English faculty in 1988. In 2004, he founded *ImageText*, an online journal dedicated to the advancement of "the academic study of comic books, comic strips, and animated cartoons." Although clearly interested in the development of Comics Studies, Ault was primarily known outside of the comics community as a scholar of William Blake, a British Romantic poet whose illuminated poetry undoubtedly played a major role in Ault's personal and professional interests in comics, particularly when it came to using literary theory and interdisciplinary approaches of studying visual literature. The name chosen for the track, "Comics *and* Visual Rhetoric," is telling since comics are, literally, a form of "visual rhetoric," but the phrase was likely added to the name of the program to bridge the theoretical gulf that still existed between Comics Studies and more established fields of academia, especially in the United States. The program's website makes it clear that students coming into the Comics and Visual Rhetoric track should be thoroughly prepared for a theory-heavy experience:

- As a new discipline, Comics and Visual Rhetoric embraces contemporary theory more rapidly and thoroughly than almost any field in the humanities. Students without a strong theoretical background will not be competitive in job searches.
- Historically, the most important foreign language for Comics and Visual Rhetoric Studies has been French. Unless a graduate student has a particular reason for needing a different language, French should be the first choice.
- Because many media studies jobs appear in English departments, students should develop an additional concentration in literature, composition, or theory. (University of Florida, 2015)

The emphasis on theory, present in each bullet point, highlights the fact that the Comics Studies program at UF relies heavily on literary theory, which is not unexpected in a graduate program from a school of UF's size and reputation. There are no specific course requirements in the M.A. and Ph.D. programs, and courses vary from year to year. Students in both programs are required to take at least two courses in the area of Comics and Visual Rhetoric (three for the non-thesis version of the M.A.) and at least two additional courses in another area of concentration (theory and cultural studies are preferred). The remainder of the coursework is made up of electives.

Also in 2011, the University of Dundee in Scotland started its own graduate program in comics with an MLitt (Master of Letters) in "Comics and Graphic Novels," a one-to-two-year program designed to give students a deeper "understanding of the comics medium and the comics industry, and their relation to the different genres, national cultures, and various media" (University of Dundee, 2015). The MLitt degree was largely created through the efforts and expertise of Chris Murray, a faculty member in the Department of English with considerable experience in Comics Studies, including serving as one of the founding editors of *Studies in Comics* and as the Director of the Scottish Centre for Comics Studies. Students enrolled in the "Comics and Graphic Novels" program at the University of Dundee must take two core classes. The first, Critical Approaches to Comics and Graphic Novels, "introduces students to critical approaches to comics and graphic novels" to help students "apply a range of theoretical perspectives to the study of comics, as well as considering the development of Comics Theory" (University of Dundee, 2015). As the course description implies, this class gives students a broad overview of literary and visual theory (gender studies, historicism, modernism, psychoanalysis, structuralism, etc.) with special emphasis given to how those traditional modes of critical theory apply to Comics Studies. The second core class, International Comics Culture, "introduces students to a variety of comics emerging from different national traditions, facilitating an understanding of the differences and similarities between those comics cultures" (University of Dundee, 2015). Students must then choose from a list of optional modules (such as "Creating Comics," "Digital Comics," "Comics and Film," "Science Fiction Comics," and "Autobiographical Comics") before ultimately attempting the dissertation, which can focus on either English Studies or Creative Writing. Although heavily rooted in English Studies, the MLitt degree at the University of Dundee is not designed like traditional graduate programs in the United States. Instead, students are given ample opportunities to participate in a variety of creative workshops and events with access to professionals in the field. In particular, the university relies heavily on D. C. Thomson & Company, a local publisher with strong ties to the comics industry, for instruction, recruitment, and job opportunities for graduates. Under Murray's supervision, interested students can also continue their education at the University of Dundee and pursue a master's degree or a doctorate in English with an emphasis on Comics Studies.

In 2012, Ben Saunders at the University of Oregon founded an undergraduate minor in "Comics and Cartoon Studies," another first of its kind and, once again, another comics-related program with roots in an English department. Saunders, like Ault, began his academic career not in comics but in the field of English Renaissance Literature; he is the author of a book-length study of John Donne's poetry and several articles on Shakespeare. However, in 2011, Saunders published *Do the Gods Wear Capes? Theology, Fantasy, and Superheroes*, a book that relies on various forms of literary theory to examine the metaphysical nature of the superhero genre; in 2015 he co-edited (with Charles Hatfield) *Comic Book Apocalypse: The Graphic World of Jack Kirby*, a combination exhibition catalog and critical anthology surveying Kirby's long career. He has also curated a number of comics-related art exhibitions at the University of Oregon's Jordan Schnitzer Museum of Art, and in 2013 he was instrumental in securing a significant private endowment of $200,000 to support the further development of Comics Studies at the University of Oregon. Although the majority of the faculty members at Oregon University who participate in the comics minor are from the Department of English, a number of classes are taught by faculty members from other areas, such as Art, Comparative Literature, East Asian Languages and Literature, Journalism, and Romance Languages. The interdisciplinary goal of the program is to offer students "an international, historical, and critical perspective on the art of comics, from editorial cartoons to comic books to graphic novels" (University of Oregon, 2015). Students minoring in Comics and Cartoon Studies must complete six four-credit courses from a list of approved classes updated each semester on the program's website. The only mandatory class that all minors must take is Introduction to Comics Studies.

One year after the University of Oregon started offering their students an opportunity to minor in Comics Studies, the Department of Humanities at West Liberty University created the first undergraduate English major in what it calls "Graphic Narrative," a four-year degree for students interested in the study and analysis of comics as literature. Wally Hastings, the Chair of the Department of Humanities, chose the name for the degree after considering several other options, including Comics Studies, but the use of the word "Narrative" was particularly important for the department to distinguish itself from the broader multidisciplinary nature of more traditional forms of Comics Studies. First and foremost, the Graphic Narrative major at West Liberty is an English degree, and although students are required to take courses in other disciplines as part of the program (especially in Art), the resources and expertise of the faculty dictated that the program be grounded in the literary tradition. Like the graduate degrees offered at the University of Florida, the Graphic Narrative major at West Liberty University is an optional track within the English program. Students who choose Graphic Narrative must still take the same core classes and electives as other English majors, including surveys in American and British literature, but students majoring in Graphic Narrative must also take an additional 15 hours of coursework in classes specifically dedicated to comics studies, including "Principles of Graphic Narrative," "History of Sequential Art and Literature," "Writing for Comics," and at least two special topics courses related to Comics Studies. Over the years, examples of such courses have included "Autobiographical Comics," "The Dark Knight Mythos," "The Extraordinary (and Hairy) Worlds of Alan Moore," "Tales of the Supermen," and "Women in Comics." In the fall of 2015, West Liberty University added a 15-hour minor in Graphic Narrative for non-English majors interested in studying comics.

Two of the newest comics-related programs, Portland State University's post-baccalaureate certificate and Henderson State University's minor in Comics Studies, both began in 2015. Susan Kirtley, a composition and rhetoric specialist who won an Eisner Award in 2013 for *Lynda Barry: Girlhood through the Looking Glass* in the Best Educational/Academic Work category, directs the post-baccalaureate program at PSU. Like many of the other Comics Studies programs mentioned above, the graduate certificate at PSU is housed in the English Department but utilizes the expertise of faculty members across the curriculum as well as industry professionals. Although students must complete 24 hours of coursework, the only required class is a special topics course in English subtitled "Comics History & Theory." The other 20 hours must come from a pool of approved electives from various departments such as Art and Philosophy. Rotating special topics in English such as "Editing Comics," "Focus on Frank Miller/Will Eisner," "European Comics," "Autobiographical Comics," "Superheroes and Society," and "Censorship and the Comics Code" have also been offered as electives. The relatively limited number of specialized courses at Portland State University devoted to comics is largely supplemented by the program's "access to professional expertise," which the program's website refers to as the "cornerstone of the program" (Portland State University, 2015). Like the University of Dundee, PSU benefits greatly from nearby comic book industry, specifically Dark Horse, Oni Press, and Top Shelf, all located just a few miles from campus. Visiting instructors from these publishers provide much of the "hands-on practice" in courses that deal more with the creative side of comics, while instructors like Kirtley handle more of the theory-oriented courses. Beyond the classroom, some of these publishers also provide internships that can be counted toward the Comics Studies certificate, meaning students have several opportunities to gain unique insights while also making valuable connections in the field. Billed as a "truly interdisciplinary" program, the Comics Studies certificate at Portland State University strives to offer its students "a vibrant, dynamic program on the cutting edge of contemporary literature and art practice" to prepare them for "work in the field of comics and cartoon art as writers, artists, and scholars" (Portland State University, 2015).

Even though Henderson State University did not start offering a minor in Comics Studies until the fall of 2015, faculty members from the school had been teaching comics-related courses for years, making HSU one of more progressive and nationally renowned organizations in relation to Comics Studies. Unlike many of the other colleges and universities with Comics Studies programs, HSU's minor is not housed in a specific department like English. Instead, the minor is an interdisciplinary program with courses in art, communication, English, and even psychology. In fact, Randy Duncan and Travis Langley, the two professors who currently run the Comics Studies program at HSU, are from two seemingly unrelated disciplines. Duncan earned his doctorate in Communication before becoming a pioneer for Comics Studies while Langley, a professor of psychology, used his lifelong obsession with Batman to become HSU's resident "superherologist."

Before becoming a Professor of Communications and Theatre Arts, Duncan did not have many options to study comics himself as a graduate student at Louisiana State University in the 1980s, but he did convince his professors that he could adapt film theory to the storytelling methods he admired most in comic books, especially Frank Miller's run in *Daredevil*. It was, he admits, a fairly novel approach to comics at the time: "I thought Miller was doing things with the story panels in the comics that were like cinema techniques, like the Expressionist filmmakers.... LSU was bold enough to let me do a paper with comics, [and] I am not sure I could have had a subject like that accepted in the 1980s at many schools" (qtd. in Bryan, 2012). Duncan would go on to become one of the leading proponents of Comics Studies in the United States, co-founding the Comics Arts Conference at the San Diego Comic-Con with Peter Coogan in 1992. But for many teachers, his most important contribution to the field of Comics Studies is arguably *The Power of Comics: History, Form, & Culture,* which he co-wrote with Matthew J. Smith in 2009. One of the first successful textbooks designed specifically to be an introductory study of the medium, *The Power of Comics* provided students (and teachers) with an accessible yet comprehensive overview of the history and theories that make up the foundations of Comics Studies.

Although Duncan and Smith are both primarily professors of communication, their textbook freely integrates scholarly approaches from a wide variety of disciplines, "including art, history, sociology, economics, psychology, and many more" (Duncan & Smith, 2009, p. vii). Travis Langley, Duncan's colleague at HSU, was undoubtedly a helpful resource when it came to writing about the psychological aspects of comic culture. In 2012, Langley published *Batman and Psychology: A Dark and Stormy Knight*, a "superhero textbook" that was as much an in-depth analysis of the Caped Crusader as it was a general introduction to psychology. In his acknowledgments, Langley admits that he might never have been able to write such a book had he not been "fortunate enough to teach at a university that respects and supports comics scholarship" (Langley, 2012, p. viii). Langley originally prepared much of the material that would ultimately make its way into *Batman and Psychology* while he was teaching an upper-level psychology course at HSU that focused on the characters and plotlines from the Batman mythos. The success of such courses eventually led to the minor at HSU, which, according to the program's website, offers students the opportunity to:

> *Appreciate* the diversity and potential of the comics art form; *Understand* comics as a unique medium of communication; *Discover* the governing principles of the comics art form; *Apply* knowledge of the medium to the creation of graphic narratives; *Analyze* the role of the comics medium in various cultures; and *Evaluate* graphic narratives.
> *(Henderson State University, 2015)*

Like many of the programs discussed above, the Comics Studies minor at Henderson State University is just the latest example of academic organizations accepting the study of comics as a viable and worthy field of inquiry. More will undoubtedly follow but, for now, four-year colleges and universities are still somewhat reluctant to create majors and minors devoted to the medium of "comic books." Still, today it would be difficult to name *every* college and university currently offering courses on comics, which is a far cry from the "deeply entrenched ideological opposition" to the study of comics that Donald Ault faced in the 1980s (Ault, 2003, p. 250).

Art Schools

There are, of course, other approaches to Comics Studies than those that deal with the analytical or theoretical sides of the art. Comics, after all, are by design created by artists who must employ more than one mode of expression. Consequently, many art schools have played significant roles in legitimizing comics as an art form while, at the same time, necessarily providing practical structure and order to the hands-on applications of comics art. Of the institutions currently teaching the practical skills of comic-book art, the program with the longest and arguably richest history is the School of Visual Arts (SVA) in Manhattan. Founded by Silas H. Rhodes and Burne Hogarth in 1947, the school was originally called the Cartoonist and Illustrators School, a name that reflected the founders' initial goal of providing professional instruction to would-be cartoonists and comic-book artists. In 1955, Rhodes changed the name to more accurately reflect his belief that "there is more to art than technique and that learning to become an artist is not the same as learning a trade" (School of Visual Arts, 2015). Nevertheless, as the school expanded its curriculum, "cartooning" maintained its status as one of SVA's most prolific programs. Thomas Woodruff, the Cartooning Department Chair, notes that industry experts have been known to call SVA the "Harvard of Cartooning," a nickname he thoroughly endorses: "The curriculum is rigorous. There is a focus on eye/hand training (perspective, page, layout, inking, etc.), but there is also a focus on the theoretical, and discussion of how to take this medium into the new millennium…Here, the intellectual and the technical are wed" (School of Visual Arts, 2015). In addition to the foundational courses that all students enrolled in the School of Visual Arts must take, students seeking a Bachelor of Fine Arts in Cartooning must also choose from a selection of courses from the Cartooning curriculum, such as "Digital Coloring for Cartoonists," "Drawing with Ink for Cartoonists," "Foundations of Visual Computing," "History of Cartooning," "Principles of Cartooning,"

"Storytelling," and "Writing for Comics." During their freshman year, students are expected to focus more on basic drawing, painting, graphic design, and humanities classes before moving on to upper-level courses in the Cartooning program during their sophomore year.

Just as SVA welcomes the opportunity to promote itself as the "Harvard of Cartooning," the Savannah College of Art and Design (SCAD) is often referred to as the "Harvard of Comics." SCAD started offering its students comics-related courses as electives in 1993, and now the school offers both undergraduate and graduate degrees in "Sequential Art," with the aim to prepare students "to be leaders and entrepreneurs in visual storytelling" (Savannah College of Art and Design, 2015). Undergraduates seeking a B.A. in Visual Communication at SCAD can choose Sequential Art as their concentration of study, which requires 45 hours of coursework dedicated to the study and practice of comics in courses such as "Introduction to Sequential Art," "Drawing for Sequential Art," "Survey of Sequential Art," "Materials and Techniques for Sequential Art," "Comic Book Scripting," and "Visual Storytelling." Students choosing the B.F.A. in Sequential Art take most of the same courses as the B.A., but, with fewer hours in General Education, B.F.A. students take more classes focused on the technical aspects of creating comics. The M.A. and M.F.A. require 45 and 90 hours, respectively, taken from a pool of classes designed specifically for the graduate degrees in Sequential Art such as "Digital Design in Sequential Art," "Drawing Strategies for Sequential Art," "Exploring the Narrative," "Theories and Practices of Sequential Art," "Visual Story Development," and "Writing for Sequential Art."

Although not as well known as SVA or SCAD, other art schools, such as the Memphis College of Art (MCA) and the Minneapolis College of Art and Design (MCAD), offer comics-related tracks in their M.F.A. programs as well. The only class at MCA specifically dedicated to comics, however, is "Illustrative Story," a class offered in four levels: "Illustrative Story 1," "Illustrative Story 2," etc. The comics courses offered at MCAD are more diverse, featuring classes such as "Introduction to Comics," "History of Comic Art," "Comic Media and Concepts," "Comic Book Publishing and Web," "Experimental Comics," and "Comic Storytelling." MCAD started its B.F.A. in "Comic Arts" in 1996, and, much like SVA, students choosing this major must complete the same foundational electives as other students but with an additional 39 hours from the courses directly related to the study of comics. Students majoring in Comics Arts at MCAD "are taught to gain command of line, color, and composition, as well as character development, storyboarding, and plot to create complex works that pull readers in" (MCAD). Like students at SVA, students in the Comics Arts program at MCAD spend most of their freshman year taking classes designed to teach or fine-tune basic art skills before taking more advanced classes in the Comics Arts program the following year.

One of the comic book industry's most iconic artists, Joe Kubert, along with his wife Muriel, founded another famous school dedicated to the study of cartooning in 1976, The Joe Kubert School of Cartoon and Graphic Art (later renamed The Kubert School). Over two decades earlier, Kubert and Joe Maurer created the *Comic Book Illustrators Instruction Course*, a planned series of 16-page lessons sold and marketed through comic books written and drawn by Kubert and Maurer themselves. In "Lesson One," the two artists introduced themselves to the readers in comic-book form, telling them:

> We intend to go into every aspect of producing comic books from the point where the artist pencils his first line to finished comic book on your local newsstand!...

> In forthcoming lessons we'll go into detail and pass on to you the many tricks of the trade we've learned! And we'll teach you to skillfully use the hundreds of varied materials available to help **you** make a good comic strip!
>
> *(qtd. in Thomas, 2001, p. 63)*

Unfortunately, although Kubert and Maurer advertised plans to produce 12 lessons in all, "Lesson One" was the only pamphlet to ever make it into print. Kubert, however, did not give up on the idea of instructing would-be cartoonists, and so, when the opportunity arose to purchase Dover's old high school, the Kuberts bought the building and some adjacent properties and officially opened the school's doors to students in the fall of 1976. The original curriculum at the Kubert School required students to take ten classes over the course of two years, with an emphasis on practical application, but the program was expanded to three years in 1978. Early graduates of the program included several future comic-book luminaries such as Stephen Bissette, John Totleben, Thomas Yeates, and Rick Veitch. Today, the school bills itself as "an intense 3-year program that strongly emphasizes methods and materials utilized in the profession as well as the refining of artistic and creative abilities" (The Kubert School, 2015). First-year courses include many basic art and comic-art courses such as "Basic Drawing," "The Human Figure," "Narrative Art," "Layout," "Design," "Digital Production," and "Lettering." In the second and third years, students take more advanced versions of many of these courses, but each year includes new offerings such as "Color Illustration," "Advertising Illustration," "Sketching and Layout," and "Advanced Technique and Creation of Style: The Graphic Novel." Somewhat in the tradition of the *Comic Book Illustrators Instruction Course*, Kubert's first foray into education, the Kubert School offers a series of correspondence courses with books and DVDs designed to instruct students on topics such as "Heroes and Superheroes," "Story-Graphics," "Penciling," and "Inking." Students who cannot commit to the three-year program can attend workshops and night classes, many of which are designed especially for children. Although not authorized to grant degrees, the Kubert School is an approved member of the New Jersey Department of Labor and Workforce Development and is accredited by the Accrediting Commission of Career Schools and Colleges, a body charged with accrediting schools that "are predominantly organized to educate students for occupations, trade and technical careers, and including institutions that offer programs via distance education" (US Department of Education, 2016). The primary mission of the school, in other words, is to prepare students for careers in cartooning and illustration.

In 2004, James Sturm and Michelle Ollie founded what is arguably the closest thing to a college focused exclusively on the study of comics, The Center for Cartoon Studies, a two-year institution in White River Junction, Vermont. After receiving his M.F.A. from the School of Visual Arts in 1991, Sturm went on to become an award-winning comic book artist, art director, and educator. From 1997 to 2001, he was an instructor in the Sequential Art program at the Savannah College of Art and Design, and *Time Magazine* named his graphic novel *The Golem's Mighty Swing* the "Best Graphic Novel of 2001." Michelle Ollie studied art and graphic design at the University of Wisconsin before working for several years in the publishing industry, specializing in print technology. In 1998, she joined the faculty at the Minneapolis College of Art and Design where she met Sturm while he was applying for a faculty position in the school's Comics Arts program. There, Sturm and Ollie discovered that they shared a mutual concern about the future of teaching the art of comics.

There was a need, they believed, for a school focused entirely on the practical education of comic art without the broader, generalized training provided at most traditional art schools. According to Sturm, "A lot of schools see cartooning as more of a pre-professional thing... I felt like I could create a better program" (qtd. in Vine, 2012). Years later, when the Center for Cartoon Studies was founded, Sturm and Ollie made their focused mission clear:

> The Center for Cartoon Studies (CCS) is dedicated to providing the highest quality of education to students interested in creating visual stories. CCS's curriculum of art, graphic design, and literature reflect the wide array of skills needed to create comics and graphic novels. CCS emphasizes self-publishing and prepares its students to publish, market, and disseminate their work.
>
> *(Center for Cartoon Studies, 2015)*

Though not accredited, the Center for Cartoon Studies is authorized by the Vermont Department of Education to confer M.F.A.s (Master of Fine Arts and Master of Fine Arts in Applied Cartooning) and certificates (a 2-Year Certificate, a 2-Year Certificate in Applied Cartooning, and 1-Year Certificate). Although each program has its own requirements, almost all students take the same core classes: "Cartooning Studio," "Life Drawing Session," "Publication Workshop," "Survey of the Drawn Story," and "Visiting Artists Seminar." Although Sturm still teaches many of these courses himself, CCS also prides itself on the reputation of its faculty, including Stephen Bissette, a "pioneer graduate" of the Kubert School, best known for *Saga of the Swamp Thing* and for co-creating the character John Constantine with Alan Moore.

In truth, students looking to learn more about the practical study of comic arts have many options that simply were not available just a few decades ago when the School of Visual Arts and the Kubert School were practically the only viable programs dedicated to the field. Even without enrolling in one of the two- or four-year schools mentioned above, would-be comic book artists can attend conferences or workshops or enroll in any number of well-respected online programs dedicated to the study of comics. In 2007, former Marvel and IDW editor Andy Schmidt founded the Comics Experience, an online series of courses and workshops "for people who want to make comics, people who want to work in the comic industry, and those who just want to know more about the fantastic medium of comics" (Comics Experience, 2015). Originally something Schmidt planned on doing in his spare time, the Comics Experience proved to be so successful that he and a team of industry professionals offer classes year-round on virtually every aspect of the industry, including coloring, drawing, editing, lettering, writing, and even comic-book law.

Conclusion

Historically, and perhaps by definition, organizations dedicated to the study of comics have almost all shared the common goal of fostering a greater appreciation of the artistic and cultural value of the medium, be it comic strips, comic books, graphic novels, or something in between. Whether organized by fans, academics, or the artists themselves, each organization has played a role in increasing the public's awareness of Comics Studies, further advancing the field and legitimizing the art form by creating the infrastructures needed to carry Comics Studies forward into its next stages of development.

Bibliography

Alter Ego: The Comic Book Artist Collection, Raleigh: TwoMorrows.
Ault, D. (2003) 'In the trenches, taking the heat: confessions of a comics professor', *International Journal of Comic Art,* 5 (2): 241–60.
Browne, R.B. (1989) *Against Academia: the history of the Popular Culture Association/American Culture Association and the Popular Culture Movement, 1967–1988,* Bowling Green: Bowling Green University Press.
Browne, R.B. and Marsden, M.T. (1999) *Pioneers in Popular Culture Studies,* Bowling Green: Bowling Green State University Popular Press.
Bryan, W. (2012) 'Randy Duncan: creating a class filled with costumes, iconic characters and CRASH!', *ArkansasOnline* [Online] Available from: http://www.arkansasonline.com/news/ 2012/oct/14/randy-duncan-creating-class-filled-costumes-iconic/?f=trilakes. [Accessed 8 September 2015].
Cassel, D., Sultan, A. and Trimpe, H. (2015) *Incredible Herb Trimpe,* Raleigh: TwoMorrows.
Center for Cartoon Studies. (2015) *Center for Cartoon Studies.* [Online] Available from: http://www.cartoonstudies.org/. [Accessed: 8 September 2015].
Center for Cartoon Studies (2016). [Online] Available from: http://www.cartoonstudies.org/. [Accessed 14 September 2016].
Chute, H. (2008) 'Comics as literature? Reading graphic narrative', *PMLA,* 123 (2): 452–65.
Comics Experience. (2015) 'Andy Schmidt: instructor and founder', *Comics Experience* [Online]. Available from http://www.comicsexperience.com/staff/andy-schmidt/. [Accessed 8 September 2015].
Comics Studies Society. (2015) *Comics Studies Society.* [Online] Available from: http://www.comicssociety.org/. [Accessed 8 September 2015].
Davis-Stofka, B. (2015) 'Studying superhero costumes', *ComicBookBin.* [Online] Available from: http://www.comicbookbin.com/fashionandfantasy001.html. [Accessed 8 September 2015].
Duncan, R. and Smith M. J. (2009). *The Power of Comics: history, form, and culture,* New York: Continuum.
Duncan, R. and Smith, M.J. (2015) 'Learning from film studies: analogies and challenges', *Comics Forum.* [Online] Available from: http://comicsforum.org/2011/07/15/learning-from-film-studies-analogies-and-challenges-by-randy-duncan-and-matthew-j-smith/. [Accessed 8 September 2015].
Groensteen, T. (2007) *The System of Comics,* trans. B. Beaty & N. Nguyen, Jackson: University Press of Mississippi.
Grove, L. (2010) *Comics in French: the European Bande Dessinée in context,* New York: Berghahn.
Hatfield, C. (2010) 'Indiscipline, or, the condition of comics studies', *Transatlantica* [Online]. Available from: https://transatlantica.revues.org/4933. [Accessed 8 September 2015].
Henderson State University. (2015) *Comics Studies Minor.* [Online] Available from: http://www.hsu.edu/Academics/EllisCollege/Communication-and-Theatre-Arts/Comics%20Minor.html. [Accessed 1 June 2015].
Institute for Comics Studies. (2015) *Institute for Comics Studies.* [Online] Available from: http://www.instituteforcomicsstudies.org/. [Accessed 8 September 2015].
International Comic Arts Forum. (2015) *International Comic Arts Forum.* [Online] Available from: http://www.internationalcomicartsforum.org/. [Accessed 8 September 2015].
Jenkins, H. (2012) 'Introduction: should we discipline the reading of comics?', in M.J. Smith and R. Duncan. (eds.) *Critical Approaches to Comics: theories and methods,* New York: Routledge.
Kannenberg, G., Srinivasan, S.A. and Witek, J. (2013) Illustrations or quotations? Permission & rights for publishing comics scholarship. [Online] Available from: http://gator.uhd.edu/~kannenbg/permissions.html. [Accessed 8 September 2015].
The Kubert School. (2015) *History of the Kubert School.* [Online] Available from: http://www.kubertschool.edu/about/history.html. [Accessed 8 September 2015].
Lacassin, F. (1972) *The Comic Strip and Film Language,* trans. D. Kunzle, *Film Quarterly.* 26(1): 11–23.
Langley, T. (2012) *Batman and Psychology: a dark and stormy knight,* Hoboken: John Wiley & Sons.

Lent, J.A. (2010) 'The winding, pot-holed road of comic art scholarship', *Studies in Comics*, 1 (1): 7–33.
Lopes, P.D. (2009) *Demanding Respect: the evolution of the American comic book*, Philadelphia: Temple University Press.
Magnussen, A. and Christiansen, H.C. (eds.) (2000) *Comics & Culture: analytical and theoretical approaches to comics*, Copenhagen: Museum Tusculanum.
MCAD (Minneapolis College of Art and Design) (2016). [Online] Available from: http://mcad.edu. [Accessed 14 September 2016].
Miller, A. (2007) *Reading Bande Dessinée: critical approaches to French-language comic strip*, Chicago: Intellect.
Modern Language Association. (2015) *Comics and Graphic Narratives: the MLA discussion group*. [Online] Available from: http://graphicnarratives.org/. [Accessed 8 September 2015].
Popular Culture Association/American Culture Association. (2015) *Comics and Comic Art*. [Online] Available from: http://pcaaca.org/comic-arts-comics/. [Accessed 8 September 2015].
Portland State University. (2015) *College of Liberal Arts & Sciences: Comics Studies*. [Online] Available from http://www.pdx.edu/comics-studies/. [Accessed 19 October 2015].
Roach, D. and Cooke, J.B. (eds.)(2001) *The Warren Companion: the definitive compendium to the great comics of Warren Publishing*, Raleigh: TwoMorrows.
Savannah College of Art and Design. (2015) *Sequential Art*. [Online] Available from: http://www.scad.edu/academics/programs/sequential-Art. [Accessed 8 September 2015].
School of Visual Arts. (2015) *Cartooning*. [Online] Available from: http://www.sva.edu/undergraduate/cartooning. [Accessed 8 September 2015].
Thomas, R. (2001) Draw for comic books! Learn and earn in your spare time—at home!!"
University of Dundee. (2015) *Comics Studies MLitt*. [Online] Available from: http://www.dundee.ac.uk/study/pg/comics-studies/. [Accessed 8 September 2015].
University of Florida. (2015) *Department of English*. [Online] Available from: http://www.english.ufl.edu/. [Accessed 8 September 2015].
University of Oregon. (2015) *Comics & Cartoon Studies*. [Online] Available from: http://comics.uoregon.edu/. [Accessed 8 September 2015].
US Department of Education (2016). [Online] Available from http://www2.ed.gov/admins/finaid/accred/accreditation_pg6.html. [Accessed 14 September 2016].
Vessels, JE. (2010) *Drawing France: French comics and the republic*, Jackson: University Press of Mississippi.
Vine, A. (2012) 'Michelle Ollie delivers comics and a serious vision', *Vermont Woman*. [Online] Available from: http://www.vermontwoman.com/articles/2012/0212/comics.html. [Accessed 8 September 2015].
Wright, B.W. (2001) *Comic Book Nation: the transformation of youth culture in America*, Baltimore: Johns Hopkins University Press.

A PIONEER'S PERSPECTIVE: JOHN A. LENT

During the past generation, Comics Studies institutions have made remarkable progress as organizations, conferences, journals, galleries, museums, and presses dedicated to the field have proliferated, in the process breaking down the sacrosanct walls of academia.

A look back to the pre-1990s reveals a sparse presence of institutions in the United States; there was the comics section of Popular Culture Association but not much else; conferences and journals were not to be seen (though fanzines and trade periodicals existed); galleries and museums were generally empty of cartoons and comics in their exhibitions and collections; libraries actually were known to reject donations of comics materials and, in other cases, toss out newspaper comics supplements once they were

(Continued)

microfilmed; and presses shied away from publishing comics-related books. Researchers studying comics often were laughed at, scorned by the media and faculty colleagues, and hard pressed to find outlets for their work.

Other parts of the world fared considerably better. In Europe, already in the 1960s, associations that fostered comics study functioned in France, Italy, and Sweden, and, during the 1970s, dozens of intellectuals, writers, and artists dipped into comics scholarship; a chair of theoretical Comics Studies existed at the Sorbonne, and books about comics appeared in England, France, Germany, Italy, Netherlands, and Spain. Japan, during the same period, had a number of scholars studying comics from various academic disciplines and at least two manga journals, and in China, the first histories of cartooning were published early in the 1970s. Comics Studies in Latin America began in Argentina in the late 1960s, with the short-lived *LD* magazine and an International Biennial of Comics, and in Brazil in the 1970s, with the publication of books and a journal and the creation of courses.

Interest in comics scholarship was rejuvenated in the late 1980s and escalated throughout the 1990s and beyond. In the United States, the Comics Arts Conference was started at the San Diego Comic-Con in 1992, joining the longer-established Comic Arts and Comics area of the Popular Culture Association, and three years later what is now the International Comic Arts Forum was spun from a 1995 manga symposium in Washington, D.C. The Ohio State University Festival of Cartoon Art, a triennial event since 1983, also has a scholarly dimension. These were followed by other regular conferences or programs of comics presentations at the University of Florida and within the Modern Language Association. More formal Comics Studies periodicals appeared, such as *Target*, *WittyWorld*, *INKS*, *International Journal of Comic Art*, *ImageText*, and others; University Press of Mississippi, in the late 1980s, began its comics series, followed by others such as Westview, Hampton, McFarland, Routledge, Bloomsbury, and more, and libraries, museums, and centers sped up building comics collections, actually soliciting cartoonists', academicians', and collectors' papers. Prominent among them are Ohio State University, Library of Congress, and Michigan State University; other university collections are at Florida, Columbia, Kansas, Pennsylvania, Yale, Boston, and Syracuse, to name a few. Also, in the 1990s, research sources were gathered and systemically compiled and published in bibliographies, encyclopedias, online databases, and anthologies.

Worldwide, Comics Studies were boosted by the sprouting of institutions—full-fledged academic organizations with their own journals in Australia, Japan, Korea, and Brazil; other scholarly periodicals coming out of Argentina, England (three), and Scandinavia, and regularly scheduled Comics Studies conferences in Argentina, Brazil, Scotland, and Japan. Kyoto Seika University in Japan operates the International Manga Research Center.

Assuming present trends continue to grow, Comics Studies institutions will have a bright future. We can expect to see institutions splinter into specialized areas—e.g., a conference on comics and disability, freedom of expression, or medicine; gallery exhibitions more theme oriented and journals defined by various comics forms (e.g., a journal on comic strips), areas (e.g., one on comic theory), or genres (e.g., one on superhero or autobiography). Let's hope this subdividing does not overrun the strength of Comics Studies or neglect necessary overview perspectives.

With a discipline as relatively young as Comics Studies, there are gaps to be filled and precautions to be taken. As indicated, national Comics Studies organizations exist, including a new one in the US; perhaps an international body will materialize as well. Size should not be the goal of these groups and their conferences, making them unwieldy, costly, and even intimidating. More loosely structured groups are preferred, where sharing of ideas on the field of study (not how many articles the organization's constitution requires) and putting a bit of fun into study are the focus. We hope that conference organizers will maintain their distance from online "gatherings" that obliterate real-face-to-real-face communication and opportunities for social mingling.

A good start has been made concerning journals, and the field can expect additional academic periodicals, ideally in non-English languages and including articles on countries where the comics scene is little known. Though recent efforts have materialized in that direction, more translated and other international content, especially covering the southern hemisphere nations, needs to appear in English-language journals. The range of comics topics, genres, and formats must be broadened beyond US superheroes and comic books and graphic novels. Genres slighted in the scholarship are adventure, romance, detective, sports, religion, and teenage life; along the same lines, journals need to increase concentration on newspaper comic strips, editorial cartoons, caricature (portrait), magazine gag cartoons, cartoons used in advertising, humor/cartoon periodicals, cartoon leaflets, posters, and postcards, and comics paraphernalia.

Still other "hope-fors" in comic art-related journals are more of a mix of quantitative and qualitative methodological approaches; the stimulation of theoretical formations from non-Western, non-Judeo-Christian, and non-capitalist perspectives to better fit a large part of the globe; the use of political economy frameworks, especially to study production, distribution, and ownership of comics industries; more audience studies with larger, more systematically developed samples; increased use of the many archives and collections set up; referencing literature that extends beyond the 1990s; and increased use and updating of established bibliographies. The recent trend of non-comic art journals carrying symposia and articles of interest speaks well of the maturation of the field, as do the number of galleries and museums dedicated to comics and the plethora of book publishers issuing related books.

These all are major accomplishments for a field still in a relatively infant stage; whatever patterns that evolve now are likely to set the standard for years. Let's hope they are the most beneficial ones.

A PIONEER'S PERSPECTIVE: PETER M. COOGAN

Late, very late, one night in the summer of 1992, a screaming Canadian called me. Vicki Green (M.Ed., University of Saskatchewan, 1974) had received the call for papers for the first Comics Arts Conference in the newsletter *Comic Art Studies*. Vicki had completed her thesis, *The Role of the Indian in the Western Comic Book*, in 1974 and was teaching at Okanagan College in Vernon, British Columbia. After finishing her thesis, she didn't have

(Continued)

a community of scholars to join. Vicki was screaming with joy because until she saw the newsletter announcing the conference she thought she was alone in the academic universe. But in 1992, there was a newsletter, a new conference, and a new doctoral student (me) who wanted to build that community.

Randy Scott, the Special Collections Librarian at Michigan State University, started the newsletter *Comic Art Collection* in 1979 to inform donors and interested parties about the library's growing comics collection. The newsletter had fallen out of regular publication; the indicia for issue 45 (December 1991) indicated "periodicity unknown." But the budget line survived, and I had the idea of using it to "spark a 'polylogue' among comics scholars, librarians, retailers, professionals, and enthusiasts."

To jumpstart this polylogue, we launched a survey of comics scholars. The questionnaire was my attempt to pose, in a "large 'democratic' context," questions about the field. On topics like gender, audience, industry, and history, I offered insightful questions like, "What work needs to be done on gender issues?" "What audience surveys have been done and need to be done?" "What about the industry has been and needs to be studied (independent publishers, censorship, creators' rights, etc.)?" and "What histories have been written?" These seem like basic questions (they *are* basic questions), but that was the point—Comics Studies as a field had no sense of itself. I did raise more substantive questions—asking "What is the definition of comics?" "What are the extremes in terms of balancing words and pictures that are acceptable as comics?" and "Do we need a rhetoric or poetics of comics?"

I presented preliminary results of the survey at the Popular Culture Association conference in Louisville, KY, on March 20, which Randy Duncan (too many Randys!) missed, which led to him calling me at Special Collections (pre-cell phone days), which led to us agreeing that there should be a comics conference on its own that wasn't part of the PCA and that we should hold it at a comic book convention, which led to the Comics Arts Conference.

Over the next three years, until *Comic Arts Studies* #55 (December 1996), the newsletter did play the role I had imagined for it. Reading back over those survey results, I see questions that are still being discussed today, albeit within the context of an established body of scholarly articles and monographs, journalistic reporting, pop scholarship, and all sorts of other discussions on the Web, in podcasts, and on YouTube.

Randy Scott and I set out to identify comics scholars and their areas of interest through the Directory of Comics Scholars starting in #48. The entries came back from established professors, a lot of graduate students, librarians, small press and mini-comics publishers, APA and fanzine publishers, comics journalists, and comics collectors, all of whom had some interest in reaching beyond their particular bailiwick and making a connection with others who had chosen to treat comics as a legitimate art form and were starting to build careers on the idea that comics could be an academic field. Other announcements in *CAS*—the formation of the Sequential Art Department at Savannah College of Art and Design, the founding of the Center of Research on Comics in Brazil, the creation of the Grand Comics Database, and the rejection of a panel on comics proposed by Luca Somigli (SUNY Stony Brook) to the MLA (rejected because the proposal "academicizes this subject in just the wrong way"). In these days of the Internet, sometimes we forget how crucial these paper postal publications were in sharing news and making contacts.

As part of being the editor of the newsletter, I also responded quite often to people looking to make those contacts. I have a whole file of letters I sent out to scholars, which quickly shifted to emails, helping them to connect with each other. Due to reviewing Comics Studies bibliographies and editing the survey, the directory, and the newsletter, I had a pretty good grip on the field and wanted to share this knowledge by acting as a nexus of comics scholarship—to be the person who knew or knew about everyone in our small field—it seemed like a reasonable goal at the time; thank goodness it would be impossible now due to the growth in the field. I sought out and took pride in this role. Once at the Popular Culture Association, Randy Duncan overheard me talking to a graduate student about who she should contact regarding her topic. Although I don't remember this meeting (maybe because it was a fairly common occurrence), I must have had the hook up she needed because according to Randy, I said, "My Rolodex kung fu is strong." I'm glad the field has grown so much since then and now has conferences, journals, courses, study centers, a few programs, and maybe a department on the horizon. I'm just happy I was in a place where, with the support of an existing institution (the MSU Library), I could play a small role in helping comics scholars advance their studies. Vicki is no longer alone.

17

THE GALLERIES

Kim Munson

Eleven-year-old Charles Schulz was stuck. He spent every available moment copying drawings from his favorite Sunday funnies at the dining room table, but he still didn't feel he was getting anywhere with his art. He recognized that something was lacking in his drawings but had no way to identify what was missing. According to Schulz biographer David Michaelis, Charles' mother, Dena, wanted to be supportive of her son but felt powerless to help him with his odd obsession to become a cartoonist, until she noticed an ad in the local newspaper for an exhibition of art by professional comic strip artists at the St. Paul Public Library (77–83). Visiting the exhibit in February of 1934, young Charles was able to closely scrutinize original drawings by working cartoonists, including pages by Ham Fisher (*Joe Palooka*), Milt Gross (*Dave's Delicatessen & Count Screwloose*), Harold Knerr (*Katzenjammer Kids*), Roy Crane (*Wash Tubbs*), and Percy Crosby (*Skippy*). He had been terrified of making mistakes, yet here he saw the fascinating leftover minutia of the production process; the notes in blue pencil, the bits of paper covering over mistakes, the blots and registration marks. More importantly, he observed the life and confidence showing through in the brushwork of these professionals, and finally recognized the spark that was missing in his own drawings.

Shows of comic art, like the one that helped Schulz break through his artistic plateau, were not uncommon. Comic strips were the prime mass entertainment in the era before WWII, and people loved to see drawings by their favorite artists. Over the decades, it has not always been easy to get comic art into museums and galleries for public viewing, despite its popularity. This chapter collects the stories of some of the pioneers that advanced the study of comics art by showing it publicly in new contexts and the resulting catalogs, reviews, and criticism that helped shape comic art into an appropriate topic for serious exhibition and scholarship.

One attempt to put comics in a scholarly context was mounted in the early 1940s; a major exhibit on the history of comics sponsored by the American Institute of Graphic Arts, organized by Miss Jessie Gillespie Willing (Program Chairman of AIGA) with Gerald McDonald (New York Public Library) and the cartoonist James Swinnerton. It opened at the National Arts Club in New York, and then toured the U S. This exhibition was discussed in detail in a lavish pair of 1942 articles by the publisher M. C. Gaines in *Print* called "Narrative Illustration: The Story of the Comics" and "More about the Comics." According to Gaines, the work was organized in several sections: Ancient art, beginning with a tracing of a cave drawing from prehistoric Spain; caricatures and satirical cartoons from the 18th and 19th centuries, such as William Hogarth, George Cruikshank, and Rodolphe Töpffer; cartoonists working between 1894 and 1920, such as R. F. Outcault, Winsor McCay, and George Herriman, and over 20 cartoonists working in the 1940s, such as Ernie Bushmiller, Al Capp, Chester Gould, and Frank King.[1] Gaines gives special mention to Milton Caniff, who was voted the favorite by visitors to the originating exhibition at the National Arts Club. As an individual, Caniff had previous exhibitions of his work from *Terry and the Pirates* at both the Dayton Art Museum (1939) and the high-end Julien Levy Art Gallery in New York (1940) (Caniff & Harvey, 2002, p. xxv).

Censorship and Disapproval of Comics

From the infancy of comics in the mid-1890s, some critics feared that reading comics contributed to illiteracy by pandering to children and working-class immigrants. Building on this demeaning concept, the idea of comics as "low art" (in contrast to "high" fine art) became the dominant opinion in the upper circles of the art criticism and museum establishment, especially after the influential critic Clement Greenberg proclaimed it kitsch or "rear-guard art" in his 1939 *Partisan Review* article "Avant-Garde and Kitsch." Comics, and most forms of what we now think of as popular culture (for example, movies, jazz music, and commercial illustration), were thought of as commercially constructed genres that depressed intellectual contemplation and advancement, and as such came to be ignored by the major modern art museums (especially in New York), which focused on the cerebral and highly lucrative art of the Abstract Expressionist, High Modernist, and Minimalist movements in the late 1940s, '50s, & '60s. Al Capp, the out-spoken cartoonist famous for his long running strip *Li'l Abner*, returned the art world's contempt, complaining that abstract art was "produced by the talentless, sold by the unscrupulous and bought by the utterly bewildered." (Schumacher & Kitchen, 2013, p. 251)

The critical opinion of comics reached a new low in 1954 with the publication of psychologist Dr. Fredric Wertham's book *Seduction of the Innocent*, which persuaded the general public that comics (particularly crime, superhero, and horror comic books) caused juvenile delinquency by depicting crime, violence, and sexual situations, which led to censorship, book burnings, and content-regulating agencies like the Comics Code and the Newspaper Comics Council. The tension between the fine arts and comics artists escalated when the superstars of the 1960s Pop Art movement, such as Andy Warhol and Roy Lichtenstein, used appropriated comics characters, panels, and elements in their work because they thought of it as ironic, campy or trash used conceptually much like Duchamp used a urinal as a "readymade" in his 1917 work *Fountain*. Opinion about the Pop Art phenomenon among comics creators varied wildly. Some felt that the comics were a successful genre defined by their own rules that needed no validation from the fine art world. Many felt it was simple theft, as they watched fine artists raking in millions of dollars from paintings that featured their panels or characters as the comics artists themselves slaved away for syndicates or for comic book publishers at low page rates.

The art business had no serious interest in comic art. Many Modern Art museums and galleries had been redesigned as spaces to display the large heroic canvases of the Abstract Expressionists and those vast white walls seemed to swallow standard-sized pages of black & white comics art originals, which were further compromised by being removed from their primary narrative context with no reference to the printed version that was the final product. In general, comics artists and their supporters faced a disapproving, disinterested art world that thought of comics as trash without artistic merit or financial value. When comic art was allowed into the Modern Art museums as contextual examples of source material for Pop Art paintings, little care was taken in how it was displayed. It was in this challenging era that many of the curators, artists, writers, collectors, and historians who wanted to advance the artistic recognition and study of comics art entered the picture.

A Cavalcade of Cartoons

Although many of the Modern Art museums were dismissive of comics and comic art, some of the major U S encyclopedic institutions, such as the Library of Congress, the Smithsonian, and New York's Metropolitan Museum of Art (MMA) recognized the importance of comics and displayed them often. One such show was *American Cartooning*, an exhibition of original drawings on view at the MMA May 11-June 10, 1951. Works by 239 artists were chosen by a committee of MMA curators and members of the National Cartoonists Society, meant to "best represent each artist's work, and at the same time provide a broad picture of contemporary cartooning in this country" (Metropolitan Museum of Art, 1951). An announcement about this show in the March 1, 1951, issue of *Art Digest* describes an intriguing range of work:

> While primarily a cross-section of contemporary cartooning, with such representatives as Carl Anderson's *Henry*, Milton Caniff's *Steve Canyon* and Al Capp's *Li'l Abner*, the Exhibition also contains comic strips popular earlier in the century. Among them are *Happy Hooligan* by F. Opper, *Little Nemo* by Winsor McCay and *Krazy Kat* by George Herriman. Representing other contemporary fields are such editorial cartoonists as F. O. Alexander, Daniel R. Fitzpatrick and Tom Little; magazine cartoons from *The Saturday Evening Post*, *Collier's* and *The New Yorker*; and animated cartoons by Walt Disney and Paul H. Terry. (1951)

Another exhibition of note was *The Cavalcade of American Comics*, which was produced by The Newspaper Comics Council (NCC) and the American Newspaper Publishers Association. It was launched in October 1963 at the RCA Exhibition Hall in New York, displayed at the New York World's Fair in the Better Living Center (1964) and at the RCA Pavilion (1965). After that it toured to the Smithsonian (1966) and to at least 20 other locations around the U S through the 1970s & '80s. According to the inventory supplied by the NCC to the World's Fair committee, the contents of this show consisted of 61 laminated tear sheets from the Gordon Campbell collection (art director of the Newspaper Printing Corp of Nashville, TN), one laminated *Yellow Kid* 1896 tear sheet from the NCC's collection, and 32 original drawings (1965). The work was arranged chronologically, and a newsprint brochure was given away that outlined the evolution of newspaper comics and their historical relevance. Cartoonists Milton Caniff (*Steve Canyon*), Mell Lazarus (*Miss Peach*), Irwin Hasen (*Dondi*), Al Smith (*Mutt & Jeff*), and Dick Cavalli (*Morty Meekle*) participated in a "Chalk Talk," drawing before an audience at the World's Fair, and similar events were held with other artists at the Smithsonian and other locations.

Comics at the Louvre

Meanwhile, a group of French fans of U S comics decided to directly respond to Pop Art and the need for serious scholarship with the show *Bande Dessinée et Figuration Narrative*, which was on display at the Musee des Arts Decoratifs (a specialty museum within the Louvre), Paris, from April through June 1967. The exhibition was organized by members of the Civil Society for the Study of and for Research into Drawn Literature (SOCERLID), whose mission was to gain recognition for comics as an art form and to advance scholarship. Led by Pierre Couperie, a professor at l'École pratique des Hautes Études, Claude Moliterni, Édouard François, Proto Destefanis, and Maurice Horn, the group curated three small exhibitions in 1965 & 1966 at the gallery of the French Society of Photography featuring the works of Burne Hogarth, Milton Caniff, and a retrospective of American comic strip art.

FIGURE 17.1 Promotional Poster for *Bande Dessinée et Figuration Narrative* at the Musee des Arts Decoratifs, 1967.

Source: Image courtesy Maurice Horn.

In a detailed article about the 1967 exhibition (in French) on Thierry Groensteen's site *Neuvieme Art 2.0,* Couperie tells Antoine Sausverd about approaching the Louvre, whose board eventually accepted their proposal, but not without forcing them to accept the addition of a group of modern paintings selected by the art critic and theorist Gérald Gassiot-Talabot. This was a sore spot because Couperie despised Pop Art in general and Lichtenstein in particular and saw this show a specific response to it. "At that time the cartoon was seen only through his [Lichtenstein's] eyes, he had shown the emptiness and futility... taking the worst pictures and expanding enormously," Couperie tells Nicolas Galilard of *Reverse Angle*. "We wanted to show that comics were something else; that they possessed aesthetic values of their own" (1997, cited in Sausverd, 2014).[2]

The Louvre exhibition, like the preceding three, displayed high-resolution photographic enlargements instead of hand-drawn originals, with the idea that this method would free the images from their usual small format and show them to people in a way that they were used to seeing works of art. As seen in the series of exhibition photos included by Paul Gravett in his introduction to *Comics Art* (2013), the idea of breaking away from panels carried over into the plan by exhibition designer Isabelle Chavarot. She affixed the reproductions to a maze of orange tulle hangings and to several sculptural forms made up of cubes. The display explored themes of narrative structure and image, vocabulary and conventions and how specific meanings are combined in the narrative technique. A wall display about comics history was also included.

Couperie told Sausverd that the show had attracted a great deal of press and public attention (the Louvre extended the run of the show), and he felt that it helped comics gain recognition as an art form. Groensteen notes in the same article that he questioned many of the assumptions made in this show, and looking with hindsight, I agree. In this exhibition, comics lost their sequential nature. Exhibitions of comics art have evolved to value the things that make comics unique: the layout, the interplay between word and image, and the idea that part of the story is going on in the space between the panels. Blow ups are sometimes used for emphasis, but not featured. Still, this breakthrough show and its extensive print catalog (in French, and in English under the title *A History of the Comic Strip*, Couperie & Horn, 1968) began the dialog that has led us to a greater understanding of the comics art form.

Key Exhibitions of the 1970s

By the late 1960s, U S Modern Art museums were still ignoring comics artists, but several academic art departments and smaller galleries were inspired to seriously explore both comics as an art form and their cultural context (perhaps inspired by the U S publication of Couperie and Horn's *A History of the Comic Strip*, which was quite popular). In 1969, Stephen S. Prokopoff curated *The Spirit of the Comics* at the University of Pennsylvania's Institute of Contemporary Art Gallery. Although this was a fine art show that included no comic art, Prokopoff's introductory catalog essay includes a serious discussion of comics history and cultural context and why comics iconography had become such a key element in modern art.

The Comics as an Art Form, a 1970 survey of comic strip and comic book art representing the work of over 70 artists, was organized by Peter L. Myer, the chairman of the Art Department at the University of Nevada, Las Vegas. Myer described the exhibit to the *Colorado Springs Gazette-Telegraph* as "a statement of belief in the validity of the comic art form." The opening event at UNLV featured a symposium on comics with Charles Schulz, Harvey Kurtzman, Will Eisner, and Jack Kirby. The show toured in 1971 to the Colorado Springs Art Center.

Also in 1971, Judith O'Sullivan organized *The Art of the Comic Strip* at the University of Maryland Art Gallery, an ambitious survey show that placed comic art in a proper artistic and cultural context, pointing out the dream-like Art Nouveau line work in McCay's *Little Nemo* and how Herriman's brushwork, language, and composition add to the sense of fantasy in *Krazy Kat*. This show was circulated by the Smithsonian from 1972 to 1974.

Maurice Horn, one of the collaborators on the Louvre show, organized an exhibition called *75 Years of the Comics* at the New York Cultural Center at 2 Columbus Circle in August 1971. This show displayed over 300 drawings tracing the history of comics from 19th century classics by Töpffer and Outcault, through generations of comic strips, to underground comix by R. Crumb, Gilbert Shelton, and Art Spiegelman. "Comics," Horn told Lesley Oelsner of the *New York Times*, "were experiencing a rebirth in the form of underground comix," and "more and more critics and intellectuals should be concerning themselves with it." (54) This may have been one of the first New York shows to include work from underground comix.

In the exhibition catalog, Horn argued for comics not only as a literary genre, but also as an art form that needs serious study. He answered critics that called comics "non-art, non-literature, and non-significant," stating:

> A thorough knowledge of the field must be obtained, with the same assiduity as is required of any other discipline; the a priori judgment that this is an inferior form only deserving of inferior scholarship is an especially galling piece of tortuous reasoning. Only by serious study can we arrive at an understanding of the underlying structures of the comics, without which no critical conclusion can emerge. (14)

Lawrence Alloway, the art critic for *The Nation Magazine*, agreed with Horn in his review of the show, concluding with a plea for more serious scholarship: "One of the requirements of future comics research, now that the artists are known and characterized, is the interpretation of the comics as a part of culture, drawn by artists but also shaped by the socially formed expectations of the audience" (1971, p. 57).

The exhibition attracted nationwide attention from the media, including an appearance on the local NY talk show *Straight Talk* on October 22, 1971, with Horn, Burne Hogarth, Stan Lee and Bob Kane. Horn continued on to write or edit several influential histories of comics, including *The World Encyclopedia of Comics* (1976), *Women in the Comics* (1977), *Comics of the American West* (1977), and *100 Years of American Newspaper Comics* (1996).

The New York Cultural Center hosted an exhibition by Al Capp shortly before the venue closed in 1975. Capp tried to cash in on the Pop Art craze by creating life-size Warhol style paintings and lithographs of his famous characters. As Michael Schumacher and Denis Kitchen report in their Capp biography *Al Capp: a Life to the Contrary*, Capp was proud to see his work displayed…

> A work of art is a work of art, regardless of form, size or material. People have been brainwashed into thinking that if it appears in a comic strip and in your daily newspaper, and done with pen and ink, it is a contemptible trifle, it isn't art. That is self-swindling snobbishness. (252)

His work sold well, but the critical acclaim he desired eluded him, and his refusal to take the mainstream art business seriously eventually made his foray into the fine arts a losing enterprise.

The First Cartoon Museum, 1974

Mort Walker, an award-winning cartoonist best known for his long-running comic strips *Beetle Bailey* and *Hi & Lois*, founded the first museum in the US exclusively dedicated to comic and animation art in collaboration with his son, author, and comics historian Brian Walker, who started out painting the building and soon became the primary curator of the museum. The Museum of Cartoon Art had all the functions we expect of a traditional museum: a growing collection, an ongoing slate of exhibitions, events, and educational programming. It opened at the Mead Mansion, Greenwich, Connecticut on August 11, 1974. It continued there until the museum lost its lease then relocated to Ward's Castle in Rye Brook, New York, opening November 12, 1977. Building repairs compelled the museum to move again on June 30, 1992. On March 8, 1996, it reopened as the International Museum of Cartoon Art as the anchor entertainment attraction for a large planned development in Boca Raton, Florida. A perfect storm of financial difficulties forced the museum to close in 2002. After a fruitless attempt to reopen the museum as a major attraction within the Empire State Building in New York in 2006, Mort Walker accepted an offer from Lucy Shelton Caswell to merge the collection with the Cartoon Library and Museum at The Ohio State University. After 34 years, the Mort Walker Collection had finally found a home, which opened at OSU's Sullivant Hall with two spectacular exhibitions in 2009 and is still producing great exhibitions as the Billy Ireland Cartoon Library and Museum today.

Like Charles Schulz, Mort Walker became obsessed with comics as a child; at 12, he was writing to cartoonists to get samples of their work for his collection. In the exhibition catalog celebrating his collection at Ohio State, Mort explains that over the years he kept collecting, and by the time he was 50, he "had a collection of several thousand pieces of favorite art with no place to show it except my studio walls" (15). It was this need to publicly share his collection that inspired the museum concept:

> I felt that there should be a museum devoted to cartoons, so I decided to create one. At the time, there weren't any cartoon museums in the whole world and people were skeptical. "Why would you need a museum for cartoons once you've read them in the paper?" they would ask. I would answer, "You've seen pictures of the Mona Lisa in books. Why would you go to the museum to see the original?" (2009, p. 15)

Moving into the Mead Mansion with seed money from the Hearst Corporation, Mort tasked Brian, who had just graduated from Tufts University with a major in East African Studies, to remodel and revitalize the place. Helpful collectors, like Rick Marschall, soon arrived to fill the walls. In the early years, the museum created its own standard for display of the art, attaching drawings to matte board with photo corners and then protecting them with plexiglass. They made captions and wall labels with an old Photostat machine. They soon mounted ambitious exhibitions of the work of three comics superstars, Walt Kelly, Hal Foster, and Jack Kirby and a touring exhibit called *The Story of America in Cartoons*, pulled together from the collections of the Library of Congress and Yale University for the

FIGURE 17.2 Brian Walker Standing Outside of the Museum of Cartoon Art at the Mead Mansion, circa 1974.
Source: Photo by Robert Stewart.

US Bicentennial. The collection swelled to 30,000 originals due to donations from artists, other collectors, and syndicates.

Over time Brian and the museum staff developed a seasonal exhibition schedule. During the winter months they organized retrospectives of major artists and important periods in comics history. These special exhibitions grew very ambitious; eventually every major cartoonist and conceivable genre of cartooning was represented. They mounted the first retrospectives of the work of Winsor McCay and George Herriman, and *Women and the Comics*, the first-ever show of female cartoonists, guest curated by Trina Robbins in 1984. During the summer they scheduled crowd-pleasing shows like *Archie: America's Favorite Teenager* and *Bugs Bunny: A Fifty Year Retrospective,* as well as movie tie-ins with Disney Animation, Warner Brothers, DC Comics, and Marvel.

Brian Walker did not relocate with the museum when it moved to Florida. His experience running the Cartoon Museum from 1974 to 1996 had made him one of the most knowledgeable curator/historians in the U S. He taught, wrote two substantial comics history volumes for Abrams in 2002 and 2004 (*The Comics Since 1945* and *The Comics Before 1945*), and curated shows for the Barnum Museum, the Belgian Center for Comic Arts, the Charles Schulz Museum, and others. He was the co-curator for the blockbuster *Masters of American Comics* (2005) shown jointly at the Hammer Museum and the Museum of Contemporary Art in Los Angeles, which also toured to Milwaukee and New York. In 2015, he curated the massive *King of Comics: William Randolph Hearst and 100 Years of King Features* exhibition at the Billy Ireland Cartoon Library and Museum.

The First Comics Museum on the West Coast, 1987

In the mid-1980s one of the longest-lasting independent comic art museums was born on the West coast, due to the efforts of the Troubador Press publisher and author Malcolm Whyte and a crew of his fellow comic art collectors. The Cartoon Art Museum opened in 1987 in a 1500-square-foot gallery in the San Francisco Print Center at 665

Third Street, surrounded by book binders, designers, printers, and discount clothing outlets. After a few years, they moved into the old Call-Bulletin newspaper building at 814 Mission Street. The museum moved from there to a prime spot in the museum district at 655 Mission Street; a long storefront with a lobby, a large bookstore, two galleries used for temporary exhibits, one long gallery dedicated to the permanent collection, and small spaces for animation art and work by emerging local artists. Curator Andrew Farago and Executive Director Summerlea Kashar maintained an ambitious exhibition schedule showing all genres of comic and animation art, as well as artist signings, educational programs, and workshops. In October 2015, the Cartoon Art Museum fell victim to the skyrocketing rents in San Francisco, forcing the museum and its collection into a nomadic existence while the organization raised money and looked for an affordable space (Mayton, 2015). In October, 2016, the museum announced that it would re-open in 2017 at 781 Beach Street, a historic building in the Fisherman's Wharf area (Hartlaub, 2016). In a 2015 phone interview, Whyte recounted the story of the founding of the museum. Returning with his wife, Karen, to their motel after dinner on a fall 1981 weekend in Monterey, Whyte scrawled on a cocktail napkin a rough outline for a Cartoon Art Museum in San Francisco. Whyte floated the idea of a West Coast museum devoted exclusively to comics at a 1983 luncheon at the Bohemian Club in San Francisco hosted by William Kent IV, where he found enthusiastic support from Kent, Larry Rugiero (Development Director for the Oakland Museum), Herb Stansbury of SF Federal Bank, and cartoonist Phil Frank.

The following year, the author/collector Bill Blackbeard was speaking at a meeting of the Northern California Cartoonists and Humorists Association, a group of Bay Area cartoonists and collectors who would meet monthly for dinner, a speaker, and an art auction. Whyte was asked to introduce Blackbeard as they had recently co-authored the book *Great Comic Cats* (1981), and he took this opportunity to mention to the group that he was interested in starting a cartoon art museum. He built a board of directors out of the six members that expressed an interest, filed for non-profit status, and created a full business plan. The directors selected 20 favorite pieces from their collections, and began to offer these as a temporary exhibition for the lobbies of office buildings and other venues as a means of raising funds toward a permanent space.

Their first exhibition was in February 1985, in a corridor at the San Francisco International Airport. The airport matted and framed the work and allowed the Cartoon Art Museum founders to keep the professional matting for the price of the materials. The collection toured northern California, until they had enough income to rent gallery space in the Print Center building. It opened in 1987 during the National Cartoonists Society's annual meeting. Encouraged by the positive response from the cartoonists and the press, Whyte, cartoonist Phil Frank, and board member Ken Kirste met with Charles Schulz at his Santa Rosa studio to see if they could raise enough seed money to make the museum a permanent thing. Describing his meeting with Schulz, Whyte said:

> We had been open long enough that our feet were steady, but our future wasn't completely solid. We mentioned all of that and said we'd like to keep going. Finally, Schulz leaned back in his chair and said, "Well, what do you want?" in that very direct way he had. After catching my breath, I said "We'd like two hundred thousand dollars," and I showed him the outline of our five-year plan. Then he asked, "When do you want it?" I said, "As soon as possible." "Get your proposal over to my accountant," Schulz said. "He'll look it over, and I'm sure he'll agree and get you a check soon." (2015)

They got the money, which was the beginning of a close ongoing relationship with the Charles Schulz Museum in Santa Rosa, CA, including the annual presentation of The Sparky Award, a lifetime achievement award given to a person who has made an outstanding contribution to the comics genre.

Whyte curated many shows and wrote exhibition catalogs, notably *Out of Chaos: Art of the Brothers Crumb* (1998), *Gorey World* (1996) and *Zap to Zippy: The Impact of the Underground* (1990). He is also the author of *Great Comic Cats* (with Blackbeard 1981, updated in 2001) and the *Underground Comix Family Album* (1998). He is proud that the museum has helped to preserve comics history, given young cartoonists a showcase, and contextualized the comic genre for so many people.

Masters of American Comics and the Comics Canon

In 1983, a group of individuals that helped advance comic art into the major U S fine art museums was brought together by *The Comic Art Show,* which opened in New York City during the summer of that year. It was a production of the Whitney Museum's Independent Study Program at their Downtown Gallery at Federal Hall on Wall Street. The show celebrated the new wave of Pop Art erupting in the streets and subways of the East Village and the new alternative comics appearing in *RAW Magazine,* as well as original classic comic strip drawings and work from the first wave of Pop Artists. The comics artists included in this show were: Ernie Bushmiller, Milton Caniff, Al Capp, R. Crumb, Will Eisner, Lyonel Feininger, H. C. Fisher, Rube Goldberg, Chester Gould, Harold Grey, Bill Griffith, Milt Gross, George Herriman, Bill Holman, Bob Kane, Walt Kelly, Frank King, Harvey Kurtzman and Wally Wood, Stan Lee and Jack Kirby, Winsor McCay, Richard Outcault, Gary Panter, Alex Raymond, E. C. Segar, Joe Shuster, Art Spiegelman, Cliff Sterrett, and Garry Trudeau.[3] *The Comic Art Show* was enthusiastically received by the public, and it attracted a great deal of positive press, with the notable exception of a disparaging review in the prestigious magazine *Art in America,* which may have signaled the attitude of the New York museum establishment and critics toward comic art.

John Carlin and Sheena Wagstaff co-curated *The Comic Art Show,* with advice and assistance from Brian Walker and Art Spiegelman, co-publisher of *RAW* and future Pulitzer Prize winner (for the graphic novel *Maus*). Carlin would go on to curate the blockbuster *Masters of American Comics* show, and Wagstaff would return to the UK to curate *Comics Iconoclasm* at the Institute of Contemporary Arts in London and become Chief Curator at the Tate (and then return to the Metropolitan in New York). Ann Philbin, who saw *The Comic Art Show* as a graduate student, eventually shepherded the *Masters of American Comics* show into existence in 2005 after becoming the director of the UCLA Hammer Museum in Los Angeles.

John Carlin was always interested in the inter-connected nature of American pop culture. He saw jazz, comics, art, and amusement parks as expressions that all fed from the same ideas and emotions. He received a very traditional education in art history and comparative literature at Yale, where he was able to teach a class about these ideas, but had to move outside of Yale to explore them, which he did in the Whitney's Independent Study Program and later through the PBS film and subsequent book *Imagining America.* His artistic vocabulary was also shaped by the East Village Punk scene of the 1980s, where he hung out at the CBGB punk rock nightclub and befriended artists like Keith Haring and David Wojnarowicz. After *The Comic Art Show,* he curated *Darkness Visible* (1992, with Mark Beyer, Charles Burns, Sue Coe, Gary Panter, Suzan Pitt, Gig Wailgum, and Sue Williams) at the Drawing Center, where Ann Philbin had become the director, as well as *Comic Power*, a 1993 show at Exit Art featuring the work of over 75 comics artists.

Art Spiegelman may be best known for *Maus*, but he has also been one of the chief innovators of the comic art form. His early works like *Ace Hole: Midget Detective* and *Prisoner from Hell Planet* incorporated post-modern art concepts into comics, and he has been one of comic art's most fearless champions. Along with Brian Walker of the Museum of Cartoon Art, this core group believed strongly in the artistic potential of comics, finally getting the chance to do the comics show they had always talked about when Philbin was hired by the Hammer Museum.

Masters of American Comics was exhibited jointly by the Hammer Museum and the Museum of Contemporary Art, Los Angeles in 2005, touring afterward to the Milwaukee Art Museum and then displayed jointly by the Jewish Museum in New York and the Newark Museum in New Jersey. This exhibition of works by 15 American comics artists was curated by Carlin, with Walker as co-curator and Spiegelman as a senior consultant. Popular and controversial, it was the team's attempt to define a canon of comics artists in the traditional art historical manner, and it was intended as a direct rebuttal to the New York Museum of Modern Art's 1990 show *High & Low: Modern Art, Popular Culture*, which paid lip service to the importance of comics but still displayed them solely as source material used by pop art superstars like Warhol and Lichtenstein. The *High & Low* show so provoked Spiegelman that he took an activist role, writing a scathing review in cartoon form in *ArtForum* magazine and inviting curators to his studio to teach them how to think about comics.

After much heated debate, Spiegelman, Walker, and Carlin ultimately picked 15 artists as the masters, with Winsor McCay, Lyonel Feininger, George Herriman, E. C. Segar, Frank King, Chester Gould, Milton Caniff, and Charles Schulz representing the evolution of the comic strip at the Hammer Museum, and Will Eisner, Jack Kirby, Harvey Kurtzman, R. Crumb, Art Spiegelman, Gary Panter, and Chris Ware representing the evolution of comic books at the Museum of Contemporary Art. Critics were quick to notice that there were no females or people of color other than Herriman represented in the show. Carlin was no stranger to controversy and provocative projects; aware of the lack of diversity in the canon they ultimately selected, he told Leslie Jones of *Art on Paper* magazine, "This is an old-fashioned type of art exhibition that I would never organize or curate if I were working in the art field.... I really felt that the canon hadn't been established in a coherent way. This attempts to do that and to create something that people can then criticize and move beyond." He continued on to explain that to be a "master" for the purposes of the show, the artists had to fulfill a combination of two criteria, "one was the highest level of craftsmanship and technical mastery... the other was a kind of formal innovation that added something to the medium so that everybody that comes after him, whether they imitate him or not has to pay homage to his work" (Jones, 2006, p. 46).

The *Masters* show was a pop culture phenomenon: it may have been the most reviewed and discussed exhibition of comic art that has occurred so far. Everything stirred controversy. Do we still need canons? Why only 15 out of so many? The show was attacked, sometimes vehemently, about the lack of diversity, especially that no women were chosen. In *Comics versus Art,* author Bart Beaty debates many of the issues surrounding the *Masters* show and brings it back to one of the essential dilemmas every curator faces when working with comics material, observing: "The biases of the curatorial selections particularly highlight the fact that the emphasis has been placed predominantly, some might say exclusively, on comics as visual culture... displaying frustratingly partial stories in the midst of the white cube as if they were paintings" (2012, p. 198). He goes on to point out that the museums placed the benches in the gallery too far away from the art to read the comics.

In interviews, both John Carlin and Brian Walker reported that they were not only focused on comics as visual art, but they sought out the best possible examples of each artist's work. The presentation was beautiful, with each artist's work in a mini-gallery and a thorough explanation of the artist's style and importance. Beaty's comments make me wonder: what do we want to see when we view comic art in an art museum? It is a rule of thumb in exhibition design that people will read a maximum of 250 words on a wall panel before they tire and their attention is lost. Yet the relationship between word and image is one of the unique strengths of comics and an important balance in an exhibition.

The curators of *Masters* emphasized visual form and technique to make their point that comic artists are worthy of elegant, big budget art museum treatment. Denis Kitchen and Jim Danky, in their 2010 underground comix survey *Underground Classics* at the Chazen Art Museum in Madison, Wisconsin, successfully solved the problem of narrative by limiting their selections to cover art and one- to two-page short stories. On the other extreme, *R. Crumb's Genesis* displayed his entire 207 page illustrated *Book of Genesis*, which toured to 5 U S cities (2009–2011), Paris, France (2011), and the 55th Venice Biennale (2013), and Art Spiegelman's retrospective *Co-Mix* featured his complete *Maus* as its centerpiece, beginning at the Pompidou Center in Paris (2012) and continuing to Cologne, Vancouver, New York, and Toronto (2013–2014). In each case, the decision about how much to include was right for the artist and material being presented.

The Feminist Canon

The exhibition *Pretty in Ink*, a display of newspaper clips, original drawings, and other works by female cartoonists from the collection of the comics creator and pop culture historian Trina Robbins, was on view in June, 2014, at the Cartoon Art Museum in San Francisco. Ranging from the Kewpies and *Brenda Starr* to *Miss Fury*, the show is a good example of the way that Robbins, through her writings, presentations, and exhibitions, has helped to establish an informal "canon" of important female artists. Her collection is very much a reflection of her personal tastes and research, and she has never claimed that her writings and exhibitions establish a canon, but arguably they have. Through their public display and publication, Robbins' collection bestows a sense of legitimacy on the selected artists and highlights the important artistic and social impact of these women in the history of comic art. Over the last few years, Robbins' collection has traveled to galleries in Germany, Portugal, Austria, Spain, and Japan and to Pittsburgh, New York, Illinois, and San Diego in the United States.

Robbins has long fought for equal representation of women's art in both publications and exhibitions. In an article by M. K. Czerwiac (2006) on the *Sequential Tart* blog, Robbins explained her theory of why women are frequently not selected for shows like *Masters*:

> My conclusion is that men have been the tastemakers and arbiters of what is "important art" for over 2,000 years and what they consider "important" is, of course, what they (men) like. What women like is considered fluffy, lightweight, not important.

And I argue that there is a difference between men's and women's art, and although the male tastemakers don't set out to intentionally exclude women, they see the signs that tell them something is women's art and subconsciously dismiss it as unimportant.

Robbins presented this argument in person at the Hammer Museum on March 8th, 2005, along with a presentation on the "herstory," and again in New York. In an inspired stroke of counter-programming, she arranged for the Museum of Comic and Cartoon Art in New York to display *She Draws Comics* (2006), an exhibition of historical works by female artists from her collection at the same time the all-male *Masters* show was being exhibited in New York at the Jewish Museum.

Robbins' book, *Pretty in Ink: North American Women Cartoonists 1896–2013*, is intended to be the definitive version of the "herstory" of female cartoonists, fulfilling her ongoing mission to document the work of female cartoonists and finally get them the recognition they deserve. Robbins has expanded her research on a few particularly influential artists, writing a separate biography of Lily Renée and developing two books and a solo exhibition on the work of Nell Brinkley, the glamorous superstar newspaper cartoonist of the early 1900s.

"God Save the Comics"

Much like Robbins and Carlin, the work of the London-based curator, author, and comics historian Paul Gravett has formed a canon of British comics through publications and large survey shows such as *God Save the Comics* at the la Cité internationale de la bande dessinée et de l'image, Angoulême, France (1990); *Strip Search: the New Breed of Comics in the UK* (UK touring exhibit, 1990), and *Comics Unmasked: Art and Anarchy in the UK* (2014), which was a massive survey of material from the collections of the British Library in London. From 1992 to 2001 he was the director of the Cartoon Art Trust, a UK charity dedicated to promoting and preserving the best of British cartoon art. He has been the director of Comica, London's international comics festival, since 2003.

FIGURE 17.3 Lily Renee (left) and Trina Robbins signing *Pretty in Ink* at San Diego Comic Con, 2015.
Source: Photo by Marc Greenberg.

Similar to Charles Schulz, Gravett formed his fascination with the hand-made, human qualities of original comics art while attending an exhibition, *AAARGH!* at the Institute of Contemporary Arts in London in 1971 when he was about 14 years old. He marveled over the power of Jack Kirby originals, such as the opening double-page from *Forever People*, and the last whole page from *New Gods* #1. In 1976, he made a pilgrimage to the Walker's Museum of Cartoon Art in Rye Brook, New York, to see originals by McCay, Herriman, Segar, and others.

He was honored to curate one of the inaugural shows for the la Cité internationale de la bande dessinée et de l'image in 1990, *God Save the Comics*, which still stands as one of the most extensive surveys of British comic art. When I asked Gravett if he'd ever had to convince anyone that comics are art, he recounted his experience with this project and the significance of working with a cultural institution that recognizes the importance of comics history and scholarship:

> Working in France and at a prestigious new comics centre, which is a project of President Mitterand, opened by his culture minister Jack Lang, the issue of "So are comics art?" never came up. Of course they are! I was lucky to work with such inspired, creative designers, Philippe Leduc and Marc Antoine Mathieu from [design firm] Lucie Lom. Between us, but led by their genius for playful installation and symbolism, we came up with settings for the artworks, such as a typical classroom but set on the moon—to combine the school-themed slapstick and the heroic sci-fi and sheer fantasy of children's comics. It would not have been possible without the great support of the Festival team as well on the administration side in France and the help of artists, publishers and collectors.

Aside from celebrating the best of comics in the UK and internationally, another area where Gravett has been pushing the envelope of innovation is a category he calls "gallery comics," comics that are created for exhibition, not reproduction. Perhaps taking a cue from his research on the 1967 Louvre show, Gravett has experimented with breaking sequential comics drawings out of books and pages. In these exhibitions, the white box of the gallery itself is the comic, with the sequential images hung around the room telling a story (or alternate stories) depending on how the visitor moves to view them, such as Lars Arrhenius's project *The Man without One Way* (first Biennale Internazionale Arte Giovane, Turin, 2000). One hundred and seventy square wordless prints of a man walking are arranged around the gallery from left to right, where they encounter doors or other events that affect the story. "Each decision he takes represents some of the myriad possibilities every moment brings," Gravett explains in *Comics Art*. "As with the internet's zooming interface, the visitor could scope out the overall project by looking from a distance around the gallery and then choose where to enter the sequences close up" (2013, p. 131).

Gravett's books, such as *Manga: Sixty Years of Japanese Comics* (2004) and *Graphic Novels: Stories to Change Your Life* (2005) and his exhibitions, for example, *Alan Moore* (2004), *Manhua! China Comics Now* (2009), *Moomin: The Dream World of Tove Jansson* (2010), *Jack Kirby: The House that Jack Built* (2010); *Comica Argentina* (2010), and *Hypercomics: The Shape of Comics to Come* (2010), have broken new ground for exhibitions and have introduced the public to a wide range of new comics material.

SIDEBAR: YOSHIHIRO YONEZAWA

Jaqueline Berndt

On the backside of Meiji University's Surugadai Campus in Tokyo, there is a small building, due to its surroundings easily overlooked despite its seven floors over ground. This building houses the *Yoshihiro Yonezawa Memorial Library of Manga and Subculture*. Opened in the fall of 2009 by Meiji University, which had just established its School of Global Japanese Studies, this facility leans in the main on the collection left by manga critic and Comiket co-founder Yoshihiro Yonezawa (1953–2006). At the time of his death, the materials, ranging from officially published comics magazines and books to fanzines, manuals, and documents, had been scattered over several storage facilities in the metropolitan area. Yonezawa's widow, Eiko, donated them to her husband's alma mater in the hope that the contents of the more than 4,000 boxes would be cataloged and made available to researchers. In actual fact, the *Yoshihiro Yonezawa Memorial Library* has become a mecca for the growing number of young academics who are engaged in the study of initially or partly manga-related Japanese fan cultures. Yonezawa himself is mostly remembered for his contributions to these fan cultures, as one of the Four Heavenly *otaku* Kings, along with critics Toshio Okada (b. 1958) and Shūichi Karasawa (b. 1958) as well as anime director Hideaki Anno (b. 1960).

In 1975, Yonezawa—together with Jun Aniwa and Nakao Harada—launched the Comiket (abbr. Comic Market), Japan's first fan-only convention dedicated to the sale and exchange of self-published materials [*dōjinshi*]. From 1980 to 2006 he served as the representative of the Preparatory Committee and, after the transformation of the event first into a joint-stock corporation and later into a special limited liability company, as managing director. Closely related to the administrative work, he published how-to books for potential participants in the Comiket, using the pseudonym Shun Ajima, and he documented the history of *dōjinshi* culture in a way that makes his compilations immensely important as resources for today's fan culture research. But Yonezawa is acknowledged not only with regards to the increasingly participatory culture of manga; he also bridged domains that do not easily converge in 21st century Japan, namely manga and science fiction. When still in high school, he participated as a staff member in the 8th SF Convention, and upon enrolling in the Engineering Department of Meiji University in 1972, he joined the university's SF Study Group instead of the Manga Club, as he was interested in criticism rather than creating manga by himself. This connection to the SF community was to become beneficial to the Comiket in the late 1970s and early 1980s, linking the older type of convention to the new one.

Yonezawa's accomplishments as a pioneer of manga studies, on the other hand, tend to be overlooked. Younger researchers of *otaku* [nerd] and *fujoshi* [literally, rotten girls] cultures do not often take an interest in manga as a distinct medium of expression, and manga researchers who focus on so-called formalism or "manga's expression" [*manga hyōgenron*] rarely reference his books, although it was he who laid the ground for the attention to line work, style, and form in manga, namely with the collection titled *Manga Hihyō Sengen* [*Manifesto of Manga Criticism*, 1987]. Film historians Yomota Inuhiko (b. 1953) and Katō Mikirō (b. 1957) contributed seminal essays to this volume, as did manga critics such as Takeuchi Osamu. Yonezawa himself addressed the responsibility of his generation, that is, the first cohort in Japan that grew up with manga, to develop a language for grasping and communicating readers' peculiar fascination with that medium of expression. But the manga-studies publications he is most widely known for are data-rich historical surveys, which record an enormous number of artists and titles against the backdrop of contemporaneous trends in media and readership. In these publications, the emphasis is put on saving the facts from falling into oblivion and not on critical interpretation or advocating a specific notion of "manga"—which almost everyone in the field is inclined to, even senior collector-historian Isao Shimizu (b. 1939). Like the other critics of the "manga generation"—Murakami Tomohiko (b. 1951), Takeuchi Osamu (b. 1951), and Natsume Fusanosuke (b. 1950), among others—Yonezawa accentuated the privacy of reading manga, the highly personal experience against the previously dominating ideological accounts. But as distinct from his fellow critics, he was not selective with respect to specific artists, periods or genres, neither as collector nor writer. This comprehensive approach manifested itself already in his earliest monographs, the trilogy he published in 1980 (and which was reprinted in pocketbook format after his death): *Sengo SF mangashi [Postwar History of SF Manga]*[5], *Sengo gag mangashi [Postwar History of Gag Manga]*, and *Sengo shōjo mangashi [Postwar History of Girls Manga]*.

Yonezawa's restraint toward taking a verbally explicit stance has led people to assume a general lack of stance, but his very choice of subject matter speaks its own language. At a time when girls comics occupied a highly marginal position within the manga industry and did not attract attention beyond the female realm, Yonezawa was one of the first male critics to appreciate that genre, not only with regards to the extraordinary Magnificent 49ers of the 1970s,[6] but in its historical entirety, introducing also earlier and more mainstream-oriented artists. In addition to manga's gender- and age-specific genres, he focused on thematic categories such as SF, gag, and, during the last years of his life, even *ero-manga*, leaning in part on personal involvement. Notably, he served as an editor of *Gekiga Alice*, one of the three major adult-comics magazines, and after its discontinuation in 1980, of the quarterly *Manga Kisō Tengai*, an offshoot of the important SF magazine. His commitment to manga in all of its facets led him eventually to take a tough stance for the freedom of expression and a reconsideration of copyright law. His primary legacy is the inclusive attitude, which applied to both manga and people.

Trends in Exhibitions

Over the course of this chapter, we've seen comic art evolve from a castoff genre striving for recognition to an art form accepted in the museums of Paris, London, New York, and Los Angeles. There are archives and specialty museums devoted to comics around the world.[4] Yet ten years later, there has not been another blockbuster group show in the U S like *Masters of American Comics*. At this time, the energy seems to have shifted to stories of individual artists, with major retrospectives of R. Crumb and Art Spiegelman attracting big budget productions and positive press. Is the time of the large contextual art museum show over? Was John Carlin right? Did we argue over his canon and move on? I asked the Canadian cultural journalist Heet Jeer this question, and he replied:

> I think the *Masters* show represented the culmination and end of a way of thinking about comics history as a story of linear progress from McCay to Ware that has now been exhausted. Post-*Masters* there is much more interest in looking at individual cartoonists as their own thing or part of a scene – the grand narrative of comics history seems too large. As artists like Ware, Spiegelman, and Crumb get canonized, they are seen as their own thing and divorced from their comics context. So, shows like *Masters*, which provide context are less valued. (2014)

Ann Philbin, director of the Hammer Museum, responded in an e-mail by explaining how difficult the *Masters* exhibition was, and that everyone involved had originally planned to produce more than one show. She discussed the complexities of the curatorial choices and then said:

> But that is what curating is! Every exhibition of art is a point of view and a certain take on history or a contemporary moment. You have to start somewhere and there is no such thing as a comprehensive show. The Whitney show and *Masters* gave a context to comics that had not been offered before. It's the catalogues and writing that are important in the end – the scholarship that surrounds such exhibitions is important and lasting. (2014)

Philbin's comment about scholarship circles back to Maurice Horn's insistence in 1971 that comics as an art form were worthy of serious scholarship and study. Catalogs are the chief record left of an exhibition's existence. Exhibitions not only show art of specific periods, but also reveal the cultural points of view and biases of the curators, institutions, and critics that produce and comment on them.

Building on Philbin's comments, publisher/cartoonist/curator Denis Kitchen told me in an e-mail interview about the influence of the *Masters* catalog from his own point of view:

> The catalog for *Masters of American Comics* reproduced the originals as they actually appear, with white-out, paste-overs, marginal notes, smudges, etc., instead of the sanitized versions always shown in prior books and even earlier art museum catalogs about comics. So that was the model we used for *Underground Classics*, and it's now the model most used since, when actual original comic art is reproduced in any scholarly context. (2015)

Kitchen continues his commentary about exhibitions of comics art from his long-view perspective:

> It's truly gratifying to see more and more museums and institutions recognize the best comic art as bona fide Art deserving of exhibition and study. I've seen the field go from almost universally disparaged or ignored to this respectful stage in my lifetime. It's sobering to see the relatively rapid change. Part of me preferred it when we were an outlaw art form, but on balance I probably prefer being taken seriously. (2015)

Notes

1 According to Gaines, the work was organized in several sections: Ancient art, beginning with a tracing of a cave drawing from prehistoric Spain, and including panels from Ancient Egypt, a ninth century Bamberg Bible, and a Japanese Kozanji scroll by Tôba SôJô (1053–1140); European paintings and etchings by Hieronymous Bosch, Peter Bruegel the Elder, and Hans Holbein the Younger; caricaturists of 18th and 19th century Britain and Europe such as William Hogarth, James Gillray, Thomas Rowland, George Cruikshank, Honoré Daumier, Gustave Doré, Rodolphe Töpffer and Wilhelm Busch; cartoonists working between 1894 and 1920, such as R. F. Outcault, Frederick Burr Opper, T.S. Sullivant, Rudolph Dirks, Edwina Dumm, H.H. Knerr, Winsor McCay, Carl Schultz, E.D. Kemble, Norman E. Jennett, F.M. Follett, Fred Nankivel, George McManus, George Herriman, Sidney Smith, T.A. Dorgan, Bud Fisher, Wallace Morgan, Tom Powers, Fred Cooper, Milt Gross, Harry Hershfield, Clare Briggs, H.T. Webster, Rube Goldberg and Billy de Beck; and contemporary (1940s) artists Carl Anderson, Walter Berndt, Martin Branner, Ernie Bushmiller, Dick Calkins, Milton Caniff, Al Capp, Roy Crane, Percy Crosby, Ham Fisher, Harold E. Foster, Chester Gould, Frank King, Elzie Crisler Segar, Otto Soglow, C. A. Voight, Russ Westover, Fran Willard and Chic Young, as well as comic book creators Jerry Siegel and H. G. Peter.
2 In the original French: "À cette époque la bande dessinée n'était perçue qu'au travers de son regard, il en avait démontré le vide et l'inanité... en prenant les plus mauvaises images et en les agrandissant démesurément. Nous voulions montrer que la bande dessinée était autre chose, qu'elle possédait des valeurs esthétiques qui lui étaient spécifiques."
3 Painters and sculptors included Roger Brown, Ronnie Cutrone, Stuart Davis, Oyvind Fahlstrom, John Fawcett, Vernon Fisher, Steve Gianakos, Keith Haring, Jess, Jasper Johns, Roy Lichtenstein, Jim Nutt, Claes Oldenburg, Suzan Pitt, Lee Quinones, Mel Ramos, Robert Rauschenberg, Ad Reinhardt, David Salle, Kenny Scharf, Alexis Smith, Saul Steinberg, Andy Warhol, John Wesley, Karl Wirsum, Ray Yoshida and two anonymous works, plus additional works by Henry Chalfant (first display of his subway graffiti photographs), The Hairy Who & C. Comics.
4 I can only scratch the surface of this topic in such a short chapter, I hope someday to include Francis Groux, Jean Mardikian and Claude Moliterni, who founded the Angoulême Festival in 1974; Thierry Groensteen's *Masters of European Comics* at the Bibliotheque Nationale in Paris; the display of local comic artists at the Brooklyn Museum in 1976; the Toonseum; Words & Pictures; *Misfit Lit*, the 1991 Seattle show that brought the Hernandez Brothers into the museum; the Belgian Comics Center in Brussels; the work of Brazilian curator Alvaro de Moya, and others. Thanks to Brian Walker and Carol Tilley for their help and to everyone that shared their memories with me for this article.
5 In contemporary Japanese discourse, "postwar" (*sengo*) signifies often not only the immediate postwar period, but rather the decades following the end of WWII.
6 Or Year 24 Group (Jap. *Hana no 24-nen gumi*), that is, artists such as Moto Hagio, Keiko Takemiya and Ryōko Yamagishi, who introduced cutting-edge subject matter (boys' love, SF, etc.) and groundbreaking ways of graphic storytelling into the genre of Japanese girls comics, but were much too innovative to create a whole new school. They were received as a group by critics.

Bibliography

AAARGH! Bumper Souvenir Catalogue. (2009) *Bear Alley Books Blog*. [Online] Available from http://bearalley.blogspot.com/2009/07/aaargh-bumper-souvenir-catalogue.html. [Accessed 29 June 2015].
Agreement between the New York State Pavilion at the New York World's Fair and the Newspaper Comics Council, Inc. (1965) Newspaper Feature Council Records. Billy Ireland Cartoon Library & Museum. Series V. Exhibits, Subseries 1. Cavalcade of American Comics. Columbus: The Ohio State University Libraries.
Alloway, L. (1971) 'Art/Lawrence Alloway', *The Nation*, 30 August: 157.
Beaty, B. (2012) *Comics versus Art*, Toronto: University of Toronto Press.
Boime, A. (1972) 'Review: The Comic Stripped and Ash Canned: a review essay', *Art Journal*, 32 (1): 21–25, 30.

Canaday, J. (1971) 'Art: huge Andy Warhol retrospective at Whitney', *New York Times*, 1 May 1: 21.
Caniff, M. & Harvey, R.C. (2002) *Milton Caniff: conversations*, Jackson: University of Mississippi Press.
Carlin, J. (1992) *Darkness Visible*, New York: The Drawing Center.
Carlin, J., Karasik, P. and Walker, B. (2005) *Masters of American Comics*, New Haven: Yale University Press.
Carlin, J. and Wagstaff, S. (1983) *The Comic Art Show: cartoons and paintings in popular culture*, New York: Whitney Museum of American Art.
Comics Symposium. (1970) *The Rebel Yell* (University of Nevada, Las Vegas). 15 April: 19.
Couperie, P. and Horn, M. (1968) *A History of the Comic Strip*, New York: Crown Publishers.
Crumb, R. (2009) *The Book of Genesis Illustrated*, New York: W.W. Norton & Company.
Czerwiac, M.K. (2006) 'The women masters', *Sequential Tart*. [Online] Available from: http://www.sequentialtart.com/article.php?id=126. [Accessed 3 June 2015].
Danky, J. and Kitchen, D. (2009) *Underground Classics: the transformation of comics into comix*, New York: Abrams.
Deitcher, D. (1984) 'Comic connoisseurs', *Art in America*: 101–107.
Gaines, M.C. (1942a) 'Narrative illustration: the story of the comics', *Print: A Quarterly Journal of the Graphic Arts*, 3 (2): 25–38.
Gaines, M.C. (1942b) 'More about the comics', *Print: A Quarterly Journal of the Graphic Arts*, 3 (3): 19–24.
Gravett, P. (2013) *Comics Art*, London: Tate Publishing.
Gravett, P. and Dunning, J.H. (2014) *Comics Unmasked: art and anarchy in the UK*, London: The British Library.
Greenberg, C. (1939) *Avant-Garde and Kitsch*. [Online] Available from: http://www.sharecom.ca/greenberg/kitsch.html. [Accessed 28 June 2015].
Groensteen, T. (2011) *Comics and Narration*, Jackson: University of Mississippi Press.
Hartlaub, P. (2016) 'Cartoon Art Museum finds new home in SF', *SFGate*. November 2, 2016 http://www.sfgate.com/art/article/Cartoon-Art-Museum-finds-new-home-in-SF-10538292.php? Accessed Nov. 2, 2016.
Herdey, W. (1972) *The Art of the Comic Strip*, Zurich: The Graphis Press.
Hignite, T. (2006) 'Masters of American comics: an interview with exhibition co-curator Brian Walker', *American Institute of Graphic Arts*. [Online] Available from http://www.aiga.org/masters-of-american-comics/ [Accessed 7 October 2015].
History of Comics Exhibit at Arts Center. (1971) *Colorado Springs Gazette-Telegraph*, 28 August: 34.
Horn, M. (1971) *75 Years of the Comics*, Boston: Boston Book & Art.
Horn, M. (2002) 'How it all began, or present at the creation', *International Journal of Comic Art*, 4 (1): 6–22.
Hughes, R. (1990) 'Upstairs and downstairs at MOMA', *Time*, 22 October: 94.
Institute of Contemporary Art. (1969) *The Spirit of the Comics*, Philadelphia: University of Pennsylvania.
Jeer, H. (2014) Facebook message with author.
Jones, L. (2006) 'Cracking the comics canon', *Art on Paper*, 10 (2): 44–49.
Kitchen, D. (2015) Email interview with author.
Mayton, J. (2015) 'San Francisco's latest high-rent victim: the Cartoon Art Museum', *The Guardian*. [Online] Available from: http://www.theguardian.com/artanddesign/2015/sep/14/san-francisco-latest-high-rent-victim-cartoon-art-museum [Accessed 7 October 2015].
Met Surveys U.S. Cartooning. (1951) *The Art Digest*, 25 (11): 17.
Metropolitan Museum of Art. (1951) *American Cartooning*. John Pierotti Collection, Special Collections Research Center. Syracuse: Syracuse University Library.Michaelis, D. (2007) *Schulz and Peanuts: A Biography*. New York: HarperCollins Publishers.
Michaelis, D. (2007) *Schulz and Peanuts: a biography*, New York: HarperCollins Publishers.
Munson, K. (2012) 'Revisiting the comic art show', *International Journal of Comic Art*, 14 (2): 264–88.

The Newspaper Comics Council. (1963) *The Cavalcade of American Comics: a history of comic strips from 1896–1963*, RCA Exhibition Hall, New York City.

O'Sullivan, J. (1971) *The Art of the Comic Strip*, College Park: University of Maryland Department of Art.

Oelsner, L. (1971) 'A retrospective on the comics opens (Pow!)', *New York Times*, 8 September: 54.

Philbin, A. (2014) Email with author.

Robbins, T. (2013) *Pretty in Ink: North American women cartoonists 1886–2013*, Seattle: Fantagraphics Books.

Sausverd, A. (2014) Bande dessinée et figuration narrative: la contribution de pierre couperie. *Neuvieme Art 2.0*. [Online] Available from:http://neuviemeart.citebd.org/spip.php?article752 [Accessed 3 June 2015].

Schumacher, M. and Kitchen, D. (2013) *Al Capp: a life to the contrary*, New York: Bloomsbury.

Shepard, R. (1963) 'Comics will stir memories (sob) at show', *New York Times*, 12 October: 13.

Smith, R. (1993) 'Art; The Comics Underground: where the funnies aren't', *New York Times*, 8 October: C25.

Spiegelman, A. (1988) 'Commix: an idiosyncratic historical and aesthetic overview', *Print*, 42 (6): 61.

Spiegelman, A. (1990) 'High art lowdown (this review is not sponsored by AT&T)', *Artforum*, 30 (29): 115.

Spiegelman, A. (2013) *Co-Mix: a retrospective of comics, graphics, and scraps*, Montreal: Drawn & Quarterly.

Varnedoe, K. and Gopnik, A. (1990) *High and Low: modern art, popular culture*, New York: Museum of Modern Art.

Walker, M. (2009) 'History of the Cartoon Museum', in *Celebrating the International Museum of Comic Art Collection*, Columbus: The Ohio State University Cartoon Library & Museum.

White, D.M. and Abel, R.H. (1963) *The Funnies: an American idiom*, London: The Free Press of Glencoe (Collier-Macmillan).

Whyte, M. (2015) Phone interview with author.

18
THE CONFERENCES

Julia Round and Chris Murray

Over the last several decades, there has been a steady rise in the number, size, and frequency of scholarly comics conferences. The character and purpose of these gatherings has changed considerably during this time, in part due to the establishment of Comics Studies as an academic field and partly due to their relationship with fan events, which have grown to huge proportions in recent years. This chapter will first set out a historical overview of the rise of scholarly comics conferences before offering a number of case studies of the key global events, with an emphasis on academic events, wider academic events with comics strands, and finally the emergence of scholarly comics strands within public and fan-based events. Surveying the history demonstrates that while the number of comics events has increased, this has come at the cost of some diversity and that the relationships among fans, practitioners, and scholars are mutually beneficial but sometimes problematic.

In *Arguing Comics: Literary Masters on a Popular Medium* (2004) editors Jeet Heer and Kent Worcester demonstrate through a range of writing about comics by the likes of e.e. cummings, Gilbert Seldes, Dorothy Parker, Irving Howe, and Delmore Schwartz, that serious interest in the medium predates the formulation of Comics Studies or even the formal academic study of popular culture. Such writings, many of them from the first half of the 20th century, celebrated the mass appeal of comics, and sometimes their artistry, but few sought to understand the mechanics of the medium or its history. A similar point is made when John Lent, in his article "The Winding, Pot-holed Road of Comic Art Scholarship" (2010), identifies the barriers that have existed in academia and the fact that much of the early critical work happened outside of the academy and much historical research was done by fans and collectors. Some of this appeared in fanzines, which were far from scholarly publications. Mark Evanier (2003) notes that the dictionary gives 1949 as the year of first usage for the term *fanzine* but also argues that the year the first science fiction fanzine came out was probably 1932, which was, as he says, "the year two science fiction aficionados—Mort Weisinger and Julius Schwartz—published the first issue of *The Time Traveller*" (p. 29). He concedes that dating the first comics fanzine is more difficult, but observes that "the EC comics of the early fifties spawned a number of homemade publications but they were preceded by other contenders for the honor—mostly science fiction zines whose fannish enthusiasms led them occasionally into the questionable realm of funnybooks" (p. 31). The likely point at which comics fanzines appeared in America is in the mid-1940s, around the same time that collectors and fans were organizing some of the first comic marts. Although the work done by fans and collectors was not scholarly, as such, they established a network for advancing knowledge about the medium. Combined with the "literary masters" that Heer and Worcester identify, these fans and collectors brought critical attention to comics long before Comics Studies existed. Indeed, it is only recently that a few established scholarly networks and dedicated events have come into being. Therefore, in order to understand how comics conferences did start to emerge, it is necessary to appreciate the difficult journey Comics Studies has had and the attitudes that have had to be challenged in order to make this possible.

The scholarly interest in comics, and indeed in popular culture as a whole, started to emerge, albeit very slowly, in the 1960s and the early 1970s. Prior to this there had been an interest in mass culture, largely from the point of view of mass observation studies and work that examined the presumed negative effect of mass culture on its intended audience (usually conceptualized as the lower classes), as opposed to the supposedly edifying effects of "high culture." Work of this kind, which emphasized the dichotomy between what was regarded as high and low culture, was quite widespread, appearing in many countries, and occasionally comics were cited in such studies. Indeed, much of the early critical work on comics, such as that by Fredric Wertham in the 1950s, was negative and proceeded from the view that such material was damaging to its readers. The methodologies and assumptions of such studies were often flawed and frequently tied to moral panics and censorious hysteria that looked to blame popular culture for social ills rather than seriously investigating these texts. Things started to change with the "cultural turn" in the arts, humanities, and social sciences in the late 1960s and early 1970s. This posited a shift toward an appreciation of popular culture as art and focused on the production of meanings, rather than supposing that pop culture was meaningless entertainment, whose only use could be how it satisfied the base needs of its lowbrow audience. Instead, popular culture started to be seen as relevant and interesting in its own right.

The roots of this "turn" were seen in the 1950s and 1960s, when some studies of popular culture appeared, such as the work of French philosopher Roland Barthes and Italian novelist and philosopher Umberto Eco. Barthes' collection of essays, *Mythologies* (1957), adopted a semiotic approach to popular culture, which was a great leveler. Semiotics argued that everything was a mode of communication and therefore contained codes and myths that we interpret as readers. This makes a magazine or a comic just as rich with meaning as a film or a novel, therefore invalidating prejudices between mediums and a sense of a high or a low culture. Eco wrote his 1972 essay "The Myth of Superman" also using a mode of semiological analysis. Comics were also sometimes mentioned by the likes of art historian Ernst Gombrich and Marshall McLuhan, the father of media studies, both of whom were positive about the potential of the medium. In 1960's *Art and Illusion,* Gombrich stated that comics achieved a kind of iconic power through their use of basic cognitive skills to link narrative with visual shorthand. In *Understanding Media* (1964) McLuhan argued that comics were a "cool" medium, requiring active participation for the reader, whereas media such as film were "hot," allowing the viewer to be relatively passive. In works such as this comics started to enter academic discourse, but they were not yet seen as a subject area in their own right, and there were no dedicated academic conferences as yet.

In the 1970s, the academic study of popular culture became firmly established, and it was not long before scholars turned their attention to comics. However, this was still not without risk to their reputations and prospects. British historian David Kunzle's *The Early Comic Strip* (1973) was attacked by his fellow art historians (Lent, 2010, p. 10), and by the mid-1980s important academic works were emerging and routes to publishing had been established by pioneers such as Donald Ault, Arthur Asa Berger, and M. Thomas Inge, but there was little in the way of formal support in terms of conferences and academic fora.

Inge reflects that, at the first few years of the Popular Culture Association conference (which began in 1971 at Michigan State University in East Lansing), "no one was talking about comics […] (television was all the rage)" (2015). But in 1973, at the PCA's third meeting, he proposed a panel on "Comics as Culture" with presentations on comics as art, as literature, and as drama, which "got things rolling." That was the same year as Berkeley Con 1973 (also known as the Underground Comix Con), which featured an early presentation by Donald Ault, who gave a presentation on Carl Barks and wrote an essay on Barks for the program book. In addition to Ault's contributions, there were panels on "Sex and Sexism in the Comics" and "Women's Comics." In December of 1978 Inge organized the first panel on the subject of comics to be held at a meeting of the Modern Language Association in New York, which featured comics creators Will Eisner and Art Spiegelman—foreshadowing the increasing involvement of practitioners in comics scholarship. The following year Inge edited a special issue of the *Journal of Popular Culture* (Volume 12), which included Robert C. Harvey's influential essay "The Aesthetics of the Comic Strip." Later scholars acknowledge Inge's key role in creating "the first sense of Comics Studies as a field and the first sense of community among comics scholars [which] developed at the PCA conferences in the 1980s" (Duncan, 2015). It is also worthwhile noting that some of the first academic papers published on comics were presented at library science conferences, so this network was also key to the early formation of Comics Studies.

There was also increasingly a space for comics scholars (of which there were only a few) at fan organized public events like comics conventions. Roger Sabin recalls the situation in the UK:

> There were some forerunners to the academic comics conference per se. First you had academics giving "serious" talks at fan conventions, in the late 1980s. UKCAC (UK Comic Art Convention), for example, would always have space in its timetable for this, and the "small press" conventions would follow suit, e.g. Caption, a little later (from 1992). The speakers would inevitably be Martin Barker, Dave Huxley, and then myself. Martin was always a star at those events, because he was a natural performer and talked about censorship – the fans loved him.

Despite the fact that there were scholars of comics and scholarly works on comics emerging in the 1970s and 1980s, and even though popular culture studies were thriving across many disciplines, notably in social sciences and humanities, the resistance to comics in academia persisted into the 1990s. This hindered the development of fully-fledged comics conferences, although there were certainly panels and papers on comics at conferences on popular culture, and in other areas. This led to the "academicization" of comics, and the beginnings of comics papers and panels appearing on conference programmes. By the mid-1990s several academic comics conferences started to appear. This was driven by the fact that certain comics scholars who had been laboring in what Lent calls "Sisyphean conditions" (2010, p. 8) for many years, were reaching a time of influence and seniority in their careers, just as a new generation was entering academia who felt unhindered by the prejudices of old. These two factors combined. It felt like Comics Studies had a history and an old-guard, as well as in infusion of new blood. Roger Sabin's recollection of the change in attitude in the UK reveals that there were many who were pushing for change:

> The origin point for academic comics conferences was the mid-late 1990s, on the back of interest in the "graphic novel." The background had to do with the gradual acceptance of comics in academia. For example, in the 1970s, there were lots of accounts of student comics projects being "allowed" as submissions for BA and MA courses at art colleges (Brian Bolland did his first strip this way), so clearly there were some progressive tutors. Then, in the 1980s academics like Martin Barker in Bristol and Dave Huxley in Manchester started incorporating comics into the curriculum. (Dave was teaching a history of comics course from 1981, and got his Ph.D. in comics studies in c.1988 – a first of its kind in the UK – and Martin's book *A Haunt of Fears* came out in 1984.) There were other lecturers, their efforts now forgotten, who had an interest in certain aspects of comics, who incorporated them – for example, Barry Curtis, in London, who taught classes about Robert Crumb in the early 1980s; Hugh Starkey, based at Leicester University, who published an important essay about BD in 1987; and Paul Dawson, at Manchester University, who incorporated graphic novels onto his literature courses, again in the late 1980s. No doubt there were others. I think this phase had a lot to do with the rise of Cultural Studies and the idea that "everything was culture", and that pop culture, especially, was worth studying.

Alongside the broadening of the study of popular culture, with interests in Television Studies and computer games, comics no longer seemed quite so exposed and exceptional. As Kent Worcester points out "the field [...] benefited from the construction of a scholarly infrastructure, as exemplified by the founding of the Comic Art and Comics area of the Popular Culture Association in [...]; the establishment of the International Comics Art Forum in 1995; and the launching of *The International Journal of Comic Art* in 1999" (Worcester, 2010, p. 111). Roger Sabin (2015) notes that

> in the late 1990s and 2000s there were academic events going on in London, Manchester, and Leeds, not to mention the burgeoning scene in the US [...] and what was happening in Europe (Jan Baetens' conference on 'The Graphic Novel' in Leuven in 2000 was an important one, as was Anne Magnussen and Hans Christian Christiansen's conference 'Comics Culture' in Copenhagen in 1998). Later, conferences in Japan came into the picture, where European (and a few American) academics started to "talk to" Japanese critics – conferences tended to be organised by Jaqueline Berndt at the University of Kyoto.

With these developments came a growing number of dedicated comics conferences, and the associated apparatus of comics courses, research grant applications, collections of comics and artwork in university collections, and ultimately, dedicated peer-reviewed journals and special issues of respectable journals that helped to form purely academic events.

However, perhaps due to the fact that comics scholarship initially emerged under the umbrella of fan events, there is still a strong academic presence at many such events. This mixed economy of purely academic events and academic strands within public events has become a boon for Comics Studies, especially as academic work steers increasingly toward public engagement as a key metric of success and impact. It is not unusual to see a major comics convention accompanied by a satellite academic event or to have creators and industry professionals participating in academic events. Indeed, in recent years the popularity of fan events such as San Diego Comic-Con International has exploded, partly due to cross-promotion of film, television, and computer games at these events; the nature of the comics fan community, which is vocal and passionate about what they like, making such events key in the marketing of popular culture. Comics scholars have therefore found themselves having strands at huge events and potentially reaching different audiences, sometimes in much larger numbers than would attend a traditional academic conference. The potential for public engagement and bringing academic work out into a wider community is therefore considerable, especially with widespread coverage of such events on the Internet through the comics industry press.

This article now proceeds to a discussion and case studies of key global events, focusing on dedicated academic events, wider academic events with comics strands, and finally the emergence of academic comics strands within public and fan-based events. Of course, it would be impossible to give a comprehensive account of all the comics events occurring internationally, so the selection below is chosen to give a flavor of the variety and diversity of activities.

Case Studies: Academia

The development of Comics Studies as a field is still ongoing. There are research centers, networks, and even dedicated degree programs, but as yet there are no departments of Comics Studies, much less an established presence in the university curriculum. What exists is often ad hoc or the exception rather than the norm, but this is slowly changing. As suggested above, what has come to unite comics scholars, across a range of disciplines, is their participation in an international network of scholarly fora and events. Dedicated comics conferences are an important part of this.

There are now a number of academic events dedicated to comics, taking many forms. There are multiple one-off events that take place in many countries around the world, often on a very small scale (around 25 participants or less), and are hosted by universities or other institutions. These are really too numerous to count; however, larger recurring events are emerging, in many cases from these small-scale events. In South America, Buenos Aires hosts Viñetas Serias [Serious Comics] at the Department of Social Sciences in the Universidad de Buenos Aires, which has been held biennially since 2010. Approximately 80–100 papers are presented to an audience three or four times that size, alongside book presentations, multimedia performances and a comic book fair. Viñetas Serias grew from a public event (Viñetas Sueltas) whose aim was to connect the European and Argentine comics industries. In North America examples of large-scale academic events include the MSU Comics Forum (Michigan State University, East Lansing, MI) aimed at academics and practitioners; Page 23 Lit Con (Denver, CO), aimed at academics, aca-fans and fans; and the International Comic Art Forum (ICAF) Conference, which takes place in multiple locations and aims to be annual. The University of Florida has, since 2002, held an annual conference on comics. This started as a symposium on Will Eisner and has become a consistent presence in the Comics Studies calendar, bringing together artists and scholars to discuss a different theme each year.

The Bande Dessinée conference started by Billy Grove in Glasgow in 1999 also started small but laid the groundwork for the IBDS (International Bande Dessinée Society). The IBDS conference is a bilingual event, and this is another challenge facing comics conferences in a global context. However, such liaisons can produce spectacular results: one organizer, Maaheen Ahmed, cites this as one of the greatest strengths of comics events "since Anglophone and Francophone scholars do not mingle much." Translation delays have had an impact on Comics Studies and contributed to the Anglo-American bias that has dogged the field. Bilingual conferences have the potential to break down such divisions and further enable a global dialogue between critical theory traditions. An additional bilingual event is the Canadian Society for the Study of Comics Annual Conference (CSSC), which has been running annually since 2012, and typically attracts around 40–45 presenters. Some years after its inauguration, the CSSC began to hold regular meetings as part of the annual New Narrative Conference organized by Andrew Lesk, which coincided with the weekend that the Toronto Comic Arts Festival was held in Toronto, ultimately taking over the established relationship between the two events when New Narrative ceased. Although a separate academic event, as organizer Barbara Postema notes, the connection with TCAF "adds interest and potential for joint guests. Some people who would not travel to Toronto for only the CSSC come because they can combine it with attendance of an excellent small press expo" (2015). As seen in Leeds Thought Bubble (discussed below), such strategies are becoming increasingly common as targeting the cross-over audience of academics, fans and professionals is a particularly attractive one. This also reflects the aforementioned long-standing relationship between fan/public events and academic ones.

It is notable that many of these dedicated events have a public side. The ICAF began in 1995 as a one-off festival in Washington D.C., founded and initially chaired by Guy Spielmann of the Georgetown University French Department. ICAF first focused mainly on comics professionals, but it has expanded its scope in subsequent years, taking place over multiple venues and bringing together a combination of academic presentations and a more general public day on Saturday. A similar arrangement is apparent in the UK: the Thought Bubble festival (which takes place in Leeds as part of the annual Leeds Film Festival in November) is preceded by Comics Forum: a two-day academic event launched in 2009. Taking place in the run-up to the main Thought Bubble festival, Comics Forum is more academically focused than an academic programming strand within the main event might be expected to be. It has been held at a number of public locations (rather than within the university) such as Leeds Town Hall and the public library and is open to all. The event is just one facet of the larger Comics Forum project, which includes a network and website. Organizer Ian Hague notes the biggest challenge is to be as globally inclusive as possible while working with a volunteer staff, and parallels can be seen here with the origins, host locations, and aims of Viñetas Serias (connecting international comics industries and taking place at public and academic locations such as the National Library of Argentina).

In Europe, large-scale academic events are also on the rise, again, often based around a network of researchers, but frequently with a public-facing element. Harmsen (2013) explains that in Germany academic research into comics is a very recent development, which gained much of its momentum from *Comic-Kunst* ("comic art"), an exhibition of work from over 130 comics artists and illustrators organized by Dietrich Grünewald in 2004. This was followed by an initial conference that led to the founding of *Gesellschaft für Comicforschung* (ComFor) in 2005. Devised as a means to connect with other scholars, the network organizes an annual conference hosted by various universities (beginning in 2006, with a first volume of conference proceeds published in 2010). Similarly, the Nordic Network for Comics Research (NNCORE) was founded in 2011 with a two-year grant from the Danish Council for Independent Research and, since hosting its first conference at the University of Helsinki in Finland (2013), has continued as an independent association, with a second conference in June 2015 at which the election of officers went forward. NNCORE has also been involved in individual conferences, for instance "Aesthetics in Comics" at the University of Aarhus in 2011 and a seminar on comics and didactics in Malmö in 2012.

Another membership organization that runs along similar lines is the International Bande Dessinée Society (who also produces the scholarly journal, *European Comic Art,* published by Berghahn and edited by Laurence Grove, Ann Miller, and Mark McKinney) who hosts a biennial conference that began in 1999. Since 2011 the IBDS conference runs jointly with the International Conference for Graphic Novels and Comics, which is organized collaboratively by the editors of *Studies in Comics* (edited by Julia Round and Chris Murray and published by Intellect Books) and the *Journal of Graphic Novels and Comics* (edited by Joan Ormond and David Huxley and published by Routledge). First held at Manchester Metropolitan University in 2010, and always with input and support from Roger Sabin of Central St. Martins College of Art, the IGNCC is transnational and mobile; it has since been held at Bournemouth, Glasgow, Dundee, the British Library in London, and Paris. These examples show that support from ongoing networks or publications such as academic journals often underpin recurring events and that collaboration and consolidation are key factors in keeping them going.

There are also many conferences that, while not in and of themselves comics conferences, have long been sympathetic to comics and have featured panels on this topic. Examples include the International Association of Word and Images Studies (IAWIS) triennial conference that has been running since 1987 and the Scottish Word and Image Group (SWIG), which started in Aberdeen (1994–2003) but moved to Dundee (2004–present). These events focus on the relationship between words and images and have routinely featured sessions on comics. Dundee is also the home of Dundee Comics Day, which is part of Dundee Literary Festival and organized by Chris Murray and Phil Vaughan, who are based in the School of Humanities and Duncan and Jordanstone Art College, respectively. Held in October, this event brings the public, comics scholars, and students at the University of Dundee together in discussion with top comics creators and industry professionals. This has been partly a response to academic imperatives like public engagement and the support of practice-based learning, but "the event also serves to provide access to the insights of professionals in an academic setting, though with the informality of a talk at a fan event. The result is a dialogue with creators that is informed by scholarly concerns, in which the public, scholars and students contribute equally, combining the best of both worlds," says host Chris Murray (2015).

There have also been several academic conferences at which the work of a single creator has been explored, such as the "Magus" conference at Northampton in 2010 which invited papers on the work of Alan Moore, and "Grant Morrison and the Superhero Renaissance" in Trinity College, Dublin, in 2012, which focused on the work of Grant Morrison. Interestingly, Moore attended the Northampton conference, after the formal academic papers had been delivered, and participated in an interview, chaired by comics impresario Paul Gravett. Being separate from the delivery of the formal papers, this was something closer to a fan event in some ways and is another demonstration of the ways in which the two types of activity can blend together. The Trinity conference on Morrison was not attended by the creator himself, but the fact that it took place in the prestigious Trinity Quad gave the conference a certain visibility and prestige that would have been unthinkable a couple of decades earlier.

Given that there are now so many academic events and huge public/fan events, it is notable that some smaller, more focused events are starting to reappear. Occasionally the larger events are so crowded with parallel sessions and headline guests that there can be little time for detailed discussion, planning, and even just socializing. Perhaps in response to this a number of activities and meetings have emerged that offer a less hectic schedule, focus on shared interests and enterprises, and offer time for a detailed discussion of issues. Good examples of this are Laydeez do Comics, Graphic Brighton, and a number of so-called "unconferences." All offer spaces for sharing ideas and providing mutual support for a growing number of comics research students and young academics, as well as practitioners, readers, and others interested in advancing comics studies in ways that do not fit into the traditional format of academic conferences. Damon Herd, one of the organizers of the 2015 Comics Unconference in Glasgow, says that the aim was to

> provide a forum for those interested in engaging seriously with comics to debate and share experiences in a format that was similar to, but outside of, the formal structure of a traditional academic conference. There was no timetable or schedule decided in advance, but rather a running order of moderated talks, events and happenings decided in collaboration with the participants at the start of the day in a democratic fashion. (2015)

Slightly more focused but providing a similar function are small reading groups, like The British Consortium of Comics Scholars (BCCS), which started in 2012 as a reading group at the University of Sussex, led by Ph.D. student Paul Davies, which quickly expanded to include research students interested in comics theory from the University of Sussex; University of Brighton; University of the Arts London, Central Saint Martins; Open University, and Loughborough University. These kinds of grassroots Comics Studies events are very important, as they are often student led. Comics Studies, being a relatively young area of study, and one that (happily) draws on a convergence (or collision) of methodologies and disciplinary perspectives, needs to remain attentive to the complex needs of the next generation of comics scholars, and they in turn need to have a hand in shaping the subject area through events that they organize.

Moving further East, the Israeli Museum for Comics and Cartooning (founded in 2007) has an annual conference (June/July) that is purely academic and has partnered with various universities, research institutes, think tanks and so forth. In Singapore, the International Scholarly Conference (currently held at ITB Bandung) has taken place since 2009.

By contrast, India is described by Debarghya Singh as having a "sheer dearth" (2015) of comics events, instead relying primarily on small one-off department-specific lectures or single sessions on comics in a larger umbrella conference or, most commonly, one or two papers in a particular session. Some larger annual conferences may have a year themed around comics, such as the annual English department conference, Metaphor, at Sri Venkateswara College, University of Delhi, for which the 2013 theme was "Superheroes: The Masking and the Unmasking."

The challenges facing these academic events within the bigger landscape of congresses, conventions, and festivals are many. Speaking about the CSSC, Barbara Postema (2015) comments that it is difficult to build the required social media presence (which would keep members connected and involved throughout the year, rather than just at the conference) when all involved are teaching academics or graduate students. Similarly, funding is always a concern: how much can be charged and what kinds of costs are necessary (for example, should scholarly events be paying for website design, logos, and so forth). Finally, there are calls and pressures to make such events more professional, for example the CSSC is considering joining the Federation of Humanities and Social Sciences (a Canadian group that organizes Congress every year, where all the annual conferences are held) which would have the benefit of making the CSSC and Comics Studies in general more established within the academy but on the other hand would remove the connection to TCAF and some of the society's independence.

Based on this very brief survey, it seems that for academic comics conferences to survive they must carefully consider notions of ownership and support, with many taking place under the aegis of wider societies, journals, or other bodies. Those that do not are typically one-off events. The success of those that can obtain some funding demonstrates that there is certainly a demand for regular, recurring academic events and an emotional reaction to their lack: Spanish scholar Roberto Bartual (2015)described it as a "wasteland" with one-offs dominating the academic landscape. Sustaining academic-only conferences seems primarily reliant on cost and commitment. Finance is the dominant issue, with very few free events taking place. A notable exception to this is Transitions, held annually at Birkbeck, London, since October 2010. Initial organizer Tony Venezia attributes this success to "connivance and goodwill" as the conference relies on the institution's providing free rooms and a little money to cover refreshments and on its supporters and the academic community to volunteer their services for free poster design, keynote talks, and so forth (2015). He thus stresses that the conference is "not as settled as it looks" and also that it has become increasingly difficult over the past few years "as universities quantify everything."

Given these issues and the changing academic landscape, it is not surprising that comics now also have an entrenched place within larger academic conferences and congresses. In North America, comics strands appear in events such as the MLA (and its various subsidiaries, like NEMLA and SMLA), and the annual Popular Culture Association conference. The latter features around 27 separate programming tracks of which comics and graphic novels are one, but in addition to this comics and comics adaptations appear in multiple various tracks (adaptation, fan studies, queer studies, and so forth). Comics strands also come into play within different disciplines, such as the SCMS (Society for Cinema and Media Studies), the SLSA (Society for Literature, Science, and the Arts), the ASA (American Studies Association), and so forth. The extent to which comics appear is growing exponentially: as Kathleen McClancey (2015) comments: "comics are so hot right now, every conference is trying to do at least a panel or two on comics."

Case Studies: Conventions

In spite of the huge rise in comics conferences, the most visible comics events (due to size, scope, and publicity) remain the fan conventions. A convention is an event at which a number of comics dealers, creators, and publishers meet with fans and collectors. The emphasis is usually commercial. The creators are usually there to promote new work and may give talks, which attracts fans. Dealers sell everything from back issues to original artwork and merchandise. Cosplay is a common feature of many conventions, with fans dressing as their favorite characters. The first conventions were likely in the late 1940s in America, and were largely a place for collectors and enthusiasts to meet and buy and sell comics. They were organized by these same fans and collectors. Later these events became much larger and reached a huge size. Many conventions are run by professional businesses and include a much wider range of attractions, with an emphasis on blockbuster films, television, and computer games. Many countries have at least one large-scale annual event devoted to comics and popular culture aimed primarily at the general public. As noted above, many such events started out as quite small fan gatherings and have grown to massive proportions, whereas many others have sprung up in recent years due to the considerable profits that can be made. Increasingly these are run by professional companies, rather than fans, and academic strands are perhaps less welcome at these professionally run events, where the emphasis is on making every available square foot pay for itself in terms of exhibitor/commercial space or a high profile guest. Nonetheless, the Institute for Comics Studies was, for a time, very active in negotiating for academic tracks at major conventions such as Dragon Con, the New York Comic Con, and so forth. Despite the drive for profit, it currently seems that there is enough diversity in the kinds of events that are being run that there is still space for academic strands in many events, especially the larger ones.

The largest of the fan/public events is Comiket held biannually (as NatsuComi and FuyuComi) in Tokyo, Japan, since 1975. Each lasts around three days and attracts over half a million attendees (an estimate since no registration is required). Comiket is a grassroots event selling self-published works from individual booths. In Europe, Lucca Comics and Games (Tuscany, Italy) is held every October, grown from the launch of the Salone Internazionale de Comics in 1965, with an attendance of 240,000 by 2014. Angoulême International Comics Festival is the third largest event in the world, held annually in Angoulême, France, every January since 1974, attracting over 200,000 guests each year. Angoulême has a more formal academic focus than the rest, with prestigious prizes for cartooning awarded. The challenges of such events are, of course, hosting and security. Angoulême takes place over an entire region; Lucca has been moved in and out of the city center; and Comiket has begun introducing strict rules for early arrival (although these are not always followed).

In North America, large-scale annual events such as San Diego Comic-Con International (CCI), New York Comic Con (New York City), C2E2 (Chicago), Wizard World (multiple events every year held all over North America), Dragon Con (Atlanta), and numerous other Comic-Cons spread across multiple cities (Denver, San Antonio, and so on) dominate the convention circuit. As noted above, many of these have an academic track, such as the Comics Arts Conference (CAC), which is held twice yearly, CCI taking place in San Diego (summer) and WonderCon in Anaheim (spring). According to co-organizer Peter Coogan, the CAC is "the largest and longest running academic conference on comics in the states," featuring around 100 presenters across four days and drawing in an audience of anywhere between 40 and 500 (their room capacity) per panel (2015).

The 1970 founding of the event that would become Comic-Con International by Shel Dorf, Ken Krueger, and Richard Alf (amongst others) is well known (see www.comic-con.org/about for details). The CAC was founded in 1992 by Peter Coogan and Randy Duncan, who recognized how much comics scholarship was in dialogue with the creators themselves and so thought an actual comic book convention would be a good place to have a conference. They first held the CAC in the hotel nearby, with CCI's blessing, but the original plan was to move the conference around the country alongside multiple conventions. The CAC had been held at Chicago Comicon and was negotiating with DragonCon in Atlanta when CCI offered a partnership and made the CAC into an official programming track. Finance was a key issue here as the organizers had been subsidizing the event from their own pockets.

The Comics Arts Conference focuses exclusively on comics (comic books, strips, graphic novels, sequential art, digital/web comics) and rejects panels that only deal with film or television adaptations without a discussion of comics. As Coogan notes, its remit is to "bring together scholars and professionals to engage in a discussion of comics with the public [...] we reach beyond the typical academic audience and spread research findings to the convention audience (fans, general audience, and aca-fans [those who consider themselves both scholars and fans of comics]) and spread the idea that studying comics is legitimate" (2015). The CAC is open to all convention attendees, although the audience self-selects toward aca-fans, or those just wanting a quiet place to sit down amidst the melee (attendance of San Diego CCI has risen to over 130,000 in recent years).Co-organizer Kathleen McClancey (2015) describes the event as "Basically a subset of Comic-Con at large, with a slight bias towards the more academically inclined."

As McClancey notes, CAC has a specific mission: "to bring together academics with pros and the public" and the resulting "cross pollination between academics, pros, and the general public" is one of the event's greatest strengths and "allows for a variety of opinions and viewpoints that don't come into contact with each other nearly enough" (2015). However, the situation also comes with its own set of challenges; for example, McClancey points out that "it can be difficult for presenters who have been acculturated by academia to remember to leave the jargon at home and remember that they are speaking to a more diverse audience than all Ph.D.s" (2015). McClancey and Coogan say that the biggest challenges of organizing such an event are logistical, with around double the required amount of proposals received and more being submitted every year. McClancey points out that while receiving too many proposals "is actually pretty nice, as far as challenges go," due to Comic-Con International's rising popularity the CAC now also receives a large number of proposals "that are less worthy, from people who just want to go to Comic-Con, and don't actually care about the CAC at all, which can be hard to identify" (2015).

These logistical struggles have their roots in cultural shifts, and it is interesting that, as part of a wider event, the CAC's main struggles are identical to the things that CCI more broadly is struggling with: recent explosion in popularity in "geek culture" has made it enormous and hard for attendees to get tickets, accommodations, and so forth (badges sell out in seconds, and the race for San Diego hotels is just as frantic). However, the "comics-only" focus of the conference sits at odds with the rest of the event and indicates a growing ideological distance between the two.

Similar set ups are apparent worldwide. In Canada, the Calgary Comics and Entertainment Expo and the Edmonton Comics and Entertainment Expo have a similar academic track, launched in 2011 by Ofer Berenstein based on his experiences with similar tracks at conventions in both Europe and Israel. A key challenge with these events is attracting an organizational team: Berenstein (2015) notes that, except for a "core team," everyone involved in the Canadian events is a volunteer. Contributing to these bigger events is yet another academic labor of love. However, due to sitting within larger events that have comics as just a small fraction of their focus, a widely varied audience is possible, and this variety enables inter-disciplinarity. Berenstein points out that it becomes impossible to distinguish between the general public/fan/academic/aca-fan: "Geologists in oil and gas companies are academics when sitting in a 'The Geoscience of *Star Trek*' talk, but total general public when listening to a talk about manga culture, for example" (2015). This variety can also be used to enable further research: Matthew J. Smith runs an ethnographic research class at Comic-Con International where undergraduate students conduct small-scale research projects using the attendees (e.g., focusing on the disabled experience of Comic-Con, cosplay, etc). The Canadian Expos go a step further and offer a "social lab" track in which researchers are assigned a room to conduct focus groups or circulate surveys to attendees on pop culture-related research.

In Europe, the various comics festivals also often have a panel/academic day, for example Helsinki Comics Festival, Tampere Comics Festival, and Kemi Comics Festival (Finland); Raptus Festival, Bergen, OCX: Oslo Comics Expo (Norway), Malmö seriefestival, SPX: Stockholm Comics Festival (Sweden); and Copenhagen Comics Festival, Art Bubble Festival, Horsens (Denmark). This might take the form of a single programming strand, or a whole academic day (for example, the Copenhagen comics festival has a biennial academic day, e.g., 2012 discussed comics and teaching and 2015 focuses on documentary comics). A similar arrangement is used by GRAF, a semi-annual congress/fair held in Madrid in December and Barcelona in May, which is structured around one day of presentations and debates and another day of fanzine, comics, and illustration market and described by Roberto Bartual as the "Best thing related to comics in Spain. Ever" (2015).

In Israel, I-Con festival for Sci-Fi and Fantasy has been running since 1998 and covers everything sci-fi/fantasy related (including comics, role playing, gaming, cosplay, fringe theatre, and so forth) and includes general tracks (aca-fans and fans) and an academic track. A similar, smaller event named The Olamot ("worlds" in Hebrew) takes place in the spring, and there are numerous other creator-driven events year round, such as the Israeli Comics Animation and Cartooning Festival (August), which, as Berenstein notes, revolves around lectures, workshops, Q&A panels with creator guests and so on, delivered by aca-fans, professionals, and scholars.

The crossover between professional and scholar is becoming more apparent in many countries, largely due to initiatives such as 24 Hour Comics Day (launched by Scott McCloud in 1990 as a personal challenge to himself and Steve Bissette: to draw a complete comic—24 pages, or 100 panels—in 24 hours). In 2004, Nat Gertler organized the first public event, which has since spread all over the globe. Cheng Tju Lim organized the first Singapore event in 2010, and the numbers involved have grown into the hundreds ever since the event was tied in with La Salle College of the Arts in 2013. Lim (2015) describes its biggest strength as motivational—"getting artists and writers off their ass. [...] Some of them have talked about their great concept for years. At most, they have done some character design or cover art/splash page. But no actual comics. This event forces them to take that step in doing a complete story." Here event and practice combine and produce amazing results; however, Lim notes that the main challenge is still the quality of work: "We need editorial processes" (2015). Perhaps the answer is that critical analysis could become part of these events in the future, bringing academia and practice still closer together.

Other large-scale events in the East seem less inclined to engage with academia. The Singapore Toy, Game and Comics Convention used to have an academic strand (2010), but this has been excised in recent years. Malaysia's Comic Fiesta; Indonesia's Pop Con, and the Philippines' Komikon are all large-scale events aimed at fans without academic tracks. India recently inaugurated Comic Con India, held annually at New Delhi, Hyderabad, Mumbai, and Bangalore, but this has a strong popular culture focus that goes well beyond comics and no academic track.

Conclusion

The vastly increased crossover between fan conventions and academic study is probably one of the most distinctive elements of Comics Studies. While academics have frequently been participants at such public events, chairing interviews or panels or delivering keynote talks, Berenstein (2014) notes that a formal approach (from the academic side) is generally needed to produce serious crossover, such as a dedicated academic track, citing examples such as the Canadian Expos and Christopher Harrison's involvement with Oz-Con in Perth. However, the reverse also holds true; for example, in the UK the Lakes International Comic Art Festival has recently been reaching out to academics to create and sustain an academic track. Berenstein argues that one possible explanation for this increased liaison is the pressure on academia to engage more with ideas of impact and outreach. Economic imperatives have also been already noted as another factor: countries with smaller fan and academic communities seek to bolster numbers by combining the two. However, the liaison is not always easy: Berenstein comments on the need for an "academic initiator" to mediate between the fan convention and academia and who must be committed to "fans, academic standards and the practicalities of the convention" as well as having "a good social-network that supplies good contents." As Roger Sabin (2015) notes, "currently there are comics conferences everywhere. It is typical for comics creators to be invited as keynotes—which is a reversal of the days when academics were invited to the fan events, so that's a neat twist. And now we are seeing niche conferences—manga studies split away a while back, but now we are seeing specialised conferences about digital comics, comics and medicine, comics and the law, etc." Sabin also argues that in some ways the development of Comics Studies has resulted in a loss of inter-disciplinarity:

> In the mid to late 1990s, even when comics started to be named in conference titles, other topics were included. There would always be somebody talking about William Blake's poems, for example; the kind of stuff that we wouldn't now include on a comics programme, but which at the time felt quite natural and connected. (Also, there simply wouldn't have been enough academics working in Comics Studies to fill, say, a two-day event, so help had to come from somewhere.) I have to say, I enjoyed the broad mix of those early conferences – which mashed-up Superman, zines, manga, Hogarth, hieroglyphics, etc. In other words, you had a situation with speakers talking about all aspects of word-image interaction, which arguably we're losing in the 21st century as Comics Studies fractures into niche interests.

As argued above, the health and growth of Comics Studies is inextricably tied to the continued health and vitality of the academic fora and the networks and events that support it. Fortunately, there are now more dedicated comics events than ever before, but as Sabin notes, that has come at the cost of some diversity. Moreover, the relationship between fandom and comics scholarship is a strong one, as evidenced by the ongoing presence of academic strands at high-profile fan events worldwide. This has a long tradition in comics scholarship, and the relationship is one that often proves mutually beneficial but could be made more so. The benefit to academics who are increasingly required to show the wider impact of their research and to demonstrate public engagement is clear. The increase in the professionalization of such events does present something of a risk to the place of academic strands, but this is perhaps balanced by the continuing involvement of practitioners in academia, and the moves to embrace practice-based Ph.Ds and the fact that comics professionals are increasingly moving between the two audiences, pointing to the close relationship between the creation and reception of comics and the academic analysis of the medium. There are risks that the pressure from much bigger, commercially driven events could swamp academic events or could distort them into something they are not designed to be, but there are also opportunities to develop a healthy relationship between the two and comics scholars are well-placed to rise to these challenges.

Acknowledgments

The authors would like to offer their sincere thanks to Maaheen Ahmed, Roberto Bartual, Bart Beaty, Ofer Berenstein, Esther Claudio, Rikke Platz Cortsen, Peter M. Coogan, Randy Duncan, Amadeo Gandolfo, Ian Hague, Damon Herd, M. Thomas Inge, Cheng Tju Lim, Kathleen McClancey, Monica Okomoto, Barbara Postema, Roger Sabin, Debarghya Singh, Matthew J. Smith, Daniel Stein, Laura Vazquez Hutnik, and Tony Venezia. We would also like to apologize for the no-doubt numerous omissions and many worthy events that have gone unnamed here due to the constraints of space.

Bibliography

Ahmed, M. (2015). Personal email to Julia Round.
Barthes, R. (1957) *Mythologies*. 2007 edn, Paris: Editions du Seuil.
Bartual, R. (2015) Personal email to Julia Round.
Beaty, B. (2015) Personal email to Julia Round.
Berenstein, O. (2014) Let's Get Serious—changing the programming rational in fan conventions. A paper presented at the annual Popular Culture Association of Canada conference. Calgary.
Berenstein, O. (2015) Personal email to Julia Round.
Bolling, B. and Smith, M.J. (eds.). (2014) *It Happens at Comic-Con: ethnographic essays on a pop culture phenomenon*, Jefferson: McFarland.
Claudio, E. (2015) Personal email to Julia Round.
Coogan, P.M. (2015) Personal email to Julia Round.
Cortsen, R.P. (2015). Personal email to Julia Round.
Duncan, R. (2015) Personal comment to authors.
Evanier, M. (2003) *Wertham Was Right!*, Raleigh: TwoMorrows.
Gandolfo, A. (2015) Personal email to Julia Round.
Gombrich, E., (1960) *Art and Illusion: a study in the psychology of pictorial representation*, Princeton: Princeton University Press.

Hague, I. (2015) Personal email to Julia Round.
Harmsen, R.C. (2013) Alma Mater Comicensis—Comic Studies in Germany. [Online] Available from: http://www.goethe.de/kue/lit/prj/com/ccs/iuv/en11919135.htm. [Accessed 17 July 2015].
Heer, J. and Worchester, K. (eds.). (2004) *Arguing Comics: literary masters on a popular medium*, Jackson: University Press of Mississippi.
Herd, D. (2015) Personal email to Chris Murray.
Inge, M.T. (2015) Personal email to Julia Round.
Kunzle, D. (1973) *The Early Comic Strip,* Berkeley: University of California Press.
Lent, J. (2010) 'The winding, pot-holed road of comic art scholarship', *Studies in Comics,* 1 (1): 7–33.
Lim, C.T. (2015) Personal email to Julia Round.
McClancey, K. (2015) Personal email to Julia Round.
McLuhan, M. (1964) *Understanding Media,* London: Routledge.
Murray, C. (2015) Personal email to Julia Round.
Okomoto, M. (2015) Personal email to Julia Round.
Postema, B. (2015) Personal email to Julia Round.
Sabin, R. (2015) Personal email to Chris Murray.
Singh, D. (2015) Personal email to Julia Round.
Stein, D. (2015) Personal email to Julia Round.
Vazquez Hutnik, L. (2015). Personal email to Julia Round.
Venezia, T. (2015) Personal interview with Julia Round.
Viñetas Sueltas. (2012). *Viñetas Sueltas.* [Online] Available from: http://www.vinetas-sueltas.com.ar/. [Accessed 16 July 2016].
Wertham, F. (1954) *Seduction of the Innocent.* 1999 ed., Laurel: Main Road Books.
Worcester, K. (2010) 'Comics scholarship', in M. K. Booker (ed.) *Encyclopedia of Comic Books and Graphic Novels Vol. 1, A-L,* Santa Barbara: Greenwood.

A PIONEER'S PERSPECTIVE: M. THOMAS INGE

Both the Popular Culture Association and its official publication, *Journal of Popular Culture,* have clearly played a major part in the development of Comics Studies in the United States. The PCA came into being because of an academic snub. The American Studies Association, which began in 1951, was busy during the 1960s attempting to establish itself as a legitimate area of study. As one wag put it, "American literature is a pigmy standing on the shoulders of giants." The group's scholarship was largely devoted to the question "Does American Studies have a methodology?" Those who wished to study popular culture were denied space on the conference programs on the assumption that this would only trivialize their argument. Thus a group, led by Pulitzer-Prize winning historian Russel B. Nye and folklorist Ray B. Browne, established the PCA in 1971, which would be open to all forms of cultural study. Other scholars who led the movement included literary scholar Carl Bode, critic John G. Cawelti, cultural historian Marshall W. Fishwick, American humor and comics historian M. Thomas Inge, and feminist critic Emily Toth, a list that rapidly expanded in the next few years.

The first national conference of the PCA was held in East Lansing at Michigan State University in 1971. The earliest panel discussion devoted to comics was organized by Inge at the third conference in Indianapolis, Indiana, in April 1973. Under the title "Comics as Culture," three papers were presented on comics as art, literature, and drama by colleagues, none of whom became comics scholars. Soon after, panels on the comics began to appear on a regular basis. Once area chairs were established under the strong leadership of Donald Palumbo and later Amy Kiste Nyberg, the number of panels on the subject literally exploded. Many years there were more panels on comics than any other subject area, competing with science fiction.

The *Journal of Popular Culture* anticipated the association and was founded by Ray B. Browne in 1967. The first essay to appear in the journal on comics was by Arthur Asa Berger on "Peanuts: An American Pastoral" in 1969. Berger, a media specialist at San Francisco State University, would go on to publish a book about Al Capp's *Li'l Abner* in 1970 and a general study in 1973, *The Comic-Stripped American*. William H. Young of Lynchburg College in Virginia, who wrote one of the earliest doctoral dissertations on comics, began to contribute with "The Serious Funnies: Adventure Comics During the Depression." His essays would continue to appear in later issues. Harvey Pekar published "Rapping about Cartoonists, Particularly Robert Crumb" in 1970. The first special "In-Depth" section devoted to comics was edited by Berger in *JPC* 5.1 (Summer 1971) with six essays, and the second was edited by Inge in *JPC* 12.4 (Spring 1979), which included among its eight essays Robert C. Harvey's influential "The Aesthetics of the Comic Strip." Harvey, a cartoonist, also did original illustrations for the essays. Both the PCA and the *JPC* remain at the center of critical and scholarly work on the comic arts.

Bibliography

Berger, A.A. (1969) 'Peanuts: an American pastoral', *Journal of Popular Culture*, 3 (1): 1–8.
Berger, A.A. (1970) *Li'l Abner: a study in American satire*, New York: Twayne.
Berger, A.A. (ed.) (1971). 'Comics and culture', *Journal of Popular Culture*, 5 (1): 164–240.
Berger, A.A. (1973) *The Comic-Stripped American: what Dick Tracy, Blondie, Daddy Warbucks and Charlie Brown tell us about ourselves*, New York: Walker.
Harvey, R.C. (1979) 'The aesthetics of the comic strip', *Journal of Popular Culture*, 12 (4): 640–52.
Inge, M.T. (ed.) (1979) 'In depth section: the comics as culture', *Journal of Popular Culture*, 12 (4): 630–754.
Pekar, H. (1970) 'Rapping about cartoonists, particularly Robert Crumb', *Journal of Popular Culture*, 3 (4): 677–88.
Young, W.H. (1969) 'The Serious Funnies: adventure comics during the Depression', *Journal of Popular Culture*, 3 (3): 382–427.

19

THE JOURNALS

Alec R. Hosterman

If academia is thought of as a grand dining table where disciplines come together to share knowledge, exchange information, and perhaps share a drink or two, then Comics Studies is one of the latest to pull up a chair and raise its glass. Like other fields, Comics Studies earned a spot at the table and continues to do so by, among other things, publishing quality scholarship that advances the field.

Comics Studies came about as many other academic fields did, by scholars asking questions, making connections, and validating its worth to those who may have seen it merely as a sub-set of other disciplines. Today, books are published and papers are presented at regional, national, and international comics conferences. Courses are taught in undergraduate degree programs, and some institutions offer graduate degrees. But most importantly (at least in regards to this chapter), original scholarship is published in peer-reviewed academic journals devoted to studying comics. This, I could argue, is one of the key elements that constitute scholarly legitimacy.

This chapter is about the forgotten, or perhaps overlooked, history of the journals that have helped legitimize Comics Studies. I will begin by briefly discussing the purpose of journals in academia, how they are produced, and the impact of digital technologies. From there, I will discuss four contexts of journals as I see them: early journals that laid a foundation for comics scholars, journals that currently publish comics scholarship, journals solely devoted to comics, and journals with a specific niche in comics research. I have interviewed several editors of these journals and will also give their insight where possible.

Print vs. Digital Publishing

Since the first academic journals created a forum for scholars to bring new research to the forefront of their disciplines, the way they reached their audience was through print. The first use of a journal can be found with the Royal Society, "the world's oldest scientific publisher, with the first edition of *Philosophical Transactions of the Royal Society* appearing in 1665" (The Royal Society, 2011). However, even today journal publishers are continuously under scrutiny for their lengthy (and often delayed) publishing process, regardless of discipline. The review, assessment, re-review, and editing process can take up to a year before an article is set for publication in a journal. Additionally, it takes time to print and send out the journals. As Bjork and Solomon remark, "Traditional paper publishing in particular creates significant delays both due to the need to bundle articles into issues and backlogs created by page limits resulting from the high per page cost of this type of publishing" (n.d., p. 2)

As you can imagine, publishing in 1650 was a far more labor-intensive process than it is today. Up to the 1990s, print was considered the dominant mode of publishing scholarship. However, with the advent of digital culture and online resources, print publishing has a new competitor: open access (OA) digital publishing. OA publishing is done online digitally rather than through traditional print venues. Likewise, access is not usually limited to members of a particular society, but rather open to all with Internet access. Yet, most OA publishers use peer-review and assessment measures similar to print publications. Only the medium, through which the scholarship is available, changes.

Print has been the dominant (but arguably flawed) mode of disseminating scholarship. The traditional print process does not allow for *opportune* discussion of important issues. For example, if I wrote a critique of the controversy surrounding canceling the variant cover for the 2015 DC Comics' *Batgirl #41*, it would likely come out one to two years after it was submitted and accepted. Commentary on the article would then take another cycle to get published, thus making a timely discussion hard to accomplish.

The digital age has accelerated the publishing process and is undergirded by scholars' desire to share information and grow the field. In a personal interview, Aimee Valentine (2015), the founder and editor of *inkt|art*, notes that

> Online comics journals have a great opportunity to crossover with one another, to advance (in real time) the work done by others, to reference articles and publications, and perhaps even collaborate in terms of covering particular comics themes, issues or artists.

This real time approach is something we strive for in academia, especially given the dispersed nature of our home institutions. Digital publishing provides this outlet, and some notable journals in Comics Studies are taking advantage of this trend, including *Image [&] Narrative, The Comics Grid, ImageText, Tebeosfera, Comics Forum, SANE Journal: Sequential Art Narrative in Education*, and the *Scandinavian Journal of Comic Art*.

Cutting edge? Perhaps. I would argue that Comics Studies is reactive to the needs and interests of scholarly communities and creators in order to develop an open, critical discussion of the medium and the message. Comics Studies is coming to fruition in a time when technology has given users new modes of communicating with mass audiences, connecting people and ideas in ways not done before. As Valentine (2015) remarks: "I'd say that the online community for comics journals has a definite advantage over print journals these days. There's room for discussion forums, videos of public talks, [and] updates." The challenge is to imbue digital forums with an ethos equivalent to that of print journals for the sake of the academic tenure process.

"What's Past Is Prologue"

In Act 2, Scene 1 of Shakespeare's (2000) *The Tempest*, Antonio famously proclaims: "Whereof what's past is prologue." In doing so, he rationalizes that all that has happened previously in the play led his colleague Sebastian and him to do what comes next: commit murder. Take that same sentiment (but not the murdering part) and think about it in the context of our journals. This section will look at some of those ground-breaking early journals that published scholarship on comics. Doing so will provide context in both time and location.

In 1971, Jacques Glénat founded *Les Cahiers de la bande dessinée [The Notebooks of Comics]*, a French magazine that studied comics in all forms, publishing from 1971 to 1990. It began as a fanzine but quickly grew in scope to include a more theoretical direction and intellectual rigor, facilitating interactions between scholars and producers of comics. This move became more prevalent when Thierry Groensteen took over as editor from 1984 to 1988.

In the mid-1970s, Thomas A. Durwood published a series of journals dedicated to "pictorial fiction." The first iteration came in 1974 under the title *Harvard Journal of Pictorial Fiction* (Abe Books). It ran essays, scholarship, and interviews with industry legends like comic book artist Jack Kirby and cartoonist turned editor Harvey Kurtzman.

In 1975 the journal changed its name to *Crimmer's: The Harvard Journal of Pictorial Fiction* (DTA Collectibles) featuring a front cover and interview with Burne Hogarth, as well as interviews with illustrators like Paul Szep (Boston Globe editorial cartoonist) and Disney Studios artists John Hench and Marc Davis. In 1976, the journal changed titles once more and became *Crimmer's: The Journal of the Narrative Arts* (Abe Books). Critical analyses were introduced, including analytical pieces like the "Politics of Comics" and "A Thematic Analysis of Undergrounds." No issues were published after 1976.

1976 also saw Gary Groth and Michael Catron acquire *The Nostalgia Journal* and re-launch it in 1977 as *The Comics Journal* (TCJ) (The Comics Journal, n.d.). *TCJ* is a magazine about the comics industry with both print and online presences. Initially, the magazine featured sections common to industry trade publications: letters to the editor, industry news, featured columns by regular contributors, reviews of books and conventions, and illustrations from artists. As the magazine evolved, it began to include more criticism and critical essays about the comics industry. For instance, the March 1986 issue included an essay by R. C. Harvey entitled "Wertham Revisited: Seduction in the Eighties." That trend continues into the present. The November 2006 issue included a critical look at the conversations of Will Eisner and Frank Miller; the April 2004 issue included Bart Beaty's "The Americanization of Angouleme?" while a January 2015 article looked at the controversy surrounding the Danish cartoonist's drawings of Muhammad in 2006. Beginning in 2010, *TCJ* publishes a daily online magazine and an annual print edition.

TCJ also includes interviews with significant industry leaders, including Alan Moore, Alison Bechdel, Daniel Clowes, Lynda Barry, and Bill Watterson. Regular contributors and editors to *TCJ* were Groth himself, Kim Thompson, R. C. Harvey, Anne Moore, and Tom Spurgeon. Guest editors include Dave Sim and Trina Robbins. *TCJ* is unique in that it is seen as an industry magazine rather than as an academic journal. However, this blend of practice, art, and criticism makes it a significant contribution to comics journals.

The 1980s saw John Lent and Joseph Szabo establish an international cartoon magazine called *WittyWorld*: "That Summer 1987 edition set the standard for *WittyWorld*, with interviews, articles, and profiles on all genres of comic art and representing nine countries" (WittyWorld, n.d., para. 6). *WittyWorld* grew in scope to include regular editorials and commentary, critical articles on the state of comics in the world, historical articles, and interviews. Scholarship appeared in various forms, from "Focus on the Environment: Political Cartoons Juxtaposed from around the World" to "Scatalogical or Satirical? Response to a

Time Magazine Article about the Hungarian Festival." *WittyWorld* also held international editorial meetings, sponsored conferences, published directories, and was one of the first to take advantage of the World Wide Web and go online in 1998. Whether it was seen as a traditional academic journal or not, *WittyWorld* was a pioneer in offering an outlet for all aspects of Comics Studies. The magazine suspended activities in 1999 but re-emerged at the end of 2001 with a focus on being an international syndication service.

And then there's *Hogan's Alley,* debuted by Rick Marschall and Tom Heintjes in 1994; the publication bills itself as a magazine of the cartoon arts (Scoop, 2015). Since its inception, *Hogan's Alley* has showcased some of the significant historians and scholars of the discipline, including R. C. Harvey, and Allan Hotz. Likewise, it includes interviews with significant individuals, like Will Eisner and Gus Arriola. *Hogan's Alley* still publishes in digital and print formats.

At the end of the 20th century *L'Indispensable [The Indispensable]* (n.d.), debuted as a French magazine that published critical analyses of comics, news on the industry, and interviews. The publication began in 1998 by Franck Aveline and ceased publication in 2000, but a new version of the journal emerged in 2011.

These publications are not all journals in the traditional academic sense, but they are outlets that tried something new for Comics Studies. In them you will find some of the early threads of academic journals: criticism, inquiry, scholarship, discussion, and reviews. Some of them were very strategic in their titles. For instance, *Crimmer's: The Harvard Journal of Pictorial Fiction* brought together some of the elements that constitute an academic journal, the Harvard name, and articles that focused on comics artists and criticism. This was a bold move, especially when institutions like Harvard have a long tradition of espousing traditional academic disciplines.

We owe a great debt of gratitude to those that came prior. Without them, the journals we have currently may not have come about or would not have the longevity they enjoy today. They opened doors and provided forums to the critical culture of comics scholarship.

Journals Publishing Scholarship on Comics

Any discussion of foundational journals would not be complete without mentioning, albeit briefly, related disciplinary journals publishing articles pertaining to comics. The list is long for sure. My goal here is not to mention them all, but rather to give a sampling of the breadth to which comics articles appear in publication. By no means are these offered in any order of preference.

Some journals publish special issues that focus on one particular aspect of comics. The spring 2015 issue of *Composition Studies* ran a special issue called "Comics, Multimodality, and Composition." Articles included composing with comics, course designs with comics, rhetorics of comics, and others. Other journals publish articles related to their mission. For instance, *Critical Studies in Media Communication* published "A Fantasy Theme Analysis of Political Cartoons on the Clinton-Lewinsky-Starr Affair" (Benoit et al., 2001) and Rockler's (2002) "Race, Whiteness, 'Lightness', and Relevance: African American and European American Interpretations of *Jump Start* and *The Boondocks*."

From a broader perspective, *Transformative Works and Cultures* and *The Journal of Popular Culture* (*TJPC*) regularly publish scholarship that engages comics as part of the interdisciplinary nature of popular culture. From *TJPC*'s inception in the late 1960s, it offered an outlet for comics scholarship. For instance, in 1969 William Young Jr. published an article that examined the "The Serious Funnies: Adventure Comics in the Depression, 1929–1938." More recently, *TJPC* published Jesus Gonzalez's (2014) article "'Living in the Funnies': Metafiction in American Comic Strips." Similarly, niche journals like *20th Century Studies, English Language Notes, Print: America's Graphic Design Magazine, Philosophy Now, PS: Political Science and Politics, SubStance, Studies in American Humor, Adaptation*, and *Animation Journal* have all published comics scholarship that fits within their editorial scope.

Finally, there are established journals—both in print and online—that examine comics as one aspect of the visual/verbal or text/image relationship. For instance, the French online magazine *textimage* emerged in the spring of 2007 and is still publishing online as of this writing. Each issue of the journal has a particular theme that looks at the intersection of image and text and the meaning produced. For instance, the first issue examined marginal/border illustrations while the third focused on lettering/typography.

Similarly, *Image [&] Narrative* is an open-access, "peer-reviewed e-journal on visual narratology and word and image studies in the broadest sense of the term" (n. d.). With their first issue debuting in 2000, the journal featured a selection of comics-themed scholarship, including "Narration in Comics," "The Publication and Sizes of Comics, Graphic Novels, and Tankobon," "Educational Comics – Text-Type or Text-Types in Gold in a Format?", "Manga Story-telling / Showing," and "Richard Castells and Contemporary Comic." (Each title was translated from French). Their most recent issue's theme blends comics and photography: "The Narrative Functions of Photography in Comics."

Likewise, *Word & Image: A Journal of Verbal/Visual Enquiry* "concerns itself with the study of the encounters, dialogues, and mutual collaborations (or hostility) between verbal and visual languages" (n. d.). Begun in 1985 and published by Taylor and Francis, the journal periodically publishes scholarship on comics, such as Richard Watts' (1989) widely referenced article "Comic Strips and Theories of Communication." Although these journals are broadly focused on the role of images and text in visual culture, they include comics as an aspect worth exploring.

I believe it is important to note these journals reference comics as being part of an interdisciplinary field approach to scholarship, whether it is in English, Political Science, Philosophy, or Media Studies. This interdisciplinary approach is the crux of what makes this field truly diverse. Embracing these publications inevitably lends more legitimacy to the field of Comics Studies and acknowledges that comics are of importance to fields of study beyond one's own.

Journals for Comics Studies

The objective for any journal is to advance the academic study of its discipline. At the same time, journals also serve to help legitimize an academic movement and move them into a fully formed field of study. In a personal interview, Mark McKinney (2015), co-editor of *European Comic Art*, told me that: "The creation of scholarly journals solely dedicated to comics helps demonstrate that the art form is worthy of study in its own right, as opposed to being only a subset of a larger field (e.g., popular culture, French studies or American studies)."

The mid-1990s saw one of the first attempts at founding a formal, academic journal for comics scholars: *INKS: Cartoon and Comic Art Studies*. With *INKS*, founder and editor Lucy

Shelton Caswell gave scholars a place for "lively articles about printed cartoon art and … a forum for new concepts and debate" (1994). The journal ran from 1994 through 1997. Whether cognizant of the wording or not, using "comic art studies" in the journal's title helped the legitimization process. *INKS* also offered a forum for articles about editorial cartoons, comic strips, comic books, and various other forms of comic art. Caswell brought together an editorial board of scholars and practitioners that bridged the divide between two worlds, including the talents of practitioners such as Will Eisner, Art Spiegelman, Frank Stack, and Kenneth Baker.

Lucy Shelton Caswell is also known for her work at Ohio State University, specifically as the founder and curator for one of the largest collections of cartoon art in the United States. She began in the 1970s by establishing a two-room library at OSU that has grown into a considerably larger facility in what is now known as the Billy Ireland Cartoon Library & Museum. Caswell retired from the Museum in 2010.

Another journal that led the way for scholars was the *International Journal of Comic Art* (*IJoCA*). John Lent, now-retired Professor of Mass Communication at Temple University, was the founder and is still publisher and editor-in-chief of *IJoCA*. He remarked that *IJoCA* came about after hearing his graduate students say that they needed a journal just for Comics Studies because there was nowhere for them to publish (2015). In 1998, he presented a one-page mimeographed document at the International Comic Arts Forum and declared to anyone interested "there is now an international journal of comic art." The actual first issue of *IJoCA* appeared in the summer of 1999 and true to its name covered issues ranging from obscenity in Japanese comics to women cartoonists of American magazines to the philosophy of Sudanese cartoonist Khalid Albaih. Since then the journal has given students and scholars an opportunity to work as part of the editorial board, publish scholarship that extends the boundaries of what we know about comics as a field and as an art, and bring to the forefront artists and their work. *IJoCA* currently publishes twice a year with an open focus on any or all issues related to Comics Studies, something John is especially proud of since it helps speed along the publication process and scholarly discussions.

Because of Lent's contributions to the field of comics scholarship, in 2007 a parody of *IJoCA* was presented to him for his 70th birthday. *The Interplanetary Journal of Comic Art: A Festschrift in Honor of John Lent* was edited by Michael Rhode (2007) and includes art by Ralph Steadman, a British cartoonist who collaborated with journalist Hunter S. Thompson on the artwork for several articles and books.

IJoCA is a print publication that has an Internet presence. Two others with similar foci are *Studies in Comics* and the *Journal of Graphic Novels and Comics*. Like *IJoCA*, *Studies in Comics* is international in scope and allows contributions from a variety of methodologies or perspectives. Begun in 2010, *Studies in Comics* comes on the heels of such journals as *European Comic Art* (discussed in the next section) and *The Journal of Graphic Novels and Comics* (discussed below). Editors Julia Round and Chris Murray open the journal to criticism from a variety of methodologies and reviews of comics and couples it with an online space for emerging work.

In May of 2001, editors Antony Johnston, Alasdair Watson, and Andrew Wheeler published *Ninth Art*, an all-digital journal that offered a forum for comics scholarship. Their website notes: "The critical and analytical literature of comics has always been in drought. On both an academic and journalistic level, there has always been little for the aficionado or casual reader to refer to. Our library shelves are bare" (*Ninth Art*, 2001). They also declare: "We make no claim to being a newsmagazine. Rather, *Ninth Art* is a journal of the medium. It is our aim to create an expanding repository of ideas, analysis and contemporary thought, exploring every aspect of the arts and industry of comics." In doing so, the journal targeted a specific niche of literary and critical readers—a growing audience that includes academics. The journal ran from 2001 to 2006.

Similarly, the *Journal of Graphic Novels and Comics* is a Taylor and Francis published journal that began in 2010 and is international in scope. The journal's founding editors, Julia Ormrod and David Huxley, focus on the "production and consumption of comics in their cultural, institutional and creative contexts" (n.d.).

Comics Studies has seen several contemporary journals emerge embracing the OA publishing model. In the spring of 2004, the English Department at the University of Florida debuted *ImageText*, a peer-reviewed, OA journal dedicated to the interdisciplinary study of comics and related media. The journal is free to the public on their website. Founded by emeritus editor Donald Ault, the journal publishes digital texts that include original research and analyses, presentations given by scholars, and reviews of comics, graphic novels, and books related to comics. The University of Florida also offers both MAs and PhDs in Comics and Visual Rhetoric, hosts the Comix-Scholars Discussion List, and is a driving force in helping legitimize Comics Studies.

OA journals are becoming increasingly popular, especially ones that are peer-reviewed as those hold more academic clout. The French-based *Comicalities: Etudes de culture graphique (Comicalities: Graphic Culture Studies)* debuted in 2010 and ran until 2014. This OA journal, published in Paris at the Universite Paris XIII, focused on the evolution and modes of expression that were specific to comics, illustrations, caricatures, and cartoons. The OA journal *The Comics Grid: Journal of Comics Scholarship* began in England in 2012, edited by Ernesto Priego for Ubiquity Press. It is inclusive of scholarship from a wide range of authors, including graduate students, scholars, artists, curators, and librarians from varied backgrounds. Like those journals prior, *The Comics Grid* believes knowledge and comics scholarship should be open to a wider audience and available digitally.

Comics Studies Journals with a Niche

As Comics Studies has grown, so has its ability to add niche-oriented journals to provide scholars with specific research foci an outlet for their scholarship. This is advantageous on several levels. First, it implies that Comics Studies has grown large enough to sustain niche research (e.g., feminism in comics, manga). Second, it implies scholars are meeting needs that have not been fully addressed prior, an important tenant, I believe, of establishing disciplinary scholarship. This section recognizes journals that offer scholars an outlet for specific areas of expertise.

Aimee Valentine began *inkt|art* as a way for readers and contributors to "appreciate and examine critically the medium of text and image as represented by women currently working in the field" (2015). She brought *inkt|art* to the digital frontier in 2007 but, by Valentine's own admission, it was "lost to the ether"; however, the response to it was promising. She re-launched it in 2012 in a more user- (and designer-) friendly format: "When you see a gap, you try to fill it–whether you're the best person for the job or not!" *inkt|art* is a platform to explore women in comics: "In a publishing community which has been dominated by males for decades, we focus on the creative and critical talents of contributors who may be otherwise overlooked due to their gender or the genres of narrative which they tackle" (2015).

The *SANE Journal: Sequential Art Narrative in Education* is another example. This journal's goal is to "add significantly to the global knowledge associated with all aspects of graphica (comics, graphic novels, and its related forms) and education" (SANE Journal, n.d.). Founded in 2010 by James "Bucky" Carter, *SANE Journal* is one of the few online platforms that addresses comics, education, and pedagogical techniques. As Carter notes in a personal interview: "SANE's aim is specific in that it seeks to help teachers and scholars consider comics and pedagogy" (2015). The connection is logical, especially given the many different uses for comics and graphic novels in education: to teach English composition, history, political science, communication, and so forth.

Those critiquing the Japanese form of comics rely on a group of well-known journals (some mentioned in this chapter), including: *The Journal of Japanese Studies*, *The Journal of Popular Culture*, *Science Fiction Studies*, *Journal of Fandom Studies*, *Journal of Japanese & Korean Cinema*, *East Asian Journal of Popular Culture*, and *Studies in Comics*. One scholarly outlet that is gaining popularity is *Mechademia: An Annual Forum for Anime, Manga, and the Fan Arts*. Begun in 2006 and published by the University of Minnesota Press, this journal focuses on fan and academic communities' reactions to manga and anime. In addition, it includes such topics as game design, fashion, packaging, toys, and the cultural/critical approaches to fan communities. More on manga can be found in Nicholas Theisen's chapter earlier in this book.

There are several other niche journals that have grown out of a desire to understand the complexity and reach of the medium. For instance, *Deutsche Comicforschung [German Comic Research]* was first published in 2005 and focuses on the cultural expressions and history of German comics, while the *Scandinavian Journal of Comic Art* is an OA journal that published four issues beginning in 2012. It is rooted in scholarship from the Nordic countries of Denmark, Finland, Iceland, Norway, and Sweden (although they will publish research regardless of regional boundaries). More broadly, *European Comic Art* is devoted to the study of graphic novels, comic books, and caricature from not just the French *bande dessinée* perspective, but contributions provided by all European countries (European Comic Art, n.d.). Edited by Laurence Grove, Mark McKinney, and Ann Miller and published by Berghahn Journals in England, *European Comic Art* debuted in 2008 and is a bi-annual publication of the International Bande Dessinée Society.

Finally, Spanish-language journals have come about in recent years. *Historietas: Revista de estudios sobre la Historieta [Cartoons: Journal of Studies on Cartoons]* published one issue per year between 2011 and 2013. It featured scholarship focused on a variety of topics but offered multiple articles based around the idea of femininity in comics. *Nona Arte: Revista Brasileira de Pesquisas em Historias em Quadrinhos [Ninth Art: Journal of Research in Comics]* was first published in 2012. The journal mainly publishes research from Brazilian scholars, such as an article on science fiction in Brazilian comics, but it does include pieces from outside of South America. Finally, *Tebeosfera* highlights the study of comics produced in Spain, Mexico, and South American countries. The first issue debuted in 2001 and was published until December of 2005 (Tebeosfera, n.d.).

Final Thoughts

There you have it: the (somewhat) secret origins of the academic journals that have helped advance the field of Comics Studies. But trends being what they are, I would guess that by the time you read this there will have been more strides in the journals. The editors interviewed all had their own ideas of future strides for Comics Studies. Julia Round of *Studies in Comics* advocates for online publishing and open access, which "allow[s] for quick turnaround and accessibility" (2015). Going further, James Carter believes that online comics journals need to be multi-modal in order to hyperlink to images and inset panels or even video clips of comics in the page. Similarly, John Lent said online journals could utilize non-traditional formats or be similar in presentation to what Scott McCloud did in constructing *Understanding Comics*. Doing so could harness more of the creative nature of both digital designers and traditional comic artists, something that harkens to the old, classic adage "practice what you preach." Partnerships between scholars and artists raise both awareness of the medium from a practical perspective and a critical/cultural perspective.

From a content perspective, Mark McKinney and his co-editors Laurence Grove and Ann Miller believe a trend toward transnationalism in comics is needed, "whether in our understanding of historical and current evolution of the form, or in collaboration between comics scholars in different countries and on far-apart continents" (2015). Likewise, Aimee Valentine feels comics journalism would benefit from online real-time, open-access publication venues where scholars and practitioners would discuss world events: "How great would it be, for readers, creators, and scholars to have several critical points of reference on a singular topic, across the board at the same time? The ability to host and promote a worldwide dialogue about comics is an invaluable advantage in the era of online publishing" (2015).

The future of journals in Comics Studies is with those scholars and publishers willing to embrace what technology can offer to promote scholarly dialogue, push the boundaries of how scholarship is presented to the academic community, and work to extend the body of knowledge we have in our discipline. It is through this that Comics Studies continues to emerge as a more fully recognized field of study.

Bibliography

Beaty, B. (2004) 'The Americanization of Angouleme?', *The Comics Journal*, April: 12–13.
Benoit, W.F., Klyukovski, A.A., McHale, J.P., & Airne D. (2001) 'A fantasy theme analysis of political cartoons on the Clinton-Lewinsky-Starr affair', *Critical Studies in Media Communication*, 18 (4): 377–94.
Bjork, B. and Solomon, D. (n.d.) 'The publishing delay in scholarly peer-reviewed journals', *Research on Open Access Publishing*. [Online] Available from: http://openaccesspublishing.org/oa11/article.pdf. [Accessed 15 June 2015].
Carter, J. (2015) Interview [Email] Message to: Hosterman, A. 22 June 2015.
Caswell, L.S. (1994) Editorial. *INKS: Cartoon and Comic Art Studies*, 1 (1): 2–3.
Comics Journal, The. (n.d.) *Wikipedia*. [Online] Available from: http://en.wikipedia.org/wiki/The_Comics_Journal. [Accessed 10 June 2015].
Durwood, T. (1975) *Crimmer's: The Harvard Journal of Pictorial Fiction*.
Durwood, T. (ed.) (1976) *Crimmer's: The Journal of the Narrative Arts*.
European Comic Art. (n.d.). *Aims & scope*. [Online] Available from: http://journals.berghahnbooks.com/eca/index.php?pg=home. [Accessed 24 June 2015].
Gonzalez, J.A. (2014). 'Living in the funnies': Metafiction in American comic strips. *The Journal of Popular Culture*, 47 (4): 838–56.
Image [&] Narrative. (n.d.). *Focus and scope*. [Online] Available from: http://www.imageandnarrative.be/index.php/imagenarrative/about/editorialPolicies#focusAndScope. [Accessed 5 May 2015].
Indispensable, The. (n.d.) *Wikipedia*. [Online] Available from: http://fr.wikipedia.org/wiki/L%27Indispensable. [Accessed 10 June 2015].

inkt|art. (n.d.) *About us.* [Online] Available from: http://inktart.org/about-us/. [Accessed 21 May 2015].

Journal of Graphic Novels and Comics. (n.d.) *Aims & scope.* [Online] Available from: http://www.tandfonline.com/action/journalInformation?show=aimsScope&journalCode=rcom20#.VZQxuVOD6QY. [Accessed 28 January 2015].

Lent, J. (2015) Interview [Email] Message to: Hosterman, A. 22 June 2015.

Les Cahiers de la bande dessinée. (n.d.). *Wikipedia.* [Online] Accessed from: https://fr.wikipedia.org/wiki/Les_Cahiers_de_la_bande_dessin%C3%A9e. [Accessed 10 June 2015].

McKinney, M. (2015) Interview [Email] Message to: Hosterman, A. 19 June 2015.

Miller, A. (2015) Interview [Email] Message to: Hosterman, A. 19 June 2015.

Ninth Art. (2001) *What is Ninth Art?* [Online] Availble from: http://www.ninthart.org/about/what_is.php. [Accessed 10 June 2015].

Rhode, M. (2007) *The Interplanetary Journal of Comic Art: A festschrift in honor of John Lent.* [Online] Available from: http://www.lulu.com/shop/Michael-rhode/interplanetary-journal-of-comic-art-a-festschrift-in-honor-of-john-lent/paperback/product-726984.html. [Accessed 15 June 2015].

Rockler, N.R. (2002) 'Race, whiteness, 'lightness," and relevance: African American and European American interpretations of *Jump Start* and *The Boondocks*', *Critical Studies in Media Communication*, 19 (4): 398–419.

Round, J. (2015) Interview [Email] Message to: Hosterman, A. 23 June 2015.

Royal Society, The. (2011) *The Royal Society journal archive made permanently free to access.* [Online] Available from: https://royalsociety.org/news/2011/Royal-Society-journal-archive-made-permanently-free-to-access/. [Accessed 20 June 2015].

SANE Journal: Sequential Art Narrative in Education. (n.d.) *Aims & scope.* [Online] Available from: http://digitalcommons.unl.edu/sane/aimsandscope.html. [Accessed 21 May 2015].

Scoop. (n.d.) *A walk through Hogan's Alley.* [Online] Available from: http://scoop.diamondgalleries.com/Home/4/1/73/1017?articleID=45988. [Accessed 10 June 2015].

Shakespeare, W., Vaughan, V.M., & Vaughan, A.T. (2000) *The Tempest,* London: Arden Shakespeare Press.

Tebeosfera. (n.d.) *Completes.* [Online] Available from: http://www.tebeosfera.com/editorial/num_13.html. [Accessed 5 May 2015].

Valentine, A. (2015) Interview [Email] Message to: Hosterman, A. 18 June 2015.

Word & Image. (n.d.) *Aims & scope.* [Online] Available from http://www.tandfonline.com/action/journalInformation?show=aimesScope&journalCode=twim20#.VMk_u76q6M4. [Accessed 5 May 2015].

WittyWorld. (n.d.) *A fascinating story that mirrors life itself.* [Online] Available from: http://www.joeszabo.us/wittyworld/history.html. [Accessed 10 June 2015].

Young, W.H. (1969) 'The serious funnies: adventure comics in the depression, 1929–1938', *The Journal of Popular Culture,* 3 (3): 404–27.

20
THE PRESSES

Joseph Michael Sommers

As I type these words on the page, Comics Studies, as a field, a set of practices, and a discourse community has entered brave new days. It is no longer relegated to a niche community of persistent scholars fighting for space at an academic publishing house for a contract justified by a spurious set of reasons masking an intense love and desire to publish on sequential art. With the advent of comics and comics-related intellectual properties dominating the cultural landscape since, at least, the mid-1980s (in popular mention of books such as Frank Miller's *The Dark Knight Returns* and Alan Moore and Dave Gibbons' *Watchmen*), the 1990s (in film), and the post-9/11 period (in virtually everything else), Comics Studies has become a dominant force on the academic press's kiosk at every major academic convention and a welcomed prospectus to the cultural studies or literature editor at most all trade or academic presses. However, by no means were warm greetings as such always the case.

The publication of comics scholarship by academic presses, in some manner or another, can be traced back in America well into the early 20th century. It simply depends on the definition of Comics Studies employed. For example, Fredric Wertham's odious *The Seduction of the Innocent*, a study replete with "falsifications" in regards to the comics community and the comics reader, was published in 1954 by Rinehart and Company[1]; and, while not the proudest moment in American comics scholarship, it may be one of the earliest. If one considers a collector's motivations in comics, then one could not discount some of the earlier guidebooks such as 1965's *Argosy Price Guide* by Michael Cohen and Tom Horsky and Jerry Bail's self-published *Collector's Guide: The First Heroic Age* in 1969, itself a predecessor to, arguably, the vaunted work of Robert M. Overstreet's *Comic Book Price Guide* from the eponymously entitled Overstreet Publications in 1970 (Miller 2005).[2,3] And while that might appear to be self-publication, by 1976, Overstreet had achieved national distribution and began to carry historical and critical essays valuable to comics scholars (Scoop, 2015). One could even find the burgeoning scholarship at the bastion center of American academics, the University of Chicago, in both John Twomey's 1955 master's thesis *The Anti-Comic Book Crusade* and Annette Fern's 1968 master's thesis, *Comics as Serial Fiction*, both some of the earliest 'official' academic studies into the medium.[4]

The scare quotes in the last statement are not designated for emphasis; trying to target a discussion surrounding the origin of academic Comics Studies in America is a daunting task with no clear point of ingress. For, what defines 'Academic Comics Studies' proper in a field that, by most accounts, has been classified as pop culture and not covered as literary or cultural studies for a great duration of its publication history? Do the more encyclopedic histories such as Maurice Horn's *World Encyclopedia of Comics* (Chelsea House, 1976) merit as starting point (followed up by works such as Ron Goulart's *The Great Comic Book Artists* [St. Martins, 1986]), or would more formalist studies by comics creators qualify, such as Mort Walker and his tongue-in-cheek *Lexicon of Comicana* (Museum of Cartoon Art, 1981)? *Lexicon* served as a repository of originally satirical reference terminologies for all the idiosyncratic visual elements of comic strips that became adopted by academics for, essentially, being a working language of the formal elements of the craft. And what about formalist studies *proper* completed not by academics but by those whose studies would later be considered as *the* academic resources such as the great Will Eisner's *Comics and Sequential Art* (Poorhouse Press, 1985) and its mammoth self-reflexive expansion on the effort, *Understanding Comics*, by cartoonist Scott McCloud[5] (Tundra Publishing, 1993[6]). And does one focus on the press or the people? The academic trade presses or the university presses (not to mention the niche and vanity presses that oft gave rise to later publication in either trade or academic presses)? In many ways the topic is underpinned by so many questions that any single point of radiation seems insufficient.

No single essay can account for this history of academic Comics Studies presses in America, let alone abroad, with a historical trajectory tracing back to its Franco-Belgian comics roots; however, there may be a germ of a thought in consideration of press types. Recently, Kenneth Kidd brought forth a notion in regards to another younger academic field of study "not generally held in high regard" (2007, p. 167), children's literature, and a term he dubbed "prizing" (2007, p. 166). Quoting James English, he writes that "the prize":

> *is* cultural practice in its quintessential contemporary form. The primary function it can be seen to serve—that of facilitating cultural "market transactions," enabling the various individual and institutional agents of culture, with their different assets and interests and dispositions, to engage one another in a collective project of value production—is the project of cultural practice as such. (2007, p. 166)

This is to say, prized work "generates what [English] calls a 'logic of proliferation' within the relational field of culture. Each new prize makes possible yet another" (2007, p. 166), or, to rearticulate: each prized study, crafts and encourages the possibility for further, better, more valuable, and less "crudely utilitarian" (2007, p. 167) studies. For my purposes, Kidd's assertion holds that prized studies, in this case, prized Comics Studies, past any simple Marxist considerations, crafts an "economy of prestige" (2007, p. 169) amongst the academic community whereby it can be regarded in the same manner of academic scholarship of more entrenched and accepted forms and fields within greater academia.[7]

Using this theory as sight-line, the essay will attempt to track a trajectory from a period when professionals, whether within the field of comics or academics, did not casually make in-roads into comics scholarship; rather, this essay will begin from the point where Comics Studies was considered a "serious field" within the American academic community using presses, both academic trade and university, to put scholarship into circulation along routes of literary, pop cultural, and cultural anthropological forms.[8] Given that rubric, it might not be surprising to note that this discourse community's roots were planted in the international soil of the Franco-Belgian appreciation of the medium as a form deserving study.

Be it in their interests in making the format worthy of appreciation with academic journals (*Les Cahiers de la Bande Dessinée*) or within museums such as the *Musée des arts decoratifs* in 1967 or major comics publishers such as Casterman,[9] the European community, particularly the Franco-Belgians, seems to have first "championed the appreciation of comics" (Duncan & Smith, 2015, p. 364) and produced scholars who found reprint in America concretizing the field's scholarship in an established tradition. Visionaries like Thierry Groensteen (*Töpffer, l'invention de la bande dessinée*, Hermann, 1994 and *Systéme de la bande dessinée*, Presses Universitaires de France, 1999) and Thierry Smolderen who were publishing both academically and creatively in France and Belgium would find reprint with one of the single greatest academic presses in Comics Studies: The University Press of Mississippi.

Founding an American Comics University Press System

Sponsored by eight distinct universities in Mississippi, The University Press of Mississippi was founded and located in Jackson in 1970 with the expressed purposes of publishing "scholarly books of the highest distinction that interpret the South and its culture to the nation and the world" (Meet the Press). One such acquisition came by way of M. Thomas Inge, then possibly foremost known as an Americanist scholar with a fondness for popular culture; he donated a large volume of papers to Virginia Commonwealth University "from the 1950s onward [...] made up of many unique items collected by Inge covering the history of the comic arts [... .] contain[ing] correspondence with a number of noted artists and writers, including Art Spiegelman, Mort Walker, Bruce Duncan, and Harold Foster, and comic arts scholars" (A Guide, 2003). Inge happened to conflate his interests in Americanist studies and culture and his love of comics and humor into one of UPM's first forays into comics studies: *Comics as Culture* in 1990. He followed that up the next year by writing the introduction to a new entry in their Studies in Popular Culture Series, a reprint of *The Comics* written by Coulton Waugh in 1947, in addition to crafting a short volume entitled *Anything Can Happen in a Comic Strip* (1995) and beginning the press's ever-growing interview series *Conversations* with the initial entry *Charles M. Schulz: Conversations* in 2000.

The press has since become known as the standard bearer amongst university presses for publishing work related to comics studies, or as Jeet Heer put it:

> Scholarship often flourishes [in] unexpected and [out] of the way places, tucked in the corner of remote cities and universities [... .] When the history of comics studies is written great attention will be given to the work of a few editors in Jackson, Mississippi. That's the hometown of the University Press of Mississippi (UPM), which has been at forefront of publishing scholarly books about comics for nearly two decades. (2008)

Heer attributes the success of UPM's role in Comics Studies to a chance meeting between Inge and former acquisitions editor and eventual press director Seetha Srinivasan at a meeting of the South Atlantic Modern Language Association. Alongside Inge's *Comics as Culture*, Srinivasan acquired Joseph Witek's *Comic Books as History* (1989) looking, according to Heer, to establish a unique identity for the press. And while Heer praises Srinivasan, Srinivasan praises Inge for helping her come to a list of intellectual properties of out-of-print books, translations, and other ephemera in an effort to raise an identity in America of material deemed somewhat academically dubious by other presses. Says Srinivasan:

> There was resistance from some of members of our editorial board who questioned whether UPM wanted to be known as a publisher of books on the comics. Were these worthy of consideration of attention from a scholarly press? It is to the credit of these members that they were willing to be persuaded of the central role comics played in a culture and to take a risk on the first titles.
>
> *(Heer, 2008)*

Ironically enough, that resistance permeated not just through the press but the English Department of Ole Miss as well; James "Bucky" Carter writes that, as late as 2007, fliers for his own courses on comics and young adult literature were inexplicably removed, he contends, by department faculty (Carter, 2008). The irony here, of course, as Kathleen Roeder argues, is that crafters of comics studies in America largely "fall traditionally to English departments" (Dueben, *Kathleen Roeder,* 2014).

There is a major difference in publication strategy between the United States and continental Comics Studies; art history and design flourish in both places, yet, in America, per Roeder, "you tend to be more concerned with narrative as opposed to the visual analysis of the images" (Dueben, *Kathleen Roeder,* 2014). Heer concurs but also notes that while UPM made ingress with a more traditional route, it brought in independent scholars and art historians, such as R. C. Harvey and David Kunzle, to diversify its offerings and manners of analyses. Speaking on Kunzle, Heer says: "There are a few people like David Kunzle, who did a valuable history of comics, but it's very rare for someone in art history to do comics. That's something we'll probably see more of. It's a valuable perspective we need" (Dueben, A Conversation, 2014). Walter Biggins, another former acquisitions editor for UPM, noted a distinct emphasis on biography and art history as crucial to the press's success "because that largely hadn't been done, and thus there was a need to establish a lineage, a tradition of comics that interacted with, and departed from, the worlds of literature and 'high' art" (Heer, 2013). Meanwhile, as UPM established a line of books with both names and reputation cementing a tradition,[10] Biggins expanded the offerings to ones that investigated "global issues with comics" and ones that "placed a stronger emphasis on comics theory and grammar–i.e., '"What is a comic, exactly?' 'What are its core elements, and the "rules" for using them?' 'What is comics as a form, and how is that distinct from other art forms, including those (literature and painting) with which it is forever linked?"' (Heer, 2013). As he notes, this brought American comics publishing more in line with the European model as well as firming up the American base of international scholarship with further translations of international work.

Since UPM's groundbreaking establishment of multiple Comics Studies series, other major university presses have begun to follow suit: The Ohio State University Press Studies in Comics and Cartoons (founded in 2013) proffers a "focus exclusively on comics and graphic literature, highlighting their relation to literary studies" (The Ohio State) continuing that connection to English and narratological study. Rutgers University Press has also begun a Comics Culture series (2014) looking to publish books "intended to contribute significantly to the rapidly expanding field of Comics Studies, but are also designed to appeal to comics fans and casual readers who seek smart critical engagement with the best examples of the form" (Comics Culture). Other prominent university presses such as the Pennsylvania State University, The University of Iowa, The University of Chicago, Duke University, New York University, University of Liege, University of Texas, and Yale University, regularly publish works in comic scholarship while not having an established series in place. As Biggins argues, "the publishing terrain's looking rich for comics studies," both in the present moment and certainly in the future (Heer, 2013).

From the University to the Academic Trade Presses

A great deal of that present and future, however, comes not necessarily within the university system anywhere near as much as it does with the academic trade presses. For example, Routledge, who publishes the anthology in which this essay appears, has many series that have published comics scholarship over the years across several disciplines including key texts such as the Robert Pearson and William Uricchio-edited *The Many of Lives of the Batman* (1991), Roger Sabin's *Adult Comics: An Introduction* (1993, 2010) and Angela Ndalianis' edited *The Contemporary Comic Book Superhero* (2008).

If the University Press of Mississippi is the gold standard in Comics Studies with the university community, Bloomsbury Publishing's Continuum division, formerly Continuum International Publishing Group, may be the forerunner at present, if only based upon critical remarks given to the press by professionals within the field. In shorthand, Bloomsbury acquired Continuum in 2009 while Continuum had been founded in 1999. It is by no means uncommon for larger publishing houses to acquire smaller houses; however, it does make discussion of them more difficult by comparison to university presses. While often couched under popular culture studies or literary studies, comics scholarship (housed, for the record, in the larger set of books in their Literary Studies catalogue) coming out of the Bloomsbury Publishing Group is voluminous by comparison to almost every competitor, boasting key texts (either through absorption of Continuum's catalogue or their own continued publishing) such as Geoff Klock's *How to Read Superhero Comics and Why* (2002), Rocco Versaci's *This Book Contains Graphic Language* (2007), Danny Fingeroth's *Disguised as Clark Kent* (2007), Randy Duncan and Matthew J. Smith's *The Power of Comics* (2009), Matthew Pustz's *Comic Books and American Cultural History* (2012), etc. While the names of the scholars at hand is key, Biggins reminds the reader that what makes Bloomsbury such a power press in Comics Studies is that it "consistently does interesting work [...] some scholarly, some more general-interest—and this looks to be a growing field for that press" (Heer, 2013). Bloomsbury's consistency in publication of noteworthy titles that have received critical praise elevates it among competing presses who put forth a greater volume of scholarship.

Marxist constructions of academic trade presses, as such, cannot be dismissed; a major difference that must be acknowledged between a university press and a trade press of any sort is the published book's capacity to be sold and bought by a consumer, often a lay person to the subject matter. A university press can, to some extent or another, publish at a fiscal loss bolstered by a university system with a variety of funds and endowments helping to secure the bottom line, or as Peter Givler put it, "university presses [are] an indispensable component of the modern research university itself [...] Commercial publishing [is] a highly competitive business" (2002). Accordingly, the trade press must actually *sell* its product.

One of the most prominent trade presses equaling (if not surpassing) the output of the Bloomsbury group and rising in academic prestige is McFarland and Company.[11]

The Jefferson, North Carolina, press was founded in 1979 and is particularly renowned for its work in pop culture studies; the work in their dedicated series in graphic novels has become increasingly and regularly recognized by Eisner Award nominations in recent years. Works such as Sarah Lightman's *Graphic Details: Jewish Women's Confessional Comics in Essays and Interviews* (2014), Nathan Vernon Madison's *Anti-Foreign Imagery in American Pulps and Comic Books, 1920–1960* (2013), and Joseph Darowski's ever-expanding set of *The Ages of...* anthologies (*Superman* [2012], *Wonder Woman* [2013], *X-Men* [2014], *Avengers* [2014], *Iron Man* [2015]) have become increasingly noteworthy to the prizing community in addition to being recognized as prestige scholarship coming out of a traditionally recognized trade house. Most recently, this has culminated with McFarland and Company's first Eisner win for Sarah Lightman's *Graphic Details: Jewish Women's Confessional Comics in Essays and Interviews* in 2015.

The Independent and Comics Presses

One of the distinct advantages Comics Studies seems to offer scholars comes in its inherent connection to popular culture *and* literary studies; this connection to more established academic fields opens avenues to presses that were once considered "intermediate" by standards of academic *rigour* in matters such as the acquisition of tenure and promotion. While popular academic columnists such as Karen Kelsky oft pooh-pooh trade presses "like Ashgate, Rowman and Littlefield, and Palgrave [Macmillian] and so on" as being of "an indeterminate rank and will count at some universities and departments more highly than at others," their earned cache in popular and cultural studies has made them prestige presses within the field of Comic Studies (Kelsky, 2012). Or, as Tanya Maria Golash-Boza contextualizes the debate between the university press and the academic trade press with a bit more context:

> In addition to university presses, there are trade academic presses such as Routledge, Rowman and Littlefield, Palgrave Macmillan, [...] Whether or not you should publish in these presses depends a lot on your field and your department. In some departments, these presses are seen as not as prestigious as the university presses, and any university press would be better. However, in other fields, it does not make a difference, and a book with one of these presses is perfectly fine. (2012)

While it might seem somewhat odd to devote a distinct amount of time and space to the decision of whether to publish within the university system or the many further presses who publish academic fare, as Philip Nel, author of the Eisner Award-nominated *Crockett Johnson & Ruth Krauss: How an Unlikely Couple Found Love, Dodged the FBI, and Transformed Children's Literature* (UP Mississippi, 2012), puts it: "in academe, publications are the coin of the realm, and we academics get to print our own money. There's pocket change [and] there are the Really Big Bank Notes—books. The book increases your cultural capital more than any other kind of publication" (2010). Within the distinct market of Comics Studies, academic trade publications not only help establish and build up a relatively young field with a greater and more distinct collection of material, but they provide the mechanisms for working academics to continue to ply their trade in the industry.

Likewise, as Nel notes, one of the more unique facets of Comic Studies is that scholars working within the field are often called upon to edit or collaborate with professionals within the comics industry to do archival work. Nel, while working on the aforementioned autobiography of Crocket Johnson, began to work with Eric Reynolds, series editor at Fantagraphics Books,[12] the Seattle-based publishers of alternative comics and graphic novels since 1976, on a series of anthologies collecting the classic Johnson strip *Barnaby* in 2012 (Cushlamochree! 2010). Such anthologizing and historical editing of classic comics, particularly newspaper comics strips, that are either out-of-print or relegated to microfiche is as much an academic process as crafting histories and argumentative pieces, and it is not uncommon in any way for a company such as IDW, Sunday Press Books, or Fantagraphics to hire an established scholar such as Heer or Charles Hatfield to serve as an editor of an archival collection. Fantagraphics has made quite an impact in this regard, publishing archival series of classic comic strips such as *Pogo* (2011–), *Peanuts* (2004–), *Dennis the Menace* (2005–), etc. They are by no means the first to participate in this tradition as, to examine the list of publishers connected with Walt Kelly's *Pogo*, for example, yields a collection of houses big and small ranging from Crest Books (1964) to Andrews McMeel (1976) to Spring Hollow (various points, most recently 2001), before landing at Fantagraphics. The difference between a smaller press such as Fantagraphics and myriad other presses, in terms of academic publication, generally comes not just in the academic prestige associated with its name (A Short History, 2015)[13] but in the consistent quality of the product the press turns out over its history.

Some of those histories, themselves, are worthy of academic study. One such case, *Drawn and Quarterly: Twenty-five Years of Contemporary Cartooning, Comics, and Graphic Novels* (Drawn and Quarterly, 2015), edited by Tom Devlin, celebrated the Montreal-based micro-press's 25 years of publishing under the eye Chris Oliveros. Not unlike Fantagraphics, Drawn and Quarterly's successes largely come from the repository of comics they produced of remarkable quality, both in art and artifact, lauded by experts like Heer and Canadian scholar Bart Beaty; likewise, their dedication to publishing archival work of artists like Chester Brown and Chris Ware, who came to international acclaim through original publication with the house. Similarly, San Diego-based IDW, founded in the same year as Drawn and Quarterly by Ted Adams and Robbie Robbins (both 1999), publishes both creative and academic content by way of renowned collections such as *The Library of American Comics* imprint. Chronicling everything from *The Amazing Spider-Man* newspaper strips by Stan Lee and John Romita to the work of Chester Gould (most notably *Dick Tracy*) and Archie Comics, IDW, as much as it collects comics for the consumer, collects a bevy of prominent academics to edit and anthologize work that might otherwise not be available to a consumer short of a visit to a museum or rare books auction. As much as any academic project, the collection of rare comics manuscripts remains as prominent a piece of Comics Studies as anything else. And this discussion could not be closed without consideration of presses like Sequart (founded in 1996), which blurs lines between academic studies and fandom as part and parcel to its editorial policy as a mission statement. Who in this case, scholar or fan, is the actual expert is of less interest than producing scholarship that can be read by everyone to increase the greater knowledge of comics for any who would seek it.

At essay's end, it is difficult to conclude with so much that *has not* been covered. Where are the mentions of presses such as Basic Books, Fireside Books, or Pantheon who have put forth critical volumes? How can one discuss the history of comics presses without mentioning seminal titles such as Douglas Wolk's *Reading Comics and What They Mean* (Da Capo Press, 2007) or *From "Aargh!" to "Zap!": Harvey Kurtzman's Visual History of the Comics*

(Prentice Hall Press, 1991, edited by Howard Zimmerman)? In the annals and collections of the hundreds and thousands of comics writers, scholars, historians, and librarians, with a "publishable" history that could, arguably stretch back to the sequential depictions seen in Egyptian hieroglyphs, Trajan's Column, or endless Greek friezes—some names will be lost. Or, at the very least, they will not fit into this essay's word count. However, that speaks only to the increasing depth of field that Comics Studies approaches; this essay is the beginning of a conversation that must continue as the discourse field expands into brave new territories. Much of the discussion here has covered known topics such as literary history, narratology, and art design, yet the future of academic publishing in Comic Studies continues to branch out in expansive manners and considerations such as educational theory (Dale Jacobs), composition studies (Gunther Kress), and, perhaps most prominently, cognitive linguistics when academics like Neil Cohn are researching the idea of comics as a language unto itself. In a field that once struggled to gain foothold in the halls of the academy, now, the study of comics has become something one could major in at the baccalaureate level in America (University of Florida) or visit in several museums (notably, the Billy Ireland Cartoon Library and Museum at the Ohio State University) dedicated to the art form.

Notes

1 And it would not be publicly denounced as untrue possessing "manipulated, overstated, compromised, and fabricated evidence," until 2012 by Carol Tilley, a contributor to this volume, in her landmark essay "Seducing the Innocent: Fredric Wertham and the Falsifications that Helped Condemn Comics."
2 Arguably, an even more important publication from his era is Reinhold Reitberger and Wolfgang Fuchs (1972) *Comics: Anatomy of a Mass Medium*, New York: Little Brown & Co. It is one of the earliest academic studies to appear in English.
3 Now with well more than 40 annual editions, the *Overstreet Comics Price Guide* was acquired by another publisher, Gemstone, in 1994.
4 Astoundingly, there are earlier dissertations connected to comics scholarship such as Etta Karp's *Crime Comic Book Role Preferences* (1954) and Sol Davidson's 1959 work *Culture & the Comic Strips*–both from New York University. There are earlier studies still: William Drummond's Master's Thesis: *Comic Book Reading in the Secondary Schools of a Rural Community* (1948) among them, but the prestige accorded to the University of Chicago not just nationally but globally separates it from most other institutions by the parameters this essay establishes for inclusion.
5 The title, itself, is a homage to Marshall McLuhan's 1964 study *Understanding Media: The Extensions of Man*, New York: McGraw-Hill.
6 Later Paradox Press and Kitchen Sink also in 1993 and HarperCollins in 2004.
7 This might be a good place to note comics' own equivalent to the major prizing and awards celebration, the annual Will Eisner Comic Industry Awards, first conferred in 1988; academically, the Eisner's awarded books in the categories of Archival Projects (comics strips) and Comics-Related Publication for a momentary period before moving toward more fixed categories of Best Archival Collection/Project - Comic Books, Best Archival Collection/Project - Comic Strips, Best Comics-Related Book, and Best Educational and/or Academic Work.
8 A major caveat, University of California Press published an impressive study of early comic strip history covering a remarkable timespan of nearly 400 years with David Kunzle's (1973) *The Early Comic Strip: Narrative Strips and Picture Stories in the European Broadstreet from c.1450–1825*, Berkley: University of California Press.
9 This is not to be confused with Franco-Belgian publishers of comics, of which there are considerable numbers such as *La Martinière Groupe* (1993), particularly since their acquisition of Abrams Books in 1997; Futuropolis, which began in the 1972 as a bookstore, published comics outright in the 1980s under Robial and Florence Cestac, and is the direct predecessor of *L'Association* before going moribund and being reinvigorated recently as a direct antagonist to the that press; *Skira Flammarion,* A French arm of the Swiss Skira press; and, of course, *Presses Universitaires de*

France—The French university system's publishing arm founded well back in 1921 in addition to several other prominent presses and houses connected with institutions (Such as CNBDI: The National Center of Comics and the Image).
10 And, as quickly as a prized tradition could commence, UPM was at the head of the awards community: when the Eisner's began accepting nominations for their new category of Best Scholarly/ Academic Work" in 2011, UPM authors Charles Hatfield and Susan E. Kirtley took home the award in consecutive years for *Hand of Fire: The Comics Art of Jack Kirby* (2012) and *Lynda Berry: Girlhood Through the Looking Glass* (2013).
11 Full disclosure: I have published two anthologies with McFarland and Company.
12 And prizers in their own right: Fantagraphics helped construct and manage the Jack Kirby Awards, a predecessor of a sort to the Eisner's, from 1985–1987, and after those awards ended, founded the Harvey Awards under Gary Groth, then the president of Fantagraphics Books (Newswatch, 1988).
13 Besides being a forerunner in underground comix and connected to some of the foremost names within the industry, Fantagraphics has been the publisher of the vaunted *The Comics Journal*, a critical trade magazine on the industry, since 1976. Additionally, the press has been ranked as one of the "five most influential publishers in the history of comics" for its myriad venues of work both critical and creative (A Short History, 2015).
14 However a few languages such as Spanish, French or German may have somehow a slightly higher chance to be read by the Anglophone scholars.
15 Of 46 English language books on comics of 2014 in the Bonn Online-Bibliography almost a third (13) is dedicated solely to superheroes, various (6) focus on social issues (such as representation of 'minorities'), or (5) are dedicated to only one creator.

Bibliography

A Guide to the Thomas Inge Papers, 1879–2001. (2003) Available from: http://ead.lib.virginia.edu/vivaxtf/view?docId=vcu-cab/vircu00103.xml;query=.
A Short History. (2015) [Online] Available from: http://fantagraphics.com/flog/about-us/.
Carter, J.B. (2008) *The University of Stupid Mississippi.* [Online] Available from: http://ensaneworld.blogspot.com/2008/08/university-of-stupid-mississippi.html. [Accessed 5 August 2008].
Comics Culture. [Online] Available from: http://rutgerspress.rutgers.edu/pages/seriesdescription.aspx#Comics_Culture. [Accessed 2 August 2015].
Cushlamochree! Fantagraphics Nabs Collected Barnaby; Dan Clowes To Design Long-Anticipated Project. (2010) [Online] Available from: http://www.comicsreporter.com/index.php/fantagraphics_signs_complete_barnaby/. [Accessed 3 December 2010].
Devlin, T. (2015) *Drawn and Quarterly: twenty-five years of contemporary cartooning, comics, and graphic novels,* Montréal, Québec: Drawn and Quarterly.
Dueben, A. (2014a) *A Conversation with Jeet Heer.* [Online] Available from: http://www.tcj.com/a-conversation-with-jeet-heer/. [Accessed 13 October 2014].
Dueben, A. (2014b) *Kathleen Roeder is "Wide Awake in Slumberland."* [Online] Available from: http://www.comicbookresources.com/?page=article&id=54054. [Accessed 15 July 2014].
Duncan, R., Smith, M.J. and Levitz, P. (2015) *The Power of Comics.* 2nd edn., New York: Bloomsbury.
Givler, P. (2002) *University Press Publishing in the United States.* [Online] Available from: http://www.aaupnet.org/about-aaup/about-university-presses/history-of-university-presses.
Golash-Boza, T.M. (2012) *How to Publish an Academic Book—Why Choosing a Publisher Is Important and How to Choose One.* [Online] Available from: http://getalifephd.blogspot.com/2012/04/how-to-publish-academic-book-why.html. [Accessed 21 April 2012].
Heer, J. (2008) *The Rise of Comics Scholarship: the role of University Press of Mississippi.* [Online] Available from: https://sanseverything.wordpress.com/2008/08/02/the-rise-of-comics-scholarship-the-role-of-university-press-of-mississippi/. [Accessed 2 August 2008].
Heer, J. (2013) *An Interview with Walter Biggins.* [Online] Available From: http://www.tcj.com/an-interview-with-walter-biggins/. [Accessed 8 March 2013].

Kelsky, K. (2012) *Does the Status of the Press Matter?* [Online] Available from: http://theprofessorisin.com/2012/09/21/does-the-status-of-the-press-matter/. [Accessed 21 September 2012].
Kidd, K. (2007) 'Prizing children's literature: the case of Newbery Gold', *Children's Literature*, 35: 166–90.
Meet the Press. [Online] Available from: http://www.upress.state.ms.us/about. [Accessed 2 August 2015].
Miller, J. (2005) *The 1900s: The Century in Comics*. [Online] Available from: http://www.cbgxtra.com/knowledge-base/for-your-reference/the-1900s-the-century-in-comics. [Accessed 12 December 2005].
Nel, P. (2010) *How to Publish Your Book; or The Little Manuscript That Could*. [Online] Available from: ttp://www.philnel.com/2010/08/11/how-to-publish-your-book/. [Accessed 11 August 2010].
Newswatch: Kirby Awards End in Controversy. (1988) *The Comics Journal*, 122: 19–20.
Scoop. (2015) *The Semi-Secret Origins of the Overstreet Comic Book Price Guide*. [Online] Available from: http://scoop.diamondgalleries.com/Home/4/1/73/1017?articleID=42897. [Accessed 2 August 2015].
The Ohio State University Press. [Online] Available from: https://ohiostatepress.org/index.htm?/books/series%20pages/scc.htm. [Accessed 2 August 2015].
Tilley, C. (2012) 'Seducing the innocent: Fredric Wertham and the falsifications that helped condemn comics', *Information & Culture: A Journal of History*, 47 (4): 383–413.

A PIONEER'S PERSPECTIVE: PASCAL LEFÈVRE

Anno 2015, the academic study related to graphic narratives bears some striking features. First, due to the widespread use of English as *lingua franca* in academic publishing and the dominant position of Anglophone academic publishers, non-native English academia and its presses are to various degrees disadvantaged. In general, scholars who do not publish in English will largely remain under the radar of the English speaking academics, because they usually don't make the effort to learn other languages or take into consideration non-English sources.[14] The consequence is that scholars publishing in other languages (and whose work isn't translated into English) will generally not be read, will not be studied, and will not be cited within the dominant Anglophone academic publishing area. For evidence one can look at the bibliographies or notes of English language publications on graphic narratives—exceptions are, of course, English publications (like in the work of John Lent, Mark McKinney, or Ana Merino) that are dealing with productions of other countries (like France or Mexico). The citation impact (for instance measured by *h*-index) plays nowadays an increasing role in the career of a scholar, so the unbalanced condition is becoming a vicious circle in which English language scholars are enjoying many advantages and the others foremost disadvantages.

Concerning graphic narratives some countries have a more developed production or tradition, so there is often a correlation between the amount and the prestige of the (national) production and of the academic study in that country. This brings along a second striking feature of the academic study of graphic narratives, which remains, figuratively spoken, till today foremost a collection of "islands," each being dedicated to a specific part of a local production. Some islands such as the superhero studies are,

(Continued)

comparatively, extremely expanded.[15] Maybe the articles in English academic journals offer a more nuanced portrait. Most academic studies, also outside the Anglophone area, are still strongly tied to the production within a particular language or country.

This restricted perspective is a partly distorting one, because as the scarce comparative research has shown, there are often a lot of transnational evolutions in the field of graphic narratives. It started already in the nineteenth century with the influence of European—and especially German—graphic culture on the development of the American illustrated journals and of the comic strips in the newspapers. Later, after the boom of comic strips in the U S, conversely the North American production was strongly influential on the European production: not only were some characters such as *Mickey Mouse* widely enjoyed, but also specific genres or graphic styles and the concept of the speech balloon were copied or transformed and incorporated in the European production—especially from the 1930s on (with a brief interruption during the war). Various publication formats crossed borders: think for instance of the adoption of the Japanese reading direction in Western translations of manga (since the late 1990s various Western countries publish translations of manga in the Japanese reading direction—thus from right to left). While the Japanese and the North American graphic narratives market are rather oriented toward their own national production, various markets of continental European countries offer a more diverse composition regarding the origin of the published graphic narratives. For example, in 2014 more than half of the published comics (5410) in France had a foreign origin: in total 31 different countries, but some countries are already quantitatively more important than others. Translations of Japanese manga account for almost 38% of the French titles; translations of American comics (80% of them being superheroes) take about 10% of the titles launched on the French market.

So, there are urgent and heavily weighted reasons to take comparative research more seriously. Certainly, there are collaborations over borders, like books or conferences with an international gathering of academics from various countries, but seldom do we see an intensive collaboration and interaction.

However, as the scope of comparative approaches is generally quite broad, the risk of dilettantism is lurking. Every artifact contains to a certain degree a lot of references to its own culture, which may not be well understood by outsiders. For this reason I've argued already at the Kyoto conference of 2009 (*Comics Worlds & the World of Comics: Towards Scholarship on a Global Scale*) that international teams of researchers should collaborate on the same topics (Lefèvre, 2010). Such international collaborations are in other research domains (like psychology) already quite common, but in the field of graphic narratives—where single author articles are dominating—they remain extremely scarce. Of course international collaboration and comparative studies are challenging, because they pose several problems, but never before were the conditions so affordable (easy and cheap international travel and communication means like email, Skype, etc.). I'm convinced that such international collaboration will even foster a better and more explicit methodology of research in the field of graphic narratives; if you're working in such a diverse team an unambiguous methodology is necessary and evident.

In the end, we will get a better understanding of the development of graphic narratives worldwide through history. We will be able to understand, for instance, the similarities and differences of particular genres (like the Western) across borders. As I stated earlier at the Kyoto conference: *"To learn more about ourselves, we will have to cross borders!"* (Lefèvre, 2010, p. 88).

Bibliography

Lefèvre, P. (2010) 'Researching comics on a global scale', in J. Berndt (ed.) *Global Manga Studies, Vol. 1 Kyoto Conference Proceedings Comics Worlds and the World of Comics: towards scholarship on a global scale*, Kyoto: International Manga Research Center. Also available online http://imrc.jp/2010/09/26/20100924Comics%20Worlds%20and%20the%20World%20of%20Comics.pdf.

Ratier, G. (2014) 2014 - L'année de contradictions [Online] Available from: www.acbd.fr/wp-content/uploads/2014/12RapportRatier_ABCD2014.pdf. [Accessed 26 May 2015].

CONTRIBUTORS

José Alaniz, Associate Professor in the Department of Slavic Languages and Literatures and the Department of Comparative Literature (adjunct) at the University of Washington-Seattle, published *Komiks: Comic Art in Russia* (2010) and *Death, Disability and the Superhero: The Silver Age and Beyond* (2014), both with the University Press of Mississippi. He chairs the Executive Committee of the International Comic Arts Forum.

Kane Anderson (Ph.D., University of California at Santa Barbara) is a Murphy Visiting Fellow in Literature and Language at Hendrix College where he teaches courses in acting, directing, and theatre. His scholarly research looks at the intersections of performance and popular culture and includes the results of his ethnographic studies of cosplayers at Comic-Con International and superhero-themed gay events.

Jaqueline Berndt is Professor of Japanese Language and Culture at Stockholm University and, until March 2017, Professor of Comics Theory at the Graduate School of Manga, Kyoto Seika University, Japan. Her publications include the co-edited volume *Manga's Cultural Crossroads* (2013) as well as the monographs *Phänomen Manga* (1995) and *Manga: Medium, Art and Material* (2015). See also: http://kyoto-seika.academia.edu/JaquelineBerndt.

Christina Blanch has taught courses to various audiences both on campus and online, most recently teaching two massive, open, online courses through Ball State and Canvas about comics to over 11,000 students. In addition to publishing chapters in *The Comics of Joss Whedon* and *Graphic Novels in the Classroom*, she also writes the comic book *The Damnation of Charlie Wormwood* as well as other comics. She is currently finishing her dissertation in Ball State University's Educational Studies program, researching the personal and professional identities of comic scholars.

James "Bucky" Carter studied the intersections of comics and literacy while teaching at the University of Southern Mississippi, the University of Texas at El Paso (UTEP), and Washington State University. He founded *SANE Journal: Sequential Art Narrative in Education*.

Among his publications are two edited collections on comics and pedagogy: *Building Literacy Connections with Graphic Novels* and *Rationales for Teaching Graphic Novels*.

Peter M. Coogan is the director of the Institute for Comics Studies, co-founder of the Comics Arts Conference, and author of *Superhero: The Secret Origin of a Genre*. He teaches comics, superheroes, and visual literacy at Washington University in St. Louis, where he also works as the Communication Lab Coordinator in the Brown School of Social Work.

Beth Davies-Stofka (Ph.D., University of Toronto) is Chair of Liberal Studies and College Prep at Colorado Community Colleges Online, teaching courses in religion and philosophy. She also serves as Adjunct Faculty in the Master of Arts in Liberal Studies program at Excelsior College in New York, where she teaches courses in globalization, culture, and conflict resolution. She is actively involved in social justice programs, focusing on hunger and clean water initiatives, and providing help for people rescued from modern-day slavery.

Julie Davis (Ph.D., University of Kansas) is an Associate Professor in the Department of Communication at the College of Charleston, Charleston, South Carolina. She has written about such popular culture icons as Dilbert, Scooby-Doo, and various Marvel superheroes. Her research also examines sport rhetoric and organizational crisis. E-mail: davisj@cofc.edu.

Randy Duncan is Professor of Communication and Director of the Comics Studies Minor at Henderson State University. He is co-editor, with Matthew J. Smith, of the Eisner-nominated *Critical Approaches to Comics: Theories and Methods*. He is a co-founder, with Peter M. Coogan, of the Comics Arts Conference and received the Inkpot Award for contributions to Comics Studies.

Wolfgang J. Fuchs, M.A., co-authored *Comics: Anatomy of a Mass Medium* which gave an important impetus to the appreciation and study of comics. Fuchs contributed to Maurice Horn's *World Encyclopedia of Comics* and to Jerry Bails' *The Who's Who of American Comic Books*. Among his own works are an "autobiography" of Mickey Mouse and contributions to radio, TV and print media in various capacities and countries. He also is the German translator of *Prince Valiant* and *Garfield*.

Ian Gordon is a cultural historian at the National University of Singapore where he is the Convenor of American Studies. His latest book is *Superman: The Persistence of an American Icon*.

Ian Hague is a Lecturer in Contextual and Theoretical Studies at the University of the Arts, London. His main research interests include materiality, sensory theory, and comics and graphic novels. He is the author of *Comics and the Senses: A Multisensory Approach to Comics and Graphic Novels* (2014) and the co-editor of *Representing Multiculturalism in Comics and Graphic Novels* (2015), as well as being the founder of Comics Forum (www.comicsforum.org). His most recent research concerns the materiality of digital media. For more information please see www.ianhague.com.

Charles Hatfield, Professor of English at California State University, Northridge, is author of *Alternative Comics* (2005), *Hand of Fire: The Comics Art of Jack Kirby* (2012), and many articles and book chapters; co-editor of *The Superhero Reader* (2013); and founding President of the Comics Studies Society. He has been active in Comics Studies since the mid-1990s, presenting papers, moderating panels, and organizing events for the Popular Culture Association, the Comic Arts Conference, the International Comic Arts Forum, the Modern Language Association, and other conferences.

Maurice Horn is the editor of *The World Encyclopedia of Comics*, *The World Encyclopedia of Cartoons*, *100 Years of American Newspaper Comics* and of the multi-volume *Contemporary Graphic Artists*. He is co-author of *A History of the Comic Strip* and author of *75 Years of the Comics*, *Women in the Comics*, *Sex in the Comics* and *Comics of the American West*.

Ian Horton is a Senior Lecturer at London College of Communication, University of the Arts London. His Ph.D. focused on the codification of British architectural education and issues of national identity. His present research is focused in three related areas: experimental typography, Dutch graphic design, and comic books. He has published work on oral history and text-based public art; multiculturalism and stereotypes in comic books and British war comics. He is currently working on a book about the Dutch graphic design group Hard Werken to be published in Spring 2017.

Alec R. Hosterman (Ph.D., Texas Tech University) is an Assistant Professor of Communication Studies at Longwood University. He teaches courses in public relations, social media, and visual communication. Alec is a prolific consumer of pop culture and longtime photographer.

M. Thomas Inge is the Blackwell Professor of Humanities at Randolph-Macon College in Ashland, Virginia, where he writes and teaches about American humor, animation, graphic narrative, Southern culture, Walt Disney, and William Faulkner. His latest book is *The Dixie Limited: Writers on William Faulkner and His Influence*. Inge serves as the general editor of two series of books from the University Press of Mississippi: "Great Comic Artists" and "Conversations with Comic Artists."

Henry Jenkins is the Provost's Professor of Communication, Journalism, Cinematic Arts, and Education at the University of Southern California. He is the author and/or editor of 15 books on various aspects of media and popular culture.

David Kunzle, educated at Cambridge and London Universities, since 1965 has taught in the US, since 1977 as Professor of the History of Art at UCLA. His books include a two volume *History of the Comic Strip* (1456–1825, 1826–1896); *Posters of Protest; Murals of Revolutionary Nicaragua; Che Guevara Icon, Myth and Message*; and *From Criminal to Courtier: the Soldier in Netherlandish Art* 1550–1672. His *Fashion and Fetishism* (2004) is going into a Chinese edition. His recent books are two on R. Töpffer—a monograph and a facsimile edition, with complete translation of the complete comic strips—and one on the comic strips of Gustave Doré. Just out in three languages: *Chesucristo, the Fusion in Word and Image of Che Guevara and Jesus Christ*.

Travis Langley is a Psychology Professor at Henderson State University. He authored the book *Batman and Psychology: A Dark and Stormy Knight*. He edits and writes for books including *The Walking Dead Psychology: Psych of the Living Dead*; *Wonder Woman Psychology: Lassoing the Truth*; and *Captain America vs. Iron Man: Freedom, Security, Psychology*. *Psychology Today* carries his blog, "Beyond Heroes and Villains," and he is one of the ten most popular psychologists on Twitter (@Superherologist).

Jeremy Larance is Chair of the Department of Humanities at West Liberty University where he teaches classes on British literature, sports literature, and comics. His publications include essays on the symbolism of the English cricketer and the influence of Alan Moore's early works on the Modern Age of comics. Kimota!

Pascal Lefèvre is special guest Professor in the arts at LUCA School of Arts, campus Sint-Lukas Brussel & KU Leuven (Belgium). He has published in eight different languages and on graphic narratives from various national productions (especially Belgium, France, US and Japan). For an overview of his work, see sites.google.com/site/lefevrepascal/home.

John A. Lent is founding publisher/editor-in-chief of *International Journal of Comic Art*, author or editor of 80 books/monographs, and for long terms edited *Berita* and *Asian Cinema* and chaired international popular culture, comics, film, and Malaysian studies groups, all of which he founded. He retired as Professor Emeritus after 51 years teaching in universities in the US, Canada, Malaysia, China, and the Philippines.

A. David Lewis is a Faculty Associate with MCPHS University where he teaches an array of Humanities electives including "Comic Books and Cancer" and "Islam in Contemporary Fiction." He is co-editor of *Graven Images: Religion in Comic Books and Graphic Novels*, *Digital Death: Mortality and Beyond in the Online Age*, and *Muslim Superheroes: Comics, Islam, and Representation*. His *American Comics, Literary Theory, and Religion: The Superhero Afterlife* was nominated for a Will Eisner Comics Industry Award, and he is an Executive Board member of the Comics Studies Society. Lewis is a founding member of Sacred & Sequential, an Editorial Board member of both *INKS* and *The International Journal of Comic Art (IJoCA)*, and a graphic novelist.

David McConeghy is an independent scholar living in Massachusetts. He holds a Ph.D. in Religious Studies from the University of California, Santa Barbara and has taught World Religions at Chapman University. He is an active member of the American Academy of Religion's Religion and Science Fiction Group and Teaching Religion Section.

Gert Meesters is Associate Professor of Dutch language and culture at the University of Lille, France. He holds a Ph.D. in Dutch linguistics from the University of Leuven and is a founding member of the Liège-based comics research group Acme. He co-edited *L'Association, une utopie éditoriale et esthétique* (2011) and *Comics in Dissent: Independence, Alternative, Self-publishing* (2014). Most of his most recent articles are based on case studies of comics by Brecht Evens and Olivier Schrauwen.

Ann Miller is a University Fellow at the University of Leicester, where she was formerly Director of Studies for French. She is the author of *Reading Bande Dessinée: Critical Approaches to French-Language Comic Strip* (Intellect, 2007), and co-editor of *Textual* *and Visual Selves* (2011) and *The French Comics Theory Reader* (2014). She is co-editor of *European Comic Art*.

Kim Munson is an art historian based in the San Francisco Bay Area. She is the author of *Dual Views: Labor Landmarks of San Francisco, On Reflection: The Art of Margaret Harrison*, and several articles on comic art and exhibitions.

Chris Murray is a Senior Lecturer in Comics Studies at the School of Humanities, University of Dundee. He is course leader of the Masters in Comics and Graphic Novels (MLitt) and Director of the Scottish Centre for Comics Studies and Dundee Comics Creative Space. He is co-editor of Studies in Comics and UniVerse Comics. Dr. Murray is author of several articles and chapters on British and American comics, horror comics, and on the work of Grant Morrison and Alan Moore. He has written two books, *Champions of the Oppressed: Superhero Comics, Popular Culture* and *Propaganda in America During World War Two* (2011) and *The British Superhero* (forthcoming 2017).

Barbara Postema is an Assistant Professor at Concordia University, where she teaches contemporary literature and comics. She is working on a book about silent comics. Her monograph *Narrative Structure in Comics* came out in 2013, and she has published articles in *Image & Narrative*, the *Journal of Graphic Novels and Comics*, and elsewhere.

William Proctor is a Lecturer in media, culture and communication at Bournemouth University, UK. He is currently writing a single-authored monograph on comic book and film reboots for Palgrave Macmillan (2017). William has written on various topics such as The Walking Dead, Batman, Spider-Man and Star Wars. He is co-editor of the forthcoming anthologies, *The Scandinavian Invasion: Critical Perspectives on Nordic Noir* (2017), the two-volume *Disney's Star Wars* (2017) and *Transmedia Earth: Critical Perspectives in Global Convergence Cultures* (2017). William is Director of 'The World Star Wars Project'.

Brad Ricca is a SAGES Fellow at Case Western Reserve University, where he earned his Ph.D. in English. He is the author of the award-winning *Super Boys: The Amazing Adventures of Jerry Siegel and Joe Shuster – The Creators of Superman* (2013).

Jenny Robb is Curator and Associate Professor of The Ohio State University Billy Ireland Cartoon Library & Museum, the largest academic research institution dedicated to cartoons and comics. Before coming to Ohio State in 2005, she served as Curator of the Cartoon Art Museum in San Francisco for 5 years. She holds masters' degrees in History and Museum Studies from Syracuse University.

Julia Round (MA, Ph.D.) is a Principal Lecturer in the Faculty of Media and Communication at Bournemouth University, UK, and co-edits the academic journal *Studies in Comics* (Intellect). Her research and teaching interests include gothic, comics, adaptation and children's literature. She has recently published a monograph entitled *Gothic in Comics and Graphic Novels: A Critical Approach* (2014) and the co-edited collection *Real Lives Celebrity Stories* (2014). For further details please visit www.juliaround.com.

Matthew J. Smith is Professor and Director in the School of Communication at Radford University in Virginia. Along with Randy Duncan, he is co-editor of Routledge's Advances in Comics Studies series. Previously, the two writing partners teamed with former DC Comic President and Publisher Paul Levitz to produce *The Power of Comics: History, Form, and Culture (2nd ed.)*.

Joseph Michael Sommers is an Associate Professor of English at Central Michigan University where he teaches coursework and publishes in children's and young adult literature, Comics Studies, and popular culture. Some of his works include *Sexual Ideology in the Works of Alan Moore*, *Game on Hollywood: Essays on the Intersection of Video Game and Cinema*, and *The American Comic Book*. He has several book length projects forthcoming on the life and art of Neil Gaiman.

Nicholas A. Theisen teaches rhetoric at the University of Iowa. He is recently the author of *[Comics] as Reading, or A Theory of Alternate Textuality* and is the sole proprietor of the weblog What is Manga?, where he posts essays on Japanese comics as well as translations of comics from Japan's prewar/kindai era.

Carol L. Tilley is an Associate Professor in the School of Information Sciences at the University of Illinois, where she teaches classes on youth services librarianship, media literacy, and comics reader's advisory. Her current research focuses on how young people in the United States engaged with comics in the mid-twentieth century.

Waldomiro Vergueiro is Professor of the Escola de Comunicações e Artes of Universidade de São Paulo (ECA-USP) in Brazil. He holds a master's and doctoral degrees in Communication Sciences and is founder and coordinator of the Laboratório de Histórias em Quadrinhos (Laboratory of Comics) of ECA-USP, a research center on comics culture. He has been teaching and researching on comics since 1983, having several articles and books published in Brazil and abroad. He is also editor of the electronic journal *9a Arte* (9th Art), founded in 2012, and a member of the international committee of the *International Journal of Comic Arts*.

Robert G. Weiner is Popular Culture/Humanities Librarian at Texas Tech University Library. He is the co-editor of the *The Joker: A Serious Study of the Clown Prince of Crime* and *Graphic Novels and Comics in the Classroom: Essays on the Educational Power of Sequential Art*. He lives in Lubbock with a couple of prairie dogs named Lee and Kirby. He has published on a wide variety of popular culture topics.

Robert Westerfelhaus (Ph.D., Ohio University, 1999) is an Associate Professor in the Department of Communication at the College of Charleston, Charleston, South Carolina. He has also written about popular culture icons in film, television, and comic art form, including Marvel superheroes, Scooby-Doo and *Fight Club*. E-mail: westerfelhausr@cofc.edu

INDEX

100 Bullets 96
24 Hour Comics Day 257
99, The 115

Abbott, Lawrence L. 93
Abel, Jessica 30, 136, 143–5, 147
Abrahams, Roger D. 138
abstract comics 29
Academy of Comic Book Arts and Sciences (ACBAS) 207
aca-fan 250, 256–7
Action Comics 6, 121, 164
Adams, Neal 207
Adams, Ted 278
Ahmed, Maaheen 251
Alaniz, José 125–8
Albaih, Khalid 267
Aldridge, Alan. xvi
Alexander, F. O. 228
Alf, Richard 256
Alley Awards 207
Alloway, Lawrence 231
Alter Ego xiii, 35–6
alternative comics 23, 139
Amar Chitra Katha 113
American Monomyth 108–9
American Studies Association 254, 260
Anderson, Carl 228
Andrae, Thomas 15–16, 39, 123–4, 128
Angoulême International Comics Festival 206, 238, 255
Aniwa, Jun 240
Anno, Hideaki 240
Anselmo, Zilda Augusta 27
Araújo, Francisco 26

Archie 71
Archie Comics 13
Argosy Price Guide 272
Aristotle 9
Arrhenius, Lars 239
Arriola, Gus 265
Art Bubble Festival 257
Asad, Talal 114
Astérix 101
Ault, Donald xxv, 15–16, 208, 212, 216, 248, 268
autobiographical comics 179, 222
Avatar 114
Aveline, Franck 265
Avengers 122

B., David 127
Baetens, Jan 95–7, 153–4, 158, 249
Bails, Jerry 35–6, 272
Baker, Kenneth 267
bande dessinée 40–1, 54, 59–60, 95, 269
Bande Dessinée et Figuration Narrative xv–xvi, 55, 58, 206, 229
Barker, Martin 18–19, 63, 125, 128, 174–7, 248–9
Barks, Carl 15–16, 39–40, 123, 248
Baroni, Raphaël 95
Barrier, Michael 125
Barry, Lynda 94, 97, 145–7, 181, 164
Barthes, Roland 94, 107, 247
Bartual, Roberto 254, 257
Baskind, Samantha 111
Batman (1966 TV series) xiii, 167, 185
Batman (1989) 168
Batman xxiii, 13, 16, 39–40, 50, 122, 126, 139, 167–8, 170, 183–4, 186, 215–16
Batwoman 185

Bayeux Tapestry 56, 60, 119, 140
Beaty, Bart xxiv, 57, 64, 93, 129, 134, 236–7, 264, 278
Bechdel, Alison 181, 183, 264
Becker, Stephen 131
Beetle Bailey 81, 135, 232
Belgian Center for Comic Strip Art 83
Bell, John 83
Benayoun, Robert. 101
Bender, H. Eric 170
Berenstein, Ofer 257–8
Berger, Arthur Asa xvi–xvii, xxiii, 118–19, 122–3, 127–8, 248, 261
Berger, James 127
Berger, John 141
Berkeley Con 1973 248
Berlatsky, Eric 97
Berlatsky, Noah 186
Berndt, Jaqueline xxv, 190–1, 194–5, 198, 240–1, 249
Best, Mark 184
Bettleheim, Bruno 168
Beyer, Mark 236
Biggins, Walter 275–6
Billy Ireland Cartoon Library & Museum 41, 76, 79, 81–2, 198, 232–3, 267, 279
Birdwell, E. Nelson 124
Bissette, Stephen 50, 218–19, 257
Bitz, Michael 21
Bjork, Bo-Christer 263
Blackbeard, Bill 74–6, 208, 234
Blair, Glenn 7
Blake, William 152
Blanch, Christina 38–9, 183
Blanchard, Gerard 59
Bloomsbury Publishing 276
Blumberg, Marvin L. 166
Blyth, Reginald H. 198
Bode, Carl 260
Bolland, Brian 127, 249
Boltanski, Luc 57
Bolton, Christopher 198
Bordwell, David 134
Boujut, Michel 41
Bowling Green State University xiv–xv, xvii, 17, 72–3, 85, 208
Brabner, Joyce 127
braiding 94, 96
Bramlett, Frank 103
Brazilian Comics Studies 25–8
Bredehoft, Thomas A. 96
Brenda Starr 237
Brinkley, Nell 38, 238
British Cartoon Archive 82
British Consortium of Comics Scholars (BCCS) 253
Brown, Chester 278
Brown, Jeffrey A. 181

Brown, Wendy 114
Browne, Pat xvii
Browne, Ray xiv–xv, xvii, 13, 72–5, 208, 260–1
Bruner, Jerome 138
Brunetti, Ivan 145–7
Bryant, W. M. 4
Buhle, Paul 110
Burch, Noel 141
Burns, Charles 236
Busch, Wilhelm 54
Bushmiller, Ernie 145, 227, 235
Buster Brown 25
Butler, Judith 114, 179, 186
Byrne, Olive 165

C2E2 255
Cagnin, Antonio Luis 26–7
Cahiers de la bande dessinée, Les 264
Calazans, Flávio 27
Calgary Comics and Entertainment Expo 256–8
Campbell, Eddie 94, 96
Campbell, Joseph 107–9, 112, 138, 168
Canadian Society for the Study of Comics Annual Conference (CSSC) 251, 254
Caniff, Milton 34, 39, 79–80, 100, 136, 228–9, 235–6
Capp, Al 118–19, 227–8, 231, 235, 261
Captain America 165
Captain Marvel 35, 109, 165
Captain Marvel Jr. 127
Cardona, Josué 171
Carlin, John 235–38, 242
Carter, James "Bucky" 28–30, 269–70, 275
Cartoon Art Museum 233–4, 237
cartooning clubs 4–5
Cartoonist PROfiles 37, 39
Cartoonmuseum Basel 82
Caruth, Cary 126
Caswell, Lucy Shelton 74, 76–7, 79–82, 232, 266–7
Catron, Michael 264
Cavalcade of American Comics, The 228
Cavalli, Dick 228
Cawelti, John G. 260
Center for Cartoon Studies 218–19
Centre d'études des littératures d'expression graphique (CELEG or CBD) 57, 206
Centre national de la band dessinée et de l'image (CNBDI) 208
Chabon, Michael 40, 110
Cham 153
Chandra, Nandini 113
Chapman, James 63
Charles Schulz Museum 235
Charlie Hebdo 115
Chavanne, Renaud 156
Chavarot, Isabelle 230
Chicago Comicon 256
Chomsky, Noam 103

Christiansen, Hans Christian 249
Chute, Hillary 91, 181–2, 210
Cirne, Moacy 26–7
Cité international de la bande dessinée et de l'image, la 83, 239
Clarke, Jack A. 73–4
Classic Comics 46
Classical Hollywood Cinema 137, 144
Classics Illustrated 7, 18
closure 157
Clowes, Daniel 264
Club des Bandes Dessinées 57
Coe, Susan 236
Cohen, Michael 272
Cohn, Neil xxiv, 97, 103, 156, 169, 279
Comic Art Collection 224
Comic Art Studies 223–4
Comic Art xiii
comic book conventions xiii; *see also* Berkeley Con, Chicago Comicon, Comic Con India, Comic Fiesta, Comica, Comiket, Dragon Con, Edmonton Comics and Entertainment Expo, I-Con, Komikon, New York Comic Con, Oz-Con, San Diego Comic-Con International, Singapore Toy, Game and Comics Conventions, WonderCon
Comic Book Price Guide 208, 272
Comic Book Project (CBP) 21
Comic Con India 258
Comic Fiesta 258
comic shops xiii, xiv, 142
comic strip xii–xiii
Comica 238
Comicalities: Etudes de culture graphique 268
Comic-Kunst 252
Comics and Visual Culture Center 83
Comics Arts Conference (CAC) 144, 169–70, 215, 223–4, 255–6
comics as myths 106–9
comics as religion 112–14
Comics Code xiii, 49, 93, 108, 120, 167, 227
Comics Experience 219
Comics Forum 251, 263
Comics Grid, The: Journal of Comics Scholarship 263, 268
Comics Journal, The xvii, 37, 82, 141, 264
Comics Reader, The 37
Comics Studies Society xix, 211
Comics Unconference 253
Comic-Scholars Discussion List 211, 268
Comiket 84, 240, 255
Composition Studies 265
Consortium of Popular Culture Collections in the Midwest 85
Continuum 276
Coogan, Peter M. 124, 209, 215, 223–5, 255–6
Copenhagen Comics Festival 257
cosplay 255

Couch, N. C. Christopher 124
Couperie, Pierre xxv, 57–60, 64, 206, 229–30
Crane, Roy 226
creators xiii, xviii, 33, 180, 190
Creekmur, Corey 113
Crest Books 278
crime comics 167, 227
Crimmer's 264–5
Critical Studies in Media Communication 265
Crosby, Percy 226
Cruikshank, George 227
Crumb, Robert 37, 57, 69, 158, 231, 235–7, 241–2, 249
cultural imperialism 123
cummings, e. e. 246
Curtis, Barry 249
Cutright, Jr., Frank 9

Daniels, Les xvii, 39, 45, 49–50
Danky, Jim 237
Daredevil 127, 215
Dark Horse Comics 21, 214
Dark Knight Returns, The 19; *see also* Batman
Darowski, Joseph J. 182, 277
Davies, Paul 253
Davis, Marc 264
Davison, Al 127
Dawson, Paul 249
DC Comics xiii, 13–14, 17, 21, 36–7, 39, 49–52, 114, 124, 144, 165, 167, 170–1, 178–9, 185–6, 232, 263; *see also* National Comics
DeKoven, Marianne 91
Delsarte, Francois 138
Denecke, Lena 7
Dennis the Menace 278
Destefanis, Proto 229
Deutsche Comicforschung 269
Devlin, Tom 278
Dierick, Charles 63
digital comics 142–3, 159, 161
disability *see* trauma and disability
DISC theory 166
disciplinarity xi, xii, xviii–xx; anti-discipline xi, xix–xx
Discourse 124
Disney 15–16, 70, 120, 123–5, 232, 264
Disney, Walt 34, 228
Ditko, Steve 167
Donald Duck 71, 92
Doom Patrol 127
Dorf, Shel 256
Dorfman, Ariel 69–70, 92, 123, 125, 128
Dr. Mid-Nite 127
Dragon Con 255–6
Drawn and Quarterly 278
Drechsler, Debbie 126
Druillet, Philippe 155

Duncan, Brian 274
Duncan, Randy 205, 211, 215, 224–5, 248, 256, 276
Dundee Comics Day 252

EC Comics 144, 246
Eco, Umberto 100, 106, 108, 112, 118, 122, 206, 247
Edmonton Comics and Entertainment Expo 256–8
Eisner Awards 28, 50, 277
Eisner, Will 15–16, 30, 34–5, 40, 45–6, 91–2, 105, 109–10, 135–40, 144, 146–7, 151, 231, 235–6, 248, 251, 264–5, 267, 273
Eliade, Mircea 106
Elkisch, Paula 166
Ellis, Allen 71, 74
emanata 135
English, James 273
Esquire 12–13
European Comic Art 63, 252, 266–7, 269
Evanier, Mark 50, 246
Everett, Bill 37
expressive anatomy 147

Fables 96
Famous Funnies 34, 110
fans xiii, xvi–xviii, xxiv, 8, 16, 33–6, 44, 49, 72, 134, 179–84, 187, 269, 278, 195, 207, 240, 246–7, 250–1, 253–5, 257–9
Fantagraphics 278
Fantastic Four 170
fanzines 47, 60, 131, 206, 221, 224, 240, 246–7, 258, 264
Farago, Andrew 234
Faust, Wolfgang Max 120–1
Fawaz, Ramzi 186
Fawcett Comics 8
Feiffer, Jules xiii, xv, 34, 45–9, 109–10, 157
Feininger, Lyonel 235–6
Felix the Cat 120
Feminist Studies 180
Fern, Annette 272
Festival of Cartoon Art 80, 222
Film Studies 205
Finger, Bill 35, 39
Fingeroth, Danny 109–10, 121–2, 168, 170, 276
Finnish Comics Society 83
Fiore, Quentin 141
First International Comics Exhibition 25
Fischer, Craig xvii, 94, 96
Fisher, Bud 34
Fisher, H. C. 235
Fisher, Ham 226
Fishwick, Marshall W. 72, 260
Fitzpatrick, Daniel R. 228
Flash, The 109, 167
Flash Gordon 34

folklore 121
Fonlladosa, Tristan 208
Forceville, Charles 103
foreign language instruction 6
Forney, Ellen 127
Foster, Harold "Hal" 114, 232, 274
Franc, Régis 153
François, Édouard 229
Frank, Phil 234
Frankfurt School xiv
Franquin, André 154
Frasca, Marilyn 146
Fremok 127
Fresnault-Deruelle, Pierre 94, 100–1, 107, 154
Freud, Sigmund 108, 166
Frey, Hugo 97, 153
Friedmann, Werner 130–1
Fuchs, Wolfgang J. xvi, xxv, 106–8, 112, 119–20, 123–5, 128, 130–2
Fujikawa, Chisui 194
funny animals 23, 124
Fusanosuke, Natsume 241

Gabilliet, Jean-Paul xxiv, 49
Gaiman, Neil 110
Gaines, Max C. 6, 165–6, 171, 226–7
Gardner, Jared 91, 95–6
Garrett, Gregg 112
Gasca, Luis 102
Gaskill, Frank 171
Gassiot-Talabot, Gérald 230
Gaudreault, André 94
Gauthier, Guy 153–4
Geertz, Clifford 111
Gender Studies 178–87
Genette, Gérard 94, 96–7
Gertler, Nat 144, 257
Gesellschaft für Comicforschung 252
Gibbons, Dave 272
Gibson, Mel 182
Gifford, Denis 47–9
Giff-Wiff 57, 59–60, 206
Gilroy, Andréa 185
Givler, Peter 276
Glasser, Jean-Claude 59
Glénat, Jacques 264
Gloeckner, Phoebe 126, 181
Goblet, Dominique 154
Goddard, Jean-Luc 141
Goggin, Joyce 64
Golash-Boza, Tanya Marie 277
Goldberg, Rube 235
Gombrich, Ernst H. 60–1, 634, 68, 138, 247
Gondō, Susumu 194
Gonzalez, Jesus 266
Gorner, Peter 50–1
Goulart, Ron 273

Gould, Chester 227, 235–6
GRAF 257
Grand Comics Database, The 36, 224
Graphic Brighton 253
Graphis 58
Gravett, Paul 57, 110, 230, 238–9, 253
Green Lantern 109, 122
Green, Justin 97, 127
Green, Vicki 223–5
Greenberg, Clement 152, 227
Grey, Harold 235
grid 155, 157
Griffith, Bill 235
Groensteen, Thierry 40–1, 57, 61, 93–5, 101, 103, 134, 150–2, 155–9, 185, 230, 264, 274
Gross, Milt 226, 235
Groth, Gary 37, 264
Grove, Laurence 63, 206, 252, 269–70
Grünewald, Dietrich 252
Gubern, Román 102
Gumps, The 5

Hague, Ian 159–61, 251
Hammer Museum 236, 238, 242
Hanley, Tim 166
Happy Hooligan 140
Harada, Nakao 240
Haring, Keith 235
Harmsen, Rieke C. 251
Harris, Albert 7
Harrison, Christopher 258
Harvard Journal of Pictorial Fiction see Crimmer's
Harvey, Robert C. xvii, 39, 76, 134, 151, 153, 248, 261, 264–5, 275
Hasegawa, Machiko 194
Hasen, Irwin 228
Hastings, Wally 214
Hatfield, Charles xi–xxii, 20, 41, 82, 94, 96–7, 152–3, 157, 160, 210–11, 213, 278
Havlik, E.J. 102
Hawley, John Stratton 113
Heer, Jeet xxiv, 242, 246–7, 274–5, 278
Heintjes, Tom 265
Helsinki Comics Festival 257
Hench, John 264
Henderson State University 214–16
Herd, Damon 253
Herge 20, 41, 154–5
Herman, David 91, 95–6
Hernandez, Gilbert 97
Herriman, George 34, 71, 97, 122, 126, 227–8, 231–2, 235–6, 239
Hi and Lois 135, 232
Highsmith, Doug 51, 71
Historietas: Revista de estudios sobre la Historieta 269
historiography 125
Hogan's Alley 265

Hogarth, Burne 59, 216, 264
Hogarth, William 54, 63–4, 67–8, 134, 157, 227, 229, 231, 258
Holman, Bill 235
Homlberg, Ryan 197
Hopkins, David 83–4
Horn, Maurice xv, xxv, 45, 50–1, 54–5, 58–9, 64, 206, 229–31, 242, 273
Horrocks, Dylan 141
horror comics 167, 174–5, 227
Horsens 257
Horsky, Tom 272
Horstkotte, Silke 96
Hosokibara, Seiki 191, 193, 196, 199
Hotz, Allan 265
Houstion, Alicia 84
Howard, Robert E. 33
Howe, Irving 246
Howe, Sean 40
Human Torch, The 109
Hünig, Wolfgang K. 93
Hurd, Jud 37
Hutchinson, Katherine 9
Huxley, David 17–18, 248–9, 252, 268

I-Con 257
IDW 219, 278
Image [&] Narrative 95, 266
Image Comics 114
ImageText xxv, 15, 212, 222, 263, 268
infinite canvas 142
Inge, M. Thomas (Tom) xiv, xvii, xxv, 14, 111, 208, 248, 260–1, 274–5
ink | art 263, 268
INKS: Cartoon and Comic Art Studies 81, 222, 266–7
Inness, Sherrie A. 180, 183
Insitutes für Jugendbuchforschung 82
Institute for Comics Studies (ICS) 209–10, 255
Institution-building xvii–xviii
International Association of Word and Image Studies (IAWIS) 252
International Bande Dessinée Society (IBDS) 251–2, 269
international collaboration 282–3
International Comic Arts Forum (ICAF) xii, xvii, 21, 151, 208–11, 222, 249–51, 267
International Conference for Graphic Novels and Comics 252
International Journal of Comic Art (IJoCA) 21, 37, 160, 267, 209, 222, 249
International Museum of Cartoon Art *see* Museum of Cartoon Art
International Scholarly Conference 253
Inuhiko, Yomota 240
Ippei 190, 192
Iron Man 127, 168
Ishiko, Jun 193

Ishiko, Junzō 194–5
Islam 114–15
Israeli Comics Animation and Cartooning Festival 257
Israeli Museum for Comics and Cartooning 253
Itō, Gō 196–7

Jack Chick Tracts 113
Jackendoff, Ray 103
Jacobs, Dale 30, 279
Jacobs, Edgar P. 156
Jason 157
Jenkins, Henry 211
Jensen, Richard and Renee 127
Jewett, Robert 106, 108–9
Jews and comics 109–11, 121–2
John Constantine 219
John Ryan Collection 83
Johnson, Crocket 277–8
Johnston, Antony 267
Jones, Gerard 40, 110
Jones, Leslie 236
Journal of Educational Sociology 7–9
Journal of Graphic Novels and Comics 17, 252, 267–8
Journal of Popular Culture xiv, xv, xvii, 14, 62, 72, 75, 120, 260–1, 265
Judge 119
Jung, Carl 108, 168
Justice Society of America 35, 165

Kaiji, Jun 194
Kambam, Praven R. 170
Kane, Bob 16, 35, 39, 231, 235
Kane, Gil 37, 136
Kannenberg, Gene, Jr. 19–20, 29
Kaplan, Arie 110–11
Karasawa, Shūichi 240
Karasik, Paul 136, 145
Kartalopoulos, Bill 82
Kashar, Summerlea 234
Katsushika, Hokusai 190
Katzenjammer Kids 140
Keaton, Russell 124
Keen, Suzanne 96
Kelly, Walt 16, 71, 131, 232, 235, 278
Kelsky, Karen 277
Kemi Comics Festival 257
Kent, William IV 234
Kidd, Chip 39
Kidd, Kenneth 273
King, Frank 227, 235–6
Kinneman, Fleda Cooper 7
Kinsella, Sharon 198
Kintsch, Walter 101
Kirby, Jack 35, 39, 136, 141, 153, 167, 231–2, 235–6, 239, 264
Kirste, Ken 234
Kirtley, Susan 214–15

Kitazawa, Rakuten *see* Rakuten
Kitchen, Denis 231, 237, 242
Kiyama, Henry Yoshitaka 198
Klock, Geoff 276
Knerr, Harold 226
Knowles, Christopher 112–13
Kolehmainer, Kristine 83
Komikon 258
Kominksky-Crumb, Aline 181
Korean Manhwa Contents Agency (KOMACON) 84
Kōzan-ji 191
Kraemer, Christine Hoff 114
Kraft, Ulrich 93
Krazy Kat 34, 71, 97, 122, 126, 231
Kress, Gunther 279
Krueger, Ken 256
Kubert School, The 217–19
Kubert, Joe 37, 136, 217–18
Kukkonen, Karin 96
Kunzle, David xvi, xxv, 17, 40, 56, 59–64, 67–70, 92, 118, 123, 143, 146, 157, 206, 248, 275
Kurtzman, Harvey 231, 235–6, 264, 278
Kyoto International Manga Museum 84
Kyoto Seika University 198, 222

L'Association 159
L'Indispensable 265
La Barre, Kathryn xxiv
La Capra, Dominick 126
La société civile d'études et de recherches des littératures dessinée (SOCERLID) 57–9
Lacassin, Francis xxiii, 57, 59, 64, 206
Lakes International Comic Art Festival 258
Lamarre, Thomas 199
Langley, Travis 169–70, 215
Lapacherie, Jean-Gérard 154
Larance, Jeremy xxiii
Larsen, Gary 114
Lawrence, John Shelton 106, 108–9
Laydeez do Comics 253
Lazarus, Mell 228
LD 222
Le Cahier de la Bande Dessinée 57
Leduc, Phillippe 239
Lee, Stan xxiii, 12–14, 153, 167, 207, 231, 235
Lefèvre, Pascal xxiv–xxv, 63, 95–6, 153, 158, 160, 166, 281–3
Legman, Gerson 166
Lendrum, Rob 185
Lent, John xxv, 20–1, 37, 207, 221–3, 246, 249, 264, 267, 270, 281
Lepore, Jill 40, 51–2
Les Cahiers de la bande dessinée xvi, 264, 274
Lesk, Andrew 251
Lessing, Gotthold Ephraim 152
Letamendi, Andrea 170
Lévi-Strauss, Claude 107

Levitz, Paul 50
Lewis, A. David 105–6, 108, 111, 114–15, 121–2
Li'l Abner 118–19, 227, 261
Library and Archives Canada 83
Library of American Comics 278
Library of Congress 72, 76–7, 222, 228, 232
Lichtenstein, Roy xiii, 227, 230, 236
Lieber, Steve 144
Life 119
Lightman, Sarah 277
Lim, Cheng Tju 257–8
Lima, Herman 26
literacy xii
Little Orphan Annie 68
Little, Tom 228
Lloyd, David 20
LoCicero, Don 112
Lom, Lucie 239
Louvre 51, 131, 229–31, 239
Lovecraft, H. P. 33
Lucca Comics and Games 255
Lund, Martin 115
Lunning, Frenchy 198
Lupoff, Richard (Dick) xv, 35
Luyten, Sonia Maria Bibe xxiii, 26

MacWilliams, Mark Wheeler 113
Mad 144
Madden, Matt 30, 136, 143–5, 147, 161
Madison, Nathan Vernon 277
Madrid, Mike 181
Magnussen, Anne xxiv, 101, 249
Mahmood, Saba 114
Maigret, Éric 150, 152
Mainardi, Patricia 64
Malmö seriefestival 257
Maltret, Olivier 41
manga 41, 51, 54, 83–5, 94–5, 113–14, 141, 158, 222, 240–1, 257–8, 266, 268–9, 282
Mansat, André 101
Marion, Philippe 152
Marques de Melo, José 26–7
Marschall, Rick 232, 265
Marston, William Moulton 39–40, 52, 164–6, 171, 186
Martin, Jacques 154
Marvel xiii, 12–13, 15, 17, 21, 36, 45, 47, 49–52, 109, 114, 120, 144, 167, 185–6, 219, 232
Marxist xiv, xvi, 17, 120, 123, 273, 276
Masson, Pierre 154, 157
Masters of American Comics 233, 236–8, 241–2
materiality 159–61
Mathieu, Marc Antoine 239
Mattelart, Armand 69–70, 92, 123, 125, 128
Mattu, Ali 170
Maurer, Joe 217–18
Maus 19, 57, 93, 126, 139, 235–7
May, Rollo 168

Mazzuccheli, David 145
McCay, Winsor 126, 134, 155, 227–8, 231–2, 235–6, 239, 242
McClancey, Kathleen 254, 256
McCloud, Scott 3, 30, 56, 60, 92, 135, 139–44, 146–7, 151, 157, 257, 270, 273
McDonald, Gerald 226
McFarland and Company 276–7
McGilchrist, Ian 146
McKinney, Mark 252, 266, 269–70, 281
McLain, Karline 113
McLuhan, Marshall 52, 54–5, 138, 141, 247
McMahon, Mike 156
McMeel, Andrews 278
McRobbie, Angela 176
Mechademia: An Annual Forum for Anime, Manga, and the Fan Arts 198, 269
Medhurst, Andy 184
media effects xii–xiii
media studies xvii
Melo, José Marques de 26–7
Memphis College of Art (MCA) 217
Menu, Jean-Christophe 134, 159
Merino, Ana 281
Messnick, Dale 38
meta-panel 137
Metaphor [conference] 254
Metropolitan Museum of Art (MMA) 228
Michaelis, David 40, 226
Michigan State University 222–5, 248, 250, 260
Mickey Mouse 282
Mikirō, Katō 240
Mikkonen, Kai 95–6
Milestone Comics 181
Miller, Ann xvi, 58, 93, 134, 252, 269–70
Miller, Frank 215, 264, 272
Mills, Tarpe 38
Minneapolis College of Art and Design (MCAD) 217–18
Miodrag, Hannah 92, 97, 100
mise-en-scéne 157
Miss Fury 38, 237
Mitchell, W.J.T. 101, 152
Miyamoto, Hirohito 191, 194, 196
Miyao, Shigeo 193
Miyazaki, Hayao 197
Mizuki, Shigeru 194
Modern Language Association xvii, 210–11, 222, 224, 248, 254
Moliterni, Claude 57–8, 64, 206, 229
Molotiu, Andrei 29
Moore, Alan 20, 97, 113, 127, 219, 253, 264, 272
Moore, Anne 264
Moran, Barbara 74
Morgan, Harry 95, 155, 157–8
Morris, Jon 51
Morrison, Grant 96, 253
Moskowitz, Sam 34

Mosse, Hilde 166
Moya, Alvaro de 25–7
Ms. Marvel 45, 115, 122
MSU Comics Forum 250
Mu group 101
Muhammad 114–15
Munson, Kim xxv
Munsterberg, Hugo 164
Murakami, Tomohiko 195
Murray, Chris 213, 252, 267
Musee des Arts Decoratifs 229, 274
Musée des Beaux Arts 206–07
Museum of Cartoon Art 81, 135, 232–3, 236, 239
Museum of Comic and Cartoon Art 238
Musturi, Tommi 158
Myer, Peter L. 230

Nachbar, Jack 16–17
Nakajima, Azusa 195
Nakano, Haruyuki 197
Nakazawa, Keiji 126
Nancy 145
narrative sequence 154–6
National Cartoonists Society 80, 228, 234
National Comics 4–8; *see also* DC Comics
National Council of Teachers of English (NCTE) 4, 6
National Diet Library 83
Natsume, Fusanosuke 195–6, 199
Ndalianis, Angela 276
Neaud, Fabrice 158
Nel, Philip 277–8
Nemo 124
New Fun Comics 34, 43
New Narrative Conference 251
New York Comic Con 255
New York World's Fair 228
Newgarden, Mark 136, 145
Newspaper Comics Council 227–8
Nick Fury, Agent of S.H.I.E.L.D 35, 47, 120
Ninth Art 267–8
Nobleman, Marc Tyler 40
Nona Arte Revista Brasileira de Pesquisas em Histroias em Quadrinhos 269
Nordic Network for Comics Research (NNCORE) 252
North, Sterling 160
nostalgia xiii–xv
Nyberg, Amy Kiste 180, 261
Nye, Russell xiv, xvii, 72, 77, 260

O Tico-Tico 25
O'Connor, Patrick 171
O'Hearn, Martin 36
O'Neill, Rose 38
O'Sullivan, Judith 231
objective historians 43–4

Oelsner, Lesley 231
Ohio State University 222, 232, 267, 275, 279
Okada, Toshio 240
Okamoto, Ippei *see* Ippei
Olamot, The 257
Oliveros, Chris 278
Ollie, Michelle 218–19
Omer-Sherman, Ranen 111
Ong, Walter 121–2
Oni Press 114, 214
onomatopoeias 101–2, 104, 154
open access (OA) publishing 263, 268–70
Open Court Publishing Company 169
Opper, Frederick 228
Oracle 127
Ormond, Joan 252
Ormrod, Julia 268
Oropeza, B. J. 112
Osamu, Takeuchi 241
Oslo Comics Expo (OCX) 257
Ōtsuka, Eiji 196
OuBaPo 161
Outcault, Richard Fenton 25, 34, 150, 227, 231, 235
Overstreet Price Guide xv
Overstreet, Robert M. 272
Oz-Con 258

Packer, Sharon 170
Page 23 Lit Con 250
Palais du Louvre xv
Palumbo, Donald 261
Panofsky, Erwin 61, 63–4
Panter, Gary 235–6
Parker, Dorothy 246
Peanuts 81, 94, 100, 120, 157, 261, 278
Pearl, Barry 44–5, 48
Pearson, Roberta 276
pedagogy xii
Pedri, Nancy 95–6
Peeters, Benoît 40–1, 94–5, 101, 134, 155–7
Peirce, Charles S. 101
Pekar, Harvey 93, 96–7, 110, 127, 261
Pellitteri, Marco 160, 198
Perec, Georges 161
Perry, George xvi
Petrovic, Paul 185
Phénix 58, 206
Philbin, Ann 235–6, 242
Pitt, Suzan 236
poetry comics 29
Pogo 71, 278
political economy 121
Pollman, Joost 102
Pop Art xiii, 55, 58, 227–31, 235
Pop Con 258
Popeye 34

Popular Culture Association xii, xiv–xv, xvii–xviii, 13, 72, 74, 208, 221–2, 224–5, 248–9, 254, 260–1
Popular Culture in Libraries 74
Portland State University 214–15
Postema, Barbara 95, 251, 254
Potts, Carl 21–2, 144, 147
Power, Natsu Onoda 41
Pozios, Vasilis 170–1
Priego, Ernesto 160, 268
Prince Valiant 114
Pritchett, Frances W. 113
Proctor, William 174–7
Prokopoff, Stephen S. 230
psychoanalysis 16
Puck 119
pulp magazines 33, 35, 52, 120
Pustz, Matthew 111, 276

qadrinho 54
Queer Studies 178–87
Queneau, Raymond 144, 161

Rakuten 190–3, 199
Raptus Festival 257
Rashid, Hussein 115
RAW 57, 145, 235
Rawhide Kid, The 185
Raymond, Alex 235
Regaldo, Aldo 124
Reitberger, Reinhold xvi, xxv, 106–8, 112, 119–20, 123–5, 128
Renée, Lily 238
Rey, Alain 93
Reynolds, Eric 278
Reynolds, Richard 106–8
Reynvoet, Jean-Pierre 101–2
Rhode, Michael 267
Rhodes, Silas H. 216
Richler, Mordecai 109–10
Robbins, Robbie 278
Robbins, Trina xxv, 37–9, 110, 233, 237–8, 264
Roberts, Tom 20
Robicek, Dorothy 165
Robinson, Jerry 37, 39
Roeder, Kathleen 275
Rogers, Buck 34
romance comics 49, 223
Rommens, Aarnoud 95
Rosenberg, Robin S. 170
Round, Julia 252, 267, 270
Rowlandson, Thomas 54
Royal Society, The 262
Rubin, Lawrence 171
Rugiero, Larry 234
Rutgers University Press 275
Ryan, Mari-Laure 95

Sabin, Roger 19, 62–3, 128, 248–9, 252, 258–9, 276
Sacco, Joe 126
Sakai, Shichima 197
Salon Internationale de Comics 255
San Diego Comic-Con International 215, 222, 250, 255–7
San Francisco Academy of Comic Art 76, 81
Sandman 96
SANE Journal: Sequential Art Narrative in Education 263, 269
Sanpei, Shirato 194
satire 123
Satō, Tadao 194
Satrapi, Marjane 126, 181, 183
Saunders, Ben 113, 213
Saussure, Fernand de 100
Sausverd, Antoine 230
Savage, William W., Jr. 71
Savannah College of Art and Design (SCAD) 217–18, 224
Scandinavian Journal of Comic Art 263, 269
Scarlet, Janina 171
Schelly, Bill xiii
Schmidt, Andy 219
Schneider, Greice 158
Schodt, Frederik 197–8
School of Visual Arts (SVA) 216–19
Schuiten, François 155
Schultz, Carl 273
Schulz, Charles M. 14, 37, 40, 81, 131, 226, 231–2, 234, 236, 239
Schumacher, Michael 231
Schurk, William 73
Schwartz, Barthélémy 134
Schwartz, Delmore 246
Schwartz, Julius 246
science fiction 34, 48, 124, 240–1, 246
Scorsese, Martin 141
Scott, Randall "Randy" 74, 77–9, 85, 224
Scottish Word and Image Group 252
Screech, Matthew 41
Scrooge McDuck 123, 125
Scully, Richard xxiv
Sedgwick, Eve Kosofsky 184
Segar, E. C. 235–6, 239
Seldes, Gilbert 246
semiotics 106, 118, 150, 152–4, 157
Sequart 278
sequence 156–8
Serieteket 83
Serrano, Julia 186
Severin, Marie 13
Sfar, Joann 110
Shaffer, Laurance 5
Shamoon, Deborah 198
Shazam! (Brazilian book) 26–7
Shelley, Mary 124

Shelton, Gilbert 231
Sheridan, Martin xv, 33–4
Shimizu, Isao 196–7, 241
Short, Robert 112
Shreve Simpson, Marianna 64
Shuster, Joe 34–5, 39–40, 124, 235
Siegel, Jerry 34–5, 39–40, 124
Sim, Dave 264
Simon, Joe 136
Singapore Toy, Game and Comics Convention 258
Singer, Marc 96
Singh, Debarghya 254
Small Press Expo (SPX) 208
Smart, Ninian 111
Smith, Al 228
Smith, E. E. "Doc" 33
Smith, Greg M. 136
Smith, Jonathan Z. 113
Smith, Lewis Jr. 5
Smith, Lena Roberts 5
Smith, Matthew J. 205, 211, 215, 257, 276
Smithsonian 228, 231
Smolderen, Thierry xxiv, 63–4, 93, 134, 151, 274
SOCERLID xv, 51, 57–8, 206, 229
social justice 28
Société civile d'étude et de recherché des littératures dessinées see SOCERLID
Society for Cinema and Media Studies 254
Society for Literature, Science, and the Arts 254
Solomon, David 263
Somigli, Luca 224
Sones, W. W. D. 8
sound effects 101–3
Sousanis, Nick xxiv, 30
specialty shops see comic shops
Spider-Man 71, 108, 110
Spiegelman, Art 57, 70, 71, 93, 97, 126, 136, 139, 144, 231, 235–7, 241–2, 248, 267, 274
Spielman, Guy 208, 251
Spirit, The 34–5, 45, 109–10, 136–7, 139
Spirou 101
Spring Hollow 278
Spurgeon, Tom 37, 50, 264
Squier, Susan 126
Sreenivas, Deepa 113
Srinivasan, Seetha 274–5
Stack, Frank 267
Stanfill, Mike 114
Stansbury, Herb 234
Starkey, Hugh 249
Starr, Brenda 38
Steadman, Ralph 267
Stefanelli, Matteo 151
Steranko, Jim xv–xvi, 35–7, 39–40, 45–9
Sterckx, Pierre 156
Stern, Roger 13
Sterrett, Cliff 235
Steve Canyon 68, 79, 100

Stevenson, Gordon 73–4
Stewart, Bhob xv
Stewart, Ron 192
Stockholm Comics Festival (SPX) 257
structuralism 107–8
Strum, James 218–19
Studies in Comics 213, 252, 267, 270
Stuller, Jennifer K. 182
Sunday Press Books 278
Supergraphics 47
superhero xiii, 12, 16, 21, 23, 27, 34–5, 39–41, 45–6, 48–9, 106–9, 112, 114–15, 119, 121–2, 124–7, 131, 139, 165, 167–71, 179, 181, 184–5, 213, 222–3, 227, 281–2
Superman 6–9, 18, 34, 39–40, 45, 50, 92, 100, 106, 108–10, 118, 121–5, 164, 179, 183, 186, 206, 258
Suzuki, CJ 194
Swinnerton, James 226
Szabo, Joseph 264
Szep, Paul 264

Tabachnick, Stephen 23, 111
Takahashi, Mizuki 195–6
Takeuchi, Ichirō 193, 196
Takeuchi, Osamu 196–7
Tampere Comics Festival 257
Taniguchi, Jiro 158
Tardi, Jacques 41
Target 222
Tarzan 5, 34, 59
Taylor, Lara 171
Tebeofera 263, 269
Terry and the Pirates 68, 79
Terry, Paul H. 228
Texas History Movies 4
textimage 266
Tezuka, Osamu 113, 191–4, 196–7, 199
Thalheimer, Anne H 183
Theisen, Nicholas xxiv, 134, 269
Thing, The 127
Thomas, Graham 82
Thomas, Jolyon Baraka 114
Thomas, Roy 35–6
Thompson, Don xv, 35, 41
Thompson, Kim 264
Thor 127
Thorn, E. V. 192
Thought Bubble 251
Tilley, Carol xxiv, 8–9, 167
time 140, 142, 157–8
Time Traveler, The 246
Tintin 20, 41, 101, 155
Tom Strong 96
Tomohiko, Murakami 241
Top Shelf 214
Töpffer, Rodolphe 17, 40, 54, 61, 63, 68, 133–4, 146, 150, 153, 157, 159, 227, 231

Toronto Comic Arts Festival (TCAF) 251, 254
Toth, Emily 260
Totleben, John 218
Toussaint, Bernard 154
Tracy, Dick 34
Transformative Works and Cultures 265
Transitions [conference] 254
trauma and disability 125–8
Trondheim, Lewis 157
Trostle, J. P. 82
Trudeau, Garry 70, 235
Tsurumi, Shunsuke 193–5, 197
Turner, Victor 111
Twomey, John 272
Tysell, Helen Trace 103

underground comix 15, 19, 37, 93, 97, 125, 145, 179, 184, 231, 237
University of Dundee 212–14
University of Florida 211–12, 222, 251, 268, 279
University of Oregon 213–14
University Press of Mississippi 41, 107, 208, 222, 274–6
Uricchio, William 276
Uslan, Michael xxiii, 12–13

Vacca, Carlo 6
Valentine, Aimee 263, 268, 270
Van Dijk, Teun 101
Van Lier, Henri 157
Vaughan, Phil 252
Vaughn-James, Martin 159
Veitch, Rick 218
Venezia, Tony 254
Vergueiro, Waldomiro xxiii, xxv, 25–8
Versaci, Rocco 276
Vessels, Joel 206
Village Voice 45
Viñetas Serias 250–1
Voloshinov, Valentin 176

Wagner, Dave 125
Wagstaff, Sheena 235
Wailgum, Gig 236
Waldman, J. T. 110
Walker, Brian 232–3, 235–7, 239
Walker, Mort 81, 135–6, 232, 273–4
Walsh, John xxiv
Walsh, Richard 96
war comics 49, 184
Ware, Chris 57, 96, 145, 154, 156–8, 236, 242, 278
Ware, Hames 35–6
Warhol xiii
Warhol, Andy 227, 231, 236
Warner, Michael 178
Watchmen 19, 155, 158, 272
Watson, Alasdair 267

Watterson, Bill 264
Waugh, Coulton xv, 34, 135, 274
Weiner, Robert G. xxiii, 8
Weisinger, Mort 34, 36, 246
Wertham, Fredric xiii, 52, 108, 114, 119–20, 131, 138, 164, 166–8, 170–1, 174, 184, 186, 227, 264, 272
West Liberty University 214
Western comics 48, 184–5
Wheeler, Andrew 267
Wheeler-Nicholson, Malcolm 4, 6
Whyte, Malcolm 233–5
Wiegand, Wayne A. 74
Wiley-Blackwell 169
Williams, J. H. 185
Williams, Sue 236
Willing, Jessie Gillespie 226
Wilson, G. Willow 115
Wilson, H. E. 4
Witek, Joseph xi, xiv, 15, 93, 151–2, 274
Witty, Paul 8
WittyWorld 222, 264–5
Wizard World 255
Wojnarowicz, David 235
Wolk, Douglas 278
Wolverine 139
Wonder Woman 37–9, 50–2, 122, 165, 167, 178, 186
WonderCon 255
Woo, Benjamin xxiv
Wood, Wally 144–5, 235
Woodruff, Thomas 216
Worcester, Kent 246–7, 249
Word & Image: A Journal of Verbal/Visual Enquiry 266
word v. image 152–4
Workshop on the Cartoon Narrative 8
Wright, Bradford 207

Xero xiii, 35
X-Men 127, 170, 182, 186

Yamane, Sadao 194
Yeates, Thomas 218
Yellow Kid, The 34, 43, 50, 150, 228
Yomota, Inuhiko 195–6
Yonezawa, Yoshihiro xxv, 195, 240–1
Yoshiharu, Tsuge 194
Yoshihiro Yonezawa Memorial Library of Manga and Subcultures 84
Young, William H., Jr. 261, 266
Yronwoode, Catherine 37

Zap Comix 69
Zimmerman, Howard 279
Zimmerman, Ron 185
zines *see* fanzines
Zorbaugh, Harvey 7–9